DATE DUE			

POLITICAL THEORY

POLITICAL THEORY

THE FOUNDATIONS OF
TWENTIETH-CENTURY
POLITICAL THOUGHT

By Arnold Brecht

PRINCETON, NEW JERSEY
PRINCETON UNIVERSITY PRESS

IN HONOR OF

THE NEW SCHOOL FOR SOCIAL RESEARCH

WHICH

TWENTY-FIVE YEARS AGO

ESTABLISHED

THE GRADUATE FACULTY

OF POLITICAL AND SOCIAL SCIENCE

GRANTING IT

SHELTER AND FREEDOM

PREFACE

WHEN a sizable new book has as its subject not some particular questions of political theory, some area, type, or aspect of it, but political theory itself; when, to some extent at least, it promises to supply and to teach this strange thing; when it boldly announces these intentions by presenting itself under the very title *Political Theory* (monumental, perhaps, but slightly challenging too); and when, surprisingly enough, this even seems to be the first full-size American book ever published under that title and the first of its kind to appear in any country—then a decent respect for the raised eyebrows of those who may pick it up requires that the author explain at the outset to what theory they are treated. Or is there only one political theory?

If we use the term in its nonscientific sense there is, of course, no system of thought that could be called simply *the* political theory of the twentieth century, or of all times. We are then confronted, rather, with many highly diversified so-called theories, antagonisms among them running so deep that internal revolutions or revolts, external conflicts, and even global wars have resulted therefrom. None of these competing systems of thought, however, not even those dearest to us, are theories in the scientific sense of the word, or at least not entirely so. They all are based, in good measure, not on science but on other sources of human scheming, good or bad, such as religious revelation, intuitional conviction, world views held in common, national tradition, nationalistic or group ambitions—in brief, on ways of thinking or feeling that do not claim scientific rank or, if they do, are not fully warranted in this pretense.

The present book is concerned with *scientific* political theory. This does not mean that nonscientific thinking will be haughtily ignored. It is one of the functions of science to examine human ideas with its tools, and hence scientific political theory deals critically with all nonscientific theories it meets on its path. Nor would it be possible to base government and politics exclusively on science. Every political system, for example, must have some goal or goals, and science alone and by itself cannot set goals. This is no good reason on the other hand for reversing the matter, turning a cold shoulder on science. For scientific theory, although unable to set goals, can contribute a great deal to the making of political decisions, even those by which goals are set.

Scientific political theory has been going through a crisis of unprecedented magnitude in this century, and is still in the midst of it. Why this is so, the reader will find explained in the introductory chapter. I shall limit myself here to a few remarks on what my purposes have been in writing this book.

There exists today no comprehensive treatise to familiarize serious students, both systematically and genetically, with the fundamental turn that scientific political theory took in the early part of this century; to initiate them, with adequate clarity and depth, into the theoretical and philosophical problems involved; and to make them fully understand both the positive and the negative implications of what is going on in political theory today. It is this volume's first purpose, at once humble and ambitious, to provide such a guide.

There are excellent texts on scientific method in the social sciences, some enthusiastic and some critical; there are books and articles in many languages on political ends and means, on values and on relativism, some pro-relativistic and some anti-; there are plenty of essays dealing with jurisprudence as if the theory of justice were something that could be separated from political theory, and vice versa; there are studies on the philosophical basis of science and others on the scientific basis of philosophy; and there are many brilliant asides on basic questions in papers that deal with practical problems. Yet there is no book, within any of the social sciences, that deals with these various, intrinsically interrelated, aspects and problems on the same level, giving each its full measure of attention, and all of them a well-integrated and entirely consistent presentation. Such a book, I believe, is needed.

What is missing is not only a comprehensive *systematic* presentation, but likewise a satisfactory description of the recent *genesis* of thought on these matters. This book tries to fill the genetic as well as the systematic gap.

There was, however, from the beginning another, an ulterior motive in my mind. The systematic and genetic study I set out to write was to serve as a well-organized basis for me to add, chapter by chapter, what as the result of fifty years of work, about evenly divided between political theory and practice, I felt able to contribute to the advancement of theoretic thinking. I had previously written a considerable number of papers in this field, but had come to see that in the present state of theory such piecemeal procedure is not adequate. So much had to be presupposed in each article, or to be expressed indirectly by mere allusions, that no generally useful purpose could be served; the actual outcome was at best an esoteric exercise for a few addicts, with little meaning for a general public. The situation would perhaps differ, I felt, if I could permeate a fully coherent presentation with whatever I had to say. Incorporating my own thoughts *in their proper settings,* I could elucidate dark regions and show the merits of over-all consistency. Lack of clarity and consistency has been a creeping evil in political theory. In human relations, even in practical politics, such a lack may at times be quite pleasant; but in scientific understanding it is one of the greatest handicaps. It is not difficult to write much and intelligently, wittily and even fascinatingly, on political issues; but to be consistent in one's thinking, both clear and consistent, is not easy, if I may understate the case.

Finally, with the foundations thus firmly established, it was my purpose to deal with the main subjects of political practice in the light of an advanced theory that has found its bearings.

These have been my aims, or rather my vision—the ideal of perfection toward which I have been steering. I am far from claiming that I have attained these goals, or any of them, to full satisfaction. Yet I am reasonably confident that the reader will find a good deal of information and stimulation here, and teachers and students a much-sought-for coherent presentation, satisfactory for advanced students, but understandable even to the beginner, if he is sufficiently intelligent to submit to theoretic discussion.

The present volume deals primarily with *general* theory, including the philosophic and scientific foundations of scientific political theory; its methods; its uses; its strength and its limitations; and what may be called its *wisdom.* Each of its chapters also discusses a goodly number of specific political issues, showing the enormous practical bearing of advanced basic research. But this is done in an incidental manner, by way of illustration. The alphabetical subject index at the end may serve to locate such treatment for any particular problem. I plan to have this volume followed by a companion volume, devoted to *special* topics in a more systematic manner. The second will lean heavily on the first. But the first, as here presented, must stand on its own merits. Additional remarks on its plan will be found at the end of the introductory chapter.

Some of my former articles have been used, as it were, as preparatory studies. But more than four-fifths of the present book is new, and where sections of former writings are incorporated, hardly a paragraph has been left unchanged.

I have dispensed with the venerable practice of submitting all parts of my work to the advance critique of numerous colleagues. Yet I did ask two philosopher friends to read early drafts of Chapters I and II on Scientific Method because of the philosophical material here included. They are William Ernest Hocking, professor emeritus at Harvard, now of Madison, N.H., and Alfred Schutz, of the Graduate Faculty of the New School for Social Research, men as different as friends can be. Their questions and comments were of great value. I am sad that I could not ask also two of my former colleagues at the New School, the late Felix Kaufmann and Max Wertheimer—two more great scholars representing different types of approach—for the same service, which they too would have generously rendered, my occasional deviations from their views notwithstanding.

I have drawn a great deal of stimulation for all chapters of this book from discussions with many others, including present and former students, colleagues of various universities and departments, my brother Gustav, formerly of Cologne and now of Bad Wiessee, Bavaria, steeped in astronomy and the foundations of natural science, and Clara, companion of many joys and sorrows in two continents, deeply interested in philosophical questions.

In a more general sense, I wish to express the debt of gratitude I owe, in maturing as a scholar, to the General Seminar which the Graduate Faculty of the New School for Social Research has held every Wednesday night for twenty-five years (only recently limited to the first semester of each academic year), with all members of the faculty in regular attendance. Except when absent from New York I have hardly missed a session through this quarter of a century.

So I offer this book, not as a perfect achievement, but as a service I wish to render to others on what is a winding, and sometimes stony, but always fascinating road, sparing them part of the time and stress they otherwise would have to expend. If they feel helped by this essay, and encouraged to go on from where it leaves off, my labors will be most happily rewarded.

A.B.

New York, N.Y.
December, 1958

PREFACE TO THE FIFTH PRINTING

THE first edition of this book was published in 1959. A second printing became necessary in 1960, and a third and fourth in 1963 and 1966. By that time foreign-language editions had appeared in German, Spanish, and Portuguese.

In this fifth printing nothing has been omitted or abridged; rather, the present edition renders the complete text with its entire apparatus of notes, appendices, and indices. A new "Supplementary Notes on Literature" section has been added, listing selected recent publications as well as a few older references.

Apart from minor corrections, no changes in the text have been made. Abstention from major alterations was justified by the fact that from the outset the book had been planned to give the fairest possible account and analysis of the numerous divergent views on the problems discussed in the four parts of the book: *systematic, genetic, polemic,* and *at the borderline of metaphysics.*

The strong and wide acclaim that the book has received, and continues to draw, is naturally most gratifying to the author; it confirms his own impression that there had been a disturbing gap in our political–philosophical–scientific literature that needed filling. Of course, amidst the lavish praise, occasional reservations have not been absent. But these reservations have rarely done more than present variations of alternative opinions already extensively discussed here, and therefore have necessitated no changes in the original text. Neither did any major revisions seem indicated in the light of subsequent publications that have come to my knowledge. On only one book, Michael Polanyi's *Personal Knowledge* (Chicago, 1958), which came out almost simultaneously with mine, shall I insert a few words of comment, because they may serve to clarify one of the basic problems.

Dr. Polanyi reaches the conclusion that not only are value judgments (evaluations) based on personal "belief" or "commitment," but so are other types of knowledge, even scientific knowledge. This thesis is kindred to the views (discussed pp. 266 ff., below) held by John Dewey and Felix Kaufmann, both of whom denied methodological differences between facts and values. The thesis should also be considered in the context of Chapter VII, Section 9, entitled "More, Not Less Relativity Contended" (p. 298). If the thesis were entirely true, and if, moreover, the purely personal elements within the process of acquiring knowledge, even scientific knowledge, were equally significant in every area (which Polanyi did not say), then the attempts made here to distinguish between knowledge scientifically transmissible *qua* knowledge and (alleged) knowledge not so transmissible (or to distinguish at least degrees of scientific transmissibility) would be futile.

No doubt, in a sense all knowledge is personal. It is "someone's" knowledge. What else could it be? "Truth" in one sense of the term may be nonpersonal, objective, universal, and even eternal (see pp. 49 ff.). But "knowledge" is necessarily personal unless we use the term in a broad sense with vague boundaries—such as "common" or "collective" knowledge, knowledge by "inherited instinct," "advanced" knowledge, or even "objectivated" knowledge (the knowledge historically accumulated or packed in encyclopedias or textbooks, ready to be had for the asking).

The personal nature of even scientific knowledge in the area of facts is particularly striking in the category of decisions which I have treated here under the generic name of "decisions to accept"—namely, the decisions to accept observations as sufficiently exact, or descriptions as sufficiently precise, or results of observations as actual facts ("reality"), or hypotheses of causal interrelations as valid (see pp. 28, 32 ff., 38 ff., 48 ff., 80 ff., 280, 469). Significantly, it is from this category that most of Polanyi's illustrations are taken.

However, shifting the emphasis on the personal element in such decisions to the nondifferentiated emphasis on the purely personal character of all knowledge tends to neglect or obfuscate the difference that obviously exists between the scientific decision to accept the *adequacy* of supporting data offered and the knowledge of the supporting data *themselves* (that is, of the "evidence")—data which generally can be freely transmitted *qua* knowledge even where their adequacy is in doubt, as can the reasoning about the significance of the data (see pp. 113-114).

Nondifferentiated emphasis on the personal element, furthermore, fails to take into account not only the *quantitative* but the *qualitative* difference that distinguishes the degree of nontransmissibility of knowledge in the area of moral values from that in the area of facts. In the former area, scientific transmission of alleged knowledge *qua* knowledge to persons committed to other values fails far earlier than it does in the latter area, or, indeed, fails altogether (see pp. 193 f. and 268 f., below).

Even so, science need not abdicate in the area of values, as this book should make abundantly clear. The factual assumptions on which evaluations are based (such as the alleged poisonous nature of a thing), the biological and psychological factors accounting for subjective differences in evaluation (as in racial controversies), and the consequences and risks to which the pursuit of cherished values or their neglect is bound to lead, lend themselves to intersubjectively transmissible examinations. Full exploitation of these approaches can do much to reduce the ideological cleavage between the fighting schools of thought in the social sciences (see pp. 121 ff., and 568 f.).

It is with great regret that I have to admit my failure thus far to present a systematically arranged second volume devoted to special problems as adumbrated on pages 22 and 23. Its completion has fallen victim to my resolve to give priority to another project: deposition of my testimony, scientifically embroidered, as a participant–observer in a most consequential period of human history. Meanwhile, Deutsche Verlags-Anstalt, Stuttgart, has published in German two volumes of about five hundred pages each: *Aus nächster Nähe, Lebenserinnerungen, 1884-1927* (1966) and *Mit der Kraft des Geistes, Lebenserinnerungen zweite Hälfte, 1927-1967* (1967). This work, although frankly autobiographical, examines a great deal of what I would discuss in the special theoretical volume regarding the rival forms of government, the topic that was to constitute its first part. My article "Political Theory" in the forthcoming *International Encyclopedia of the Social Sciences* expands the implications of the ideas here developed for the scientific treatment of special problems and provides a somewhat more detailed outline.

A. B.

New York, N.Y.
May, 1967

ACKNOWLEDGMENTS

Teamwork has been the key to great achievements in the social sciences. But it is no panacea fit to serve all needs. The integrating aims I had set myself could not well be satisfied but, rather, were certain to be missed, by cooperative efforts. Hence the writing of this book had to be and has been a one-man job.

In the last, the editorial, stage I have received valuable help, though, which I wish to acknowledge here. Mrs. Jane Haydu typed the final copy of the main text, and Mrs. Gertrude Lederer that of the complicated Appendix B, both working with equal care and understanding. A carbon went to Miss Janet Rosenwald, formerly an editor in the Research Division of the New School and now of Santa Fe, N.M., to check on my use of English grammar and style, a precaution which I have reason not entirely to omit. She did not find much to object to, fortunately. Still, with a sure hand, she proposed the change of a word or of its position here or there, always to the advantage of form, clarity, or idiomatic expression. Numerous pages were added later that she did not see. Miss Elizabeth Todd, managing editor of *Social Research,* who had done such reviewing with many of my earlier articles when that was a harder job to do, graciously read the introductory chapter. Miss R. Miriam Brokaw, managing editor of Princeton University Press, put the final editorial touches on the book, patiently accepting late alterations and additions. Mrs. Lederer took care of the index of names and assisted me in compiling the subject index. To all of them I present my cordial thanks.

As regards the free use I have made of ideas and formulations that originally were incorporated in some of my scattered earlier articles, I duly acknowledge my sincere gratitude to the *Harvard Law Review Association* and to the editors of *Social Research, American Political Science Review,* and *California Law Review* for the permission granted me to do so. The articles are cited in Appendix B, notes to Chapter VII. The permission included the use of passages from my reviews of books by Jacques Maritain, in *American Political Science Review,* vol. 35 (1941) p. 545, and by Eric Voegelin, in *Social Research,* vol. 20 (1953) p. 230.

I am likewise indebted to several publishers for permission given me to quote excerpts of some length from works of other authors, as indicated hereafter:

Harvard Law Review Association: Oliver W. Holmes, "Natural

Law," *Harvard Law Review,* vol. 40 (1918) pp. 32 ff. Copyright 1918, Harvard Law Review Association.

The Macmillan Company, New York: Alfred N. Whitehead, *Science and the Modern World.* Copyright 1925, The Macmillan Company.

Oxford University Press: Felix Kaufmann, *Methodology of the Social Sciences.* Copyright 1944, Oxford University Press.

The Free Press, Glencoe, Ill.: Max Weber, *Methodology of the Social Sciences,* translated by Edward A. Shils and Henry A. Finch. Copyright 1949, The Free Press.

The Beacon Press, Boston, Mass.: John Dewey and Arthur F. Bentley, *Knowing and the Known.* Copyright 1949, The Beacon Press.

University of Chicago Press: Leonard D. White, ed., *The State of the Social Sciences.* Copyright 1956, University of Chicago Press.

The estate of the late Professor Ralph B. Perry permitted quotations from his book, *The Thought and Character of William James,* published 1935 by Little, Brown & Co., Boston, Mass. (briefer version, 1948, Harvard University Press); the editors of the *Journal of Philosophy,* from an article by Alfred Schutz, published in vol. 51 (1954), pp. 257 ff., under the title "Concept and Theory Formation in the Social Sciences." The quotation on p. 275 from the *Collected Plays* of William Butler Yeats, New York 1939, was authorized by The Macmillan Company.

I have quoted extensively also from several German texts. Although scientific quotations of this character do not require special permission under German law, I would like to express my gratitude to the authors or their heirs and to the publishers.

CONTENTS

POLITICAL THEORY

INTRODUCTORY

1. Political Theory about 1900

I F today, rapidly advancing into the second half of the twentieth century, we try to recapture some of the characteristic traits that distinguished nineteenth-century political theory (or "theory of the state" as it was then generally called) from our own, we naturally become aware of a great variety of problems examined and approaches used in either period. All major contributions, however, up to the beginning of our century had one feature in common that is less frequently encountered in typical scientific writings thereafter. They focused attention on questions such as these: What are the ends of state and government? What are the proper means toward these ends? and, above all, What is the best form of government?

In asking and answering questions of this kind—and scholars would feel it their professional duty to answer them—pronouncements were freely advanced on good and evil, just and unjust, morally right and wrong, worthy and unworthy (detestable or wicked), laudable and reprimandable, desirable and undesirable, valuable and nonvaluable. In support, the writers would refer to a number of "first principles," derived in various ways—sometimes from religion, sometimes from nature, sometimes from philosophical speculations, sometimes forwarded as self-evident postulates, sometimes distilled from the history of political ideas, sometimes based on the historical evolution of Western civilization, and not infrequently taken, directly or indirectly, from the positive law, in particular the constitution, of the respective country or countries.

Among the sources of such principles, Christianity and the Law of Nature played an especially important role. They continued to do so in political science at a time when other branches of the sciences had learned to distinguish more carefully between scientific and religious sources, and when Natural-Law doctrines had been all but crushed under the blows suffered at the hands of critical philosophers, utilitarians, historians, and positivists.

As a result, publications in the field of political theory up to the turn of the century, if not beyond it, included many statements, meant to be scientific, as to what were the proper ends and means of organized human life; for example, states and governments ought to serve the interests of the individuals or of the greatest number of them; all men should be treated as equal *because* they were born equal; everyone

3

should fulfill some useful function in society; the Ten Commandments should be obeyed; states properly so called must be sovereign; and many more maxims of this kind. While some of them recurred in all writings, others came out differently according to the particular theories of the author. The doctrine that state and government should serve the individual would frequently cede to the older maxim that the interests of the individual must be subordinated to those of the group. The Ten Commandments were ignored by some, or were considered principles that on occasion had to yield in some measure to the interests of the state, the *raison d'état;* although not all writers said so explicitly, many did implicitly.

Even when scholars were seemingly agreed on the principles, they often meant different things by them. Thus all were sure to enumerate justice, security, order, and the general welfare among the proper ends of state and government, and many would add freedom and equality. But they would interpret these ideals in various, often highly contradictory, ways, from the most conservative to the most revolutionary meaning.

The important point here is not that these questions were being raised and discussed in political writings. They are today and will always be. The point is that up to the end of the nineteenth century writers in the field of political theory, or the theory of the state, would present their answers as *scientific* contributions on the same level as other scientific contributions which they felt able to render.

2. *Triumph and Tragedy of Twentieth-Century Political Theory*

Around the beginning of the twentieth century, however, methodological scruples began to interfere with this kind of argument. Scholars became more generally aware of limitations in the nature of science. The principal tools of science *qua* science, they found, were observation of facts, measurement, and logical reasoning. Anything that could not be done with such tools should not be presented under the pretense of being scientific but be frankly put forward as the personal opinion of the writer, or as a piece taken out of a religious creed, or as a tentative assumption, or the like.

Although there remained ample room for debate on which tools were scientific and which were not, what their proper use was, and how they could be refined and supplemented or superseded by better methods, a marked trend toward methodological awareness has been notable during the last fifty or sixty years. It is not saying too much that ours has become the methodological century in the social sciences.

This trend has proved to be of incalculable benefit in some respects, but to imply grave drawbacks in others. The benefits were many. Instead of indulging in the establishment of first principles a priori, the validity of which was not proven but from which detailed postulates had nevertheless been derived, twentieth-century political science gradually came to focus research on actualities, that is, on the disclosure of facts and of their interrelations, basing its findings on painstaking observation and measurement, especially on a rapidly growing stock of pertinent statistics. No greater revolution has ever taken place in the routine work of scholars in the social sciences.

Scientific books as well as articles in scientific journals began to be filled with examinations about the conditions of life as they actually were, in industry, commerce and agriculture, in large cities, small towns, and in the country—employment and unemployment, wages and hours, housing and food, slums and crime, wealth and misery, growth and decay, competition and corruption, etc. They tried to find out how government actually worked in all its branches and on all levels; how governmental offices were manned, what the background of men and women in public office was, what their interests and their expectations were; how parties were run, campaigns financed, elections manipulated, pressure groups organized, influence exercised; how conditions and institutions at home compared with those abroad; what the net effect of governmental efforts was and what the waste; and sometimes also, what alternatives there were for what was being done or planned.

Actualities were found to differ greatly from what had been postulated under the old maxims. In generalizing observed facts or explaining them no more than tentative hypotheses were scientifically accepted, ever subject to tests by further observations. The trend thus was away from "dogma"—from religious dogma as well as from dogmas of national tradition or of personal conviction—and on to "reality." Many facts were revealed that had not been brought to public consciousness before, either at all or in full measure. By the mere weight of such disclosures often the foundation was being laid for practical reforms. Unprecedented progress ensued in many fields, especially in those of social welfare in the broadest sense of the term.

At the same time, however, the new insistence on scientific methods had a negative effect of tremendous bearing. As now understood, such

5

methods did not enable a scientist to determine the superiority of any ends or purposes over any other ends or purposes in "absolute" terms. He could only examine their "relative" superiority as means in the pursuit of other, ulterior or ultimate, purposes or ends. Which of several antagonistic ultimate purposes or ends were superior to the others appeared to be beyond the scope of scientific determination. Therefore, what occurred was more than a mere shift in emphasis of scholarly work; the new methods if strictly observed compelled scientists to withdraw *completely* from all statements that expressed evaluations and preferences in absolute terms and thus from all those questions that had played a dominant role in former writings—the "best" form, the "proper" ends and means of government, right and wrong, good and evil, just and unjust.

Such topics, therefore, gradually disappeared from typical scientific essays. Unable to make scientific statements concerning them, conscientious scientists felt they had only the choice of either abstaining from offering such statements or forwarding them as merely personal opinions or at best as philosophical "speculations." Scientifically, they could build their analysis or research on some "assumption" of goals or values; but in this case one assumption was scientifically as good as the other, even though practical purposes or environment might induce the scholar to accept one rather than the other as a working hypothesis. Thus "Scientific Method" led automatically, at the beginning of the twentieth century, to "Scientific Value Relativism." The two were necessarily tied together; they were two aspects of the same approach to science. (See Chapters III and IV on the theoretical problem, and Chapter VI on the historical genesis.)

The rapid increase in descriptive and analytical scholarly contributions soon brought the good effects of modern scientific methods to general recognition. Their negative implications, however, i.e., withdrawal from value judgments and consequently the emergence of Scientific Value Relativism, were hardly noticed outside the academic world during the first two decades of this century. If observed at all, relativism was ridiculed as an ivory-tower product of no practical significance.

This lack of attention was chiefly due to the historical coincidence that around 1900 a broad practical agreement on basic values and principles still prevailed in Western civilization. This agreement, which seemed to be ever expanding, included such important political principles as: that government should be based on respect for the dignity of man and on freedom of conscience; that there should be independent judges, equality before the law, no slaves, no torture, no cruel punishment; that the principles of habeas corpus should give every arrested person the right to be heard by a judge who could, if detention was not warranted under the law, free him with or without bail; and that science, art, and press must go uncensored. The doctrine that government should serve the greatest happiness of the greatest number, too, was generally accepted. What did it matter, then, that science did not consider itself competent to buttress any of these basic principles, generally recognized as they were?

There happened once more what had happened so often before in the history of science—a chronological gap appeared between theory and practice. Theory was twenty years ahead of the practical consequences implied in it. The withdrawal of science from ethical value judgments on purposes and means had established a *scientific void*. While for some time this vacuum was filled by practical agreement, such agreement was no longer scientifically necessary; it could no longer be defended by science. Yet only after the First World War did this fact dawn upon the amazed world.

At that time all the agreed-upon principles mentioned above were being abandoned one by one, first by Communism (Bolshevism), next by Fascism, then by National Socialism. All three proclaimed that no respect for individual persons should hinder the government from doing what it considered good for the group—the group meaning, to Communism, the toiling masses; to Fascism, the state; and to National Socialism, the German *Volk*. No freedom of conscience, no independence of judges, no equality before the law, no principle of habeas corpus, no freedom of art, of science, and of the press were to be tolerated in opposition to official policy. Even torture, enslavement, cruel punishment, and outright "liquidation" were proper means to enforce government purposes in the service of ends thought to be beneficial to the group. Only one item in their creeds all three seemed still to have in common with Western democracy—that government should serve the greatest happiness of the greatest number, or at least of the greatest number within the respective country. But Communism, Fascism, and National Socialism accepted this standard only in the sense that their dictatorial governments were to decide what the greatest happiness was and which minorities were to be excluded—the capitalists, the liberals, the Jews, etc. Agreement on the essence of the principle had broken down.

There was no doubt, of course, among the apostles of scientific method and scientific relativism that none of the totalitarian doctrines, including Marxism, had scientific proof for its own validity (See Chapter v). Yet under the severe standards of twentieth-century science none of them seemed to be subject to scientific disproof either, because admittedly science could not verify ultimate principles of right and wrong, of just and unjust. It appeared, therefore, that science was unable to defend Western civilization by reference to fundamental principles. Scholars could state what the necessary implications and probable consequences were of totalitarian value systems when practically applied by the government and supported with all its powers. They could possibly predict also that cruel means of repression used against opponents would not lead people to the happiness they had been promised. Better use could have been made of these legitimate weapons than was actually done (see Chapter xii). Yet even so, science as now understood was not in a position to state in absolute terms, i.e., without reference to a specific value system, that the new creeds were to be condemned because they were "immoral," "unjust," and "evil."

Its inability morally to condemn Bolshevism, Fascism, or National Socialism in unconditional terms was to become the tragedy of twentieth-century political science, a tragedy as deep as any that had ever occurred before in the history of science. The personal fate of a considerable number of modern scholars who had been foremost in advancing scientific methods and relativism illustrates the dilemma. Paradoxically, they were among the first victims of all three totalitarian regimes, although their teachings had weakened the defense against totalitarianism in a world that had come to rely on science. Yet while feeling unable to disprove totalitarian value judgments with scientific means, relativists equally refused to support these doctrines. And so they had to go.

Under the impact of totalitarian experiences new methodological controversies flared up (see Chapters vii and viii). Yet they were not able to overcome the tragic rift. Five years after Hitler's ascendancy to power in Germany, the senior of the American philosophers, John Dewey, still wrote: "Approach to human problems in terms of moral blame and moral approbation, of wickedness or righteousness, is probably the greatest single obstacle now existing to development of competent methods in the field of social subject-matter."[1] Professor Hans Kelsen, Austrian-born refugee from Germany, where he had held the chair of public law at Cologne University, after his arrival in the United

[1] John Dewey, *Logic, The Theory of Inquiry*, New York 1938, p. 495.

8

States made it clear that he was "still a relativist."[2] Albert Einstein, creator of relativism in physics, but deeply religious and he, too, a refugee from National Socialism, wrote in 1940, "If someone approves, as a goal, the extirpation of the human race from the earth, one cannot refute such a viewpoint on rational grounds."[3]

3. Popular Confusion about the Nature of the Crisis

When asked what he regards as the crisis of scientific theory in the field of politics within the twentieth century the average student is likely to point to the antithesis between democracy and totalitarianism. This answer would be quite correct if, at the time when the totalitarian doctrines arose, Western scientific theory had supported the democratic value system to the exclusion of others. Actually, however, as has just been intimated and will be brought out in more detail in Chapter vi, this was no longer the case. While most scholars who lived under constitutionally limited forms of government were most happy to do so, the superiority of the ultimate democratic values over contradictory standards was no longer supported by them *qua* scientists, and could not be under the rules of scientific method as now understood. The democratic system of values like all others had become, scientifically speaking, merely a "dogma," an "ideology," or—as Professor MacIver called it in a book crowned with a prize by the American Political Science Association[1]—a "myth." Whoever claimed *scientific* authority for his value system—even for democracy—was scientifically *in error*. Support for value systems as such was considered beyond the reach of science; critique was permitted only in the form of statements on the system's predictable consequences or on its logical inconsistencies, if any.

The real crisis in Western *scientific theory,* therefore, is not to be sought in the emergence of different ideologies, but in what preceded this event by about two decades—the rise of the theoretical opinion that no scientific choice between ultimate values can be made. That this withdrawal remained unnoticed by the general public when it began in a period of a far-reaching practical agreement on ultimate values and of

[2] See Arnold Brecht, "Beyond Relativism in Political Theory," report on a round-table, *American Political Science Review,* vol. 41 (1947) p. 471, note 2 (letter to the chairman), and Kelsen's later publications, as quoted in Chapter vi below.

[3] Albert Einstein, "Freedom and Science," in Ruth Anshen, ed., *Freedom, Its Meaning,* New York 1940, p. 382.

[1] *The Web of Government,* New York 1947, especially pp. 39 and 51, where the term "myth" is explicitly used for the democratic value system also. See Chapter vi, Section 5, below.

economic prosperity, and that only the ensuing crisis in practice became a matter of universal consciousness when it followed many years later in a period when both harmony of ideas and economic prosperity had collapsed—all this is theoretically irrelevant. Even the fact that new systems of government, based on violence, were actually being established did not by itself indicate a crisis in scientific theory; had theory still offered absolute standards under which the different policies could be critically judged, there would have been just another clash in practical politics. But at the time when the battle was joined, scientific theory had ceased to offer such standards, and the older theories had become suspect as not being scientific. *This* constituted the real crisis in theory, as distinct from the crisis in practice.

4. *Professional Escapes*

What, then, was the reaction of professional social scientists when the crisis in theory revealed itself in its full magnitude? As the totalitarian governments smashed everything within reach that had been dear to democratic traditions, the temptation was great indeed, and was widely succumbed to by teachers of the social sciences, simply to deride scientific relativism and to brand it as a kind of obvious absurdity (see Chapter vii, Section 1). Derision, however, is no scientific argument. If justified, it must be possible to explain in scientific terms what the error was and how the methodological difficulties that had led to it could be overcome.

The "revolters" can be roughly divided into two groups—those who have tried to get around scientific relativism without refuting it, and those who have attempted to refute it. In these introductory remarks I am dealing only with the first group, by far the larger one; the second will be treated in the main body of this book (Chapters vii ff.).

There are at least ten typical routes of escape within the first category. Some are legitimate as long as they are not used to divert attention from the real problem, but none contributes to its solution. I shall enumerate them briefly, adding references to later chapters where that may be helpful.

The most usual behavior is to ignore the problem. This, if I may insert a value judgment here as a short-hand characterization (see Chapter vii, Section 1), is unworthy of a scholar. Or, to speak without a value judgment, it fails to solve the problem and it veils its very existence.

Some have taken refuge in religion. This is by no means unworthy of a scholar (see Chapters VII, Section 4, and XIII), provided he does not present his personal convictions as science. Yet in referring to religion we acknowledge our impotence to solve the problem by science.

A third group resorts to "assumptions." Well aware of the methodological problem, they avail themselves of the permission granted by scientific method to "assume" the eminence of values which they actually hold in highest esteem, as a "working hypothesis," or to assume the pursuit of these values as a political fact, actually given at a certain place and time. Then they proceed in line with scientific requirements to examine how these values can be materialized. A prominent illustration is offered by the late Charles Merriam who, in 1938, published a celebrated article on the "Assumptions of Democracy,"[1] and proceeded on the basis of his pronounced assumptions in this and other works (see Chapter VI, Section 5). This is perfectly legitimate as long as the assumptions are stated as such, as they generally were by Merriam. Yet it fails in controversies with adherents of different assumptions; the crisis in theory remains unresolved and raises its head as soon as the debate shifts to the assumptions.

In the neighborhood of this category runs the escape route of, fourth, those who refer to "general agreement." There are two weaknesses in this approach. Agreement does not necessarily prove the validity of a theory; human history is to a considerable extent a history of erroneous agreements.[2] At any rate, reference to agreement does not help us where there is no agreement, that is, in controversies with dissenters.

Others (fifth) refer to their country's constitution or traditions or to the historical traditions of Western civilization. Within this area they are able to engage in many scientifically unimpeachable examinations and to make many scientifically correct statements, some of great importance otherwise but none that would present a relevant argument in the debate with adherents of different principles.

The sixth group includes many of our finest scholars. They seek their asylum in the history of political ideas. Research upon research can be done, and statement can be piled upon statement, on what Plato,

---

[1] *Political Science Quarterly*, vol. 53 (1938) p. 328. See also the remarks by Benjamin E. Lippincott at the Round-Table "Beyond Relativism in Political Theory"; my report in *American Political Science Review*, vol. 41 (1947) p. 479.

[2] "A proposition does not gain validity because of the number of persons who accept it," John Dewey, *Logic*, p. 490, n. 4. "The general intellectual atmosphere of the time is always determined by the views on which the opposing scholars agree," F. A. Hayek, *The Counter-Revolution of Science*, Glencoe, 1954, p. 191. "Each generation criticizes the unconscious assumptions made by its parents," A. N. Whitehead, *Science and the Modern World*, New York 1925, p. 36. See also below, Chapters I, Section 7 (acceptance) and VI, Section 3 (Max Weber).

Aristotle, St. Thomas, Locke, Rousseau, Kant, Hegel, and a hundred others of the great philosophers have thought about values and about what science can do regarding them. There is no end of delight for the scholar, and no end of discovery or rediscovery of deep observations, penetrating arguments, appealing speculations. No relativity need tune down our statements about what others said and what their theories were. Yet what we are then dealing with is *history*—history of ideas, and history of science; it is not science unless we accept their ideas as still scientifically valid today; and if we do so, it is our responsibility to say how through the old ideas, and through which of them, the present crisis in theory can be overcome. Otherwise we merely ignore the problem in a particularly sophisticated manner.[3]

To many others (seventh group) the solution is very simple. It is a democratic principle, they say, that on all political controversies the majority must decide after free discussion through free elections; hence it is also up to the majority to decide on controversial values. Living in the westernmost part of the Western world, we may be sold body and soul on this principle; but we should be able to see that it does not tell the majority which values to prefer, and even less does it help us in a debate with people who reject the principle that majorities should have the final say on all values or on some. Free elections and decision by the majority are among the most successful devices ever invented to prevent a crisis in theory from becoming one in practice. Yet they do not resolve the former or necessarily prevent the latter. All three, Russia (Kerenski), Italy, and Germany, had been governed democratically before the totalitarian regimes there arose, and so had Spain. Ancient Athens, too, was a democracy before her fall.

Others again (eighth) have chosen to escape into the fields of biology, psychology, and psychoanalysis. Instead of asking which evaluations are valid they examine how people came to their evaluations, beginning from inheritance and childhood impressions and repressions, and leading up to the influences exercised by advertising, propaganda, and other mass manipulations. This is in itself an entirely legitimate scientific endeavor, of course, and one of great importance too. Science has made particularly large strides in this area during the twentieth century.[4] But whenever this approach is used to veil the limitations that

[3] See on this point Andrew Hacker's witty attack on the wrong use made of the so-called "Great Books," in his article "Capital and Carbuncles: The Great Books Reappraised," *American Political Science Review*, vol. 48 (1954) pp. 775 ff.

[4] See Harold D. Lasswell's report in UNESCO, *Contemporary Political Science* (Paris 1950, pp. 526 ff.) and Gabriel A. Almond's remarks at the Round-Table "Beyond Relativism in Politi-

hamper science in its attempts to establish the *validity* of value judgments, it is detrimental to theory, and merely amounts to another refined form of ignoring the crisis. So many people, even of scholarly reputation, have succumbed to this confusion between a theory's origin or genesis and its validity that I may insert here two drastic illustrations as an antidote. In a doctoral examination, the candidate had given the name of Lenin among ten political philosophers on whom he proposed to be examined. When I asked him, "Why did Lenin think it impossible to carry through socialism with democratic means in the Western sense, that is, by free elections and majority decisions?" he answered that what had made Lenin think in terms of dictatorship was the fact that his brother had been hanged by the Czar; this event warped his thinking in the direction of radicalism. When I tried to induce the candidate to distinguish between the psychological genesis of Lenin's theory and its content and validity, he repeated his answer with increasing emphasis. But, then, *is* it possible to carry through socialism with purely democratic means, or not? (See Chapter xii below.) The other illustration is fictitious. Suppose a young astronomer publishes a theory according to which there must be a star at some place indicated by him. It may be fully in accordance with truth when you say that he went in for astronomy only because he loved a girl who did not like businessmen but wanted a husband with more lofty interests. But this biographical contribution does not refute his theory. What about that star? Is it there, or not? You do not refute a man's theory by telling me stories about his nurse, or his father, or his girl. It is as elementary as that; still, this type of argument crops up time and again in scientific writings, and even more so in teaching.[5]

Then there is the large (ninth) group of those who refer for knowledge of values to "intuition." In our context this amounts to an escape unless the scholar either admits the impossibility of demonstrating the validity of one intuition over against the other—then it does not help us resolve the crisis in theory, but keeps us at least aware of it—or shows how that demonstration can be effected. Much more will be said of this approach later on (see Chapters ii, Section 5, and vii, viii).

Finally (tenth), there remains the most popular escape: "from theory to practice." There can be no quarrel with it if it means only that we

---

cal Theory" (*op.cit.*, pp. 482–83). Almond did not use this as an escape from the basic problem, though; see *ibid.*, p. 474. Regarding Lasswell, see below, Chapter vi and Appendix b.

[5] Other illustrations: Marx's carbuncles made him vitriolic, Rousseau's constricted bladder made him less coherent, Machiavelli's bad temper explains *The Prince* (Hacker, *op.cit.*, p. 777). See also Chapter viii, Section 6, below on Julian Huxley's *Evolutionary Ethics*.

should not lose valuable time on theoretical squabbles when we have urgent practical goals before us on which we are agreed and in the pursuit of which we can use available knowledge to good effect. But even then we are applying theory. Practice, unless it starts helplessly from scratch, is applied theory. Just as the building of a bridge or of an atomic pile is applied mathematics and physics, so is any act of government applied political theory, although the theory, instead of being well prepared in advance, is often rather clumsily being formed while we are going ahead. The better our theory, the better it is for our practice (see Section 6 below). The decisive objection, however, is another one. Practice presupposes a goal but does not tell us which goal to choose—building bridges, constructing atom bombs, effecting more equality rather than preserving liberty, or vice versa, etc. It does not, therefore, resolve the crisis in theory regarding goals.

Many illustrations of all these types of escape could be given, and some will be found in subsequent chapters. The crucial test is always reached when we leave the area of agreement among persons with similar convictions and proceed to an actual or anticipated debate with persons who in good faith cling to different convictions. What scientific argument is left us in such controversies? No complacent restatement of our own convictions among people with similar persuasions is—whatever else it may be—a contribution to political theory.

5. *Philosophy, Science, and Theory*

The twentieth-century use of the terms "philosophy," "science," and "theory" is not definitely settled. It could not be, precisely because the interrelation between philosophy, science, and theory is one of the fundamental problems in the present crisis of scientific thinking.

This is not to say that there is complete disagreement about the use of the three terms. In several respects there is no argument about it. Thus, "theory" is always used to designate attempts to "explain" phenomena, especially when that is done in general and abstract terms (see Appendix B). It is quite usual also to admit that theory may be "scientific" or "nonscientific" according to whether or not scientific rules are followed. What these rules are is highly controversial, but it is not controversial that there is a difference between scientific and nonscientific theorizing.

In explaining phenomena a theory may refer to some general "law," in the sense of "regularity," or to several such laws. These laws may have been discovered earlier, the theory merely referring to them as known; or the theory may consist of the suggestion that some previously hidden general law explains the respective event. In the latter case, the suggested law may need further corroboration, of course. New theories often combine references to long-established laws with the suggestion of some additional law.

Therefore, a "theory" is never a "law"; it *refers* to laws and may suggest the existence of additional laws, but it is not itself a law. It may try to "explain" a law, of course; but if that is the intention the theory must refer to some more general law. Exactly speaking, a law can never be deduced directly from a theory; it can be deduced only from a more general law offered in a theory.[1]

Conversely, a "law" is not a "theory"; it is, rather, a "fact," namely, the fact that certain constituent facts or factors are always associated or, in a less strict sense of the term "law," that they are associated "as a rule" or "generally." In again another sense, to be considered later, the term may be meant to refer to a legal, moral, aesthetic, or procedural "norm."

Just as there is general agreement that not all theory is necessarily scientific, so there is agreement that not everything scientific is necessarily theoretic. Observation and description of facts, important steps in science, are not theory, since they do not explain facts. Even when carried on under some definite theory about the manner in which they should be handled in order to lead to scientifically useful results, they do not in themselves constitute theory. Whether every statement of facts can be called "science" is questionable; yet whenever factual research is done with the intent of contributing to our knowledge of the universe, it may be "scientific" in character without being "theoretic." This, too, is not controversial.

As regards philosophy, there is agreement that it deals with ideas about world, men, and God, and also that the term has had many different meanings in the history of ideas. Originally its meaning was all-inclusive and coextensive with that of science. From its classical beginnings, however, the term philosophy implied a universalistic reference. Every theory, as we have said, tries to explain something. Philosophy tries to explain, not *some*thing but *every*thing—the universe, the macrocosmos and the microcosmos. It examines not only what

---

[1] Norman Campbell, *What Is Science?* 1921, Dover Publ., New York 1952, pp. 89, 91, formulates incorrectly when he says that every theory must be such "that the laws which it is devised to explain can be deduced from it." The words "from it" should read: "from the laws which it suggests."

is but also what *ought to be,* or ought to be done, or to be approved. It is not limited to the physical world but entitled and even supposed to meditate also about metaphysical questions. Nor is it limited by the rules of preestablished scientific procedure, or by the requirements of exact proof, but it is entitled and even supposed to engage in speculation beyond the reach of observational tests. All this has remained the generally accepted meaning of the term.

This is not to say, on the other hand, that philosophy deals *only* in speculations. Inquiries into the possibility, the conditions, and the limitations of knowledge have been considered part of philosophy at all times. More especially, the most exacting scientific disciplines of logic and methodology have always been regarded as its legitimate subjects.

There is, finally, agreement that philosophy, insofar as it tries to explain phenomena, is theory, and insofar as it applies scientific methods is science. The trouble begins when it is asked whether everything that philosophy does is science, and every theory it produces is scientific theory. Originally the three terms were used interchangeably. Today they are no longer, at least not by the majority of twentieth-century scholars.

The decisive change did not occur in the meaning of either theory or philosophy but in that of science, which in the course of time became ever more exacting. The details of this development are the topic of the first two chapters of this book. Here it may suffice to note that the more exacting the demands for precision and control grew in science, the more did it become necessary to distinguish between science and philosophy. Philosophy could, of course, continue to remain perfectly scientific in the limited sense that its speculations did not conflict with the results of science, that all its reasoning proceeded logically, that inconsistencies were avoided, that in support of the argument observations were referred to, and so forth. Yet it could no longer stay *only* scientific without giving itself up, so it seemed. To live on it must go beyond what today we call science.[2]

This entire development, it is true, led to two antagonistic cross-currents of thought. Some scholars, like Edmund Husserl, tried to

---

[2] It was in line with such ideas when, for instance, W. Ernest Hocking in his remarkable book, *Science and the Idea of God,* Chapel Hill 1944, p. 4, recommended a "jurisdictional agreement. Science withdraws from making assertions about the whole of things, admits that its knowledge does not reach the whole, adding in parentheses a doubt whether 'the whole' is a knowable object. Religion (together with philosophy) responds that it is just the whole of things which is—if I may put it that way—its special province . . ."

make philosophy more fully "scientific" (see Chapter ix, Section 6). Others, like Maritain and Voegelin, proposed to do the opposite, namely, liberate science from its narrow rules and make it "philosophic" once more, so as to include metaphysics (see Chapter vii, Section 3). Both of these movements, however, run clearly counter to the use of the terms philosophy and science as it prevailed in the first half of this century, and continues to do.

From what has been said it follows regarding political questions that political philosophy, political theory, and political science are no longer interchangeable terms as they were in the past. Sometimes, as in university curricula, the term political science is still used in a very general sense to cover all three. Yet when used specifically, with the emphasis placed on science and on distinction from philosophy, political science now refers to efforts limited by the use of scientific methods, in contrast to political philosophy, which is free to transcend these limits.

Likewise, political "theory," when opposed to political "philosophy," now is usually meant to refer to *scientific* theory only, in distinction from political philosophy. Any speculative thesis that is proposed by political philosophy can be made part of (scientific) political theory only as a "working hypothesis," an auxiliary tool in the scientific kit, and not—or not yet—as a piece of scientific knowledge (see Chapters ii, Sections 6 and 7, and vii, Section 3).

6. *The Importance of Theory*

To speak of theory contemptuously, or at least ironically, is a habit so widely spread that the brief remarks inserted on this matter in Section 4 call for elaboration.

The relation between practice and theory is well indicated in the popular saying that we learn best through "trial and error." Trial is practice; error refers to theory. When a theory miscarries in practical trials it needs correction, and the proverbial maxim supposes that we do correct it and do not act a second time under the same erroneous theory we had applied before. Frequently we come to think, after our first trial—in the political field, for example, after trying out a new electoral system—that we might well have avoided the error from the outset had we invested a bit more of hard thinking before the trial. In matters of no great consequence trial may facilitate theoretical thinking, and accelerate the attainment of desired results. But where a person's, or a nation's, entire fate is at stake, or where the negotiation of a second trial meets with great practical difficulties—as, for instance, in the case of electoral systems, where, in order to get the erroneous theory corrected, the representatives elected under the first trial must be persuaded to change the system under which they had been elected— there is no justification for the postponement of better thinking until after the trial. The price of "trial and error" may then become too high, and even prohibitive.

It is often believed that theoretical thinking is an ivory-tower affair that flourishes only under luxury conditions and that our political foes care little for theory. Rather the opposite is true. As an illustration it is well worth quoting from Stalin's lectures of 1924 on *The Foundations of Leninism* which, anti-Stalinist proclamations in other spheres notwithstanding, have remained the basic Communist statement on the importance of theory to the present day.[1]

Some think—thus Stalin begins his chapter on Theory—that Leninism signifies the supremacy of practice over theory, in the sense that the chief thing is the translation of Marxist principles into the realm of fact, the "fulfillment" of these principles. "My business here," he continues, "is to show that this view is utterly wrongheaded. It is quite out of touch with the world of reality. The endeavor of 'practical' persons to have no truck with 'theories' runs counter to the whole spirit of Leninism and is a great danger to our cause."

Of course, theory out of touch with revolutionary practice is like a mill that runs without any grist, just as practice gropes in the dark unless revolutionary theory throws light on the path. But theory becomes the greatest force in the working-class movement when it is inseparably linked with revolutionary practice: for it, and *it alone can give the movement confidence, guidance, an understanding of the inner links between events* . . .

He quotes Lenin, who said again and again: "Without a revolutionary theory, there cannot be a revolutionary movement."[2] "Lenin knew better than any one else the immense importance of theory. . . . As far back as 1902, foreseeing the special role of our Party, he thought it necessary to point out that 'Only a party guided by an advanced theory can act as a vanguard in the fight.' "[3]

[1] Reprinted in *House Document* No. 619, 80th Congress, 2nd Session (Report of Subcommittee No. 5 of Committee on Foreign Affairs, "The Strategy and Practice of World Communism") pp. 87 ff. Italics not in the original.
[2] Lenin, *Works*, Russian ed., vol. 5, p. 133.
[3] *Ibid.*, p. 136.

The immense importance attached by Lenin to theory is perhaps best shown by this, that he himself undertook the great task of generalizing . . . the main achievements of science since the days of Engels . . .

Stalin then lashes out against those who think in terms of what he calls the "theory of spontaneity," that action must be left to spontaneous reactions of the people without a preconceived theory. He calls this the theory of opportunism. "It is the theory of those who underestimate the importance of the thinking elements, the theory of those who cling to the tail instead of leading." (The Russian text uses the word *"hvostism,"* i.e. "tailism," instead of the last words.)

In reading this praise of theory, let us make no mistake. Marx and Lenin did believe in their own theories! So, at least to a certain extent, did Stalin; and so did Hitler and Mussolini. If their theories are not correct, scientists must say why, and fight them with better theories. The apocalyptic Armageddon will be, in the first place, a battle of theories.

The dislike many persons feel for theories as "impractical" must be distinguished from an entirely different kind of aversion based on the confusion between scientific theories and mere propagandistic ideologies, in the sense of constructs framed for the purpose of driving the masses in the direction which their leaders wish them to take. It is quite wrong to dismiss all theories of our opponents as ideologies in this sense. Faced with a propagandistic ideology we may ask seriously whether it is effective, but as a rule not whether it is correct. When faced with a scientific theory, however, the first question for science is whether that theory is correct, i.e. scientifically warranted or not. If it is not, the next function of the scientist is to oppose it with a better theory. To meet an incorrect theory with a correct one is a process very different from that of meeting one propaganda with another. We may, of course, entertain some scientific theory about the type of propaganda that will best attain the desired results or will fail in its purpose. Yet the propagandistic ideology as such is not meant to be a scientific theory.

The works of Lenin and Stalin are indeed a blend of scientific theories and propagandistic ideologies. But the fact that much in them is schemed merely to manipulate the masses and to confound enemies should not lead us to overlook the underlying theories that are meant to be scientific and in which the communist leaders themselves do or did believe. While science cannot refute the propagandistic super-structure, only expose it as such, it can refute the underlying scientific theories to the extent that they are invalid.

To illustrate, Leninism rests on two theoretical contentions, both of which are meant to be scientific but are scientifically unwarranted when examined with twentieth-century scientific methods. The one is the old Marxian doctrine that a definite historical course of events is necessary and inescapable, and that it will include—as a consequence of capitalistic exploitation and imperialism—the collapse of economic systems based on free enterprise and their subsequent succession by socialist systems; the other—in its extreme form Lenin's own addition —is that it is impossible to achieve a socialist system and to carry it through, with the means of free elections and parliamentary government. A truly scientific theory will admit that certain dangers are inherent in the system of free enterprise and that its failure in the course of history is "possible" and even "probable" unless effective action is taken to meet these dangers; but will not maintain that its complete elimination in the course of history will necessarily and inescapably occur, as radical Marxism teaches. Again, it is good theory to state that a parliamentary democracy will meet with new problems if it tries to carry through full-fledged socialism with non-totalitarian methods; but not that it is "impossible" to solve them without recourse to totalitarian means, as Lenin teaches. These questions will be discussed more thoroughly in Chapters v, Section 5, and xii.

Conversely, science can predict a number of undesired effects which the espousal of totalitarian value systems and their pursuit with totalitarian means is bound to entail, and also that certain ends envisaged by Communism cannot be reached by totalitarian dictatorship (Chapter xii). Finally, science can construct plans better capable of reaching, or at least approximating, some of the desired effects.

It is the function of the political theorist to see, sooner than others, and to analyze, more profoundly than others, the immediate and the potential problems of the political life of society; to supply the practical politician, well in advance, with alternative courses of action, the foreseeable consequences of which have been fully thought through; and to supply him not only with brilliant asides, but with a solid block of knowledge on which to build.

When political theory performs its function well, it is one of the most important weapons in our struggle for the advance of humanity. To imbue people with correct theories may make them choose their goals and means wisely so as to avoid the roads that end in terrific disappointment. Illustrations of the importance of theory will be multiplied in further chapters.

7. *The Plan of This Book*

If we want fully to utilize the resources and potentialities of science for enlarging our knowledge and deepening our wisdom-of-action in political affairs, and in so doing to overcome the handicaps with which political science like any other branch of the social sciences is saddled by the severe postulates of scientific as distinct from nonscientific approaches, we must first fully understand these postulates, learn to look at them without exaggeration and without emotional blindness, carefully examine the arguments pro and con, resolutely evade escapism in all its forms, and finally weigh what we find on our scientific Pegasus' back, and cannot remove. Legitimate interest in the negative side of the matter should not permit our attention to be diverted from the great positive contributions scientific political theory is able to render to the practical needs of human society.

This volume is divided into four major parts, the first and the last systematic in treatment, the second historic, and the third polemic. Part One, more voluminous than the others, is to lay the cornerstone of the entire enterprise. In a systematic manner it presents, logically intertwined, the theories of Scientific Method (Chapters i and ii), of Scientific Value Relativism (iii) and of Justice (iv). A good deal of what it includes is, or should be, common property today of advanced students in either the social sciences or in philosophy, but rarely is so of students in one of these fields alone. The integration here attempted may, therefore, be welcome not only to beginners. But there is more in these four chapters than information otherwise available and conveniently put together. I hope to have, in each of them, shed new light on some of the fundamental questions there treated. Moreover, as a gratifying reward for the systematic handling extended to the whole area and for the logical consistency in its pursuit, a number of significant results fall into our laps like ripe fruit from a tree in September. New buds too can be seen sprouting forth.

The systematic discussion is interrupted in Part Two, which presents the historical genesis of twentieth-century Scientific Method—and of its offspring, Scientific Value Relativism—in politics and justice, with one chapter (v) to examine precursors in the nineteenth century and parallel movements in the twentieth; the other (vi), the rise and spread of Scientific Value Relativism in Europe and America in this century. This, to my knowledge, is the first comprehensive narrative of what happened, and when, why, and how it happened; I believe it fills a vital need and should do away with many unsubstantiated legends.

Part Three is devoted to critique, and to the critique of critique. It deals with the revolt against scientific abstinence in questions of valuation, one chapter (vii) examining methodological objections, the other (viii) political top values that have been offered as scientifically established by contemporary writers. Here the preceding systematic and historic groundwork leads to concrete results.

Part Four resumes the systematic treatment on a different plane. It reconsiders questions that have generally been discarded in twentieth-century scientific literature as metaphysical or transcendental. Yet it tries to deal with them on a strictly scientific basis. The initial chapter (ix) probes more deeply into the question of factual, as distinct from logical, links between Is and Ought, such as are intimated by alleged voices speaking from without (revelation) or within (conscience). The next (x) pursues the idea that there may be universal and invariant ideas of justice; the following (xi) singles out for separate treatment the interrelation between justice and truth; another (xii) deals with the category of "impossibility," or rather limited possibility; and the last (xiii) is a reminder of the latent alternative with which we are confronted in science no less than in our private lives and political decisions—the existence or nonexistence of God.

In distributing the vast material over the four parts I have not been too pedantic. Thus some of the most practical questions—impossibilities, genuine or imaginary, in the argument between democracy and totalitarianism—are handled within the "metaphysical" part (Chapter xii), because they are closely interwoven with other matters there discussed.

A summary of Results, with concluding reflections, terminates this volume. A sequel, still in its early stages of preparation, is planned to handle specific topics in a more systematic manner than could be done here, where many of them are touched upon (see Subject Index) but merely in the incidental context of general theoretical problems. The follow-up volume's first part, tentatively numbered Part Five to indicate the unity of the whole plan, is to examine the rival forms of government. Part Six is to deal with power, rights, goals, and techniques, including masses, parties and elites, revolution and resistance, equilibrium, order, and general welfare; Part Seven, with government organization, federalism, public administration and bureaucracy; and Part Eight, finally, with sovereignty, international organization, and world government. I shall occasionally refer to the scheduled continuation as "second volume" or "vol. 2."

Pending completion of the second volume—in view of the possibility that completion may not be granted me within my quickly shortening lifespan—I may be permitted to refer in Appendix A to some of my published writings that deal with subjects relegated to the later book. Although some of these publications concern specific areas only, all have been written with a view to the general theoretical and practical problems involved, and have utilized a broad comparative material. And all have followed the methods expounded in the present book.

A few remarks should finally be added on the literature. This volume is not meant to replace a comprehensive bibliography of the social sciences. Some chapters, especially VI and sections of VII and VIII, try to cover all important contributions up to the point where they become repetitious. Others, however, in particular those in the systematic parts, have been purposively limited to a highly selective treatment of literature; generally only a few representative authors have been chosen for a more extensive discussion, and citations have been restricted to writers who originated the ideas and to a few of the most recent contributions. To do more would have interfered with the primary purpose of the book. It would have made it impossible to preserve continuity of presentation and would have delayed completion beyond reason. The fact that some book or article has not been mentioned does not at all indicate, therefore, that I consider it of minor quality, or even that I have not known it—although the latter may have happened, of course, and especially in sections where I deal with questions that have not been in the focus of my own life work. Appendix B supplements the references given in the text, without disturbing the flow of the argument in the main body of the book.

As mentioned in the preface, no major American book, if any, has yet appeared under the title *Political Theory*. Within the entire range of Western literature only two smaller studies that bear this label have come to my knowledge, quite different from mine in scope and design. The one, written by a Britisher, the late Professor Guy C. Field of the University of Bristol, an authority on Plato, starts out from a historical analysis of political theories from Plato to Rousseau and the Utilitarians, and then adds chapters of great democratic acumen commenting on some of the traditional topics (London 1956, 297 pp.). The other, by

23

the Dutch professor of public law at the University of Leiden, R. Kranenburg (tr. by R. Borregaard, London 1939, 268 pp.), is more systematic in structure. Good as the two essays are otherwise, both handle chiefly specific problems of a type here referred to the second volume, where their contributions must be duly discussed. Neither gives more than a few incidental remarks to the foundations of scientific political theory to which this book is primarily devoted. The authors escape from these issues *via* Route One (ignoring them), Three (making moral and political assumptions), Six (history), or Nine (intuition). Within the narrow space of their books they could hardly have acted differently. To do that requires a full-size volume.

PART ONE

SYSTEMATIC

CHAPTER I

THEORY OF SCIENTIFIC METHOD: FACTS AND LOGIC

1. *The Meaning of Scientific Method*

(a) SURVEY OF SCIENTIFIC ACTIONS

THE term "scientific method" can be used in more than one sense. In its broadest meaning it sets off any method that is considered "scientific" from any other that is considered "non-scientific," without indicating what makes it such. When used this way the term designates a problem—the problem of what is scientific—rather than an answer to it.

In its more specific sense, however, the term refers to a definite type of method. Hereinafter, when so used, the words "Scientific Method" will be capitalized. There still remain two alternative possibilities. Scientific Method may be considered the only method that can claim to be scientific, all others being called unscientific; or it may be singled out only because it is well defined and scientific beyond doubt, without the claim that it is necessarily the only scientific method. These alternatives will be taken up at the end of Chapter II.

Universities in English-speaking countries have long dealt with subjects other than the natural sciences under the title of arts ("liberal arts") rather than sciences. Scientific Method, therefore, carries in English some connotation of methods used in the natural sciences, which, for instance, the literally corresponding German term *wissenschaftliche Methode* would not necessarily have. To suggest it one would have to speak of *naturwissenschaftliche Methode* (method of the natural sciences); but then there would be more than a mere connotation or suggestion; it would be explicitly postulated that the method is actually used in the natural sciences, while the English term is broad enough to allow for adaptations and additions appropriate to other subject matter. In other words, the question whether elements not used in the natural sciences may enter Scientific Method in the social sciences is not entirely prejudged by the English term, as it would be by the German *naturwissenschaftliche Methode*.

To begin a book on the foundations of scientific political theory in the twentieth century with a theoretical analysis of Scientific Method is justified not only on the ground that this method has dominated scientific work; it is advisable also for several other reasons. It provides us with a clearly defined model of scientific operations, and with un-ambiguous terms of reference for any basic remarks in later chapters, apt to throw them automatically into sharp relief as being either in line with or in opposition to this model. It supplies an appropriate framework within which fundamental philosophical problems of science can be discussed, each in a setting that indicates the relevance of such examinations. And it offers the welcome opportunity for clarify-ing the meaning of Scientific Method, as understood in this book, re-garding points where clarity is lacking or opinions are not yet unified. But nothing said in this chapter or in the beginning of the next should be considered prejudicial to the question whether there are other, better, or at least supplementary, scientific methods. This question will be thoroughly treated in Chapter II, Section 7, and later on (especially in Chapter VII). The reader is requested to restrain his understandable impatience in this respect, because the issue can be successfully handled only after it has been made clear what is here understood by Scientific Method.

The following brief survey is offered as a convenient introduction to the subsequent, more detailed analysis. Be it noted at once, however, that this summary presentation is subject to several qualifications and modifications, which will be brought out in due course.

In every inquiry—and that means inquiry within the social as well as the natural sciences—Scientific Method concentrates on the follow-ing "scientific actions," "scientific operations," or "steps of scientific procedure:"

1. *Observation* of what can be observed, and tentative acceptance or nonacceptance of the observation as sufficiently exact.

2. *Description* of what has been observed, and tentative acceptance or nonacceptance of the description as correct and adequate.

3. *Measurement* of what can be measured; this being merely a par-ticular type of observation and description, but one sufficiently distinct and important to merit separate listing.

4. *Acceptance* or nonacceptance (tentative) as *facts* or *reality* of the results of observation, description, and measurement.

5. *Inductive generalization* (tentative) of accepted individual facts (No. 4), offered as a "factual hypothesis."

6. *Explanation* (tentative) of accepted individual facts (No. 4), or of inductively reached factual generalizations (No. 5), in terms of re-lations, especially causal relations, offered as a "theoretical hypothesis."

7. *Logical deductive reasoning* from inductively reached factual

generalizations (No. 5) or hypothetical explanations (No. 6), so as to make explicit what is implied in them regarding other possible observations (No. 1), or regarding previously accepted facts (No. 4), factual generalizations (No. 5), and hypothetical explanations (No. 6).

8. *Testing* by further observations (Nos. 1–4) the tentative acceptance of observations, reports, and measurements as properly made (Nos. 1–3), and of their results as facts (No. 4), or tentative expectations as warranted (No. 7).

9. *Correcting* the tentative acceptance of observations, etc., and of their results (Nos. 1–4), of inductive generalizations (No. 5) and hypothetical explanations (No. 6), whenever they are incompatible with other accepted observations, generalizations, or explanations; or correcting the previously accepted contributions.

10. *Predicting* events or conditions to be expected as a consequence of past, present, or future events or conditions, or of any possible constellation of such, in order either

(a) to test factual or theoretical hypotheses (Nos. 5 and 6), this being identical with steps 7 and 8; or

(b) to supply a scientific contribution to the practical process of choosing between several possible alternatives of action.

11. *Nonacceptance* (elimination from acceptable propositions) of all statements not obtained or confirmed in the manner here described, especially of "a-priori" propositions, except when "immanent in Scientific Method" or offered merely as "tentative assumptions" or "working hypotheses" (Chapter II, Sections 5 and 6).

Before we discuss these scientific actions, operations, or steps in detail,[1] several points should be made perfectly clear. In the first place, our enumeration is not meant to express the postulate that Scientific Method proceed exactly in the given order. On the contrary, actual procedure will generally begin with a tentative working hypothesis ventured upon not infrequently on the basis of an as yet most cursory knowledge of facts and used as a trial balloon to guide more systematic research. In the absence of conclusive data, the inquiry may even start out from a purely factual assumption.

We must go even further and recognize that in order to engage in scientific work at all, as distinct from other activities, the investigator

---

[1] F. S. C. Northrop, *The Logic of the Sciences and the Humanities,* New York 1947, p. 18, uses the term "scientific method" for each individual step (observation, description, forming a hypothesis, etc.). Then, of course, "There is no one scientific method" (pp. ix, 19, 107). I follow here the prevalent usage, epitomizing its meaning by capitalization. As regards other scientific methods, see Chapter II, Section 7.

must always begin by forming in his own mind some tentative *ideas* about (1) the objective of his inquiry, i.e. the question for which the answer is sought, (2) the relevance of this question for human knowledge in general, as distinct from a merely private interest of the investigator, and (3) the relevance of the scientific actions the investigator is about to take for his purpose of finding the answer.[2]

We shall see later what great importance this initial mental stage of every scientific inquiry has for the scientific process (see, e.g., below, b, on the role of genius; Section 2, on observation; Chapter II, Sections 3, on tests, and 6, on working hypotheses). All this is not denied but strongly vindicated by Scientific Method as here understood, although it has often been overlooked by its most enthusiastic apostles. Yet with that much granted, it remains characteristic of Scientific Method that it concentrates on the actions, operations, or steps enumerated above.

Secondly, it should be noted from the beginning that the various steps here enumerated are not always neatly separable in actual scientific working practice. Frequently the forming of a hypothesis and its testing by observation, the engaging in inductive and deductive reasoning, in generalization and specification, follow one another so quickly that they seem to constitute a whole rather than a sequence of actions. However, analytically the various steps can and must be distinguished (see below, Section 6).

(b) THE ROLE OF GENIUS

Scientific Method must not be understood as a merely mechanical procedure of indiscriminately gathering data and of processing them in line with prescribed steps, leaving every progress to assiduity and little if anything to genius. Rather the opposite is true. Even the mere selection of a problem, i.e., of a question for worthwhile inquiry, is as a rule no mechanical act but an act of the creative mind, and in the most important cases, one of genius. There is no rule of procedure to describe how the creative mind hits on such a question, except that it

---

[2] Similarly, John Dewey (*Logic, The Theory of Inquiry,* New York 1938, *passim*) held that inquiry begins, neither with facts nor with hypotheses, but with the recognition of a "problematic situation," and F. S. C. Northrop (*op.cit.,* pp. 18, 28), that "analysis of the problem" is a second important step, equally preceding the forming of a hypothesis. Both views are in line with those expressed above. However, finding that a situation is scientifically problematic, and engaging in its analysis, are two steps that in turn must be preceded by the investigator's forming some idea or "working hypothesis" that the situation *may* conceal a significant problem and that its analysis may be relevant for human knowledge in general. "Analysis" is merely one of various steps in the complex process of either forming definite hypotheses for the solution of a "problematic situation" or discovering that, after all, it is not problematic.

must be guided by curiosity, inquisitiveness, and independent creative imagination. Furthermore, most events we observe are the results of a confusing multitude of factors, as the curved path of a hurled stone is the result of the initial impulse, of the force of gravity, and of air resistance. To isolate the constituent factors and to select those that are suitable for tentative generalization are the work of a creative mind, not merely mechanical operations. Most of all, the first conception of a theoretical explanation (No. 6) is a creative act. Absurd ideas along with promising ones may incessantly pass through the mind of a creative thinker. This very play of imagination is creative. So is the act required to select among these ideas one or several that are more promising than others. The thinker's capacity for using analogies, for combining courage with disciplined humility, may be decisive for the effect. Data already available, including the scholar's total experience, of course play a considerable role at every stage; but neither knowledge nor assiduity can replace the part played by the creative mind.[3]

In other words, Scientific Method offers no substitute for the creative mind; nor does it tell a person how to be creative. It merely insists—at least in its exclusive interpretation (see Chapter II, Section 7)—that all ideas, however hazardous, mechanical, or creative in their origin, must finally be processed in line with Scientific Method in order to become a part of the body of science; until then they are at best preparatory in character. This does not deny that the preparatory work may be that of a genius and the processing quasi-mechanical. It should be understood by every scientist that to put a fertile idea through the mills of Scientific Method is often merely the last act of the total process, even though it be the one that gives it the stamp of science.

(c) THE RELEVANCE OF RELEVANCY

Data and hypotheses are selected scientifically according to their potential relevance for the solution of a problem that is under actual or potential inquiry.

To amass trivial data indiscriminately is no science. But sometimes a most trivial question can become extremely relevant in scientific re-

---

[3] See also Max Weber's comment on this question, quoted below, Chapter VI, Section 2, Max Wertheimer's *Productive Thinking*, New York 1945, and the careful report on the manner in which some of the greatest contributions to science have actually been reached, given in James B. Conant's fine book, *Science and Common Sense*, New Haven 1951, in particular, pp. 48, 122, 183, 193. Dr. Conant overshoots his mark, however, when on this ground he scoffs at speaking of *a* scientific method; as will be shown in the text (see Chapter II, Section 7, below) certain elements are characteristic of every scientific procedure.

search. Generally it would be scientifically irrelevant to investigate in what year some Greek orator suffered his first fit of gout. But under special circumstances this did become a highly significant question. The Acts (18:12) relate that when Paul arrived in Greece, one Gallio was Roman proconsul of Achaia. In order to know when Paul came it is important to learn when Gallio was proconsul. One of the few links was the casual remark in the writings of an insignificant but prolific Greek orator, who referred to Gallio as becoming proconsul in the fourth year of his, the orator's, gout.[4] Hence, in order to check upon the date when Paul came to Greece, it became relevant to know in what year this orator incurred gout, to him the starting point of an era. So, genius and triviality may blend in scientific procedure. We shall have frequent occasion to discuss questions of relevance in the course of this book.

Turning now to particular questions regarding the several scientific actions, operations, or steps, I would like to say that those familiar with Scientific Method may skip large portions of the first two chapters, but may do well not to omit what will be found in various sections (2, 3, 5, 7) of the first on "acceptance," and in the second on "consequences" (4), on "a priori" (5), and on the exclusive or nonexclusive character of Scientific Method (7). Everywhere the emphasis is on theory rather than on mere description, yet the former cannot be treated without the latter.

2. *Observation*

(a) GENERAL

Empirical observation of even the simplest fact is a complicated process. In its course the mind is not merely a receiving instrument; it cooperates in various ways, intentionally singling out the objects and subobjects of observation, using many conceptions and experiences previously piled up in it, and affecting—sometimes sharpening, sometimes corrupting—the accuracy of observation through expectations or through some preconceived shape or configuration. Twentieth-century phenomenology (see Chapter IX, Section 8) and Gestalt psychology (Chapter VII, Section 7) have done much to clarify this process. Logicians have emphasized that, strictly speaking, there is no such

---

[4] I am following here a report given long ago by the late theologian, Professor Adolf von Harnack, Berlin, in a circle of friends; as to the number of years, I may be incorrect.

thing as "immediate" empirical knowledge.[1] We shall revert to special aspects of this problem later.

An empirical observation may be limited to a single situation or be repeated in essentially similar situations. It may be "extrospective," focusing on the outside, or "introspective," focusing on the inner self. It is always, strictly speaking, observation by a person, and by one person only. Other persons may make similar observations, but never identical ones, because the terms "I" and "HERE" refer to different persons and places in each case.

Even though observations by two or more persons are never identical, the "what" observed may, of course, be so, if due allowance is made for the different "angle" or "perspective." However, to accept identity of the object (the "what") observed by several persons means to accept a fundamental presupposition: the truth of the common-sense assumption that one and the same thing often causes parallel impressions in different human beings, and that, therefore, there is a broad sphere of what is best called (Hocking) "consubjectivity."[2] This term is more graphic, and more to the point here, than the more familiar "intersubjectivity," which alludes to the process of intercommunication and is best reserved for that process. Without consubjectivity there can be no intersubjectivity, and without intersubjectivity there could be no science.

In permitting the scientist to accept consubjectivity, Scientific Method makes its first and greatest concession to common sense. For Scientific Method is unable by the formal steps of its own procedure to prove that consubjectivity exists; this it presupposes, or rather, permits the scientist to accept. The theoretical meaning of such presuppositions or permissions to accept will be discussed in later sections, especially Chapter II, Section 5.

An observation may be more or less exact. It may attain the maximal

[1] See, e.g., John Dewey, *Logic,* New York 1938, pp. 139 ff.; Felix Kaufmann, *Methodology of the Social Sciences,* New York 1944, pp. 33 ff.; Charles Sander Peirce, *Collected Papers* (as cited below, Chapter V, Section 6), vol. I, No. 38: "All significant observation involves interpretation. Reasoning begins before observation is over, not only afterwards." Also, Howard Becker, *Through Values to Social Interpretation,* Durham, N.C., 1950, p. 24, n. 12; Ernest Nagel, *Sovereign Reason,* Glencoe, Ill., 1954, pp. 72, 190 ff. (arguing against Bertrand Russell). For Kant, see Chapter II, Section 5; for Northrop, Appendix B.

[2] William Ernest Hocking, *The Coming World Civilization,* New York 1956, pp. 27 f., 31 f., 72, 107. He uses "consubjectivity" as a synonym of "intersubjectivity." Yet, as explained in the text above, the former is rather the presupposition of the latter, since it refers to the parallelism of subjective perceptions, ideas, and feelings regardless of whether or not it constitutes the basis of intersubjective communication. It is precisely because it makes this relevant distinction in terms possible that I accept Hocking's term "consubjectivity" for the parallelism.

exactness possible, or at least sufficient exactness to justify accepting the observation as relevant; or it may not be considered sufficiently exact to be taken into account. This distinction is independent of a second relevant distinction, namely, whether the observer's report on what he has observed is accurate or not (see below, Section 3); and of a third one, namely, whether the results of the observation correspond to reality (Section 5).

Every empirical observation is, therefore, first of all subject to a challenge of its exactness. It may or may not be *accepted* by the scientist as exact. Although criticism of exactness is, of course, practically limited where corresponding observations have been made by many and can be repeated in similar constellations—as can the extrospective observation of falling bodies or the introspective one of the feeling of hunger—the exactness of any empirical observation always remains open to challenge in science.

Whether, and in what circumstances, an observation is to be accepted as exact is not governed by absolute rules (see below, Section 7). The decision may be of the common-sense type, granting acceptance to observations often corroborated and even to a singular observation made by a reliable person and considered entirely plausible as to its nature; or acceptance may be critically withheld until the most refined controls devised by modern technology and psychology justify it. Acceptance may be generally agreed upon by all scholars or by a special group; or it may be the singlehanded acceptance by an individual scholar, who is building his own work upon the observation in question. In every case, acceptance is tentative only; it may be withdrawn on better grounds at any time.

Our means of observation are limited by our human structure. Waves of more or less than a certain length and corresponding frequency, for example, are not registered by our senses directly. We may, however, tentatively infer from observable data facts or events that are not directly sensed, such as the operation of larger or smaller waves, the inner structure of an atom, or the operations of the "unconscious" in human beings. Such inferences are clearly theoretical conjectures that belong in the category of tentative hypotheses formed to explain the more directly observed data (No. 6 of our survey). Strictly speaking, there is no scientific observation, however direct, that does not contain, for reasons discussed at the beginning of this section and to be elaborated in Chapter II, Section 6, some sort of hypothesis.

(b) INTROSPECTIVE OBSERVATION

Introspective observation presents special problems. Its peculiarity does not lie in the fact that it is performed by one individual person only, since that, as we have seen, is true also of every extrospective observation. The real difference is that the *object* of inner observation, the "what" observed, is accessible to only one person. This fact gravely limits the possibility of control. On the other hand, it does not impede intersubjective (i.e., interpersonal) communication. We do "understand" reports on each other's inner observations extremely well in the great majority of cases. This understanding does not rest on identity of the observed object, as may our common knowledge of a particular tree, or eclipse of the moon, or Joe entering the corner store last night; it is grounded in "analogy." Other persons' reports on the results of their self-observations, whether made in orderly language or in gestures or other bodily reactions, so precisely resemble what we have to report on the basis of our own introspection that this analogy enables us to "understand" others. In other words, a considerable amount of con-subjectivity is generally supposed by common sense to prevail regarding objects of inner observation; Scientific Method follows common sense in this respect. "Man is that which we all know," as Democritus said.[3]

Analogy often leads us to accept complete equivalence of the inner phenomena perceived by others and by ourselves. We claim to know exactly what a person means when he says he is feeling hunger or thirst, or pain in pricking his finger, and possibly also when he speaks of such complex and mysterious sensations as sexual orgasm. In other cases however, we may doubt full similarity, as when we feel love or enjoy art or religious edification in our own way. There are many reasons why our understanding of another person's inner phenomena may be more or less limited. Our own experience may date far back, as in later-life memories of childish exuberance, or of our first great sentimental love, or of how it feels to be very drunk, but it may still enable us to understand, faintly at least, what happens in others who are going through these stages now. Conversely, we may be able to anticipate feelings of a later age by the strength of our imagination, as a young person may be able to act old King Lear or Hans Sachs with great delicacy, finding in his own younger experiences germs of such feelings as older men may have. We may to some de-

[3] H. Diels, *Die Fragmente der Vorsokratiker*, 4th ed., Berlin 1922, vol. 2, p. 94. F. A. Hayek, *The Counter-Revolution of Science*, Glencoe, Ill., 1952, p. 79.

gree understand crimes and vices which we have avoided committing, because we do know at least some undercurrents or cross currents within our own experience that make us understand them. "There, but for the grace of God, go I," we may mutter, seeing a criminal brought to justice, or, *Homo sum, humani nil a me alienum puto* (I am human; nothing human I believe alien to me—Terence) when we are philosophizing. But sometimes we may hear reports on self-observation for which we discover no analogy even in the germ within ourselves and which, therefore, we find difficult to understand, as a man born blind finds it hard to comprehend the phenomena of seeing, color, or perspective.

The fact that we have no immediate access to the inner world of others limits our means of checking on the results of their self-observation and of separating truth from deception or illusion, both so prevalent in this sphere. This difficulty came to the support of the most radical of all American-born schools in the social sciences, that of Behaviorism, which, entering the scene in the second decade of this century, has influenced practical methods of research more deeply than theoretical thinking.[4] In its extreme form Behaviorism rejects any operation with concepts such as consciousness, soul, mind, purpose, and introspection. It substitutes the careful observation of bodily phenomena, in particular of responses of the human body to stimuli, including both external responses (doings) and internal ones (visceral, muscular, glandular, etc.), but only those of a physical character. The object of behavioral research in the social sciences is what men really do when faced with situations rather than what their alleged opinions or feelings are.[5]

It is generally admitted that behaviorist methods provide us with relevant data and invaluable checks. Nevertheless most scholars refuse to abandon reliance on inner observation entirely, since that would deprive us of an important source of potential knowledge and understanding. Scientific Method, as here interpreted, is not tied to Behaviorism, i.e., behaviorist taboos are not mandatory within Scientific Method.

---

[4] Basic, John B. Watson, *Behaviorism*, New York 1924. As to the influence of behaviorism on present-day research methods, see, for instance, Leon Festiger and Daniel Katz (eds.), *Research Methods in the Behavioral Sciences*, New York 1953.

[5] The behaviorist "dropped from the scientific vocabulary all subjective terms such as sensation, perception, image, desire, purpose, and even thinking and emotion as they were subjectively defined." Watson, *op.cit.*, p. 6. "Don't you get the idea, please, that the inside of our body is any different or any more mysterious than the outside of our body." *Ibid.*, p. 12. Behaviorism is "intrinsically interested in what the whole animal will do from morning to night and from night to morning." *Ibid.*, p. 11. See Appendix B on later modifications of Behaviorism.

The scientist, in other words, is not forbidden by the rules of Scientific Method to "accept" self-observation, either his own or that of others, as exactly performed and relevant to his goal, although this acceptance may be exposed in every concrete case to criticism as not sufficiently guarded. Modern psychology has done a great deal of work in this field.

The freedom of the scientist to accept self-observation for what it can offer does not entitle him to assume that what he observes within himself, and what he finds corroborated by reports of others, occurs in essential similarity within *all* human beings. Whether and in what circumstances he is justified in drawing this inference from introspection is an entirely separate question, which will occupy us extensively at various places of this inquiry; see Section 6 of this chapter (inductive logic); Chapter ix, Sections 7 (Kant) and 8 (Husserl); and Chapters x and xi.

In order to understand another person's behavior adequately I must know, not only what he is doing, but the subjective meaning his own observations and his doings or omissions have for him. The fact that similar observations or actions would have a different meaning for me must not be allowed to dominate my inquiry. I must try to put myself in his shoes and to think in his way, not in mine. If I do that, then I no longer conclude by simple analogy that the other fellow feels the way I feel, or did feel in similar situations; rather, I conclude that he feels differently because he is in a different situation. Some of the illustrations given above, such as anticipation of the feelings of an old person by someone who is still young, are of this nature. Here we may speak of a second degree of understanding others. No behaviorist technique can help us to reach this important stage of insight.

Understanding of the second degree will often be facilitated if the scientist shares the life and the experiences of the observed persons. This idea has led to the technique of the "participant observer."[6] Participant observation has proved equally fruitful in the observation of people living in primitive or otherwise uncommon stages of culture,[7] and of employees working in modern industrial enterprises.[8]

---

[6] The name was first used, it seems, by Eduard C. Lindeman in his *Social Discovery, An Approach to the Study of Functional Groups*, New York 1924, pp. 193–97.

[7] Bronislaw Malinowski, *Argonauts of the Western Pacific*, London 1922.

[8] As in the "Hawthorn experiments" conducted at the Hawthorn Works of the Western Electric Company in Illinois by Professor Elton Mayo and associates. and described by Fritz J. Roethlisberger and William J. Dickson, *Management and the Worker*, Cambridge, Mass., 1930. See the brief summary given in John Madge, *The Tools of Social Science*, London 1953.

A special type of observation is that made by an interviewer in research on private data inaccessible to direct observation by outsiders. This type is so closely connected with the process of description that we shall deal with it in that context in the following section.

3. *Description, Spontaneous or in Answering Questions.*
The Interview

(a) GENERAL

Any description by an observer of his observation can be transcribed into the basic form: "I, *N.N.*, was at place *p* at time *t* and thought then and there that I saw (heard, felt, smelled, etc.) *a*." This is best called a "report proposition," a term that seems to me preferable to "protocol proposition," introduced about 1930 by positivists like Otto Neurath and Rudolf Carnap.[1] Protocol, in continental Europe, means the written record kept of formal proceedings, a meaning not so generally associated with it in English, where "record" is used instead. At any rate, both protocol and record carry a connotation of formal proceedings; the informal report of the common man on what he has observed is not generally understood by these words. Therefore, "report proposition" seems to me less ambiguous.

Report propositions constitute, so to speak, the documentary primary source of every empirical work in science; in communicating about empirical work we must ultimately refer to them (see Chapters II, Section 7, and V, Section 3, below). This raises all questions regarding the correctness of the reports we use to particular importance. No observer can describe what he has seen without using conceptions or pictures that refer to things he had seen before. Language itself consists of memories incorporated in words, the latter serving as symbols for the former. It is not feasible to construct a primary report style of speech that contains no reference to things thought or seen before.[2] The best we can do, apparently, is to analyze the meaning of the words actually used in a report by reference to whatever other data are available to clarify their meaning. Thus the interpretation of a report prop-

---

[1] Otto Neurath, "Soziologie im Physikalismus," *Erkenntnis*, vol. 2 (1931) p. 393, and "Protokollsätze," *ibid.*, vol. 3 (1932) p. 204; Rudolf Carnap, "Die physikalische Sprache als Universalsprache der Wissenschaft," *ibid.*, vol. 2 (1931) p. 432, "Psychologie in physikalischer Sprache," *ibid.*, vol. 3 (1932) p. 107, und "Über Protokollsätze," *ibid.*, vol. 3 (1932) p. 215. Also Felix Kaufmann, *Methodology of the Social Sciences*, New York 1944, Chapter IV.

[2] Carnap postulated such a language ("Die physikalische Sprache," *op.cit.*), whereas Neurath rejected this postulate as "metaphysical" ("Protokollsätze," *op.cit.*). See also Chapter V, Section 3, below.

osition, or its translation into a more precise scientific language, becomes a practical problem.[3] Furthermore, anyone, and that includes the scientific observer, who tries to describe what he has observed, is confronted with the problem of whether what he first noticed was a number of details which next he combined into larger units; or, first, larger units ("wholes"), which he dissolved into details afterwards—the latter view forming the foundation of Gestalt psychology.

Scientific Method, as here understood, does not claim to have a ready answer to these questions. It should be noted, however, that a report proposition must always be interpreted so as to include the words "I thought" before the assertion "I saw, etc." This is significant for the distinction between the acceptance of the report as correctly made and the acceptance of the results of the reported observation as actual facts (see below, Section 5). Indeed, to be quite exact, the report should be read to have this pattern: "I do think (believe) *now* that I was at place *p* at time *t,* and that *then and there* I *did* think (believe) I saw *a*."

The scientist who studies another person's report on an observation may or may not accept the report as correct and adequate (see below, Section 7). Even when the observation reported upon was performed as exactly as could be, its verbal communication may be incorrect or inadequate. There may be conscious or subconscious intent to deceive, to modify or to exaggerate, and even with the sincerest of intentions the expressions used may be ambiguous or otherwise inadequate. Adequate description does not depend alone on the mind of the observer and what is in it when he reports; it is contingent also on the mind of the report's receiver. Words may have a different meaning for the writer and the reader, the speaker and the hearer.

(b) REPORTS ON SELF-OBSERVATION. THE INTERVIEW

Special problems of accuracy and adequacy, and therefore of acceptance or nonacceptance, are involved in the use of reports on self-observation. The informant himself may put down such a report, and he may do so either spontaneously, as in a diary or letter, or in answering questions, as in filling out a questionnaire; or the report may be put down by another person, as in the case of an interview.

Carefully planned questionnaires and interviews have in this century come to play a major role in directed mass observations. Some-

---

[3] It is typical of the ambiguity of the term "protocol" that Carnap apparently uses it for the naïve report; Neurath, however, for a purified report, i.e., one stripped of metaphysical terms and the like.

times they have focused on "facts," sometimes on "opinions."[4] What matters in the present context is that, whenever the interview is being used, another link is added in the chain of possible sources of error. Not only may the respondent's self-observation regarding his actions, opinions, or feelings be inexact or, if exact, incorrectly communicated to the interviewer; even if exact and correctly communicated it may be incorrectly noted down and passed on by the latter. The interviewer's presence may make the informant's self-observation less exact or his report less adequate than it might have been otherwise. The interview may have this disturbing effect whether it proceeds in a spirit of formality and lack of personal rapport or, though for other reasons, the interviewer first tries to establish a friendly personal contact with the respondent.[5] Furthermore, the accuracy of the observations made by the interviewer may be marred by bias and by preconceived ideas about the respondent's opinions, if, e.g., the interviewer entertains definite expectations on the ground that the respondent belongs to a certain group, say colored people, bureaucrats, or the like.

It has been shown that even the mere order in which questions are put in questionnaires or interviews may influence the informant, as when he is asked whom he prefers for President, A or B, or which he considers the chief reasons for his preference, $a, b, c, d,$ or e.

Questionnaires and interviews are exposed to the particular source of error that most respondents are motivated by a tendency toward reporting "respectable" views or facts rather than the views or facts as they actually are or were, or that at least they try to give their statements a respectable slant or explanation. Furthermore, whether in actual situations a person will act the way he says he would, always remains doubtful. Not only may he get different ideas when faced with reality, but intervening events may cause him to change his mind; e.g., new speeches of the candidates in elections or even the bandwagon effect of the published results of pre-election polls may cause

---

[4] For general orientation see, especially, George Gallup, *A Guide to Public Opinion Polls*, 2nd ed., Princeton 1948 (1st ed. 1944); Hadley Cantril *et al., Gauging Public Opinion*, Princeton 1944; National Opinion Research Center, Chicago (formerly Denver), *Interviewing for N.O.R.C.*, rev. ed., Denver 1947; Herbert Hyman *et al., Interviewing in Social Research*, Chicago 1954; William J. Goode and Paul K. Hatt, *Methods in Social Research*, New York 1952; John Madge, *The Tools of Social Science*, London 1953, Ch. IV; and the articles cited below. We shall revert to other problems involved in the use of interviews in other contexts, as for instance in Sections 4 (classification) and 6 (inductive logic) of this chapter and in Section 6 (hypotheses) of Chapter II.

[5] Well discussed by *Goode and Hatt, op.cit.*, pp. 164 ff., and Hyman, see next note.

the respondent to vote differently from the way he would have voted not many days before.[6]

All errors may be magnified by the inadequacy of the prepared questionnaire which is to form the basis of an interview, or of the "coding" which the interviewer may be directed to use in noting and classifying the answers. The meaning of the questions may be very different for the respondent from that intended by the designers of the questions, and it may be different for various respondents and interviewers.[7] Even when all goes well so that the report of the interviewer is entirely valid, it cannot be seen from the report that it is; the "reliability" remains in doubt.

Refined techniques have been devised to avoid the most obvious pitfalls:

Instead of asking the informant point-blank what one wants to know, indirect questions have been formulated that avoid betraying the investigator's purpose. But this may only put the respondent the more on his guard.

Instead of asking preformulated questions, whether of the direct or the indirect type, and noting down the informant's answers to them without paying attention to his entire personality and to his particular frame of reference, we may be more patient, letting him do most of the talking on whatever comes to his mind in connection with the general topic. This technique (somewhat grandiloquently referred to as "depth interviewing"), which may or may not be followed up by specific questions, is far more reliable in the individual case, but its use in mass interviewing is limited on the double ground that it consumes a great amount of time and, therefore, of cost, and that the results are not fit for statistical calculations unless they are first coded and thereby once more bereaved of all or some of their "depth."

An intermediate technique uses "open-ended" questions, where only the question is fixed in advance but the respondent is left free to answer it in whatever form he chooses, in contradistinction to the simple yes-

---

[6] For the foregoing see the critical analysis of interviewing methods in the literature mentioned above, and in the excellent article by Herbert Hyman, "Interviewing as a Scientific Procedure" in D. Lerner and H. D. Lasswell (ed.) *The Policy Sciences, Recent Developments in Scope and Method,* Stanford 1951, pp. 203 ff. His appraisal is basically favorable, however. "To find out a person's thoughts one must sometimes ask him a question!" (p. 205).

[7] As an illustration one may think of the many different meanings the question put to post-Hitler Germans whether they would like to have "a leader" could convey. Other telling illustrations are given by Rensis Likert in "The Sample Interview Survey as a Tool of Research and Policy Formation" in Lerner and Lasswell, *op.cit.,* pp. 233 ff. (p. 238).

or-no question, or the multiple-answer question, where the answers too are precoded.

A more ambitious scheme, called "latent structure analysis," has been devised in order to find out, by a battery of indirect questions, some underlying structure of thinking and feeling that dominates all the answers, or many of them, of the individual respondent. Such underlying structure of mind, for example, may be found in a strong type of patriotism (e.g., "America first").[8]

To counteract the influence of the order in which questions are put (see above) various clients were asked the same questions in different order.

Techniques that are too time-consuming or too difficult to handle for statistical purposes in mass research may still have great merits in the preparatory stage, as they can serve to make the planner wary of inadequate hypotheses regarding the complex he wants to investigate (see Chapter II, Section 6, on working hypotheses and types).

In spite of the many dangers lurking on the paths of interview surveys, and of serious mistakes that have been made in a goodly number of cases,[9] the well-designed mass interview has had such spectacular success in many others that it has won an important place as a scientific tool,[10] and will probably retain and even strengthen its position as our interviewing techniques become further refined and we learn *not* to use them where they cannot be helpful. Their ascendency can only serve, however, to epitomize the significance of the decision on acceptance or nonacceptance required of the scientist who uses such material. Nor are we justified in neglecting other methods out of an undue enthusiasm for the, after all, limited value of mass interviews (see Appendix B).

The specific problems of "sampling" in mass interviews will be discussed below, Section 6, in their proper context of inductive reasoning, and those of "classification" and "typification" hereafter in the immediately following section on measurement, and in Chapter II, Section 6, in the context of working hypotheses.

[8] Basic, Paul F. Lazarsfeld, "The Logical and Mathematical Foundations of Latent Structure Analysis," in S. A. Stouffer and Assoc., *Measurement and Prediction*, Princeton 1950, and "A Conceptual Introduction to Latent Structure Analysis," in P. F. Lazarsfeld (ed.) *Mathematical Thinking in the Social Sciences*, Glencoe, Ill., 1954, Ch. VIII.

[9] See also Lindsay Rogers, *The Pollsters*, New York 1949.

[10] More than one-third of John Madge's book on the *Tools of Social Science* and almost one-half of Goode and Hatt's *Methods of Social Science* deal with questionnaires, interviews, and scaling techniques.

4. Measurement and Classification

(a) GENERAL

Quantitative magnitudes have the great advantage over qualitative ones that they often lend themselves to exact measurements, capable of correct communication. It is, therefore, important to transform qualitative into quantitative descriptions wherever possible, as for example in stating the quality of food by counting its nutritional value in terms of calories, vitamins, and other factors. Many qualitative values, however, such as the pleasant or unpleasant taste of food, resist attempts to measure them in quantitative terms. Then other methods may be tried to state differences in the most precise manner available. This can sometimes be done through relative propositions, such as: P prefers a to b, to c, and to d, but e to a; he prefers a also to $(b + d)$ or $(c + d)$, but $(b + c)$ to a. To some extent, therefore, qualitative differences, too, can be measured. Much work has been done within the last ten or twenty years to refine qualitative measurement by techniques of classification (see below) and of typification (see Chapter II, Section 6). Yet the possibilities of measurement in the social sciences have remained, and will continue to remain, limited because of the great number of variables, all of which cannot be included in scientific analysis and, insofar as they can, are not all measurable. A potential factor of "disturbance" must, therefore, generally be taken into account. It has been suggested to note this factor in equations by a special symbol (u);[1] see Section 6, below, on mathematical expression.

(b) CLASSIFICATION

To classify phenomena means to form several categories, systematically arranged if feasible, in each of which all observations covered by its description are to be lumped together.

Whatever we cannot explain we can at least try to classify. Men early began to classify stars, plants, animals, and other things. Classification was the backbone of Aristotelian and Scholastic science. The mere collection of facts and their classification has been called the "natural history stage" of scientific inquiry.[2] "If only the schoolmen

---

[1] See Trygve Haavelmo, "The Probability Approach in Econometrics," *Econometrics*, vol. 12 (1944) Supplement. More briefly, K. J. Arrow, *op.cit.*, p. 151, and Jacob Marschak, "Economic Structure, Path, Policy, and Prediction," *American Economic Review*, vol. 37 (1947) No. 2, p. 81.

[2] F. S. C. Northrop, *op.cit.* (Section 1, above) p. 173.

had measured instead of classifying, how much they might have learnt," exclaimed A. N. Whitehead.[3]

However, classification is necessary also in an advanced stage of science. In the social sciences today, classification plays an important role in directed mass observation (general census, sampling through questionnaires, interviews, and the like). When qualitative factors are involved, classification can serve purposes of measurement to some extent. First, the various categories may be so devised as to constitute a scale of measurement, with the order of the categories providing a serial order of ranking, as in the rating of examinations. Second, the number of observations listed in each category may yield useful figures, either absolute or relative (e.g., percentage).

What is lumped in the categories may be whole units (things, persons, groups, etc.) or attributes. Attributes may be either quantitative, i.e., "continuous variables" (such as size, weight, age), or qualitative. Qualitative attributes may or may not permit of a serial ranking of some kind (such as relative intelligence, relative command of language, relative pleasantness or desiredness; highest third, middle third, lowest third, and the like). There may be only two categories or there may be three or more. If only two (yes or no, citizen or noncitizen, under twenty-one or twenty-one and over) we speak of "dichotomous," otherwise of "multiple," classification.

Various techniques can be used to improve serial ranking. One is the establishment of "standards" for comparison. Before the brightness of stars could be measured in quantitative terms through appropriate technical devices, some stars of distinctly different brightness were used as standards for the comparative classification of all others. This primitive method led to surprisingly valid results, as was demonstrated when quantitative checks had become available. In similar manner, standards for intelligence rating, for the rating of social distance or social proximity, or of pleasantness or unpleasantness, etc., can be set. A special application is the construction of "ideal types" (*Idealtypen*), introduced by Max Weber.[4] Ideal types of bureaucracy, of feudalism, of parliamentary democracy, of capitalism, or any other historical phenomenon can be constructed. Then the observational material is classified according to its greater proximity to one of the types than to

---

[3] A. N. Whitehead, *Science and the Modern World*, New York 1925, p. 43.

[4] See Max Weber, "Die 'Objektivität' in sozialwissenschaftlicher und politischer Erkenntnis," *Gesammelte Aufsätze zur Wissenschaftslehre*, Tübingen 1922, Section II, pp. 161 ff. Engl. transl., see below, Chapter VI, Section 2.

the others. More will be said on this technique in Chapter II, Section 6.

Another device is the use of "indicators," i.e., of easily observable single data indicative of a broader attribute, as the institution of *habeas corpus* or its equivalent is indicative of a system of government built on respect for freedom, or corporal punishment may be indicative of an authoritarian paternal attitude, or the fact whether a soldier on furlough prefers to wear uniform or civilian clothes may be indicative of the degree to which he identifies himself with the army.[5] Several indicators may be combined in various ways. One is the combining of a number of simple indicators in an "index" which is to serve in turn as a summarizing indicator for some broader concept, as, e.g., a cost-of-living index, based on the cost of some typical elements of consumption, serves as an indicator for the entire cost of living. Another is that of fitting individual indicators together in characteristic "profiles," i.e., typical combinations.[6]

In order that observations can be properly listed in classifications all categories must be clear, unambiguous as to their meaning, and mutually exclusive. Special care must be taken that all attributes involving an essential difference are listed separately. Once a complete list of categories has been logically constructed, it can often be "reduced" by omitting combinations that have no practical importance; e.g., if two attributes will always be present together they need not be listed separately, and if they will never be present together they need not be listed in combination, or if different attributes have no different weight regarding the purpose of the inquiry (e.g., the specific nationality of an alien) they may be lumped together.[7]

Where preferences play a role, classification may follow a "utility index." Theoretically speaking, an individual may set up a list of all alternatives of action with all their foreseeable consequences spelled out, arranged in the order of his preferences regarding the consequences. He would then act rationally if among those actions possible for him

[5] The last illustration is taken from Samuel A. Stouffer *et al., The American Soldier* (Studies in Social Psychology in World War II), 2 vols., Princeton 1949, vol. 1, p. 64.

[6] See Paul F. Lazarsfeld and Allen H. Barton, "Qualitative Measurement in the Social Sciences: Classification, Typologies and Indices," in D. Lerner and H. D. Lasswell, *The Policy Sciences, op.cit.,* pp. 155 ff., and Hans Zeisel, *Say It with Figures,* with an introduction by P. F. Lazarsfeld, New York 1947.

[7] On the importance of logical completeness and of the process of reduction see Lazarsfeld and Barton, *op.cit.,* pp. 173 ff. "It can be safely stated that most progress in measurement consists in taking this step: the substitution, for an impressionistic rank order, of a systematic process of reduction [of a scheme] logically representing the definition of a serial." This step the authors call "substruction" (p. 175).

in a special situation he selected that which is highest on the list.[8] Such a list, however, is hard to draw up, and preferences are often so unstable that the list would quickly lose its usefulness; furthermore, the consequences include reactions of others and are therefore enmeshed with the preferences of others. Yet in spite of these difficulties, the utility index is a valuable tool in the scientific approach to qualitative measurement.

Forming categories of classification is, of course, no part of the observations themselves, but a theoretical process. More exactly speaking, the scientist assumes as a "working hypothesis" that useful conclusions can be drawn from the criteria according to which he proposes to group observations (see Chapter II, Section 6 below). Whether the categories actually will be useful for the purposes of the inquiry depends on the correctness of this hypothesis, which in turn depends on its logical soundness and on its realism, i.e., its accordance with reality. To form a useful classification, the scientist must have an adequate advance idea of all the elements that may play a role for the purpose of the inquiry; e.g., in drafting a questionnaire on the reasons for surprising election results he must be aware of all the various motives that may have caused a voter to act in the election the way he did. Self-observation, totality of experience, and constructive imagination are among the sources from which the tentative picture that underlies the first draft of a classification must be drawn. Careful exchange of views with other experts can serve to improve it. It is best, whenever feasible, to conduct a practical tryout, which may even be organized in two stages: first, "informal interviewing" of some informants only ("pilot study," in Great Britain called "pre-pilot"),[9] and next, a formal "pretest" (pilot survey), resembling the final test as planned in every respect except in that it is administered only to a more limited number of people.

(c) QUANTITATIVE CONTENT ANALYSIS

Quantitative content analysis, developed since about the mid-thirties, deserves special mention among newer devices designed to objectify qualitative comparison. Instead of relying merely on subjective im-

---

[8] This point was forcefully made by Vilfredo Pareto, *Manuel d'économie politique,* transl. from the original Italian ed. (Milano 1919) by Alfred Bonnet, 2nd ed., Paris 1927, pp. 150 ff.; see Kenneth J. Arrow, "Mathematical Models in the Social Sciences," in D. Lerner and H. D. Lasswell, *The Policy Sciences* (*op.cit.*) pp. 129 ff. (p. 135). See also Felix Oppenheim, "Rational Choice," *The Journal of Philosophy*, vol. 50 (1953) pp. 341-50.

[9] See John Madge, *op.cit.,* p. 216. For the American usage, Goode and Hatt, *op.cit.,* p. 145.

pressions regarding differences in political climate, governmental tactics, the peoples' behavior, or the like, in different countries, or at different times in the same country, the quantitative content analyst subjects the content of newspapers, public speeches, state documents, radio announcements, private letters, or other means of communication to a painstaking scrutiny regarding the frequency with which certain subjects have been mentioned or key words have been used, or have been referred to in a favorable or in an unfavorable context, or with a different meaning, or in coordination with other terms (e.g. democracy in coordination with freedom or with equality, respectively). This is expected to supply a more objective basis or test for hypotheses about the differences or changes in question than subjective analyses can give.[10] Research projects of this type have been carried through, e.g., on the amount of, or the space devoted to, foreign news in newspapers,[11] the use of various verbal devices in German radio propaganda during World War II,[12] changes in the use of ideological symbols in the world's leading newspapers,[13] and other topics.[14]

Quantitative content analysis is hardly practicable unless some rather specific hypotheses have already been formed which it is designed to test. Often the quantitative analysis will merely confirm the obvious, and then may appear unnecessarily cumbersome and costly. But some-

[10] See Harold D. Lasswell, *The Analysis of Political Behavior,* New York, London, 1948, p. 296; H. D. Lasswell, N. Leites *et al., The Language of Politics: Studies in Quantitative Semantics,* New York 1949; and especially, Bernard Berelson, *Content Analysis in Communication Research,* Glencoe, Ill., 1952.

[11] For the United States, see *Recent Social Trends in the U.S.,* New York 1933, vol. 1, p. 382; for Great Britain, *Report of the Royal Commission on the Press,* Cmd. 7700.

[12] Ernst Kris, Hans Speier and associates, *German Radio Propaganda, Report on Home Broadcasts during the War,* Studies of the Institute of World Affairs, New York 1944. The thirty-six graphs of this remarkable work present the relative frequency in the use of a great variety of verbal propaganda means, such as the use of truth-falsehood stereotypes in reference to communications, the use of predictions, of references to victories, of Hitler's name, of references to German culture, to enemy weakness or immorality, "intense" vilifications of the various enemies, mention of the various enemy leaders, praise of Japan, attention given to Hitler-Mussolini meetings, references to social disunity in England, nonmilitary items in communiques of the German High Command, reference to reasons for British doom, use of words connoting bravery, medal awards, etc., etc., and all this carefully separated for the various periods of the war.

[13] So-called RADIR project ("Revolution and the Development of International Change") conducted by the Hoover Institute on War, Revolution and Peace, Stanford University. This project sought to measure the changes in the ideological symbols used in such leading organs as *The Times* of London, the *New York Times, Le Temps,* and *Izvestia* as well as in major political speeches of chiefs of governments. The group drew up a list of some 400 key ideological symbols of our time, such as democracy, communism, free enterprise, nationalism, constitutionalism, and Soviet, and counted how often these symbols occurred and whether they were used favorably or unfavorably (I. de Sola Pool, Daniel Lerner and G. E. Rothwell, "On Measurement of Ideological Change," paper read at the Hague Congress of the International Political Science Association, September 1952, mimeographed).

[14] Illustrations, see John Madge, *op.cit.,* p. 112.

times it may draw attention to significant traits that have been over-looked. It may become more important when we learn to use it more discriminately.

5. *Acceptance as "Fact" and the Concept of Truth*

(a) FACT

Even when an observation is accepted as exactly made and adequately communicated, it remains to be decided by science whether the conclusion can be drawn that the phenomenon which was subjectively observed corresponded objectively to an actual fact. The report may say that at some definite place and time the observer saw something that *looked to him* like a chair, or a star, or an unusual type of airship, "resembling a flying saucer," or a steamship on the high seas approaching from the left side, or *A* shooting *B,* or soldiers of country *P* entering country *G* across the border and killing people there. The scientist may not question the exactness of the observation and the correctness of the report ("looked to me"); still it requires a separate decision on his part to the effect that he does or does not accept the conclusion, whether or not it has been explicitly drawn by the observer, that there *was* a chair, a star, an unusual type of airship, a steamer approaching from the left side, or that *A did* shoot *B,* or that the men costumed as soldiers of country *P* actually were such. There may be other grounds than lack of exactness in observation or description for questioning the apparent results, e.g., defects of tools used, as of a telescope or radar screen; the limited range of observability; disturbing influences, such as atmospheric conditions or reflections; inconclusiveness; or outright deception. Even the fundamental philosophical problem of the certainty and nature of reality is involved in every decision on the acceptance of the results of observation as facts. This acceptance is, therefore, a step that must be clearly distinguished from the acceptance of the processes of observation and description as correctly performed.[1]

There are again no strict rules to tell the scientist whether and when the apparently observed fact can or must be accepted as an objective fact. There are rules of a negative nature forbidding the unmodified acceptance of facts that are incompatible with previously or simultaneously accepted other facts, factual generalizations or theoretical explanations without the correction of the latter (see step No. 9); but

---

[1] On acceptance as "fact" see the pertinent remarks by Felix Kaufmann, *Methodology of the Social Sciences,* New York 1944, pp. 57, 58. He failed, though, to mention that two other stages of acceptance (exactness of observation, adequacy of communication) must precede this third one, although he would hardly have denied it.

there are no positive rules saying precisely whether and when an apparently observed fact has to be accepted as an actual fact. See Section 7, below.

Proof of facts by observation, therefore, depends on more than observation, description, and measurement. It depends on (1) acceptance of the observation as sufficiently exact to support the report made on it; (2) acceptance of the report as sufficiently correct and adequate; and (3) acceptance of the apparently observed facts as actual facts.

(b) TRUTH

These relative elements in the meaning of "proof by observation" play a role in the difficulty which besets the philosophical task of clarifying the concept of truth. It is not necessary to discuss here all aspects of this problem. "Logical" truth and the truth of "causal relations" will be dealt with in subsequent sections. In the present context, however, that of the truth of alleged "facts," it must be made clear that the term truth here may be used either with direct reference to the actual occurrence of an event (Caesar truly *was* assassinated, Hitler truly *did* commit suicide, Jesus truly *was* crucified, truly *did* rise from the dead) or to the truth of a statement made (the *statement* that Caesar was assassinated, that Hitler committed suicide, that Jesus was crucified, that he rose from the dead, is true, or is not true). If used in the first sense, the historical fact may have truly occurred without being observed and with no statement ever being made on it; e.g., the emission of light by a star from which it requires a thousand years to travel to the earth and to meet our observing eyes was a truth even before we could observe it. If used in the second sense, however, the term truth has no meaning except in reference to statements made, and the statements may be erroneously accepted as true although the alleged historical fact did not occur, and vice versa.

These two different meanings that may be given the term truth are paralleled by two different theories about the interrelation between science or knowledge, on the one side, and truth, on the other. If we start from the first meaning, a proposition is true when it corresponds to reality. This "correspondence theory" of truth is the older of the two and has also been used by what is likely to be the majority of twentieth-century scholars, including Bertrand Russell,[2] J. M. Keynes,[3]

---

[2] Bertrand Russell, *An Inquiry into Meaning and Truth*, New York 1940 (critically discussed by Ernest Nagel, *Sovereign Reason*, New York 1954, pp. 205 ff.); also, *Power*, London 1938, pp. 267–73.

[3] J. M. Keynes, *Treaty on Probability*, London 1921.

and R. Carnap.[4] Starting from the second meaning, truth has been equated with "warranted assertibility" (Dewey[5]) or "empirical validity" (Felix Kaufmann[6]) or the like. This approach is often equated with positivism but is not necessarily associated with all the connotations of that term (see below, Chapter v, Section 3); nor is it held by all positivists, for example, not by Carnap.

It is important to see that the difference of approach just mentioned has two sources. One is the mere choice of the meaning we are going to associate with a word when we use it—here, the word truth. In this choice we are free. The other is a difference in philosophical speculation about reality and in the scientific approach to it. So long as we do not abandon the speculative idea that there is a reality which no human senses have yet observed or may ever be able to observe—be it a star whose light has not yet reached us or has not yet been made noticeable and may never become noticeable, or be it some metaphysical reality—so long do we need in our vocabulary for this reality a term that is independent of the state of our knowledge; unless we use truth for this we need some other word. I shall, wherever necessary for the sake of clarity, capitalize Truth when emphatically used in this sense.

An intermediate view would include in the meaning of truth not only the aggregate of what can be asserted in a scientifically warranted manner *today*, but also what may be so assertible at some future time, and what might have been asserted in the past had *possible* observations been made. In extending this intermediate view so as to include observability by beings other than human, like God, the two ideas of truth and Truth merge; still the definition would remain different.[7]

---

[4] Rudolf Carnap, "Truth and Confirmation," in H. Feigl and W. Sellars, *Readings in Philosophical Analysis*, New York 1949, pp. 119 ff.

[5] John Dewey, *Logic*, pp. 7, 104, 118–19, 139 ff., 262.

[6] Felix Kaufmann, *op.cit.*, pp. 20 ff., 64 ff., 128 ff. He proposes to speak of "empirically valid" instead of true, and "empirically counter-valid" instead of false. Propositions that are neither empirically valid nor counter-valid he calls "undecided" (p. 66).

[7] Kaufmann, *op.cit.*, pp. 64 ff. (and in an earlier article, "Truth and Logic," *Philosophy and Phenomenological Research*, 1940, pp. 59–69) suggests limiting the use of the term truth to propositions whose assertibility is warranted not only today, but that "once accepted, could withstand all possible controls" also in the future. This definition would make truth an *ideal*, he said, which we can never be sure to have attained. Yet even this concept of truth refers exclusively to statements or propositions; it has no reference to the alternative of a Truth that is real although no statement has been made to assert it. Similarly, Dewey (*Logic*, p. 345 n.) quotes for what he considers the best definition of truth C. S. Peirce, who said (*Collected Papers*, vol. 5, No. 268) that truth is "the opinion which is fated to be ultimately agreed to by all who investigate," and that reality is "the object represented by this opinion." Here, too, the term truth is related to opinions only, not to something irrespective of any opinions held thereupon.

5. FACT, TRUTH, PROOF, REALITY

The important point for us here is that Scientific Method is not necessarily tied up with a definite choice among these views. As far as this method is concerned only such truth as is empirically ascertainable counts, has a standing, *in science*. If there be any Truth beyond it, it is no part of science as this term is used within Scientific Method. Whether such other Truth is accessible through other methods, and whether these can be called scientific in some other sense of the term, cannot be decided within the framework of Scientific Method (see Chapter II, Section 7).

Any acceptance of propositions about alleged facts as being true, corresponding to reality, empirically valid, verifiable, or warranted—whichever term is preferred by the individual scholar—is only tentative or provisional within Scientific Method. This is one of the differences between belief or faith on one side, and science on the other, because belief or faith may be meant to be final and irrevocable. Psychologically speaking, belief or faith plays a powerful role also in science; it often determines the acceptance by the scientist of reports on empirical observations. Nevertheless, the distinction remains logically important. While an objection to, or doubt regarding, the alleged truth of some particular report may be considered inadmissible and a sin from the religious angle, scientifically it can never be ruled out of order. In scientific procedure such objection can be rejected only *with scientific means,* and reference to belief or faith is no scientific means. The nature of the apparent conflict between religious faith and scientific doubt will be discussed in Chapter XIII.

(c) PROOF

In the strictest sense of the term, full empirical proof is never available under Scientific Method, since on principle any empirical proposition is unendingly subject to attack. Only analytical judgments can present full proof; yet they do not deal with the "truth" of propositions, only with their "meaning" (see next section). It has been said, therefore, that in empirical questions we can speak only of probability of a high degree, or of plausibility, and had better replace the term proof, like that of truth, with some other term. This warning is quite appropriate wherever we deal with inductive generalizations of observed events (to be discussed in the next section) or with statements about causal relations (Chapter II, Section 1). Yet with all due respect for precision, when the question is of particulars only, we need not always be so shy. It would indeed be foolish and misleading if with regard to every particular event social scientists spoke of there being no more than a high degree of probability that it happened. That, for example, a man named Hitler did live and assume a leading political role, is both true and fully proved, and so is it fully proved, going back in history, that Lincoln and Washington, Caesar and Cicero, Plato and Socrates did live. To counter such statements with Pilate's question, "What is truth?" is not appropriate in scientific discourse. Here again it appears that Scientific Method is to a considerable degree based on common sense. To be sure, it reserves to everyone the right to challenge empirical evidence, but only on good grounds, and the philosophical question, "What is truth?" is not considered a good ground in the presence of overwhelming empirical evidence. This distinguishes Scientific Method from radical Skepticism (see Chapter v, Section 2, below).

We need not, therefore, be pedantic in avoiding the use of the term proof, and actually it is generally used in both the natural and the social sciences whenever the empirical evidence appears fully adequate. When this is not so, however, it is more appropriate to express the limited nature of the evidence by using other terms, such as "confirmation" or "corroboration."

(d) REALITY

The questions of truth and proof are closely interconnected with the problem of "reality." Although, as we have seen, there is no strict code of rules about when to accept an apparently observed fact as real and when to deny acceptance, there is agreement that acceptance is not barred by philosophical doubts about reality. This is not to say that Scientific Method is able to demonstrate whether there is reality and what it is, whether the things that appear real are so, or whether something back of them or nothing at all is real. It is only to say that acceptance of the results of observation as facts irrespective of philosophical doubts about reality is not considered a violation of the rules that govern acceptance in scientific inquiry. On the contrary, Scientific Method expects the scientist to accept reality, unless he has weighty grounds for withholding acceptance. It can be said that, in a sense, the observable world *is* the real world to Scientific Method. But this must not be mistaken to mean that Scientific Method claims ability and competence to judge what reality is. It makes no such claim.

Indeed, the old philosophical question of reality, insofar as it aims at the ultimate Truth behind all possible astronomical, physical, chemical, and biological discoveries, is beyond the province of Scientific Method by definition, since it is metaphysical in character and Scientific Method does not answer metaphysical questions (see Chapter II, Section 5 and 7). In some other way, nevertheless, Scientific Method has greatly contributed to clarifying the problem of reality. It has led to profound investigations about the modes in which reality is *subjectively* experienced by human beings. Important psychological and phenomenological contributions regarding this aspect have been made by such men as William James, Henry Bergson, George H. Mead, Edmund Husserl (see below Chapter IX, Section 10), and more recently, by Alfred Schutz.[8] The latter's analysis seems to have probed even deeper than did his precursors, but it still keeps strictly within the sphere of *subjective* experience of reality.

Speculations by scholars on the *objective* nature of reality, beyond the discoveries made by the natural sciences, have become rare in this century, at least outside the older schools of metaphysics. Such examinations fall into the general field called "ontology" by the philosophers. This is the science that deals with "Being as Being," the subject of inquiry put in the center of Aristotle's *Metaphysics*. It examines, not particular things, but Being as such, as distinct from not-Being, and the difference between propositions such as *that* something is (i.e., that it has Being) and *what* it is. In the broadest sense of the term, ontology refers by no means only to the metaphysical aspects of Being but also to the mere clarification of the meaning of a proposition that asserts the Being of something, and to observable data about Being and the modes of Being. Some such questions can be examined with the tools of Scientific Method. But the major interest of ontological investigations in the past was metaphysical. Considered one of the most important branches of science from Aristotle until deep into the modern age, ontology dealt freely with the Being of matter, of "ideas" and of "essences," of things, of men, of angels, and of God. This entanglement with metaphysical speculations proved fatal to the discipline in modern universities. For a hundred years or more it lay all but dormant.

In the second quarter of this century, however, scientific interest in ontological questions was revived. The ontology that has emerged is not just the old one, however. It has become essentially new, because now serious attempts are being made to keep away from metaphysics, so as to present an exact account of observable facts and relations. It has,

[8] Alfred Schutz, "Multiple Realities," *Philosophy and Phenomenological Research*, vol. 5 (1945) pp. 533–576, with an illuminating discussion of the literature on the question.

in particular, assumed the character of a scientific effort to describe the "categories" in which Being is known to man. In this sense, Nicolai Hartmann's *New Ways of Ontology* is representative.[9] The author tries to discern the spheres, or "layers" (*Schichten*), of Being: inorganic matter, organisms, the psychic sphere, the sphere of the mind (*Geist*) in its objectivated workings, the sphere of the community, and the sphere of history. He analyzes typical characteristics (categories) of each sphere, and fundamental ones common to all.[10] He further examines their mutual interpenetration and the limits of interpenetration, upwards and downwards; the relative "strength" and "height" of the different spheres according to objective criteria; dependence and autonomy in each sphere; and whatever else can be stated about the various modes of Being on the basis of human experience. Such inquiries can be carried through, let me repeat, in a manner that is entirely in keeping with Scientific Method, provided the temptation of presenting personal speculations as scientific data is effectively resisted. In this effort Hartmann succeeded in his *New Ways* better than in some of his earlier works.[11]

The neglect of metaphysical questions in inquiries based on Scientific Method has been under attack. This, and the possible solution of the methodological problem involved, will be discussed in Chapters VII, Section 3, and IX ff.

[9] *Neue Wege der Ontologie,* Stuttgart 1942 (tr. by R. C. Kuhn, *New Ways of Ontology,* Chicago 1953). This is a reprint of a contribution to Hartmann (ed.) *Systematische Philosophie,* and is based on Hartmann's former books, especially *Zur Grundlegung der Ontologie,* Berlin, 2nd ed., 1941.

[10] In view of the general lack of familiarity with ontological categories, the following illustration may be helpful, taken from Hartmann's *Neue Wege,* pp. 248, 249. *Fundamental* categories of Being (in common to all spheres) are, for example: unity and manifoldness, accord and discord, disjunction and continuity, form and matter, determination and dependency; also, the qualitative categories of identity and difference, universality and individuality; and the modal categories of possibility, actuality and necessity and their contraries. Categories of the *inorganic* sphere: space and time, process and condition, substance and causality; of the *organic* sphere: the structure of something as an organic whole (*Gefüge*), metabolism, self-regulation, reproduction, constancy of the species; of the *psychical* sphere: consciousness and nonconsciousness, pleasure and displeasure; of the sphere of the *mind*: thought, knowing (*Erkennen*), willing, freedom, valuation, personality.

[11] *Neue Wege,* pp. 239 ff. ("The new ontology is no speculative metaphysics, and Kant's theory on the limits of what can be known [*Erkennbarkeitsgrenze*] applies to it not less than to every serious science.") But see below, Chapter VII, Section 5, on Hartmann's *Ethics.* The series of new writings of an ontological character was opened by Heidegger, *Sein und Zeit* (*Jahrbuch für Philosophie und phänomenologische Forschung,* vol. 8, 1927; 8th ed., Tübingen 1957). Heidegger is dominantly interested in that hypothetical Being which is back of all particular Being, and this has given his writings a metaphysical and speculative touch.

6. *Logical Reasoning*

(a) DEDUCTIVE

Logical reasoning is accepted as *full* proof by Scientific Method when, and only when, it is strictly analytic. It is analytic when it adds nothing to the meaning of a given term or proposition, but merely makes explicit what is implied in that meaning. To say that, if all men are mortal and Socrates is a man, Socrates too is mortal, is a strictly analytical statement. It does not say that all men are mortal, or that Socrates is, or that Socrates is a man; it says merely that according to the *meaning* of the statement "all men are mortal," Socrates, if a man, also is mortal. Deductive logic, in the sense in which the term is used in this book, is strictly analytic. It deals with meaning (*Sinn*).[1]

Whenever a proposition adds something to the meaning of a given term or proposition it is not analytic but synthetic. It then cannot be arrived at by deductive reasoning from the given term or proposition. Whether a proposition is meant to be analytic or synthetic cannot always be seen at once; it depends on the meaning (definition) of the terms used. "All men are mortal" is an analytical proposition if the concept of man is so defined as to include certainty of death; otherwise, the statement is synthetic. Likewise, "all stones fall to the ground unless supported" is analytic if stones are defined as bodies having weight, and weight as a quality which makes things fall unless supported; the same statement is synthetic if stones are defined without reference to weight or heaviness. When we say that justice requires equal treatment of what is equal, we are making a merely analytical statement, if we have defined justice as regard for equality, whereas our statement is synthetic if we have defined justice otherwise. One and the same statement may be true, if analytic, and false, if synthetic. "All swans are white" would be a true proposition if swans had been defined as being white; it is false, if not, because there are black animals that have all the characteristics of a swan otherwise.

Are mathematical statements analytic or synthetic? Kant considered

---

[1] The word "meaning" can be used in different ways (see Charles K. Ogden and I. A. Richards, *The Meanings of Meaning*, New York 1923; 10th ed., 1952). I shall generally use it only in the sense (or senses) in which we speak of the meaning of a word, of a sentence, of a proposition. In English usage—different from the German use of *Sinn*—the term is often applied figuratively to causal relations; we ask what clouds "mean," what a sudden going up of prices "means," in the sense of what has caused a phenomenon and what may be expected from it (so-called "material meaning"). This sense is not intended in the text here. See Appendix B.

them synthetic, because to say that five plus seven is twelve adds something that is not contained in five and seven.[2] The matter looks different, however, if we consider mathematical propositions as logical deductions from a small number of basic postulates or, in other words, if we *define* mathematics by such postulates. Then arithmetic statements, for example, have some form like this (slightly oversimplified) scheme:

"If (1) we assign symbols called whole numbers to units that for the purpose at hand are considered equal among themselves (fingers, or sheep, or human beings, etc.) or to classes of such units (fingers of one hand, members of the House of Commons); and if (2) we devise an endless chain of whole numbers so that each number differs from the preceding and from the subsequent one by one unit; and if (3) the individual numbers in the chain are assigned the symbols 0, 1, 2, 3 . . . in this order, 0 standing for the absence of any unit, *then* . . ."

All implications following from these premises—which may be refined by adding others, such as the concept of infinite—are strictly analytic. That applies to simple implications such as $5 + 7 = 12$ as well as to the most intricate ones, such as that whole numbers or fractions of whole numbers multiplied by themselves may be equal to 4, 9, 16, etc., but never to 2; or that, if a and b signify any number, then $(a + b)^2 = a^2 + 2ab + b^2$, and $(a + b)(a - b) = a^2 - b^2$. In other words, the logical reasoning in arithmetic is strictly analytic, and it is for this reason that it can and must be accepted as absolutely true.[3]

What has been said here of arithmetic is basically valid for geometry as well. Geometry too is strictly analytic, and not synthetic, apart from its basic postulates, which can be neatly formulated as such (if-then). The selection of the postulates in either branch may be grounded on the belief that they reflect existential reality or self-evident truth. If so, such "axiomatic" belief may or may not be correct. Or, the selection may be based on sheer expediency and even on arbitrary choice. All this makes no difference for the main point just made. Whatever were the motives that prompted the choice of postulates, the mathematical operations based on them are correct when, and only when, they are

[2] *Prolegomena zu einer jeden künftigen Metaphysik* (1785) pp. 28 ff. (*Gesammelte Schriften*, Academy ed., Berlin 1900–42, vol. 4, p. 268; Cassirer ed., Berlin 1912–22, vol. 4, p. 16.)

[3] Basic, Alfred North Whitehead and Bertrand Russell, *Principia Mathematica*, 3 vols., Cambridge, 1910–13, and Bertrand Russell, *Introduction to Mathematical Philosophy*, 1st ed. 1919, 2nd ed. 1920, reprinted 1938. Good presentation, Alfred Tarski, *Introduction to Logic, and to the Methodology of the Deductive Sciences*, New York 1941 (originally in Polish, 1936, then in German: *Einführung in die mathematische Logik und die Methodologie der Mathematik*, Leiden 1937). See also Appendix B.

strictly analytic in drawing implications. To that extent, and only to that extent, are they absolutely and demonstrably true.

Although analytical deductions add nothing to the premises that is not implied in their meaning, they are by no means always an irrelevant play with words. They may be relevant for the purpose of inquiry because often all the implications of a statement, especially of a sweeping one, are not immediately seen: they may, if made explicit, add considerably to our knowledge, and often be strikingly surprising in character, as arithmetic shows.

That analytical deductions if correctly made can be said to be "absolutely true" gives deductive logic, whether used in mathematics or in any other context, its singular place in science. But this quality of absolute truth refers only to the analytical inference as such, i.e., to the statement that the meaning of proposition a implies the proposition b. Whether the proposition a is true, and consequently, whether b is true, is not guaranteed by the fact that b is implied in the *meaning* of a. These are the most elementary facts about logic.[4] Consequently, statements such as "If God is almighty he can square the circle, or make wrong right and right wrong" are strictly analytic, and therefore necessarily true, once we have defined "almighty" as meaning "able to do or effect anything without any exception." Once made explicit, however, the implications may lead us to question the truth of the premise or to modify the definition of the terms used ("almighty").[5]

Clarity and unambiguity of all terms used are the first requirement of logical reasoning. Most words (verbal symbols) are ambiguous; they cover a great variety of facts or values, or of both. This is especially so in the political field, where terms such as freedom, equality, democracy, socialism, patriotism, loyalty, power, authority, order carry many different meanings. It is sometimes advisable to eliminate these difficulties by the use of symbolic signs the meaning of which has been exactly stated. We shall make frequent use of this device. Its radical acceptance might make it possible to express our scientific knowledge about political questions in mathematical form and with mathematical clarity; yet this presupposes, of course, that all variable factors are correctly treated as such and any other unknown elements that may be involved, too, are symbolized and included in the equation.[6] While

---

[4] See e.g., Felix Kaufmann, *op.cit.*, p. 25.

[5] See Chapter x, Section 2.

[6] See Paul F. Lazarsfeld, ed., *Mathematical Thinking in the Social Sciences*, Glencoe, Ill., 1954, and Kenneth J. Arrow, "Mathematical Models in the Social Sciences" in D. Lerner and H. D. Lasswell, *The Policy Sciences*, *op.cit.*, pp. 129 ff.

economists have long been developing mathematical economics (including econometrics), there are hardly any beginnings yet of a mathematical political science (including "politicometrics").[7] Greater clarity of thought might be achieved in many questions by the development of such a technique.

That the meaning in which a term is used has been made unambiguously clear is no guarantee, however, that the concept it covers is scientifically "useful." To be clear and to be useful are not the same thing. The meaning of "centaur" may be made perfectly clear; but the concept of a centaur would remain irrelevant for political science. The terms "happiness" or "power" may be defined clearly, but either so broad or again so specific that the concepts covered by them are utterly inadequate for scientific purposes (see Chapter VIII, Sections 8 and 12). As every other branch of science, political science too would wish to have a few *basic* concepts that are both clear and useful, i.e., serviceable as building stones within a logically developed theory. To be useful they must be "realistic" in the sense that they themselves, or their analytical derivations, correspond to carefully observed facts. Consequently, the selection of scientifically useful concepts, or their new formulation, is a function that cannot be performed by "analytical" (deductive) logic alone. A concept's usefulness can be tested only when it forms part of "synthetic" propositions, as does, e.g., the concept "power" of the synthetic proposition, true or false, that "All men have a lust for power," or "All power corrupts," etc. (see Chapter VIII, Section 12).

The need for adequate basic concepts has led to a quest for "conceptualization" of political theory. By mid-century, attention had come to center on attempts to use as basic such concepts as "power," "groups," "equilibrium," "elites," "action," "decision-making," "game," "field,"[8] in addition to the basic concepts of psychology and psychoanalysis, and in preference to the older concepts, like formal or informal government, institutions, freedom, equality, etc. The fashionable vogue enjoyed by the new approaches, shifting from one to the other, has not been so helpful, however, as had been hoped. It has even done some harm, because it has tended to detract attention from political problems that require different approaches, as for instance clarification of the

---

[7] An interesting essay of this type is Helmuth Unkelbach, *Grundlagen der Wahlsystematik, Stabilitätsbedingungen der parlamentarischen Demokratie*, Göttingen 1956.

[8] For literature, see Appendix B.

specific consequences and risks implied in the various types of governmental institutions (see Chapter XII).

I shall deal with basic concepts each in its proper context, partly in this, partly in the second volume. At present I merely wish to make it clear that the scientific usefulness of a concept depends not on analytical reasoning alone but on the truth of "synthetic" propositions that are meant to reflect reality.

(b) INDUCTIVE

Synthetic statements, too, may be true; but whether they are depends on something more than mere deductive, analytical logic, and this "something more" is always subject to scientific challenge. Kant held that in some cases synthetic statements too were certain to be absolutely true, independently of all experience (a priori). As regards mathematical statements, to which he referred as his first illustration, we have just seen that their absolute truth is due to the fact that, what is necessarily true in them, is analytic and not synthetic in character. As for metaphysics, we shall see below (Chapter II, Section 5) that Kant's metaphysical a-priori propositions for which he claimed absolute truth were chiefly negative, and that to this degree they are not in conflict with the principles of Scientific Method.

Modern science, as ushered in by men like Francis Bacon (1561–1626), Galileo Galilei (1564–1642), Johannes Kepler (1571–1630), and Isaac Newton (1643–1727) in the natural sciences and, more than a hundred years before them, by Niccolo Machiavelli (1469–1527) in the social sciences, has tended to reach its generalized synthetic propositions not a priori from reason, from religion or from the depth of convictions, but by "inductive" reasoning from observed individual facts.[9] This movement has led up to, and culminated in, Scientific Method as presently understood. Whenever we generalize some synthetic statement—saying, for instance, that all stones, unless supported, fall to the ground, because we have observed many doing that and none behaving differently; or that all human beings feel some urge toward the good as distinct from the evil, because there are millions of observations to this effect by millions of people; or that all power corrupts, because we have seen power corrupt people very often—then we are applying so-called in-

---

[9] Bacon was the first to center scientific work in the process of induction, but Galileo actually used induction (see A. N. Whitehead, *Science and the Modern World, op.cit.,* pp. 57 ff.). So did, to some extent, Machiavelli.

ductive reasoning. How can this type of reasoning be justified, and if at all, under what conditions? Are we proceeding "logically" in such reasoning?

Inductive reasoning can be considered logical in the analytical sense in two ways, of which only the first has been generally noted. This first approach interprets inductive reasoning as an elliptical (abridged) form of deductive reasoning where the suppressed first premise is supposed to be "What has been observed once (or often) will always be observed under essentially like conditions." If we base our reasoning on this major premise, then, having observed many unsupported stones falling to the ground without exception, we arrive at the proposition that all stones will do so, in a strictly analytical manner. The trouble is only that the validity of the major premise "Once-equals-always," or "Often-equals-always," is not accounted for in this type of reasoning and that, in the second version, the major premise says nothing about the number of cases to be observed, and in neither is it expressed what conditions are essentially alike.

How, then, can the major premise be verified, and if at all, to what extent? If we turn for proof again to analytical deduction we must have recourse to some higher premise from which our major premise can be derived. Such higher premise has been sought in the proposition that all events in the universe follow universal laws. But then we are only pushed one step farther back. How do we know that all events in the universe follow universal laws? Should we try to answer this by saying we know it because we have observed uniformity in many instances without exception. and because what has been found often with no exception must be universally true, then we would move in a circle. The thesis of the uniformity of the universe cannot be proved; it must be accepted as a kind of religious creed, as an ultimate "assumption" or "axiom."

This regress to the axiom of uniformity of the universe is the way John Stuart Mill argued the case of inductive reasoning.[10] It forces us, as we have just seen, to go from contentions we cannot prove, up to higher premises we can prove even less, and finally to accept as an axiom what we can prove least. Nor does it tell us anything about the number and essential equality of cases that must be observed to warrant generalization.

The second approach to an analytical transformation of inductive

---

[10] See his *System of Logic*, 8th ed., London 1889, pp. 200 ff.; abridged ed., Ernest Nagel, *John Stuart Mill's Philosophy of Scientific Method*, New York 1950, pp. 181 ff.

reasoning starts, not from the uniformity of the universe, but from accepted rules of scientific procedure. Having watched certain regularities in nature in general, and in some special field of scientific research in particular, we derive from the results of such observation tentative *rules* regarding "warranted types of generalizations." These rules do not merely say "Once-or-often-equals-always," they do say something about the conditions of observations required to warrant some cautious generalization. Abstracted from previous experience they do not necessarily go beyond what is required for the case at hand.[11]

If we look at inductive generalizations in this way, then they are not derived deductively from the general premise "Once-or-often-means-always-everywhere-in-nature" but from the specific procedural rule that a generalized statement of fact in field F_1 of science is warranted after a single observation, accepted as exactly made and correctly reported; in another field (F_2), after corresponding observations repeated in a small number of cases under varying conditions, or (F_3) in millions of cases, or (F_4) not even then. In physics, for example, a single test like that of the atomic explosion in New Mexico in 1945 may be considered enough for a scientist (and possibly for all of them) to warrant some generalized statement—tentative, of course, as are all scientific empirical statements—whereas in the social sciences many more observations are required; there it may be necessary to extend research to tremendous numbers of observations before generalizations, if any, are warranted.

John Dewey took a far more radical view. He did not care for analytical justification of inductive reasoning. To him, logic had no pre-eminent position or rank in science; it was an integral part of scientific method, nothing more and nothing less, and like any other abstract rules in scientific method was abstracted from what men had found operationally useful for getting results where they wanted them. The only justification of the rules of logic, then, lay in their usefulness, and accordingly, logical rules changed with their changing usefulness for inquiry.[12] Secondly, inductive and deductive logic were so closely inter-

---

[11] The chief representative, and the most consistent one, of this approach is Felix Kaufmann, *op.cit.*, pp. 77 ff. He aptly emphasizes the distinction between generalized *empirical* propositions ("all men are mortal," "all have a sense of justice") and of generalized *procedural* propositions ("warranted statements that all men are mortal or have a sense of justice can be made when . . ."). Unfortunately and quite unnecessarily he has marred his otherwise clear exposition by introducing for procedural rules the term "theoretical laws," highly misleading here and in its constant further use by Kaufmann because neither are these rules "laws" in the usual sense of the term nor are they the only "theoretical" rules or laws.

[12] *Logic*, pp. 139 ff. and 419 ff.

woven in operations of inquiry that one could not serve without the other. It was no longer tenable, then, to teach that there is one logic of induction and another of deduction and that the two logics are independent of each other, Dewey said. *Both* require "familiarity with material, sagacity in discrimination, acuteness in detection of leads or clews, persistence and thoroughness in following them through, cherishing and developing suggestions that arise." And he ended by insisting that there are no "rules" to be followed. "The only 'rule,' it might be said, is to be as intelligent and honest as lies within one's power." [13]

The close interplay between inductive and deductive reasoning is recognized today by all empirical schools. Dewey's more extreme views, however, going as they do beyond this point, lie open to criticism on two counts. Regarding operational usefulness as the only criterion of logic, it is well to note that the usefulness sought after in *science* is that for discovering the truth ("warranted assertibility"), not for any other interest as such, and even in conflict with other interests. [14] As regards the distinction between deductive and inductive reasoning it can be answered that when deductive logic is understood, as it has been here, as the analytical explication of the *meaning* of propositions rather than of their truth or validity, its distinction from inductive reasoning cannot be rejected as unwarranted.

For our present purpose, however, it does not matter which of these theories we follow. Whether, in justifying inductive generalizations, we refer to the axiom of uniformity of nature (Mill), to rules of procedure (Kaufmann), or to operational usefulness (Dewey), it is recognized today that inductive reasoning can lead only to tentative hypotheses, whose truth may always be exposed to scientific challenge. Mill was still obsessed by the idea that it might be possible to develop the general theory of induction to a stage of perfection where we would obtain general laws of induction. Sighed he:

> Why is a single instance, in some cases, sufficient for a complete induction, while, in others, myriads of concurring instances, without a single exception known or presumed, go such a very little way toward establishing a universal proposition? Whoever can answer this question knows more of the philosophy of logic than the wisest of the ancients and has solved the problem of induction. [15]

[13] *Ibid.*, and pp. 484–85.
[14] See Dewey's own pertinent remarks on this point in his and A. F. Bentley's *Knowing and the Known* (Boston 1949, pp. 278 ff.), where he writes that "knowing should be conducted without pre-determination of the practical consequences that are to ensue from it" (p. 284).
[15] J. S. Mill, *op.cit.*, p. 206, Nagel ed., p. 186.

This dream has been abandoned. The tendency now is to single out, in each individual case, the most plausible generalizations for a choice among them.[16]

The theory of inductive generalizations has greatly benefited from the mathematical theory of probability. Grounded on mathematically exact (i.e., strictly analytical) probability calculations, laws of "statistical inference" have been developed [17] with results that have proved very fruitful for the social sciences as we shall see presently. But it is no longer claimed that such analytical aids can spare the scientist the decision when to accept and when to reject inductive generalizations in his work. There are no strict rules of this kind (see also Section 7, below).

(c) SAMPLING AS A CASE IN INDUCTIVE REASONING

Sampling in mass observation is a special case in applied inductive reasoning. In order to find out the approximate distribution of individual attributes (physical or mental, opinions, preferences, intentions, habits, etc.) within a great number of people, it is often sufficient to explore the distribution within a relatively small number of samples and then inductively to infer, from these findings, the distribution of the same attributes over the "universe" (country, group, profession, etc.) under investigation. Special problems here involved are how to find out which individuals are "representative" of others, and of how many they are representative. These two questions cannot be answered by analytical reasoning but only on the basis of empirical inquiry. They must be carefully distinguished from a third question of how to get correct reports on self-observation from the interviewed individuals, a question discussed in Section 2, above.

The rapid development of sampling tests, especially from the nineteen-thirties on, has led to a constant refinement not only of the questioning techniques (Section 2) but also of the inductive reasoning involved.[18] Great efforts have been made to single out groups of in-

---

[16] See, e.g., Kenneth J. Arrow, *op.cit.*, pp. 129 ff.

[17] See George A. Yule and M. G. Kendall, *Introduction to the Theory of Statistics*, 14th ed., London 1950; Sir Ronald A. Fisher, *Statistical Methods for Research Workers*, Edinburgh, 1st ed. 1925, 11th ed. 1950; A. Wald, *On the Principles of Statistical Inference*, Notre Dame Mathematical Lectures, No. 1, 1942; Arrow, *op.cit.*, p. 138.

[18] On sampling methods, see Frank Yates, *Sampling Methods for Censuses and Surveys*, London 1949; John Madge, *op.cit.*, and the literature on statistical inference, cited above; also the publications of the Survey Research Center, Institute for Social Research, University of Michigan, especially those by Roe Goodman. The theoretical interest in the probability aspects of sampling seems to have found its first expression in the United States as late as 1938 in an article by Jerzy Neyman, "Contributions to the Theory of Sampling Human Population," *Journal of the American Statistical Association*, vol. 33 (1938) p. 101 ff.

dividuals who were thought to be particularly representative; but therewith bias, preconceived ideas, and inadequate knowledge on the part of the research planners found a broad entering wedge in the base of inductive inference. In order to improve the representative character of samples, efforts were made to fix the samples in exact proportion to the total number of people in the categories from which the samples were drawn, such as categories determined by age, sex, race, profession, income, geographical section, etc. But this still left leeway for unwarranted selections *within* each category, e.g., overemphasis on college or high-school students, present or past, because they were more easily accessible, and underemphasis on sections of people who were difficult to interview or underrated in their significance. It has consequently been found that the probability of correct inferences frequently increases if in picking the samples—at least those within the various categories—more reliance is placed on truly random selections than on guesswork about representative character. In other words, wherever our knowledge of who is representative of whom leaves off, we often do better to rely on random sampling than on loose reasoning. We may, for instance, divide the country into regions and each region into small sections of similar size and characteristics, then pick *by lot* sections in each region, and query there *all* the people of the type (age, etc.,) in which we are interested.[19]

Inference statistics (see the preceding subsection) helps us to be more precisely aware of both the strength and the weakness of inferences drawn from random samples. Statistical probability calculation tells us, e.g., which error we must expect when we infer the composition of some "universe" (such as a country's population) from random samples. It tells us that, when the factors under inquiry are evenly distributed in a large population, errors in about two-thirds of our sampling experiments (meaning sampling surveys fully carried through) will stay within the range of what is called the "standard error," and in about nineteen-twentieths within double that range of error. Yet in the remaining twentieth (i.e., in one out of twenty sampling experiments) the error may go to the extremes.

---

[19] See Rensis Likert, "The Sample Interview Survey as a Tool of Research and Policy Formation," in Lerner and Lasswell, *The Policy Sciences* (*op.cit.*) pp. 233 ff.; Angus Campbell, "Measuring Public Attitudes," *Journal of Social Issues*, vol. 2 (1946) pp. 1 ff. When samples are chosen from samples, e.g., samples of families from samples of regions, we speak of "multistage" sampling. When first some informants are asked more details than are later the broader samples (or the entire population), we speak of "multi-phase" sampling. See John Madge, *op.cit.*, pp. 208–09.

The standard error is surprisingly small. Even when we take only 100 samples from a large population, the standard error is no more than 5 percent where the actual percentage of the special group we want to count in the population is 50 percent; no more than 4 percent where the actual percentage is 80 or 20 percent, and no more than 3 percent where it is 90 or 10 percent. This is to say that in two out of three experiments in sampling we would get from 45 to 55 where we should get 50; from 16 to 24 where we should get 20; and from about 7 to 13 where we should get 10. If we took 1,000 samples the standard error would shrink further to about 1.6 percent, 1.26 percent, and .95 percent respectively, i.e., among the 1,000 samples we would get 484 to 516 instead of 500; about 187 to 213 instead of 200; and about 90 to 110 instead of 100.[20]

Yet all this holds true only where the factors are evenly distributed within the population. Where they are not, as when we go about counting Negroes or Catholics in an area where most of them live in one section while the whites or the non-Catholics live in another, the error involved in the use of random sampling can grow infinitely. Even where the factors are evenly distributed the error must be expected to be greater than the standard error in one-third of our sampling experiments (see above). Furthermore there are types of research, as in election statistics, where even small errors of less than 1 percent can be decisive.

Sampling has been one of the greatest contributions of twentieth-century social science toward improvement in our knowledge of conditions and opinions of man in contemporary society. It has, within the last two or three decades,[21] been applied in a great variety of research. Business has used systematic sample interviews for consumer market research, e.g., for finding out what the reaction of the population will be to new models, what the motives are back of consumers' preferences, and the like. In the United States, the Census Bureau, the Department of Agriculture, the State Department, the Defense Depart-

---

[20] If the actual proportion of an evenly distributed group with certain characteristics within a large population is p percent over against q percent that do not have these characteristics, and n samples are examined, then the "standard error" we must expect in the results of the sampling is the square root of $\frac{p.q}{n}$. The square root of $\frac{50.50}{100}$ is 5, of $\frac{20.80}{100}$ is 4, etc.; the square root of $\frac{50.50}{1000}$ is only about 1.6, etc. See Madge, *op.cit.*, and the other references given above.

[21] The decisive year was 1935, when the first Gallup and Roper polls appeared and the first modern bibliography in the field was published. See Bernard Berelson, "The Study of Public Opinion" in Leonard D. White, ed., *The State of the Social Sciences*, Chicago 1956, pp. 299–318.

ments, the Treasury Department, and others have made multifarious use of sampling interviews, e.g., for exploring possibilities in financing public expenditures and for influencing people in buying and holding government bonds. Similar use has been made of sampling interviews in other countries, as in Great Britain by the technically well advanced Social Service Division of the Central Office of Information. Much more can be achieved. Sample interviews can bring to light the differences that prevail between various individuals, or categories of individuals, as to their conditions or attitudes—differences that remain hidden in the aggregate figures of the general census or of general election statistics. In the field of political science, public attitudes, opinions, preferences, and intentions can be probed by sample interview surveys, not only regarding elections, where this is done regularly nowadays, in constantly refined procedures,[22] but on many other questions of political concern.[23]

Yet after all this has been said, it must be stressed that we are dealing here with purely *descriptive* methods. Generalizations from individual factual data do not yield theories of causal explanation; they do not give us anything more than general factual data, which at best may serve as suitable raw material for the establishment of theories about causal relations but do not by themselves supply such theories. A clear distinction must be made between *facts* on one side, and their *explanation* on the other, and therewith between two different objectives of inductive reasoning. One objective is the establishment of general factual statements; this is the inductive "generalization of accepted individual facts," just discussed. Another quite different one is that of presenting a causal explanation for generalized facts, such as the law of gravity in the case of falling bodies; this is the "theoretical explanation of generalized individual facts," to be discussed in the next chapter.

(d) LOGIC IN NATURE AND IN HISTORY?

Logic, as the term has been used here, may be defined as the method, art, or technique of either (deductively) making explicit what is im-

---

[22] See, in addition to the American literature on the sample interviews survey studies of election results, for Great Britain, e.g. R. S. Milne and H. C. Mackenzie, *"Straight Fight,"* special issue of *Parliamentary Affairs,* vol. 8, no. 1 (winter 1954–55).

[23] Berelson, *op.cit.,* p. 308, enumerates as possible research subjects of opinion research through sampling: attitudes, values, patterns of morality, modes of child rearing, religious observances, family practices, sex behavior, leisure-time activities, morale, "happiness." See also Likert, *op.cit.* We shall give further illustrations in other chapters of this book.

plied in the meaning of propositions, or (inductively) so formulating general propositions that the implications of their meaning cover a definite or indefinite number of specific propositions. In both alternatives, therefore, it deals with meaning.

It has often been said that this is not all, and that, far from dealing only with the meaning of statements, logic partakes of Being and Reality, that it is itself *real*.[24] This is said to be shown by the fact that nature herself follows the rules of logic, quite irrespective of whether man watches her and makes meaningful statements about her behavior. In other words, not only do all phenomena of nature, e.g., the movements of the stars, obey general laws, but they do so with the most immaculate logic. Logic, therefore, must be part of the ways of nature.

This manner of arguing, however, is based on a fallacy. In the first place, it is very doubtful whether we are scientifically justified in saying, except figuratively, that the phenomena of nature are "ruled" by general laws, and that nature "obeys" or "follows" these laws. For we cannot state scientifically that the general laws are something separate from the behavior of nature. As far as scientific knowledge goes they may well be nothing but the ways of nature, as described by man in general terms, owing to the fact that they actually are describable in such terms. But, however that may be, it is certainly not warranted to say that nature, in her obedience to general laws, behaves "logically." If nature behaves differently from what we expect under the general propositions which we call general laws and suppose to be descriptive of the actual behavior of nature, then the trouble is not that nature acts illogically but that the alleged general laws are not general laws, that they need modification or scrapping. Likewise, when nature behaves in line with our expectations, it is not because she performs logically, but because to that extent the general laws describe the behavior of nature correctly. When men die it is not because they behave logically under the general proposition that all men are mortal, but because this proposition expresses the actual phenomena correctly. Stars are not ill-behaved if they deviate from their expected course, but our descriptive formula has been incorrect.

Sometimes the behavior of nature seems indeed to be highly illogical. When, e.g., we note that light rays always pass across moving bodies with the same speed, as measured in terms of these bodies, no matter whether the body moves against the rays (upstream) or with them (downstream), the result seems to be so illogical that it is hard to be-

---

[24] See, e.g., Nicolai Hartmann, *Zur Grundlegung der Ontologie,* as cited above.

lieve; whereas the water of a river appears to act logically in needing more time for passing a boat that goes downstream than one moving up. Actually, the respective energies and masses perform neither logically nor illogically in either case; they merely act according to their nature or to the nature of the fields within which they move, and we, in formulating universal laws from our primitive observation of streaming water and the like, have been mistaken; the alleged laws did not describe the behavior of nature adequately.

It cannot even be said with assurance that the general laws themselves are "logical" in character. There is no particular logic in the fact that light moves with the speed of just about 186,000 miles a second, or that effective quantums of energy[1] are always a multiple of the absolute and invariant magnitude of just 6.55 times 10^{-27} (which is 6.55 times one-billionth of one-billionth of one-billionth, or 6.55 divided by a denominator with twenty-seven zeros). These are simply facts, provided they have been correctly stated. Only when we use the term "logic" in quite a different sense—for instance in the sense in which the ancients used the Greek term *logos,* or more especially that in which the latter term is used in the New Testament—are we justified in saying that the universal laws may be descriptive of the *logos,* or of the word of God. But it is beyond science to verify that this is so and that what we call general laws are indeed "orders" given to nature. Science can do no more than state that general laws describe the way in which nature actually behaves. It is for man to deduce the implications from these supposedly descriptive general statements and watch whether all implications are in line with nature's actual behavior; it is not for nature to keep in line with our descriptive general statements.

Likewise, when we examine the sequence of events in history, we cannot with scientific authority say that history moves "logically," except in the sense that the sequence of events is logically in line with general propositions formulated by man, such as those regarding causal interrelations, swing of the pendulum, progress from thesis through antithesis to synthesis, or with more specific ones. Like nature, history can never move "logically" or "illogically," but can only reveal that our insight into the general laws or our knowledge of the contributing factors was either correct or defective. We shall say more about historical laws in the following chapter.

---

[1] Measured in erg, the unit used in Physics for measuring *work.* One erg is the work done by one unit of *force* (one dyne) acting through the distance of one centimeter.

7. *Excursus on Acceptance of Propositions*

From the standpoint of a logician it is possible to divide all synthetic propositions into two classes—"accepted" and "nonaccepted"—and then define Scientific Method as that method by which propositions are allocated to the one or to the other class according to presupposed rules of procedure. Any allocation, then, of synthetic propositions to the body of science must ultimately be justified through a deductive (analytical) inference of the following form: "*If* a synthetic proposition is to be considered part of the body of science when, and only when, it is to be accepted according to code-of-rules-of-procedure C, and if the proposition p is to be accepted according to C, whereas p_1 is not to be accepted according to C, *then* p but not p_1 is to be considered part of the body of science."

Felix Kaufmann in his *Methodology of the Social Sciences* did indeed adopt such an approach.[1] However, while to define science and procedure this way is not logically objectionable, it is not advisable, because the "grounds of acceptance" have no well-determined status in science. As we have seen in Sections 2 through 6, above, whether an observation is accepted as exact, its reporting as adequate, the results as facts, and the inductive generalization of individual facts as warranted, depends greatly on the judgment of scholars, singularly or in groups, so as often to lead to a situation where some accept while others do not. The same holds, as we shall see in Section 1 of the next chapter, for the acceptance of a causal explanation as warranted. There are, to repeat, some negative rules of a strict character that govern the step of acceptance, such as that no proposition can be kept in the accepted category after one of its implications has been shown to be false, and that no new proposition may be accepted that is incompatible with another one previously or simultaneously accepted unless the incompat-

[1] *Op.cit.*, pp. 39 ff. (division "into two disjunctive classes, accepted propositions and nonaccepted propositions"); p. 48 ("From the point of view of the logician, the procedure of an empirical science consists in the acceptance or elimination of propositions in accordance with given rules," it "will result in changing the corpus of his science" . . . "the rules of procedure state the conditions for an exemption from the general prohibition against changing the corpus of a science"); p. 50 (it is inconsistent "to deny the givenness of rules and at the same time to declare the objective control of every scientific decision to be essential for science. For the rules are presupposed in control"); p. 51 ("The rules of procedure exhaustively determine the exception to the general prohibition"); p. 65 (". . . the rules of empirical procedure and a scientific situation being given, the correctness of scientific decisions is provable by pure reason"); and p. 229, No. 2 ("By scientific procedure we decide whether given propositions should be considered parts of the corpus of a given science"). Kaufmann did not spell out the logical syllogism, as has been attempted in my text, but that is what his theory amounts to.

ible factors are eliminated at the same time. Yet beyond such negative rules there are few, if any, rules of a strict character according to which acceptance is to be granted. The logician is free to build his definition of science on the premise, presupposition, or postulate that there are, or should be, such strict rules; but as there are not, the definition would be unrealistic.[2]

Furthermore, to define scientific procedure with reference to a body of science to which propositions are being added or from which they are withdrawn presupposes that there is a well-defined body of science at any one time.[3] But this again is not a realistic assumption. Not even is there always such a thing as a "prevailing opinion" about what *is* the "established knowledge" at the time; and if there were, to let numbers decide would make little sense, although it would be logically possible. Galileo's propositions, although they were won through what we now call Scientific Method, were not accepted by prevailing opinion for some time to come. Lavoisier's discovery of oxygen and his explanation of combustion as a process of oxidation, achieved about 1776, was not generally accepted until at least the end of the eighteenth century; the majority of scientists, including great James Watt, continued to cling to the older phlogiston theory, which explained fire as the escape of some mysterious element.[4] Does Darwin's theory of evolution constitute no part of the body of science when not accepted by prevailing opinion, and vice versa? Are not controversial acceptances of facts, of generalizations and explanations important ingredients of science—of science considered as a living, dynamic thing, not static at any time except in a state of either decay or heavenly perfection? We could, then, speak of a "body of science" only in the sense of a body with pretty hazy boundaries.

The unsuitability of using the two classes of accepted and nonac-

---

[2] Kaufmann himself says (*op.cit.,* p. 49): "For example, the rules of induction contain the condition for the acceptance of universal propositions, *but the scientist is never bound to incorporate such propositions;* he is always free to wait for additional corroboration" (italics not in the original), and he emphasizes (pp. 63, 66) that "there are undecided propositions at every stage of scientific inquiry." Then the dichotomy "accepted" and "nonaccepted" can be maintained only by putting all "undecided" propositions in the nonaccepted class; but this still yields no strict rules on what must be accepted.

[3] Kaufmann speaks of a "scientific situation," which he defines as "the totality of synthetic propositions accepted at a particular time" (p. 52), or "the knowledge considered as established at the time of a scientific decision" (p. 230, No. 6b). He anticipates the objection that "it is arbitrary to draw a sharp line of demarcation between accepted and unaccepted propositions," but answers that this objection "may be met by pointing out that the procedure of scientific control presupposes such a strict division" (p. 54).

[4] See James B. Conant, *Science and Common Sense,* New Haven 1951, p. 189, on the obstinacy with which the older doctrine was being defended.

cepted propositions as the criterion of science is particularly striking in the social sciences, where acceptance is even more controversial than in the natural sciences.

These disputes about the logical structure of science are, however, of little practical importance in our general context. For there is no controversy among the adherents of Scientific Method that, in making a decision on acceptance at the various stages where such a decision is required, the scientist, while not bound by prevailing opinion, is not free in every respect to follow his hunches, dispositions, intuitions, and the like. We have already seen that he must not accept incompatible propositions, etc. We must add here another grave limitation. The scientist is not free in his decision on *what can be legitimately accepted or offered for acceptance*. In this respect he is bound by the rules of Scientific Method as long as he acts as a scientist in that sense; he cannot, e.g., as such a scientist accept a-priori propositions as final (see Chapter 11, Sections 5 and 7). Furthermore, his decision to accept or not to accept what has been legitimately offered for consideration must, of course, be used judiciously, that is not in an arbitrary way but with a feeling of responsibility toward the purpose of science to follow the truth (see Chapter vii, Section 1). He must not ignore contradictory observations, although he may explain the seeming differences away if he can. His decision is exposed to being rejected by all others, or by the majority, or by some, on grounds that are not in conflict with Scientific Method. All decisions on acceptance, those of individual scholars as well as those of the majority, are subject to constant control and to change; scientifically speaking, they are only tentative in every case. On all this the adherents of Scientific Method are agreed. Yet within this framework, to repeat, there remains a considerable area of freedom for the individual scientist to grant or refuse acceptance.

The great physicist Heinrich Hertz said in 1889 at the annual meeting of German natural scientists that the truth of the wave theory of light "is, humanly speaking, certainty."[5] Less than twenty years later, Planck's quantum theory put this statement out of date. Someone (in this case, Einstein) started with denying acceptance. Someone must always start. The others will not always follow suit at once. Such are the ways of science.

These considerations also show that the tentative acceptance or non-acceptance of propositions gained in accord with Scientific Method—

[5] See Arnold Hildesheimer, *Die Welt der ungewohnten Dimensionen*, with a preface by Werner Heisenberg, Leiden 1953, p. 234.

if they are so gained—is the responsibility of each individual scientist; its legitimacy is not contingent on approval by the majority of all scientists or of any special group of them. Objections raised are relevant if they show that the proposition is not acceptable under the rules of Scientific Method. But whenever acceptance is not barred, the decision is up to the individual scientist. Only for purposes of historical description is it permissible, and sometimes appropriate, to speak of a body of science in the sense that acceptance by all or by the majority of scientists within a definite historical period determines what was part of it. Science, seen as a dynamic concern of humanity, moves on irrespective of what the majority of scientists at any given time is ready to accept, as our illustrations show. The body of science is living, not petrified. It includes all tentative acceptances, or refusals to accept, that are legitimately offered by any scientist. It embodies controversial theories as well as noncontroversial ones; and the controversial theories do not merely surround an otherwise firm and petrified body of science like an atmosphere or aura but sometimes reach deep down to its very core.

CHAPTER II

THEORY OF SCIENTIFIC METHOD (CONTINUED):
CAUSALITY, TESTS, PREDICTION

An Introductory Note on Explanation

To "explain" something scientifically may mean one of several things, according to whether one tries to explain (1) what it "means," or (2) why it is "true" or "false," or otherwise compatible or incompatible with some norm, standard, or rule, or (3) how it has come to "be there," what it "is" (not what it "means"), and what the consequences of its being there may be. A few words will be added here on each of these types of explanation before we turn to a more detailed account of the third.

If we try to explain the "meaning" of a word, signal, symbol, or other sign, or of a sentence, proposition, or mathematical formula, we seek either to express the same meaning in other, more familiar words or signs, or, going beyond such mere translation, to point out some or all of the meaning's implications. This was discussed in Chapter 1, Sections 5 and 6, and will be taken up, with regard to the meaning of life and of history, in the present chapter.

If, instead of explaining the "meaning" of a proposition, or after explaining it, we try to explain why we hold the proposition to be "true" or "false," we may do so by showing either (a) that it is logically implied in the meaning of other propositions which have been accepted or assumed to be true or false, or (b) that acceptance of the proposition as true or false is in line with other rules of scientific procedure.

Likewise, we may try to explain why some behavior, attitude, etc., is "right" or "wrong" by showing that it is or is not in accord with presupposed norms, standards, or rules. This type of explanation will be dealt with specifically in Chapters III and IV.

If, however, we try to explain neither the meaning of something nor its compatibility with norms, standards, or rules, but simply the fact that it "is there" or that it "happened"—an "existential" fact or event, as we may call it—and "what" it is that is there or happened, then the two forms of explanation mentioned before will not do. To explain an existential fact or event means to present it as a link in the chain of cause and effect, or, if we are unable to assign it a place in some pattern of cause and effect, at least to give it a place in some other pattern of existential regularity. The physician who tells his patient that he is suffering from rheumatism, and is asked to explain how rheumatism comes about and what it is, may himself not know that exactly; but he feels able to arrange the symptoms and effects of rheumatism within some pattern of regularity, and that is as far as he may be able to go in explaining it. This is less satisfactory, scientifically, than is an explanation in terms of cause and effect. To an inquiry into the particular relationship of causation the first section of the present chapter will be devoted.

The "meaning" of an existential fact must always be distinguished from the fact itself. Any fact (event) may be regarded as a sign carrying a definite meaning; for example, a star as a message telling of God's greatness, or a rotten egg thrown at a campaign speaker as a message expressing contempt. Such interpretation may be correct or incorrect. Unquestionably, many facts, such as letters of an alphabet used in communication, *are* signs, carrying some meaning. Conversely, every sign made is also a fact, something that "is there" or "happens." In explaining facts which I regard as signs, I may limit myself to explaining the sign's alleged meaning, and stop there. Such explanation, however, always implies a rudimentary explanation in terms of cause and effect. For when I say that stars are signs of God's greatness, this implies the meaning that the existence of stars is causally interrelated with God's existence, and when I say that a rotten egg is a sign of contempt, that implies the meaning that the egg hits the speaker because someone had thrown it. But the two types of explanation here interwoven—explaining the meaning of something and explaining how it happened—must be clearly distinguished in scientific inquiry.

1. *Causation*

(a) CAUSING AN EFFECT

Cause-and-effect is the conventional name for the interrelation between two successive events where the occurrence of the earlier is regarded as a condition for that of the later.

Whether causality rules the universe and what causality really is has remained a matter for scientific controversy. Hume insisted that reason alone—reason a priori, see Section 5, below—could never establish that all events must have been caused by others or that any event actually had been so caused; he denied our ability to state more than that, according to our sense experiences, certain conjunctions of events did take place. It was on the basis of experience alone, and not of a-priori reasoning, that we reached this conclusion, he said; our experience, however, did not extend to the causal relation as such but only to the conjunction of events.[1]

Kant, greatly impressed by Hume's argument and proceeding from it, saw the solution of the problem of causality in a reversal of the approach. Conceding that neither pure reason nor experience can reveal the reality and the nature of causal relation, he taught that nonetheless the human mind cannot operate—or, at least, cannot acquire generalized empirical knowledge—but in terms of the idea that every change in phenomena must have a cause. If the universe did not project this principle into reason, then it was reason which projected it, as a necessary form of its own functioning, into the universe. This was Kant's Copernican revolution.

To be precise, Kant did not go so far as to base his theory exclusively on the contention that men are absolutely unable to think differently, although he has often been interpreted in this manner. Whatever may have been his original thoughts on this question, at any rate he inserted some unequivocal passages to the contrary into the second edition of his *Critique of Pure Reason* (1787).[2] There he objected to an interpretation of his theory in the sense that the notion of causation was "solely founded in some arbitrary necessity implanted in us of combining certain empirical notions according to such [causality] rule of relation." People would not be lacking, he added, who would deny that they felt this necessity. But he still insisted that the category of causality was a "first principle, product of our own thought (*selbstgedacht*), a priori to our acquisition of empirical knowledge." This must be considered along with his doctrine that only *appearances* in the sensory world (phenomena), not what he called "things-in-themselves," could be objects of our cognition. Thus, even in the second version, Kant maintained that our knowledge has access only to the subjective sources of the generalizing law of causality: the idea that some cause must underlie every change in appearances was, according to him, determined a priori, either by our mental make-up, or, if not that, at least (later version) by necessary regulative principles of our own making.

The exact meaning of the development in Kant's thought on causal-

---

[1] On Hume see also Appendix B, notes to Chapter V.

[2] In the section titled "Transcendentale Elementarlehre," No. 27. The first edition appeared in 1781.

ity, and whether there was any development in it, is controversial.[3] I hold that Kant never gave up the idea that men cannot help thinking in causal terms (see the word "solely" in the quotation above), but that he only tried (1) to protect himself from the objection that some people might claim they were able to think of changes without a cause, and (2) to emphasize that the phenomena corresponded to the expectations formed on the basis of the generalizing principle. However that may be, it is important to notice that from the beginning to the end Kant's thesis referred to appearances in the sensory world only. He explicitly rejected the inference that the "things-in-themselves" too were subject to the law that every event must have a cause. Whether that was so we could not know, he said, and we had no way of finding out. This was the decisive factor in his argument that "causal determinism" in the realm of appearances (phenomena) might be coexistent with "freedom" in the realm of things in themselves, a question to which we shall revert later.

More recently, quantum physics has led to a revival of the debate. Atoms and their constituents have proved inaccessible to attempts at explaining them in terms of cause and effect; their structure, behavior, different life periods, and their very existence defy such explanation. People interested in the latest developments of physics are, therefore, often heard to say that quantum physics has dethroned causality, or at least destroyed belief in it. As a matter of fact, however, there are few physicists, quantum or other, who would doubt that even microcosmic occurrences have "causes" in *some* sense of the term, or who would positively maintain that anything in the physical world can happen without any cause.

What has actually evolved in quantum physics is something else. It has been found—and this much without a possible doubt, it seems—that microcosmic occurrences cannot be revealed by human observation beyond a limiting point, because factors that are inevitably connected with the observational procedure, such as the turning of light beams or other forces on the object, so greatly influence microcosmic events that what we observe is the effect of our disturbing interference rather than the occurrence without that effect. We are, therefore, unable fully to explore microcosmic structures and events. Only the tremendous number of atoms and their constituents and the velocity of their move-

---

[3] Literature: Ernst Cassirer, *Determinismus und Indeterminismus in der modernen Physik, historische und systematische Studien zum Kausalproblem*, Göteborg 1937, pp. 74 ff., 128, 141, 202.

ments, together with their mutual operation as obstacles to one another's free movements, permit the calculation of the results of their *combined* behavior in processes that are sensorially observable by us. The regularities of these observable processes, then, can be scientifically explained only with the aid of the laws of probability as applied to very great numbers of events, i.e., through "statistical" laws, and not through *recognizable* "causal" laws.

But this does not preclude the possibility—or, as many physicists (including Einstein) would say, the probability [4]—that the microcosmic events too have causes. Only if causality is defined, not objectively, as the ubiquity of causal relations, but subjectively, as our *knowledge* about such relations—e.g., the possibility of our predicting the effects after knowing the existing conditions—is it correct to say that microphysics has destroyed belief in causality. But then the fault may be in our lack of knowledge as to existing conditions, and not necessarily in the absence of causal interrelations. Werner Heisenberg stated this side of the matter well in his famous paper of 1927, in which he presented the Incertainty (or Indeterminacy) Principle: "What is wrong in the sharp formulation of the law of causality (if we know the present exactly we can predict the future) is not its second part but the condition. It is impossible, on principle, for us to obtain knowledge of the present in all its determinants." [5]

Doubt may be carried one step further, it is true, so as to involve the objective nature of causal interrelations. It might be said, and actually has been, that the apparently erratic and unpredictable behavior of individual atoms and their consituents—with respect to the direction in which they move individually, their individual life span in the case of radioactivity, and the like—raise the question whether this individual behavior reflects any *universal* (if hidden) laws, or in other words whether, even if we knew all about the individual behavior, it could be described in universal terms. But this is no more than a *question*, which for the reasons just stated can hardly ever be answered. It is far from being definitely established that microcosmic events fail to be

[4] See the discussions among Einstein, Planck, and James Murphy in the appendix to Max Planck, *Where is Science Going?* New York 1932.

[5] Werner Heisenberg, "Über den anschaulichen Inhalt der quantentheoretischen Kinematik und Mechanik," *Zeitschrift für Physik,* vol. 43 (1927) p. 172. See on this passage Cassirer, *op.cit.,* p. 152, and Arnold Hildesheimer, *Die Welt der ungewohnten Dimensionen,* Leiden 1953, p. 312. The latter adds, "No quantum physicist will contend that anything can happen that has no cause at all" (p. 317), and again, "No quantum physicist has ever contended that anything could occur that has no cause at all" (p. 321). But see the following paragraph in the text above.

ruled by universal laws, any more than that they are so ruled; and even if it were, which it cannot be, there would still be room left for assuming that every individual microcosmic occurrence has, nevertheless, always "some" cause, though possibly one of an individual type, not universal in character. All this is mere speculation, however, in contrast to the limitation of microcosmic observability. This limitation is now generally held to be the inevitable result of scientific thought.

The impact of quantum physics on the causality principle is also frequently overrated because of a confusion with another issue, namely, the tendency of some scholars to deny "meaning" to any hypothesis that cannot be scientifically verified. From this point of view, the hypothesis that all events have causes has no meaning, since it cannot be verified by observation. But then neither has the opposite contention meaning that there are events which have no causes, since that too cannot be verified.[6] This way of putting it is no result of quantum physics but a mannerism of a special type of scientific language, with which we shall deal in Chapter v, Section 3 (Neopositivism). It fails to answer the question whether every event has a cause, either affirmatively or negatively, and even avoids confessing to our ignorance.

Whether the human mind is so structured as to be unable to think that changes have no causes still remains an open question. Even if Kant did not rest his theory on this thesis, or not on it alone, there is much to be said in its favor. It should be noted, in particular, that explanation of microcosmic events in terms of statistical probabilities rather than of cause and effect does not refute it, because our ability to discard causal explanations in theoretical calculations does not testify to our ability really to *imagine* that some occurrence, even in the microcosmic sphere, has no cause.

A special difficulty in the conception that one event is caused by another arises from the fact that, even apart from atoms and happenings within them, events cannot be neatly separated into "units" that follow each other like the units of an alphabet, distinctly identifiable as separate. Every detail of what occurs is so inseparably intertwined with what had occurred before and will occur after, and even with what occurs simultanously, that any lumping together of occurrences into

---

[6] See, for instance, Max Born, who, in the manner of the Neopositivists, thinks it empty talk to say that every event has a cause if it is impossible on principle to know all the conditions (causes) of any event (*Atomic Physics,* London 1944), but who does not contend that on this ground there are events that have no causes. Most consistent in Neopositivistic language regarding causality: Philipp Frank, *Between Physics and Philosophy,* Cambridge, Mass., 1941, pp. 55 ff., 151 ff., especially 155.

bigger units called "events" is utterly arbitrary, except where we do so for some special purpose, as for example a scientific one; then it may be a reasonable, and even the best possible, procedure in the pursuit of this particular purpose. Apart from such purposive human selections, the apparently separate and independent events are, to use John Dewey's words, "integral constituents of one and the same continuous occurrence." [7] It follows that we cannot label separate clusters of minute events "the cause" or "the effect," except for our convenience in the pursuit of some inquiry or the like. We step on the gas lever—event No. 1—and off goes the car—event No. 2; so we like to think. Yet how many "events," about which the average driver does not care, lie between the two, and how many others must have preceded them to make the car move!

This impossibility of neatly culling out definite clusters of events as causes and others as the effects of the causes does not, however, seem to preclude the possibility that within the total flow of the "continuous occurrence" causal influences do operate. Hume and Kant merely said we do not know. Dewey went further. These considerations of continuity led him to guess that causation was no ontological reality at all, but *merely* a "functional means of regulating existential inquiry," i.e., a means we use for the purpose of our scientific inquiries into what actually happens. He held that just as "essences," "purposes" (on these, see below), and "simplicity" are no longer considered ontological properties of nature today, as they were once thought to be, but are now recognized as mere means of inquiry, so also should causation be recognized as no ontological property of nature but merely as a means of inquiry.

Actually Dewey adduced no evidence why we must pass from the modest agnostic doubts of Hume and Kant to his own bolder denial of causation. Nor did he expect that his views would be readily accepted.[8] For all his critical attitude, however, he did not question the value of the causal category as a means of inquiry; on the contrary, he called it a "leading principle" of inquiry and insisted that as such it cannot be affected even by experimental findings that lead to question-

---

[7] *Logic,* p. 445.

[8] *Ibid.,* p. 462. He makes much of the fact that the so-called "causal laws," which must be formulated in *if-then* form (if *a*, then *b*) themselves contain no temporal sequences of events, i.e., no temporal antecedents and sequents; the sequence of events comes in only in the application of these abstract laws (pp. 442 ff.). Yet even if this were correct, which I doubt, it would still not preclude the possibility that causality operates in the flow of events irrespective of our formulating laws about it.

ing causation as an ontological reality.[9] This brings Dewey's view close to Kant's, putting the laws of causality into the human mind rather than in nature, although Dewey would have denied more definitely than Kant that men *must* think in the category of causality; to him it was sufficient that it is useful for them to do so.

The important point here is that, despite philosophical doubts about the ontological reality of causation (Hume, Kant, and more radically, Dewey) and of the particular difficulties with which the problem is beset in the explanation of microcosmic events, twentieth-century Scientific Method continues to work with the concept of causal relationship or its equivalent in both natural and social sciences, at least outside microcosmic research. This does not mean that Scientific Method is able to establish the reality and the nature of causal laws; it means only that in "accepting" such relations in the many decisions required of the scholar about acceptance of data and of their explanation (Chapter I, Sections 2, 3, 5, and 7), he does not violate rules of scientific procedure, at least not unless the nature of the causal relation is his specific subject of research.

It is now generally recognized, however, that whenever we say "event *b* is the effect of event *a*," we are making an assumption which scientifically is hypothetic in character. The assumption is even twofold, because we assume (1) that under like conditions an event of the nature of *a* will always be succeeded by an event of the nature of *b*, and (2) that this is to be ascribed to some influence or impact of *a* on *b*. Both these hypotheses, based as they are on the results of observations in particular cases only—though very many of them [10]—are reached inductively in our mind; they are not immediately observed. It follows that every explanation in terms of cause and effect, or of other regularities, is exposed to potential challenge in science. But the philosophical doubt of causality is not of itself considered a good enough ground under Scientific Method for challenging empirical evidence, any more than is the philosophical doubt of reality (Chapter I, Section 5, above). To this extent Scientific Method is grounded in common sense (see Chapter V, Section 2, on skepticism).

[9] P. 462.

[10] "The causal law represents the special form of statistical correlations holding for 100 percent of the cases," Hans Reichenbach, "Probability Methods in Social Science," in D. Lerner and H. D. Lasswell, *The Policy Sciences, Recent Developments in Scope and Method*, Stanford 1951, pp. 121 ff. See also Reichenbach's *Theory of Probability, an Inquiry into the Logical and Mathematical Foundations of the Calculus of Probability*, 2nd ed., Berkeley 1949 (in German: *Wahrscheinlichkeitslehre*, Leiden 1935).

Several types of causal interrelation are traditionally distinguished. The first event may have been a "necessary" condition in the sense that the second could not have occurred otherwise, or it may have been only one of several alternative conditions, each of which could have produced the later event. It may have been a "sufficient" condition, in itself alone enough to explain the effect, or it could have produced the effect only along with other events or conditions. The effect may or may not have been "foreseeable," and this may have a great bearing on the question of responsibility. Such distinctions, important as they are, do not yet concern us here where we are engaged in an inquiry of a more fundamental character into the causal relationship.

(b) EFFECTING A CAUSE. MOTIVATION AND FREE WILL

If an effect depends on a mechanical cause, as the propulsion of a bullet on the snapping of a trigger or the motion of a car on the lowering of a gas lever, one can often intentionally make the cause occur, for example, by pulling the trigger or stepping on the lever. Then the acting person "effects a cause." Instead of performing the necessary act himself, he may be able to induce another person to do it, and thus effect the cause in an indirect manner. What makes him act, and what makes the other person act that way?

Human behavior is motivated by a number of factors, whose systematic classification presents considerable difficulty. Among them are need, various kinds of "drives," conscious and subconscious ones, habits, emotions, and thoughts. There is no necessity for us here to engage in a fundamental discussion of these factors. From the viewpoint of Scientific Method, motivation is a special type of causation, distinguished by two particular characteristics. The first is that scientific observation, in the form of self-observation, has more direct access here to the process of causation than in physical and chemical reactions. The second is that the cause-effect relation presents itself as less compelling, less necessary, here than there. Free will seems to interfere at times. Sometimes, free will seems even to be able to start a new line of causation. (See Chapter XII, Section 1.)

Whether or not there is free will, and, if so, where lies the line between necessity and free will, continues to be a controversial philosophical problem. Scientific Method is not generally concerned with it, unless it is the special subject of research. This is not to say that Scientific Method has the answer, or assumes one, this way or that. It means only that the scholar who in his various procedural steps of "acceptance" assumes some human freedom to operate in the common-sense interpretation of reality does not necessarily violate the scientific rules governing acceptance (Chapter 1, Section 7; also, XII, Section 1).

Much as is dark in this field, one thing is certain. The human will is not so free that it is immune to outside influences. Motivations can be "manipulated" to a great extent. That is to say, men can bring about events that foreseeably set inner drives in other men in operation, arouse emotions or prompt thoughts in them, or otherwise affect the process of motivation. This "manipulability" of motives is a factor of the greatest importance in the political field, as it is in other fields of the social sciences.

Scientific knowledge of motivation and of its manipulability has increased considerably during the last fifty years, especially through research done on the great role played by the subconscious, by repressed drives and emotions, by other irrational factors, by the influence of in-group, out-group, and mass situations, and by the various techniques of advertising, propaganda, and terror ("brain-washing"). The comprehensive work done within this whole area by psychologists of various schools, including psychoanalysts, and by sociologists constitutes an inseparable part of the tools with which political science must try to discharge its own specific function. Much remains to be done to establish better cooperation between psychologists, sociologists, and political scientists. Many illustrations of this need will occur as we go along. Special problems of motivation within the political field will be taken up in the further course of this work.

(c) EFFECTING A CAUSE (CONTINUED). ENTELECHY

Can the order of cause and effect be reversed? Can the end effect its own cause? Can the future shape the past to suit it?

We need not ponder here about the conflicting readings of time that would result if time were measured in separate cosmic systems that move in different directions or at a different speed (Einstein's relativity). We are dealing here only with life on our little planet, where cosmic relativity does not interfere with our common-sense concept of time, and time flows in only one direction. It might, however, seem that, though the flow of time cannot be reversed, the order of cause and effect can, in two ways, because (1) future events often influence man's actions, and (2) the future seems to be incorporated in the very nature of many things.

The first of these two arguments presents no particular difficulty. Motivation of man's action by future events does not really affect the order of cause and effect, since in this case the fact that a person pursues certain purposes and harbors certain expectations is the cause of his action and antecedes it in time. But the second argument confronts us with a grave problem. The order of cause and effect may appear reversed in a most puzzling manner—with no human anticipation serving as a connecting link—on the ground that the seeds of plants, animals, and human beings seem to carry their own future in them, and every organ of a living body seems to be the incarnation of a purpose, and to act for that purpose. Even some inanimate matter, like crystals, seems to develop toward a goal.

This way of looking at things is called "teleological." It is more beautifully and most graphically expressed in the Greek term *en-telécheia* (Engl., entelechy), which is composed of *en,* meaning "in," *telos,* meaning "end" or "goal," and *echein,* meaning "have." [11] If life could *only* be explained in teleological terms, because things or organs that have no mind capable of anticipating the future act as if they did anticipate it, then either the future is the cause of the past, or a "goal" or "purpose" is incorporated in things, and that would logically require that there is, or was, someone who conceived the goal or purpose and did incorporate it. If no one has done that, we cannot logically say that a goal or purpose is contained in a thing, unless we mean by this —in some type of pantheistic thinking—that the thing itself sets the goal, or forms the purpose, which it pursues.

The striking appearance of entelechy in nature has, therefore, always been one of the strongest arguments for the belief in a Creator. From antiquity until the middle of the nineteenth century—and that means from Plato and Aristotle until Kant and Hegel—even the most unorthodox scholars generally felt they had no reasonable choice but to accept some divine explanation of nature, because up to that late date no plausible alternative to entelechy had been offered. When we study the harsh measures of intolerance directed against atheists in earlier periods, we should not forget that the apparent obviousness of goal and purpose in nature seemed to give such reaction some scientific justification.

Only when, one hundred years ago (1859), Charles Darwin published his theory on the origin of species "by means of natural selec-

[11] It should be noted, however, that the term *entelécheia* has been used with various meanings in the course of the history of philosophy, owing to the fact that *telos* means end not only in the sense of end-in-view (goal, purpose) but in that of terminating-end (close) as well.

tion" was the human mind offered a carefully substantiated scientific alternative which does not necessarily require that plants, animals, or human beings, seeds, or living organs have a purpose, a goal, an end put into them.[12] The alternative is that only those organisms grew and survived which could stand the astronomical, geographical, physical, chemical, and other conditions of the universe, and more particularly, the competitive conditions of existence on the earth. Among the innumerable variations that came into being through the play of chance, there gradually arose, in the course of many millions of years (according to the present state of research our galaxy is about four and one-half billion years old), variations that were better adapted to conditions than others. In other words, things grew without any purpose, and those which were best adapted to existing conditions grew better and multiplied more than others. The fact that the seeds and organs of living beings seem to have a purpose, then, would be a mere illusion. When there finally arose beings that developed a mind, *they* could form a goal or purpose. But there may be no other goal or purpose except that which they form and pursue.

Let it be clearly stated, however, in view of many misinterpretations, that Darwin himself drew no atheistic conclusions from the results of his research. He did not teach that life developed from matter. The evidence displayed in his great book led him only to the far more modest conclusion "that animals are descended from at most only four or five progenitors, and plants from an equal or lesser number." He added: "*Analogy* would lead me one step further, namely, to the belief that *all animals* and *plants* are descended from some *one* prototype." He conceded that "analogy may be a deceitful guide." None the less, "it does *not seem incredible* that from some such low and intermediate form both animals and plants may have been developed; and if we admit this, we must likewise admit that all the *organic* beings which have ever lived on this earth *may* be descended from some one primordial form. But this inference is chiefly grounded on *analogy,* and it is immaterial whether or not it be accepted"—immaterial, that is, for his less radical main thesis, mentioned above.[13] There, however, he

[12] Charles Darwin, *The Origin of Species by Means of Natural Selection, or, the Preservation of Favored Races in the Struggle for Life,* 1859. There had been earlier attempts to explain the existence of higher forms of life through a process of natural evolution, either in a purely mechanistic manner, or (Antoine de Lamarck, 1744–1829) by assuming the inheritance of acquired traits. But these theories lacked the evidential strength mustered by Darwin for his, and most of them, including Lamarck's, relied on the cooperation of teleological factors or "tendencies" in the process of evolution.

[13] Sixth ed., p. 500. Italics mine.

stopped, explicitly admitting "that science as yet throws no light on the far higher problem of the essence or origin of life." [14]

Incidentally, Darwin confessed to his own continuing belief in a Creator. "I see no good reason," he wrote, "why the views given in this volume should shock the religious feeling of any one." He quoted with approval a letter he had received from a "celebrated author and divine," who stated that "it is just as noble a conception of the Deity to believe that He created a few original forms capable of self-developing into other and needful forms, as to believe that He required a fresh act of creation to supply the voids caused by the action of His laws." [15] Indeed, the book ends with these religious words: "There is grandeur in this view of life, with its several powers, having been originally breathed by the Creator into a few forms or into one; and that, while this planet has gone circling on according to the fixed laws of gravity, from so simple a beginning endless forms most beautiful and most wonderful have been, and are being evolved." [16]

It is fitting, on the centenary of Darwin's publication, that these passages be quoted. The important point in our present context, however, is that after 1859 the mere *appearance* of entelechy has lost its old force of providing conclusive scientific evidence for the truth of the assumption that there *is* entelechy. There now are, rather, two alternative explanations. Either there is incorporation of goals or purposes in nonconscious entities like seeds and organs, and this presupposes some kind of divine Creator; or things behave as they do merely as a result of chance and survival, and then the existence of a Creator is not presupposed, although it is not excluded either.

Scientific Method provides no answer to the question which alternative is correct. Biological research and experimentation based on Darwin's hypotheses and Mendel's laws have had phenomenal results, it is true, especially in plant and animal breeding. It is, therefore, today considered a matter of course in biological research to accept Darwin's hypotheses as a starting point. But this must not blind us to the fact that the evidence is still limited to what has been specifically proved through observation. There surely is an overwhelming evidence in favor of the thesis that plant and animal forms have undergone a process of gradual evolution in the course of millions of years; many geological and embryonic findings cannot be explained in any other way.

[14] *Ibid.*, p. 496.
[15] *Ibid.*
[16] *Ibid.*, p. 505.

But there is no conclusive evidence yet, as Darwin himself recognized, that the origin of all life, or of any life, is traceable to natural evolution alone, nor that the evolution of higher forms of life from lower ones has proceeded, as Darwin did believe, in line with his hypotheses, and exclusively so. There are scientific counterarguments, such as that the earth is not old enough to explain the evolution of the highest forms of life with all their wondrous interaction of organs and cells, or even only a single cell (one egg-cell contains trillions or quadrillions of atoms, arranged in billions or trillions of molecules, it has been figured), merely through chance variations, selection, and survival of the fittest in the struggle for existence.[17]

Furthermore, although many appearances of entelechy have now lost their former evidential force under the weight of the Darwinian arguments, there are other such appearances which obstinately resist attempts to explain them away, e.g., the growth of the whole form out of each part of artificially halved or even quartered sea urchin eggs (Hans Driesch, 1867–1941). Many philosophers, therefore, while otherwise accepting Darwin's basic hypotheses, have tried to salvage the traditional distinction not only between stones and plants (recognized by Darwin, see above) but also between plants and animals and between the latter and men. They have assumed that life, nonconscious soul, and conscious, self-reflecting mind did not evolve through natural evolution each from the next lower form but, rather, through one, two, or three additional infusions coming somehow from somewhere, which successively added these gifts to the preceding base (Neovitalism); or, that the whole of every cell directs some influence to its parts, and that the whole of the cosmos has some directive influence on all that is in it. In the course of this discussion, the "creative" character of evolution has been stressed (Bergson, Whitehead, and others), and emphasis has been put on the "emergent" and "novel" feature (the *novum*) that appears on each higher level and that cannot be derived from the next lower level (Lloyd Morgan, Samuel Alexander, Nicolai Hartmann, Arthur O. Lovejoy, and others). Whitehead was even more radical. He suggested that all "concrete enduring entities," such as molecules and their combinations, are "organisms," so that "the plan of the whole influences the characters of the various subordinate organisms [even

[17] This objection has been eloquently illustrated by Lecomte du Noüy, *The Road to Reason*, ed. by Mary L. d. N., New York 1948. Debate of this point is not yet terminated, though. The rebuttal has been that under conditions as may have existed on earth some two billion years ago the chances (probabilities) of live cells emerging from purely fortuitous combinations of atoms were far greater than they are now.

chemical ones, etc.] which enter into it"; an electron in a living body, then, would be different from an electron outside it.[18]

On the other side of the fence, many twentieth-century scholars, going far beyond the cautious inferences drawn by Darwin himself, believe in the emergence not only of higher forms of life from lower ones, but ultimately of all life from physical, inorganic events; or they insist at least that this alternative should not be dismissed too easily.[19]

The important point here is that neither Darwin's evolutionary theory nor the ensuing debate has made possible a solely scientific choice between the two alternatives—divine forces, or not. Great as are the difficulties that beset the scientific pursuit of the thesis of natural evolution, especially if extended to the evolution of life from inorganic matter, it can hardly be denied that the same holds true for the divine alternative, assuming a Creator who was not created, and who has no cause for "being there" outside of his own will.

Scientific Method can only point to procedure for inquiry, and as we have seen in Chapter 1, Section 1, it cannot even provide us with the most promising questions suitable for further research, nor with advice how best to pursue it; this remains a matter for human genius to determine, or for good luck to hit upon. Scientific Method must, however, insist that when we speak of "goal" or "purpose" and of their embodiment or the like, we must say what we mean by these terms. It must point out that, if we mean by them, as we generally do, ideas which some mind has formed and pursues, then the assumption of goals and purposes in plants, seeds, sperms, eggs, organs, etc., implies the assumption of a suprahuman mind.[20] When the same terms are used in a different sense, e.g., in the sense that nonconscious organisms act *as if* they pursued a purpose,[21] Scientific Method must demand that this other sense be clearly stated and not ambiguously veiled by terms that carry a connotation to a conscious and planning mind. Scientific Method must insist, on the other hand, that the reality of natural evolu-

---

[18] A. N. Whitehead, *Science and the Modern World,* New York 1925, pp. 115, 157 ff.; *Process and Reality,* New York 1929.

[19] John Dewey was in this category, it seems. See William Savery in R. A. Schilpp, ed., *The Philosophy of John Dewey,* New York 1939 and 1951, pp. 510 ff.

[20] The fact that the human mind conceives of purposes and goals and human beings strive after them, making means or ends of everything there is, actually or potentially, has rightly been said by Whitehead and by Hocking (*Science and the Idea of God, op.cit.,* p. 108) to make the entire universe purposive to a degree, since human existence is part of the history of the universe. Yet this does not prove that any goals or purposes outside those formed by the human mind are operative in the universe. It may make us inclined to think so; but if it was true, then it would no longer be the human mind alone that formed purposes.

[21] See e.g., F. A. Hayek, *The Counter-Revolution of Science,* Glencoe, Ill., 1952, pp. 80 ff.

tion is not proved by a demonstration of its theoretical possibility alone. Even if fully verified, natural evolution would fail to explain how the entire chain of events that led to such miraculous results was set going and to establish whether or not that was done by a Creator with a purpose—a purpose incorporated, not perhaps in individual things, but in the entire chain of events and the evolutionary laws governing them.

In other words, the theory of evolution does not *eliminate* the divine alternative. It merely makes us aware of the fact that there are *two* alternative explanations, neither of which has been scientifically verified. See Chapter xiii for a further discussion of this point, especially regarding the chances of verification and the degree of "likelihood" to be allotted to either alternative.

(d) MAN-MADE LAWS AND INSTITUTIONS

The course of human events, i.e., their causal interrelation, is influenced not only by natural laws but, as everyone realizes, quite strongly also by man-made laws and institutions. They carry great weight in motivating human beings, and success and failure often depend on them. It can be said assuredly, for example, that the causal sequence of events will generally differ according to whether a man tries to carry through his plans within the framework of the country's constitution and other laws or in violation of them. The obstacles that are placed in his path in the latter case may be unsurmountable and, even if not, will constitute a relevant factor in the course of events. To the political scientist, therefore, man-made laws and institutions have an importance that is often hardly less relevant to his inquiries than that of natural laws. But there always remains this difference, that man-made laws *can* be disobeyed while natural laws cannot. We shall revert to this topic more specifically in Chapter iv.

(e) HISTORY

History, seen as the sequence of events, reveals effects, not causes, at least not directly. It is generous and even merciless in putting effects before our eyes, in the long run if not at once. Yet as to causes, history is often cryptic or ambiguous. It needs interpreters who trace the individual events or clusters of events to particular other events or clusters as their causes.

That task is made difficult by the fact that each historical situation is unique, both in many details of the external conditions and in the individualities of the persons participating in the event. History never repeats itself *completely*. Scientifically speaking, such repetition is impossible, at least during the life span of our planetary system, because of the myriads of variables involved, which can never be expected to arrange themselves in the same order.[22] Nietzsche, it is true, figured that if dispensing with the idea of a Creator we took the concept of eternity (*infinite* time) seriously, there was a mathematical probability that after a very, very long time the arrangement of the (large but *finite*) number of smallest particles in the universe would be the same as it had been once before. This was one of the foundations of his belief in "perpetual recurrence" (*ewige Wiederkehr des Gleichen*).[23] But before this process of repetition could ever start, the entire universe must have disintegrated; "entropy," as we would say now, must have been completed. Even then, the mathematical probability that things will repeat themselves—either at once, or after many trillion swings of the full circle—exactly as they had been, is infinitesimally small. Nor does mathematics authorize us to assure (although many probability theorists indulge this fallacy) that whatever *can* happen, even though it may have only the slightest chance, *must* happen in the long run. However that may be, political science deals with history *prior* to the disintegration of this earth.

Every historical situation being unique, it is always perilous to expect the repetition of what, seen from afar, may appear as a set historical pattern. History does not weave patterns, or write laws, of her own. But she too follows—or rather, registers the working of—natural laws or regularities, at least those of cause and effect, which have their source not in history but in the factors that go into history, the raw material of history. These laws or regularities are being disclosed, not by the sequence of events as such (history), but by scientific observation and scientific hypotheses. History merely illustrates, corroborates, or invalidates these hypothetical laws; it does not produce them.

Different as each historical situation is from any other, particular features may be, and often are, similar in character, and this similarity may be more relevant to the scientific problem under inquiry than is the difference. Every physical or chemical experiment also is an historical occurrence, taking place at a definite time and running through a definite, if brief, period. But the factors relevant for the physical or chemical inquiry are alike and the differences in the unique historical

[22] See, e.g., W. E. Hocking, *Science and the Idea of God, op.cit.*, p. 112.
[23] Nietzsche, *Werke*, vol. XII, pp. 51, 61, 63; XVI, pp. 396, 400. Karl Löwith, *Nietzsches Philosophie der ewigen Wiederkehr des Gleichen*, Stuttgart 1956, pp. 93 ff.

situations may be irrelevant for the problems under inquiry. In much the same way, the consequences of specific political events, such as the introduction of some particular constitutional clause, electoral system, or administrative set-up, are factors that may lend themselves to valid comparison with similar events, at other places and times. Above all, in every unique situation of human history there is always *man,* with his characteristic peculiarities that have remained fundamentally the same through all recorded history.

Hence it is by no means unusual that regularities and parallelisms in historical sequences of events can be pointed out and plausibly explained in terms of cause and effect. But many obstacles obstruct the successful pursuit of such endeavors, especially if undertaken large-scale as a causal interpretation of what we may call "macro-history" —whole periods of history, the entire history of individual nations or civilizations, or history altogether. While it is often quite possible to demonstrate that a certain event was likely, and even bound, to have a certain effect, there is no scientific law, either logical or empirical, that enables us to infer from posterior events which of a plurality of possible causes produced them, although many people argue as if there were. Furthermore, even where it can be shown that some specific human action constituted an essential link in the chain of causation, it often remains open to question whether the actor can be considered "responsible" for the outcome, because this depends, among other circumstances, on whether he could have foreseen the effect, and what the possible alternatives of his behavior were. External causation is not enough for placing responsibility; a causal interrelation must be shown to exist between not only the action but between the "guilt" of the actor and the untoward effect. This type of causal nexus might be called "culpa-causation," to distinguish it from external causation.[24]

Limited knowledge of relevant events, plurality of possible causal factors, limited possibility for actors in history to foresee the effects, and the limited ability of the historian to list all the possible alternatives of action and their potential effects, plus the immense number of other variables involved in the analysis of history—all this makes the causal interpretation of macro-history a free field for almost unlimited adventures in speculative thought, while the possibilities of verification are narrowly limited. Owing to these limitations such interpretations

---

[24] The name "culpa-causation" was suggested in one of my earliest papers, "Die einfache und die wiederholte positive Vertragsverletzung," *Jherings Jahrbücher,* vol. 54 (1909) p. 85, note 1, but has not been adopted, as far as I can see. I have found no better word in the meantime.

can rarely claim a *scientific* status higher than that of "working hypotheses." As such they may, however, in fortunate cases fulfill an important function, opening our eyes to causal interconnections that we might otherwise overlook (see Section 6, below, and Chapters VII, Section 3, VIII, Section 12, and XIII). Consequently, large-scale interpretation of history has proved to be a field not only for amateurs, charlatans, and quacks but also for men of true genius. It so happens, however, that most of the great interpretors of history have been part-genius and part-charlatan. The scientist should expose all unjustified claims to scientific certainty of historical interpretations and predictions (see Chapter V, below, for illustrations), but should heed relevant suggestions. In condemning what is scientifically unwarranted he should not overlook or minimize what remains, and what *may* be true.

Within more narrow and specific limits, inquiries into causal interrelations are apt to yield better results, scientifically speaking. Frequently, proper inquiries can trace causal interrelations with sufficient accuracy to expect acceptance of conclusions cautiously drawn. To that extent, the study of history is among the best substitutes for experimental laboratories in political science (see Section 3, c, below).

The fact that the study of history supplies "case histories" which reveal and illustrate causal relations may justify our speaking of "lessons of history," if by that we mean no more than just this illustrative service we can obtain from history for the consequences produced by certain types of actions, institutions, etc. But this is not equivalent to saying that history herself "teaches" us lessons, or that history has a "meaning" in the sense that a word has meaning. Whether that is so depends on whether history is more than merely the sequence of events produced by causal laws or by mere chance, and in particular, whether back of the sequence of events there is a Mind that intentionally expresses some meaning through the events, in order to teach us lessons. As Scientific Method is unable to demonstrate either that there is such a Mind or that there is none, speculations about history as such having a meaning are not apt to reach a scientific status higher than that of a working hypothesis, with no chance of its conclusive confirmation by the results of inquiries. See Chapter XIII for a further pursuit of this reflection.

2. *Deduction as a Tool of Control*

Whenever we make a statement to the effect that *all* things of a certain class have a certain quality, for example, that all men are mortal or that all power corrupts, it follows that *according to this statement* (i.e., according to its *meaning*) some individual thing of the class described also has this quality. It is an important step in Scientific Method that, when we have ventured upon any generalization of observed facts, we make its logical implications explicit, because this enables. us to check on the correctness of the generalization by testing individual examples to which it applies.

Likewise, once we have tentatively explained a fact in terms of cause and effect, we take an important next step in scientific work when we state the logical implications of the causal law which we have assumed to operate. When we explain the fact that a stone which is exposed to sunshine is warmer than one which is not, on the theory that the rays of the sun make all things exposed to them warmer, then it follows deductively that boiling water, too, will be made warmer when hit by the rays of the sun. If logically correct inferences are invalidated by tests, then the general statement of causal relationship is wrong, or is at least in need of modifications.

It is utterly false, therefore, to say what is so often heard, that Scientific Method has replaced deductive (analytical) with inductive reasoning. Actually, deductive reasoning has remained one of the most important tools in modern science. What has been discarded is not deductive reasoning; it is the acceptance in scientific procedure of major premises (generalizing statements) as true or valid on ultimate grounds other than inductive reasoning carefully checked. In other words, Scientific Method objects to the acceptance of "a-priori" propositions, about which more will be said in Section 5, below; it does not object to a correct statement of their logical implications. On the contrary, one of the methods used scientifically to refute false propositions, a-priori or other, is to state deductively all their logical implications in order to submit them to tests of observation and of compatibility with other propositions.

If there be any order of rank between inductive and deductive reasoning, then the latter still deserves first prize as to logical validity. Inductive reasoning from mere samples, if ever so numerous, is never fully valid; and yet, in order to obtain a major premise from which deductive reasoning can be done and which is meant to correspond to reality and not merely to express a postulate, inductive reasoning is, generally speaking, the most reliable method available whenever we care to transmit the reasons for our conclusions to others (see below, Section 7). Such inductive generalizations are, however, of little scientific value unless they are followed by deductive derivation of their logical implications and subsequent testing of the latter. Induction and deduction are so closely intertwined, therefore, in modern science that the mind of the scientist operates like the hands of the weaver thrusting the thread of thought upward and downward in quick succession. But the quickness of movements is no excuse for confounding them; they remain logically different operations. Clear distinction between the question whether a premise is true (i.e., whether its assertibility is warranted), and the question whether deductive reasoning from the premise is correctly done, is essential for all scientific work.

3. *Testing and Correcting*

(a) GENERAL

The tentative acceptance of observations, reports, and measurements as properly made (Nos. 1–3 of our survey, Chapter 1, Section 1) and of their results as facts (No. 4) is tested by additional observations. Likewise, hypothetical generalizations of tentatively accepted facts (No. 5) and hypothetical explanations (No. 6) are tested by observations. When invalidated by test observations, the tentative decision must be withdrawn or corrected.

Careful tests constitute an essential element in Scientific Method on two grounds. They fortify the operating scientist's own acceptance of observations and conclusions; and they increase the intersubjective (interpersonal) transmissibility of scientifically acquired knowledge (see Section 7).

The need for tests is well expressed in the common-sense saying that "the proof of the pudding is in the eating thereof." Strictly speaking, however, the scientist does not test the pudding; he tests the hypothesis (using this term here in its broadest sense, see Section 6), formed on sight, that the thing before him *is* a pudding, and not a fake made of dirt or of something else that should not go into a pudding. Nor does he test his hypothesis just by eating a piece; he tests it by observing his sense experiences in eating, or in making other experimental tests. It is observation that counts in verifying a hypothesis.

To insist that the scientist tests not things but hypotheses may appear pedantic. Yet the difference is significant. There can be no scientific observation unless it be to some degree a test of a hypothesis previously formed, because to observe scientifically means to observe with a specific purpose. There are also nonscientific and prescientific observations on the part of a scientist, and plenty of them, in his everyday life. Yet the very moment he begins to pay "scientific" attention to what he observes, he must at least have some idea in his mind about the potential relevance of the observed fact or event for some scientific purpose, and in carrying on his observation in this mood he is already testing a hypothesis, at least the hypothesis of relevance, if not a more specific one he had formed in the past or is forming on the spur of the moment. Many types of scientific observation, such as mass observation by means of questionnaires and interviews, can hardly have any scientific significance at all unless the hypotheses to be tested thereby have already assumed a rather specific character in the mind of the scientist.

In other words, a clear line of demarcation between nonscientific and scientific observation can be drawn, but there is no such sharp line between an original scientific observation and subsequent tests.

All that has been said about observation, description, measurement, logical reasoning, and explanation in the preceding sections of Chapters I and II applies to tests as well as to the original observation.

(b) EXPERIMENTAL TESTS, PURE TYPE

The ideal test is the pure-type experiment, in which two situations essentially alike in every respect but one are brought about and their outcome is watched in the expectation that it will reveal the influence of the one different element. Yet rarely, if ever, is it possible to concoct such favorable experimental conditions in the social sciences. Even when external conditions can be arranged in line with strict postulates, many variables enter the experiment because of the human factor involved. For no two human beings are entirely alike.

Some carefully prepared experimental tests with school children, college students, or other relatively homogeneous groups have tried to come close to a pure-type experimental situation. Generally they have followed the scheme that two groups are formed, as similar in composition as it is humanly possible to achieve, and then one of them is exposed to the particular condition whose influence it is intended to test, while the other serves as a so-called control group. It is desirable that the subjects themselves do not know to which of the two groups they belong. We shall occasionally refer to such experiments. Yet as they never reach the pure type fully, their validity often remains questionable.

(c) EXPERIMENTAL TESTS, LESS SEVERE FORMS

Even in less severe varieties, nevertheless, experimental tests play a great role in political science, and indeed a far greater than is generally recognized. Novel governmental institutions or administrative devices may be, and often are, deliberately tried out in some limited geographical areas, with all others serving as it were as control groups. The large number and relative independence of local government units offer particularly favorable opportunities in this respect. The evolution of the commission and manager types of city government in the United States presents a striking illustration; their workings in large and small communities under various conditions have shed a great deal of light on causal relationships in this field. The federal system allows competitive experimental tests also on the state level; this is rightly considered one of its merits. The national government, too, may single out limited areas for experimental tests, as was done, for instance, when the Tennessee Valley Authority was established in the United States. As a matter of fact, at all levels of government novelties can be tried out by every department in pilot units, and this too is generally done with good effect. Experiences in other countries are seriously studied at home. Indeed, the entire history of government and institutions supplies an almost inexhaustible source of tested hypotheses.

The development of the theory of electoral systems may be cited as a good case in point. Various techniques of holding general elections have been used in such numbers since the ascendancy of constitutional government that we now know much more about the causal nexus in this field than even the most ingenious thinker could have found out without the benefits of these tests. How primitive appear today, in retrospect, most of the ideas that prevailed about proportional representation (P.R.) before the growing number of practical tests drew the scientific observer's attention to many unforeseen factors that enter into the sum total of effects—features including the influence of P.R. on the selection, type, age, loyalty-feelings, and tactical behavior of the candidates, before and after election, differences in the strength and coherence of the cabinets formed, and other consequences.

American interest in the comparative study of government and institutions has been overshadowed recently by the keener interest aroused in newly developed methods, such as sample surveys and controlled experiments. It would be a great mistake, however, if this should lead to a neglect of the careful study of the many kinds of experiments, both large- and small-scale, that have been made by governments here and abroad. Comparative government, including comparative administration, is still today the most important substitute for laboratory tests in political science. Much remains to be done here. Better utilization of comparison for theoretical progress would require acquaintance with many details that have never been written up.[1]

No mechanical generalizations, of course, are warranted. Different conditions may lead to different results from the same type of institutions at different places or times. If, for example, popular elections of the chief of state have good results in the United States, where people are practically unanimous in their support of the Constitution, similar procedures are likely to lead to very different experiences in countries where the basic loyalties of the people are split among different types of government (France in 1849, interwar Germany, South American republics). Such differences in conditions must be taken into account; otherwise predictions will go astray. But theory *qua* theory profits from practical experiments even when they have been based on imperfect inductive reasoning, though the price may be heavy.

4. *Predicting Consequences and Risks*

The scientific actions so far discussed (Nos. 1–9 of our survey) are unable to convey an adequate impression of the range of Scientific Method, unless we add to them the legitimate function of science to predict what can be scientifically predicted about future events. Such predictions are part of every testing procedure, as just discussed. But testing is not the only legitimate purpose of scientific predictions. In predicting the outcome of an action that has not yet been taken, the scientist may influence the decision on whether or not to take it. In predicting the different results of alternative actions, he may influence the choice among them.

Any prediction may, of course, be challenged on several counts, such as, first, that the alleged facts or events on which the prediction is based have not occurred or will not occur; second, that there are other alternatives of action (this is only a special case of the first challenge); third, that the hypothetically accepted causal law is not valid;

[1] See Arnold Brecht, "Three Topics in Comparative Administration," *Public Policy*, vol. 2 (1941) p. 289, and "Smaller Departments," *Public Administration Review*, vol. 1 (1941) p. 363; also, *The Art and Technique of Administration in German Ministries*, with Comstock Glaser, Cambridge, Mass., 1940.

and fourth, that additional factors will interfere with the predicted events.

Considering that in the social sciences human behavior plays a decisive role and that the assumption of a certain amount of human freedom obstructs all our efforts to formulate strict laws wherever human behavior in the future is a factor, it might seem that predictions in this field can have no practical value. But this would be a fallacious conclusion. It is true that exact predictions are not, as a rule, possible because of the great number of variables that have to be taken into account.[1] Wherever a large number of people are involved, however, predictions based on probability of human behavior can often be made with great accuracy. Just as in economics we can to some extent (and only to some extent) assume that the guiding motivation of the average businessman is that he prefers gain to loss, so in political science we can assume, for example, that it is the desire of the average representative in a legislature that he be reelected. There are many other situations in the political field where behavior of people can be predicted to some extent on a similar basis.

Furthermore, it is often possible to state with scientific precision that a certain action, if taken, will alter the range of possibilities, either enlarging or narrowing it; or that it is *impossible* to reach a certain goal at all or to reach it with the means proposed; or that, if event *a* occurs, it will be impossible to prevent *b* from following suit, as for instance if workers or soldiers are given no food or rest they will collapse or revolt, whatever severe disciplinary actions may be taken against them. In other cases, it can at least be stated that certain actions will imply some particular *risk,* that is, the probability, high or low, that an actually undesired effect will occur. The importance of the categories of "impossibility" (limited possibility) and "risk" in scientific predictions will appear more clearly in later chapters (especially XII).

Sometimes the statement of a consequence is not synthetic but purely analytic in character. Then we shall speak of "implication" in preference to consequence. When a dictator is appointed and is given "unlimited power," it is merely an implication of such an arrangement that *in terms of his appointment* he has been given the power to put people into concentration camps, and to whip, shoot, hang, or gas them without trial, although no one may have thought of this in ad-

---

[1] On the mathematical problems involved here, see especially Harald Cramer, *Random Variables and Probability Distribution*, Cambridge 1937.

vance, and that on those terms he can be deposed against his own will only by a violent revolution or revolt. Whether he will use these "implied powers" cannot be predicted with certainty, but it can be stated that a "risk," or an increased risk, is implied in the vesting of a person with such powers.

Fully to exploit all scientific capabilities at our disposal for predicting consequences, risks, or necessary failures of action, and for displaying in advance a broad choice of possible alternatives of action, gives us the greatest chance we have to overcome the drawbacks of Scientific Value Relativism (see next chapter).

Prediction in the face of a great number of variables can sometimes be facilitated by the construction of a simplified "model" of the situation to be studied, including only the most plausible variables; see Section 6 below.

5. Elimination of A-Priori Reasoning. Kant and Scientific Method

(a) A-PRIORI REASONING

The preceding sections, referring to our survey Nos. 1–10, have stated in positive form which steps of inquiry are considered scientific under Scientific Method. Negatively speaking, Scientific Method eliminates all propositions that have been arrived at otherwise or have been invalidated through it, as nonscientific in its terms. This is not to say that no other propositions correspond to reality; they may do so, just as someone's prediction that there will be no rain in Washington, D.C., on the next ten Fourths-of-July may prove to be correct in terms of subsequent experience, and one's personal conviction that there is a God may correspond to Truth. It is only to say that such statements are "not-scientific-in-terms-of-Scientific-Method." Whether they may be called scientific in other terms depends on the claim to exclusiveness of Scientific Method, whereof we are going to speak in Section 7 of this chapter.

The elimination of all arguments that are extraneous to Scientific Method from science has three negative implications of great bearing. It shuts the front door of science to (1) a-priori judgments, (2) metaphysical propositions, and (3) absolute value judgments. These three are only admitted, if at all, through the back door of "working hypotheses" and "assumptions" (see Section 6, below). We shall deal with metaphysical propositions and value judgments, both of which may be regarded as special types of a-priori propositions, in later chapters. Here we are limiting ourselves to a general discussion of a-priori reasoning.

A-priori propositions have played a tremendous role in the history of science, up to the very beginning of this century and beyond. The postulate of their elimination in science marks, on the one hand, the culmination in the development of modern Scientific Method, the climax of its triumphal achievements, and on the other, the point of crisis. To understand this fully is made difficult by the fact that the term "a priori" has assumed different shades of meaning in the history of thought according to the context in which it has appeared. These various meanings must first be distinguished.

In the most firmly established classical sense the term "a priori" points to notions, propositions, or postulates that are considered true or necessary irrespective of experience or anterior to it; in other words, not derived from experience and yet considered valid. This I shall call the *classical (scientifically accepted) a priori*. Illustrations will be given below.

In a second, more modern sense the term is now often used for all notions, propositions, or postulates that are extraneous to the system or method of thought under which the inquiry is conducted. Thus, in terms of Scientific Method, any proposition not introduced in line with it is a priori in this second sense. I shall call this the *methodologically repudiated a priori,* or the *alien-to-the-method a priori*. It is "off limits," "off rules," "out of order," "taboo."

Closer analysis reveals, however, that Scientific Method itself, like any other conceivable method, privileges certain a prioris, if only a small number, that are not ruled out of order but, rather, underlie the method's operations, although they too cannot be reached or verified through the latter. Such accepted or acceptable (see below) a-priori assumptions of Scientific Method include: consubjectivity; the ability of observations to disclose "facts"; causality or, at least, regularity; and some human freedom of will (see above, Chapters I, Sections 2 and 7, and II, Section 1). This third type I shall call the *immanent methodological a priori*. Strictly speaking, Scientific Method does not as such accept or incorporate these assumptions, but it permits the scientist to accept them without being on that ground guilty of violating the rules of procedure.

An immanent methodological a priori might also be dubbed a "methodological axiom," if that were not too ambiguous a term. An axiom is a synthetic proposition that is accepted as the basis for logical deductions without being itself logically derivable. The concept is ambiguous because it may mean either an a-priori truth, which would not be acceptable under Scientific Method, or an expedient postulate or assumption, use of which would be permissible if openly declared. This ambiguity counsels against the use of the term. I shall, therefore, generally avoid it, replacing it with terms that in each individual case describe more precisely what is meant.

Fourth, some writers have called all things that are "given" or "simply there" a priori; i.e., the things that constitute, so to speak, the raw material of scientific research. They are neither accepted nor repudiated; they are to be processed. In this sense, for example, all things we watch are a priori. This I shall call the *a priori of givenness*. See Chapter IX, Section 6, on phenomenological research.

Our present analysis of Scientific Method is particularly concerned with the second and the third meaning, i.e., with the two types of methodological a priori, that which is ruled out of order, and that which is immanently accepted. Historical continuity suggests, however, that we start from the classical a priori, the more so because it will appear that some aspects of it have been preserved in the "immanent methodological a prioris" of Scientific Method.

(b) KANT AND SCIENTIFIC METHOD

The philosopher whose name is most closely associated with the term a priori is Kant. It is often believed, therefore, that the fight of the adherents of Scientific Method against a-priori principles is primarily directed against Kant and the Kantians. But this is true only in a very limited degree, especially with regard to Kant's later books (see Chapter V, Section 7). The actual use he made of a-priori reasoning in his first two great critical works, *Critique of Pure Reason* (1st ed. 1781) and *Prolegomena to Any Future Metaphysic That May Be Presented As a Science* (1783), is hardly, if at all, in practical conflict with Scientific Method as now understood; on the contrary, these works have essentially contributed to its development. The great influence Kant's thinking has exercised on philosophical thought, and which is far from exhausted, makes it advisable to present his teaching on the subject in some detail with a view to clarifying the meaning of present-day Scientific Method.

Kant's classical a-priori notions were of three types, which he called (1) of the sensual sphere, (2) of the intellect, and (3) of reason. The names sound awkward to twentieth-century ears,[1] but the substance of his argument has remained influential and can be made clear to modern readers.

1. "Elemental a-priori notions of the sensual (sensory) sphere" (*Elementarbegriffe der Sinnlichkeit*) is the classification used by Kant for the notions of space and time. They dominate our sensual (sensory) perception to the extent that we are unable to think of something as not being or occurring at some place within space and time, or to think of a state of affairs where there is no space or time, he said. The Copernican revolution in his thinking as compared with pre-Kantian thought—here as in the field of causality (above, Section 1)—was Kant's idea that we projected our a-priori notions of space and time, which actually were merely inherent "forms" of our sensory experiences or of our way of thinking, into the universe as if we had found them there, while we could not really know whether they applied to the "things-in-themselves" (*Dinge an sich*). The only fact we could state with certainty was that we were unable to think of sensory perceptions outside of space and time.

Scientific Method has no quarrel with this first type of Kant's a-priori notions. Scientific Method itself allows references to space and time without much ado about their nature, unless the latter is the special subject of scientific inquiry, as for instance in examinations of the difference between inner and astronomical time. More precisely speaking, the scientist who accepts results of observation as "facts that have occurred in space and time" does not violate scientific rules governing acceptance; rather he would be expected to give reasons if he did not accept space and time as terms of reference. This is another illustration of the common-sense basis of Scientific Method (see Chapter 1, Section 5, about reality, and Section 1, above, about causality). Furthermore, Kant's thesis that human beings are unable to imagine events occurring outside of space and time is a factual contention, which might be submitted to empirical testing, and should be, if anything depended on its accuracy. As a rule, nothing seems to depend on it. For both these reasons there is no conflict here between Scientific Method and Kant.

2. "Intellectual notions-a-priori" (*Verstandesbegriffe*) in Kant's language were those notions that make experience "at all possible"

---

[1] See Carl J. Friedrich, *The Philosophy of Kant—Immanuel Kant's Moral and Political Writings*, edited, with an Introduction, by C. J. F., The Modern Library, New York 1949, p. xxxii. This is a handy collection from Kant's writings in good, if occasionally boldly free, translations. I am using my own translations here.

(*überhaupt möglich*). To understand this we must first know that Kant used the term "experience," not for every sensory perception (*Sinneswahrnehmung*) as such but—much in line with recent investigations (see Chapter 1, Section 2)—only for perceptions on which the human mind had operated. This the mind did, according to Kant, by "subsuming" the sensory perceptions under notions. To illustrate, my sensory perception that a stone is hot becomes an "experience" only when I subsume my impressions under such concepts as "stone," "is," and "hot." Some notions of this kind are a priori, Kant taught, that is, independent of any experience. In our example, the notions "stone" and "hot" are not a priori, since we know their meaning only by experience; but "is" and "is not" are, according to Kant, notions a priori; they are two out of a dozen categories of thinking in which the mind alone is able to form any judgments at all in the realm of "being" and into one of which every sensory perception must fall to become an experience. Aristotle had enumerated such categories before Kant in a list of ten or, in other places, fifteen. Yet Kant criticized Aristotle's list as "unsystematic" and merely "rhapsodic"; instead, he offered one of twelve which he considered systematic and complete. These twelve were "logical functions," he said, and they corresponded to forms of verbal expressions in the grammars of human languages. But the important point to him was that they were a priori of any experience; without them, no experience, as distinct from the sensory perception as such, was even possible.

In rendering hereafter Kant's twelve categories I shall add to each an illustration of the corresponding grammatical forms which serve to express it. Conclusions drawn by the human mind, Kant said, could only be:

1-3   (according to quantity): general, special, or individual (expressed by such terms as "all," "some," or "this," respectively)

4-6   (according to quality): affirmative, negative, or infinite (expressed by such terms as "are," "are not," or "are infinite" [2])

7-9   (according to relation): categoric, hypothetic, or disjunctive (expressed by such terms as "always, under all circumstances," "if . . . then," or "either-or, but not both")

10-12   (according to modality): problematic, assertative, or apodictic (expressed by such terms as "possibly," "actually," or "necessarily").

---

[2] Kant distinguished "The soul is immortal" (infinite) from "The soul is not mortal" (negative). The meaning of this category is controversial; its logical justification has frequently been questioned.

The significant thing here to note is that these "intellectual notions a priori" offer no definite answer regarding any particular question. They merely set up a *formal* scheme of all possible answers to questions regarding "being." They may be challenged, and they have been, insofar as they were meant to be complete, which would imply the contention that no other statements were possible. This negative contention is the only substantive point in Kant's listings with which present day Scientific Method could ever come into conflict. It is a relatively minor point, because if some other type of statement should appear necessary and possible, it would be made irrespective of Kant's thesis. The regular work of science is not hampered by Kant's categories, whether or not they are a priori.

3. "A-priori notions of reason" (*Vernunftbegriffe*). While the a-priori notions of the intellect serve only to make experience at all possible—by offering intellectual categories under which to subsume sensory perceptions—and thus keep entirely within the range of possible experience, human "reason" (*Vernunft,* a term used by Kant only in its more lofty sense) asks questions beyond any possible experience, i.e., metaphysical questions. The asking of such questions was characteristically human, as if this urge had been put in the human mind for some purpose, Kant said. "Experience never satisfies reason fully" (*Erfahrung tut der Vernunft niemals völlig Genüge*).[3] In order not to remain entirely unsatisfied, reason could freely speculate on metaphysical questions and form "notions of reason," such as the notion of a soul or of some immaterial highest being. Instead of doing this in an undisciplined manner, which was scientifically irrelevant although it could be very important emotionally, human reason may try in a disciplined way to ascertain some a-priori principles of absolute certainty. Such principles could indeed be found, Kant continued, with regard to the *limits* of all possible experience. Reason could, he said, state a priori that no sensory experience could ever give us certainty about the "thing-in-itself" which had caused the experience, nor about the real nature of causation or about that of space and time. In all these respects, our experience was limited to phenomena as they *appeared* to us. The manner in which they appeared to us was determined by the forms of thinking to which we were restricted by human nature; these inevitable forms of our thinking included space and time and the notion that every event must have a cause. In other

---

[3] *Prolegomena zu einer jeden künftigen Metaphysik, die als Wissenschaft wird auftreten können* (1783), Academy ed. (1919) p. 351; Cassirer ed. (1922) p. 105; skipped in Friedrich transl.

words, one thing which reason could make out a priori was that we could not know nor learn by experience whether the forms of space and time and causality pertained also to the things-in-themselves. Nor could we find out anything else concerning the things-in-themselves; we could do so only concerning their appearances. "The mind does not take its laws from nature but prescribes them to nature" (*Der Verstand schöpft seine Gesetze nicht aus der Natur, sondern schreibt sie dieser vor*).[4]

In particular, we could not know the reality or nature of a higher being, which our reason postulated for its own satisfaction. Yet we could at least state with certainty that here was a limit to our possible knowledge. In addition, we could speculate about the relation (*das Verhältnis*) that might pertain between such a higher being and the world of appearances, even though we could describe this relation only in symbolic language, using as symbols or analogies notions of the sensual world, such as "creator" or "father."

In addition to its negative insights, pure reason (i.e., a-priori reason) could form what Kant called "transcendental ideas" about conceivable answers to metaphysical questions, just as our mind had been able to form a-priori categories of the intellect into which our statements or conclusions in the realm of sensory experiences would fall (see above). But, here as there, reason could not state with certainty which answer was right.

As we have just seen, Kant emphasized that our occupation with metaphysical questions is a natural disposition (*Naturanlage*), which apparently no human being can abstain from using (*sich entziehen*). He went on to say that it is, therefore, natural for us to examine for what "purpose" this disposition may have been laid in our nature and that we may do so under the hypothetical assumption that everything *has* some purpose. If we follow this line of thought we may reach the conclusion, he said, that we have been endowed with this particular disposition in order to keep us away from three errors, namely (1) *materialism,* since our transcendental ideas about psychological phenomena (our "psychological transcendental ideas," as he called them) point to the inadequacy (*Unzulänglichkeit*) of empirical concepts for an explanation of the "soul"; (2) *naturalism,* since "cosmological" transcendental ideas show us that no possible empirical exploration is able to explain nature; and (3) *fatalism,* since "theological"

[4] *Prolegomena, op.cit.,* Academy ed., p. 320; Cassirer ed., p. 72; Friedrich transl., p. 91.

transcendental ideas indicate that causality can never explain either necessity or freedom unless we assume some "highest intelligence" as a final cause.[5]

These passages must be interpreted within their general context so as to mean that, although it is natural for us to speculate about the purpose of our natural disposition, it cannot be stated scientifically whether our natural disposition *has* any purpose. But Kant was definitely a pre-Darwinian philosopher. As such he saw little choice for the human mind, in explaining reality, but to assume the operation of divine forces in the universe, with no alternative conceivable (see above, Section 1). Indeed, he went so far as to call the reality of a highest immaterial being, or God, a *necessary* notion of reason. "We are compelled to regard the world *as if* it was the work of some highest mind and will" (*Wir sind genötigt, die Welt so anzusehen, als ob sie das Werk eines höchsten Verstandes und Willens sei*).[6] But there he stopped. Definite statements about God's reality were to Kant beyond knowledge (science).

Kant's a-priori principles of pure reason, then, were essentially negative. They tell us what pure reason can *not* do. Reason may speculate freely, and may do so also to good practical purposes, but it cannot lead to any definite statement about things beyond the possibilities of sensual experiences. He once stated the essence of his doctrine as follows: "All acquisition of knowledge (*Erkenntnis*) about things through the pure intellect alone, or through reason alone, is nothing but mere sham (*Schein*), and truth is only in experience."[7]

This brings us back to Scientific Method as generally understood today and so also in this book. Kant's negative a-priori principles of reason, i.e., those which limit our possible knowledge, are in line with the basic principles of Scientific Method that science must rely on observation. His formal principles, regarding the categories into which answers must fall, do not practically restrict Scientific Method; whether they are a priori in the sense that they constitute inescapable elements of our human way of thinking is a problem that Scientific Method would have to leave to special phenomenological, psychological, or anthropological research (see Chapters IX and X). As to space, time, and causality, we have seen above that Scientific Method permits the scholar to use these concepts without much ado as to their nature. In

---

[5] *Prolegomena*, Academy ed., p. 363; Cassirer ed., p. 118; Friedrich transl., p. 108.

[6] *Prolegomena*, Academy ed., p. 357, see also p. 359; Cassirer ed., pp. 111, 114; Friedrich transl., p. 106. Italics here added.

[7] *Prolegomena*, Academy ed., p. 374; Cassirer ed., p. 129; Friedrich transl., omitted.

sum, there is no practical conflict between Scientific Method and Kant's a-priori principles.

The practical accord between Scientific Method and Kant's approach is well illustrated by the following passage from the *Prolegomena:* [8]

Natural science will never disclose to us the inner nature (*das Innere*) of things, i.e., that which is not phenomenon (*Erscheinung*) but might serve as the ultimate explanatory ground (*Erklärungsgrund*) of the phenomena; nor does it need that [knowledge] for its purpose of physical explanation. Yes, even if natural science should be offered such explanation (e.g., the influence of immaterial beings) from some other quarter (*anderweitig*), it should reject (*ausschlagen*) it and not include it into the process (*Fortgang*) of its own explanations, but should base these at all times exclusively on that which as an object of the senses pertains (*gehört*) to experience and can be brought into connection with our actual perceptions according to rules of experience (*nach Erfahrungsgrundsätzen*).

On the other hand, Scientific Method, by limiting its concept of science the way it does, itself accepts a number of rules which must be classified as "immanent methodological a prioris" since they themselves are not reached through Scientific Method and cannot be derived from it. Their justification, as will be discussed in Section 7 below, rests, in the last analysis, on the practical ground that only such knowledge as is supported by experience and logical analysis is capable of a conclusive transmission from person to person (hereafter called "intersubjectively transmissible knowledge," a term which will be explained in Section 7).

Summing up, the fight of Scientific Method against a-priori principles is not primarily, if at all, directed against those chiefly negative and formal principles of which Kant in his first two critical books stated that they had a-priori character. It is rather directed against a-priori propositions of a positive and substantive character, as they are forever being encountered in quasi-scientific discussions, including propositions of the most hallowed type, such as "There is an almighty God," or "All men are equal," or "All power corrupts," or "All states must be sovereign," or "No government ought to be held bound by any principle not of its own recognition." Scientific Method does not admit these and similar principles into science a priori, irrespective of

[8] Academy ed., p. 352; Cassirer ed., p. 107; Friedrich transl., p. 101.

experience. They are, in strictly scientific discussions, "out of order." They are admitted merely to the extent that they either have been won with the tools of Scientific Method, or are proposed as mere "assumptions" or "working hypotheses" (see next section).

Kant's "categorical imperative," the basic moral law presented in his later writings, will be discussed in Chapter v, Section 7, and especially in Chapter ix.

6. *Assumptions, Working Hypotheses, Types, and Models*

(a) ASSUMPTIONS AND WORKING HYPOTHESES

Assumptions and working hypotheses are tentative propositions that have not yet been, and may never become, definitely accepted, but are employed as useful tools in the course of a scientific inquiry. The assumption or working hypothesis may concern: (1) a fact or event, past, present, or future—the latter, for instance, when we assume the death of a ruler, a change in election figures, a poor harvest, or the outbreak of a war; (2) a goal, as when we assume that a certain goal, like preserving peace, ought to be achieved on the ground that our country's government has decided to pursue it, or on any other ground; or (3) a law of causal relationship or other regularity, as when we assume that an increase in density of population will increase per-capita public expenditures, or that the use of atomic bombs by one party in a war will cause their use by the other.

The term "assumption" is more often used for facts and goals, the term "working hypothesis" for causal interrelations, but there is no definite regularity in the limitation of either term to the one or the other category. In a narrower sense, however, the term "working hypothesis" is reserved for causal theories provisionally adopted on the ground of their presumptive correctness or plausibility. We may call them "working hypotheses of higher order."

In contrast to classical a-priori propositions, which were considered absolutely true or necessary, no such claim is made for assumptions, nor for hypotheses of any kind, whether "accepted" or "working," of lower or of higher order. All are merely tentative and subject to challenge whenever they do not meet tests of empirical observation. The working hypothesis, however, like any assumption, differs from an accepted fact or an accepted causal explanation of facts (Nos. 4, 5, and 6 of our survey; Chapter i, Section 1) in that it has not been sufficiently confirmed through the procedural steps of Scientific Method. This difference remains important, although we have seen there are no strict rules as to when a scientist must accept facts or laws; the "working" hypothesis or assumption is not accepted as scientifically established even by the scientist himself who uses it.

It has sometimes been said that, to be acceptable as a working hypothesis, a theory must offer at least some chance of empirical verification, and that a theory whose empirical verification is not possible should not be admitted even as a mere working hypothesis (see Chapter v, Section 3, on Neopositivism). However, there is no necessity for excluding a working hypothesis on the ground that it does not permit of full verification, provided it serves scientific research in some other way, e.g., by directing our attention to facts that have been overlooked (see Chapter xiii for illustrations).

As a rule, an assumption will of course be so chosen as to promise as much correspondence to reality as possible. In exceptional cases, however, one that is obviously contrary to fact or to previously established laws may be useful for some indirect purpose, as when we imagine that men had only two dimensions in order to consider how then they would conceive of a three-dimensional being that should come their way, so as to get an idea by analogy of what would happen when three-dimensional beings meet with four-dimensional ones.[1] Likewise, when the occurrence of a future event or the desirability of some goal is assumed, this is not necessarily meant to express that the event (death of the ruler, poor harvest, etc.) within the respective period is probable, or that the goal (peace or war) is actually being pursued; it merely limits the range of the investigation, the findings of which may be expected to be valuable for preparedness or motivation.

(b) TYPES OF PERSONS, ACTIONS, AND ATTITUDES

In order to master the vast amount of variables with which they are confronted, social scientists make use of a number of particular devices in forming their working hypotheses. One is the grouping of persons, actions, or attitudes in a limited number of *types* according to features considered relevant for the inquiry at hand. We have already noted that human actions cannot be adequately described and explained unless we have understood the meaning they have for the actors themselves (above, Chapter i, Section 2). In view of the impossibility of dealing with every actor individually, the social scientist, having good reason to assume that similar actions have similar mean-

[1] See also Appendix B.

ing for many people, is methodically led to "typify" human beings. He then operates with these types, i.e., with constructs of his own mind, instead of with the actual human beings. Such types are, e.g., the "economic man," whose actions have for the actor the meaning that they are to bring him profit or avoid loss; or the *bona fide* official, appointed or elected, whose actions have for him the meaning that he therewith fulfills a useful function in society, but who at the same time has certain typical conceptions regarding his own importance, etc.; or some type of politician, whose actions have for him the meaning that they are to secure his election or reelection; or the vacationist, who is out for recreation, and so forth.

Such typification, however, can have scientific merit only if based on some hypothesis according to which the distinction between the various types is relevant for the solution of some scientific problem. It can be fruitful only when the types chosen are realistic, i.e., true to life. Whether they are so is subject to observational tests.

Yet not the scholar alone, but the common man too, engages in a constant process of typification in order to understand the world around him and to pursue his own interests and purposes. The typifications constructed by the social scientist, therefore, are as it were produced on a second level, above those formed by the common man. They are more refined, and scientifically more exact; but in order to reflect reality they must take account of the types constructed by the common man. Alfred Schutz, who deserves credit for aptly having brought this interrelation to attention, describes the procedure of the social scientist in the following words, worthy of direct quoting:

> How does the social scientist proceed? He observes certain facts and events within social reality which refer to human action and he constructs typical behavior or course-of-action patterns from what he has observed. Thereupon he coordinates to these typical course-of-action patterns models of ideal actor or actors, whom he imagines as being gifted with consciousness.[2] Yet it is a consciousness restricted so as to contain nothing but the elements relevant to the course-of-action patterns observed. He thus ascribes to this fictitious consciousness a set of typical notions, purposes, goals which are assumed to be invariant in the specious consciousness of the imaginary actor-model. This homunculus or puppet is supposed to be inter-

[2] "Model" refers here to individuals. As we shall see below, the term is nowadays used more often with reference to society and the conditions of group life. Schutz himself so uses it a few lines later.

related in interaction patterns to other homunculi or puppets constructed in a similar way. Among these homunculi with which the social scientist populates his model of the social world of everyday life, sets of motives, goals, roles—in general, systems of relevances—are distributed in such a way as the scientific problems under scrutiny require. Yet—and this is the main point—these constructs are by no means arbitrary. They are subject to the postulate of logical consistency and to the postulate of adequacy. The latter means that each term in such a scientific model of human action must be constructed in such a way that a human act performed within the real world by an individual actor as indicated by the typical construct would be understandable to the actor himself as well as to his fellow-men in terms of common-sense interpretation of everyday life.[3]

Types of attitudes may be so constructed as to supply a serial scale of classification for the purpose of measuring qualitative differences (see Chapter 1, Section 4), as for example when attitudes of social proximity or distance are being typified according to whether or not people would admit members of another nationality or race into their families through marriage, and in the negative case, whether they would admit them into their club, or at least into civic neighborhood in their street, or, if not even that, then to citizenship in their country, or whether they would exclude them from citizenship also.[4]

As a rule, the social scientist, preparing for tests through questionnaires or interviews, will construct his types as economically as possible by singling out merely one particular feature, or a small number of features, that alone are relevant to his problem at hand. All other personality traits he may choose to ignore. Typification may, however, be used also to describe personalities more fully. This leads to the construction of what Max Weber has called the *Idealtyp,* literally "ideal type." The term "ideal" here is meant to designate, not some *moral* ideal, but the perfectly representative construction of the type in question, though in this combination of qualities and attitudes it

[3] Alfred Schutz, "Concept and Theory Formation in the Social Sciences," *The Journal of Philosophy,* vol. 51 (1954) pp. 257–273, especially, p. 271.

[4] Such a scheme was first suggested by Emory Bogardus, see Gardner Murphy, Murphy, L. B., and Newcomb, Th. M., *Experimental Social Psychology: an Interpretation of Research upon the Socialization of the Individual,* New York 1931, 2nd ed. 1937, p. 900. See also John Madge, *op.cit.,* pp. 188 ff., on the attempts made by L. L. Thurstone and others to refine this highly subjective method of building scales by leaving the process of arranging attitudes in a scale to a number of people working independently of one another *after* the interview reports are in.

may exist only in our own minds. Thus we may construct the "ideal type" of a National Socialist, of a Bolshevist, of a militarist, of a bureaucrat, or even of a gangster or a tramp, just as well as that of an American family, of a social worker, or of a democratic party boss—not the moral ideal in any of these categories, but an abstraction from reality. Such ideal types—or, as Howard Becker has called them, "constructed (or constructive) types"—may be used to good effect especially in historical retrospect, when the relevant data are in hand. Yet there always lurks the danger that, unless the social scientist is a man of unusual caliber, caricatures rather than human beings are presented. Especially, it is often forgotten that no type is true to life unless we take full account of the meaning which the attitudes of its members have for themselves. Sometimes, the ideal-type construct may be useful as a mere standard of reference for the purpose of qualitative measurement (see Chapter 1, Section 4).

Typifications, like questions in questionnaires, often reveal more about the author than about the people he tries to describe. Yet when applied with great skill, a skill that must be little short of genius, typification of persons and of events or situations can become first-rate tools in the social sciences.[5] We must never forget, though, that the construction of types is no more at the outset than the construction of a working hypothesis and like any other such construction of questionable value until its realism has been proved by observational tests with careful avoidance of wishful thinking and logical pitfalls. Nor can it be emphasized enough that all typification is merely *descriptive;* it does *not explain* (although it may be used or misused to explain) the facts it reveals, or their consequences. Neither does it tell us what action can or should be taken.

(c) TYPES OF SOCIETY; SOCIETAL MODELS

An assumption, or a working hypothesis, may be so chosen that it assumes a particular "structure of society" as existing at a certain time and place, including, for instance, the composition of the population, the distribution of economic conditions and of political opinions, a

---

[5] In addition to Max Weber (as cited Chapter 1, Section 4), see especially Howard Becker, *Through Values to Social Interpretation,* Durham, N.C., 1950, pp. 93 ff. (chapter on "Constructive Typology in the Social Sciences"). Becker's "constructive types" are essentially identical with Weber's "ideal types," although Becker puts greater emphasis on the requirement that the construct must be "objectively probable," not merely "possible"; he insists on finding close empirical approximation (see pp. xi, 107, n. 5; 160, n. 62; 172, n. 91; 173, n. 94). But to all practical intents and purposes Weber meant about the same.

specific political system, and so on. On this assumed basis the special problem under investigation may then be approached.

Instead of choosing one particular structure as a starting point, the scientist may try to cover a whole class of potential structures, but still reduce the infinite variety of all possible structures and situations by limiting those taken into account to a certain class. Such a "model" differs from the selection of a particular structure in that it comprises several alternative structures, and the problem to be solved may be that of singling out the optimum structure, either descriptively (what structure corresponds best to the aggregate of all observations) or normatively (what structure would best serve a definite purpose).[6] The validity of the results depends, of course, on whether the model was well chosen, i.e., in accord with reality.

Models may be so constructed as to refer only to a definite time, past, present, *or* future; or they may be speculative constructs of a dynamic character so as to depict the development of society in an entire epoch, comprising past, present, *and* future ("stage" or "development" model); for instance, the development of a revolution in an entire epoch where it changes its original character but still appears to be an identifiable historical unit.[7]

The choice of a constructive working hypothesis or assumption is often the most creative act in science. I may refer here to what I said about the role of genius in science in Chapter 1, Section 1. It is, however, an important postulate of Scientific Method, and one frequently violated even by its most ardent adherents, that all working hypotheses or assumptions should be avowed explicitly and not smuggled in as self-evident truths.

The line between "accepted" and "working" hypotheses is not always as sharp as it might seem. It sometimes happens that a working hypothesis of higher order is so carefully built and appears so plausible even to the most exacting view of the expert that the circumstantial and costly procedure of systematic tests is dispensed with in practice, or indefinitely postponed. We shall meet with illustrations in later chapters. Yet even then must we remain conscious of the significant

[6] See the publications by scholars connected with the Cowles Committee for Research in Economics at the University of Chicago; especially Trygve Haavelmo, "The Probability Approach in Econometrics," *Econometrica*, vol. 12 (1944) Supplement; introductory, Jacob Marschak, "Economic Structure, Path, Policy and Prediction," *American Economic Review*, vol. 37, No. 2 (1947) p. 81; Arrow, *op.cit.*, p. 150.

[7] Lasswell in D. Lerner and H. D. Lasswell, *The Policy Sciences, op.cit.*, p. 11; E. R. Hilgard and D. Lerner, "The Person," *ibid.*, pp. 36 ff.

theoretical distinction between an a-priori principle and a mere working hypothesis. Examples where this distinction has not been clearly drawn will be found in Chapter IX, Sections 7 (Kant) and 8 (Husserl) and elsewhere in this book.

7. Exclusiveness of Scientific Method?

We now shall take up the discussion, thus far postponed, of the exclusive or nonexclusive character of Scientific Method. All scientists, both in the natural and in the social sciences, agree that Scientific Method *is* scientific, i.e., that contributions made according to its principles are contributions to science. Objections are raised solely against claims that it *alone* is scientific and that results reached through other methods, unless checked in line with Scientific Method, apart from being "nonscientific-in-terms-of-Scientific-Method," are nonscientific also in every other sense, so as not to add to science in any reasonable sense of the term. These objections are tantamount to denying that the elements of Scientific Method are *necessary* elements of every scientific procedure.

The leading adherents of Scientific Method have indeed raised the claim to exclusiveness for it. Felix Kaufmann, for example, calls certain basic rules (see below, note 3) "invariable"; they are common to all sciences *qua* sciences and, therefore, "a priori for science because science is defined in terms of them," he said.[1] This is a good illustration of what we have called an "immanent methodological a priori."

The decisive question, of course, is not whether science *is* defined in these terms, but whether it *must* be so defined and not otherwise, since it is our purpose here to present a *theory* of Scientific Method and not just a description of it. Consequently, it is not sufficient for us to insist on the a-priori character of the rules of procedure. The question remains, Why must these rules be so? Why can they not be otherwise? Or is there "no ultimate justification of these rules," as Kaufmann said, adding that "we cannot go beyond them in discriminating between correct and incorrect scientific decisions"?[2]

If there were no justification, how then could insistence on Scientific Method be defended in view of the manifold attacks that have been leveled against its claim to exclusiveness? Yet there is one distinguishing merit of Scientific Method, among others that are less relevant in the present context. It supplies knowledge that can be transmitted

[1] *Methodology of the Social Sciences*, pp. 45, 47.
[2] *Ibid.*, p. 230, No. 4.

from person to person *qua* knowledge (here called "intersubjectively transmissible knowledge," or briefly "transmissible knowledge"). To transmit knowledge *qua* knowledge is more than merely to communicate the assertion that I have such knowledge, or even to add how I came by it. This latter type of communication is always possible, of course, where the usual means of communication are at our disposal; with their aid we can relate to others anything that we consider part of our own subjective knowledge and the fact that we do so consider it and why, limited only by the shortcomings of language and the receptiveness of the hearer or reader. But mere communication does not transmit our subjective knowledge to others *qua* knowledge. To do that requires more, and Scientific Method supplies this more regardless of individual beliefs. Indeed, it supplies a type of knowledge that can be transmitted from *any* person who has such knowledge to *any* other person who does not have it but who can grasp the meaning of the symbols (words, signs) used in communication and perform the operations, if any, described in these communications. It submits observational testimony, refined as far as feasible by testimony on the conditions under which the observations were made, in order to enable ourselves and others the better to appraise the exactness of the observations made and the plausibility of the conclusions derived therefrom. Yet, as we have seen in Chapter 1 (Sections 2, 3, 5, and 7), Scientific Method does not insist that any other scientist must "accept" as unchallengeable either the exactness of the observations or the validity of the conclusions, beyond the purely logical implications of meaning. Such acceptance is ultimately left to the judgment of the receiver of the communication. What is intersubjectively transmitted *qua* knowledge is the evidence, not the conclusions therefrom. Scientific Method, quite consistently, is zealous to exclude evidence that cannot be transmitted.

This justification of the claim to exclusiveness seems to me to provide a good ground as far as it goes. Couched in terms of logical reasoning it would read, "*If* we decide to call scientific only those methods which supply intersubjectively transmissible knowledge (as defined above), *then* only such and such methods are scientific." But placing ourselves on this ground we must not ignore the fact that there has been at all times in the world a considerable amount of subjective knowledge not intersubjectively transmissible *qua* knowledge yet still firmly held, and frequently on excellent grounds, such as childhood remembrances no longer shared by any other person, or the knowledge of a wrongly condemned person that he has not committed the crime, or reminiscences by a statesman of important political conversations he had with others none of whom is still alive or willing to tell the truth about it. There may be such correct yet non-transmissible knowledge also in metaphysical questions, if there be metaphysical agents that reveal knowledge to us, or to some of us. But, although all this must, I think, be conceded, we cannot lump these types of knowledge indiscriminately with knowledge that is intersubjectively transmissible. Should someone want to use the term "science" for both types of knowledge (as some do, see Chapter VII, Section 3) then there would be an obvious need for distinguishing them in some other manner, giving them either different compound names—such as "science in the sense of intersubjectively-transmissible-knowledge" and "science in the sense of not-intersubjectively-transmissible-knowledge"; or different symbols, such as S_1 and S_2, respectively. To these two categories a third might be added, "science in the sense of speculations-not-considered-knowledge," or S_3.

The problem, then, of the exclusive character of Scientific Method boils down to that of whether there is "intersubjectively transmissible knowledge" (S_1) outside of Scientific Method. We shall take up this question in Chapters IX ff., where some proposals will be made that lead to broadening the conception of transmissible knowledge by including the category of "universal and inescapable" elements in human thinking and feeling to the extent that their existence can be empirically ascertained. By and large, however, with due reservation for these proposals, I consider the claim of Scientific Method to exclusiveness in category S_1 justified.

All rules of procedure enumerated at the beginning of Chapter 1 are essential for science as a supplier of intersubjectively transmissible knowledge, except that No. 10 b (prediction) is optional, of course, and that some of the others may be omitted when, *but only when,* the strength of the grounds provided by the other steps suffices for intersubjective transmissibility.[3]

[3] Felix Kaufmann (*op.cit.,* pp. 39 ff.) singled out seven fundamental rules as "invariable." These are, briefly summarized: (1) Distinction between "accepted" and "non-accepted" propositions; (2) transfer from one to the other class not to be arbitrary; (3) such transfer to be based only on grounds accepted at the time of the decision on the transfer; (4) no decision irrevocable; (5) no incompatible propositions to be tolerated within the "accepted body of knowledge"; (6) no proposition that falls within the subject-matter of a science to be a priori excluded from acceptance; and (7) results of observation to play a key role as grounds for acceptance.

The last four are generally recognized by all adherents of Scientific Method. As to the

From what has been said, it is plain why I did not propose to speak of intersubjectively "verifiable" knowledge. We actually do not through Scientific Method "verify" the data and conclusions on which our knowledge relies, at least not all of them, either to ourselves or to others. In the strictest sense, no empirical data and inductive inferences can be fully verified (see Chapters I, Sections 5 and 6, and V, Section 3, b). We can merely transmit them with the evidence, leaving acceptance ultimately to the recipient. True, as we have seen, the evidence is sometimes so strong that acceptance is practically necessary and inescapable, but not always. On the other hand, we shall meet with examples (Chapter x) where acceptance is necessary and inescapable without special steps toward verification being required as evidence. For both these reasons the term "intersubjectively transmissible" seems to be more exact. This question will be further discussed in Chapter VII, Section 3.

The need in many steps of scientific procedure for decisions on *acceptance* that are not fully governed by strict rules keeps the body of science flexible, without interfering with intersubjective transmissibility, since the data on the basis of which the decisions on acceptance or nonacceptance have been made are transmissible.

---

first three, concerning acceptance, I have expressed my criticism in Chapter I, Section 7. Kaufmann himself is compelled to admit that some rules can be "modified and changed"; these are obviously those which govern acceptance, not the other principles. On the other hand, his seven invariable rules omit any special reference to tests and to logical reasoning, criteria that are generally held to be essential for empirical science, but seem to be drowned in Kaufmann's broad requirement of submission to the rules governing acceptance. Limitation of his list to its last four items would, therefore, not be satisfactory either. This explains why I have considered it necessary to refer to all the eleven steps enumerated in our initial survey, subject to the modifications mentioned in the text above.

CHAPTER III

THEORY OF SCIENTIFIC VALUE RELATIVISM
(VALUE ALTERNATIVISM)

1. *Value Relativism, the Seamy Side of Scientific Method*

A GREAT deal of nonsense has been spoken and written about relativism—not that every comment was wrong, of course, or that it was wrong with regard to every one of the types of philosophy that go by that name. Yet the trouble is that rarely have the various types of relativism, historic and contemporary, been clearly distinguished in attacks on it, even by great scholars.

Only one type will be dealt with in this chapter, within the systematic part of this book. Others will be discerned in the historical and polemic parts (Chapters v and vii). Here we are concerned only with that type of relativism which is implied in the acceptance of Scientific Method. In order to distinguish it from all others, it will be called "Scientific Value Relativism." This is a clumsy name, yet it is at least sufficiently distinctive without making a complete break with the traditional nomenclature. What other names might be used instead will be discussed at the end of the historical part (Chapter vi, Section 7); there, "Scientific Value Alternativism," or briefly "Alternativism," will be suggested as more expressive and less exposed to misinterpretation. Yet I do not think it honest, nor conducive to the achievement of full clarity, to use another name at this point before the issues involved have been squarely faced.

Compactly formulated, Scientific Value Relativism (or Alternativism) holds that:

(1) The question whether something is "valuable" can be answered *scientifically* only in relation to
   (a) some goal or purpose for the pursuit of which it is or is not useful (valuable), or to
   (b) the ideas held by some person or group of persons regarding what is or is not valuable;
   and that, consequently,
(2) it is impossible to establish scientifically what goals or purposes are valuable *irrespective* of

(a) the value they have in the pursuit of other goals or purposes, or

(b) of someone's ideas about ulterior or ultimate goals or purposes.

According to Scientific Value Relativism, "ultimate," "highest," or "absolute" values or "standards of values" are "chosen" by mind or will, or possibly (see Chapter VII, Sections 3 to 5) "grasped" by faith, intuition, or instinct; but they are not "proven" by science—excepting, however, that science can help a great deal in clarifying the meaning of ideas about such values and the consequences and risks entailed in their pursuit. In other words, science can approach values only indirectly, not directly. What this means will be discussed in this chapter.

In a sense, Scientific Value Relativism represents the seamy side of Scientific Method. Many social scientists who speak of Scientific Method with great esteem, and even with enthusiasm, refer to relativism with contempt or ignore its problematic nature or are inconsistent regarding its gravest implications or ignorant of its history, failing even to mention the term and Weber's work.[1] And yet, Scientific Value Relativisim is the logical implication of Scientific Method. They are merely two sides of the same thing: the positive and the negative side, so to speak.

On the positive side, as discussed in the preceding chapter, Scientific Method is entirely amenable to a common-sense acceptance of reality. It concentrates, without undue skepticism, on sober observation and description of facts and on constructing hypothetic theories regarding causal relations. It may be extremely bold in forming such hypotheses and then testing their validity. It may describe the most intricate and hidden ramifications of facts, as for instance in the various branches of psychology, this great passion of our century. It may be keen and efficient in observing and describing the evaluations bestowed by different people on things, properties, events, and the like; in ferreting out the biographic origins of these evaluations; and in analyzing the consequences of actions based on them. But when it comes to the point where the question is which ultimate evaluations are right and which are wrong, which are laudable and which reprehensible, Scientific Method must consistently refuse to take a stand, beyond describing the consequences and the like, because it can do no more.

[1] Barbara Wootton, *Testament for Social Science—An Essay in the Application of Scientific Method*, New York 1951, able apostle of Scientific Method, exemplifies the last two objections. Her exaltation of the value of health (pp. 119 ff.) keeps strangely silent about the morally decisive point why we should respect this value in *others*, even in people we dislike. See below, pp. 124, 311 ff., 569.

Confronted with this impotence of Scientific Method to take an unconditional stand in matters of value judgment, many social scientists have come to develop something like a feeling of shame, a kind of guilt complex. This feeling, as discussed in the introductory chapter, grew almost unbearable when Bolshevism, Fascism, and National Socialism were successively taking possession of the area that had been abandoned by science. Before we speak of the ensuing revolt (Chapters VII ff.) we must first study the meaning of Scientific Value Relativism (Alternativism) more closely, because a great many of the objections raised against it are based on misunderstandings or distortions and on a gross underestimation of the contributions it can render to a fertile discussion of values.

2. *What Is Valuable?*

Several branches of science have an obvious relation to specific values, as medicine has to health, economics to commodities in demand, and law to justice. The meaning and the grades of value in these special branches have been intensively examined, especially so in economics. But these disciplines as such do not deal with the ultimate criterion of what is valuable; they use the term in a definite setting. Here, however, we are concerned with the general aspects of the concept of value, the more so since politics and political science deal with values in many fields: health, economics, justice, religion, culture, labor, recreation, reproduction, and others. A few general remarks will lead us quickly to the critical points.

Whenever things, conditions, properties, events, actions, or judgments are useful for the achievement of some purpose which we are actually pursuing, or may eventually pursue, we call them "valuable," meaning that they are conducive to that purpose. A chair is a valuable thing because we can sit on it; food, because we can eat it; freedom is a valuable condition or institution because it permits us to do what we like; patience, a valuable property because it serves peaceful coexistence; rain, a valuable event because it is conducive to the production of food, or ·contrariwise because it spoils our trip; a stateman's speech, a valuable action because it promotes peace or trade; an opinion of the Supreme Court, a valuable judgment because it serves the purpose of abolishing racial segregation, or of maintaining the Constitution, or of simply preserving "justice."

Then, however, there arises the next question as to whether the purpose we are pursuing is itself valuable, and if we think so, then why? We may answer by showing the usefulness of our immediate purpose for some other, "ulterior," purpose. Sitting down is useful for the purpose of resting, eating for preserving health. Resting and health, in turn, are useful for our enjoyment of life, for our ability to work, for reaching old age. There seems to be always another purpose for which the achievement of the former is useful. Freedom, we have just said, is useful because it enables us to do what we like. To be able to do that seems useful for whatever other purpose we pursue. And so in every one of the examples we have given the first purpose may always be considered conducive to the achievement of another, ulterior purpose.

Then we reach a third stage. The purpose we are pursuing at present, say, enjoying a number of hard drinks, may be in conflict with another purpose which we also pursue, say, preservation of health or of ability to work. In this case our freedom, while helping us to achieve one purpose, threatens the other. Among conflicting purposes we may cherish one—enjoying the drink—over all others at one time, and another—health, or a good conscience, or life after death—at another.

Our argument here arrives at a fourth stage. While the pursuit of changing purposes is going on in our own lives and we see it going on in the lives of others, we may, and generally do, feel that some purposes ought to be pursued and others ought not. We thus distinguish between what we *do* cherish and what we *ought* to cherish. Nevertheless we may relapse at any moment into a state where we do cherish something, for instance, a drink, which at other times, or even at the same time, we feel we ought not to cherish. Yet there is not always such a conflict. Sometimes we feel that what we actually do like, we also ought to like, say, the starred sky, great art, some religious experience, our own hard work; and that what we do hate we also ought to hate, such as a flagrant injustice.

This leads up to the fifth problem. Are there "ultimate" purposes, purposes not to be explained by further ulterior ones for the achievement of which they are a mere means? If so, are ultimate purposes only to be found at the end of a whole range of purposes—immediate, ulterior, ultimate—or may some immediate purposes be at the same time ultimate? Furthermore, is there always only one ultimate purpose, or may there be a plurality? We can ask these questions in two ways, namely (1) whether people actually pursue ultimate purposes, and (2) whether they ought to do so.

Finally, there emerges even a sixth question. Must everything have a purpose at all, or be pursued as one, in order to be considered valuable? May not something be valuable without its either serving any purpose or being pursued as one, such as the most unselfish type of love or an aesthetic enjoyment that overcomes us without our having purposively looked for it and with which we do not pursue any purpose while we are experiencing it?

If values are sought merely because of their usefulness for the attainment of ulterior or ultimate ends, they are sometimes called "extrinsic"; and "intrinsic," if they are appreciated for their own sake, as ultimate ends or irrespective of any purpose.

3. *What Scientific Method Can Do Regarding Values*

In view of this complicated interplay between means and purposes, purposes and ulterior purposes, ulterior purposes and ultimate purposes, purposes and conflicting purposes, purposes we are pursuing and those we ought to pursue, values sought for and values that are independent of any purpose—what can science do? Obviously, many inquiries can be made to good effect on all six questions in line with Scientific Method. Briefly indicating topics for such inquiries hereafter, I shall add in parentheses references to chapters or sections of this book where some of them are treated in more detail.

Regarding the first four questions the scientist can try to find out in line with Scientific Method:

i. PURPOSES

(1) What the *immediate* purposes are which people actually are pursuing at some definite place and time;

(2) what their *ulterior* purposes are, what the purposes back of their ulterior purposes, and so forth (Chapter VI);

(3) whether there are *conflicting* purposes, pursued by the same person at the same time or at different times (Chapters IV, VI, and XII);

(4) in case the goals pursued are ideals, such as justice, freedom, equality, general welfare, what is the *meaning* of these purposes in the minds of those who pursue them, and what other meanings have been, or might be, associated with these abstractions (Chapters VI, VIII, and XII);

(5) what the biographical or biological *origin* of the person's espousal of the purpose was, i.e., what has made him pursue some partic-

ular purpose, especially what role has been played, in the formation of his value judgments, by inheritance, by environment, by childhood experiences, and so on, down to immediate motivations, including the question whether his choice of purpose was influenced by moral ideas and how he arrived at them (Chapter VIII, Section 6);

(6) the possibility, probability, improbability, or *impossibility* of achieving the purpose at all, by any means used (Chapter XII);

(7) what are the foreseeable *consequences and risks* involved in the pursuit of the purpose at hand, irrespective of the choice of means (Chapters VI, VIII, XII);

(8) how people might be *influenced* to pursue some particular purpose, or to drop its pursuit, especially through a switch to other purposes (to be discussed in Vol. 2);

(9) what is the *function* of purposes, and of exercising an influence on their selection (manipulating them), in the various spheres of social life, political, economic, etc. (to be discussed in Vol. 2).

ii. MEANS

(10) The *suitability* of the means to achieve the end, i.e., the possibility, probability, improbability, or impossibility of achieving the purpose by the means at hand (Chapter XII);

(11) whether there are *other means* whereby the purpose could be reached more quickly, more thoroughly, or at a lower price in money or in sacrifice of conflicting purposes (Chapters VI and XII);

(12) what are the foreseeable *consequences and risks* of applying the means at hand or any alternative means especially regarding conflicting purposes pursued by the same person or by others (see Chapters VI, VIII, XII);

(13) how the choice of means can be *influenced* (see above, No. 8);

(14) what is the *function* of the selection of means and of influencing it in social life (see above, No. 9)

iii. QUALITIES

(15) If a *quality* is cherished, such as a person's courage or patience, or a knife's property to cut well, whether the person or thing actually has that quality and in what degree.

The scientist may make relevant statements and inquiries also on our fifth and sixth questions, whether there are or ought to be ultimate purposes and whether something may be valuable without serving a purpose. On these two points some comments will be added here.

As regards "ultimate" purposes, if a person always looks for his own enjoyment, then enjoyment may be called not only his ulterior but his ultimate purpose, underlying all others. It may also be maintained that other people have different ultimate purposes, such as attaining eternal life. But it would be obviously unrealistic to assume that every person always pursues only one ultimate purpose, and that he does so consciously. Many people seem to form their concrete purposes as they go, and to pursue them alternately without actually having one ultimate purpose in their minds all the time. An immediate purpose, like the highest possible degree of sensual satisfaction, may become ultimate at the moment, with no ulterior purpose back of it. The next moment, other purposes may become immediate, ulterior, or ultimate. Normally, nothing seems to force us to select one ultimate purpose to the exclusion of all others. To enjoy eating and drinking in a moderate way is quite compatible with, and even conducive to, preserving our health and raising a family, and both are, as a rule, not in conflict with the purpose of serving our country, nor are all three with that of serving our ideals or God. But any day some conflict may arise, as between the desire for heavy drinking and all the other purposes, or between eating enough ourselves and feeding our family, or between raising a family and volunteering for military service, or between abiding by our country's laws and being faithful to God or to our ideals—the typical dilemma of religious persons, liberals and humanists in a fascist or communist country, or of communists in a liberal one, the conflict of Socrates, who deliberately chose obedience to the Athenian laws, drinking the cup. Scientists may point to these possible conflicts and examine which purposes people actually give priority to in situations of conflict, and whether a person consciously pursues one ultimate purpose and which, and how consistently he does so (see Chapter VII, Section 2, on Dewey).

Furthermore, the scientist may be able, with the means of Scientific Method, to corroborate that human beings are sometimes overcome by feelings of appreciation and high emotional valuation of things they had not looked for and which they do not consider a mere means to some end, and what the significance of such experiences is in their own minds and in its influence on their behavior.[2] Whether others

[2] The difference between purposive (*zweckvolle*) and nonpurposive (*zwecklose*) responses underlay the philosophy of Walther Rathenau (1867–1922, assassinated as German foreign minister). He made it the distinctive mark between the intellect (purposive) and the soul (nonpurposive). See especially his *Zur Mechanik des Geistes*, Berlin 1913, reprinted in vol. 2 of *Gesammelte Schriften*, Berlin 1929; and Arnold Brecht, "Walther Rathenau and the German People," *Journal of Politics*, vol. 10 (1928) pp. 21–48, also in German, *Walther Rathenau und das Deutsche Volk*, München 1950. See below, Chapter VIII, Section 13.

have intentionally pursued the purpose of impressing them this way —for example, the artist, or the priest, or God—that, the scientist will discern, is another question.

Sometimes people think it obvious that certain values, such as health, are supreme and absolute. Then the scientist may point to the fact, likely to have been merely overlooked in such statements, that there are contradictory views. A nurse who voluntarily goes to a leper colony or ministers to cholera-stricken people holds other purposes higher than the preservation of her own health. So, obviously, did Christians and Jews in the Roman empire, who accepted martyrdom for the sake of their faith, and liberal, humanist, or religious people who went to torture, starvation, and death in concentration camps in Nazi Germany rather than complying with Hitler's orders. More generally, illness and physical suffering have been considered by many, and not only religious, persons conducive to our spiritual growth and hence more valuable than constant health. People have consciously impaired their health in order to increase their wealth, to help their families or their country, or even to climb a mountain or to satisfy other aims. Not all do care for the health of strangers.

The scientist himself may influence the choice of purposes and means by his strictly scientific work, whether or not he intends to, in particular by his clarification of meaning (No. 4 above), of possibilities and impossibilities (Nos. 6 and 10), of consequences and risks (Nos. 7 and 12). His inquiries may also influence ideas about what a person ought to do. This influence of science will be discussed more closely in Chapters VI, XI, and XII.

4. *What Scientific Method Cannot Do*

After what has been said there is so much for science to do regarding values that one might be satisfied with this work load. Yet it cannot be denied that there is something important left beyond the reach of Scientific Method. This method does not enable us to state, in *absolute terms,* whether the purpose pursued by us or by others is good or bad, right or wrong, just or unjust, nor which of several conflicting purposes is more valuable than the other. It only enables us to answer these questions in relative terms, with reference to some purpose that is actually being pursued, or which the scientist in some "working hypothesis" assumes ought to be pursued, or with reference to ideas that are actually held or might be held. In particular, Scientific Method cannot state in absolute terms which of several conflicting ultimate purposes is better than others except in relation to some presupposed goal or idea. In short, it does not enable the scientist to render an unconditional scientific value judgment, and especially not a moral one. It cannot set the goal.

The reason for this impotence is closely connected to the inability of Scientific Method to provide conclusive scientific evidence for or against the reality of God and for or against the validity of the opinion that the world in general, and life on earth in particular, has any purpose apart from that we give it (see Chapters II, Section 1, and XIII). Could we answer these questions scientifically we would also have an answer to questions regarding moral values. Ever the discussion of values slips back into arguments based on the "higher purposes" of man and of the entire creation; but that world and men have been endowed with a purpose by some act of creation is a religious creed, not within the reach of Scientific Method to be either confirmed or refuted. Strong as the subjective evidence for it may appear to many of us according to our personal experiences and convictions, there is no intersubjective evidence of a conclusive nature, and none is yet in sight (see Chapters VII, Sections 3 and 4, and XIII). Scientific Value Relativism, therefore, insists that references to ultimate goals or purposes of human life must be debarred as evidence from scientific discussion, except in hypothetical forms. This is a hard demand indeed, and to live up to it requires a great deal of discipline. Yet science is no child's play.

No confusion, however, should be allowed to creep in regarding the following fundamental point. The commonplace saying that relativists deny there is anything of absolute value is entirely incorrect with regard to Scientific Value Relativism. Scientific Method does not lead to a denial that there *may* be a God or that something, for instance an unselfish action, *may* be of absolute value. Although no "scientifically warranted assertion" can be made under the rules of Scientific Method that there is a God, none can be made either that there is no God. The only assertion warranted in this respect is that God's reality cannot be either proved or disproved through Scientific Method (Chapter XIII). Likewise, Scientific Value Relativism does not say that there *is* nothing of absolute value; it merely says it cannot be proved intersubjectively that there is or is not.

The chief technical ground for the withdrawal of science from moral value judgments has been the logical difference ("gulf") between Is and Ought, which will be discussed in the next two sections. In the

concluding section the objections commonly raised against the resigna-
tion of science from this field will be taken up.

5. *The Logical Gulf between Is and Ought*

Far into the nineteenth century, and in part even into the twentieth,
writers on ethical and legal questions derived their doctrines of what
ought to be, or what ought to be done, from the factual data on what
is. Human beings are, therefore they ought to be; they ought not to
be killed. They have a natural impulse to preserve their lives; therefore they ought to have the right of self-defense. They are born equal;
therefore they ought to be treated as equal. Society exists, and is useful to the maintenance of life; therefore there ought to be society.

It was this blending of statements couched in forms of Is and Ought
that aroused the special scorn of scientific critics around 1900. Deductive analytic logic, as we have seen in Chapter 1, Section 6, can add
nothing to the meaning of propositions; it can merely make explicit
what is implied in that meaning. Inferences of what "ought" to be,
therefore, can never be derived deductively (analytically) from premises
whose meaning is limited to what "is"; they can be correctly made
only from statements that have an Ought-meaning, at least in the
major premise. All human beings ought to have the right of self-
defense; Doe is a human being; hence he too ought to have the right
of self-defense—this would be a logically valid syllogism. But the fact
alone that human beings exist does not logically justify the inference
that they ought to exist, any more than the fact that there are mosquitoes or man-eating sharks logically justifies their continued existence. Nor does the fact that there is society and a state of mutual dependence among its members logically imply, as has been argued by
the French professor, Léon Duguit, that we ought to fulfill our functions in society.[1] Only a number of additional premises would imply
logically that a person ought to exist, or ought to fulfill a function.
This will be shown in more detail in the next section.

Ordinarily people do not think in terms of formal syllogisms. It is
often difficult to make a beginner see that if something is, it does not
follow that it ought to be. The mere fact of existence, he would strongly
feel, gives a thing some warrant of life "because otherwise God would
not have created it or allowed it to exist." But then the conclusion

---

[1] Léon Duguit, *L'Etat, le Droit Objectif et la Loi Positive* (1901). This has been translated: *Theory of Objective Law Anterior to the State*, in *Modern Legal Philosophy Series*
vol. 7 (1916). See pp. 135, 258, and 290 of the translation.

that the thing ought to exist is not derived from the fact that it does exist but from the conviction that it has been created by God, which constitutes the basis for the major premise that "all that is, ought to be," namely, according to the will of the creator. In order to verify the conclusion, therefore, one would have to verify the reality of God and of creation; that, however, cannot be done with Scientific Method, nor otherwise intersubjectively with scientific means.[2]

Short cuts that omit the Ought-premise have crept not only into daily parlance but also into scholarly literature. Objecting to such omissions in deductive syllogisms, scientific purists have only called to our attention old and established principles of logic (see Chapter VI, Section 1). The matter is less obvious if one turns to *inductive* generalizations. In order to establish the required major premise in the Ought-form (e.g., all men ought to be treated as equal) even scholars of great competence have slipped into deriving it from facts in the realm of Is (all men are born equal, or in an equal state of helplessness). Such inductive conclusions, though very popular, are scientifically not warranted. In order to give our demand for "equal treatment of what is equal" a scientific basis, we must have recourse to something more than mere logic (see Chapters VIII, Section 2, and X, Section 5). In logic there is, as some have expressed it, an "unbridgeable gulf" between Is and Ought.[3]

This "Gulf Doctrine," as we shall call it in further references, has far-reaching consequences because, if logical derivations from facts are barred, no transmissible proof can be presented for nonhypothetical propositions in the form of Ought beyond the demonstration that human beings themselves insist or urge that something ought to be done. That, of course, can be verified by science in many cases.

It is often thought that "values" constitute a bridge over the logical gulf between Is and Ought. True, we often speak of values as if they were things in the realm of Is that can be simply "observed." But what we can really observe in keeping with Scientific Method is "evaluations," not "values." We can, of course, also observe the things, properties, etc., which people actually consider valuable and which, therefore, they even call "values" in a concrete sense, such as jewels or money or health. But whether these things are really valuable, apart from the

---

[2] Even Rommen (*op.cit. infra*, p. 138n) p. 186, writes simply: "That which is, so far as it is, also ought to be," as though this followed from its being, irrespective of the will of God or man.

[3] See the quotations from Max Weber, Emil Lask, and Hans Kelsen in Chapter VI. All three have used this phrase.

purposes they can serve and from the consequences they can produce, is not a thing we can inspect in the realm of Is. In calling ultimate purposes or moral qualities "values" apart from our own appreciation, we mean that they ought to be achieved, or be approved; and whether something ought to be achieved or be approved cannot be established through Scientific Method, except in relation to some ulterior human purpose, or some human evaluation.

This identification of ethical values with postulates of Ought-form has been questioned (see Section 5 of Chapter VII) and so has the claim that Scientific Method is the only scientific approach possible (see below Section 7, and Chapter II, Section 7). But that Scientific Method does not warrant absolute statements on values is hardly denied by anyone.

6. Merits of Formal Logic

Strict obedience to the rules of formal analytical logic in the sense discussed in Chapter I, Section 6, has great merits. Not only does it help us to beware of unwarranted inferences, it also teaches us how to make implicit ideas explicit. This often leads to quite surprising results because it may end in our discovering unsuspected assumptions under the surface of propositions that bore no reference to them.

It is worthwhile to illustrate this gravely underrated value of logical analysis by some graphic example. Let us choose the derivation, already referred to, offered by Léon Duguit for his thesis that everyone has the duty to fulfill a useful function in society. For the matter of the present analysis his deduction may be put in the following form:

1 (a) All members of society profit from society
   (b) Hence, all ought to fulfill useful functions in society

The effect of this thesis on the average reader is that of an entirely logical conclusion drawn from a plausible statement of fact. Critical analysis shows, however, that much must be added in order to make the argument logically valid. To begin with, the premise has Is-form whereas the conclusion has Ought-form. To correct this defect the syllogism would have to be enlarged in about the following manner:

2 (a) Those who profit from an institution of which they are members ought to fulfill useful functions in it
   (b) All members of society profit from society ($=$ 1a)
   (c) Hence, all ought to fulfill useful functions in society ($=$ 1b)

With 2a thus made explicit we may ask how it can be verified. Why should I fulfill a function in a body that does not need my doing so to keep going? The answer might be given by dissolving syllogism 2 into the following two syllogisms:

3 (a) All those who profit from an institution ought to share the burden of it
  (b) All members profit from society ($=$ 2b $=$ 1a)
  (c) Hence, all ought to share the burden of society [1]
4 (a) All members ought to share the burden of society ($=$ 3c)
  (b) Those who do not fulfill useful functions in society do not share the burden of it
  (c) Hence, all members ought to fulfill useful functions in society ($=$ 2c $=$ 1b)

If we then go on asking why all those who profit from an institution should share the burden (3a), we are pushed back to statements such as

5 (a) All those who are by nature equal ought to be treated equally
  (b) All members of society are by nature equal (in proportion to their physical and mental abilities)
  (c) Hence all members of society ought to be treated equally (in proportion, etc.)

This conclusion (5c) together with the syllogisms 3 and 4 then would yield the result that everyone ought to fulfill some useful function in society (4c $=$ 1b). There would remain other vague factors, some of which are discussed by Duguit. The important point here is that Duguit's thesis requires for its logical precision a number of further statements, including one on human equality, although at first sight there was nothing in it to refer to this basic problem. When we challenge the equality statement because human beings have different characteristics, we need a refinement, such as inserting the word "essentially" before "equal" and explaining it in detail (see Chapter VIII, Section 2). At any rate, the contention of equality as a fact, and the postulate of equal treatment of what is equal should be made explicit and not be left implicit only. Whether and to what extent we are ready to accept Duguit's conclusion depends on whether and to what extent we recognize human equality, both as a fact and as a postulate for man's treatment in society. Formal logic, rigidly applied,

[1] Syllogism 3 was suggested to me in a class discussion.

brings this out and enables us to conduct an orderly scientific discussion.

It may be entirely possible to derive Duguit's thesis in other, equally logical, ways. But he who prefers another deduction must again be requested to make his premises explicit. To compel us to do so is one of the merits of formal logic. No reproach of pedantry should be permitted to prevail when we insist on compliance with logic in scientific arguments.

7. *Cannot Science Prove Absolute Values in Some Other Way?*

If Scientific Method is unable to establish in absolute terms, beyond a description of consequences and the like, which of two conflicting ultimate purposes is more valuable than the other (see above, Section 4), can we not prove that in some other way?

This challenge, at first sight, appears deeply justified. To hell with Scientific Method, one might be tempted to exclaim, if it cannot tell us, for example, that moral purposes are superior to immoral ones. Yet here we are in danger of falling into logical traps. All depends on what we mean by "moral" and by "superior." If we define "moral" purposes as those which are pursued in the interest of others, or of society, and if we further define "superior" again as that which is of greater use to others, or to society, then we have given the answer to our question in advance by our definitions. We then have defined "moral" purposes and "superior" purposes in identical terms, and we can, therefore, assert the superiority of moral over immoral purposes with full scientific assurance (see Chapter 1, Section 6). There is then no failure of Scientific Method.

Another logical trap threatens us on the ground that the purpose of a public debate is, as a rule, precisely that of examining which of several proposals is better for the community or for society, and not which is better for some particular person. This very purpose of public debate prejudges the answer to the question whether in case of a conflict between public and private interest the former or the latter is to be considered more valuable.

Only when we insist on asking (which people rarely do in public but not so infrequently in private) whether it is not more reasonable to pursue one's own interests—even if under the guise of an activity in the public interest—instead of sacrificing them in the interest of others, only then does the question of superiority become a scientific problem. Even then, as we have seen, science can contribute a great deal by examining the consequences which the pursuit of selfish plans is likely to have, and whether we can expect really to reach our own ultimate purpose (enjoyment of life or the like) by whatever selfish steps we are planning, and also the risks we are going to run of meeting with counteractions we don't desire to attract on the part of society. On the other hand, we may scientifically examine whether and to what extent the pursuit of selfish interests actually does serve public interests indirectly, as Adam Smith was sure it would in the economic sphere, and as Hegel even more generally assumed to be the case in history as a whole, owing to the "ruse of the idea," with the World Spirit using our selfishness as a means within its wider plans. Such questions Scientific Method can examine within its own rules of procedure to a large extent (though not including Hegel's World Spirit). But there remains an area of scientific impotence if in the debate about "public vs. private interests" science is requested to say simply which of the two it is better to pursue. Science *qua* science cannot say that it is better to act for others than to act for oneself without first defining "better" in terms that are capable of verification.

This painful area of scientific impotence is more noticeable when the topic is not that of "public vs. private" interests but rather which of several purposes is more in the public interest. Material progress or contemplative life? Equality or liberty? Peace or expansion? The national interest or international idealism? Scientific Method can do a great job in clarifying the meaning and the implied consequences of each, but cannot say unconditionally which ought to be preferred. It can do so neither on logical grounds nor on any other within its range. In short, it provides many an indirect, but no direct, approach to values.

This thesis has been challenged, as we shall see in Chapters VII and VIII, with references to intuition, to revelation, to objectivity, to psychology, and otherwise. But as we shall see there also, these objections have not been able to refute the assertion of Scientific Value Relativism that there is no "intersubjectively transmissible proof" regarding the validity of ultimate value judgments beyond the clarifications of their implications and consequences.

This leads up to a final question. Is it at all necessary to supply full evidence? Is it not sufficient to provide "approximate" proof, some high degree of "probability" or "plausibility"? As we have seen in Chapters I and II, Scientific Method *never* leads to full empirical proof; everywhere it is compelled ultimately to rely on tentative "acceptance" on the side of the scientist—his acceptance of the results of observation as "facts," of generalizations of facts as "warranted," and of explanations in causal terms as "correctly done." Why should we not deal in the same tentative manner with moral values, declaring ourselves satisfied by tentatively accepting them on the ground of their plausibility?

It is true that under Scientific Method we may grant or refuse acceptance to the apparent results of observations, to generalizations and explanations. There is, however, this decisive limitation to our discretion. Under Scientific Method we are not free to accept as a "fact" *every* assertion we opine to be true, or consider "plausible." Scientific Method permits us to accept as scientifically established only what has been offered in line with its rules of procedure, and that means, in an intersubjectively transmissible manner (Chapter II, Section 7). Unless we present our hunches merely as "working hypotheses," we must have final reference to observations, and these must not be contradicted by the results of other observations.

Here is the rub with regard to value judgments. Not that we were forbidden to accept individual reports on self-observation, including opinions, feelings, and intuitions regarding values (Chapter I, Section 2); but in matters of value judgments we are faced, as a rule, with *contradicting* observations about opinions, feelings, and intuitions. Thus there is nothing we can generalize in line with scientific principles of induction, unless there should be elements on which all reports agree; even then, what we get would not necessarily be "values" *per se,* but only "universal opinions about values." Chapters IX and X will revert to these questions.

8. *Types of Relativistic Behavior*

Scientific Value Relativism leaves room for various scientific behavior patterns. It may, and does, appear in various forms. In order to identify the subtypes it is advisable to give them distinctive names.

In the first place, relativism is either "positivistic" only, or "transpositive" as well. Only in the latter case can we speak of Scientific Value Relativism at all. Legal positivism is positivistic by definition. It considers only such laws binding as are in force in some particular country at some particular time; it has no truck with transpositive questions about values (see on legal positivism, below, Chapter V, Section 3). The relativism of Scientific Value Relativism, by contrast, is primarily "transpositive." It investigates values irrespective of their acceptance or nonacceptance by government and positive laws.

Likewise, we must distinguish between "historical" and "transhistorical" relativism. Historical relativism deals with the historical conditions of value judgments and of science; it either denies or neglects the possibility that there may be transhistorical values (see below Chapter v, Section 4). The relativism of Scientific Value Relativism, by contrast, is primarily "transhistorical." It investigates the problems of values that are thought of as independent of historical conditions, or at least it refers to them also.

While these distinctions set off Scientific Value Relativism from other types of relativism (legal positivism, historicism), it is our chief point here that Scientific Value Relativism itself appears in different forms. First of all, it may be either "latent" or "overt." As a matter of historical record it had been latent long before it became a formulated, well-defined, publicly established school of thought. Many legal positivists and many historicists were "latent" relativists with regard to transpositive and transhistorical values as well, before overt Scientific Value Relativism entered the scene. The relativism of American social scientists is to this day as a rule "latent" only. Not alone because they shun the name relativism, referring instead to other designations (see Chapters v, Section 6, and vi, Sections 5 and 7); they avoid entanglement with the theoretical problem, trying to evade it in many ways. Yet closer analysis reveals that, even so, most of them are scientific value relativists in all but name.

Next, Scientific Value Relativism may be either "partisan" or "neutral." If the former, the relativist like any nonrelativist takes sides on values within his scientific work, and may do so no less decidedly than in private life. He espouses those goal-values which appear highest to him, and devotes science to their service. His choice of ultimate values may be religiously founded, or nonreligiously based on the deeply felt ground of human responsibility from man to man; or it may be frankly personal and egotistic. His chosen values may be political or—such as those of art or charity—nonpolitical. He may justify his carrying partisanship into scientific work by reference to man's being a "whole man," not to be divided into a bloodless scholar on duty and an unscholarly human being living his own life in his off hours. Yet, in spite of his partisanship, he is a scientific relativist because he acknowledges that we must "choose" our values and cannot prove them in an intersubjectively transmissible manner. He honestly avows his chosen values and admits to their indemonstrability, unless in the heat of the argument he inadvertently forgets to do so, which frequently happens. He despises neutrality in science as much as everywhere else, considering it a useless waste of time and energy, doomed to failure anyway, and encourages his disciples to use science with all vigor at their disposal in their effort to bring their self-chosen goals nearer to realization. His favorite subject is "applied theory," not "pure theory."

His opposite number, the "neutral" relativist, recognizes the right of the partisan relativist to behave as he does, provided he never fails in his duty to avow his underlying value judgments and to admit to their nonscientific basis and never abuses his authority as a teacher for purposes of indoctrination under the cloak of academic freedom. But although the neutral relativist on these conditions allows partisan relativism to proceed, he considers it only the second best choice of scientific behavior. He thinks he is no less a whole man by abstaining from mingling his own value judgments in his scientific work than is the surgeon who tries to keep all his other human instincts out of his mind while performing an operation. He thinks that in his scientific work he serves mankind best by bringing into play everything that science can contribute to its problems without blending scientific and personal interests. He thinks science can do a unique service by impartial research on the consequences of value judgments, and also on their origins. And above all he thinks that only neutral relativism enables science to make any scientific contributions in the case of conflicting systems of values.

Finally, another distinction is needed. Neutral relativism, in turn, may be "passive" or "active" ("aggressive"). The passive relativist keeps out of the political fight, which he considers a matter for politics and not for science, devoting himself exclusively to scientific theory (pure or applied) and to research, in particular to the investigation of conflicting value systems. The aggressive type of neutral relativist, by contrast, enters the political arena in a fighting spirit that pits him against all those who try to sell their own value systems under the false flag of science, whether they be religious organizations who claim their religious dogmas to be scientifically established or verified, or political movements, such as Marxism, based on a pseudo-scientific prediction of the course of history; or old-fashioned monarchism, based on quasi-scientific theories of natural law and divine rights; or National Socialism, based on quasi-scientific doctrines of the superiority of violence and of racial prerogatives. The aggressive relativist is, in principle, militant even against adherents of democracy who absolutize democratic values as if the latter could be scientifically established beyond a comparative examination of risks and consequences. Yet by fighting dogmatism, he actually supports the democratic principles of freedom, tolerance and equality. On the relations between Scientific Value Relativism and democracy more will be said in Chapter VIII, Section 8.

Many illustrations for these various types of relativistic behavior will be found in later chapters of this book. For example, Roscoe Pound and Felix Cohen (Chapter VI, Section 5) may be classified as "latent" relativists; Charles Merriam and Harold Lasswell (*ibid.*) as "overt, but partisan" relativists; Max Weber and Radbruch (*ibid.,* Sections 2 and 3) as "overt and neutral" relativists; the early Radbruch of the "passive" variety, later however an "aggressive" neutral relativist (Chapter VIII, Section 8), as Kantorowicz (Chapter VI, Section 3) had been from the beginning. Radbruch finally came to recognize some absolute elements; but to that extent he ceased to be a scientific relativist (see Chapter VIII, Section 16).

9. *Summary*

In the present chapter, Scientific Value Relativism, or Scientific Value Alternativism, has emerged as the "seamy side" of Scientific Method (Section 1). Examination of the various meanings of the term "valuable" (Section 2) has led to an extensive table of significant steps which under Scientific Method can be legitimately and successfully taken regarding values (Section 3). Yet there remains a gap which Scientific Method is unable to close: the validity of the ultimate standards that underlie value judgments cannot be established through Scientific Method (Section 4). This is due, in part, to the logical gulf between what Is and what Ought to be (Section 5). Formal logic remains an important tool in the scientific discussion of values, but it is unable to bridge the gulf (Section 6). Scientific Value Relativism insists that neither can any other method close the gap scientifically (Section 7). A later chapter of this book (VII) will focus on objections that have been raised against this view. At present, several types of relativistic behavior have been distinguished: transpositivistic vs. positivistic, trans-historical vs. historical, overt vs. latent, neutral vs. partisan, and aggressive vs. passive relativism (Section 8).

We now turn to a special case of the theory of value—the impact of Scientific Method and Scientific Value Relativism upon the theory of justice.

CHAPTER IV

THEORY OF JUSTICE AND THE IMPACT ON IT OF SCIENTIFIC METHOD AND VALUE RELATIVISM

WHAT is just, what is unjust? Sometimes a voice within us claims to know. Whether or not we are trained as lawyers, that voice likes to announce, at times even to cry out: this is just, this is unjust. Not always, it is true, will this inner voice speak so decidedly. Sometimes it will remain indifferent, or waver, or even hold contradictory answers in readiness. But in many cases it will respond clearly and distinctly to a fact. What voice is this? Is it God who speaks? Is it nature? And if nature, is it the nature of things or that of the human mind, or of human emotions and passions, or of some other instrument, such as man's soul or his conscience? What is the "idea" or the "feeling" of justice which announces itself in these ways?

These questions are basic for political and juridical thought. They encompass, or reflect as in a mirror, most of the other problems of social life on earth. They are, therefore investigated here in advance of more specific topics.

1. The Role of Justice in Political Science and in Jurisprudence

Among the proper ends of state and government, justice has been given a high, if not top, rank at all times. Two axioms have been generally accepted without question: first, that the government's own actions ought to be just; second, that governmental institutions, such as law courts, ought to ensure the preservation of justice.

Basic principles of justice were, up to the beginning of the nineteenth century and in part even until its end, chiefly derived deductively from four grounds not always kept strictly separate but clearly distinguishable. These were, first, Divine Law; second, some Law of Nature, which prescribed not only the movements of the heavenly bodies but also the proper relations between human beings; third—often treated as a mere specimen of the second, but sometimes as a separate ground —Reason; and fourth, some kind of Social Contract, either postulated as a historic event or constructed as the only theoretical justification for government.

It was generally recognized, however, that these four grounds failed to supply *all* the norms necessary to provide and preserve justice and that, therefore, lawmaking was a proper function of organized society. As a lawmaker the government stood under the postulate that all its actions ought to be just. Ideas of legal justice hence appeared on two levels according to whether they referred to the making of laws or to their application, with the term justice occurring in both, but in a different setting: the laws laid down by governments ought to be just laws; once laid down, they ought to be administered justly. The lawyers' minds have generally been fixed on the second aspect, the political scientists' on the first. But the basic question is the same for both: what is just, what is unjust?

During the last hundred years, political philosophy and the philosophy of law have often been treated as though they were two distinct fields of thought. However, for the reasons just given they cannot be so separated. This was quite correctly understood during the Natural-Law period, when they were always handled together. In law schools the positive law may properly constitute the primary subject of study. Yet to *philosophy* of law, exactly as to political philosophy, the law as it stands is only a matter for either critique or justification. Whenever we ponder what "ought" to be law, we necessarily turn to the question whether there are eternal, or absolute, or at least objective, standards of justice. If there are, they are relevant to both policy and law. If there are not, philosophy of law as well as of policy must establish and defend this negative contention, and thereafter either resign—as seems to have been the case widely with Anglo-American philosophy —or investigate, in a relativistic manner, the political purposes to which legislation might be made subservient.

Thus both "absolutists" and "relativists," in either branch of philosophy, are bound to deal with the principles of justice underlying legislation. Absolutists have always done so quite elaborately. Whether building on revelation, intuition, reason, comparison, or speculation, they have put forward dogmas on proper ends and means of legislation. Among the relativists in legal philosophy, their late leader, Gustav Radbruch (see below, Chapter VI) presented a thorough analysis of the ideas held by typical political parties, because the goals they consider highest determine their ideas of justice. He went so far as to say that "one may call the theory of political parties the subject proper of the relativistic philosophy of law."[1]

It follows that philosophy of law is necessarily political philosophy,

[1] Gustav Radbruch, *Grundzüge der Rechtsphilosophie,* 1st ed., 1914, p. 96.

and vice versa. So perfect is this ultimate identity that we are justified in speaking of "political and legal philosophy" in the singular form. Granted that there may be questions that belong only to the one or the other; in dealing as we do in this chapter with common ground, references to one alone would be inadequate.[2]

2. *Eclipses and Revivals of Natural-Law Ideas*

The idea that there is an immutable, universal, absolute Law of Nature that directs the proper relations between men had clearly developed by the fifth century B.C. and, although often declared to be dead, it never died completely; some time earlier or later after each apparent demise it was always resuscitated, although in ever new forms. Within the twenty-five hundred years from its first inception to the end of the nineteenth century, we can count at least three eclipses and three revivals.[1]

The zigzag of this movement, graphically illustrated in the accompanying table, is a model of historical dialectics in the realm of ideas. Each subsequent stage was not simply a negation of the preceding one but incorporated some of its thought. This fact gives the story the typical Hegelian appearance of a movement from thesis through antithesis to synthesis. It should be noted, however, that ideas of previous stages have to some extent kept on living side by side with the theories succeeding them.

The first eclipse of Natural-Law ideas occurred when around 400 A.D. their "pagan" approach caused them to be pushed into the background, if not entirely superseded, by the growing emphasis on Divine Law in the sense of the declared divine will (St. Augustine). The first revival was effected eight hundred years later when, in the thirteenth

[2] The last three paragraphs are reprinted, with minor changes, from the introductory pages of my article "The Impossible in Political and Legal Philosophy," *California Law Review*, vol. 29 (1941) pp. 312 ff. In the meantime, similar ideas have been variously expressed by others, especially Jerome Hall in a paper "Unification of Political and Legal Theory," read at the annual meeting of the American Political Science Association in 1953. An "American Society of Political and Legal Philosophy" has been founded, which issues an annual publication under the title *Nomos* (vol. 1, *Authority*, Cambridge, Mass., 1958).

[1] Literature on the history of Natural-Law ideas, see Appendix B. An excellent overall presentation from the pre-Socratics to date is Eric Wolf's short book in German, *Das Problem der Naturrechtslehre, Versuch einer Orientierung*, Karlsruhe 1955. The best total survey in English, written from the Roman Catholic viewpoint, is A. Rommen, *The Natural Law, A Study in Legal and Social History and Philosophy*, St. Louis and London 1947, translated and annotated by Thomas R. Hanley from Rommen's *Die ewige Wiederkehr des Naturrechts*, Leipzig 1936. See further, Leo Strauss, *Natural Right and History*, Chicago 1955 (German translation, *Naturrecht und Geschichte*, Stuttgart 1956), a very careful study. My few remarks above follow independent ways for a more modest purpose; they are not meant to replace intensive historical studies.

century, reason and faith—and thus Natural Law and Divine Law, Aristotle and the Bible—were pronounced compatible approaches to truth (St. Thomas, and later Suarez and Leibniz).

The second eclipse followed three hundred years later, in the sixteenth and seventeenth centuries, when after the birth of the doctrine of sovereignty the legal authority of each country's positive law was enhanced so as to supplant that of both Divine and Natural Law (Bodin and, more radically, Hobbes). The second revival came, still within the seventeenth century, with the doctrine of Natural *Rights,* by which an attempt was made to demonstrate that certain rights of the individual could not be eliminated by the positive law. In its weaker form this theory contended that, notwithstanding the existence of such rights, the sovereign power could disregard them without acting unjustly (Hobbes, *Leviathan,* ch. vii); in its more familiar, stronger form it insisted, however, that any violation of natural rights which was not designed to preserve them was unjust (Locke).

The third eclipse was more thorough. Formidable blows were struck at Natural Law and Natural Rights in the eighteenth and nineteenth centuries from at least six sides: (1) from the philosophers of skepticism, such as Hume; (2) from Kant's theory of knowledge which criticized, although less radically than Hume's, the excessive use of "pure reason" (see above, Chapter ii, Section 5); (3) from moralists, such as Burke who, while fundamentally still recognizing a law of Nature, stressed duties and tradition rather than natural rights; (4) from utilitarians, like Bentham and the Mills, who put their standard of "greatest happiness of the greatest number" as an extinguisher over the flame of Natural Law, although that standard was a bit of natural law itself (see Chapter v, Section 7); (5) from modern positivists who, again like Bentham and more particularly John Austin, assigned to the sovereign parliament the exclusive power to determine rights and duties; and (6) from the historicists, such as von Savigny and Sir Henry Maine, who declared that law must be allowed to "grow" from the national ground and cannot be "made." These schools were in conflict among themselves, but they were all aligned against the old confidence in Natural Law.

At the end of that period appeals to Natural Law had become more and more dispensable because of the rapidly increasing practical agreement on political values, in particular the wide acceptance of the utilitarian formula and of certain basic principles of civilization, such as the abolition of torture and slavery, the postulate of judicial independence, and the remedy of habeas corpus or of its Continental equivalent against unwarranted detention (see Introductory, Section 2). The democratic ideals of popular sovereignty and majority decision as ultimate political judges on the priority of values were constantly spreading. Thus the nineteenth century closed with a wide practical consent on highest values, but with Natural-Law theories in a state of disintegration and the former interest in them all but extinct.

Yet in the meantime there had taken place one more, a third, revival. Kant himself had introduced it by recognizing "necessary regulative principles" of the use of reason and the "categorical imperative" of the moral law, efforts that led him at the end of his life to ideas closely related to Natural-Law doctrines (see Chapters v, Section 7, and ix, Sections 1 and 5). Hegel, in his conception of the World Spirit, exalted reason once more to an objective and creative position. Neo-Kantians and Neo-Hegelians carried such ideas on in refined versions. And still another delicate crescent had appeared in the philosophical skies, visible only to a few; this was Kant's idea, taken up by English and German idealists (T. H. Green, Radbruch), that moral duty is a generator of rights, since it is one's right to do his duty (see Chapter viii, Section 16).

Side by side with these new approaches the earlier schools, in particular those of Thomas Aquinas and Locke, continued to live. In fact, the belief in Natural Law and Natural Rights has never ceased to loom large as a full moon in the popular skies, even after it had lost credit with the leading philosophical schools as an adequate ground for scientific theory.

Finally, around 1900, Scientific Method in association with the Logical-Gulf Doctrine (separation of Is and Ought) and, as their common offspring, Scientific Value Relativism began to make its impact felt. The result was a fourth eclipse of Natural Law, more fundamental than any of the former. This time the eclipse had all the appearances of being final, with no hope left for another revival. What historicists and positivists had begun piecemeal, centering attention on one people, one period, or some definite positive law, was now being carried on by Scientific Value Relativism in wholesale fashion: a definite system of reference, the validity of which was beyond scientific proof, was held to be necessary as a starting point for every consideration of justice. As we saw in the preceding chapter it was no longer regarded as scientific to argue that men ought to exist and not to be killed "because they did exist"; that their right to defend themselves

GRAPH

ECLIPSES AND REVIVALS OF THE NATURAL LAW DOCTRINE

Stage	Time approx.	Origin and Revivals	Eclipses
Origin	prior to 400 B.C.	Greek philosophy (Sophists, Plato, Aristotle, Stoics). Cicero	
1st Eclipse	400 A.D.		"Divine Will," overshadowing Natural Law, St. Augustine
Revival	1270	"Divine Will plus Natural Law" "Faith plus Reason" "The Bible plus Aristotle" St. Thomas (d. 1274)	
2nd Eclipse	1576		"Sovereignty," "Positive Law," Bodin (Six Livres de la République, 1576); Hobbes (Leviathan, 1651)
Revival	1690	"Inalienable Human Rights," Locke, 2nd Treatise of Gov't, 1690	
3rd Eclipse	after 1740		"Skepticism," Hume "Critique of Pure Reason," Kant I "Traditionalism," Burke "Utilitarianism," Bentham, Mill "Positivism," (revived), Bentham, Austin "Historicism," von Savigny, Maine (Ch. v)
Revival	late 18th & 19th c.	"Categorical Imperative: Moral Law Within Us," Kant II (Ch. ix) German Idealism, Fichte, Hegel "Duty, a source of Rights," Kant, T. H. Green	
4th Eclipse	1900		"Scientific Method," "Scientific Value Relativism," Simmel, Rickert, Jellinek, M. Weber, Radbruch, Kelsen; Holmes, Merriam, Lasswell, MacIver, etc. (Ch. vi)
Revival	1920–	Revolt against Relativism (see Ch. vii, viii) Universal elements of human thinking and feeling? (Ch. ix-xii)	Defense of "Scientific" Value Relativism (Ch. vii, viii)

ought to be recognized "because they did have an impulse to do so"; that they ought to be treated as equal "because they were born equal"; that they ought to fulfill some useful function in society "because they did depend on society." These and similar inferences from Is to Ought lacked logical validity. Other reasons, then, had to be found in order to establish the justice of the propositions in question, if it could be established at all in a scientifically tenable manner.

3. *Scientific Method and the Nature of Things*

But then, what *is* just, what *is* unjust? What *is* that inner voice, sometimes so strong and powerful? If this eternal question, with which advisedly we have started the present chapter, is asked of a twentieth-century scholar who follows the rules of Scientific Method, he has no easy time in answering it.

The one answer, which through the ages has come most naturally to most people, It is God's voice, must be debarred from the tribunal of science as being beyond its jurisdiction. It *may* be God's voice; but whether there is a God cannot be verified with the means of Scientific Method. While the inner voice may be considered a possible signpost in that direction, it is no conclusive proof in scientific terms; what seems to speak within us may be the memory of the father's voice, or reflect habits of thinking formed by the environment, or it may be our mind's reaction to a disturbance of its expectations (see Chapter IX).

The same limitations also forbid final scientific statements on the human "soul" as the source of the sense of justice. Whether there is a human soul as a sphere of immediate contact with God or as an immortal part of man or otherwise as an entity distinct from mind, will, and emotions, and what is its origin, essence, and purpose, these are questions of greatest concern to men. But to provide an answer to them is beyond Scientific Method. Reflections thereon have yielded a rich harvest of "intersubjectively not transmissible knowledge," either real or alleged (S_2, see Chapter II, Section 7), and of "speculations" (S_3), but no conclusive type of "intersubjectively transmissible knowledge" (S_1).

Far more accessible to scientific examination is the suggestion that in deciding on what is just or unjust we respond to the *nature of things*. It is under this more subtle title that Natural-Law ideas have staged a comeback recently. Let us see, then, what Scientific Method can here contribute.

It can certainly do two things. It can, first, try to clarify to what extent the nature of things makes a successful human interference with a definite course of events either altogether impossible or more or less costly in terms of the price that must be paid for the interference or of the consequences involved. This approach will be pursued in Chapter XII. Second, Scientific Method can investigate to what extent the nature of things is certain or likely to elicit some definite type of human responses. To this aspect, although it is somehow interwoven with the first, it is appropriate to turn at this point.

Many illustrations can be given for interrelations between the nature of things and human conceptions of what is just and what is unjust, what ought to be done or approved and what ought not to be done or approved. It is quite obvious, for example, that conceptions about maternal duties after childbirth have something to do with the physical conditions of mother and infant, and conceptions of "appropriation" and "property," as Locke recognized in his *Second Treatise,* with the gathering and consumption of fruit. The natural requirements of agriculture are reflected in a great number of widely recognized customs and institutions, such as land property and tenancy, the typical organization of family relations, and conceptions of the proper use of animals,[1] and also in associations for the common use of meadows, woodlands, and tools.[2]

Such interrelations are frequently close enough to permit the scientific prediction that legal institutions which correspond to them will be received as "natural" by most people with approval, while legal orders that disregard them will meet with disapproval and resistance as being "unnatural." Sometimes the interrelations are so close as to make their effective disregard by the lawgiver actually or virtually "impossible" (Chapter XII).

A particularly striking illustration of the interrelation between the nature of things and human ideas of justice is offered by the principle that promises must be fulfilled. Scientific Method can verify by logical analysis and observation that a "promise" generally arouses the "expectation" of its being fulfilled and resentment if it is not, that this concatenation gives rise to concepts of "obligation" and of "claim" and of their expiration when fulfilled, and that it leads to possible measures of "enforcement" and demands for the payment of "dam-

---

[1] See Alexander Rüstow, *Ortsbestimmung der Gegenwart,* vol. 1, Stuttgart 1951.

[2] This was the basis for Gierke's thesis that rural associations had an origin independent of the state. See Otto von Gierke, *Deutsches Genossenschaftsrecht,* cited in Appendix B.

ages" in case of default.[3] Not only can we observe that this chain re-action actually follows a promise in innumerable cases; we can also state that the *meaning* of the sentence, "I promise you to do this," im-plies the meaning of "You may expect fulfillment," and so on. It is, therefore, possible to state with full scientific assurance that, *according to the meaning of my promise,* I "ought" to do what I promised.

But stating scientifically that such was the "meaning" of my promise is not the same as stating that I really ought to do what I said I would. If someone makes promises to a child to take it away from its parents, or to his sweetheart to divorce his wife, or to an addict to supply him with heroin, or if a fascist promises his leader to torture or kill a prisoner, or a politician makes sweeping promises in his campaign speeches, then it may have been the "meaning" of the promise that he who made it ought to do what he promised; but it does not follow from this fact that he actually ought to do it. Likewise, in a different category of cases, when a workman promises to work ten hours every day, or in a fully socialized country to serve as a private laborer at all, or if one producer promises another not to sell below a definite price, or if someone promises never to marry, or having made such a vow later promises a girl to marry her, then the question whether justice demands fulfillment of the promise is in doubt. Elements other than the meaning of the promise enter into the scientific analysis. Society can successfully deny binding force to promises, disregarding that it is "na-tural" to expect fulfillment and that to arouse this expectation is the meaning of a promise. Whether and when society is "justified" in interfering is obviously determined by ideas that cannot be subsumed under the vague concept of the nature of things.

At any rate, the nature of things does not of itself warrant the con-clusion that it should not be interfered with, provided interference is possible and the price is not considered too high. To reason otherwise involves a logically unwarranted inference from Is to Ought. To be sure, if conciously or subconsciously we start from the premise that God created world and man, then a conclusion to the effect that the nature of things should not be interfered with might be logically justi-fied. But then we derive our postulates from God, not from nature, which merely serves us as an announcer of God's intentions. Without the divine premise it is much the same with the nature of things as

[3] See Arnold Brecht, "System der Vertragshaftung," *Jherings Jahrbücher,* vol. 53 (1908) pp. 213–302; Adolf Reinach, *Die apriorischen Grundlagen des bürgerlichen Rechts,* Jahrbuch für Philosophie und phänomenologische Forschung, vol. 1, Halle 1913 (also published separately, republished München 1953).

with a man's beard—we observe that it is growing by nature, but it does not follow that we ought to let it grow; men may decide to shave, disregarding the remonstrations of those who prefer naturally-bearded faces (the nature of things), unless the naturalists force us to comply with their value judgments. So in every case where nature seems to suggest but not to enforce some human attitude we cannot, without interposing ideas of a divine will or of other overriding premises, logically deduce that we ought to abstain from interference. Whenever there is a choice between two alternatives, namely, either to let nature take its course, or—as in irrigation projects, elimination of mosquitoes, surgical operations, the use of anesthetics, birth control, or the shaving of beards—to subjugate it to the human will, there the nature of things alone cannot tell us how to choose. It is after all an essential part of the nature of things that man frequently can interfere with them by using the nature of other things, such as a shaving knife.

Nevertheless, the theory that the nature of things determines what ought or ought not to be done has cropped up time and again. Professor Gustav Radbruch, who had done so much to establish Scientific Value Relativism in legal philosophy (see Chapter VI, below), referred to the nature of things with a growing emphasis in his last period, when after Hitler's barbarian rule he tried to discover some scientific limitations to relativism.[4] Yet the nature of things is no way out of the dilemma. No strictly scientific reasoning can prove that a lawgiver must respect the nature of things, except to the extent that interference is either impossible or entails consequences which he himself wants to avoid. Religious and even juridical arguments (see below, Section 8) may be able to go further. But scientifically, here is the end.

Any sanctification of the nature of things beyond this measure is merely one of the many instances in which the same divine forces whose existence has just been declared scientifically undemonstrable are subconsciously assumed to be operative when it comes to some special question such as that here discussed. This inconsistency we should be severe and honest enough not to let pass. If we think that

[4] Radbruch, *Vorschule der Rechtsphilosophie,* Heidelberg 1947, pp. 19 ff.; and, "Die Natur der Sache als juristische Form," *Festschrift für Rudolf Laun,* Hamburg 1948; also, the remarks by Erik Wolf, editor, in Radbruch's *Rechtsphilosophie,* 4th ed., Stuttgart 1950, p. 70, and in his article "Revolution or Evolution in Gustav Radbruch's Legal Philosophy" *Natural Law Forum,* vol. 3 (1958) p. 1 ff., and Fritz von Hippel's valuable presentation in his *Gustav Radbruch,* Heidelberg 1951, pp. 40–45. For the United States, see Lon L. Fuller, *The Law in Quest of Itself,* Chicago 1940. He speaks of the "natural order" underlying group life, which it is the task of the judge—and of lawyers in general—to discover; see also below, Chapter VIII, Section 5, end.

there is sufficient interpersonal proof for the existence of a divine will back of the nature of things, or if we propose to establish science on such a basis although there is no interpersonal verification, or if at least we want science to pay respect to the "potentiality" of God's existence (Chapter XIII), then we should say so, and not today deny demonstrability, agreeing on that ground to separate science from religion, and tomorrow draw scientific inferences that presuppose for their logical validity a divine will.

In the last analysis, then, the nature of things offers no more of an absolute standard of justice than did the old Law of Nature. Radbruch seems to have felt this, for he summed up his postwar remarks as follows: "The nature of things serves somewhat to mitigate the steep dualism between value and reality, or between Is and Ought, but *not to eliminate it.*" [5]

It is not the nature of things as such, but the human mind and human emotions reacting to the nature of things—functioning as an instrument of observation and reasoning, of predicting consequences, of shaping expectations, and of devising means to promote or counteract their realization, or engaging in metaphysical speculations—which we must examine, if we want to learn more about justice in scientific terms. To this approach we shall turn in the next section.[6]

4. *Ideas of Justice—Relative to the Second Power and on Several Levels*

Scientific Method enables us to reveal a great deal regarding the way our mind and our emotions operate in matters of justice. First of all, we can observe that postulates of justice are generally expressed in terms of some desired state of affairs, for instance one where equality, or "more" equality, would be established, or liberty, or more liberty, or security and order, or obedience to God's will, or all of these. Even when not expressed in such terms, postulates of justice can be translated into them. The desired state of affairs may be conceived of in an

---

[5] *Vorschule, op.cit.,* p. 21. Italics not in the original. The anti-relativist Helmut Coing is frank enough to admit (*op.cit. infra,* p. 285n; pp. 128, 147) that the nature of things yields no answer on many questions, e.g. whether one may sell a child for economic reasons. Here, he says, "a moral decision is needed, which in turn goes back to a definite evaluation." Regretfully, he sees "the spectre of relativism rise again" here, but fails to draw the logical consequences: distinction between "philosophical" and "scientific" value relativism, and acceptance, however regretful, of the latter.

[6] For additional remarks on the nature of things see Chapters VII, Section 7 (Gestalt psychology), VIII, Sections 5 (Nature) and 16 (Radbruch vs. Radbruch), and XII (impossibility and risks).

abstract manner ("equality") or concretely with regard to some particular situation ("my wages should be higher"). But whether abstract or concrete, it can be described without using the concept of justice or its equivalent. Ideas of justice, in other words, seem to express an urge for an ad-"just"-ment to some ideal state of affairs that is considered a "just" one, or "more just," but can be described without using the concept of justice.

This relation to some ideal state of affairs as a standard, therefore, is the first relative element we meet in analyzing human thinking about justice. This relative element would be present even if science could tell us which ideal state of affairs would be the really just one. Even then the idea of justice would be relative in that it referred to such an ideal state of affairs.

But this is not the end of relativity for the scientific observer because science, as we have seen in dealing with value judgments in general, is unable to decide which state of affairs *is* really just. Opinions differ, and science cannot decide between them in absolute terms. We shall find later (Chapter x) that certain elements in human ideas of justice can be said to be universal and invariant, if not absolute. But they alone do not suffice to describe the state of affairs that might deserve to be called really just. In this respect the scientist, if he follows Scientific Method, has no choice but either to "assume" some ideal standard as the really just one, or to refer to particular opinions, held by himself or by others, individually or in groups, either directly or in submission to some other nonscientific source of authority. Justice, therefore, is relative not only to some state of affairs, it is relative twice over —to the second power, so to speak—because what state of affairs ought to be preferred can be stated by science only in relation to some nonscientific source of authority.

This twofold character of relativity in inquiries on justice has not to my knowledge been noted in the wide literature on the subject. The emphasis has sometimes been on relations between the idea of justice and the desirable state of affairs, and sometimes on those between the desirable state of affairs and opinions about it, without a sharp distinction between the two kinds of relativity involved. But this is a minor point at the moment. More important is the following.

Not only do different individuals hold various ideas about the ideal state of affairs they would consider really just; every individual is capable of several such ideas. Our ideas or feelings of justice may be twofold or threefold, or even morefold, in accordance with the different systems of values to which we respond positively at different times, or even simultaneously. Justice in the light of personal ideas is, or at least may be, a barrel with several bottoms.

In particular, there are two distinct levels in our ideas of justice. Either our thinking moves strictly within the institutions of our present status of civilization—this may be called the "traditional" idea (feeling, sense) of justice; or it may transcend the traditional institutions—then we may speak of the "transtraditional" idea (feeling, sense) of justice.

The "traditional" idea of justice accepts the fundamental institutions which constitute the basis of our daily social life, takes them for granted, does not question them. Insofar as these institutions have been established by the positive law (written constitutions, legislation, judicial precedents, and the like), the traditional idea of justice is positivistic.

In contradistinction, the "transtraditional" idea of justice detaches itself from the existing institutions, either in whole or in part, and criticizes them according to principles which are taken from a transtraditional scheme of evaluation. This again may be done in dependence on group ideas that are accepted and carried on by the individual in some condition of submission, as for example ideas of a party or revolutionary junta, or merely in deference to opinions of a stronger personality, a friend, the husband or wife, or the priest.

From there the individual may penetrate to a third level, in more courageous hours, where he discovers what he "really" thinks and where he may be critical also of the transtraditional ideas of his friends. Within a single day he may move through all three levels, in his business hours living and feeling with the traditional sense of justice, in the evening joining with his friends in their criticism, and at night isolating himself also from his friends. It may even be possible for the individual to shift at will from one level to the other.

The following two sections will try to illustrate the difference between traditional and transtraditional justice as the two most important levels.

5. *Traditional Justice*

Our present Western civilization is built upon certain fundamental social institutions. One might insert into their list an infinite number of usages, long established or recently added, central or marginal ones —there is no well-defined boundary. As fundamental institutions one may think, more particularly, of the following five: Monogamy, Family (status of parents and children), Private Property, Inheritance, Contract (its freedom and its binding force).

These basic pillars of Western civilization are so familiar to everyone living in the Western world that our traditional sense of justice accepts them as given conditions. All of them might be different from what they are, as most of them have been at other times and still are in various countries. Yet within our own civilization everyday thinking and feeling about justice moves within the temple that is built upon these five pillars and supported by many smaller columns and buttresses.

The way in which the sense of justice operates in the traditional temple includes the following four distinct steps: (1) consciously or unconsciously the individual accepts the traditional institutions in his arguments; (2) he uses them as a basis for logical reasoning, drawing all implications; (3) he accepts laws and regulations that make for expediency and certainty, such as bills of exchange, statutes of limitations, fixation of the proper time for serving notice in the absence of special agreements; and (4) he argues against "abuses." In doing the latter he either contends for a modified meaning of the institutions as he interprets them, or he demands a modification for the future, which means a transition from the traditional to the transtraditional.

Logical reasoning on the basis of given institutions leads far in some cases. Suppose someone has thrown a stone through a shop window. The automatic response of the traditional sense of justice is that he ought to pay damages. For he was not the owner of the window (property!); it was the shopkeeper's property inherited from his father (inheritance!). That the doer of the act was an illegal child of the same father did not make him the owner (monogamy!). That he had been an employee in the shop and fired without cause is not relevant, the less so because he had been served notice within due time that he had to leave (contract!). That he was a poor devil was just bad luck; there is no traditional institution excluding one's having bad luck.

In other cases, however, logical reasoning on the basis of given institutions ends in a clash between contradictory implications of two institutions, and then leaves traditional feelings in confusion, our sense of justice wavering undecidedly. Freedom of contract may collide with monopolistic ownership of the means of production. In the event that someone has acquired stolen goods in good faith, property rights may collide with another recognized institution, that of protection of good faith (certainty). Whenever confronted with such collisions the traditional sense of justice loses its bearings.

It is always characteristic of traditional ideas of justice that our thinking starts from unquestioned social institutions, although in our zeal of reasoning we often forget that it does so. And yet it is obvious that wherever the traditional institutions are different from ours, or were so formerly, the traditional reactions of the sense of justice are or were different accordingly. That is to say, the traditional idea of justice is relative to something *objective,* the existing institutions.

6. *Transtraditional Justice*

We come to transtraditional justice when, instead of staying within the traditional temple, we look at it from without and judge and criticize the structure. This too we can do under the guidance of our sense of justice. The standard we are applying then, however, is no longer relative to objective factors such as offered by the traditional institutions. The relativity now is in regard to some subjective—in the sense of personal—conviction or creed as to what is the most valuable state of affairs toward which, in order to be just, society ought to move (the ultimate goal), or what are those improved conditions that should be next realized (the next step), and what is the right order in a plurality of valuable goals and in a plurality of steps toward their attainment.

Kant expressed the hypothetical view that, *if* there should be anything of absolute value on earth, it could only be the dignity of the individual. During the nineteenth century it had become customary to distinguish *two* possible highest values, the welfare of the individual and that of the group; if one chose the former, then no sacrifice of the individual for the sake of the group could ever be justly demanded unless it was to the individual's own good; if the latter, other sacrifices also could be asked for in justice. Radbruch added a third category, the "work," the achievement, or more particularly *Kultur* (spiritual civilization) as a third standard (see Chapter VI).

These three categories, hereafter called individualism, groupism, and transpersonalism,[1] offer convenient symbols for quick reference. Yet for

---

[1] There is some confusion as to the names. The first category has been generally called "individualism." The name of the second has varied. At first "universalism" was frequently used (so by Georg Jellinek, *Allgemeine Staatslehre,* Berlin, 1st ed. 1900; 3rd ed. 1914, p. 173); this is misleading if one thinks, not of mankind but of the nation, as was generally intended. Later, "supra-individualism" was substituted (Gustav Radbruch, *Rechtsphilosophie,* see Chapter VI, below); or "transpersonalism" was used for all ideas that transcend the interests of the individual, whether in the interest of the nation or of other ideals (Radbruch, *op.cit.,* 2nd ed., and Julius Binder, *Philosophie des Rechts,* Berlin 1925, pp. 282, 307; the latter

a relativist to say that it is possible to present all conceivable schemes of highest values systematically in such a small list of three items (Radbruch), or in any other exhaustive list, is inconsistent. Unless science should be able—contrary to the theory of Scientific Value Relativism —to establish absolute limits for possible ideas of justice, or at least some universal and invariant elements in human thought about justice (a question to which we shall return in Chapters ix ff.), potential creeds in this field cannot be scientifically-enumerated in advance. Indeed, what a man may treasure as superior values is so varied that classifications a priori will lead to arbitrary selections or to merely formal categories.

To give an illustration of the variety of conditions, or states of affairs, which people regard as standard goals in their ideas of justice either for the distant future or for the present moment, a few "ideal types," or characteristic patterns, of creed will be briefly sketched. Thus we have:

1. The *equalitarian,* who places equality highest in matters of justice and derives from this ultimate ideal his standards of justice. As will be discussed later (Chapter x) there is a good deal of evidence that a certain segment of equality is contained in every idea of justice. But the equalitarian wants more. He wants the whole thing. There are many kinds of equalitarian, however, depending on what they desire to make equal: wealth or income, happiness, freedom, opportunity, or what else. And further subdivisions are necessary. If, for instance, equality in wealth is the ideal, we must distinguish whether equality is desired on a per capita basis, or according to need, or according to work, and if the latter, whether quantity or quality of work is to decide. Earlier socialism held the according-to-need ideal; the Soviet Constitution of 1936, however, incorporated the according-to-work standard, which leads to different results.[2] We must also distinguish whether equality is sought on a world-wide basis or on a national or racial basis,

---

reverted to "universalism," in the specific sense of an organic theory of the state, in the 2nd ed. of his work, published under the title *System der Rechtsphilosophie,* 1937, p. 150). Transpersonalism, first introduced by Emil Lask (see Chapter vi), was best suited for the third category, however, and was so finally used by Radbruch (3rd ed.). That would leave us for the second with Radbruch's "supra-individualism," which has the disadvantage that it expresses no clear distinction from the third. I shall, therefore, use "groupism" instead. "Collectivism" is tinged by too many particular connotations to be useful as a general name for this category, within which it has come to signify one specimen only.

[2] Article 12: "In the U.S.S.R. the principle of socialism is realized: 'From each according to his ability, to each according to his work.'" Article 118: "Citizens of the U.S.S.R. have the right to work, that is the right to guaranteed employment and payment for their work in accordance with its quantity and quality." See Arnold Brecht, "The New Russian Constitution," *Social Research,* vol. 4 (1937) pp. 157, 167. It is official communist doctrine, however, that distribution according to need is the final goal.

and the like. All these propositions are actually incompatible with one another. What is justice under the one is injustice under the other. See Chapter VIII, Section 2.

2. The *libertarian,* who tends to measure everything by the yardstick of liberty. He will ardently oppose as unjust steps intruding on liberty which the equalitarian would welcome as just, and inversely. Subdivisions run from liberty as a condition of personal dignity and morality (Kant) to liberty for egoistic self-assertion.

3. The *revelationist,* whose highest aim is the execution of God's will. Whether the divine will be individualistic or national or universal in its purpose is, on principle, quite irrelevant to one of this type. Hence we might call him a transpersonalist. But if the divine intentions are individualistic, he may be an individualist as well, or he may be a group fanatic with regard to his church or sect. Subdivisions are as manifold as revelations.

4. The *conservative,* the traditionalist pure and simple, provided the temple of traditional institutions has remained unchanged long enough. Even if he regards it from outside he likes it and happily reenters it, caressing every pillar and ornament with tender hands. His transtraditional level of feeling is identical with the traditional one. If the temple has recently been changed he may want to set the clock back to former stages. Subdivisions are as manifold as traditions. In another sense of the term, the conservative is always an authoritarian and an adherent of the organic state. Then he falls under the next category.

5. The *authoritarian,* who regards leadership as a principle of highest value. To follow leadership is just, to counteract it, unjust. The different ideas on the legitimacy of leadership multiply the subdivisions of this group. Ideas on mutual relations (feudalism, *Gefolgschaft*) may further qualify each subdivision.

6. The *majority worshipper,* who holds that whatever the majority decides is the highest value to be accepted by everyone. To follow the majority will is just, to oppose its execution is unjust. It is not leadership that arouses his enthusiasm but the consent of the people through the majority.

7. The *hedonist,* who looks for individual happiness or (like Bentham and J. S. Mill, see Chapter V, Section 7 below) for the greatest happiness of the greatest number. His ideas would oppose those of the majority worshipper whenever the majority does not act for this highest end. The many different conceptions of happiness, from material egoism to immaterial altruism and transpersonalism, split this category into as many subdivisions.

8. The *group worshipper*. The group may be the family, a fraternity, team, racial group, religious sect, or a class, the territorial community, state-folk, or nation, the continent, or humanity. The group worshipper may be more or less exacting in the subordination he desires of the individual's interests under those of the group. In the relation to other groups he may be a group-libertarian or a group-equalitarian, in the latter case standing either for formal or substantial equality, according to any of various conceivable standards. In the extreme case he may be a group fetishist, ready to sacrifice any individual interest for any group interest and placing any other group outside the pale. The saying "my country right or wrong," [3] is not the extreme view, since it still admits that the controversial action may be wrong (evil) and only expresses an emotional readiness to commit even a sin if that is necessary to defend the nation. The limit was reached by the doctrine of the German National Socialists that "all that is useful to the German people *is* right, all that harms them *is* wrong." [4]

9. The *harmonizer,* who thinks of harmony as an ultimate value. Not everyone does. Thomas Jefferson wrote in 1787: "I hold it, that a little rebellion, now and then, is a good thing, and as necessary in the political world as storms in the physical." [5] . . . "God forbid we should ever be twenty years without such a rebellion [as that in Massachusetts]. . . . And what country can preserve its liberties if the rulers are not warned from time to time that the people preserve the spirit of resistance?" [6] An oppositional libertarian may prefer hell to harmony.

[3] This is generally circulated as a British phrase, yet it seems that it was coined in 1816 by an American, the United States naval commander, Stephen Decatur. In agreement on this are: Bartlett's *Familiar Quotations,* Boston 1948, p. 262 n.; Gustav Radbruch, *Kleines Rechtsbrevier,* ed. by Fritz von Hippel, Göttingen 1954, p. 63, n. 15, with references to H. Kantorowicz, *Geist der englischen Politik,* 1929, p. 120; and Büchmann, *Geflügelte Worte.* Decatur (1779–1820) rose to fame in the Tripolitan War and the War of 1812. This is what he said in a toast at Norfolk, Va., in April 1816: "Our country! In her intercourse with foreign nations, may she be always in the right; but our country, right or wrong." This wording leaves no doubt that the speaker did not intend to make his country's interests the final criterion of right or wrong. The same holds true of a speech made by John J. Crittenden, Kentuckian statesman and U.S. senator and attorney-general (1787–1863), who said during the Mexican War, which he had opposed: "I hope to find my country in the right: however I will stand by her, right or wrong" (Bartlett, *op.cit.,* p. 472); and even more so of the words used by German-born Carl Schurz in an address in the Congress of 1872: "Our country, right or wrong. When right, to be kept right; when wrong, to be put right" (*ibid.,* p. 580). About a hundred years earlier, the English writer Charles Churchill (1731–1764) wrote in his "Farewell" these words: "Be England what she will, with all her faults she is my country still." But this too is far from the snappy phrase now in use.

[4] See Hans Frank, *Nationalsozialistisches Handbuch für Recht und Gesetzgebung,* 2nd ed. Berlin 1935, p. 4: "Alles was dem Volke nützt, ist Recht; alles was ihm schadet ist Unrecht."

[5] In a letter to James Madison from Paris, January 30, 1787, in which the writer also expressed some sympathy with societies that exist "without government as among our Indians." *The Writings,* 1907, vol. 6, pp. 63, 65.

[6] Letter to William Steven Smith from Paris, November 13, 1787, *op.cit.,* pp. 371, 373.

Harmony may cover backward institutions under which people are not aware of their exploitation, misery, and lack of education. See also Chapter VIII, Section 14.

10. The *pyramid builder,* the transpersonalist proper. He may have in mind civilization or *Kultur* (civilization's spiritual part),[7] or the evolution of the folk spirit, or a more specific achievement, such as building a cathedral, completing or saving some great work of art, reaching the north pole, climbing Mount Everest, winning a battle, or giving birth to a child. Using aesthetic ideals for his illustrations, Radbruch quotes Treitschke, who said harshly, "A statue by Phidias counterbalances all the misery of the millions of ancient slaves"; but also the German socialist Kurt Eisner: "I at least do not value my life as high as I do a creation of eternal art, nor art so low as to be less valuable than living beings"; and the Britisher, Sir George Birdwood who, when asked whether in a burning house he would save a child or Raphael's Sistine Madonna if he could save only one, answered, "The painting." These may now appear to many readers as slightly fantastic examples from a period of aestheticism. Yet the same problem became most real and pressing during the two World Wars, when it had to be decided often enough whether it was more important to spare great monuments of civilization or the lives of a number of soldiers, more of whom were likely to be killed if destruction was avoided. Sometimes the decision was in favor of civilization, as when the city of Rome was spared; at other times it was in favor of the lives of soldiers, as when the sixth-century monastery of Monte Cassino was destroyed, first of the great foundations through which the survival of Latin culture, the regeneration of Western civilization and the growth of Christianity were secured.[8] Our sense of justice cannot take a stand in such conflicts without deciding on the relative value of the individual and of transpersonal civilization. War offers illustrations for many other conflicts of this type. Winning a battle may become the ultimate yardstick for just and unjust, superior to many if not all other values, including regard for soldiers even on one's own side, and this irrespective of the ultimate purpose and justification of the war at hand; once in a battle one wants to win.

11. The *man of duty,* who looks at life as a chain of duties rather than

---

[7] See below, Chapter VIII, Section 13. Writers as different as Kohler, Radbruch, Binder, and Alfred Weber of the German sector and Northrop here show a preference for Kultur as the recommendable standard, without however drawing radical conclusions in detail. See also Roscoe Pound, *Harvard Law Review,* vol. 51 (1938) p. 461.

[8] See Arnold J. Toynbee, *A Study of History,* vol. 3 (1st ed. 1934) pp. 265–67.

of rights or a struggle for survival and happiness. This view has been in common to Scholasticism, to Kant, Burke, T. H. Green, Stammler, and in functional terms to Duguit. See also Chapter VIII, Section 16, below on Radbruch. The man of duty derives rights, if any, from duties (functions), not from selfish wants; man should be given at least as much freedom as he needs to fulfill his moral duties. A subdivision, or even a separate type, is the person of soldierly mind, who thinks of discipline, courage, honor, and comradeship as ultimate values in themselves. Neither is necessarily tied up with the authoritarian type.

12. The *peace-and-order fanatic,* who places peace and order at the top, regardless of what they preserve. This is the regular state of mind of the policeman or civil servant on duty. He may not be a conservative, nor may he consider the present state of affairs to be harmonious; he may be in favor of thorough reforms, but he wishes them brought about in an "orderly" way. One can meet such views on high levels, as in international affairs (antiwar pacts), in jurisprudence (where postulates of certainty and security are often raised above other values), and among creative personalities. In the same year of 1787 when Jefferson expressed his sympathy with rebellion, Goethe in witnessing a nascent rebellion on his ship near Sicily wrote "[*Mir ist*] *von Jugend auf Anarchie verdriesslicher gewesen als der Tod selbst"* (From my youth I have loathed anarchy more than even death) [9] and a few years later: *"Ich will lieber eine Ungerechtigkeit begehen, als Unordnung ertragen"* (I'd rather commit an injustice than bear disorder).[10]

Many items might be added to this list. In every case the transtraditional ideas on what is just and unjust vary according to the subjective scheme of values. *One who changes from one conviction to the other will thenceforth have a different idea of justice.*

In addition to the pure types, which may or may not exist as such, there is an infinite number of blends. As a rule every political creed is a blend of evaluations in many varieties of juxtaposition and interrelation of the various items. In particular, almost every individualist accepts conditions in which the group ranks higher than the individual, and vice versa.

Only two of the types enumerated above—the libertarian (No. 2)

[9] "Italienische Reise" in *Sämtliche Werke,* Jubilee ed. (1902–07) vol. 26, p. 377. Auguste Comte made similar remarks; see Hayek, *op.cit.,* p. 183.
[10] "Belagerung von Mainz," July 25, 1793, *ibid.,* vol. 28, p. 251.

and the individualistic hedonist (No. 7)—can be classified under individualism; only one each under groupism (No. 8) and transpersonalism (No. 10). All others—especially the equalitarian (No. 1), the revelationist (No. 3), the conservative (No. 4), the authoritarian (No. 5), the majority worshipper (No. 6), and the harmonizer (No. 9)—cannot be adequately subsumed under any of the three.

Nor is it possible to make a definite distinction between values that are "means" only and those which are "ultimate." Values that to many people are merely means, e.g., forms of government which they regard as means for the attainment of peace, order, welfare, etc., often gain esteem as values in themselves, not derivable from others. Belief in a definite authority for the establishment of values (God, a king or leader, or the majority) may be as strong as, or even stronger than, belief in those values themselves (equality, liberty, pleasure, civilization, peace, order, etc.).

We shall see later (Chapter VIII) that almost every one of the values listed above has still been absolutized by some twentieth-century scholar in his revolt against Scientific Relativism—a fact which is of no little support for the relativistic thesis.

Another phenomenon that supports the viewpoint of Scientific Relativism is the fact that modern democratic parliaments reflect many of the ideas on justice included in our listing. This is especially true where parties are founded on ideological programs and seated from "left" to "right" in line with their basic views. There we have:

PARTIES	TOP VALUES
Socialists	Equality
Liberals	Liberty
Democrats (under various names)	Majority
Christian Democrats and other religious parties	Revelation
Moderate Conservatives	Tradition, Peace and Order
Legitimists	Authority
Nationalists	the Group
Fascists, Nazis	Leadership, the Group
Some Independents	*Kultur,* Civilization
Other Independents	Happiness
Others	Harmony

This rainbow of party ideologies is merely the logical consequence of the fact that science is unable to decide which of the several views is correct. Wherever tolerance is accepted as the basis of society, therefore, the different views will find expression side by side, each claiming at least the same respect as any other. Neutral Relativism can do no more than describe all these views impartially and, without making a decision in submission to some a-priori principle, examine the consequences and risks involved in the acceptance of each, and the actual or potential meanings of vague standards. It will appear in the further course of our discussions that such scientific contributions are apt to lead very far. The scientific relativist may also draw attention to possible alternatives that have not yet found practical advocates in the political party life, as Radbruch regretted—characteristic of his own preferences—that no party had yet been founded upon the principle of transpersonalism, with culture as the ultimate standard and value.

Radbruch and his German colleague Julius Binder, although not political scientists but professors of law and legal philosophy, presented elaborate descriptions of the tenets of the various parties, precisely because they express the various ideas of justice held by the people.[11]

7. *In Defense of Scientific Relativism*

Advanced as it was with the utmost soberness and modesty (see below, Chapter VI) Scientific Relativism has done a great deal to correct, cleanse, and refine scholarly thinking about justice. But at the same time it has thrown people into a state of bewilderment, into a feeling of helplessness. If justice can be discussed by science only in relative terms, how then can one any longer call with any certainty of language for more justice beyond the deficient existing institutions, how even oppose, with an appeal to justice, any deterioration?

Science replies to these complaints that no emotional pressure enables it to do what is beyond its reach. If by more justice you mean a little less inequality and a little more freedom, *and you say so,* you may clamor for more justice with the greatest certainty of language, and you will be readily understood. Science can help you along with scientifically established data. If you insist on more equality at the price of freedom, or on more freedom at the price of equality, and make it clear that this is what you mean by justice, you are likely to run into trouble. Your trouble cannot be fully resolved by science.

It is not for the scientist to deceive others in this important matter

[11] See below, Chapter VI, Section 3.

and to pretend being able to do what, as a scientist, he cannot do. The service to justice that he can render is chiefly to be sought for (1) in the clarification of the meaning of alternative ideas of justice, (2) in the scientific examination of the consequences and risks involved in their acceptance and practical execution, and (3) in the fight against all dogmatic doctrines regarding justice that are offered with the pretense that their general validity is scientifically established, a claim that is necessarily untenable under Scientific Method.

In addition, the scientist can and must warn against a grave misunderstanding. True, justice is always relative to some yardstick. But *that the "right" yardstick is relative to subjective ideas science does not say,* and cannot say. The right yardstick may be absolute, and it may be immutable; only whether there is one and what it is Scientific Method is unable to state. For this reason, and for it alone, Scientific Method must limit itself to dealing with yardsticks in relative terms.

Scientific Value Relativism thus takes full account of the fact that the believer may have an absolute yardstick as the basis of his thoughts on justice—absolute for him, and perhaps really absolute if his revelation is right. But science holds modestly that, precisely as God's existence cannot be scientifically proved or disproved, the absolute standard of justice, too, cannot be proved or disproved, only believed and taken for granted, or disbelieved and not so taken. If you believe in some ultimate order of values, justice will appear immutable and standardized to you according to that order. But if someone else believes in another order of values, justice will look different to him. Make your choice. Tell me, but tell me honestly, what your highest values look like and I shall tell you what justice means to you. Before you tell me the one, I cannot tell you the other. But if you speak out I may be able to tell you what the consequences of your choice will be, and what risks you are going to incur; *and then, maybe, you will alter your choice.* It may also appear that you were mistaken in your honest opinion about what your highest values were.

The problem of whether there is a "right" ultimate yardstick, and what it is, has thus been removed from science as beyond its reach. It has been left to other methods of selection, such as religious revelation and ethical intuition (knowledge of the type S_2, not transmissible *qua* knowledge, see Chapter II, Section 7), philosophic speculation (S_3), individual or political choice based on the foregoing or on utilitarian inquiry, and—last but not least—to juridical ascertainment of what is valid law today as distinct from scientific discovery of what it ought to be (see next section).

Did not Aristotle do essentially the same thing in his classical statement of the three systems of values: democracy, in which the quality of being a freeman was the measure of rights; oligarchy, in which wealth or noble birth decided; and aristocracy, in which virtue was the yardstick? Said he:

All are agreed that justice in distribution must be based on some sort of merit, but they do not all mean the same sort of merit, the democrats having in mind the quality of being a freeman; the adherents of oligarchy, wealth, or other noble birth; and the adherents of aristocracy virtue.[1]

8. *Distinction between Juridical and Scientific Validity*

One softening factor, apt to cushion the impact of Scientific Value Relativism in matters of justice, has been generally overlooked by relativists and antirelativists alike. The impotence of science to establish ultimate standards of justice does not necessarily imply that, as a matter of law, common citizens, officials, and law courts must capitulate before every dictatorial value judgment handed down to them in the shape of a positive law, however outrageous and immoral it may appear to them. It is entirely possible to argue juridically that some "fundamental" legal principles and maxims, although disregarded by the government of the day, are *juridically* valid at some definite place and time in the sense that they ought to be applied by the country's law courts, etc., even against contradictory orders clothed in the external cloak of valid law.

This is a *legal* argument, not a scientific setting of standards. It may be based on clauses of a written constitution, like the due-process clauses of the United States Constitution or the various amendment-proof clauses inserted in the Bonn Basic Law of 1949;[1] or it may, in the absence of such constitutional bases, be grounded merely on general convictions of the people, on legal traditions, or on the status of civilization reached in the country at the time. In this manner it was often

---

[1] Aristotle, *Nicomachean Ethics*, Book v, ch. iii. Note that Aristotle in his context does not go into the question which of these systems is best.

[1] See Arnold Brecht, *The New German Constitution*, Occasional Paper of the Institute of World Affairs, New York 1949, reprinted from *Social Research*, vol. 16 (1949) pp. 425, 461 ff.

argued in the France of the Third Republic that the principles of the Declaration of the Rights of Man of 1791 were still juridically valid in spite of their noninsertion in the Organic Laws of 1875. Likewise it might be argued in any other country that even after formal abrogation of constitutional guarantees certain principles or maxims continue to be juridically valid.

Such a way of pleading must not be confused with the contention that the universal or absolute validity of these principles or maxims can be *scientifically* demonstrated. It is one thing to say that a principle is juridically valid at a certain place and time, and another that it is scientifically valid in general. Lack of clarity as to this distinction has caused a great deal of misdirection in the efforts of post-Hitler jurisprudence; jurists have come to search once more for scientifically ascertainable moral Laws of Nature—as I think with dubious results (see above, Section 3, and Chapter viii, Section 5, below)—while what they should and could have done was to lay the foundations for a juridical tradition that certain principles must be considered *juridically* valid even against government orders to the contrary.

Hans Kelsen based his pure theory of law on a fictitious "basic law" according to which a country's constitution, however barbarous, is legally valid, and therefore all steps taken in line with it, too, are juridically valid (see Chapter vi, Section 3, and Appendix b). Nothing can prevent us from grounding our legal theory on the fiction of a slightly different basic law, according to which every country's constitution is valid *except so far as it authorizes violation of minimum standards of respect for human dignity*. No more than this is necessary to develop the theory of a modern Hobbes, like Kelsen, into that of a modern Locke. To take this step is a matter for juridical conviction and tradition, or for popular agreement on principles, not a scientific journey into the realm of Absolute Truth.[2] More will be said on this outlet in Chapter viii, Section 16.

9. *Summary and Reservations*

To summarize the argument of the present chapter, this is what we have seen. What is just and what is unjust is a question equally fundamental for political and for legal philosophy; these two disciplines should not, therefore, be separated (Section 1). The old idea

---

[2] See my review of W. Ebenstein, *Die rechtsphilosophische Schule der reinen Rechtslehre,* in *American Political Science Review,* vol. 32 (1938) pp. 1173–75, where I first pointed to the solution here discussed.

that some Law of Nature answers the question, at least to some extent, had already undergone no less than three eclipses, followed by three revivals, when near the beginning of this century the rise of Scientific Value Relativism seemed to mark its final eclipse in scientific thinking about justice (Section 2). Among the conceivable sources of the human sense of justice, some, like God and soul, are not accessible to scientific statements, while the "nature of things," which can be studied scientifically, does not lead to conclusive prescriptions as long as there is a choice open to man (Section 3). Science, therefore, is thrown back on human ideas or feelings about justice. These, however, have a relative character; they are relative even twice over, namely, always relative to some state of affairs that is considered desirable, and secondly, at least to a considerable extent (see below), relative also to particular ideas as to which state of affairs *is* desirable. Different ideas of justice may prevail even within the same person on several levels at different times, and even at the same time, according to whether existing institutions are either accepted or criticized, and if the latter, according to whether criticism follows group opinions or the like, or is original (Section 4).

Traditional justice is relative to something that can be objectively described—the existing institutions (Section 5). Transtraditional ideas of justice, however, reflect a great variety of preferences as to desirable conditions and goals with no possibility of an authentic choice among them to be effected by science nor even of an exhaustive scientific classification a priori; this has been illustrated by a list of twelve typical creeds, many of which are mirrored in the programs of typical political parties, whose ideas of justice differ correspondingly (Section 6).

Several points were finally made in defense of Scientific Relativism in the field of justice; in particular (Section 7) that Scientific Method cannot and does not deny that there may be absolute standards of justice, but only insists that they cannot be scientifically verified, and that science can contribute a great deal to a rational choice among standards by clarifying meaning and consequences; furthermore (Section 8) that scientific abstention from absolute value judgments does not imply the necessity for law courts, etc., to submit to every dictatorial value judgment, since jurisprudence can establish the *juridical* validity of certain basic principles at a definite place and time against dictatorial impositions even though science cannot establish their general validity.

In concluding this chapter, we shall insert two reservations here. The "inner voice," of which we spoke in the beginning of Section 3, should and will be examined further in scientific terms. In this connection, another question will be taken up. Granted that there are many particular ideas of justice among which science cannot make an authentic choice, there may in all such ideas be some universal elements that can be scientifically ascertained. These reservations will be pursued in Chapters ix ff., where the systematic treatment to which these first four chapters were devoted will be resumed.

In the next two chapters we shall, however, first turn to the postponed historical account on the genesis of twentieth-century Scientific Method (Chapters v and vi) and subsequently to the mid-century revolt against it (Chapters vii and viii), which in large part rests on grounds other than those whose examination we have just noted for future discussion.

PART TWO

GENETIC

CHAPTER V

PRECURSORS AND COUSINS

As our introduction to the foundations of twentieth-century political theory now turns from systematic presentation to the historical genesis, the reader is asked to keep in mind that this book deals, at least primarily and directly, with *scientific* political theory. It cannot, therefore, be our purpose here to describe the historic development of, say, communist, fascist, and democratic thought, with all their nonscientific elements. What we must first examine is, rather, the evolution of twentieth-century scientific political theory as such, and that means the way in which its distinction between scientific and nonscientific political theory came about. Since there are now chiefly two schools that oppose each other—the one recognizing only Scientific Method as scientific, and the other, while not denying the scientific nature of work done under that method, rejecting its claim to exclusive authority—the genesis of present-day scientific political theory is inextricably interwoven with that of these two schools. Part Two of this book will, in two chapters, concentrate on the first; Part Three, on the second. These inquiries will fully confirm, however, that this volume, although primarily concerned with scientific theory, deals actually, though indirectly, with all nonscientific political theories. They are the natural objects of its analysis and critique.

1. Genesis of Scientific Method and the Late Arrival of Value Relativism

Present-day Scientific Method is fundamentally a product of empirical and logical approaches to knowledge. The story of its genesis is, therefore, at least until the end of the nineteenth century, identical with the general history of logic and empiricism. Only a few general remarks will be inserted hereafter on developments prior to the nineteenth century. The subsequent sections of this chapter will deal with nineteenth-century precursors of twentieth-century Scientific Method, and with some related movements in the twentieth century which, although not identical with Scientific Method as understood today, may be called its "cousins" in scientific thought.

The empirical approach has never been entirely absent from the struggle for knowledge. But it was often grossly neglected, especially in the Middle Ages, and always had to fight for recognition against traditions, superstitions, the dogmatic influences of religion, and the pseudo-authority of allegedly self-evident a-priori principles. Even when—especially after the development of the experimental method by Galileo—it won growing respect, it was at first received merely as a special technique in scientific research cultivated side by side with knowledge that was grounded on other sources. Only after a long period of coexistence did the empirical approach begin to crowd out all others from the field for which the name "science" was claimed, thus growing from what originally had been no more than one among several methods into what finally was said to be the only scientific one.

This development gained momentum under the influence of Locke and Hume, of Kant's *Critique of Pure Reason,* and later, of the positivist and pragmatist schools.[1] It was not carried to its logical conclusion, however, until the theories of the "unbridgeable logical gulf" between the Is and the Ought and of the scientific impotence to establish values in absolute terms were finally added. For, as long as scholars continued to infer what ought to be done from what is and to accept judgments on ultimate values as scientific, they necessarily transgressed on in-tuitional and metaphysical grounds beyond the boundaries of a science based on observation and logical reasoning.

The historical genesis and the gradual spread of Scientific Value Relativism have never been adequately traced and described.[2] This is regrettable on several grounds: first, because of the revolutionary bear-ing its appearance had upon, or at least implied for, the social sciences, especially political and legal theory; second, because approaches and vocabularies have been very different in Continental Europe and in Anglo-Saxon countries; and third, because the basic contributions are so widely scattered that access to them is cumbersome at best.

Understanding of the genesis is made difficult by the same factor that operated as an obstacle to our systematic treatment, namely, the variety of uses to which the terms relativity and relativism have been

---

[1] The term "science" began to be used in its modern limited sense about 1830, when the positivism of the French sociologists was taking shape (see below, Section 3) and the British Association for the Advancement of Science was founded. As to the latter event, see T. Merz, *History of European Thought in the Nineteenth Century,* vol. 1 (1896) p. 89, and F. A. Hayek, *The Counter-Revolution of Science,* Glencoe, Ill., 1952, p. 207, n. 2.

[2] It seems that my papers "The Rise of Relativism in Political and Legal Philosophy," *Social Research,* vol. 6 (1939) pp. 392 ff., and "The Myth of Is and Ought," *Harvard Law Review,* vol. 54 (1941) pp. 811 ff., both reprinted in M. Forkosch, ed., *The Political Philosophy of Arnold Brecht,* New York 1954, were the first to attempt a coherent historical presentation. They still left many gaps, however, which the present discussion tries to fill.

put. Yet it is precisely this confusion in terminology which makes the historical analysis particularly rewarding and clarifying, as is strikingly illustrated by what happened in the field of justice.

If one were to call a relativist everyone who holds that *something* in justice is relative, dependent on customs, laws, history, climate, environment, or the like, there would be no writer on justice from ancient to recent times who did not deserve that description; for such observations prevail with all of them, though to a different extent. As a rule, however, it was maintained, from Plato to the end of the nineteenth century, that not *everything* in justice is relative, but that some absolute standards knowable to man lie back of and transcend all relative elements of justice.

This absolutistic position was maintained, wholly or in part, during what we have called the first and second eclipses of Natural Law (Chapter IV, Section 2). For these eclipses were not total. The shift of emphasis from Natural Law to Divine Will in the early Middle Ages —first eclipse—was far from relativistic, of course; it pointed to standards rather more than less absolute. And the turn from the resuscitated Natural-Law ideas entertained by the Scholastics since the thirteenth century to doctrines of sovereignty and positivism in the sixteenth— second eclipse—was due to the growing tendency of referring to the sovereign as legitimate interpreter of Natural Law and Divine Will in earthly matters, rather than to a complete rejection of absolute standards; the sovereign himself was expected to bow to God.

Even the multiple attack launched on Natural Law in the eighteenth and nineteenth centuries—third eclipse—did not necessarily imply an entirely relativistic attitude. Ideas of Natural Law were often merely pushed back from unduly advanced positions with no intention of discarding them completely (Burke), or supplanted by new absolutes under different names (greatest happiness of the greatest number, see below Section 3), or simply by-passed by concentration on relative aspects (historicists and positivists). Kant, who had done much to tear down the uncritical reliance on pure reason, himself resumed the scientific acknowledgment of absolutes under the name of necessary regulative principles and categorical imperative (see below, Section 7).

Actually, the whole nineteenth century was to elapse before a self-assertive and overt scientific relativism regarding ultimate values arose in political and legal philosophy. Such earlier or contemporary phenomena as skepticism, philosophical and legal positivism, historicism, materialism, pragmatism, and the general withdrawal of philosophy during the second half of the nineteenth century can be said to have each in its own way helped to prepare the minds for value relativism, and even to produce some latent types of it. Yet, as will be shown in the present chapter, they all differed essentially from Scientific Value Relativism in its overt, theoretically substantiated form, which developed only at the beginning of the present century.

2. Skepticism

In the modern use of the term, skepticism has been given the broad meaning of indulgence in doubt to the extent that the skeptic believes nothing, and in nothing, and rejects every evidence as inconclusive. If such be the meaning, modern science is skeptical in part only, since it accepts the results of carefully checked observations and measurements and of logical operations, and plausible hypotheses of cause and effect, without any particular degree of skepticism. Its radical skepticism begins where Scientific Method leaves off.

It is illuminating to realize fully what this difference implies. Skepticism might be—and sometimes has been—carried so far as to reject even sensory data, usually accepted by Scientific Method. Conversely, as Scientific Method overcomes skeptical qualms in its recognition of sensory data, why should it not do so as well in dealing with values? Why is its skepticism so selective? Basically it denies the possibility of full empirical proof and yet permits the scientist to accept carefully controlled observation as sufficient evidence; it permits him to accept reality, causation, and some human freedom of choice, although unable to prove that there *is* reality, causation, and free will (see Chapters I, Section 5, and II, Section 1). If it does not care to go the limit of skepticism in these questions, why should it refuse to accept arguments in favor of ultimate values as sufficient proof?

Nothing can serve better to illustrate the important fact, repeatedly referred to in the systematic part of this book, that Scientific Method is based fundamentally on common sense—but only on *common* sense. It is common sense to accept reality, causation, some freedom of will, and the results of careful observation. Inquiries based on these assumptions are, therefore, interdenominationally understandable in their approach. This foundation, however, disappears when we deal with value judgments. It is no "common" sense to accept controversial value judgments. When facts are controversial we can still present the observational data underlying our contention; but when it comes to value judgments, there are no data to refer to other than either personal opinions which differ or facts from which logical inferences regarding what ought to be considered valuable cannot be drawn without some implicit previous ulterior value judgment, as we have seen in Chapter III. Nor is there "common" sense concerning any method by which the validity of the one or the other opinion could be ascertained (a point which will be discussed further in Chapter VII, Sections 2 ff.). No divine source of values is either commonly accepted or accessible to scientific proof. What we are faced with here, then, is precisely the opposite of "common" sense; it is its absence. There may be some common elements also in value judgments (see Chapter X); but they are few and do not settle the major controversies. These are the reasons why Scientific Method finds itself compelled to be more skeptical in accepting value judgments than in recognizing facts.

In other words, Scientific Method, as distinct from skepticism, is based on a practical proposition, which can be formulated as follows. If we want to proceed carefully in inter-subjective scientific inquiry, but still *proceed* and not stop at every step as extreme skepticism would do, then reliance on empirical observation and on logical reasoning offers the safest procedure available. Let us, therefore, for good or bad proceed along these lines. And let us do so consistently, without swerving to the incidental use of less severe methods. What we can present then is a substantial contribution of a pure type, which can be received and used in full awareness of the methods on which it rests.

One witty opponent once remarked that Scientific Method is based on the "lowest common denominator"; he would rather see science start from the highest possible basis, even though that be attainable to only a "small elite." The answer to this is twofold. The metaphor that Scientific Method starts out from a common denominator is quite valid. The qualification, however, that it is the "lowest" common denominator is misleading. If this adjective is meant to imply a *morally* low level [1] it is entirely out of place here. The morally lowest common denominator—in terms of customarily accepted moral standards—might be found in common passions like drinking and sex, selfishness and greed. As Heinrich Heine expressed it, "Only when we met in the dirt did we understand each other at once." [2] Science is at the opposite end; it is the morally highest, not lowest, common denominator of humanity, in the absence of a common religion. If we

---

[1] In mathematics the lower denominator actually marks the higher figure, because ½ is higher than ¹⁄₂₀ (2 and 20 being denominators).

[2] "Selten habt ihr mich verstanden,/ Selten auch verstand ich euch;/ Nur wenn wir im Koth uns fanden,/ So verstanden wir uns gleich" (*Die Heimkehr*, 1823–24, No. 80).

want to proceed from some noncommon basis instead for which absolute validity is claimed by some elite we may do so at any time, provided we avow what our yardstick is and how its validity is supported. But then we abandon intersubjective transmissibility; we switch from S_1 to S_2 (see Chapter II, Section 7) and expose the rest of the people to the peril that it may have been the wrong decisions that were handed down to them as "scientific" by the wrong type of "small elite."

It should be noted, incidentally, that the present-day radical use of the term skepticism is out of tune with its original meaning. The Greek verb *skeptomai* meant to watch and search closely. A *skeptikos* in ancient Greece, therefore, was just a particularly searching and careful type of investigator. No rejection of proof on principle, no refusal to believe under all circumstances, was implied. The skeptic seeks, observes keenly, and investigates, but "that which he seeks is not doubt but truth." Skepticism, therefore, was originally "search for truth" in the sense that "the one who searches has to continue his search until he has found what removes his doubt." It was expected of the ancient skeptic, as Sextus Empiricus described him at the end of the second century A.D., that he would never give up and would persist in seeking and searching.[3] In this original sense skepticism is at the basis of all modern science.

3. Positivism

The meaning of the term positivism in matters of law and justice differs from that associated with the same term in science, general philosophy, and sociology. Political theory is caught between these two vocabularies. I shall first deal with the more general use of the concept.

(a) THE POSITIVISM OF THE FRENCH SOCIOLOGISTS [1]

Auguste Comte (1798–1857) introduced the term into the social sciences. He used it to distinguish the "scientific" approach in the "positivistic" era from "metaphysical" and "theological" speculations

---

[3] See Karl Löwith, "Skepticism and Faith," *Social Research*, vol. 18 (June 1951) pp. 219, 222, from which the above quotations were taken.

[1] Among recent publications, see especially Albert Salomon, *The Tyranny of Progress, Reflections on the Origins of Sociology*, New York 1955; Karl Löwith, *Meaning in History, the Theological Implications of the Philosophy of History*, Chicago 1949 (2nd impr., 1950) pp. 67 ff.; and F. H. Hayek, *The Counter-Revolution of Science, op.cit.*, pp. 105 ff.

in the two preceding epochs. His ideas about what constituted a scientific approach were in many respects similar to those of present-day Scientific Method, but not identical. Like his predecessors, Robert Jacques Turgot (1727–1781) and Henri de St. Simon (1760–1825),[2] Comte absolutized progress and science. Progress, or progressive evolution, was to him an ultimate law governing historic phenomena, and science a human activity able to solve all social problems, not excluding moral ones. Twentieth-century Scientific Method cannot accept either thesis. Not that science today feels unable to render any contributions in these matters; it can help a great deal, as we have seen in previous chapters, first to clarify the issues involved and, next, to examine means, consequences, and risks. Yet it cannot say with assurance that progress will necessarily ensue, nor that science will be able to solve all problems in the long run. Quite the contrary, it now appears certain that moral problems can never be solved by *science* because (1) Scientific Method cannot even state what the moral goals should be, and (2) reaching them requires moral decisions, which are not scientific ones. As regards progress, Scientific Method cannot even say what in the human situation as a whole *is* progress. It can, of course, say what is technological progress, progress in the knowledge of facts and causal relations within the universe and within human society, progress in medicine, in material social welfare, and the like. But it cannot advise us as to what progress means with regard to the human situation in its totality whenever an advance in one sphere is attained at the price of some impairment in another. At that point, ultimate value judgments are required, and to supply them Scientific Method is unable.[3]

Insistence that progress is not scientifically certain and that science is no remedy for all human troubles is in itself a very important contribution, because it impels us to abandon easy-going reliance on science and pay more attention to our own responsibility, will, and determination as indispensable factors if we want to choose worthy goals and lead our personal lives and that of society toward them. Whether we are guided in this by religious inspiration or by what we consider our own authentic decision is a secondary question here where the point is that, in any case, we must not look to science as though it

[2] For documentation, see Salomon, *op.cit.*, pp. 18, 20, and Hayek, *op.cit.*, pp. 123 ff.

[3] That the term "progress" implies value judgments was emphasized by Max Weber at some length in his paper "Der Sinn der Wertfreiheit . . ." (cited below, Chapter VI, Section 2), pp. 480 ff.

could be a guarantor of progress, a setter of ultimate goals and standards, or a substitute for making, daily and hourly, moral decisions of our own.

Comte also used the term "relativity" quite frequently. He emphasized that all concepts which had been regarded as absolute under theological and metaphysical theories had become relative under the positivistic approach. Yet the relativity he had in mind was that between the scientific knowledge of each historical period and the respective stage of progressive evolution that had been reached,[4] and not that to which modern Scientific Value Relativism refers, the relativity between value judgments and the ultimate standards guiding them, whose validity is not scientifically verifiable. The need for a scientific distinction between facts and values did not worry Comte. It never occurred to him that ultimate value judgments could not be verified by science; on the contrary, he blamed Condorcet for his exclusion of moral questions from scientific efforts.[5] His own value judgments were quite explicit, and they were closely interwoven with his entire work. Abolition of war, for example, was to Comte both, an "inevitable" result of progress, i.e., the final outcome of the law of progress, and a desirable aim, i.e., a high value, superior to the opposite. Scientific Value Relativism would reject the first proposition as nonscientific, and refrain even from the second whenever it competed with other value judgments, such as self-defense, liberation, honor, or merely the praise of soldierly virtues, much as the individual relativist might hope for a historic development toward eternal peace and would favor it even at a high price in other values.

In pointing out these distinctions I do not intend to minimize the extent to which Comte's positivism actually contributed to preparing the ground for modern Scientific Method and Value Relativism; yet the differences are important (see also Appendix B).

By 1900, under the leadership of Emile Durkheim (1858–1917), French sociologists had reached a new stage of professional eminence. They adhered more strictly now to Scientific Method than Comte and his immediate disciples had done. But they did not, as a rule, engage in original inquiries into the basic philosophical and methodological problem of whether it was possible to establish moral judgments with scientific means. Their primary interest was the descriptive investigation of sociological facts; their secondary, the explanation of these facts

---

[4] Hayek, *op.cit.*, p. 201.
[5] See Hayek, *ibid.*, and Löwith, *op.cit.*

by tracing them to scientifically determinable sociological and psychological causes. These inquiries led them, of course, to a relativistic emphasis on local and temporal differences in ethical systems. But here was the end of their professional interest. Although some accepted Scientific Value Relativism in incidental remarks, especially with reference to Simmel's *Introduction to Moral Science* of 1892 (see below, Chapter vi), they were not instrumental in establishing it, and not always consistent in applying it, and others, including Durkheim, did not entirely accept it.[6]

As an illustration I may refer to L. Lévy-Bruhl (1857–1939), *La morale et la science des moeurs* (Paris 1903; 5th ed., 1913).[7] The author took it for granted that men had moral duties (Ought), *because* that much was recognized everywhere (Is); only the details differed. This was an inference from Is to Ought. "In short, if philosophers do not *make* ethics, neither do scientists *unmake* them, and for the same reasons" (Engl. tr., p. 112). Stating as a historical fact that ethical revolutionaries, like Socrates, Jesus, and the socialists, have always been denounced as subversive, he added laconically: "That must be so" (*Celà doit être*), obviously because he was not interested in the question who was right and who was wrong but merely in the psychological concatenation of events (p. 114; French ed., p. 143). Everywhere he emphasized the descriptive task of sociology. It is "our practice itself (that is what seems to us subjectively in the conscience as a compulsive law, a feeling of respect for that law, for the rights of others, etc.) which, considered objectively, constitutes (under the forms of morals, customs, laws) the reality to be studied by scientific method in the same way as the rest of the social facts" (p. 7). "Science has no other function than to know what is" (p. 8). What is contained in the conscience "as a given reality" is an "object of science that must be studied in the same spirit and by the same method as other social facts" (p. 11). The "subject of ethics is the *practice,* objectively studied" (p. 114). He questioned the possibility of "theoretical ethics" in the sense of a normative or legislative science, calling it a "confused conception . . . destined to disappear" (p. 11). For this approach he referred to Simmel's work quoted above (p. 16) and to Durkheim's *Les*

---

[6] Lon L. Fuller, *The Law in Quest of Itself* (Chicago 1940) confirms that the sociological positivism of Comte, Durkheim, and Duguit "has never insisted on a rigid separation of *is* and *ought*" (p. 17). As regards Durkheim, he attempted to find the criterion of moral health in perfect adjustment (see also Fr. Vinding Kruse, *The Community of the Future,* New York 1952, p. 64). As regards Duguit, see Chapter iii, above.

[7] Tr. by E. Lee, *Ethics and Moral Science,* London 1905.

règles de la méthode sociologique, the second edition of which had been published in 1901. But he did not himself go more deeply into the question of demonstrability of moral questions, and what he said about it was not entirely consistent, as we have just seen.

Another noteworthy work of this period—C. Bouglé (1870–1940), *Les idées égalitaires, étude sociologique* (Paris 1899)—likewise followed an ethically neutral line (p. 15). But the author declared at the outset that it was his intention merely to inquire into the causes and consequences of egalitarian ideas (p. 19), not into the question whether egalitarianism is recommendable. "Conscience may despise what science explains" (pp. 217, 249). He did not care to inquire into the origin and the authority of conscience. Like Lévy-Bruhl, he referred to Simmel as one of those by whom he had been most immediately influenced (p. 20) without contributing original ideas of his own to the basic methodological problem. Even if egalitarian ideas were wrong, the sociologist must state to what extent they are actually held, or were held during some epochs and not in others, and which sociological institutions generate such ideas and for what psychological reasons. To find out what is right or wrong, if it can be found out at all, is not the task of sociology.

However, by their radical concentration on description and inquiries into cause and effect, with no attention paid to questions of right or wrong, modern French sociologists added strongly to the relativistic trend in the early years of this century.

(b) NEOPOSITIVISM

Some twentieth-century positivists, variously called Neopositivists or Logical Positivists, have gone to the logical extreme of positivism. Starting from the postulate that scientific inquiry should be based exclusively on what is given to perception and on strictly logical reasoning, they have made it their particular business to draw the severest conclusions therefrom. This led them, or a group of them, beyond Scientific Method as here understood to a more radical position, characterized—at least in the movement's early years (see below)—by three specific features: (1) insistence on strictly "physicalist" or behaviorist methods, which imply the rejection of any merely introspective sources of psychology; (2) elimination of metaphysical terms not only in the final stages of scientific work, but in any type of sentences, and hence especially also in preparatory steps, where they are merely used as inspiration for the formulation of problems, as working hypotheses, or as avowed assumptions; and (3) designation of any synthetic sentence which is not ultimately verifiable through perceptions as not only "nonscientific" but "meaningless" (*sinnlos*).[8]

Only statements that can be expressed in physicalist, behaviorist language, had "meaning" to the radical wing of the Neopositivists, led by Rudolf Carnap and Otto Neurath. Their theoretical ideal was that all scientific propositions should be so expressed. While readily acknowledging that this was not achieved even by themselves—who like ordinary people would sometimes say that Joe made an exciting remark, instead of pointing out that the movements of his mouth and the sound-waves reaching the listener, visibly produced a physical state popularly called excitement in the latter, etc.—they conceded "meaning" only to sentences that can be translated into such language, or at least "reduced" to it (see below). Those that can't, as, for example, that there is a God who is imperceptible to human senses, or an immortal soul, are neither true nor false but simply "meaningless."

Scientific Method as here understood does not go that far. As we have seen, it does not reject, summarily and on principle, all references to introspection; it has room for competition between behaviorist and other psychological methods in scientific research (Chapter I, Section 2). Neither does it bar recourse to metaphysical ideas in the preparatory stage of scientific research (Chapter II, Section 6; more will be said about this in Chapters VII, Section 3, and XIII). And, while it agrees that the term science is best used exclusively for intersubjectively transmissible knowledge, it does not therefore contend that all other propositions are "meaningless."

To inject the term "meaningless" here is a highly objectionable manner (indeed, a mannerism) of speech, objectionable especially on the part of scholars otherwise exacting in questions of logical precision. Naturally, once we choose to define "meaningless" as "unverifiable" it follows logically that *in terms of this definition* any sentence that cannot be verified is meaningless. Yet this definition is in most provocative, and quite unnecessary, conflict with established daily usage,

---

[8] For the beginning of this approach, see, in addition to the work of Ernst Mach (below): Rudolf Carnap, *Der logische Aufbau der Welt*, Berlin 1928; the papers by Neurath and Carnap, cited in Chapter I, Section 3; Moritz Schlick, "Positivismus und Realismus," *Erkenntnis*, vol. 3 (1932) pp. 1–31, one of the clearest presentations of the Neopositivist views; and Philipp Frank, *Between Physics and Philosophy*, Cambridge, Mass., 1941, pp. 155, 214 ff. Also Carnap, "Testability and Meaning," *Philosophy of Science*, vols. 3 (1936) pp. 420–71, and 4 (1937) pp. 1–40, reprinted, with omissions, in H. Feigl and M. Brodbeck, *Readings in the Philosophy of Science*, New York 1953, pp. 47 ff.; *Logical Syntax of Language*, New York 1951. Further, Otto Neurath, ed., *International Encyclopedia of Unified Science*, Chicago 1938, 1955.

something scientific definitions should avoid as far as possible. Moreover, it is by no means certain that we are faced here with technical language only. The formula that "unverifiable sentences are scientifically meaningless" has, rather, the appearance of a *synthetic* proposition, which *adds* something to the quality of unverifiability (see Chapter I, Section 6). Some of the Neopositivists have indeed insisted that their equation of verifiability and meaning is no arbitrary rule imposed by some especially invented scientific language. No proposition, they have said, can convey any meaning unless we can tell how it can be verified, i.e., under what conditions (tests) we would declare it either true or false; no other use of the term "meaning" is conceivable to them.[9] This was most graphically expressed in the last sentence of L. Wittgenstein's *Tractatus Logico-Philosophicus* (New York 1922, translation of his German *Logisch-philosophische Abhandlung,* 1921), "Whereof one cannot speak, thereof one must be silent" (*Wovon man nicht sprechen kann, darüber muss man schweigen*). Even this epigram was not pointed enough for some of the group. They noted that one must indeed be silent, but not "about" or "of" anything (Neurath), indicating that there *is* nothing even to be silent about. What we cannot say "we can't say, and we can't whistle it either" (F. P. Ramsey).[10]

This equation of meaning and verifiability passes too lightly by the fact that the radical wing of the Neopositivists recognizes only sense experiences in the process of scientific verification, thus ignoring two alternatives which we have no possibility of refuting: first, that there may be realms entirely inaccessible to human senses, as inaccessible as is ancient Greek history to a dog; and second, that some facts may be recognized in some nonsensory manner by some people, or by all, without being describable by reference to sensory perceptions. A priori to deny "meaning" to all sentences that are not verifiable in physical terms is a *petitio principii,* a begging of the question, because the prob-

---

[9] See Schlick, *op.cit.,* p. 25.

[10] See A. J. Ayer, "The Vienna Circle," in Gilbert Ryple, ed., *The Revolution in Philosophy,* London 1957, pp. 70 ff.; also, Frank, *op.cit.,* p. 88, where he writes that "no problems can be set up [through science] that are insoluble by its means," referring to Wittgenstein, who said, "When an answer cannot be expressed, neither can the question be expressed." Frank adds, "Hence, as understood by Carnap and Wittgenstein, the questions beloved by the school philosophy, such as whether the outer world really exists, not only cannot be answered but cannot even be expressed, because neither the positive assertion, falsely called the realistic 'hypothesis,' nor the negative idealistic assertion can be expressed through constituted concepts." Constituted concepts (Carnap) are those exactly defined by reference to physicalist verification.

lem is precisely this: whether there are, or may be, entities or events that cannot be pointed up in such terms. By simply declaring this question meaningless on the ground that it deals with unverifiable sentences the Logical Positivist proves nothing; he merely makes a metaphysical statement himself, although a negative one, without proof.

Neopositivists have countered that they declare metaphysical propositions not false but "only" meaningless. Poor excuse. Can meaningless sentences be true? "No," Neopositivists are compelled to answer, "they cannot—because they are meaningless." What kind of language is this? To give an illustration, Paul's contention that Jesus appeared to him at Damascus would be, to Neopositivists, not merely scientifically "unverifiable"—as it is also under the procedural rules of Scientific Method —but "meaningless" as well, which it is not to Scientific Method and which it was definitely not to Paul. The Neopositivist vocabulary leads to the absurd situation that the sentence, "There are visible gods on top of Mount Olympus" is meaningful (although not true), whereas the sentence, "There is an invisible God," is meaningless because no intersubjective tests can be offered. That no such tests are available is a formidable enough matter to realize (although possibly very meaningful, see Chapter xiii). How can it be justified that we complicate this dilemma, or try to resolve it, by simply denying meaning to the very question? Such absolutistic negative statements, incapable of verification themselves, resolve no problem.

Beginning with the second half of the Nineteen-Thirties, some Neopositivists have abandoned one or another of their original positions. Thus, Moritz Schlick in one of his last papers, "Meaning and Verification," [11] modified the requirement of verifiability for meaningful sentences by interpreting it as requiring only a "logical," not an empirical, possibility of verification. The empirical circumstances, he wrote, are all-important when you want to know if a proposition is *true,* but they can have no influence on the *meaning* of the proposition. The only thing necessary for a process of verification to be "logically" possible, Schlick argued, is that it "can be described." Logical possibility or impossibility of verification, therefore, is "always *self-imposed.*" If we utter a sentence without meaning "it is always *our own fault.*" [12] This leads him to concede that the proposition "Man is immortal" is mean-

---

[11] *Philosophical Review*, vol. 45 (1936), reprinted in Feigl and Sellars, *Readings in Philosophical Analysis,* New York 1949, pp. 146 ff.
[12] *Ibid.,* pp. 154–55. Italics in the original.

ingful, because it "possesses logical verifiability"; it could be verified by following the prescription "Wait until you die!" [13]

This interpretation is apt to take the sting out of the rejection of unverifiable sentences as "meaningless." There would then be little difference left between the approach to immortality used by a Neopositivist like Schlick and by a nonpositivistic philosopher like W. E. Hocking in his recent book, *The Meaning of Immortality in Human Experience* (New York 1957). Schlick went even so far as to say that immortality, in the sense of life after death, should not be regarded at all as a "metaphysical problem," but as an "empirical hypothesis." But other Neopositivists, like Carnap, Neurath, Frank, Hempel, Ayer, have maintained more strictly physicalist criteria of verifiability and thus of meaningfulness.[14] It is advisable to discuss this in some detail with regard to Carnap.

Carnap, too, has modified his original ideas considerably. In his painstaking analysis, "Testability and Meaning" of 1936–1937 (cited above) he redefined the "principle of empiricism" as requiring the language of science to be restricted "in a certain way," such that descriptive predicates, and hence synthetic sentences, are not to be admitted unless they have "some connection with possible observation." This does not go beyond Scientific Method as here understood. What is "observable" Carnap does not undertake to define, using this word as a "basic term," definition of which must come from psychology. But he refers explicitly to the "behaviorist theory of language," thus indicating his continued behaviorist leanings (No. 8).

As regards the kind of possible observation to be required, Carnap makes his first major concession by dropping the term "verifiability" on the ground that it can be accepted only as a "rough first approximation" (No. 13) and (No. 2) that universal sentences, such as the "so-called laws of physics or biology," can never be completely verified (see above, Chapter 1, Section 5). He discusses at length two conceivable substitutes, "testability" and "confirmability," the latter being the broader of the two because it admits sentences that are capable of being "confirmed" by observable events although such confirming events cannot be arranged as "tests" at our will. I take it that "confirmation" is, therefore, to include also *unrepeatable* observations. Then Carnap

---

[13] *Ibid.*, p. 160.

[14] See the papers by C. I. Lewis, "Experience and Meaning," *Philosophical Review*, vol. 43 (1934), to which Schlick's paper was the answer, and by V. C. Aldrich, "Messrs. Schlick and Ayer on Immortality," *ibid.*, vol. 47 (1938), which was a rebuttal. Both papers are reprinted in Feigl and Sellars, *op.cit.*, pp. 128 ff., and 171 ff., respectively.

distinguishes whether the requirement of testability or confirmability is to go to the limit of "completeness," or whether incomplete confirmability or testability are to suffice. He thus reaches four possible criteria, among which empiricism must choose (No. 18): the requirements, respectively, of simple "confirmability," simple "testability," "complete confirmability," or "complete testability." The latter two would be so severe as to exclude inductive generalizations and hypotheses, because their truth can never be "completely" confirmed and even less completely tested. Thus there remains a practical choice only between simple "confirmability" and simple "testability." Carnap tells us (No. 11) that he would now be satisfied with confirmability and no longer require testability, since "scientists are justified to use and actually do use terms which are confirmable without being testible." This is the second retreat, and a remarkable one, because it admits the possibility of accidental and unrepeatable observations as a basis of scientifically meaningful statements.[15]

It might thus seem as though Carnap had cut down the old requirement of verifiability to generally acceptable proportions. In all four variants, however, he maintains his former physicalist doctrine that confirmability, etc., just as the verifiability of old, must be expressed in terms of a "thing-language." He merely mollifies the harshness of this requirement by now conceding that in order to be scientific a sentence need not be fully "translatable" into physicalist language, but that it suffices if the sentence is "reducible" to such language (No. 11). This is the third major retreat. For he thus recognizes that certain sentences, e.g., those dealing with "life," may *lose* something of their original meaning by being reduced to physicalist thing-language; that they may not be fully "definable" in it. But he still insists (*ibid.*) "that every term of the language of science—including languages which are used in biology [e.g., "life"], in psychology [e.g., "introspection"], and in social science [e.g., "democracy," "freedom"]—is reducible to terms of physical language." He still says of all psychologically formulated introspective statements that "such a language is a

---

[15] The sentence "If all minds should disappear from the universe, the stars would still go on in their courses" had been regarded as "not verifiable" by Lewis and Schlick. Carnap (*op.cit.*, last page) comments that both were right if "verifiable" was interpreted as "completely confirmable." But he now admits that the sentence is "confirmable" and even "testable," though incompletely, by reference to observations that justify the acceptance of general laws. See also Hans Reichenbach, who wrote in 1951: "The theory of meaning has been emancipated for a long while from its past dogmatic version and has assumed a moderate version, which admits of modified terms of verification" ("The Verifiability Theory of Meaning," reprinted in Feigl and Brodbeck, *Readings in the Philosophy of Science*, p. 93).

purely subjective one, suitable for soliloquy only, while the intersubjective thing-language is suitable for use among different subjects" (No. 16, 2a). And, different from Schlick, he continues to admit sentences as scientific only if their confirmation is possible in terms of *this* world, not of the Beyond; the problems of immortality or of the existence of an invisible God, therefore, remain excluded from scientific work at any stage, even from mere questions asked, it seems.[16]

This perseverance, in turn, is made more palatable by Carnap's fourth retreat; he no longer insists on the equation of "confirmability," etc., with "meaningfulness." It would be advisable, he wrote (No. 13, end), to "avoid the terms 'meaningful' and 'meaningless' in this and similar discussions—because these expressions involve many rather vague philosophical assertions"; and again (No. 14): "We used to say [of a sentence like 'this stone is now thinking about Vienna,' that it is] not false but meaningless; but the careless use of the word 'meaningless' has its dangers. . . ." Consequently, he is now willing simply to say what others have always preferred that a metaphysical assertion is or is not "confirmable" (testable, etc.), instead of that it is or is not "meaningful." [17]

Other Neopositivists have continued to use the old meaning-jargon. Whether or not that is done, there remains some inherent weakness in the whole attempt first to construct a language of empiricism and then to decide what is scientific according to whether it can be expressed in this language.[18] Such procedure is "logically" possible, to be sure; but it is not necessarily the *only* logically possible procedure. The requirement that all terms used in scientific language must be reducible to physicalist terms may be incapable of doing justice to precisely that which in the process of reduction is left over, e.g., "life," or, like the concepts of "God" and "soul," cannot even partially be reduced to a mere thing-language. It is true that not all Neopositivists

[16] See the passage (No. 14) in which Carnap writes that he is among those "who would not wish to have [in scientific language] a sentence corresponding to every sentence which usually is considered as a correct English sentence and is used by learned people. We should not wish, e.g., to have corresponding sentences to many or perhaps most of the sentences in the books of metaphysicians."

[17] It should be noted, however, that sentences such as "This stone is now thinking about Vienna" are not only "not confirmable" but they are self-contradictory, if the meaning of the terms "stone" and "think" is spelled out. Metaphysical sentences, however, are not necessarily self-contradictory.

[18] Carnap (*op.cit.,* No. 15, last sentence), in laying down the rule, "Every primitive descriptive predicate of L [i.e., the scientific language to be constituted for empiricists] is observable," calls this a "decision," made by the constructor of the language. Likewise (No. 16), "Every primitive predicate of L is a 'thing predicate.' "

have insisted on thing-language. Some have accepted reference to "experience" in a broader sense of this term; but then they have frequently retained the requirement of "verifiability" in terms of such experiences, and its equation with "meaningfulness." Therefore, it is difficult now to describe in precise terms what has remained of Neopositivism.

As I have stated in Chapter 1 and will discuss more elaborately in Chapters VII, Section 3, and X, I propose to start out from the distinction between intersubjectively transmissible and nontransmissible knowledge, and then—without a-priori limitations imposed by a preconstructed language of science and without denying meaningfulness or function to assertions of nontransmissible knowledge—try to find out whether some alleged knowledge is or is not intersubjectively transmissible. Although this approach runs parallel to that of the Neopositivists to a considerable extent, it may, and does, lead to different results in areas of great significance. It is, so to speak, a more openended type of approach.

Neopositivism arose in the wake of efforts made by Ernst Mach (1838–1916) to establish the unity of all sciences through the radical elimination of metaphysics in every scientific work and through common recognition that all scientific authority must be ultimately based on perception.[19] Mach was an Austrian physicist and philosopher, who held the chair for the philosophy of science at the University of Vienna until 1901. William James had paid him a visit in Prague in 1882, and after many hours spent in lively discussion had found himself deeply impressed.[20] A small group of scholars in Vienna, starting out from Mach's work, attempted to refine it by cleansing it of unwarranted elements and by adding greater logical precision to Mach's empirical purism and to all its implications; this ended up in their equation of verifiability (testability) and meaning in science. This group, which later became known as the "Vienna Circle" (as such it made its first public appearance in 1929) included the mathematician Hans Hahn (d. 1934), the economist Otto Neurath (d. 1945 in

---

[19] Ernst Mach, *Die Geschichte und die Wurzel des Satzes von der Erhaltung der Arbeit*, 1872 (translation, *History and Roots of the Principle of the Conservation of Energy*, Chicago 1911); *Die Mechanik in ihrer Entwickelung*, Leipzig 1883 (tr., *The Science of Mechanics*, Chicago 1893; 4th ed., 1919; 5th ed., La Salle, Ill., 1942); *Beiträge zur Analyse der Empfindungen*, Jena 1885 (tr., Chicago 1914).

[20] "I don't think that I ever envied a man's mind as much as I have envied Ostwald's—unless it were Mach's," wrote James to Hugo Münsterberg twenty years later (July 23, 1902; see R. B. Perry, *The Thought and Character of William James*, Briefer Version, Boston 1948, p. 236). See also Frank, *op.cit.*, p. 211.

England), the physicist Philipp Frank, and the philosophers Rudolf Carnap, Herbert Feigl, Friedrich Waismann, and especially, Moritz Schlick. The last-named was appointed 1932 to Mach's former chair in Vienna; he was murdered by a disgruntled student in 1935. Carnap, who had begun his academic career in Vienna, later was transferred to the newly established chair for the philosophy of science at the University of Prague.

A number of other scholars came to be associated with the Vienna Circle, though not necessarily with all their ideas. Among them were Hans Reichenbach (in Berlin, later Prague); the mathematicians, Ludwig Wittgenstein (later, Cambridge, England), Kurt Gödel, Karl Menger, and Richard von Mises;[21] the physicist, E. Schroedinger; the economist, Josef Schumpeter; and the lawyer, Hans Kelsen. Several Americans, including Ernest Nagel of Columbia and Charles W. Morris of the University of Chicago, made early contacts with the Circle. A "Congress for the Unity of Science" was held in Prague in 1934 (Dr. Morris was there), followed by international congresses in Paris (1935), Copenhagen (1936), Cambridge (1938). Similarities with American pragmatism and with the operational ideas of Percy E. Bridgman (Harvard) were discovered, and mutual approaches intensified when many members and friends of the Circle (among them Carnap, Feigl, Frank, Reichenbach, Gödel, Menger, Schumpeter, Kelsen) came to this country, most of them as refugees.[22]

Not all friends of the Vienna Circle, however, subscribed to its extreme views. Many kept closer to the ideas expounded in this book. Yet the exaggerations described above have discredited the very name of positivism, and done considerable harm to the general understanding of Scientific Method and Scientific Value Relativism.

(c) LEGAL POSITIVISM

In political and legal philosophy, positivism has assumed still another, more specific sense, only loosely connected with that which it

---

[21] See Richard von Mises, *Positivism*, Cambridge, Mass., 1951, revised ed. of his German book, *Kleines Lehrbuch des Positivismus*, The Hague 1939.

[22] On the history of the Vienna Circle, see Philipp Frank, *op.cit.*, pp. 1–16, and his papers on Mach, *ibid.*, pp. 28 and 211; Victor Kraft, *The Vienna Circle: The Origins of Neo-Positivism*, translated by Arthur Pap, New York 1953; A. J. Ayer, "The Vienna Circle" in Ayer and others, *The Revolution of Philosophy*, with an introduction by G. Ryle, London 1957, pp. 70 ff. As regards Bridgman, he wrote in his *The Logic of Modern Physics*, New York 1928: "If a specific question has meaning it must be possible to find operations by which an answer can be given to it."

has in general philosophy. It designates the theory that only those norms are juridically valid which have been established or recognized by the government of a sovereign state in the forms prescribed by its written or unwritten constitution. No Divine Law and no Natural Law is juridically valid, according to legal positivism, unless so recognized by the state or its government.

This line of positivism is much older than Comte's. It was inaugurated by Jean Bodin (1530–1596) and, more radically, by Thomas Hobbes (1588–1679). After an eclipse of about one hundred years, caused by Locke's doctrine of inalienable rights, it was resumed by William Blackstone (1723–1780), Jeremy Bentham (1748–1832), and especially by John Austin (1790–1859). Thereafter it became the leading legal doctrine in most Western countries.

To examine its similarities with and differences from twentieth-century Scientific Value Relativism we must distinguish between *lex lata,* the law that is, and *lex ferenda,* the law to be made. To the question what the valid law is at some particular place and time, or in other words which commands or norms ought to be recognized then and there as juridically binding, legal positivism seems to give a relative answer, referring to the individual country. Yet the basic doctrine itself—that recognition by the government of a sovereign state, and only this recognition, makes a norm or command a valid law—is quite absolutistic in character. It has indeed no scientific basis other than the fact that this is the currently accepted doctrine and that it is practically acted upon in the individual states and in the community of nations. There is no scientific reason why this must be so and not otherwise.[23]

Likewise, when the question is not what the valid law is but what law *ought* to be made, political and legal positivism is not necessarily associated with relativity. A legal positivist, while insisting that no rule is "legally" valid before its pronouncement by the legislature or by the judge, may well be a devout Christian, or an ardent utilitarian, or a radical equalitarian, who would give a definite answer to the question what rule should or should not be made. At first glance it might seem as though utilitarians were relativistic as lawmakers too, since they measure all values relative to human happiness. Yet in so doing they actually recognize one absolute standard, happiness, or the

---

[23] See my article "Sovereignty" in *War in Our Time,* ed. by H. Speier and A. Kähler, New York 1939, pp. 58–77.

happiness of the greatest number. A utilitarian, therefore, is no relativist regarding ultimate legislative values (see Chapter xii).[24]

Legal positivism (relativistic by its reference to the law of the individual country) and legislative utilitarianism (absolutistic by its axiomatic acceptance of the goal of happiness) often go hand in hand. The father of utilitarianism, Jeremy Bentham, was a legal positivist. The leading representative of nineteenth-century positivism, John Austin, was no relativist in the transpositive sphere. It is true that in his famous lectures dedicated to positivism he made a short remark which sounded as though he extended his positivistic relativism to his legislative philosophy. He observed that Hobbes's phrase "no law can be unjust" was not an immoral or pernicious paradox, as it had often been branded, but was merely a truism expressed in unguarded terms. "Just and unjust, justice or unjustice, are terms of relative and varying import," he went on. "When uttered with a determined meaning they are uttered with relation to a determined law which the speaker assumes as a standard of comparison. . . . If positive law be taken as the standard of comparison, it is manifest that a positive law cannot be unjust. . . ."[25]

Austin clearly recognizes here that in legislation, too, justice is relative to some standard (see Chapter iv above). Yet he never went so far as to say that all standards were necessarily relative and that none had absolute validity. On the contrary, in a footnote he expressly accepted utilitarianism and the law of God as standards for lawmaking.[26] As a true positivist, however, he was interested primarily in the relation of justice to *law,* not to some translegal creed, or as one might put it, only in the relation of justice to law and not of law to justice.

Political and legal positivism simply fails to deal with transpositive questions, either in a relativistic or in an absolute manner. And yet, in recognizing the exclusive validity of any law that has been enacted in the past or might be in the future in line with the country's constitution, it makes its adherents inclined to think also of legislative ideals in terms of relativity. Hence political and legal positivism easily expands into, or entails, relativism in the transpositive sphere. Vice

---

[24] Bentham recognized that he could not give proof for the principle of utility, ". . . for that which is used to prove everything else cannot itself be proved" (*Introduction to the Principles of Morals and Legislation,* ch. i, par. 11; see G. Hall, "The 'Proof' of Utility in Bentham and Mill," *Ethics,* vol. 60, 1949, pp. 13 ff.).

[25] *Lectures on Jurisprudence,* delivered in 1826–32, ed. by R. Campbell (2 vols., New York 1875, from the 4th ed., London 1873) vol. i, p. 155.

[26] *Ibid.,* note to section 251.

versa, adherents of Scientific Value Relativism are inclined to be legal positivists since they deny the scientific verifiability of higher law, whether divine or natural. See Chapters VI, Section 3, on Kelsen and VII, Section 8, on Radbruch; but also IV, Section 8, on the distinction between juridical and scientific validity of legal principles.

4. Historicism

The case of historicism is comparable to that of positivism. The nineteenth-century historical school in the philosophy of law (Friedrich Karl von Savigny, 1779–1861, Sir Henry Maine, 1822–1888, and their followers both in Europe and America) was relativistic to a certain extent because of its emphasis on the historical growth of law, on the particular national or regional conditions of that growth, and on the particular *Volksgeist* (national spirit) that expressed or revealed itself in it—law "grows," it cannot be "made." Relativistic appearances were supported by the fact that most members of the school actually refrained from searching for absolute principles in justice. But their historical way of thinking did not necessarily reject the possibility that there *were* such absolute elements, permeating the particular laws, and knowable to men. All that can be said in this respect is that the question whether such laws existed was not in the center of the historicist's interest. Precisely as the question of transpositive (i.e., legislative) justice failed to interest legal positivists, so problems of transhistoric justice failed to interest their rivals, the members of the historical school. This lack of interest cannot be equated with a theoretical denial of any transpositive and transhistoric elements in justice. Yet it evoked or promoted tendencies toward such denial.[1]

That historicism and absolutistic ideas were indeed compatible is clearly shown in the philosophy of Hegel, where ideas of particularity and universality, of history and of absolute laws, were artfully welded within the one doctrine that some sort of objective and absolute reason —be it God or the World Spirit or simply Reason—revealed itself in history, differently in different nations and at different times, but not, therefore, reducible to a plurality. Hegel's historicism, it is obvious, was not entirely relativistic; in its ultimate references it was absolutistic.

[1] As Leo Strauss, *Natural Right and History*, Chicago 1953, pp. 14, 15, has aptly expressed it: "The historical school . . . discovered the value, the charm, the inwardness of the local and temporal . . . the superiority of the local and temporal to the universal . . . that the local and the temporal have a higher value than the universal. As a consequence, what claimed to be universal appeared eventually as derivative from something locally and temporally confined, as the local and temporal *in statu evanescendi*."

At the end of the nineteenth century, and in the beginning of the twentieth, historicism became more relativistic than before by its new emphasis on the *singularity* of every historic situation, fact, or event. This singularity seemed to preclude generalizations of the type possible in the natural sciences. While this is true to some extent, it cannot bar generalizations based on the matériel with which history works, such as the astronomic, geographic, physical, and biological conditions of human life. Whenever and wherever man lives he needs sleep and food, he is a child before he reaches maturity, and he is mortal. Even in this new stage, therefore, historicism did not necessarily negate the possibility that science might be able to ascertain some universal laws governing human external and internal life; nor did it imply a denial of God. That certain questions, such as God's reality and the validity of ultimate value judgments, are inaccessible to science does not follow from the singularity of historical events, nor was it derived from it.

In a still later stage—actually after the ascent of Scientific Value Relativism—historicism became associated with the idea that all human knowledge is historically conditioned and that human beings could not entirely disentangle themselves from the singular social conditions under which their minds had been shaped (see below, Chapter VII, Section 9). Then historicism began to imply that the social sciences could never succeed in being objective. Yet this did not entail a particular emphasis on the relativity of *values;* on the contrary, it led to the more radical theory that there is nothing peculiar to values in this respect, because man's impotence to be objective was no less present in the recognition of facts than in that of values. We shall revert to this erroneous denial of differences between facts and values in Chapter VII. Here it has been my purpose to point out only that in none of the various forms in which it appeared did historicism imply Scientific Value Relativism, although it served to prepare the mind for relativistic viewpoints.

5. Marxism

Marxists generally are disappointed, and inclined to grow indignant, if one fails to refer to Marx as an early representative, nay the creator, of modern scientific theory in political science. Other students, seriously confused and afraid of propaganda whenever this question comes up, are distrustful of arguments from both sides. To clarify affinity and differences between Marxian doctrines and Scientific Method is, therefore, particularly necessary within the general context of this book.

Marx and Engels[1] did indeed apply what we now call Scientific Method—empirical observation, description, hypothetical explanation, and so forth—to a considerable extent in their common work. Precisely by so doing, and to the extent that they did, they made great contributions to the social sciences. They drew attention to the brutal facts of social and economic life. They combated the customary glossing over of actualities with arguments taken from theology, from some custom-made ideology, or from wishful thinking, at least if not of their own making. They pointed to interrelations between political and economic factors in history that had been widely neglected. They refused to accept the ethical value judgments of their own epoch or of earlier periods, denouncing the influence of economic and class interests on moral standards.

Nevertheless, for three reasons, their methods do not stand the tests of modern scientific theory. First, Marx and Engels claimed that they could predict the general course of human history with certainty, at least in the long run. This claim is scientifically untenable because of the many variables involved. It is possible to some extent to predict what will happen if a number of conditions are fulfilled, among which there may be the assumption that in other respects everything remains as it now is. Such predictions are of the essence of genuine science (see Chapter II, Section 4). It also is often possible to state in advance that predicted developments, should they come true, will entail specific human tendencies in response, such as the tendency of capitalistic entrepreneurs in a crisis to look for new areas of favorable investments and of workers and tenants to revolt if exploited. It is unscientific, however, to ignore the possibility that conditions may develop differently and that human responses may take a different course. I refer to Section 6 of the Introductory chapter and to Chapter XII, Section 5, for additional remarks on this point.

---

[1] This is no place for a guide through the tremendous literature on Marxism. The following books are particularly valuable for political scientists: H. B. Mayo, *Democracy and Marxism*, New York 1955, a systematic presentation and analysis point by point, with a useful bibliography; Joseph Schumpeter, *Capitalism, Socialism, and Democracy*, London 1943, 2nd ed., 1947, analysis of the underlying economic and political problems, independent and profound, with a keen attempt to advance to scientifically superior predictions; and Eduard Heimann, *Communism, Fascism or Democracy*, New York 1938; *Freedom and Order*, New York 1947; and in German, *Wirtschaftssysteme und Gesellschaftssysteme*, Tübingen 1954, and *Vernunftglaube und Religion in der modernen Kultur*, Tübingen 1955; all distinguished by first-rate knowledge of the various doctrines and their history as well as by fairness of treatment, but freely abandoning Scientific Method at times, trespassing on metaphysical ground in the author's own interpretations of history. Lately, Alexander Rüstow, *Ortsbestimmung der Gegenwart*, vol. 3, Zurich 1957, pp. 291–322, equally strong in praise and blame.

Secondly, Marx and Engels projected experiences of the past into the future on the scientifically untenable assumption that in human and social affairs, just as in inanimate nature, what happened in the past will always and necessarily happen essentially the same way in the future, irrespective of changes in circumstances, improvement in scientific analysis, better awareness of implied risks, alteration of ethical standards, and new governmental methods. In pointing to past experiences they signaled many serious warnings to our own and to future generations; but again they failed to take full account of the variables, in particular the unpredictable potentialities of human ingenuity, determination, and organization. They pretended that they could offer scientific certainty where the utmost they could have done was to point to probabilities or risks. Their reliance on past experiences was the more tenuous because it was chiefly based on only three case histories—slave economy, feudal economy, and early capitalism.[2]

Thirdly, in denouncing the value judgments of their contemporaries and of former generations Marx and Engels freely expressed value judgments of their own, both negative and positive. Their polemic emphasis that the prevailing ideas of justice and morals in each epoch depended on economic factors, in particular on methods of production and class interests, and were nothing but "superstructures" erected on material interests, was relativistic in character, of course; but the relativity asserted therein did not imply for them that science was unable to ascertain the validity of ultimate value judgments. On the contrary, while teaching in the first place that history would inevitably move to the final stage of socialism anyway, whether or not that was the juster system, Marx and Engels were far from treating this course of events as a merely factual process devoid of value; it meant to them the establishment of true justice. They did not care to classify their own value judgments as a mere "superstructure" based on personal economic preferences, or otherwise as merely subjective and relative; in the transpositive, or transtraditional, sphere of value judgments their ideas were rather absolutistic in character.

From what has been said it follows that for all their incidental application of empirical research and relativistic references Marx and Engels did not obey the rules of Scientific Method, as now understood. Their belief in inevitable historical progress, their faith in science as being able to predict the course of history, and their reliance on the validity of their own value judgments bear all the typical marks of nineteenth-century thinking—and erring. Just as in regard to Comte

[2] Regarding the limited scientific value of these comparisons see Mayo, *op.cit.*

so it can be said regarding Marx and Engels that twentieth-century science has made perhaps its most important contribution by merely recognizing the nonscientific character of the unlimited trust in progress and science and of many specific predictions. For it is this contribution which, although negative only, deserves credit for having cleared the path toward our better understanding of reality in approaching the future, unhandicapped by scientific superstitions; just as at the end of antiquity the growing awareness that the traditional belief in ancient mythologies was scientifically untenable cleared the path to higher forms of religion (Acts 17:15 ff.), and in modern times the recognition that science can neither prove nor disprove the reality of an invisible God cleared the path for religion on the one side and for concentration of science on subjects and methods germane to scientific research on the other.

Yet twentieth-century science has more to offer in the discussion of Marxism than this negative contribution. It can point out ways and means by which it may be possible to meet the particular perils that threaten a liberal democratic society, perils exaggeratedly denounced by Marx; it can, conversely, lay bare the consequences and risks to be encountered in the execution of full-scale socialism; and it can try to present alternative approaches toward desired goals of human development. These matters will be dealt with further in Chapters VIII (equality) and XII (possibility and impossibility).

6. Withdrawal of Philosophy. Darwinism. Early Pragmatism

We have seen that each of the three nineteenth-century schools so far discussed—positivism, historicism, and Marxism—introduced relativistic ideas, but that the relativity they spoke of was, in each case, determined by factors other than scientific impotence to ascertain the validity of ultimate values. Actually, when members of these older schools ventured beyond the sphere of their primary interest—such as the positive law, history, or the class struggle, respectively—they often revealed absolutistic, dogmatic tendencies of thought. If in rare cases they abstained from value judgments in transpositive, transhistoric, transtraditional questions as well, this was due to some vague type of skepticism rather than to any specific theory of values. Scientific value relativism remained at best latent and passive.

(a) WITHDRAWAL OF PHILOSOPHY

General philosophy in the second half of the nineteenth century was in no position to resolve the conflict of competing relativities or to provide absolute standards. Its withdrawal from the traditional business of providing comprehensive metaphysical ontologies left the particular branches of science philosophically on their own. As Roscoe Pound has aptly put it with regard to jurisprudence: "In the last third of the nineteenth century the abandonment of philosophy had gone so far that the philosophical jurists either had been swallowed up in the dominant historical [or in the positivistic, A.B.] school or had disappeared."[1] Whitehead (*Science and the Modern World*, p. 148) calls the last twenty years of the nineteenth century one of the "dullest stages of thought" since the crusades.

Hegel, in a weird premonition, once dubbed himself the last philosopher. In this he was more right than he could know if what we mean by philosopher is a producer of metaphysical systems. When he died, the fervor for such creations seemed to have been spent for good. The decisive reason for this sudden decline, however, was not the towering greatness of Hegel's philosophy, or that of his predecessors, but the growing awareness of the scientific weakness of all metaphysics. The exacting demands put on scientific work operated as a deterrent to metaphysical speculations. That science was unable to prove the existence of God solely with scientific means was becoming a scientific commonplace. Its wide acceptance led, in a formidable move of historical dialectic, to two extreme alternative doctrines, the one personified by Sören Kierkegaard (1813-1855), who called for a "jump into faith" out of the scientifically unsolvable dilemma, the other by Friedrich Wilhelm Nietzsche (1844-1900), who declared "God is dead."[2] Caught between these extremes, scientists turned to empirical research with quickly growing success. Yet none of these tendencies kept scholars from spicing their works with value judgments. Consistent abstinence in this respect would have required a methodological clarity that did not yet exist.

(b) DARWINISM AND ETHICAL NEUTRALITY

The publication, in 1859, of Darwin's *On the Origin of Species by Means of Natural Selection* played a leading role in this development, of course.[3] It led to embittered disputes everywhere on the respective

---

[1] Roscoe Pound, *Interpretations of Legal History*, New York 1932, p. 69. See also Gustav Radbruch, "Anglo-American Jurisprudence through Continental Eyes," *Law Quarterly Review*, vol. 52 (1936) pp. 530, 531.

[2] For a lucid discussion of this historical situation, see Karl Löwith, *Meaning in History, Methodological Implications of the Philosophy of History*, Chicago 1949.

[3] See above, Chapter II, Section 1. Darwin's theory found official scientific recognition in the United States sooner than in Europe. The American Philosophical Society awarded

authorities of science and religion, and to an ever-growing tendency toward a clear distinction between religious or otherwise metaphysical doctrines and strictly scientific inquiries. The primary subject of the ensuing controversies were geological history, the origin of man, and divine intervention; not ethical questions. The latter, however, entered the debate indirectly on the ground that doubts in revealed truth placed the moral foundations of society in jeopardy. Darwin's opponents demanded, therefore, that scientists should take such moral consequences of their theories into account; his followers assailed this so-called "doctrinal moralism" as being beside the point in scientific inquiry.

In the course of this debate, some of the Darwinians, especially the positivistic American mathematician and psychologist Chauncey Wright (1830–1875), spoke of the "ethical neutrality" of science.[4] But this call had not yet the specific meaning it conveys today. It was not intended to inaugurate a relativistic theory of values, or to express a desire that ethical judgments should be abandoned outside the natural sciences as well. It was primarily directed against the demand just mentioned that the natural sciences should take the ethical effects of their theories into account.[5] To that extent it was widely acclaimed. Beyond the particular issue that had aroused it, however, it found little support, not even from the pragmatists.

(c) EARLY PRAGMATISM

The school of thought which, about the turn of the century, came closest to the nascent European theory of Scientific Value Relativism was American Pragmatism. Its rebellion against all a-priori statements, first principles, and the traditional practice of deductively deriving postulates from such principles, on the one side, and its insistence on inquiries into the *consequences* of concepts, ideas, actions, and habits, on the other, were among the most important American con-

---

Darwin honorary membership as early as 1869, ten years after publication of the *Origin of Species*, whereas Cambridge, Darwin's own university, gave him a honorary degree only ten years later, and the French Academy at first rejected Darwin's membership. See Walter P. Metzger in R. Hofstadter and W. P. Metzger, *The Development of Academic Freedom in the United States*, New York, pp. 322, 355.

[4] See Chauncey Wright, *Philosophical Discussions*, ed. by C. E. Norton, Boston 1877; the chapter on Chauncey Wright in Ralph B. Perry, *The Thought and Character of William James*, unabridged ed., Boston 1935, vol. 1, pp. 520–532; and Walter P. Metzger, *op.cit.*, p. 322. The best analysis of Wright's thinking to date is Philipp P. Wiener, *Evolution and the Founders of Pragmatism*, with a foreword by John Dewey, Cambridge, Mass., 1949, pp. 31–69.

[5] J. B. Thayer, ed., *Letters of Chauncey Wright*, Cambridge 1878, p. 118.

tributions to the formation of twentieth-century Scientific Method. They entitle pragmatism to be credited with a major share in genetic fatherhood to Scientific Method as understood today. But the early pragmatists did not follow this line of thinking through to the point where their theories would have merged with Scientific Value Relativism.

Of course, pragmatists were inimical to value judgments made *a priori,* as they were to all a-priori statements. There was, however, no outspoken tendency on their side to bar value judgments when arrived at *a posteriori.* On the contrary, they seemed to look to value judgments made *post factum* with confidence. Their major concern, in full accord with the principles of Scientific Method as now generally understood (to repeat, under contributing pragmatist influence), was the emphasis on the practical consequences of different ideas and actions. The standards finally to be applied in evaluating these consequences played little if any role. Pragmatists seemed ever to repeat, "Let us watch the consequences and *then* judge, or rejudge; let us do things and see what happens, and then revise our concepts and ideas." It generally remained obscure, or at least undecided, whether they meant to say that when it came to evaluating the consequences there could be ultimately no difference of opinion, a view that would betray absolutistic tendencies in the tacit assumption of some highest standard of judgment, such as happiness of the individual or of some group; or whether they recognized that final controversies in evaluation could not be resolved with scientific means, a view in accord with Scientific Value Relativism; or whether they would refer supra-individual evaluation to democratic procedure (majority decision after full discussion), which would be a political, not a scientific, solution of the problem and not help us in scientific controversies with those who in good faith do not agree with the majority principle (see Chapter VIII, Section 8).

Some of the fundamental statements made by William James in his *Pragmatism,* published in 1907,[6] will serve to illustrate the main point. Pragmatism, James wrote, "at the outset, at least," stands for "no particular results. It has no dogma, and no doctrines save its method."[7] What the pragmatic method means is: "The attitude of

---

[6] *Pragmatism—A New Name for Some Old Ways of Thinking,* here quoted from R. B. Perry's ed., New York 1943, which adds three essays from *The Meaning of Truth,* originally published in 1885, 1895, and 1904, and republished under that title (with a new preface) in 1909.

[7] *Op.cit.,* p. 54. Similarly, p. 51, and *passim.* The words "at the outset, at least" should not be overlooked; they left room for judgments a posteriori.

looking away from first things, principles, 'categories,' supposed necessities; and of looking toward last things, fruits, consequences, facts."
"Pragmatism is uncomfortable away from facts. Rationalism is com-
fortable only in the presence of abstractions. . . ." [8]

All this is obviously fully in accord with Scientific Method as understood today. It has helped that method become what it now is. The
difference, however, appears in passages such as the following. Pragmatists, James said, "talk about truths in the plural, about their *utility*
and *satisfactoriness,* about the *success* with which they 'work' . . ."
" 'The True,' to put it very briefly, is only the *expedient* in the way of
our thinking, just as 'the right' is only the expedient in the way of our
behaving. . . ." Truth, law and language "make themselves as we
go." [9]

The trouble here is with the terms "utility," "expediency," "satisfactoriness," and "success." Scientific Value Relativism would not pass
by these standards so quickly. Utility or expediency for what, or for
whom, it would ask. Satisfactoriness for whom, and for what kinds
of demand? Success, toward what aims or ends, attained with what
means? And it would disclaim the ability of science to provide ultimate standards, whereas James never spelt out his answer to this side
of the problem in unambiguous language. He surely was vociferous
in rejecting any need for the inquirer to recognize *a priori* that there
was only one truth. But this did not make him necessarily a relativist
when it came to looking at things *a posteriori.* Nor did he exclude
ultimate standards of value and their scientific recognition when he
said that "truth makes itself as we go."

What, then, does this formula imply regarding values as distinct
from facts and from scientific laws in the natural sciences? Is the
value of the outcome always sure to speak for itself? This belief is
widely held among pragmatists of the rank and file. It is based on a
fallacy, however, as we shall see later (Chapter VII, Section 2) in more
detail: the outcome of the destruction of Carthage does not tell us
how to judge its value or disvalue unless we side with either Rome
or Carthage, or adopt an impersonal yardstick—but which? It is hard
to believe that the great William James himself should have fallen
into this logical trap; yet at times he came fairly close to it. When,
for example, in his *Pragmatism* he spoke of expediency, he added that
he meant expedient "in the long run and on the whole, of course; for

---

[8] *Ibid.,* pp. 54, 55; p. 67; and in the essay "Humanism and Truth," *op.cit.,* p. 395. See
Appendix B, below, on the term "rationalism."
[9] *Pragmatism,* p. 67; p. 222; p. 242. See also Preface to *The Meaning of Truth.*

what expediently meets all the experience in sight won't necessarily meet all farther experiments equally satisfactorily." [10] Quite true. But can we know even in the long run what meets the experience satisfactorily without a decision regarding the type of satisfaction that matters most? In the essay "Humanism and Truth" he wrote that "abstract truth, truth verified by the long run, and abstract satisfactoriness, long-run satisfactoriness, coincide." [11] What is to be the objective standard here? Or is there none? In the same essay he said that "satisfactoriness" is a term that permits "of no definition, so many are the ways in which [this requirement] can practically be worked out." [12] But this still leaves satisfaction the decisive criterion, even in ethical questions, without saying whose satisfaction, that of the acting person or of the critical observer, and satisfaction of which of several conflicting desires. In the only paper he ever published on theoretical ethics, "The Moral Philosopher and the Moral Life," originally an address delivered at Yale in 1891,[13] he rightly stressed that ethical hypotheses may be invalidated by further experience, but again accepted final experiences without questioning the standard of judgment and its validity. There can be found "no final truth in ethics any more than in physics, until *the last man* has had his experience and his say," he wrote.[14] Yet will not even "the last man," in order to decide what had been expedient (if he should care to make such a decision) be confronted with the same dilemma as his predecessors: choice of the standard?

Be that as it may; at any rate, James did not propose to wait with moral value judgments until the last man could have his say. He admitted the possibility of different views of value and of conflicts between values.[15] But he did not stop there. He rejected what he called "skepticism," and did so explicitly even in the context of value judgments.[16] Consequently, he invited all philosophers to try their hands at ethical judgments, and tried his own. The truth that had "made itself" as *he* was going led him to definite statements in this respect, to which he attributed some objective validity. This is shown by an outline of lectures he delivered at Harvard, 1888–1889,[17] one of the few

[10] *Op.cit.*, p. 222.

[11] *Ibid.*, p. 407.

[12] *Ibid.*, p. 419.

[13] First published in *International Journal of Ethics*, April 1891, and later included unchanged in *The Will to Believe*, 1897; Dover ed., New York 1956, pp. 184 ff.

[14] *Ibid.*, p. 184. Italics added.

[15] Same paper, and the lecture notes mentioned hereafter in the text.

[16] "The Moral Philosopher . . . ," *op.cit.*, p. 184, and "The Will to Believe," *ibid.*, pp. 1 ff.

[17] Published in Ralph B. Perry, *The Thought and Character of William James*, as cited, vol. 2, pp. 263–65. Briefer version, 1948, p. 221.

notes of his that deal directly with values. There he wrote: "That act is the best act which makes for the best whole, the best whole being that which prevails at least cost, in which the vanquished goods are least completely annulled." This maxim he found good enough to repeat later almost literally in his paper, "The Moral Philosopher," just mentioned,[18] and in the latter's republication in 1897. It may be a highly praiseworthy rule, indeed, from the liberal point of view; but at present we are concerned only with the question whether it is relativistic, and that it certainly is not. It professes, not nationalism, not transpersonalism, but some sort of individualism. As Perry comments: "The principle is clear: value derives ultimately from the interests of the individual; and the social whole is justified by the inclusion and reconciliation of its individual parts. *Individualism is fundamental.*" [19] Whatever this was, it was no expression of Scientific Value Relativism.

The following reflections will serve to render this still clearer. It was, of course, entirely in keeping with scientific relativism when James traced valuations to the "mind," either a suprahuman mind, if there was one, or human minds. Good or evil, he wrote, "are objects of feeling and desire, which have no foothold or anchorage in Being, apart from the existence of actually living minds." [20] But from this relativistic starting point—relativistic at least in the absence of proof for God's existence—he proceeded to the nonrelativistic statement, italicized by him, that "the essence of good is simply to satisfy demand," and from there briskly onward to the nonrelativistic ideal that *all* demands should be fulfilled as far as possible, because the philosopher "cannot, so long as he clings to his own ideal of objectivity, rule out any ideal from being heard." "Since everything which is demanded is by that fact a good, must not the guiding principle for ethical philosophy . . . be simply to satisfy at all times as many demands as we can?" [21] Therewith he accepted a particular set of standards, including individualism and equality, against possible alternative sets, for instance those based on aristocratic ideals, religious orthodoxy, or transpersonal aims. Scientific Value Relativism would consider this a political, not a scientific, decision. James did not care to make such distinctions in this context.

[18] "The Moral Philosopher . . . ," *op.cit.*, p. 205: "That act must be the best act, accordingly, which makes for the *best whole,* in the sense of awakening the least sum of dissatisfaction. In the casuistic scale, therefore, those ideals must be written highest which *prevail at the least cost."* And he added: *"Invent some manner* of realizing your own ideals which will also satisfy the alien demands,—that and only that is the path of peace!" Italics in the original.

[19] Italics not in the original.

[20] "The Moral Philosopher. . . ," p. 197.

[21] *Ibid.,* p. 201; p. 203; p. 205.

My intention here is by no means to blame the early pragmatists for their neglect of the scientific aspects of the value problem, but merely to state the historical fact that they did neglect it. One reason was that it was not in the center of their interest, and that there was no immediate need for them to deal with it. Peirce's original thesis, for instance, that a concept's meaning is no more than the conception of its practical consequences [22] was true or false no matter how the consequences were to be evaluated; its validity had little to do with that evaluation. The same can be said of his later formulations, and those used by James and other pragmatists, who put more emphasis upon action and actual consequences than on conceptions and imagined consequences.

Moreover, both Peirce and James were distracted from the scientific aspect of evaluation by their metaphysical predilections. Neither was a positivist. Peirce's thought ran entirely counter not only to Hume's skepticism but also to the modern type of naturalistic realism which, while recognizing reality of things, yet denies that of ideas. Like Plato and a goodly portion of the Scholastics, and also like, after Peirce, the revivers of ontology in the second quarter of the twentieth century (see Chapter 1, Section 5,d), he attributed reality to ideas, though he did not regard them as independent entities, separate from the things that imitated or mirrored them, as Plato had done. Even logic had to Peirce a status of ideal reality. Altogether he tried, as Ernest Nagel puts it, "to construct a metaphysical system in the grand manner." [23] Unimpressed by Darwin, he believed that the species had been predetermined by a Creator. He devised a cosmology of evolutionary love, "which for sheer speculative audacity was a worthy rival of the absolutism of Schelling and Hegel." [24]

James, too, if in very different ways, and with little interest in logic, was deeply steeped in metaphysics, and particularly in its recognition through mystical experiences. He expressed these interests vigorously

---

[22] "Consider what effects, that might conceivably have practical bearings, we conceive the object of our conception to have. Then our conception of these effects is the whole of our conception of the object." *The Collected Papers of Charles Sander Peirce*, ed. by Charles Hartshorne and Paul Weiss, Cambridge, Mass., 1935 ff., vol. 5, no. 402. This was first published in Peirce's article, "How to Make Our Ideas Clear," *Popular Science Monthly*, January 1878, p. 293, and first referred to by James approvingly in his own paper "The Function of Cognition," Mind, vol. 10 (1885), reprinted later in *The Meaning of Truth, op.cit.*, p. 358. James's concept of pragmatism shifted later in the direction of "workability" and "satisfactoriness," in line with Dewey and Schiller, see *ibid.*, p. 360.

[23] Ernest Nagel, *Sovereign Reason*, Glencoe, Ill., 1954, p. 90. This book includes Nagel's papers on Peirce (pp. 58–100).

[24] Philip P. Wiener, *op.cit.*, pp. 76 ff.

in his publications around the turn of the century: *The Will to Believe* (1897), *Human Immortality* (1898), and above all, *The Varieties of Religious Experience* (1902); but not only during this period. In letters, like those written to Professor James H. Leuba (April 17, 1904) and to Charles E. Norton (October 17, 1908),[25] he vented them, rather more than less intensely, in his later years, when he wrote his *Pragmatism* (1907) and most of his *Essays on Radical Empiricism* (published posthumously). His belief in immortality was on the increase. We must not be misled by the fact that he greeted the far more positivistically oriented John Dewey as an ally in the cause of pragmatism. For, as Perry aptly summed up the relationship between the two, "it is quite clear that he [James] felt a deeper allegiance to the army of the mystics and intuitionalists. It was a metaphysics of vision and insight, rather than either activism or positivism, that sprang from the ancient roots of his thought."[26]

Now, metaphysical thought, while nonpositivistic by definition, need not on this ground be in conflict with Scientific Value Relativism, as here understood (see Chapter VII, Section 3); once metaphysical speculations and scientific research are clearly distinguished, even scientific relativists may take a flight toward heaven and leave dull earth behind them whenever they choose to do so, and still be consistent thinkers. But neither Peirce nor James pursued this distinction to the happy end. James explicitly rejected the differentiation between philosophy and science in lectures delivered in 1905; "both are just man thinking by every means in his power," he commented.[27] This is true enough, but ignores the difference in intersubjective transmissibility between various types of knowledge, a difference that is bound to come to the fore whenever philosophy loses contact with scientific procedure in the narrower sense of the term. And Peirce dotted down his laconic advice, "Do not block the way of inquiry";[28] sound admonition, indeed, but pretty general and in need of elaboration regarding the difference between pre-scientific speculations and scientific hypotheses and tests, and the steps that may lead from the one to the other (Chap-

---

[25] Perry, *op.cit.*, vol. 2, pp. 348, 359. See also, regarding James's opposition to Chauncey Wright's "anti-religious teaching" and rejection of metaphysics, *ibid.*, vol. 1, p. 522.

[26] Perry, *op.cit.*, vol. 2, p. 582; briefer version, p. 322.

[27] *Ibid.*, vol. 2, p. 442 (unabridged ed.).

[28] *Collected Papers*, vol. 1, no. 135. The four illustrations which Peirce added in the subsequent paragraphs (nos. 137–140) were directed against, not the preclusion of scientific value judgments, but any a-priori statements denying the possibility that certain *facts* could ever be known, such as Comte's contention that the chemical compositions of fixed stars will never be known. Peirce did not mention values here.

ter II, Sections 6 and 7, above). This elaboration was missing with regard to values in the work of both Peirce and James.

If the ethical neutrality which the Darwinists demanded for the natural sciences (see above) was to be understood as a general postulate for all sciences, including the moral and social sciences, it is quite possible, after what has been said, that this would have appeared to Peirce and James as an "emasculation of science" or a "disparagement of metaphysics," as Walter Metzger puts it in his study.[29] As far as I have been able to verify, however, they never said so with such strong words. On the contrary, there are passages in James's work which suggest that he was closer to Scientific Value Relativism than might appear from the remarks quoted above. Thus he wrote in his lecture notes of 1888– 1889, cited, that philosophy has "two subdivisions: (1) science, the principles of *fact* or what *is,* whether good or bad; (2) ethics, what is good or bad, whether it *be* or *be not.* The principles of ethics are independent of those of science. . . ." Here, then, he made exactly that distinction between science and ethics which he refused to accept between science and philosophy in the later note. He admitted, moreover, that there was no possible proof of a thing's being good. "To *prove* a thing good, we must conceive it as belonging to a genus already admitted good. Every ethical proof therefore involves as its major premise an ethical proposition; every argument must end in some such proposition to be admitted *without proof.*"[30] Then he stressed the subjective nature of valuation. "So far as I feel anything good, I make it so. It *is* so, for me." Only after these introductory remarks did he proceed to make objective proposals, saying that "Of all the proposed *summa genera,* pleasure and perfection have the best claim to be considered," and accepting Josiah Royce's "moral insight"—"consider *every* good as a real good, and *keep* as many as we can"; and only thereafter did he finally introduce his definition, rendered above, of the "best act," following it up with suggestions regarding the decision in the event of conflicts.

In view of these notes, and in the light of James's emphatic pluralism, which intimated a possible plurality of values as well; in the light, further, of his "humanistic" objections to all "absolute standards,"[31] of his individualism and of his respect for every honest belief, I venture to suggest that his pragmatism actually harbored some sort of *latent* Scientific Value Relativism (see Chapter III, Section 8), bound to come

[29] Metzger, *op.cit.,* p. 355.
[30] The emphasis on the two last words has been added here, but not that on the former.
[31] "Humanism and Truth," *op.cit.,* p. 409, and the essay mentioned in the next note.

into the open if a clearer distinction between science and philosophical speculation was to be made, as for some purposes it must be made. In support I may point to the passage in his *Will To Believe* (p. 22) in which he reiterated the distinction made in his notes of 1888–1889 between science and ethics, now putting it thus: "Science can tell us what exists; but to compare the *worths* both of what exists and of what does not exist, we must consult not science, but what Pascal called our heart." This is in line with Scientific Value Relativism. One might be tempted, also, to refer to the remark James made in a chapter on relativism in his *Meaning of Truth,* where he wrote outright, "we pragmatists are typical relativists." [32] But I do not want to make too much of this latter passage since it was directed against what James called Rickert's "absolutism" in the German philosopher's general theory of knowledge. Their controversy here was primarily about *facts,* with no mention made of value judgments (see below, Chapter vi, Section 2, a).

If, then, much of what James wrote sounded like an anticipation of Scientific Value Relativism, it was at best a latent type of it, frequently obscured by contradictory remarks. Only after Scientific Value Relativism matured in Europe and began to spread to the United States (see next chapter) did pragmatists pay special attention to the problem. There was no complete merger even then, because the surviving protagonist of the American school, John Dewey, tended to deny—incorrectly, I think—that there were fundamental differences between facts and values in scientific inquiry, a point to which I shall revert later (Chapter vii, Section 2).

7. Is-and-Ought Fusion Lingering On.
Kant II, J. S. Mill

If, in our looking back to the nineteenth century, we now concentrate on one particular element in Scientific Value Relativism, the doctrine of the logical gulf between Is and Ought, it is amazing to realize how long the logical fusion lingered. Deductively to infer a proposition of Ought-form from a major premise of Is-form was, after all, obviously incompatible even with old Aristotelean logic. How then could the fusion go on with so little inhibition?

The trouble had its source in inductive rather than deductive logic. As long as major premises of Ought-form were held to be readily avail-

---

[32] William James, *The Meaning of Truth,* ed. of 1909, ch. viii, p. 263. This entire chapter is omitted in Perry's ed. of 1943.

able in science on the basis of religious revelation (such as the Ten Commandments), Natural Law, reason, or intuition, separation of Is and Ought in deductive logic was not disturbing to academic work in morals and politics, and the need for it was hardly noticed as a handicap. Only when in the seventeenth and eighteenth centuries religion and science began to separate, when the scientific capabilities of intuitive reason were critically examined, when consequently the rich afflux of first principles or premises in Ought-form was petering out, and scholars could turn only to inductive reasoning for help, only then was the time ripe for the emergence of a maxim that insisted on a strict distinction between Is and Ought all across the board of science, and that meant also in the process of inductive reasoning.

Even then, however, such a doctrine did not develop at once. David Hume made a short sarcastic remark on the shift from Is to Ought in logical arguments. But his skepticism went far beyond the area of Ought; it included that of Is and, therefore, contributed little to the separation of the two (see Appendix B). To a greater extent, the Gulf Doctrine can be traced to Kant's two main works, *Critique of Pure Reason* (1781), dealing with Is, and *Critique of Practical Reason* (1788), dealing with Ought.[1] Yet while Kant did separate the two areas as objectives of his studies, he offered also connecting links. Inaugurating a new start in philosophical thought he contended that certain factors, such as the forms of thinking in terms of time and space and of causality, were always present in the human process of thinking (see above, Chapter II, Section 1 and 5). He spoke also of ideas we use to "regulate" our thinking, contending that some among them, too, were always present in the human process of thinking because they were necessary to it. These "necessary regulative ideas," according to Kant, included the notion that the world was a unity, and the assumption that we have a certain amount of freedom in thinking, and more specifically his "categorical imperative," the basic moral law. If this was correct, then some Ought elements had Is character because they constituted a part of our human structure. We shall deal with these ideas, and the scientifically sound nucleus in them, in Chapters IX ff. At this point we are merely concerned with the historical fact that the fusion of Is and Ought was not halted by Kant.

The most influential mid-century book on logic and scientific

---

[1] Kant, *Kritik der reinen Vernunft* (1781), in *Gesammelte Schriften* (Academy ed., 1900–42) vol. 4 (2nd ed., 1787, is in vol. 3), also in Kant, *Werke* (Cassirer ed., 1912–22) vol. 3; *Kritik der praktischen Vernunft* (1788). Academy ed., vol. 5; Cassirer ed., vol. 5. There are several English translations of both works.

method, John Stuart Mill's *System of Logic* (1843),[2] ignored the distinction between Is and Ought up to the very last pages, failing to mention it wherever one could expect to find it discussed, as for instance in the chapter on logical fallacies.[3] At the end, however, in the short last chapter dealing with the "Logic of Practice, or Art, Including Morality and Policy," [4] Mill finally turned to it, and here, on the three or four concluding pages of the entire extremely long work he put down the most discerning statements regarding the separation of Is and Ought ever written up to that time. On the merit of these pages, from which we shall quote more extensively below, Mill would deserve the title of the earliest champion of the Gulf Doctrine had he not ended this chapter, and therewith the entire book, with a few paragraphs that contained a new, and most gigantic, fusion between Is and Ought.

Before we turn to this final chapter, however, it is noteworthy that there were other features in Mill's book which contributed to the fusion. Where he dealt with deductive syllogisms he focused attention on the premises and contentions expressed in them;[5] the latter could be obtained only by induction, he said. This led him to the confusing statement that all deduction, therefore, was actually induction.[6] He reduced the significance of deductive logic still further by his—today generally abandoned—doctrine that all reasoning from observation is "from particulars to particulars." He meant by this that in the process of inductive reasoning the detour over deductive logic—i.e., first, generalization from particulars, and subsequently, deduction of other particulars from such generalization (see above, Chapters I, Section 6, and II, Section 2)—was unnecessary, irrelevant, and unrealistic. He believed that we must, could, and most often did, reason directly from particulars to particulars without the medium of general propositions; the latter we used merely as shorthand notes, or as a memorandum for our memory.[7] In this he confused psychological description and logical requirements; for whenever we infer from one particular to the other

---

[2] John Stuart Mill, *A System of Logic, Ratiocinative and Inductive, Being a Connected View of the Principles of Evidence and the Methods of Scientific Investigation,* 1st ed., 1843; 8th ed., London 1889, here referred to in quotations. Abridged edition, Ernest Nagel (ed.), *John Stuart Mill's Philosophy of Scientific Method,* New York 1950.

[3] Pp. 481 ff.; not included in Nagel ed.

[4] Pp. 616–22; Nagel ed., pp. 352–58.

[5] P. 116; Nagel ed., p. 116.

[6] P. 133; Nagel ed., p. 134.

[7] Pp. 121 ff.; Nagel ed., pp. 123 ff. Especially, p. 126 (Nagel, p. 127): "All inference is from particulars to particulars; general propositions are merely registers of such inferences already made, and short formulas for making more; the major premise of a syllogism, con-

the previous generalization is logically required even when it is psychologically omitted.

Mill did not go so far as entirely to reject generalization. On the contrary, he admitted generalizations freely as a guidance for practical purposes, even where they merely stated a "tendency" of what would happen.[8] Fascinated by the problems of the inductive process, he tended to overrate its possibilities, hoping that some day the laws of correct induction would be discovered (see Chapter 1, Section 6, above) and that induction would lead, among other achievements, to what he called an "ethology," a science of the human character.[9]

Furthermore, there was some ambiguity in Mill's ideas about intuition, as distinct from inductive reasoning. Generally speaking, he was a valiant fighter against references to intuition as a basis of scientific knowledge.[10] When he finally turned to morals, however, he did not entirely exclude intuition.[11] Since he failed to examine the sources of intuition more intensively, the logical structure of his thought about the relations between science and ethics was weakened. But all these flaws in his great work were minor as compared with his final disregard of the separation between Is and Ought when, at the end of the book, he reintroduced into the theory of morals and politics an absolute Ought which he derived from Is.

Nothwithstanding these inconsistencies, the passages dealing with the separation of Is and Ought which preceded that final relapse into fusion were so precise and clear that they shall be discussed here more fully. Mill there distinguished science from art, using the latter term in its broader sense including ethics, or morals, and policy. "Whatever speaks in rules or precepts, not in assertions respecting matters of fact," he said, "is art." [12] Art, and not science, supplies the "major premise, which asserts that the attainment of the given end is desirable." Every art "has one first principle or general major premise not borrowed from science, that which enunciates the object aimed at and affirms it to be a desirable object." Here he made an explicit distinction between Is and Ought: the propositions in question he said, "do not assert that

---

sequently, is a formula of this description, and the conclusion is not an inference drawn *from* the formula, but an inference drawn *according* to the formula, the real logical antecedent, or premise, being the particular facts from which the general proposition was collected by induction."

[8] P. 585; Nagel ed., p. 334.

[9] Pp. 562 ff.; Nagel ed., pp. 317 ff.

[10] See especially, J. S. Mill, *Autobiography,* New York 1924, p. 157; and *An Examination of Sir William Hamilton's Philosophy,* 3rd ed., London 1867; Nagel ed., pp. 359 ff. Also, Nagel's introduction, *op.cit.,* pp. xxviii ff.

[11] P. 621; Nagel ed., p. 357.

[12] This and the following quotations are from pp. 616–22; Nagel ed., pp. 352–58.

anything is, but enjoin or recommend that something should be." He called them "a class by themselves," and went on:

A proposition of which the predicate is expressed by the words *ought* or *should be* is generically different from one which is expressed by *is* or *will be* [italics in the original]. It is true that, in the largest sense of the words, even these propositions assert something as a matter of fact. The fact affirmed in them is that the conduct recommended excites in the speaker's mind the feeling of approbation. This, however, does not go to the bottom of the matter; for the speaker's approbation is no sufficient reason why other people should approve, nor ought it to be a conclusive reason even with himself. For the purposes of practice, everyone must be required to justify his approbation; and for this there is need of general premises determining what are the proper objects of approbation and what the proper order of precedence among those objects.

These general premises he called "the art of life," dividing it in three departments, morality, prudence of policy, and aesthetics. In this context he spoke of "teleology, or the doctrine of ends," and observed that the German (Kantian) name of "practical reason" was not improperly used for it. Then he continued, again fully in line with the Gulf Doctrine as understood today:

A scientific observer or reasoner, merely as such, is not an adviser for practice. His part is only to show that certain consequences follow from certain causes and that, to obtain certain ends, certain means are the most effectual. Whether the ends themselves are such as ought to be pursued, and if so, in what cases and to how great a length, it is no part of his business as a cultivator of science to decide, and science alone will never qualify him for the decision.

He emphasized, however, that those who treat of human nature and society invariantly claim this office; "they always undertake to say not merely what is, but what ought to be." He noted that in the subordinate arts we seldom need justification of the end since its desirableness is denied by noone; "but a writer on morals and politics requires those principles at every step." The most elaborate exposition of laws is of no avail if the ends to be aimed at by that art are left to the individual, or are "taken for granted without analysis or questioning." Here is the point where Mill's argument diverted from the straight path. Said he:

There must be some standard by which to determine the goodness or badness, absolute and comparative, of ends or objects of desire. And whatever that standard is, there can be but one; for, if there were several ultimate principles of conduct, the same conduct might be approved by one of those principles and condemned by another, and there would be needed some more general principles as umpire between them.[13]

The decisive point, scientifically speaking, is that Mill did not say, as any scientific relativist could say today, that there *may* be some absolute standard, and that it *may* be only one, but concluded there *must* be such standard and there *can* be only one. He also thought he had found it. In looking for it he did not rely on intuition because, he said, even if in morals general principles could be won from intuition—which possibility he did not entirely exclude—some principle or standard must still be found for the remainder of practice, that is, for policy. He ended his book by stating his conviction that this general principle "to which all rules of practice ought to conform and the test by which they should be tried, is that of conduciveness to the happiness of mankind . . . , in other words that the promotion of happiness is the ultimate principle of teleology." In this way he stopped short of drawing relativistic conclusions from his eloquent separation of Is and Ought, offering a kind of humanistic and benevolent philosophical absolutism, an absolute standard basically in line with the teachings of Bentham and of James Mill, John's father. He referred for vindication of this principle to his essay *Utilitarianism*.

What vindication did he offer there? None other than an inference from Is to Ought! Conceding that questions of ultimate ends do not admit of proof in the ordinary acceptation of that term he claimed that, nevertheless, some proof could be given. The task was that of finding out which ends are *desirable*. "Questions about ends are, in other words, questions which things are desirable."[14] The utilitarian doctrine was, he said, that "happiness is desirable, and the only thing desirable as an end; all other things are desirable only as a means to that end." Yet

---

[13] Pp. 620–21; Nagel ed., pp. 356–57. See similar observations made by Eduard Spranger in his discussion of Radbruch's list of three ultimate values, below, Chapter VI, Section 7.

[14] J. S. Mill, *Utilitarianism*, 1863, Chapter IV; Everyman's Library, London, New York, No. 482, p. 32. Mill had not always thought favorably of the utilitarian maxim; see Jacob Viner, "Bentham and J. S. Mill: The Utilitarian Background," *American Economic Review*, vol. 39 (1949) pp. 360–82. See also Fred Cort, "The Issue of a Science of Politics in Utilitarian Thought," *American Political Science Review*, vol. 46 (1952) pp. 1140 ff.; and on modern utilitarianism the fine chapter in Paul Kecskemeti, *Meaning, Communication, and Value*, Chicago 1952, pp. 292–313.

how can we know that happiness is the only desirable thing? Mill's only answer was, Because it actually *is* desired. After showing that it is generally desired, he ended up by saying:

> if human nature is so constituted as to desire nothing which is not either a part of happiness or a means of happiness, we can have no other proof, and we *require no other,* that these are the only things *desirable. It so, happiness is the* sole end of human actions, and the promotion of it the test by which to judge all human conduct; from whence it *necessarily follows* that it must be the *criterion of morality,* since a part is included in the whole.[15]

The term "desirable" in this passage permits of no other interpretation than "worthy of being desired" in the moral sense. The suffix *-able,* it is true, does not always denote that something ought to be done or approved, or is worthy of being done; "eatable" and "readable," e.g., imply merely that a thing so characterized can or may be eaten or read, not necessarily that it ought to be. Had Mill used the word desirable only in the sense that happiness *can* be desired, there would have been no logical fallacy, but merely a trivial tautology—happiness is desired, hence it can be desired. But this would not only be an entirely uncommon use of the term desirable; Mill cannot have meant it, because he explicitly spoke here of the "criterion of morality."

Thus, completely neglecting his own warning against confusion of Is and Ought, Mill presented us at the end with the supreme logical blunder that happiness *ought* to be desired because it *is* desired. Whatever the great merits of Mill's *Logic* and of his *Utilitarianism* in other respects—and they remain considerable to the present day, and will remain so beyond it—we cannot list him as the father of the Gulf Doctrine.

8. *"Natural Law with a Variable Content"* (*Stammler*)

The final transition from latent and passive to overt and active relativism in political and legal philosophy seems, at first sight, to be marked by Rudolf Stammler's thesis that there was a "natural law with a variable content," first offered in 1896.[1] For this proposition seems to suggest that, while there was a natural law above the positive law, it too was relative in character.

---

[15] *Ibid.,* p. 36. Italics not in the original.

[1] *Wirtschaft und Recht nach der materialistischen Geschichtsauffassung* (1st ed. Leipzig 1896) p. 185; see 5th ed. (1924) p. 174, also pp. 161, 168, 454.

Stammler, however, was far from being a relativist. He did not dwell on the variable content, so strikingly suggested by his formula, but, on the contrary, searched for invariable criteria of objectively justified purposes and endeavors. From historical and positivistic relativity he wished to proceed to standards of objectively "right" law.

It was actually the first time in several decades, after all scientific efforts had been absorbed by positivism, historicism, and empiricism, that scientific standards in criticism of legislation were proclaimed outside the old religious and Natural-Law schools. As a Neo-Kantian —this term was coined only later, but with special regard to him— Stammler stressed that such standards could be only formal, not substantive (material). But he was strangely inconsistent in this respect, confusing formal and substantive views. Characteristic of this is a passage declaring that it is impossible to be certain about the substantive content of any proposition concerning right, and the contradictory note attached thereto, stating that man can never be justly treated as an animal and that the idea of right demands that all men be led to community life.[2] The question here is not whether these are highly acceptable political principles, but that they are substantive rather than formal and that they are not relativistic.

In fact Stammler derived scores of other substantive implications from his alleged formal postulates, such as the rejection of slavery, despotism, and polygamy; the prohibition of contractual clauses that would restrict freedom of marriage or free choice of residence; and the postulate that the institution of divorce must be recognized.[3]

Stammler's later writings were couched in more strictly formal language.[4] But he never became a relativist; he continued to hold that there were scientifically demonstrable, absolute standards of justice. In this respect we shall revert to his teachings in Chapter VIII below.[5]

[2] *Op.cit.*, 5th ed., p. 172. The note referred to in the text is note 120.

[3] *Die Lehre vom richtigen Recht* (Berlin 1902, 2nd ed. 1926) book 3, pp. 309 ff., especially pp. 424, 434, 576; this work has been translated in the Modern Legal Philosophy Series under the title *The Theory of Justice*.

[4] See *Lehrbuch der Rechtsphilosophie* (Berlin 1922, 3rd ed., 1928); "Rechtsphilosophie" in *Das Gesamte deutsche Recht*, vol. 1 (Berlin 1931) pp. 1–88; and the instructive article in English, "Fundamental Tendencies in Modern Jurisprudence," *Michigan Law Review*, vol. 21 (1923) pp. 623–54, 765–86, and 862–903, especially p. 645. This article contains a rather superficial paragraph on relativism, but an illuminating chapter on historicism.

[5] There is a considerable American literature on Stammler. See especially: W. E. Hocking, *Present Status on the Philosophy of Law and of Rights* (New Haven 1926); Roscoe Pound, "Fifty Years of Jurisprudence" in *Harvard Law Review*, vol. 50 (1937) p. 581, vol. 51 (1938) p. 448; and Morris Cohen, *Law and the Social Order* (New York 1935) pp. 173, 194.

CHAPTER VI

THE RISE OF SCIENTIFIC VALUE
RELATIVISM

1. Birth of the Gulf Doctrine (Logical Separation of Is and Ought)

WE saw in the preceding chapter how the logical fusion of Is and Ought continued deep into the nineteenth century, and that even Kant and John Stuart Mill, who came close to establishing the necessity of logical separation, failed to do so unambiguously since both offered bridges that seemed to span the gulf, bridges grounded on the rocks of Is and allegedly leading to the realm of Ought. We shall see later (Chapter IX) that these constructs—certainly Kant's moral bridge, but possibly also Mill's happiness bridge—can be looked at in such a way as not to be in conflict with the theory of the logical gulf. Yet with neither Kant nor Mill pointing out clearly that there were two different approaches here involved, the one logically forbidden, the other permitted, the necessity of logical separation remained unestablished. It so continued until the end of the nineteenth century, when things finally became clarified.

For some time, owing to circumstances to be dealt with later, the discussion centered in Germany. In the 1860's two of the lesser German philosophical lights, Arnold Kitz (b. 1807) and Julius von Kirchmann (1802–1894), both jurists and neither a professional philosopher, writing independently of each other emphasized the fundamental difference between Is and Ought, but received scant attention. Kitz, in 1864, published a brilliant little essay under the very title "Is and Ought" (*Seyn und Sollen*).[1] His analysis of "Being" anticipated some of the vocabulary that more than sixty years later was to play a role in the writings of existentialists, who did not know him. He aptly discerned "to be," "to be something," and "to be this or that," and contrasted them with "not to be," refusing to give the latter any kind of positive meaning or special status.[2] In particular, however, he distinguished "to be" (*Sein* or, as it was then spelled, *Seyn*) and "ought to be" (*Sollen*). "From the fact," he wrote, "that something *is* may well follow

---

[1] Arnold Kitz, *Seyn und Sollen, Abriss einer philosophischen Einleitung in das Sitten-und Rechtsgesetz*, Frankfurt 1864. Also, *Das Prinzip der Strafe*, Oldenburg, 1874.
[2] *Ibid.*, pp. 65 ff.

that something else *was* or *will be,* but nevermore that something *ought* to be (*sein soll*). It is quite conceivable that something ought to be that, nevertheless, never was, nor now is, or will be in the future." [3] Union between Is and Ought, he said, could be found, not in nature or reason, but only in the will, both man's and God's. Up to this point he was a consistent apostle of logical separation. In the latter part of his paper, where he discussed the union in God's will, he impaired the scientific character of his contribution by failing to draw a line between science and religion, or science and philosophical speculation. But he stuck to logical separation.

Five years later, Julius von Kirchmann, lonely anti-Hegelian fighter for empirical realism in mid-nineteenth-century Germany (see Appendix B), published a book on the fundamental concepts of law and morals, in which he emphasized that the essential meaning of the proposition that something ought to be was its claim to having the Is "subjected" to the Ought, and that therefore it appeared impossible to derive the one from the other; not even Kantian "reason" could bridge the gulf, since reason itself is in the realm of being.[4] He clearly distinguished between the psychological origin of the notion of Ought (Thou Shalt) and its logical character. The psychological origin he saw in the respect felt for the overwhelming power of someone who expressed his will, be it the father, the king, the people, or God. The power may be real or imagined; that had no bearing on the reality of the feeling. But the logical category of Ought was independent of its psychological origin. While Kirchmann did not go so far as to develop a theory of value relativism from his approach, he deserves credit for his unambiguous pronouncement of the need for logical separation.

These occasional proclamations [5] did not yet carry the day, however. In 1882, Wilhelm Windelband (1848–1915), a philosopher of far greater influence in his time, and a leading figure in a back-to-Kant movement, to which he tried to give a progressive turn, pointed in the right direction when he reemphasized the distinction between *Naturgesetze* or physical laws (Is) and Norms (Ought).[6] Like Kant,

[3] *Ibid.,* pp. 74, 75.

[4] J. H. v. Kirchmann, *Die Grundbegriffe des Rechts und der Moral als Einleitung in das Studium rechtsphilosophischer Werke,* Berlin 1869 (2nd ed., 1873), published in *Philosophische Bibliothek,* vol. 11, see in particular pp. 48, 52 ff.

[5] Both were, more briefly, mentioned in H. Kelsen, *Hauptprobleme der Staatsrechtslehre,* Tübingen, 2nd ed. 1923, pp. 7 and 19.

[6] "Normen und Naturgesetze" (1882) in Wilhelm Windelband, *Präludien* (5th ed. 1915) vol. 2, p. 59; "Geschichte und Naturwissenschaften" (1894) *ibid.,* p. 136; "Uber die gegenwaertige Aufgabe der Philosophie" (1907) *ibid.,* pp. 1, 19 ff.; also his address on Kant, "Nach Hundert Jahren" (1904) *ibid.,* pp. 147, 160, 161, 166.

however, he made definite statements on what we ought to do. He ascribed Ought-character not only to ethics but to logic and aesthetics as well. There is a mandatory Thou Shalt, so he taught, which *demands* of us that we acknowledge not only the good but the true and the beautiful also. Without much ado he took the "necessary and general validity" of ultimate Ought-norms in all three fields for granted. This prevented him from elaborating the logical distinction between Is and Ought. With his assumptions made, there followed once more some sort of link between the two realms.

About the turn of the century, Neo-Kantians in Freiburg, Heidelberg, and Marburg took up the basic dualism. Among them was Windelband's former pupil, Heinrich Rickert (1863–1936) of Freiburg and, later, Heidelberg. He was concerned less with the line between Is and Ought than with that between Being (Is, Reality, Existence) and *Meaning*. Reality and Meaning, he said, are distinct realms not to be confused, since Meaning as such is nonreal and nonexistent, although possibly "valid" or "invalid." Whether there was a "third realm," where Reality and Meaning fused, was an issue of metaphysics, not of scientific knowledge. Accordingly, he contrasted natural science (Being-irrespective-of-Meaning) and cultural science (Meaning, and Being-related-to-Meaning).[7]

Now, Meaning is a concept broader than Norm (Ought); every Norm (Ought) incorporates some Meaning, but the converse is not necessarily true. The Ought, Rickert explained, is a "specific way" in which some values "appeal to our interest and cause it to respond."[8] The realm of Ought was not quite inaccessible to our knowledge, he taught. Like Windelband he held that we ought to acknowledge truth; and this we know. For there is one norm (Ought, *Sollen*) whose validity cannot be doubted by anyone: the "transcendent Ought" which demands of us that, within our own thinking and judging, we affirm positively (*bejahen*) our perceptions of what we do perceive. In other words, if we perceive "red" it is demanded of us that we ought to say "yes" in our inner answer to the inner question whether

---

[7] Rickert's views are now best studied in his *System der Philosophie, Erster Teil: Allgemeine Grundlegung der Philosophie*, Tübingen 1921, pp. 101 ff., 149. His main contributions were presented earlier in *Der Gegenstand der Erkenntnis*, Tübingen 1892 (2nd ed. 1904), *Kulturwissenschaft und Naturwissenschaft*, Tübingen 1899 (6th and 7th ed. 1926) and *Die Grenzen der naturwissenschaftlichen Begriffsbildung*, Tübingen 1902 (5th ed. 1929). Windelband, convinced a priori as he was of the general validity of values, considered it paradoxical to call the valid values "nonreal"; see his *Einleitung in die Philosophie*, Tübingen 1914, p. 212 (3rd ed. 1923; tr. "An Introduction to Philosophy" by Joseph McCabe, New York 1921) and Rickert's reply, *System der Philosophie*, p. 136.

[8] *System der Philosophie*, p. 116.

we do perceive "red." Rickert did not—and this is important in our particular context—derive this Ought logically from any Is. On the contrary, he said, it is logically prior to any recognition of what is; no proposition that something is has significance before we have recognized the validity of that transcendent demand. This thesis was the foundation of his "transcendental idealism." But he denied that we could penetrate any farther into the transcendent realm. Although the validity of the transcendent Ought cannot be doubted, he said, its origin cannot be explored by science; any attempt to do so leads beyond science into metaphysics, which is not science.[9]

It is not here our purpose to examine whether Rickert's "transcendent Ought" is indeed beyond any possible doubt as he thought it was. It might be argued, I think, that the inner force which compels us to recognize our perceptions is based not on a transcendent Ought but on a pure psychophysical Must—on the fact, namely, that perceptions leave their marks ("tracks," "grooves") in our cortex and that these marks obstruct subjective attempts to bypass them and to deny our perceptions (see below, Chapter XI, Section 6). But this is not here the issue. I merely want to make plain that Rickert's preoccupation, on the one hand, with the distinction between Is and Meaning rather than Is and Ought, and, on the other, with the absolute validity of some type of transcendent Ought, prevented him from concentrating on the much simpler problem whether it is logically possible to infer some Ought from some Is, or *vice versa*. No doubt he recognized that this could not be done. If every type of Meaning was to be kept strictly separated in logical reasoning from every type of Being, then certainly the specific meaning of Ought was to be kept so separated. But he did not elaborate on this. His first major work had a chapter titled "Is and Ought" (*Sein und Sollen*),[10] in which one would expect to find this logical problem treated; actually, it is not even mentioned.

Contemporaneously with Rickert, however, and more explicitly than he, another German philosopher, the sociologist and logician Georg Simmel (1858–1918) turned his scorn on the logical fusion of Is and Ought. In his magnificent work on ethics of 1892[11] he presented a triple thesis regarding the nature of Ought. In the first place, he wrote, the feeling that one "ought" to do something (*Sollen*) is an original datum (*Urtatsache*) of human experience which, just as the

[9] *Gegenstand der Erkenntnis* (2nd ed.) pp. 116 ff., 125 ff., and *passim. Grenzen der naturwissenschaftlichen Begriffsbildung* (5th ed.) p. 604. Also, *System der Philosophie*, pp. 121, 134.
[10] *Gegenstand der Erkenntnis*, pp. 116–122.
[11] Georg Simmel, *Einleitung in die Moralwissenschaft*, Berlin, 1st vol. 1892, 2nd vol. 1893.

feeling that one "wills" something, "hopes" for something, or "can do" something, and even like the feeling of "being" and "thinking," could not be described to someone who had not himself experienced it. Therefore, there is "no definition of Ought." [12] Secondly, the concept of Ought, *qua* concept, is a merely formal mode of thought, grammatically expressed by an imperative, just as the formal concepts of past and future are grammatically expressed by preteritum and futurum. No particular substantive content can be derived from a formal mode of thought; it lends itself to any type of content, denying itself to none. [13] Thirdly, *"The logical inference from what is to what ought to be, is false in every case."* [14] "In no case can we find out by a logical analysis (*Zergliederung*) of Ought why it has its particular content, nor from the particular content why we ought to do it." [15]

These were the strongest statements yet made in support of the emerging Gulf Doctrine. Simmel elaborated on them as follows. By way of logical deductions, he said, it cannot even be demonstrated that something *is,* in the sense that it exists. That "can merely be experienced and felt, and therefore cannot be deduced from pure concepts, but merely from concepts into which it had previously been incorporated somehow or other." The same was true of Ought:

> That we ought to do something can, if we wish to demonstrate logically, never be proved otherwise than by referring to some other Ought that is presupposed as certain. So conceived it is an original datum, beyond which we can ask no logical questions, though possibly psychological ones. [16]

For the same reason, jurisprudence can prove the justice of its principles "only by demonstrating that they are the logical consequence of ultimate principles which must simply be assumed as right and cannot be proved to be so." And he added that, no matter whether we speak of Is or Ought, "the last we are able to explain [logically] is the last but one." Before we can explain any Ought there must be a moral concept or feeling; "we could perhaps ask, therefore, why we are moral, but by no means why we ought to be moral." [17]

[12] *Op.cit.,* vol. 1, pp. 8, 98, 99.
[13] *Ibid.,* pp. 9, 119; vol. 2, p. 310.
[14] *Op.cit.,* vol. 1, p. 72 (italics added). It would be different only, he said, in case one used the concept of Ought merely as a duplication of the concept of Is (in the sense that all that is also ought to be, which would not tell us anything about what we ought to do as distinct from what we are doing).
[15] *Ibid.,* p. 54.
[16] *Ibid.,* p. 12.
[17] *Ibid.,* p. 16.

Switching from the (impossible) logical explanation to the (entirely feasible) psychological one, Simmel suggested that men may have "old-inherited social instincts," which had their origin in social interrelationships (*Verhältnis zur Allgemeinheit*), or derived from them as from their unconsciously effective original cause.[18] Perhaps the feeling of Ought indicated the operation of human drives that cannot be attributed to egoism and, therefore, cannot be "explained" in the usual meaning of that term in which we accept as an explanation only references to egoistic motives.[19] If looked at apart from its psychological causes, Simmel reflected, the feeling of Ought is nothing but the feeling of one's own *will,* sometimes of a weak will, at other times of a very strong one, but always of some type of will, just as the feeling of temptation is the feeling of one's own will, a weak or a strong one.[20] He used a beautiful metaphor to illuminate the psychological transition:

Just as a tree if hit by a gust of wind redresses itself as soon as the wind subsides, but if constantly exposed to winds blowing in the same direction finally bends itself in that direction and grows that way, so conditions bend man's will in their direction until he adjusts to them, feeling the constant pressure from conditions at first as an Ought and finally as [his own] unwritten will.[21]

Under the impact of Rickert's and Simmel's publications the doctrine of the logical gulf between Is and Ought began to become a scientific commonplace. The sociologist Max Weber and the jurists, Gustav Radbruch, Hans Kelsen, and others,[22] in their writings at the beginning of this century (see below, Sections 2 and 3), accepted the separation as an elementary principle of logic. Weber felt no need to elaborate on it. Radbruch did. He wrote:

Propositions of Ought, value judgments and other judgments, cannot be founded inductively upon statements of Is, but only deductively upon other propositions of like kind. . . .[23] Propositions

[18] *Ibid.,* p. 30.
[19] *Ibid.,* pp. 64, 65.
[20] *Ibid.,* pp. 20, 21.
[21] *Ibid.,* p. 321.
[22] E.g. Hermann Kantorowicz, see below, Section 2; also Kantorowicz and Patterson, "Legal Science—A Summary of Its Methodology" in *Columbia Law Review,* vol. 28 (1928) pp. 679, 683, 684; Barna Horvath, *Rechtssoziologie,* Berlin 1934, pp. 49 ff. Regarding Simmel's influence on the French sociologists, see above, Chapter V, Section 3.
[23] *Rechtsphilosophie* (see Section 3 c, below, on the various editions) 3rd. ed. p. 7; 4th ed. p. 97; Wilk transl. (not used in this book) p. 53.

of Ought can be based only on other propositions of Ought and can be proved only by them. Exactly for this reason ultimate propositions of Ought cannot be proved, are axiomatic, capable not of cognition but only of confession. Wherever there meet in dispute antagonistic contentions about the ultimate propositions of Ought, or antagonistic views of values or *Weltanschauungen,* decision between them cannot be made with scientific precision (*Eindeutigkeit,* unambiguity).[24]

And Kelsen:

The contrast between Is and Ought is formal and logical and as long as one keeps within the limits of formal and logical considerations no road leads from one to the other; the two worlds confronting each other are separated by an *unbridgeable gulf.* Logically the question as to the "why" of some particular Ought can only lead to some other Ought, time and again, just as the question as to the "why" of some Is can only receive as an answer another Is, time and again.[25]

Some European writers tried to adjust the two overlapping dualisms of Is vs. Ought and Being vs. Meaning. Science can deal, they said, either with "nature, free-of-values" (Is), or with "norms, free-of-nature" (Ought), or thirdly, with "nature, related-to-values," that is, nature affected with meaning. Any manmade piece of nature, such as a table, an engine, a cathedral, or a legal code carries a reference to values in itself and can be understood only by looking to this reference. In accord with this analysis they distinguished "natural science," "normative science," and "cultural science," accepting Rickert's term for the third category.[26] But this step from dualism to triadism did not weaken their opposition to inferences in the realm of Ought from premises in the realm of Is.

---

[24] *Ibid.,* 3rd. ed. p. 9; 4th ed. p. 100; Wilk tr. p. 56. Similarly, 1st ed. (*Grundzüge der Rechtsphilosophie,* 1914) pp. 2, 3.

[25] *Über Grenzen zwischen juristischer und soziologischer Methode,* Tübingen 1911, p. 6. Italics not in the original. See similar passages in Kelsen, *What Is Justice?* Berkeley 1957, p. 354, and frequently throughout.

[26] Radbruch, *op.cit.,* 3rd ed. p. 25; 4th ed. p. 118; Wilk tr. p. 69. Hermann Kantorowicz, "Staatsauffassungen" in *Jahrbuch für Soziologie,* vol. 1 (1925) p. 101; Rickert, *System der Philosophie, op.cit.,* p. 149, *Kulturwissenschaft und Naturwissenschaft, op.cit.;* Emil Lask, "Rechtsphilosophie" (see below, Section 3 a); Max Weber, *Wirtschaft und Gesellschaft* (Tübingen 1922; 2nd ed. 1926) p. 3; Barna Horvath, *op.cit.,* p. 54. Compare Talcott Parsons, who, some twenty years later, proposed to distinguish "nature," "action," and "culture," as basic methodological references—not a very convincing alignment of rather incongruent concepts (*The Structure of Social Action,* New York 1937, p. 762.)

Anglo-American literature around the turn of the century paid little if any attention to the logical gulf. Even avowed relativists like Viscount Haldane (1856–1928) [27] and Edvard Westermarck (1862–1939) [28] still failed to mention it in their works on relativity in the nineteen twenties and thirties. The former based his relativism on physico-philosophical reflections, the latter on the fact that "the predicates of all moral judgments, all moral concepts, are ultimately based on emotions, and that . . . no objectivity can come from an emotion"; there are "no moral truths." Most texts on logic neglected the problem. Yet there can be little doubt that, whenever the question is seriously considered in its logical setting, most Anglo-American scholars today would consider inferences from statements in the Is-form to such in the Ought-form logically inconclusive. Some writers have said so explicitly, as did Karl Llewellyn:

> Fusion or confusion of the realms of Is and Ought . . . is rooted with dire firmness in our thinking. . . ."[29] Science does not teach us where to go. It never will. To fuse Is and Ought is to confuse the gradually accumulating semi-permanent data on which any science must rest with the flux of changing opinion as to social objectives—that welter of objectives *any* of which a science can be made to serve.[30]

Stuart Rice, like Simmel, Radbruch, and Kelsen, declared that in order to prove a value one must always refer to another, more general value and that, in the last analysis "the end which is sought must be posited or assumed. It cannot be arrived at by scientific procedure." [31] And R. M. MacIver: "Science itself tells us nothing, just nothing, about the way we *should* act, about the ends we *should* seek." [32] At the round-table "Beyond Relativism in Political Theory," held at the annual meeting of the American Political Science Association, December 1946, general agreement on the logical separation between Is and Ought was expressed at the outset.[33] More references will be given in

---

[27] Richard B. Haldane, *The Reign of Relativity*, London 1921. The only vague allusion to the gulf-problem in this book seems to be the contention on p. 357 that "what ought to be and what is tend to come together."

[28] Edvard Westermarck, *Ethical Relativity*, New York 1932, pp. 60, 288.

[29] Karl Llewellyn, "Legal Tradition and Social Science Method, A Realist's Critique," *Essays on Research in the Social Sciences*, Washington 1931, pp. 89 ff. This passage, p. 98.

[30] *Ibid.*, pp. 101, 102.

[31] Stuart Rice, *Quantitative Methods in Politics*, New York 1928, p. 15.

[32] Robert M. MacIver, *The Pursuit of Happiness. A Philosophy for Modern Living*, New York 1955, p. 173.

[33] See my report in *American Political Science Review*, vol. 41 (June 1947) p. 470.

the next section. Not all twentieth-century thinkers have drawn relativistic conclusions from the need of keeping Is and Ought logically separated, as we shall see in Chapters vii and viii. Nor have all cared to mention that need. But few have attempted explicitly to doubt or to deny it. Their arguments too will be discussed in the polemic part.[34] Here, in the genetic chapters, my only purpose was to relate how the doctrine of the logical gulf between Is and Ought arose and spread.

2. *Birth of Scientific Value Relativism: The Fathers*

Once it had been seen that inferences from Is to Ought could never be validly drawn in a purely logical manner, Scientific Value Relativism was around the corner. But something else was necessary to enforce its acceptance. It had to be recognized (1) that every conscious pursuit of goals or purposes, whether moral, amoral, or immoral, contains elements of evaluation; (2) that every selective evaluation ("better than") of ultimate standards and, therefore, in particular every moral evaluation is either identical with, or at least associated with, ideas or feelings about what ought to be done or approved, whose validity cannot be logically drived from facts; and (3) that the validity of ultimate standards of evaluation is not only logically undemonstrable but cannot be proved in any other scientific manner.

It had always been clear, of course, that human purposes and the evaluations underlying them could be examined and ascertained scientifically as *actual facts,* that is, historically, or as *potential facts,* that is, hypothetically. But value relativism contends, in addition, that science can deal with purposes and evaluations *only* historically or hypothetically, and that means relative to some actual or potential will.

It is generally assumed that credit or blame for value relativism must go to Max Weber, as the theory's inventor. But this is not correct, and Weber himself would have decidedly denied his primary role in generating the doctrine. Simmel, Rickert, and Georg Jellinek preceded him. The decisive role which Simmel played in this matter has been underestimated, owing to the fact that his contributions were not presented as was Weber's basic statement in some compact article, but widely scattered through the two volumes of his essay on ethics.

[34] See Chapters vii, Section 7 (Wertheimer) and viii, Section 5, end (Fuller); also Chapter iii, Section 5 (Rommen).

(a) SIMMEL AND RICKERT

"That we put value on something at all," Simmel wrote, "is, in ultimate analysis, a matter of the will, beyond all deductions." For value "is nothing objective," he continued. This latter statement, as we shall see in Chapter VII, Section 5, went farther than was warranted and necessary for his argument, since the human will may well be influenced by objective factors without thereby losing its subjective character; and it was merely this subjective character Simmel wanted to stress, adding that "neither gold nor silver, neither food nor clothes, have any value by themselves but obtain it only in the subjective process of evaluating them."[1] "All values are merely emotional consequences of certain ideas."[2]

This evaluating activity of the human will, operating subjectively without any possible proof of its ultimate standards, is part of human nature, he held. "Human thinking is after all so constructed (*nun einmal so eingerichtet*) that something ultimate (*irgendein Letztes*) which is to serve as a criterion for everything else, both what is or ought to be, must be presupposed without being proved. This criterion can be made the object of criticism only to the extent that the question may be asked whether it has been carried through consistently or inconsistently."[3] It is impossible "to relieve the determination of the ethical Ought of the contingency (*Zufälligkeit*) of ultimate value-feelings (*letzter Wertgefühle*) and to attach it to some demonstrable rational necessity."[4] This was not meant to deny that the feeling of value could have a nonfortuitous, for example, a divine origin; but its necessity could not be demonstrated rationally.

The core of Simmel's analysis was that science cannot set values. If science attempts to go "normative and teleological" it "needs some purpose given as a fact (*als Tatsache vorgefunden*), which, as science, it cannot itself set." It cannot go beyond the psychological explanation of our choices. "*Science itself never sets a norm (normt nie)* . . . since the questions asked by science are always causal, not teleological."[5]

It is, therefore, a complete misunderstanding if one expects to gain some new Ought (*Sollen*) from a science of ethics. Such a science

---

[1] *Einleitung in die Moralwissenschaft,* as cited, vol. 1, pp. 231, 232; also vol. 2, p. 6.
[2] *Op.cit.,* vol. 1, p. 251.
[3] *Ibid.,* p. 453.
[4] *Op.cit.,* vol. 2, p. 70.
[5] *Op.cit.,* vol. 1, pp. 320–21. Italics added.

can possibly confront (*zusammenhalten*) some given norm with other, equally given, impulses, and show that we can logically pursue only the one or the other but not both. But *science cannot make the choice between the two,* or determine the value which the one or the other must have for us; it *cannot . . . set purposes,* which is always the business of the will, but only determine the means for the achievement of the purposes, or rather—more correctly speaking from the viewpoint of science—explore the causes whose effect would be the desired conditions, which to do is precisely the business of theory.

Therefore, Simmel concludes, every inquiry into ethical norms must either limit itself to an examination of the logical interrelation between their elements, or must "set some other principle as a priori valuable, as the ultimate purpose, and then merely state how far those norms are adequate means for the realization of this purpose."

The pure problem of science is: if such and such purposes and conditions are given, what must we do to realize the former, granting due consideration to the latter. Only the moral legislator, in setting ultimate purposes dogmatically, can say: this shall be so!, leaving proof alone, since the final setting of values is a fact that cuts off any [scientific] criticism. Ethical science, therefore, can but set hypothetical imperatives, in the Kantian sense; it can reveal absolute imperatives only as historical facts, it cannot set them.[6]

In the preface to the second volume Simmel summed up these thoughts in a few graphic passages. Just as an anatomist as such has to render no aesthetic judgments regarding the body on his dissecting table, he wrote there, "just so little has the student of ethical science (*der Ethiker*), as a scientist, to confound the examination of moral phenomena with moral evaluations." The fact that the scholar's own value judgments often agree with those he examines makes a blend of explaining and norm-setting activities quite understandable, indeed; but from this "there arises so much more severely the duty [for the scientist] to sever the scientific task, which is merely to state empirical and hypothetical realities impartially, from the normative one, which is to mold (*gestalten*) reality practically, and that means always onesidedly."[7]

[6] *Ibid.*, pp. 321–323.
[7] *Op.cit.*, vol. 2, p. iv.

Simmel did not use the term "relativity"; but his ideas actually correspond to what is understood in this book by Scientific Value Relativism. It will appear, however, that he understated the role which objective elements play in human value judgments (Chapter VII, Section 5, below) and the importance of the contributions which science, although unable to set values, can render in helping people to choose values, by examining risks, consequences, ulterior purposes, and the like.

Heinrich Rickert was equally unambiguous in his statements that the validity of ethical and aesthetic values can be neither demonstrated nor refuted by science. He conceded that in the *theoretical* field there was one value whose objective validity could be logically demonstrated —the value of truth. "The philosophy of theoretical problems begins with one's recognizing truth as a value," he wrote.[8] But the "objective validity of ethical, aesthetic, religious, and other a-theoretical cultural values is inaccessible (*entzogen*) to any scientific proof." [9] This, he said, followed from the very nature of the nontheoretical values. They would cease to be nontheoretical if their validity could be theoretically supported. We would destroy their character as nontheoretical values. "No one, therefore, who has once understood the specific character (*Eigenart*) of the a-theoretical values can even wish (*wollen*) to have a proof or logical demonstration of their objective validity." [10] He saw in such attempts remnants of an obsolete intellectualism. He called a man "ethical, in the widest sense of the word, if, after recognizing a value as valid [ought] *by free decision,* he does what he ought to do." [11]

As a consequence, Rickert demanded that philosophy, after clarifying the meaning of the various value concepts, finally "establish a system in which all of them find their orderly place." [12] Thus he postulated a neutral type of Scientific Value Relativism, although like Simmel he did not use this name, and although he frankly expressed his own personal belief in "objective" values—unverifiable by science beyond the value of theoretical truth. He was relentless in his emphasis on the difference between facts and values. "Only when we have come

---

[8] *System der Philosophie*, p. 112, also pp. 118, 150. See above, Section 1, and below, Chapters VII, Section 1, and XI.

[9] *Ibid.*, p. 150.

[10] *Ibid.* Similar ideas were expressed in his earlier work, *Grenzen der naturwissenschaftlichen Begriffsbildung* (*op.cit.*, 2nd ed., 1913, pp. 599 ff.).

[11] *System*, p. 327. See below, Chapters VI, Section 3, and XI, Section 3, on the question whether the recognition of values is entirely left to *arbitrary* decision.

[12] *Ibid.*, pp. 150, 155.

to see all values as values can we successfully guard against onesidedly espousing specific values" in science, he insisted.[13]

Here, however, we witness another formidable confusion in terminology. For not only did Rickert fail to call himself a relativist; there is even a chapter headed "Relativismus" in his *Gegenstand der Erkenntnis* which is nothing but one solid indictment of relativism.[14] This is explained by the fact that Rickert called "relativists" only those who denied not alone the demonstrability of specific value judgments (which he himself denied) but even the absolute nature of the demand that we ought to recognize the facts of our perceptions, i.e., who denied also the "truth of simple statements of facts." This denial which, he said, made even statements of facts entirely dependent on a relative and subjective approach—leading ultimately to the contention that "all truth is relative" or that "there is no truth at all"—seemed unbearable and illogical to Rickert; he used against it the old argument that if someone contends that there is no truth then this statement too cannot be true.[15]

William James, who read Rickert's book carefully in both editions, saw in the latter's attack on relativists one directed against his own pragmatism and pluralism. While he generally held Rickert in high esteem, he replied sharply to this presumed attack in the chapter on "Abstractionism and 'Relativism' " in his own *The Meaning of Truth*.[16] There he called Rickert an "absolutist" (p. 265) and the pragmatists "typical relativists" (p. 263). Thus we are here faced with the paradoxical situation that Rickert, now generally referred to as one of the fathers of relativism, himself used that term with contempt, because he averred the absolute duty of truthfulness in our inner recognition of observed facts, and was on this ground called an "absolutist" by James, who possibly misunderstood him, and styled himself, James, a "relativist" because he refused to recognize any absolute truth (see above, Chapter v, Section 6). But there the issue was the cognition of facts and not the validity of value judgments; when it came to value judgments,

---

[13] *Ibid.*, p. 153.

[14] *Gegenstand der Erkenntnis*, 2nd ed., pp. 132–141.

[15] "Relativism . . . as a final 'system' is one of the strangest structures known in the history of philosophy. It can only be psychologically comprehended as the product of a period which dares not look the problem of truth in the face, because it feels instinctively that any serious attempt to solve it will wreck the basis of their fashionable ideas of the day. . . . Compared with relativism, even solipsism is a most reasonable view, because the solipsist can at least consider his own theory true. The relativist cannot even do that, and therefore there has never been a genuine relativist." *Ibid.*, p. 141.

[16] Original edition of 1909 (London, New York), pp. 246 ff. This chapter is omitted in Perry's edition, cited in Chapter v, Section 6.

Rickert was a more outspoken relativist than James, as we have seen.

After all, the reader will understand why in view of this confusion in terminology I have persisted, quite pedantically, using the compound term "Scientific Value Relativism" in pointing to the type of relativism I am dealing with here. Rickert then, let me repeat, was a Scientific Value Relativist, without using that name.

(b) JELLINEK

In the sphere of political science, the first explicit statement of Scientific Value Relativism—again without using the term relativism—occurred in 1900 in the classical *General Theory of the State* (*Allgemeine Staatslehre*) by Georg Jellinek (1851–1911).[17] Political science in the sense of an applied and practical science, he wrote, is a theory of the attainment of certain state ends, and thus a teleological consideration of political phenomena. Therefore, political science has value judgments as its subject. Since these are beyond scientific proof, only inquiries of a relative character can attain scientific merit; that is to say, only inquiries which assume as a hypothesis that a definite end ought to be attained but admit the possibility of a different teleological judgment. The following quotation brings this out neatly:

> Since absolute ends can be demonstrated only by way of metaphysical speculation, no empirical political science complete in itself and endowed with universal convincing power is conceivable. Scientific merit can be attained only by political inquiries of a relative character, that is, inquiries assuming as an hypothesis that a definite end ought to be attained, but necessarily admitting the possibility of a differing teleological judgment (*Beurteilung;* the first ed. had here the term *Betrachtung,* i.e., "view" or "approach"). Therefore political examinations, as a rule, assume a partisan character, and do so the more because the confinement to empirical ends is rarely found, with the result that the contrasting variety of metaphysical ends is added to that of empirical ends and finds expression in the methods of the examinations and their results. Even a cursory glance at political literature teaches us that differences in *Weltanschauungen* (world views) and in convictions about the ultimate purposes of human community life determine the course of a great deal of political research work, and often do so subconsciously.[18]

[17] Berlin, 1st ed. 1900; 2nd ed. 1905; 3rd ed. (substantially unchanged in the pertinent passages) 1914, 5th reprint, 1929.
[18] *Op.cit.,* 1st ed. p. 12; 3rd ed. pp. 13, 14.

In another passage, Jellinek traced the controversies in the principal conceptions of the state back to the conflict between two great *Weltanschauungen*—the individualistic-atomistic way of thinking, and the collectivistic-universalistic.

These few lines of Jellinek's contain the nucleus of the dual thesis of Scientific Value Relativism that the selection of goals depends on value judgments and that the validity of the latter cannot be proved with scientific means.

Strongly as Jellinek expressed this view with regard to politics, he seemed to hesitate to accept it fully with respect to justice. He referred to the "appearance, never quite to be eliminated, that there exists a law which is binding of ethical necessity, and therefore valid because of its inner justice." Thinking in such terms, he observed, seems to be "based on our psychic makeup." But he emphasized that it is impossible to draw reliable conclusions on what is objectively just without engaging in metaphysical speculations beyond the reach of science.[19]

(c) MAX WEBER

Four years later, Max Weber (1864–1920) raised his louder and more generally noted call for scholarly submission to the limits of Scientific Method in his article " 'Objectivity' of Knowledge in Social Science and Social Policy" (1904).[20] In view of the tremendous influence this paper had, and of the superficial and incorrect ideas often expressed about its contents—including misrepresentations by great scholars (see Chapter VII, Section 1)—it is advisable here to insert a full description.

Weber's article was designed to introduce the continued publication of a socio-economic periodical (*Archiv für Sozialwissenschaften und Sozialpolitik*) that had changed its editorial staff. For eighteen years it had been edited by its founder, Dr. Heinrich Braun, a member of the German Social Democratic Party of long standing, in a most

---

[19] The substance or content of this apparent (natural) law, he wrote, "is variable according to time and space, and the conclusion drawn on the objectively just is quite as metaphysical in character as is any dogmatic assertion about an objective ethical force" (*op.cit.*, p. 351).

[20] "Die 'Objektivität' in sozialwissenschaftlicher und sozialpolitischer Erkenntnis," in *Archiv für Sozialwissenschaft und Sozialpolitik*, vol. 19 (Neue Folge, vol. 1, 1904). This essay is also available in Weber's *Gesammelte Aufsätze zur Wissenschaftslehre*, Tübingen 1922, p. 146. After more than forty years an English translation by Edward A. Shils and Henry A. Finch was published under the title " 'Objectivity' in Social Science and Social Policy," *Max Weber on the Methodology of the Social Sciences*, The Free Press of Glencoe, Illinois, 1949, p. 49. The omission of "knowledge" (*Erkenntnis*) in the title is misleading. Otherwise, the translation is ably done, but contains many misprints, especially for "casual" for "causal." It is here used with slight changes.

liberal spirit of editorial policy.[21] None of the three new editors, Max Weber, Werner Sombart, and Edgar Jaffe, was a Social Democrat (Jaffe joined the party later) although all three had an open mind toward socialist thought. Hence they felt it necessary to clarify their editorial policy and to state their conception of science, for, as the first sentence of Weber's article said: "When a social science journal, and especially one that deals also with social policy, appears for the first time or passes into the hands of a new editorial board, it is customary to ask about its line (*Tendenz*)."

What the article actually did was to lay down the principles of Scientific Value Relativism, without ever using this name or even the term "relativism." It turned immediately to this subject. Even in the prefatory note Max Weber remarked at once that the agreement of the three editors included in particular "insistence on the rigorous distinction between empirical knowledge and value judgments as here understood." But he characteristically inserted the parenthetical observation, "naturally without claiming to present anything new therewith." "We are attempting only to apply the well-known results of modern logic to our own problem," he added. "Those who know the work of modern logicians—I cite only Windelband, Simmel, and for our purpose particularly Heinrich Rickert—will immediately notice that everything of importance in this essay is tied up with their work."

The article proper began with stating that the purpose of the journal ever since its establishment had been education in judgments on practical social problems and criticism of practical social policy. In spite of this it had firmly adhered, from the beginning, to its intention "to be an exclusively scientific journal and to proceed only with the methods of scientific research." Are these two purposes compatible? Weber asked. "What has been the meaning of value judgments found in the pages of the *Archiv* . . . ? What are the standards governing these judgments? What is the validity of the value judgments which are uttered by the critic, for instance, or on which a writer recommending a policy bases his arguments for that policy? In what sense, if the criterion of scientific knowledge is to be found in the 'objective' validity of its results, has he remained within the sphere of *scientific* discussion?"

In answering, Weber pointed to the fact that the clear distinction between knowledge of what is and what ought to be had long been

[21] See Julie Braun-Vogelstein, *Ein Menschenleben*, Tübingen 1932, especially about the *Archiv*, pp. 101 ff. and 185 ff. Its original name had been *Archiv für soziale Gesetzgebung und Statistik*.

hampered by two views that were widely held about the economic life of society, namely, first, that it was governed by immutable natural laws, and more recently, that it was ruled by an unambiguous evolutionary principle. Accordingly, what was normatively right was held to be identical in the former case with the "immutably *existent*" and in the latter with the "inevitably *emergent*." Even today, he stated, "the confused opinion that economics does and should derive value judgments from a specifically 'economic point of view' has not disappeared." This view the journal must reject, he argued. "It must do so because, in our opinion, it can never be the task of an empirical science to provide binding norms and ideals from which directives for immediate practical activity can be derived."

As Max Weber's name has become a trademark for "value-free science" it is important to stress that the emphasis of his article was rather on the methods by which science *can* deal with value judgments than on full abstention. "What is the implication of this proposition?" he asked after the statement just quoted. And he answered: *"It is certainly not that value judgments are to be withdrawn from scientific discussion in general. . . .* Practical action and the aims of our journal would always reject such a proposition." This was followed by the fundamental statement that *"criticism is not to be suspended in the presence of value judgments.* The problem is rather: what is the meaning and purpose of the scientific criticism of ideals and value judgments?" [22] It is this question to which the main part of his analysis addressed itself.

Weber's argument ran as follows, and its significance justifies literal quotation:

All serious reflection about the ultimate elements of meaningful human conduct is oriented primarily in terms of the categories "end" and "means." We desire something concretely either "for its own sake" or as a means of achieving something else which is more highly desired. *The question of the appropriateness of the means for achieving a given end is undoubtedly accessible to scientific analysis.* Inasmuch as we are able to determine (within the present limits of our knowledge) which means for the achievement of a proposed end are appropriate or inappropriate, we can in this way estimate the chances of attaining a certain end by certain available means. In this way we *can indirectly criticize the setting of the end* itself as prac-

---

[22] Italics not in the original.

tically meaningful (on the basis of the existing historical situation) or as meaningless with reference to existing conditions.[23]

The last passage hinted at the category of impossibility, to which we shall return in Chapter XII of this book. Weber did not elaborate on it, but turned at once to the most important function of a critical discussion of value judgments and of ends and means, namely, the causal examination of consequences. Whenever it appears possible to reach a proposed end, he said,

> we can determine (naturally within the limits of our existing knowledge) the *consequences* which the application of the means to be used will produce in addition to the eventual attainment of the proposed end. . . . We can then provide the acting person with the ability to *weigh* and *compare* the undesired as over against the desired [24] consequences of his action.

This led him to the question of what Americans are wont to call "the price we pay." In Weber's words:

> Thus we can answer the question: what will the attainment of a desired end "cost" in terms of the predictable loss of other values.

He added that in the vast majority of cases every goal that is striven for does cost, or may cost, something in this sense. Therefore, "the weighing of the goal in terms of the incidental consequences of the action which realizes it cannot be omitted from the deliberation of persons who act with a sense of responsibility." However, the making of the decision itself—

> is not a task which science can undertake; it is rather the task of the acting, willing person: he weighs and chooses from among the values involved according to his own *conscience* and his personal view of the world.

In three more ways, according to Weber, science can help a man make his choice, in addition to examining the adequacy of means and the consequences of action. First, science can make the acting person realize that every action, and naturally also every inaction, in view

---

[23] Italics not in the original.
[24] The Shils-Finch translation, using the terms "undesirable" and "desirable" here, is incorrect. Weber spoke, quite logically, only of consequences that were actually undesired (*ungewollt,* not willed) as distinct from those actually desired (*gewollt*), advisedly avoiding the term *wünschenswert* (desirable), which would have involved a value judgment. See Chapter V, Section 7, above, on Mill.

of its consequences implies "the espousal of certain values and here-
with (what is today so willingly overlooked) the rejection of certain
others." Second, science can also make the choosing person see the
"significance" (*Bedeutung*) of what he is after, the "ideas" that either
do or may underlie the concrete end. He considered it one of the
most important tasks of any science that deals with man's cultural
life to arouse a fuller understanding of the "ideas" for which men
struggle. He admitted that the methods to be used in this effort could
not simply be "inductions" in the usual sense. But this task, he said,
cannot be omitted because "the historical power of ideas in the development of social life has been and still is so great."

Third, Weber said, science can to a certain extent judge evaluations
critically according to their consistency and by laying bare the final
axioms from which they are derived. This analysis was only formal,
to be true, but through it science could assist the choosing person in
becoming aware of the "ultimate standards of value which he does
not make explicit to himself or which he must presuppose in order
to be logical."

Yet here is the end of what science can do, according to Weber:

> The elevation of these ultimate standards, which are manifested in
> concrete value judgments, to the level of explicitness, is the utmost
> that the scientific treatment of value judgments can do without enter-
> ing into the realm of speculation. As to whether the person express-
> ing these value judgments *ought* to adhere to these ultimate stand-
> ards is his personal affair; it involves will and *conscience,* not em-
> pirical knowledge.

He summed up the essence of what he had said, in one sentence:
"An empirical science cannot tell anyone what he *ought* to do, but
rather what he *can* do, and under certain circumstances what he wishes
to do."

With all his insistence on the limitations of science, Max Weber
never ceased personally to *believe* in ultimate values, nor did he ever
underrate the importance of such belief for human personality and human dignity. He spoke of these aspects with great candor and warmth.
We do regard those innermost elements of the personality, those highest and ultimate value judgments that determine our conduct and give
meaning and significance to our life, as "objectively" valuable, he said.
"We can indeed espouse these values only when they appear to us as
valid, as derived from our highest values, and when they are de-

veloped in the struggle against the difficulties which life presents." Only on the assumption of belief in the validity of values is the attempt to espouse value judgments meaningful. He repeated, however, that "to judge the validity of such values is a matter of *faith*," and not of science.

We have "eaten of the tree of knowledge," he continued, and an epoch which has eaten of that tree must know "that we cannot learn the *meaning* of the world from the results of its analysis, be it ever so perfect; it [our epoch] must rather be capable of creating this meaning itself." Our epoch must recognize

> that general views of life and of the universe can never be the products of increasing empirical knowledge, and that the highest ideals, which move us most forcefully, always are formed only in the struggle with other ideals which are [or may be] just as sacred to others as ours are to us.[25]

Weber ended up by calling for a distinction of arguments that appeal (1) to our emotional enthusiasm, (2) to our conscience, and (3) to our "capacity and need for analytically ordering empirical reality in a manner which lays claim to *validity* as empirical truth." The differences between these three arguments he called "unbridgeable".

Yet he did not go so far as to assert, and felt rather "completely free of the prejudice which asserts," that all reflections on culture which go beyond the analysis of empirical data in order to "interpret the world metaphysically" can, because of their metaphysical character, fulfill "no useful cognitive task." He did not explain what cognitive task that might be (see below Chapter VII, Section 3), only to repeat that such truth alone is *scientific* as can claim, even for a man of different culture, "the validity appropriate to an analysis of empirical reality." If this was a hint at a possible distinction to be made between "science" and other sources of "knowledge" (see Chapter II, Section 7, above, and VII, Section 3, below), Max Weber did not elaborate the point.

In concluding the editorial comment Weber stated that the editors neither would nor could deny themselves or others the opportunity of expressing the ideals which motivated them in terms of value judgments. But in doing that all contributors must keep the readers and themselves sharply aware of the standards by which they judge reality, he warned; if they did so, then the confrontation of different standards of values in criticism could indeed be useful.

[25] See below, Section 5b on the similar phrase used by Oliver W. Holmes.

All the foregoing was condensed in the first section, covering no more than fifteen pages of Weber's article.[26] There followed a much longer second part,[27] in which Weber displayed his stimulating ideas—not necessarily shared by his two coeditors—about the construction of "ideal types" (*Idealtypen*) of historical phenomena or developments as a useful tool for understanding and describing reality. But he made it quite clear that these ideal types were mere constructs of the mind and could never be passed on as normative standards. This section, full of genius as it is, does not fall into the ambit of the present chapter (see above, Chapters I, Section 4 and II, Section 6).

Weber later resumed the discussion of "value-free" science, especially in his lecture on "The Meaning of *Wertfreiheit* [literally, value-free-ness, or abstention from value judgments; freely translated as "ethical neutrality" by Shils and Finch, *op. cit.*] in the Sociological and Economic Sciences," delivered in 1913 and published in the philosophical journal *Logos* in 1917.[28] A few words will be added here on this essay, although it appeared later than some of the papers to be discussed in the next section of this chapter. It is noteworthy in our context also because of the protest Weber raised here against the use of the term "relativism" with regard to his theory, a point to which we shall return in the "Excursus on the Term Relativism" at the end of this chapter. As regards the functions which a strictly scientific discussion of value judgments can perform, Weber presented them now (in highly involved language, here simplified) in the following order:

1. Elaboration of the ultimate value axioms from which evaluations

---

[26] Pp. 146–161 of the German reprint in *Gesammelte Aufsätze,* and pp. 49–63 of the translation, cited above.

[27] Erroneously designated as No. III in the Shils-Finch translation.

[28] "Der Sinn der 'Wertfreiheit' der soziologischen und ökonomischen Wissenschaften," *Logos,* vol. 7 (1917), reprinted in *Gesammelte Aufsätze zur Wissenschaftslehre* (Tübingen 1922) p. 451, translated in Shils and Finch, *Max Weber on the Methodology of the Social Sciences,* cited above. It will be helpful for the reader who uses the Shils-Finch translation, if he corrects the following errors:

Page 12, first sentence of last paragraph should read: "At first, I would like to make a few remarks against the view that *the adherents of scientific neutrality in ethical questions think* the mere existence of historical and individual variations in evaluations proves the necessarily 'subjective' character of ethics." The omission of the italicized passage in the Shils-Finch translation distorts the sense of the sentence in its context.

Page 15, line 16 from bottom, should read that certain aims, considered valuable, for instance in politics, can be "realized only by one who takes ethical *guilt* upon himself." Translation of *Schuld* with "responsibility" instead of "guilt" alters the meaning.

Page 17, line 2. The words "the recognition of autonomous, extra-ethical spheres" should read "the recognition of autonomous, extra-ethical *value* spheres."

Page 17, line 5 from bottom, should read that a genuine axiology could not overlook the fact "that no 'system' of values . . . is able to handle the crucial issue," rather than that "a system of 'values' is unable" to handle it. The stress is here on "system" rather than on "values."

are derived, and examination whether these axioms are consistent in themselves.

2. Deduction from the respective axioms of their implications for other value judgments.

3. Examination of the factual consequences which the practical realization of the adopted value judgments must have because of (a) the indispensable means, or (b) the undesired "by-products" (*Nebenfolgen*); which examination may, in turn, lead to findings on the impossibility or improbability of attaining the desired end, or to a reconsideration of the value judgment because of the undesired by-products.

4. The uncovering of collisions in value judgments that had not been taken into account.[29]

Comparison shows that there is nothing included here that had not been contained in the earlier paper. The general argument, however, was enriched by additional points; in particular, by a vigorous attack on the acceptance of "agreement" as a substitute for scientific proof, a short-cut that has remained a favorite stand-by to the present day in all discussions on scientific relativism. Wrote Weber:

> What we must vigorously oppose is the view that one may be scientifically satisfied with the conventional self-evidentness of very widely accepted value-judgments. The specific function of science, it seems to me, is just the opposite: namely, what is conventionally considered self-evident becomes problematic to science.[30]

Furthermore, Weber turned his most acid criticism on the frequent illogical attempts to derive the validity of alleged values from some historical *trend* toward their realization. He devoted considerable space to this question. But these and other details added little to the basic concepts that had been established in his 1904 article. Incidentally, the second essay showed once more Weber's close reliance on Heinrich Rickert, in particular on the latter's fundamental distinction between concepts that can be understood only by their inner reference to some value (*wertbezogene Begriffe,* value-related concepts) and concepts that include no reference to values.[31]

---

[29] Summarized from *Gesammelte Aufsätze, op.cit.,* p. 472. The Shils-Finch translation (p. 20) is hard to understand here. Translation of *Nebenfolgen* as "repercussions" is misleading. "By-products," I think, is both more literal and more in line with what Weber meant.

[30] *Op.cit.,* p. 464; Shils-Finch tr., p. 13, deviating in part.

[31] The Shils-Finch translation of *wertbezogen* as "value-relevant" instead of "related-to-values" or "value-related" (see Section 1, above) is misleading. The same mistranslation mars the analysis of Weber's thoughts in T. Parsons' *The Structure of Social Action* and in H. Becker's *Through Values to Social Interpretation.*

A year before his death, Weber reverted to the topic of values in one of his most admired papers, "Wissenschaft als Beruf," an address delivered before students in 1919 and published posthumously.[32] He repeated that "politics does not belong in the classroom of a university," neither on the side of the students nor on that of the professor, "least of all when he deals with political subjects scientifically." Instead, the truly scientific teacher,

> when speaking of democracy, for instance, will discuss its various forms, will analyze the way they function, will inquire what consequences for the conditions of life the one or the other has, will then oppose to them the other, the non-democratic forms . . . and try to get so far that the student is able to find the point from which *he, out of his* ultimate ideals, can take his stand (*Stellung nehmen kann*). But the genuine teacher will be careful not to impose on the student from the lectern any decision, either explicitly or by suggestion; to do the latter, by (ostensibly) 'letting the facts speak for themselves,' is of course the most disloyal behavior.[33]

He could demonstrate, Weber said, from the works of historians that whenever they brought their own value judgments into the picture their complete understanding of the facts ended. A good teacher's "first task is to teach his students to recognize uncomfortable facts (*unbequeme Tatsachen*), such I mean as are uncomfortable for their partisan opinions." [34]

In the course of the paper Weber compared conflicting ultimate values to ancient gods who, "disenchanted and, therefore, now in the nature of impersonal forces, arise from their tombs, striving for power over our lives and engaging once more in their eternal fight among themselves." [35] He resorted to this metaphor several times. "How one will go about the business of deciding 'scientifically' between the value of the French and of the German *Kultur,* I don't know. It's just the ancient gods fighting each other, for ever and ever." [36] Of course, Weber stressed again what services science can perform in dealing with values, cursorily repeating the points made in his former writings;

---

[32] *Gesammelte Aufsätze zur Wissenschaftslehre* (*op.cit.*) pp. 524–55. Not included in Shils-Finch, but separately translated in H. H. Gerth and C. W. Mills, ed., *Science as a Vocation*, New York 1946 (not here used).

[33] Pp. 542–43.

[34] Pp. 544–45. See below, Chapters VII, Section 3, and VIII, Section 13, on the difference of opinion on historical evaluations between Max and Alfred Weber.

[35] P. 547.

[36] P. 545.

this time, he especially stressed the scientific task of laying bare the "fundamental philosophical position" (*weltanschauliche Grundposition*), or the several such positions, from which some specific stand derives. If you decide in favor of one such fundamental position, he said to his hearers, the scientist must tell you that "figuratively speaking, you are serving this god and *offending that other one.*" [37] He called it a "basic fact" (*Grundsachverhalt*) that life "only knows the eternal fight of these gods with one another" and the "incompatibility of, and therefore the impossibility of settling (*Unaustragbarkeit*) the struggle among, fundamental viewpoints of life, and hence the necessity to make one's personal decision among them." [38] Only a prophet or a saviour—not science—can answer the question which gods we should serve. If that prophet or saviour "is not there, or if his pronouncements are no longer believed, then you will surely not force him down to earth through thousands of professors who as little prophets in their class rooms try to relieve him of his role." [39] In the last sentence of the entire speech there occurred another reference to Weber's figurative polytheism of values; waxing poetic rather than mystical, I think, he now spoke of "demons" rather than gods. Everyone, he said, must "find and obey the demon who holds the threads of his life." [40] We shall come back to this passage in the last section of this chapter.

The same address is noteworthy for the strong emphasis put by Weber on the role—discussed above in Chapter 1, Section 1—played by imagination and productive ideas in scientific work. "Some good idea must occur to man (*es muss dem Menchen etwas einfallen*), and indeed the correct idea, before he can achieve anything of value in science." [41] But he warned that "the good idea (*der Einfall*) normally presents itself only on the basis of very hard labor." Occurrence of a good idea is "no substitute for labor, nor is labor a substitute for the good idea, any more than is passionate zeal; both together may allure the idea, but it comes when it listeth and not when we like." [42] And he referred to the great jurist, Jhering, who said the best ideas came to him on the couch while smoking a cigar, and to the great physicist

[37] P. 550. Weber's emphasis.
[38] *Ibid.*
[39] P. 551.
[40] Howard Becker, *Through Values to Social Interpretation,* Durham, N.C., 1950, p. 165, n. 73, translates *Dämon* by "inner urge" or "genius," which may indeed render the meaning better than the English "demon."
[41] P. 531.
[42] Pp. 532–34.

and inventor, Helmholtz, who used to get his best ideas on strolls, walking up a slowly rising path. At any rate, Weber summed up, the *Einfall* plays no smaller role in science than in art.

3. *The Jurists*

(a) LASK, LINK BETWEEN PHILOSOPHERS AND LAWYERS

Rickert was a philosopher; Jellinek, although member of the Faculty of Law, primarily a political scientist; Max Weber, economist and sociologist. Their relativistic writings made no more than fleeting reference to jurisprudence. But the spark leaped quickly to the neighbor's house in Heidelberg, fanned by a young philosopher's essay on the philosophy of law.

If Jellinek's 1900 book still left some doubt about the relativity of justice, no such hesitation could be found in *Rechtsphilosophie*, published in 1905 by Emil Lask (1875–1915).[1] Fated to die early in action during World War I, this promising pupil of Rickert in Heidelberg wrote that it "would be futile to attempt a universal definition of justice. For since this term (justice) merely predicates the very absoluteness and a-priori nature of right (*des Rechts*), all those demands are condensed therein that are made on law according to the various *Weltanschauungen*."[2] Under Rickert's influence he urged strict separation between scientific inquiries in the realms of Is and of Meaning. "One can take no step ahead in the methodology of jurisprudence unless one first takes account of the methodological dualism to which all research on right and justice is subject and which one may rightly call the *ABC* of juridical methodology," he said.[3] In this context he used the phrase of the "infinite gulf that lies between Meaning and Being"[4] (see Chapter III, Section 2 above).

Lask's essay was dominated by the idea that there might be ultimate values which were not personal. While the Kantian tradition had derived all other values from that of the individual as an ethical personality, Lask suggested that social values might have another, an independent source. In this context he coined the term "transpersonal"

---

[1] Emil Lask, *Rechtsphilosophie*, in W. Windelband (ed.) *Die Philosophie im Beginn des Zwanzigsten Jahrhunderts* (2 vols., Heidelberg 1904–05), vol. 2 (1905); also in Lask, *Gesammelte Schriften*, Tübingen 1923–24, vol. 1; able Engl. transl. by Kurt Wilk in vol. 4 of *20th Century Legal Philosophy Series* (Cambridge, Mass., 1950). I have used my own translation.

[2] *Op.cit.*, p. 24.

[3] *Ibid.*, p. 31.

[4] *Ibid.*, p. 11.

values, later taken up by Radbruch and others. Transpersonal values, according to Lask, "set an objective (*sachlichen,* non-personal) type of value over against the personal one."

If justice is really understood to express some specific . . . idea, then the mere introduction of this notion breaks fundamentally through the exclusive evaluation of the personality, toward an idealization of the social life. Therefore, every philosophy of justice, even that of Kantianism and also that of Kant himself, contains the rudiments of a striving beyond personalism in social philosophy.[5]

(b) KANTOROWICZ

The decisive steps on the road to scientific relativism in jurisprudence were made by Hermann Kantorowicz (1877–1940), then in Freiburg, and especially by Gustav Radbruch (1878–1949) in Heidelberg. Of the two friends, Kantorowicz was the more passionate and fighting spirit, fighting even when the fight was for neutrality, Radbruch the wise, perseverant, and judge-like thinker.

"Science cannot spare anybody the trouble of choosing among the various viewpoints," Kantorowicz wrote in a paper of 1908 on comparative criminal law, the first legal paper I have been able to find, apart from Lask's, that espouses modern scientific relativism.[6] Yet science need neither take sides nor abdicate, he continued in Weber's footsteps. On the contrary, "in demonstrating the consequences of each viewpoint science can help everyone to find the one which is really adequate to his nature, instead of persuading him to accept the subjective viewpoints of the individual theorists, as is the case today." He urged the theorist to stay well within this neutral and detached attitude; in so doing he waxed quite enthusiastic about relativism, not aware of the misleading connotations of the term that made Rickert and Weber avoid the word (see Section 7, below). "As practical lawyers," Kantorowicz wrote, "we have long been accustomed to being conscientious trustees of other peoples' interests. As theorists we must, in severe self-discipline, assume the corresponding procedure, that is, relativism." And he went on:

Only through relativism, confining itself strictly to theory, will our science become a science. Only through relativism, sufficiently limit-

[5] *Ibid.,* p. 24.
[6] "Probleme der Strafrechtsvergleichung," *Monatsschrift für Kriminalpsychologie und Strafrechtsreform,* vol. 4 (Heidelberg 1907–08) pp. 65, 102–03.

ing the field from the outset, can results of general validity be attained. Only through relativism will the insolvable controversy on ultimate value judgments be eliminated to make room for the only worthy controversy—that on facts and relations. Only through relativism will the pernicious impulses of our discussions become their harmless topics. Only through relativism will "normative science," that fruitless hobby of zealots, become the "science of the normative." [7]

This eulogy, despite its emphatic use of the term "relativism," was basically in keeping with Weber's views, except that Weber would never have said that the controversy on facts and relations was the "only worthy controversy." For he thought it imperative that science should promote the understanding of "ideas" about which the struggle revolves—not just of their consequences but of the ideas themselves. Kantorowicz would hardly have denied that, but forgot to say so.

As to neutrality, Kantorowicz conceded, as had Weber, that the theorist could not be forbidden to take sides in the fight for legislation if he so desired, provided this did not lead him "in the manner of the objectivists to consider his view-point as the only correct one and to deny all other potentialities, or, in the manner of the subjectivists, to consider it the only interesting one and to pass over all others." [8] Yet he favored neutrality, urging the scholar to "keep strictly neutral and not to allow his basic conviction with regard to legal philosophy to come into the open any more than his political or religious convictions." [9]

Kantorowicz had to leave Germany in 1933. He joined the Graduate Faculty at the New School for Social Research in New York and later accepted a call to Cambridge, England, where he died.

(c) RADBRUCH

Whereas Kantorowicz had not proceeded to integrate relativistic ideas into a systematic philosophy of law, Gustav Radbruch did, and thereby became the head of the twentieth-century school of Scientific Value Relativism in legal and political philosophy, in particular after Max Weber's death (1920) and until his own passing almost thirty years later (1949). His *Grundzüge der Rechtsphilosophie* were pub-

[7] *Op.cit.*
[8] *Ibid.*
[9] "Der Strafgesetzentwurf und die Wissenschaft" in the same periodical, vol. 7 (1910–11) pp. 257, 265. See also his essay *Zur Lehre vom richtigen Recht*, Berlin 1909, critical of Rudolf Stammler (pp. 23 ff., 37).

lished in 1914 and reprinted unchanged in 1922. Considerably amplified, they appeared in a third edition (1932) under the title *Rechtsphilosophie* and were finally republished without essential changes
after the author's death by one of his ablest disciples in 1950.[10] Full of
penetrating and suggestive observations, the book, from its third edition on, offered the first and to the present day the only system to be
fully developed on the basis of neutral relativism.

Radbruch started out from differences between Ought and Is and
from the impossibility of proving propositions of Ought. This methodological discussion, from which I quoted in Section 1 above, led him to
the conclusion that legal philosophy, whenever it goes beyond examinations of methods and tries to "build up a system based on definite
value judgments, has to give up any scientific claim to universal
validity"; and that, therefore, if legal philosophy wishes to proceed
beyond the arbitrary presentation of individual systems, there is no
other choice than that of "developing a *system of systems* without deciding among them. To do this then, is the task of relativism in legal
philosophy." [11] Any other method can attain only illustrative significance.

Radbruch did not deny the value of subjective philosophies of law,
however. The human urge for knowledge, he wrote, will lead time
and again to new attempts "to break through this relativistic self-
denial." Relativism, he assures us, "welcomes" such attempts as a
clarification of an individual opinion and as the "personality-impreg-
nated illustration of one of the systematic possibilities." In the absence
of such illustrations a relativistic philosophy of law "would have to
remain a colorless and shapeless realm of shadows." But all this did
not affect his scientific position. "Relativism," he warned, "must insist
on rejecting the presumptuous claim to universal validity of such
attempts, and show that they are conditioned on quite definite hypotheses of *Weltanschauung*." [12]

In building up his "system of systems" Radbruch, as mentioned above

---

[10] First ed., Leipzig 1914; 2nd ed., unchanged, 1922; 3rd ed., revised and enlarged, 1932; 4th
ed., after the author's death, with 77 pp. introduction and 16 pp. glossary by Erik Wolf, Stuttgart
1950; 5th ed., essentially unchanged, 1956. The 4th and 5th eds. include several footnotes taken
from Radbruch's handwritten drafts, four of his postwar articles, and a bibliography. An excellent
translation of the 3rd ed. by Kurt Wilk was published as vol. 2 of *20th Century Legal Philosophy
Series* by Harvard University Press, 1950. I am using my own translations. On the 3rd ed., see
Roscoe Pound, "Fifty Years of Jurisprudence," *Harvard Law Review*, vol. 51 (1938), and Anton-
Hermann Chroust, "The Philosophy of Law of Gustav Radbruch," *Philosophical Review*, vol. 53
(1944) pp. 23–45.

[11] 3rd ed. p. 25; 4th ed. p. 117; Wilk transl. p. 69.

[12] *Ibid.*

in Chapter IV, Section 5, tried to classify all possible ideas on ultimate values. "There are in the whole reach of the empirical world only three kinds of things that are capable of having absolute value—human individual personalities, human collective personalities, human works," he wrote.[13] He did not prove this contention; he merely stated it. Yet the very formulation he used is reminiscent of Kant's statement on what he, Kant, considered the only absolute value—the individual as an end-in-himself. Unless one accepted the individual as an absolute value, Kant said—and this was his main proof—"nothing of absolute value could be found anywhere."[14] According to Jellinek and Lask, as we have seen, one more absolute value could be imagined—the group; and according to Radbruch a third one—human works, *Kultur*. Such claims to exhaustive classification are inconsistent with Scientific Value Relativism, as shown in Chapter IV; but here we are concerned with the historical sequence of ideas rather than with their accuracy.

Radbruch christened the three as "individual," "collective," and "work" values; the views corresponding them he called "individual," "supra-individual," and "trans-personal" (see Chapter IV, Section 6). The unique feature of his work, first developed in the third edition, was his examination, from each of these three basic viewpoints, of all the fundamental topics of legal philosophy, including the distinction between private and public law, and the concepts of the "person" in legal relations, of property, of contract, of matrimony, of penal law, of the death penalty, and of the law of nations.[15] In so doing he idealized all three sets of values and led them to heights where they almost cease to be antagonistic principles and approach a mystical transmutation from one to the other. The highest prize attainable for an individual, that of becoming a "personality," man cannot win by just striving to become one, but only by forgetting about self and engaging in honest struggle for the interests of others, or of the group, or for transpersonal values. Likewise, the supra-individualist (collectivist) cannot succeed unless he labors for individual and for transpersonal values, and the transpersonalist not unless he is inspired by individual and group values.

This mutual interpenetration of ultimate values again prompts the question, raised in Chapter IV, Section 5, whether it should not be pos-

[13] *Ibid.*, 3rd ed., p. 51; 4th ed., p. 147; Wilk tr., p. 91.
[14] *Grundlegung der Metaphysik der Sitten* in *Gesammelte Schriften* (Akademie ed.) vol. 4, p. 428; Friedrich transl., pp. 140 ff.
[15] *Rechtsphilosophie*, 3rd. ed., pp. 122, 128, 132, 141, 159, 169, 191; 4th ed., pp. 224 ff.; Wilk tr., pp. 152 ff.

sible to construct some higher level of union above Radbruch's three categories. Eduard Spranger, in 1948,[16] did indeed suggest that all three views were one-sided and that the "dialectic" conflict among them must be resolved within some higher union, although one that was not without tension. This, no doubt, is what religious faith and philosophical speculation will always postulate. But Radbruch wisely stopped where he did. For as long as we are to keep within the limitations of science in the sense of intersubjectively transmissible (verifiable) knowledge, we cannot force upon others an acceptance of our personal conception, whether religious or philosophical, of the way in which the three—and all other possible—views of highest values are to be united: we cannot do so with scientific means, although every serious person will try to find the unity for himself and may try to persuade others to follow him.

Radbruch—not of Jewish descent—was among the first professors in Heidelberg to be dismissed in 1933 after Hitler's ascent to power. He lived in "inner exile" in Heidelberg, interrupted only by one short visit in France (1934) and a longer one in England (1935–1936), until the collapse of the regime. Then he was reestablished on his old university chair, and his home became a kind of national shrine until his death in 1949. Under the impact of totalitarian experience he tried in several ways to overcome relativism. To these attempts we shall turn in Chapter VIII. But when he prepared the fourth edition of his *Rechtsphilosophie* he saw no way to incorporate his later thoughts on the subject without destroying the historically unique character of his main work. So he planned to leave it unchanged, except for some added notes. He died before executing this plan, which was ably and reverently carried through by Professor Erik Wolf, who added several postwar articles of Radbruch's in the appendix and prefaced the book with a thorough discussion of the master's life and work.[17]

(d) KELSEN

Further support came to scientific relativism in its formative stage from Hans Kelsen (b. 1881) in his first great book *Chief Problems of the Theory of the State,* published in 1911,[18] which began with the

---

[16] *Universitas,* vol. 3 (1948) p. 410.

[17] Another excellent analysis of the totality of Radbruch's philosophical thinking on law and justice, with the emphasis on the latest period, was presented a year later by Fritz von Hippel, *Gustav Radbruch als rechtsphilosophischer Denker,* Heidelberg 1951. See also Karl Engisch, *Gustav Radbruch als Rechtsphilosoph,* Heidelberg 1949, and now again Eric Wolf, "Revolution or Evolution in Gustav Radbruch's Legal Philosophy" in *Natural Law Forum,* vol. 3 (1958) pp. 1–23.

[18] Hans Kelsen, *Hauptprobleme der Staatsrechtslehre,* Tübingen 1911; 2nd ed. 1923. *Allgemeine Staatslehre,* Berlin 1925.

statement that no Ought can be derived from any Is. Kelsen entered the scene from the outset as both a positivist and a relativist. This was a novel situation. When nineteenth-century positivists limited their attention to the positive law they did so because they recognized sovereignty as the only source of valid law. They were not necessarily relativists with regard to the principles of justice that ought to control legislation, as we saw (Chapter v, Section 3, c) in the case of Austin, who was an absolutist in the transpositive sphere. It was different with Kelsen. His positivism rested on his relativistic scientific conviction. When some twenty years later (1934) he published his book on *The Pure Theory of Law* [19] he began it with the statement "The Pure Theory of Law is a theory of positive law," [20] reminiscent of the passage with which Austin had begun his *Lectures on Jurisprudence:* "The matter of jurisprudence is positive law: law strictly so called, that is law set by political superiors to political inferiors." But Kelsen followed up his opening sentence with the argument that no Ought could be derived from an Is. This theoretical foundation indirectly distinguished the meaning of his initial sentence from that of Austin's. Kelson's positivism was dictated by his concept of science, and not as Austin's by the concept of sovereignty. The exclusion of "principles of justice" from scientific inquiry was to Kelsen a matter of scientific necessity, not of mere expediency and voluntary self-limitation. Whether a law serves justice, he said, is beyond the (scientific) theory of law. It can never be the task of legal science "to justify anything. Justification implies judgment of value, and judgment of value is an affair of ethics and politics, not, however, of pure knowledge. To the service of that knowledge legal science is dedicated." [21]

The validity of the positive law can, according to the Kelsen school, be derived only from a fictitious "basic norm" (*Grundnorm*), which is postulated as an hypothesis and which prescribes that the norms contained in the constitution of the respective country ought to be obeyed.[22]

---

[19] *Reine Rechtslehre*, Leipzig and Vienna 1934. See also in English, "The Pure Theory of Law," *Law Quarterly Review*, vol. 50 (1934) p. 474; vol. 51 (1935) p. 517, chiefly an extract from *Reine Rechtslehre*, translated by C. H. Wilson. See also William Ebenstein, *Die philosophische Schule der reinen Rechtslehre*, Prague 1938 (English version, revised under the title *The Pure Theory of Law*, Madison 1945), reviewed by the present writer in *American Political Science Review*, vol. 32 (1938) p. 1173.

[20] Kelsen repeated this statement literally in many of his subsequent writings, latest in *What Is Justice?* Berkeley 1957, p. 266.

[21] Kelsen, *Law Quarterly Review*, vol. 51, p. 535; *What Is Justice?* pp. 229, 266.

[22] *Reine Rechtslehre*, pp. 62 ff.; *Law Quarterly Review*, vol. 50, p. 482; vol. 51, p. 517. An excellent more recent presentation of this doctrine can be found in his 1951 article, "Science and Politics" (cited in the next paragraph) pp. 650 ff., and in *What Is Justice?* pp. 221 ff. See also below, Appendix B.

Through the constitution the basic norm leads down, step by step, to the lower forms of law by means of delegation of authority (*Stufentheorie*).[23]

Although primarily interested in the positive law, Kelsen supported the transpositive teachings of Scientific Value Relativism in many of his writings.[24] He continued to do so after he himself had become a victim of Hitlerian positivism, which brought him as a refugee eventually to the United States. Whereas Radbruch modified his relativism and positivism after the event, Kelsen never did. He published an American edition of his theories of law and state after World War II with his old teachings on legal positivism and value relativism unmitigated.[25] In an article of 1951 on "Science and Politics" he once more repeated these teachings in strong formulations.[26] The statement, he said there, that a certain social organization guaranteeing individual freedom but not economic security "is good" and consequently "better" than a social organization guaranteeing economic security but not individual freedom, "is not a statement of fact; it cannot be verified by experiments and is neither true nor false." Science "can determine the means, but it cannot determine the ends." [27]

> To the question "Why is a particular value judgment or a particular norm valid?" the answer can be only another value judgment or another norm, never a judgment about reality—the ascertainment of fact; and thus the question must lead to a judgment about a supreme value or to a basic norm.[28]

Neither a judgment about supreme values nor one about the validity of the basic norm can be rendered by science, Kelsen concluded. Yet

[23] Founder of the *Stufentheorie* is Adolf Merkl, *Die Lehre von der Rechtskraft*, Leipzig and Vienna, 1923. See also Felix Kaufmann, *Logik und Rechtswissenschaft, Grundriss eines Systems der reinen Rechtslehre*, Tübingen 1922.

[24] See especially *Allgemeine Staatslehre*, pp. 38, 368–71; *Reine Rechtslehre*, pp. 12 ff.; *Law Quarterly Review*, vol. 50, p. 482. Consequently, Kelsen rejected all subjective rights if conceived as distinct from positive law, *Reine Rechtslehre*, pp. 39 ff.; *Law Quarterly Review*, vol. 50, pp. 492, 497. See on this problem Chapter IV, Section 8, above (juridical vs. scientific recognition of rights).

[25] Hans Kelsen, *General Theory of Law and State*, vol. 1 of *20th Century Legal Philosophy Series*, Cambridge, Mass. 1945; this is an Engl. transl. by A. Wedberg from the author's "Allgemeine Staatslehre," "Reine Rechtslehre," and other writings, revised by Kelsen. An appendix renders Kelsen's basic essay *Die philosophischen Grundlagen der Naturrechtslehre und des Rechtspositivismus* (Charlottenburg 1928) in tr. by W. H. Kraus ("Natural Law Doctrine and Legal Positivism").

[26] *American Political Science Review*, vol. 55 (1951) p. 641, reprinted in *What Is Justice?* p. 350.

[27] Pp. 642–43.

[28] P. 644. See also his "Absolutism and Relativism in Philosophy and Politics," *American Political Science Review*, vol. 42 (1948) p. 906, reprinted in *What Is Justice?* p. 198.

precisely this fact should leave us free, as I submitted above (Chapter IV, Section 8), to choose as a starting point for jurisprudence a basic norm different from that which Kelsen used.

4. *Reasons for the Germanic Origin*

At first sight it may appear puzzling that, although the practice of empirical research in the social sciences had developed earlier and more vigorously in the United States and Great Britain, the theoretical implications regarding values were first formulated not there but in Germany. Sociological factors played a decisive role in this. The original German relativists were scholars of democratic, liberal, or socialist inclinations who lived in a country run by a semi-authoritarian monarchic government. They were surrounded by a great majority of other scholars who accepted that type of government as ideal and often carried emotional patriotism and conservatism into their lectures and scholarly writings. Disinclined in their own work to bow to authoritarian forms and values, they were driven in self-defense to study the proper relation of science to political evaluations more carefully than their colleagues in democratically governed countries had reason to do. Thus they began to object to all nonscientific arguments and unavowed assumptions in scholarly work and to proclaim the principle that personal preferences were the "private affair" of the scholar, to be kept separate from his scholarly work. There was a crusading zeal in their methodological publications.

It would be a mistake, however, to ascribe the rise of relativism in Germany merely to these sociological peculiarities. Germany was, after all, the country of Kant's *Critique of Pure Reason,* and it is readily understandable that the constant reconsideration of the theory of knowledge under his influence should have led to ideas of scientific relativity of values in the social sciences. One can even wonder that they emerged so late.

A third factor was the codification of German law, then in full swing. The *Bürgerliche Gesetzbuch* (Civil Code) was enacted in 1896 and went into force in 1900. The preparation for a reform of the criminal code started soon afterward.[1] These great undertakings naturally led to fundamental discussions about the essence of justice.

Finally, the German scholars did not mean to create a fundamentally

---

[1] The Government Commission for the Reform of the Criminal Law did not meet until 1911, but the preparations began long before that. Later, Radbruch himself introduced a reform bill in the Federal Cabinet, when he became a minister of justice in the Weimar Republic. Actually, no total reform act has been passed to the present day.

new doctrine.[2] They thought they were simply giving a more exact formulation to what had been widely felt everywhere in Western countries. Parliaments with their rainbows of party ideologies had become the living expression of the relativity of ideas about transtraditional justice, grounded on the principle that—barring violent action—each ideology was to be accorded equal rights. The striking analogy between party types and conceivable types of transtraditional ideas of justice was keenly noticed by Radbruch, who offered a stimulating analysis of party ideologies.[3]

The whole tendency of the early twentieth century was toward measurement in every field of science. Although Einstein's theory of relativity in physics had no immediate connection with value relativism—the term "relativity" in the two theories refers to entirely different things—it is no mere chance that both appeared at the same time. Man's mind was bent on measurement and precision and, therefore, ready to recognize any limitations in the exactness of his own measurements. This led to a critical examination of the tools of measurement, and even to the suspicion that they might change their length and breadth under his very eyes.

5. *Spread to the United States*

(a) SPECIAL REASONS FOR THE LATE ARRIVAL HERE

Theoretical work about political value judgments remained spotty and casual in the United States until the third decade of this century. While empirical research in political science played a much earlier, and up to recent times a far greater, role here than in Europe, American professors cared less for theorizing about the foundations and the limitations of such work. Their sociological situation was precisely the opposite of that faced by the early German relativists. They found little reason to question the value judgments that underlay their country's system of government, which they approved, and to discuss other political value judgments scientifically on a basis of neutrality.

I should venture to go further. Whatever may be the anti-dogmatic attitude of Americans in other precincts of life, their acceptance of general democratic principles and ideals, such as the right to life, liberty, property, and the pursuit of happiness, is highly dogmatic in character,

---

[2] See Max Weber's introductory remarks to his 1904 article, as quoted in Section 2c above.

[3] *Rechtsphilosophie*, 3rd ed., p. 58; 4th ed., p. 156; Wilk tr., p. 97. So did Julius Binder, using his own classifications, in *Philosophie des Rechts* (Berlin 1925) p. 288.

carried over from pre-scientific and extra-scientific spheres into the realm of science.[1] This subconscious dogmatism was a very valuable antidote against totalitarian propaganda; but in the scholarly work of political scientists it made for a certain superficiality in the treatment of basic theoretical questions, and for oversimplification in historical and critical essays.

Nevertheless, a good deal of latent relativism developed when democratic principles were not at issue. It was implied in the democratic postulates of freedom of opinion and of tolerance. It was also inherent in the empiricist tendencies more deeply engrained in the character of Americans than of Europeans—owing to the conditions of life in the New World, where the dead wood of obsolete traditions could be cast off more easily than in the Old, and to the exigencies of practical co-operation among people of various creeds and national origins. A matter-of-fact approach to all problems of common concern and a ready smile at things that appeared merely theoretical were the natural consequence.

Such latent relativistic tendencies were only strengthened when, about the turn of the century, legal positivism—international training ground for relativistic thinking—finally conquered legal thought in the United States. Higher-law ideas had lingered here considerably longer than in Great Britain, where the positivistic stage was reached at the time of Blackstone, Bentham, and Austin.[2] Yet when the postulate of due process in matters of life, liberty, and property, as a principle binding upon all levels of government, state as well as federal, got incorporated in the Federal Constitution through the Fourteenth Amendment (1868), there was little need left for references to divine law or the law of nature. Thereafter, legal positivism won through here also; it became generally assumed that whenever a statute was in line with the Constitution it was valid and no appeal lay from it, or from the Constitution, to higher law in court.[3]

---

[1] Repeated from my article "The Rise of Relativism in Political and Legal Philosophy," *Social Research*, vol. 6 (1939) p. 60. Meantime, see also George H. Sabine, *Democracy and Preconceived Ideas*, a lecture delivered at the Ohio State University, Columbus, Ohio, 1945.

[2] See Rodney L. Mott, *Due Process of Law*, Indianapolis 1926, pp. 48 ff.; E. S. Corwin, "The Higher-Law Background of American Constitutional Law," *Harvard Law Review*, vol. 42 (1928) pp. 149, 365, especially 274–76; and C. H. McIlwain, *The High Court of Parliament and Its Supremacy*, New Haven 1910, pp. 336 ff.

[3] On the gradual disappearance of references to higher law in the United States, see E. S. Corwin, *The Twilight of the Supreme Court*, New Haven 1934, pp. 56 ff., 102 ff.; C. G. Haines, *The Revival of Natural Law Concepts*, Cambridge, Mass., 1930; and B. F. Wright, Jr., *American Interpretations of Natural Law*, Cambridge, Mass., 1931. More recently, references to Natural Law have again entered opinions of the U.S. Supreme Court.

Just as in England and on the Continent, however, legal positivism did not immediately lead to theories of value relativism in the trans-positive (legislative) sphere, at least not overtly. American law schools showed little interest in the philosophical problems of justice. There was a growing endeavor to study how the law and the courts could best be made to serve social improvements—the sociological school—, and also a growing tendency to examine to what extent individual ideals and class prejudices influenced the judges, and what formalistic techniques they used to allow these influences to prevail in their judicial opinions—the realist school. But neither tendency led to a thorough theoretical reexamination of the relation between science and value judgments.

What delayed the arrival of an overt type of Scientific Value Relativism in the United States more than anything else, however, was the rise of Pragmatism. The fight of the pragmatists against a-priori principles and derivations therefrom, and their insistence on the examination of consequences—identical with parallel demands of the European relativists but preceeding them by a few years—took much wind of the relativistic sails in advance in America. That Pragmatism stopped short of producing a theory of its own on the scientific feasibility or unfeasibility of scientific value judgments escaped notice. German and Austrian thought in this field remained little known here until far into the nineteen-thirties.

(b) BEGINNINGS AND GROWTH (HOLMES, M. COHEN,
       MERRIAM, LASSWELL, ETC.)

As a consequence of these various retarding factors views about the scientific relativity of all value judgments were rarely expressed in the writings of American social scientists prior to World War I. The Darwinists' insistence on their right to "ethical neutrality" can hardly be counted in this context. The phrase "ethical neutrality" did not mean then what it is understood to imply today. It referred primarily to the natural sciences and to the rejection of conservative demands that natural scientists should take the moral consequences of their inquiries and theories into account (see Chapter v, Section 6, above). It did not yet reflect any general theory of scientific relativity regarding all statements on values in the social sciences.

One isolated instance of a nascent Scientific Value Relativism—the only one, indeed, I have been able to find up to the end of the first decade of this century outside the specific Darwinian controversy—is a letter written by Oliver Wendell Holmes, Jr., to William James on March 24, 1907. "I have been in the habit of saying," Holmes wrote, frankly critical of James's metaphysical leanings, "that all I mean by truth is what I can't help thinking. . . . But I have learned to surmise that my can't helps are not necessarily cosmic can't helps—that the universe may not be subject to my limitations; and philosophy generally seems to me to sin through arrogance." He went on to compare philosophers to the old knight-errants, who promised "to knock your head off if you didn't admit their girl was not only a nice girl but the most beautiful and best of all possible girls," and ended: "I can't help preferring champagne to ditch [sic] water,—I doubt if the universe does." [4] This was relativistic, but it was not yet a precisely formulated theory.

Six years later, George Santayana used more formal language when he wrote in his *Winds of Doctrine* (1913): "But to speak of the truth of an ultimate good would be a false collocation of terms; an ultimate good is chosen, found or aimed at; it is not opined. The ultimate intuitions on which ethics rests are not debatable, for they are not opinions we hazard but preferences we feel; and it can be neither correct nor incorrect to feel them." [5]

But these were exceptions. Only after the start of the war did American writers begin to express such ideas more frequently. Among the first was Holmes again, this time in a formal paper published under the title "Natural Law" in *Harvard Law Review,* 1918. It is of special interest to compare this article with the ideas of the German prewar relativists, whom the author did not seem to know. Far from dwelling on abstract contemplations or theoretical examinations of Is, Ought, and values in the manner of the Germans, the great judge started off from childhood remembrances, dear to him but not to others, spoke of the fact that one cannot argue a man into liking a glass of beer, and of the way in which the most fundamental right, the right to live, is sacrificed to the so-called interest of society, which may not be the interest of mankind in the long run. In his own phrasing he spoke of "skepticism" rather than relativity; but his skepticism, precisely as that of the German relativists, referred to value judgments only, not to the whole scale of scientific efforts. Basic preferences cannot be proved, he said; those of the other fellow may be just as good as one's own; [6]

---

[4] Published in R. B. Perry, *The Thought and Character of William James*, Boston 1935, vol. 2, p. 459; abridged ed., 1948, p. 300.

[5] *Winds of Doctrine, Studies in Contemporary Opinion*, New York 1913, p. 144.

[6] Note the almost literal identity of this phrase with that used by Max Weber in his 1904 article, as quoted above, Section 2.

one may fight for one's own preferences, but reasoning will not solve the conflict. The article failed to go more deeply into the question of the ways that remain open to reason and scientific argument in discussing divergent value judgments, in this respect lagging behind the studies of the German relativists; but this was not its primary topic.

The following literal quotation from Holmes's article may here be inserted:

> I love granite rocks and barberry bushes, no doubt because with them were my earliest joys that reach back through the past eternity of my life. But while one's own experience thus makes certain preferences dogmatic for oneself, recognition of how they came to be so leaves one able to see that others, poor souls, may be equally dogmatic about something else. And this again means skepticism. Not that one's belief or love does not remain. Not that we would not fight and die for it if important . . . but that we have learned to recognize that others will fight and die to make a different world, with equal sincerity of belief. Deep-seated preferences cannot be argued about—you cannot argue a man into liking a glass of beer—and therefore, when differences are sufficiently far-reaching, we try to kill the other man rather than let him have his way. But that is perfectly consistent with admitting that, so far as appears, his grounds are just as good as ours. . . .[6] The jurists who believe in natural law seem to me to be in that naïve state of mind that accepts what has been familiar and accepted by them and their neighbors as something that must be accepted by all men everywhere. . . . The most fundamental of the supposed preexisting rights—the right to life—is sacrificed without a scruple not only in war, but whenever the interest of society, that is, of the predominant power in the community is thought to demand it. Whether that interest is the interest of mankind in the long run no one can tell. . . . Men to a great extent believe what they want to—although I see in that no basis for a philosophy that tells us what we should want.[7]

Three years earlier, in 1915, the philosopher Morris R. Cohen had stated that "all things cannot be proven, since proof rests on assumption" and that reason "cannot determine the ultimate ends that are a

[7] Oliver W. Holmes, "Natural Law," *Harvard Law Review*, vol. 32 (1918) p. 40; reprinted in *Collected Legal Papers*, New York, 1920–21 (last article). Copyright 1940, Harvard Law Review Association.

...tter of ultimate choice." [8] He strongly rejected Stammler's conten-
...on to the contrary:

> All metaphysical philosophies of law (like Stammler's) that pretend
> to have no empirical elements at their basis, they really attempt the
> logically impossible. You cannot construct a building merely out of
> the rules of architecture. . . . There is a downright absurdity in
> Stammler's efforts to derive substantive rules of law from purely
> formal or logical principles.[10]

Most instrumental for the introduction of Scientific Method in the
social sciences in the United States was Charles E. Merriam, professor
of political science at the University of Chicago and initiator of the Social Science Research Council. In his 1925 book, *New Aspects of Politics,*
he ably distinguished four periods in political thinking: a priori and
deductive, down to 1850; historical and comparative, 1850–1900; observation, survey, measurement, after 1900; and psychological, more
recently.[11] He demanded the development of an unbiased science leaning strictly on observation and measurement, to be separated from
political "prudence" in those spheres that had not yet been explored
by science.[12] In line with the postulates of Scientific Value Relativism,
Merriam was careful, as a rule, to avow his value assumptions, especially so in his 1938 article "The Assumptions of Democracy," [13] and
his 1945 book *Systematic Politics.*[14] He was not always consistent in
this, it is true, and could use a highly dogmatic style at times. If I may
italicize freely, he proclaimed in the last-mentioned book with finality,
"The role of government *is* . . ." (p. 30); "The purpose of authority,
it is clear, is not authority as such but freedom" (p. 60); "The ends and
purposes of government . . . may be *simply stated* as follows: external
security, internal order, justice, general welfare and freedom" (p. 31).
This enumeration occurs many times, but sometimes equality is sud-
denly inserted (pp. 211, 287, 327) as though that made no difference.[15]

---

[8] Morris R. Cohen, *Law and the Social Order,* New York 1935, p. 256, reprinted from the
essay "The Place of Logic in the Law," which first appeared in 1915 (*Harvard Law Review,* vol.
29, p. 622).

[9] *Law and the Social Order,* p. 173.

[10] *Ibid.,* p. 194.

[11] Charles E. Merriam, *New Aspects of Politics,* Chicago 1925, (2nd ed., 1931) pp. 49 ff.

[12] *Ibid.,* pp. 100, 163.

[13] *Political Science Quarterly,* vol. 53 (1938) p. 328.

[14] Chicago 1945.

[15] For further comments on Merriam's *Systematic Politics* see my review in *Social Research,* vol.
13 (1946) p. 117.

These were, however, inadvertent lapses in formulation rather th.
intentional attempts to establish absolute value judgments; he mig
have corrected the wording simply by inserting a clause .that he w.
speaking of democratic ideals, whose validity he assumed.

One year after Merriam's *New Aspects* there appeared the first American book devoted exclusively to the problems of value, Ralph B.
Perry's *General Theory of Value* (New York 1926). This book, which
bore the characteristic subtitle "Its Meaning and Basic Principles, Construed in Terms of Interest" revealed that Perry identified values
with interests; whatever a man takes an interest in, that he values.
Thus he took a basically relativistic view (see especially p. 640), though
with minor reservations, to be dealt with in later chapters. He maintained this approach also in his follow-up book, *Realms of Value, A
Critique of Human Civilization,* published almost thirty years later
(Cambridge, Mass., 1954). To the reproach that taking his view meant
to fall into relativism he replied ". . . and so what?"

> The word "relativism" has a bad sound; even the word "relativity,"
> despite its association with the latest physics. . . . But suppose that
> one substitute the word "relational" and, instead of rejecting it as
> a fault, boldly confirms it as a merit. . . . There is nothing in the
> relational view which forbids a thing's being conceived as absolutely
> valuable, that is valuable regardless of the value of anything else.
> (*Realms,* p. 12.)

The only objectionable kind of relativism was "vicious relativism,"
he continued. Relativism "is vicious only when it is concealed. Moral
judgments commonly apply a standard without stating it; as when a
hurtful act is simply pronounced 'wrong,' when it should be pronounced 'wrong-by-the-standard-of-harmonious-happiness' " (p. 121).[16]
He clearly distinguished the same two types of value judgments that
had been discerned by the early German relativists, namely, "the judgment which adopts the standard and the judgment which applies it,"
and he agreed that the "fundamental question of moral knowledge is
the question of the proof of the first or basic judgment. It is a judgment about a standard . . ." (p. 123). Unless some standard can be

---

[16] Elsewhere he defined vicious relativism as the doctrine that all statements must be introduced by the words "it seems to me at this moment" (p. 12). This is a different matter. Every
report ("protocol") on an observation must indeed be read to include such a clause (see above,
Chapter 1, Section 3). This does not exclude, however, the scientist's acceptance of the results
of the observation as facts. We must distinguish between the observational report and the acceptance of its results as facts, as discussed in Chapter 1.

proved "to be *the* moral standard, to the exclusion of other standards" on the ground of some "unique qualification," then "it will be merely one standard among many"; any other standard would be judged *"in terms of* this standard, but there would be no judgment *between* them" (*ibid.,* italics in the original). And he went on to subject all previous attempts to present proof for one paramount standard to a devastating critique, especially the intuitional proof, the rationalistic or logical proof, the metaphysical proof, and the psychological proof (pp. 223–32).

Now, all this is Scientific Value Relativism[17] as described above in Chapter III. The reader must not get confused by the fact that at the end Perry himself does recommend one standard—harmonious happiness—above all others, giving the reasons for his choice; and that in another, most eloquent chapter he praises democracy as "the optimum form of social organization" (pp. 272 ff.). To do these things is entirely compatible with Scientific Relativism as long as the reasons are not presented as a scientific proof for the ultimate values underlying the standard. It is as compatible with Scientific Relativism as is the belief in God. Every scientific relativist, unless he indulges in unlimited skepticism, will personally adhere to certain standards of evaluation, and—after stating the impossibility of presenting scientific proof for their absolute validity—may freely recommend his own choice to others, giving his reasons for it, including a scientific analysis of the consequences and risks implied in rival standards. This is exactly what Perry did. We shall revert to his particular recommendation and the grounds given for it at another place (Chapters VII and VIII).

Returning now to the literature at the end of the twenties, when Perry's *Theory of Value* was first published, we must mention English-born George E. G. Catlin, who, in a book of 1927, limited political science, in the relativistic fashion, to the examination of what one must do if one wishes to achieve a certain result.[18] Another book of his, published in 1930, distinguished itself by its cautious inquiry into alleged scientific laws in politics on the same basis.[19]

Stuart A. Rice, in his *Quantitative Methods in Politics,* from which we quoted a couple of clearly relativistic statements in Section 1 of

---

[17] However, Scientific Value Relativism distinguishes inquiries into what is desired from inquiries into what is desirable, a distinction that is blurred by Perry's identification of value and interest. See above, Section 2 (Weber), and Chapters V, Section 5 (Mill) and VII, Section 2 (Dewey).

[18] George E. G. Catlin, *The Science and Methods of Politics,* New York 1927, pp. 347–48. That science deals with means, philosophy with ends, he repeated thirty years later; see Appendix B.

[19] G. E. G. Catlin, *A Study of the Principles of Politics,* New York 1930, pp. 100 ff.

this chapter, blamed social scientists for having pictured their task as "the creation of a science of moral ends," which involved a contradiction in terms, he said. He called for a clear distinction between science and philosophy.[20]

John Dickinson, in the following year (1929), rejected, one by one, various alleged sources of higher law—such as *ratio legis,* popular custom, principles gained by induction, "science"—and referred, time and again, to the element of "desirability" and "value judgment" underlying all legislation, by courts as well as by legislatures. He made a strong point of the fact that the so-called principles of justice always appear in pairs of opposites; they are contradictory, and they clash. The choice between them is based on value judgments. Said he:

> Competing interests have an unexpected habit of expressing their conflicts precisely in the form of an apparent conflict between these accepted fundamental principles of the law. The axioms clash. . . .[21] The broad general principles of the law have a significant habit of traveling in pairs of opposites. . . .[22] All questions of law are ultimately questions of policy, or rather of opinion about policy.[23]

Karl Llewellyn, in 1931, approximated Continental terminology even more closely in emphasizing the separation of the realms of Is and Ought and the inability of science to teach us where to go (see the quotation in Section 1). Of values he said in this context that "as we move into these value judgments we desert entirely the solid sphere of objective observation, of possible agreement among all normal trained observers, and enter into the airy sphere of individual ideals and subjectivity." [24]

Felix S. Cohen, Morris' son, published a book in 1933 which was meant to be an attack on relativism but revealed him to be a scientific relativist himself (see next subsection).

In 1936, Harold D. Lasswell brought out his *Politics; Who Gets What, When, How* (New York), an almost cynically neutral application of Scientific Method and Value Relativism. Later, he took the lead in partisan (goal-orientated) relativism. In the introductory chapter

---

[20] See also Stuart A. Rice, ed., *Methods in Social Science: A Casebook,* New York 1931 (publication by a Committee on Scientific Method, appointed by the Social Science Research Council).

[21] John Dickinson, "The Law behind the Law," *Columbia Law Review,* vol. 29 (1929) pp. 113, 285; the quotation is from p. 296.

[22] *Ibid.,* p. 298, with many illustrations.

[23] *Ibid.,* p. 313, note 62.

[24] *Op.cit.,* p. 100.

to his and Lerner's collective volume *The Policy Sciences* (1951) he declared "The battle for method is won." Now the emphasis must be put on "the choice of significant problems on which to apply and evolve method." He summoned the policy scientist to become "value-orientated" by accepting or rejecting opportunities for research "according to their relevance for *all* [italics in the original] of his goal values" or by initiating research "which contributes to these goals." But this was not to say that he should sacrifice objectivity:

> The place for nonobjectivity is in deciding what ultimate goals are to be implemented. Once this choice is made, the scholar proceeds with maximum objectivity, and uses all available methods.[25]

Lasswell left no doubt about his own preferences, and ended by saying he thought it "probable" that science in the United States "will be directed toward providing the knowledge needed to improve the practice of democracy." His "special emphasis" was upon the policy sciences of "democracy, in which the ultimate goal is the realization of human dignity in theory and practice."[26]—an attitude completely in line with Scientific Value Relativism.

In 1938, Roscoe Pound, in his review of "Fifty Years of Jurisprudence"[27] called it futile to wait for a statement of absolutes, and recommended practical work on the basis of our present civilization—again an activity entirely legitimate from the relativistic viewpoint.

From 1939 to 1941, five of my own essays on relative and absolute justice appeared, which tried to make American scholars more familiar with the European theory of Scientific Value Relativism and its history. Warning against defeatism these papers attempted to show what great services science could render in the process of a prudent choice among conflicting goal-values, and they also engaged in an inquiry into universal and invariant standards—ideas resumed in Chapters ix ff. of the present book.[28]

Outstanding among the many essays of a basically relativistic character during the subsequent period is Professor MacIver's *The Web of Government* (1947), to be discussed separately hereafter.

[25] Harold D. Lasswell, "The Policy Orientation" in D. Lerner and H. D. Lasswell (ed.) *The Policy Sciences, Recent Developments in Scope and Method*, pp. 3 ff. The quotations are from pp. 9 and 11.

[26] *Ibid.*, p. 15; also p. 10: "The emphasis will be upon the development of knowledge pertinent to the fuller realization of human dignity." See Appendix B for a fuller treatment of Lasswell.

[27] *Harvard Law Review*, vol. 51 (1938) p. 460.

[28] The five papers are cited in Appendix B to Chapter VII.

(c) A RELATIVIST MALGRÉ LUI (FELIX S. COHEN)

Felix Cohen's *Ethical Systems and Legal Ideals* (New York 1933) offers a good illustration of an unsuccessful flight from Scientific Value Relativism. Examining various concepts of justice the author found that they gave us no absolute standards; nor did nature yield standards irrespective of time and place.[29] There was, therefore, relativity, he admitted. Reason does not help us to conformity; on the contrary, the more reason there is, the more disagreement. The German relativists he does not seem to have known, but in speaking of Santayana's relativism, mentioned above, he stated he had seen "no conclusive argument for or against this position."[30]

Yet Felix Cohen disliked relativism, as most people do, and offered an absolutistic alternative, the validity of which he admitted he could not prove either. This alternative, absolutistic hedonism, will be discussed in its proper place (Chapter XII). What matters here is that the presentation of this or any other absolutistic alternative, as long as it is not being claimed that its validity can be scientifically proven, is fully compatible with Scientific Value Relativism. According to Radbruch, even Stahl's conservative legal philosophy might have been written by a relativist, provided he had conceded that he had no proof for his assumptions, as Cohen admits that he has no proof for his.[31] It would be entirely unwarranted to reserve the right to propose great and comprehensive systems of evaluations to politicians and priests and to deny it to the professional philosopher who dedicates his lifework to such attempts and presents his results with due humility.

Cohen's dislike of relativism was grounded not on scientific objections but on the contention that it was an "immoral" doctrine.[32] Indeed, as we have seen, in a time where people look to science rather than to religion for guidance, the scientific abstinence of relativism has left at least a temporary vacuum. But to predicate as "immoral" this conscientious abstinence is not tenable unless relativism is wrongly interpreted as permitting a free and arbitrary option. This is not its meaning, however, as we have seen. Scientific Value Relativism is

---

[29] Pp. 93 ff., 109 ff., 118, 175.

[30] Pp. 157, 169.

[31] Radbruch, *Rechtsphilosophie* (3rd ed., pp. 12, 25; 4th ed., pp. 102, 118; Wilk tr., pp. 57, 69) stressed the need, outside scientific discussion proper, for a firm stand on basic principles and *Weltanschauung*.

[32] "It is the assertion of a real anarchy in the moral world, and an acceptance of it may well lead to a good deal of anarchy in the real world" (*op.cit.*, p. 157).

"scientific" only. And in this sense Felix Cohen is a scientific relativist too. His alternative of hedonism, avowedly unprovable, is even less free than relativism from the danger of being misinterpreted as an immoral doctrine. Not whether the scientific abstinence from value judgments is dangerous, but whether it is fully necessary, is the decisive scientific question.[33]

(d) NEUTRAL RELATIVISM IN ANOTHER GARB (MACIVER)

MacIver's book, *The Web of Government* (New York 1947), which received a prize as the best book of the year on government from the American Political Science Association, is one of the strongest supporters of Scientific Value Relativism in the United States, although the author rather coquettishly hides his neutral relativism behind another term, *myth*. This word has undergone many different uses within the last century. MacIver consummates the trend toward expanding its meaning and carries it to its logical limit by employing the term myth for all "value-impregnated beliefs and notions that men hold" (p. 4) or, as he formulates it elsewhere, for any value system outside exact knowledge (pp. 447–48, note). The author makes it quite clear that he uses the term in a *neutral* sense with regard to the quality of the value judgment. "We use the term in an entirely neutral sense. . . . We need a term that abjures all reference to truth and falsity" (p. 5).

Whether the word "myth" is an appropriate medium for abjuring reference to truth and falsity is open to question, since it has ample connotations of superstition, obsoleteness, saga, fairy tale, or primitivity. But MacIver himself has been consistent in its neutral use. Thus he speaks not only of the "myth" of sovereignty (p. 48), of feudalism (p. 48), of authority (p. 39), of racial superiority (pp. 447–48), but also of the "myth of democracy" (pp. 39 and 51), without any qualitative differentiation. He explicitly emphasizes that science cannot establish truth and falsehood in value judgments: "The value-component is strictly outside the sphere of scientific investigation" (pp. 447–48).

Thus it is obvious that, stripping the language of its new use of terms, we are meeting in the author another scientific relativist. It is neutral Scientific Value Relativism sold under a new label—myth.

The longer second part of MacIver's book is a comprehensive sociological text on government, a work of great merits, but with no relation to our present context, except for the fact that it does not keep within the limits of that neutral relativism the author had proclaimed

[33] See Appendix B on C. I. Lewis.

in the first. He definitely takes sides there for the "myth of democracy," without always proclaiming his assumptions, but with relevant analyses of cause and effect.[34]

In other books and articles, MacIver has strongly pleaded for cautiously chosen values, such as the Golden Rule (see below, Chapter VIII, Section 15), yet without a claim to scientific verification beyond the analysis of implications and consequences. On the contrary, he has repeated time and again that science "speaks of processes, not of goals; of laws, but not of values"; it "eschews evaluations"; it "cannot give us positive values." [35]

(e) PECULIARITIES OF RELATIVISM IN THE UNITED STATES.

Many more illustrations of the gradual spread of Scientific Value Relativism in the United States could be given. Most relativistic observations here have been casual, however, *obiter dicta,* logical derivations from the postulates of Scientific Method in the individual case at hand, rather than attempts to establish a general theory of relativity. Even the name of relativism, as we have seen, was rarely if ever used. No writer went so far as actually to treat various views on an equal footing in a synoptic manner, as did Radbruch in Germany—at least none except Lasswell in his *Who Gets What, When, How*. On the contrary, whenever the fundamental principles of the American way of life are at issue, Scientific Relativism in the United States has been cultivated in a partisan rather than a neutral manner. Scholars have made basic "assumptions" for the solution of their particular problems, especially regarding the desirable goal, and then applied Scientific Method to their further work. This practice, as mentioned above, was explicitly recommended by Lasswell in one of his later papers, and it prevailed also in Merriam's, Perry's, and MacIver's publications.

Thus the difference between relative and absolute views did not come so much into the open in the United States as in Europe, as there is no conspicuous difference of attitude between "partisan relativists" who assume the validity of traditional ideals as a working hypothesis, and "absolutists" who operate with the same values as absolutes. The difference, if made at all explicit, may show merely in a few lines of the preface.

This is not to say that the use of Scientific Method in the United

---

[34] See my review in *Social Research*, vol. 15 (1948) p. 244.

[35] See his profound and honest *The Pursuit of Happiness, A Philosophy for Modern Living*, New York 1955, pp. 157, 170, 173, and the quotation above, at the end of Section 1.

States has been altogether partisan in practice. Whenever the foundations of American life were not at issue, scientific research was generally carried on in a nonpartisan fashion, as for instance in the numerous scholarly analyses of elections. Most factual research, too, tried to keep away from value judgments or to use them within a clear frame of reference, as when corruption, substandard dwellings, or juvenile delinquency were investigated.

Only when after World War I the great international conflicts of ideologies—Democracy, Communism, Fascism—arose, did the theoretical problems of value relativism begin to draw more systematic attention in the American social sciences. But then the approach was frequently emotional, basically hostile, leading up to the mid-century revolt against relativism with which the next two chapters will deal.

6. Genetic Summary. One Gap in the Historical Course of the Argument

Our analysis of the historical genesis in this and the preceding chapter has shown that Scientific Value Relativism was first formulated around the beginning of this century in Germany, and that the type of relativism which emerged was fundamentally different from earlier relativistic theories. It no longer referred to evolutionary progress, historical or economic conditions, but to value judgments. It was no longer merely positivistic, it was primarily transpositive (legislative); it was no longer latent, it was overt; it was not passive but active; not partisan only, but primarily neutral. It was, on the other hand, from the outset strictly limited to the scientific approach as distinct from the religious, philosophical, or political. No postulate of relativity was raised regarding any of these other spheres. No attack was directed—with the possible exception of some extreme neopositivists—at scientific admissions that there *may* be a God or absolute values, or at personal convictions that there *are*. All the early relativists, even of the neutral type, personally believed in moral values. Weber and Radbruch frequently expressed such faith; Kelsen and Kantorowicz, like Radbruch, demonstrated their recognition by their behavior after Hitler's ascent to power, as undoubtedly Weber would have done had he been still alive. (Sections 1 to 4.)

On the American scene, Scientific Value Relativism arrived some fifteen years later, with some of its principles anticipated by empiricism and pragmatism, and the need for it less pressingly felt because of the wide homogeneity in basic political creeds at home. When it finally came, it remained more casual and more latent than its systematic and overt European counterpart, and was more often of the partisan rather than the neutral variety. But its logical necessity as a consequence of Scientific Method was hardly denied. (Section 5.)

Among the fathers of Scientific Value Relativism in Europe there was, from the outset, strong emphasis on its positive aspects, especially on the service science could render in analyzing the logical implications and factual consequences of the espousal of any particular value, and, therefore, on the practical usefulness of science in the process of choosing among conflicting value axioms (see especially Section 2 c, above, on Max Weber).

Before we conclude this historical report, one more question should be raised and the answer given by the early relativists be put on record. If all ideas of justice depend on a choice among ultimate values (goal values), is the individual entirely free with respect to the motives of his choice? Is his personal interest allowed to play a role, and an unlimited role? And if not his selfish interest, are different persons at least free to seize upon different values on the mere ground of differences in their individual temperament and character?

Weber and Kantorowicz seem to have taken the latter view, judging from Weber's figure of speech that everyone must find and obey his "demon," and from Kantorowicz' statement that science can help each individual find the viewpoint "which is really adequate to his nature" (above, Sections 2 and 3). No similar pronouncements were made by Radbruch or any of the others. There was, however, full agreement regarding the first point. All stressed that the individual is not allowed to make his choice in an arbitrary manner. He is supposed to follow what both Weber and Radbruch referred to as his "conscience," and Kantorowicz as his "feeling of right and wrong" (*Rechtsgefühl*).[1] Selfish interests, therefore, were not accepted as a legitimate guide, and the individual's search for his "demon" or his "nature" did not entitle him to act against his conscience or his feeling of right and wrong. As Radbruch formulated it: "what stand to take is left to the individual's resolve drawn from the depths of his personality and, therefore, by no means to his arbitrary choice (*Belieben*) but rather to his conscience."

---

[1] Weber, see quotations from his 1904 article in Section 2, above; Radbruch, *op.cit.,* 1st ed., p. 28; 3rd ed., p. 11; Wilk tr., p. 57; 4th ed., p. 102 and Wolf's introduction, p. 66; Kantorowicz, articles cited above, Section 3. Kelsen, too, referred to "conscience" in his farewell lecture at the University of California (1952). "It is a peculiarity of the human being," he said, "that he has a deep need to justify his behavior, that he has a conscience" (*What Is Justice?* p. 8).

This passing reference to conscience or to the feeling of right and wrong seems to involve a fundamental inconsistency. Elimination of arbitrariness and pure selfishness is generally considered the very nub of justice, and according to what has just been said this view was also accepted by the relativists. Yet if all other value judgments are beyond scientific verification, why should this one alone be excepted, why could it alone claim scientific standing? Are we, then, able to state with scientific methods whether and to what extent such a thing as a conscience or a feeling of right or wrong exists, whether it exists in all human beings, and if so, that it ought to be obeyed?

The early relativists did not go more deeply into this matter, be it because they considered it a foregone conclusion that empirical research could not lead to results here, or because they felt no avocation or professional competence to undertake it. But the question obviously requires an answer.

Closer examination reveals, furthermore, that Radbruch had included two more postulates in his teaching from the beginning without any relativistic reservations, namely, the postulate of equal treatment for what is equal and the postulate for certainty of law. His relativism, as he himself took occasion to emphasize at the end of his life,[2] had referred only to the choice among *goals*. But then again, why should scientific impotence to verify value judgments apply to some such judgments and not to others?

This problem will be taken up in Part Four of this book (Chapters IX ff.). At present our modest purpose has been only to report on the historical data. But in order to avoid leaving this chapter in a confused state of mind it is advisable that two points be stressed at once. In the first place, should these exceptions from the rule that science is unable to establish ultimate values not stand the test of critical analysis, this would by no means "liberate" us from Scientific Value Relativism; on the contrary, it would lead to more rather than less relativity. It would do nothing to refute the basic contention that other value judgments cannot be ascertained scientifically. On the other hand, the question here at issue illustrates a point made earlier in this book (Chapter IV, Section 8); namely, that relativists have not been careful enough in distinguishing between the scientific and the juridical side of the problem. Should it be impossible to establish the absolute validity of

---

[2] *Rechtsphilosophie*, 4th ed., p. 102, n. 1—one of the few notes Radbruch had prepared for the revised edition before his death. See below, Chapter VIII, Section 16 (Radbruch vs. Radbruch).

even those basic postulates scientifically, it could still be contended that they have *juridical* validity in countries of Western civilization in our time, even if opposed by dictatorial decree. So we need not be scared out of our wits, or out of our scientific honesty, by the discovery of these open questions. Fortunately, we shall see in Part Four that this is not all that can be said, but that science has indeed the possibility of approaching the problem at hand in a more positive manner, without abandoning the benefits of objectivity and intersubjective transmissibility.

Before we deal with this matter any further, however, it is urgent that we now turn to basic objections that have been raised against the theory of Scientific Value Relativism as a whole from several sides. This will be done in the two chapters of the following, the polemic, Part Three.

7. *Excursus on the Term "Relativism"*

Has the term "relativism" been wisely chosen for the views here discussed? The name is repellent to people with strong convictions and arouses suspicions and misrepresentations everywhere. In the United States it is rarely heard other than in a disparaging tone. Those here whose scientific work follows the methodological theories of Scientific Value Relativism either have no particular name for it, or simply refer to scientific requirements or to Scientific Method. In vain would one look for the term "relativism" in the indexes of the great American texts on the history of political ideas or of the philosophy of justice.

Even Max Weber lodged a sharp protest against the term. He had not used it in his first (1904) essay on the subject. That this was no accident appeared in the second (1917):

Probably the crudest misunderstanding which the representatives of this point of view constantly encounter is to be found in the interpretation of their standpoint as "relativism"—that is a philosophy of life which is based on a view about the interrelations of the value-spheres which is diametrically opposed to the one they [Weber and his followers] actually hold and which can be held with consistency only if it is based on a very special type of ("organic") metaphysics.[1]

Weber objected to the term with so much vigor because he personally believed in definite values, was engaged in a fight for them, and was aware that people generally called relativists only those who categor-

[1] *Gesammelte Aufsätze, op.cit.,* p. 470. See also Section 2, above, on Rickert.

ically denied the superiority of any value over others, not only the scientific demonstrability of that superiority. But his protest came too late. Meantime the term had been adopted, not by Weber's opponents only, but by his friends and followers as well, in order to designate the very method Weber had sponsored, and this has remained so, at least in Europe, to the present day. However, doubts about the appropriateness of the term have kept cropping up. Radbruch, too, was irked by the constant misunderstandings caused by it. In the footnote, already mentioned, which he had prepared for the fourth edition, he accepted the comment [2] that his was relativism only in part (*partieller R.*). But that did not give us a better term.

Eduard Spranger, in pursuance of his remarks reported above (Section 3) regarding the need for a higher unity of ultimate values, called Radbruch's method "dialectic"; he added that, when we are staking our entire personality on our choice among the three values and on our fight for it, then relativism obtains an "existentialist" character.[3] Similar observations were made by Karl Jaspers.[4] Radbruch, taking up this challenge, went so far as to say—at the end of the footnote cited—that in this sense his book represented not "relativism" but rather "existentialism." Now, this again does not help us to find a better term, since existentialism has many varieties of meaning and many connotations alien to our subject; it fails to express the particular point that science, being unable to verify ultimate value judgments directly, is forced to deal with them in relative terms and that in this way it can indirectly contribute much to the debate on values.

As misunderstandings continue to flourish (see next chapter, Section 1) it might still appear worthwhile to alter the terminology. Other terms have sometimes been used. Wilhelm Windelband, in Germany, spoke of "problematicism," [5] Georges Gurvitch, in France, of an "antinomic" philosophy of law,[6] and MacIver, in the United States, dubbed all ultimate value judgments "myths," as discussed above (Section 5). But none of these terms is specific enough for our purpose. Radbruch himself (in the note mentioned) offered "perspectivism" as a possible choice. This term would well express the thought that values can be judged only in the perspective of some ultimate value, or that the

---

[2] Made by Karl O. Petraschek, *Kritische Vierteljahrsschrift für Gesetzgebung und Rechtswissenschaft*, third series, vol. 27 (1921) p. 136.

[3] *Universitas*, vol. 5 (1948) p. 410.

[4] *Vernunft und Existenz*, Göttingen 1935, p. 72.

[5] *Einleitung in die Philosophie* (as cited above, Section 1) S. 219.

[6] *L'expérience juridique et la philosophie pluraliste du droit*, Paris, 1935.

ultimate values chosen involve different perspectives in which all inter-mediate questions of value appear. To make the term specific enough one might enlarge it to "Scientific Value Perspectivism." Even so it fails to indicate the possibility of scientific contributions to the choice between alternative highest values through analysis of their implica-tions and consequences. The most satisfactory name I could think of is "alternativism," or more specifically, "Scientific Value Alternativism." It would suggest that the choice is one among alternatives, that it is a matter of consequences, and that the alternatives, their meaning, range, implications, and consequences are open to scientific inquiry.

In this book, nevertheless, I have refrained from carrying this change in terminology through, though only on the ground that it would have weakened the coherence of historic presentation. Using the compound "Scientific Value Relativism," instead of simply speaking of relativism, I have at least tried to express the distinction from (1) "historical" rel-ativism or other forms of relativism, discussed in Chapter v, that are not focused on values, and from (2) any type of "philosophical" rel-ativism that asserts relativity not only within scientific work but cat-egorically beyond it. Occasionally, however, I have felt free to speak of "alternativism," at least in parentheses.

PART THREE

POLEMIC

CHAPTER VII

THE REVOLT

SCIENTIFIC VALUE RELATIVISM has, during the fifty or sixty years of its history, aroused many attempts to refute it, attempts that have often been impassioned, impatient, and even outrightly contemptuous but, for all their emotional intensity, not entirely successful. The strong emotional overtones so characteristic of the debate have not been conducive to scientific clarity and objectivity. Felix Kaufmann did not exaggerate when he wrote:[1]

> No methodological controversies in social science have been more embittered than those relating to value. Time and again, particularly in the discussion of the basic issue whether the social sciences ought to be value-free, substantial arguments have been supplanted by arguments *at hominem,* and the conscious or unconscious emotional motives "behind" the different views have been examined. . . . Those demanding value-free sciences reproach their opponents with placing obstacles in the way of a resolute search for truth for fear of possible consequences of unbiased inquiry for cherished prejudices and for vested group interests. The reply to this charge is either that social science cannot be value-free and that a particular kind of value judgment is smuggled into it under the cloak of the demand that it should be value-free, or that such a demand is a symptom of the moral callousness of those raising it. This kind of approach to methodological problems is apt to block the path to their solution.

Attempts to refute Scientific Relativism have generally taken one of several distinct paths. The broadest road has been chosen by those who describe it incorrectly and then have an easy time overthrowing it. This has been the prevailing attitude to the present day (see Section 1, below). A smaller, scientifically more important group rejects the methodological distinction between facts and values, holding that Scientific Method can deal satisfactorily with both (Section 2). A third, considerably stronger than the second, agrees with the relativists that distinctions between facts and values must be made and also that Scientific Method cannot lead to absolute statements on the hierarchy of values, but claims that a broader view of science makes available more

---

[1] *Methodology of the Social Sciences,* New York 1944, p. 199.

adequate methods for statements on values (Section 3). Some go so far as to consider the truth of Christianity scientifically verifiable (Section 4). Others, leaving the deity out of the scientific perspective, concentrate on the claims that values are "objective" and "real" rather than merely the reflection of some unverifiable Ought (Section 5). Several scholars of world fame have tried to present quasi-logical evidence for the rank of values (Section 6). Gestalt psychology has sought a new approach through its concept of "requiredness" (Section 7). An older group, conceding scientific impotence to verify substantive values, has claimed that at least formal standards can be established with absolute certainty (Section 8).

While all these are united in their striving for less relativity, others have attacked Scientific Value Relativism on the opposite ground that it acknowledges not too much, but too little relativity. They say that relativity rules science far beyond the sphere of values (Section 9). There are certain interrelations between this group and some of the others, especially the second; but the arguments are sufficiently different to advise separate treatment. We shall take the several groups up one by one.

1. *Misrepresentation*

> *. . . almost all really new ideas*
> *have a certain aspect of foolishness*
> *when they are first presented*
> —A. N. WHITEHEAD

Most revolters against Scientific Value Relativism describe it incorrectly. They do so in good faith, of course, but for that reason the more passionately. The commonest misrepresentation is to arouse the impression that "scientific" relativists are "philosophical" relativists who teach that there *is* nothing of absolute value and that all values *are* equal—a dogma that could be upheld scientifically only by someone who was not alone personally disinclined to believe in God but was positively convinced that there was none, and more than that, who thought the nonreality of God could be scientifically demonstrated. I have never met a scientific relativist who took this stand in his scientific work. If he did, it would be easy to refute him, since it is self-contradictory to deny absolute truth and in the same breath to proclaim one. Yet although this type of argument flails the air, hitting no real opponent, or no serious one, it is still the standard weapon against scientific relativists. It is presented in hundreds of classrooms time and again, even by first-rate scholars. Other misrepresentations are hardly less confusing. The questions raised by them are sure to arise for every student of twentieth-century political theory. Closer analysis will, therefore, help to clarify the entire subject.

Rather than exploit minor lights for illustration I shall refer to recent books by two eminent political scientists, born and educated in Germanic countries and well acquainted with Max Weber's work: Professor Leo Strauss of the University of Chicago, and Professor Eric Voegelin, now at the University of Munich, until 1957 at the State University of Louisiana. Both are by no means despisers of Weber; on the contrary, Strauss says of him, "Whatever may have been his errors, he is the greatest social scientist of our century," [1] and Voegelin calls him "a thinker between the end and a new beginning"—the end meaning that of the positivist approach and the beginning that of metaphysical research—who was "headed again on the road toward essence"; he also speaks of the "grandeur" of Weber's work, which is "more sensed than understood." [2]

In spite of their respect, both Strauss and Voegelin adopt the typical misrepresentation mentioned above. Strauss says that Weber "assumed as a matter of course that there is no hierarchy of values: all values are of the same rank," [3] and Voegelin, that Weber "treated all values as equal." [4] Now, Weber taught nothing of the kind, and he could not have done so, because in the first place he was not of the opinion that the absence of a hierarchy of values, and that includes the nonreality of God, could be scientifically ascertained; and in the second, the very point of his work was that values are unequal according to their different origins, implications, and consequences, and also because of their different ideal meaning. He did not treat values as "equal," but merely their validity as "equally undemonstrable" beyond the demonstrable consequences. He did not even treat all values this way but only "ultimate" values; for he recognized of course that each value can be judged scientifically as to its consistency with, and its usefulness for the

[1] Leo Strauss, *Natural Right and History,* Chicago 1953, p. 36. This book is a rich mine of penetrating analysis and thought in the field of the history of political theory and its great merits in this respect cannot be blurred by the above critical discussion in our particular context. There is a good German translation by Horst Boog, *Naturrecht und Geschichte,* Stuttgart 1956. See also Appendix B.

[2] Erich Voegelin, *The New Science of Politics,* Chicago 1952, a leading work in the mid-century revolt against relativism. See my notes, expressing my high esteem for it, in *Social Research,* vol. 20 (summer 1953) pp. 230–35.

[3] *Op.cit.,* p. 66.

[4] *Op.cit.,* p. 20.

attainment of, some allegedly ulterior value. Whether Weber was entirely right in treating the validity of all ultimate values as equally undemonstrable is not the question here; that will be the subject of subsequent chapters. Here our only purpose is to clarify what Scientific Relativism does say and what it does not say.

The next best misrepresentation is to assert that according to value relativism, science can contribute nothing to the value problem. This criticism is almost as common as the first one. Thus, Voegelin contends that Weber left the "political values of the students untouched," since "values were beyond science." [5] Actually, Weber's chief concern was not to leave political values alone but, on the contrary, to influence evaluations in a truly scientific manner by a solid discussion of their implications and consequences. As shown in Chapter vi above, his basic article of 1904 began with the statement that the implication of his proposition "is certainly not that value judgments are to be withdrawn from scientific discussion in general," and he added that "criticism is not to be suspended in the presence of value judgments." He claimed that science can "provide the acting person with the ability to weigh and compare the undesired as over against the desired consequences of his action," and to open his eyes as to the price one has to pay for their realization. That is a very different thing from leaving the political values of his students "untouched."

A third type of misrepresentation accuses Scientific Value Relativism of inconsistency. Voegelin sees inconsistency in the fact that Weber, on the one hand, considered the Marxian materialistic interpretation of history exposed as incorrect by objective historical research so that no scholar could be a Marxist, while, on the other, Weber's theory of values should have forbidden him to question the "value" of a Marxist.[6] Actually, no inconsistency is involved here. If historical research proves that the Marxian historical laws are contradicted by historical facts, then Marxism cannot be praised as valuable *on the ground of its correct interpretation of history,* just as bayonets cannot be praised as valuable on the ground that we can sit on them. No relativist has denied the right of scholars to criticize the factual contentions given as reasons for alleged values; on the contrary, such criticism is what they consider the proper scientific function.

Strauss, likewise, sees inconsistency in the fact that relativists cannot help using value judgments themselves. If they were consistent, he

[5] *Op.cit.,* p. 16.
[6] *Ibid.,* pp. 18, 19.

writes, relativists in describing concentration camps would not be permitted to speak of "cruelty" because this includes a value judgment; they could merely describe the acts actually committed, in a factual manner (which by the way might be much more graphic than speaking of cruelty, A.B.). Nor would historians be permitted to speak of "morality," "religion," "art," or "civilization," when interpreting the thoughts of peoples or tribes that are unaware of such notions or use them differently, or of "prostitutes," or "epigones."[7] Wittily he enumerates many value-impregnated expressions Weber used in his own historical papers, such as "grand figures," "laxity," "absolutely unartistic," "ingenious," "crude and abstruse notions," and "impressive achievement."[8]

These illustrations only go to show that Weber's own interpretation of his methodology was very different from Strauss'. No scientific relativist would condemn words like cruelty, civilization, prostitution, or, for that matter, crime or slums, wherever they are used within a clear frame of reference as descriptive in accordance with known standards, *as long as these standards are not themselves at issue*. Whenever the latter is the case, then indeed, according to Scientific Value Relativism, is it scientifically not correct to continue using one's own standards as though their absolute validity had been proven. Then the scientist must first analyze meaning and implications of the different standards within the possibilities of science—possibilities that, as we have seen, are by no means so limited as to exclude scientific contributions.

Others have pointed to the fact that even scientific relativists acknowledge the value of truth, which is presupposed in science.[9] We shall see in Chapters x and xi that the value of truth has indeed an absolute, or at least invariant, character. But there would be no inconsistency even if this were not so. For Scientific Value Relativism leaves us entirely free to define science as that human activity which follows the truth wherever it may lead and, therefore, to exclude work that does not follow truth from being classified as science under this definition. There would be many reasons, both utilitarian and ideal, grounded on actual human desires, for establishing such a discipline. The judgment that something is true or false is no value judgment.[10] Furthermore, when scientific relativists confess to their personal recognition of truth

[7] Strauss, *op.cit.,* pp. 52 ff., 59.

[8] *Ibid.,* p. 55.

[9] This point has been made, in a slightly different context, also by John Dewey, see next section.

[10] So rightly Kelsen, *What Is Justice?* p. 351.

as a high value, and within science the highest one, this is only a characteristic illustration of the fact that they deny neither the scholar's right to choose his own evaluations, provided he announces them, nor the potentiality of a valid hierarchy of values within which truth holds a high place.

A fourth misunderstanding equates Scientific Value Relativism with an extreme type of *historical* relativism, as when relativists are said to teach that the question of what is morally good or morally evil "has no meaning except in reference to the moral value system of a given society," and that, if two societies clash "one can only wait to see which of the two will prevail." [11] Actually, this has little to do with Scientific Value Relativism. The relativists of whom we are speaking in this book would not say that the question of good and evil *has* only the meaning given it by a particular society, but merely that its absolute meaning, if any, is beyond scientific determination. They would insist that the scholar is not compelled to apply the historically given value system; he may try to be neutral, or take his standards from accepted present-day ideas or from his own preferences or moral convictions, provided that in every case he declares what his standards are. He may criticize historical value judgments freely by exposing their origin, their opportunism, their implications and consequences. Least of all would they admit that survival in a clash determines the rank of values. When the defeated society is said to have suffered defeat as a consequence of its value system the truth of this proposition may be examined scientifically; but the answer would not decide on the value of that system except in relation to success or defeat. Furthermore, the outcome of the clash may have had consequences other than those which meet the eye—good ones for the defeated society, bad ones for the victorious one, in terms of standards chosen by the observer, or acknowledged by both parties to the discussion. This point of view is, of course, much more difficult to refute than the one presented in the above quotation.

2. *Methodological Differences between Facts and Values Denied*

John Dewey and Felix Kaufmann are protagonists of a relatively small number of scholars who deny that Scientific Method is unable

---

[11] Kurt von Fritz in his otherwise splendid paper "Relative and Absolute Values" in Ruth N. Anshen (ed.) *Moral Principles of Action*, New York 1952, pp. 94–121. On historicism see also Leo Strauss, *op.cit.* pp. 9 ff.

to establish the validity of value judgments. They hold that physical and moral inquiries can be successfully conducted according to identical principles. They do so, however, for different reasons.

To understand Dewey's argument we must first turn to his rejection of the idea of "ultimate" values. He can see no valid reason for the assumption that there necessarily must be one highest good, or one hierarchy of values, which we must either divulge through scientific procedure or, if we cannot, must choose according to our individual preferences. There is neither a practical possibility nor a theoretical need for such abstract constructions, he insists (see my own remarks on this question, Chapter III, Sections 2 and 3). Instead, he stresses the concrete situation in which we decide on values. This situation is always unique and it has, he claims, a "morally ultimate character." [1] In order to find our way in a concrete situation, all so-called principles, standards, criteria, and generalizations are merely "procedural *means*"; [2] they are no more than "intellectual instruments" in our inquiry. [3] We should abandon the presupposition of one highest good or end in favor of the belief in a "plurality of changing, moving, individualized goods and ends." [4] He rejects the idea that in the event of a moral conflict there is any predetermined hierarchy. "Action is always specific, concrete, individualized, unique, and consequently judgments . . . must be similarly specific." [5]

Hence, according to Dewey, in value judgments just as in judgments on physical questions it is the specific situation which determines the general principles, not vice versa. In this respect physical and ethical laws are alike. In both fields a selective activity is required as to what general laws should be tentatively adopted. There is no dualism of methods here. This first analogy is duplicated by a second, he says, namely, that moral factors rule physical judgments as well as moral ones, because the former presuppose at least the "sincere aim to judge truly." For this reason *any* scientific judgment is, in ultimate analysis, always a moral judgment. [6] While conceding that physical and moral judgments are otherwise different to some extent, he in-

---

[1] John Dewey, *Reconstruction in Philosophy,* enlarged ed., Boston 1948, p. 163 (ch. VII). *Logic, op.cit.* pp. 172 ff.

[2] *Logic,* pp. 173–74; italics in the original.

[3] *Reconstruction, loc.cit.,* and *Problems of Men,* New York 1946, pp. 211 ff.

[4] *Reconstruction,* p. 162.

[5] *Ibid.,* p. 167.

[6] *Problems of Men,* p. 228. This point is debatable, as we saw in the preceding section, because the exclusion of untruthful statements from science can be explained without reference to morality by agreement on the meaning (definition) of science. See also Chapter XI, below.

sists that these differences are logical, not moral, in character. What is different is only the "conditions" of the judging activity, and these differences can be objectively determined.[7]

On this basis Dewey sees no reason for relativistic abstinence from scientific judgments when the question is that of finding the most "valuable" action in the unique concrete situation. He thinks the decision can be put up to intelligence here quite as well as in any other question of science. Any other view would mean to surrender ethics to authority.[8] Nor need we rely on subjective preferences, he holds. Preferences are only the "raw material" for value judgments, and not themselves such judgments. We can find out by experimentation the consequences of values and then follow those values which have been found superior on the basis of this examination.

Much of this is entirely compatible with Scientific Value Relativism as described in this book. Indeed, it is fundamentally no more than a pointed statement of its basic ideas when Dewey emphasizes the great contribution science can make by the examination of consequences:

> The only way of . . . resolving the doubts that have arisen, is to review the existential consequences which will probably occur *if* esteem, admiration, enjoyment are engaged in. . . . There is no way to estimate their probable consequences save in terms of what has happened in similar cases in the past, either one's personal past or in the recorded experience of others. . . . We have to investigate connections—usually that of cause-effect.[9]

The difference begins where Dewey argues that the examination of consequences makes a scientific judgment possible as to which of several competing values is higher. Here he is definitely wrong. Clarification of consequences merely *postpones* the nonscientific choice, and sometimes makes it easier, but it does not eliminate the need for it. If I have found out that a certain action will impair my health, but add to my wealth, or that it will impair both, but be useful to my child, my friend, my country, or to humanity, I have still to choose according to which value I *do* consider higher, and/or which I *ought* to consider higher. When a general at war is faced with a situation in which an attack he contemplates will save the lives of a number of

[7] *Ibid.*, p. 233.

[8] This is one of the theme songs of Dewey's *The Quest for Certainty; a Study of the Relation of Knowledge to Action*, New York 1929, especially pp. 40 ff.

[9] *Logic*, p. 173. See also *The Quest for Certainty*, pp. 129, 258, 265, 298 and *The Public and Its Problems*, New York 1927, Chicago 1946.

soldiers but destroy a venerable monument like Monte Cassino
Italy, he must, after all the consequences are clear to him, still
ecide which is the higher value. Even if he knows what is more
aluable to *him*—he may not care for cultural values but may care
deeply about his soldiers, or he may be a fanatic lover of cultural
values but callous as to lives—the question remains whether he *ought*
to prefer something different from what *he does* prefer, and no argument of Dewey's relieves him or his superiors of this responsibility.
When all the information science can produce regarding the consequences of our acts is in, and let us assume that it is actually perfect
and complete, there still remain those two different questions: What,
in view of the consequences, do I desire? and, How ought I to act irrespective of my own desires? Even when sure about what I desire I
do not know on that account alone what is desirable from the ethical
point of view, unless I choose to accept plain hedonism as the only
relevant guide (see Chapter xii). No intellectual sleight of hand can
eliminate the difference, fundamentally acknowledged by Dewey,[10] in
the meaning of "desired" and (ethically) "desirable," i.e., between
what is desired and what ought to be desired. The answer to the latter
question, unless looked for in revealed commandments of the deity or
in orders given by earthly authorities, depends on a human decision, a
choice among competing ideas.[11]

The argument that scientific abstinence means surrender to some
authority is impressive, but does not make science fit to do what it is
unable to do *qua* science. It is a misplaced argument. It should be used
in the debate on the form of government, not on the methods of
science. It is indeed one of the strongest grounds in favor of democracy,
as a form of government where the choice between competing values
is not surrendered irrevocably to some particular authority but ultimately left to the people, at least in principle (see Chapters viii, Section
8, and x, Section 1).

Except for this methodological flaw, Dewey's total work presents
strong support for the thesis of the present book that by clarifying the
consequences of acts—and especially of any acts attempting to carry

---

[10] *The Quest for Certainty*, p. 260.
[11] See my remarks on J. S. Mill, Chapter v, Section 7; further, Norton C. White, *Social Thought in America: The Revolt against Formalism*, New York 1949, p. 212. Sidney Hook's defense of Dewey in the paper, "The Desirable and Emotive in Dewey's Ethics," in *John Dewey, Philosophy of Science and of Freedom*, New York 1950, pp. 194 ff., fails to meet the above criticism. I am indebted to Mr. Philip A. Slaner, who drew my attention to these references in a graduate term paper in which he took Dewey's view.

through value judgments—science can contribute so much to ▮ making and to the criticism of value judgments that it would be absu▮ to speak of value judgments being taboo for science or of all valu▮ being equal to science. However, when value judgments remain dif▮ ferent after full consideration of the consequences, Scientific Method leads to no decision; it only sharpens the antithesis. This must be fully understood before it is possible to continue with a fruitful discussion of the remaining problems.

Another abortive attempt to deny the need for a methodological dualism has been made by Felix Kaufmann in his *Methodology of the Social Sciences*.[12] Kaufmann rightly points out that whether we discuss values or facts two questions must always be distinguished: first, whether our specific judgment in the case at hand accords with the general proposition from which it is derived, and second, whether that general proposition is accurate. He claims that the two questions require no difference in method when examined for facts or for values. Regarding the first question he is right. All specific value judgments must and can indeed be checked as to their compatibility with the general value judgments from which they are deduced, exactly as any specific application of a general factual law must and can be checked as to its accord with the latter. The contention that the particular action *a* is valuable because it is "moral" can and must be checked for its consistency with the underlying general proposition regarding what is moral. To this extent there is indeed no difference in procedure.

Kaufmann was wrong, however, when he denied any methodological difference regarding the second question also, that of examining the validity of the general proposition. Here he argued that in physical science too the validity of the general proposition always rests on acceptance by the scientist. It is true, as discussed in Chapters I and II, that in physics the question whether an alleged general law of a factual character can be considered valid depends on its acceptance by scientists, since all generalizations rest on hypotheses, and the process of checking, theoretically speaking, never ends. In the same way, Kaufmann says, the validity of a general value judgment depends on its more or less general acceptance and can always be challenged. This analogy ignores the decisive difference that the scientist's acceptance of empirical laws of a factual character is based on factual observations, while his acceptance of ultimate value judgments would have to be based on a generalization, not of factual occurrences, but of

---

[12] *Op.cit.,* pp. 128–38, 199–211, and p. 238, no. 36.

opinions, and in the typical case, of conflicting opinions (see Chapter v, Section 2). The difference will always appear, therefore, when the validity of the general proposition to which the scientist refers is questioned. When the general proposition is factual, or a theory to explain facts, we can then turn to a discussion of its accordance with all known facts. When the general proposition is a value judgment, however, we cannot proceed this way; we must apply some quite different method, be it reference to ever higher principles, such as utility, obedience to God's will, or equality, and if they too are questioned, to intuition or some other final criterion, or we must give up scientific decision.

The problem is obscured by Kaufmann's peculiar use of the term value judgment. To him a value judgment is the analytic judgment on whether or not a specific case falls under a general value whose validity is accepted or assumed. But the scientific debate that has been going on for fifty years has understood by value judgments primarily the judgment on the validity of the general value from which the specific value judgment is deduced.[13]

The real problem is bypassed unless we recognize the remaining difference between inquiries into physical facts and into moral values. The particular case of universally accepted value judgments will be discussed in Chapters ix and x.

3. *Differences Not Denied, but the Concept of Science Broadened to Include Value Judgments*

Since we must ultimately choose our highest values according to nonscientific criteria, why not choose the Bible or the values there sanctified? Faith, supplemented but not replaceable by science, can give us certainty of values. Do enter, then, St. Thomas, and repeat in twentieth-century terms the consummation of the greatest union ever effected in the history of thought: the marriage between faith and reason. With science now become modest in the realm of values, the door is wide open for faith, wider than in four centuries.

So it could be argued, and quite emphatically even by scientific relativists. But there remains one important difference between such ideas in the thirteenth century and in the twentieth. St. Thomas regarded what he offered as real science, for science in the Thomist sense included supra-empirical and supra-rational kinds of wisdom. Contemporary Scientific Method, grounded on an altered concept

[13] See, for example, Felix E. Oppenheim, "The Natural Law Theory," *American Political Science Review,* vol. 51 (1957) p. 42.

of science, cannot follow him there. The Neo-Thomists urge us to return to the scholastic concept of science. Leading among them has become the French philosopher, Jacques Maritain. We should realize, he demands, "what misery it is for the mind to reduce science to the type of empiro-logical science, i.e., the physico-mathematical sciences and the sciences of phenomena." There "must" be such a nonempirical science, he exclaims, some knowledge in which the intellect is "on the inside." The intellect "sees." Metaphysics, wrongly ousted from science by Scientific Method, is science in this ampler sense, he insists. He speaks of the "mystery of abstract intuition," which he says makes the metaphysician and which Kant did not have, but St. Thomas did. Even between physics and metaphysics there is room for science; there is a "philosophy of nature" which, without entering into metaphysics, at least reaches Being itself, beyond the mere realm of phenomena.[1]

This call for a reinclusion of metaphysics, or at least of ontology (see above, Chapter I, Section 5), in science has been echoed by all those who are generally grouped together under the name of Neo-Thomists. It is raised also by non-Catholic scholars who would otherwise disclaim affinity to Thomism. Thus, Eric Voegelin, not a Thomist, in his militant book *The New Science of Politics* (Chicago 1952), combats the restriction of the term "science" to the application of Scientific Method. He calls for a "restoration" of political science, and for its "retheorization," through a revival of the attempts made by the Greek philosophers and the medieval Christian scholars to provide an ontological description of the order of values, "the theoretical orientation of man in his world, the great instrument for man's understanding of his own position in the universe." This aim, of course, cannot be reached by Scientific Method. But method should never be allowed to decide on relevance, Voegelin writes; whether a method is good or bad can be seen only from the results, retrospectively. Therefore, we should free ourselves from the positivistic approach. He states almost jubilantly that this movement today is spreading "at a breathless speed," although it is "practically unknown to the general public."

Similar objections have been raised within other branches of the social sciences. In the field of cultural history, Max Weber's brother Alfred, sociologist in Heidelberg, became their forceful spokesman. Only four years younger than Max he survived him by thirty-eight,

[1] These quotations are from Jacques Maritain, *Scholasticism and Politics*, New York 1940. Maritain has repeated his views in an impressive array of other books and articles in English and French. See especially, *The Rights of Man and Natural Law*, cited below, Chapter VIII, Section 4, and *Man and the State*, Chicago 1951.

continuing as a vigorously active member of the profession almost to his death in May 1958, a few weeks before he would have been ninety. His contributions to the concept and the history of human culture are discussed in Chapter VIII, Section 13, below; present remarks will be limited to the basic methodological issue.

Alfred Weber considers it necessary, at least in cultural questions, to renounce that insistence on "scientific dignity" (*wissenschaftliche Dignität*) for which his brother had called. He refuses to strive in all cases for a demonstrability which is "unconditionally compelling" (*unbedingt aufzwingbar*). In historical research, and especially in overall interpretations (*Gesamtdeutungen*), he would be satisfied with some "tolerable degree of evidence" (*leidliche Evidenz*), although for certain basic data, including the structure of society and the stage attained in the process of civilization, he too would insist on exact demonstration. In this context, he explicitly proclaims that (1) "intuition" is an ultimate source of reference (*ein Letztes*) to him, although its results must, of course, be checked and improved by analysis and synopsis; and (2) that, at least in the cultural sphere, all scientific activity is "entirely tied to values" (*vollständige Wertgebundenheit wissenschaftlichen Handelns*).[2] Along these two lines his criticism runs parallel to that raised by scholars like Maritain and Voegelin.

In dealing with such objections four questions, generally confounded, must be clearly distinguished: first, the terminological protest against the monopolistic appropriation of the term "science" for one particular method; second, the protest against the disregard of metaphysical or otherwise nonempirical aspects of life; third, the claim that truth can be found through intuition, and in many relevant questions can be found only in this manner; and fourth, the claim that the truth of propositions based on intuition can be intersubjectively demonstrated in some cases, or that full intersubjective demonstrability is irrelevant. I shall address myself to these four points successively.

(a) TERMINOLOGICAL PROTEST

To the extent that the criticism is merely a protest against the appropriation of the term "science" for one particular method the controversy may have a considerable practical bearing on the ground that

[2] For the foregoing see Alfred Weber, *Prinzipien der Geschichts- und Kultursoziologie*, München 1951, pp. 107–9, this part being a reprint from an article first published in *Ideen zur Staats- und Kultursoziologie*, Karlsruhe 1930.

great prestige goes with the term, but little theoretical significance, because we may use words as we choose, provided we explain what we mean by them. Should we choose to broaden the meaning of "science" so as to include personal knowledge, alleged or real, that cannot be intersubjectively transmitted in conclusive forms to others, then, as discussed in Chapter ii, Section 7, we need another term to distinguish intersubjectively transmissible knowledge from that which is not so transmissible (see below, at e).

(b) NEGLECT OF METAPHYSICS

As far as the objections are directed against the neglect of metaphysical and otherwise nonempirical questions in present-day scientific research, they do indeed hit a weak spot. But this weakness is one in the personal attitude of social scientists rather than in the basic tenets of Scientific Method and Scientific Value Relativism, which in no way *forbid* a scientist to engage in speculations about metaphysical questions, least of all when carried through with the full use of all scientific data available, but only insist that he should make it clear that what he then offers are mere speculations or hypotheses.

It is true that scientific relativists, including Max Weber, have generally abstained from this type of speculative writing. With few exceptions,[3] they chose to withdraw completely into fields that could be tilled with empirico-logical tools, and by such abstention gave food to the absurd and quite unrelativistic idea that what cannot be proved in the exact sense is either not existent or not relevant. Their abstention is humanly explainable by the fact that they were engaged in a bitter fight against the customary uncritical fusion of empirico-logical research and mere speculations. But actually it has led to the neglect of a very important field of human concern. There was no necessity for it. Why should only nonscientists have the right to satisfy the legitimate demand of the human mind for metaphysical reflections? It is, on the contrary, highly desirable, I hold, that great scholars occasionally engage in such work, because they alone are able to use all scientific resources and to draw the line between established knowledge and mere surmises or hypotheses.

The call of the Neo-Thomists for a revival of metaphysical speculation, or as Voegelin has styled it for a "new craftsmanship of meta-

---

[3] See, for example, Radbruch's fine analysis, *Theodor Fontane oder Skepsis und Glaube*, Leipzig (no date, published about 1946) and Erik Wolf's comment on Radbruch's religious ideas in the Introduction to the 4th ed. of *Rechtsphilosophie*, pp. 65 ff., and in *Natural Law Forum*, vol. 3 (1958) pp. 1 ff.; furthermore, MacIver's *The Pursuit of Happiness*, to be discussed in Chapter xiii, below.

physical speculation" (note that even he uses the term "speculation" here, not "science"[4]) and Alfred Weber's insistence that scholars should attempt to achieve an overall interpretation of cultural history although that could not be done through empirico-logical methods alone—these and similar appeals[5] are, therefore, not necessarily in conflict with Scientific Method and Scientific Value Relativism as here understood. Whether we name such speculations and interpretations "science" is theoretically unimportant.

(c) INTUITION, A SOURCE OF KNOWLEDGE

When the revolters insist that their hypotheses and interpretations are no mere hypotheses or propositions of faith or belief, but true "knowledge," although based on "intuition" or "inward seeing" rather than Scientific Method, we reach a third stage. To the contention that there is "intuitional knowledge" of factors which are beyond empirico-logical proof the answer of Scientific Method is not that there is no such knowledge, but merely that we cannot intersubjectively prove it to be correct. Intuition, if understood as the sudden rise within the human mind of an idea of plausible validity, or as the sudden grasping of interrelations and the like, far from being incompatible with Scientific Method, plays a tremendous role in preparing scientific research and giving it new direction in intermittent situations during its progress (see the remarks at the outset of this study, Chapter I, Section 1 b). Nor can there be doubt that we do have knowledge of things we cannot prove. As I have said (Chapter II, Section 7), childhood remembrances no longer shared by any living person constitute a melancholy illustration. "Study that house," says the Old Man in W. B. Yeats's *Purgatory* to his son:

> I think about its jokes and stories;
> I try to remember what the butler
> Said to a drunken gameskeeper
> In mid-October, but I cannot.
> *If I cannot, none living can.*
> Where are the jokes and the stories of a house,
> Its threshold gone to patch a pig-sty?

Many a defendant or witness in court has gone through the agony of impotence to prove what he knew well. Should there be metaphysical facts, then some or all of us may have obtained knowledge

[4] Voegelin, *op.cit.*, p. 25.
[5] See Chapter VIII, Section 5, on Northrop.

about them. People have at all times given testimony to their own conviction that they had such knowledge, and that they considered it as firmly established as any knowledge that had been verified in some intersubjectively conclusive manner. Reference to this type of knowledge, however, is scientifically exposed to the old rejoinder that different people confess to having different intuitional knowledge and that it remains for us to say whether we can decide who is right.

(d) INTERSUBJECTIVE TRANSMISSIBILITY OF INTUITIONAL KNOWLEDGE?

Whenever such reference to intuition as the ultimate source of some particular knowledge is made, there are two alternatives. There may be no claim that this knowledge is intersubjectively transmissible *qua* knowledge to others, or there may be such a claim. In the latter case, this contention, if verified, would be an event of the utmost significance; it would change the basis of twentieth-century theory in the social sciences and deserve the name of a new revolution in science rather than that of a mere revolt.

Unfortunately, the leaders of the revolt have been generally vague as to whether their challenge concerned only the other three points —terminology, neglect of metaphysical speculation, intuition as a source of true knowledge—or also this fourth point: a claim that intuitional knowledge is intersubjectively transmissible *qua* knowledge.

It is characteristic of the fluid limits the term "science" acquires when extended to intuitional knowledge to see how Maritain begins his argument with attacks, always certain to be applauded, on positivism and relativism (without a clear distinction of Scientific Value Relativism from other types of relativism); then gradually leads to the general concepts of natural law and humanism, which are at least in line with the prevailing feeling in the Western world; then proceeds to add Christianity, first as a historical fact, which no one denies, but then also as part of our scientific knowledge as to its revelations (see next section); and finally ends, in the latter part of his *Scholasticism and Politics,* by passing from Christianity in general to the doctrines of the Catholic Church—all this in the name not of religion but of science. In this process he fails to give an unambiguous answer to the question of intersubjective transmission of intuitive knowledge. It seems that he ultimately refers to "authority," which he defines as the "authentic right to be obeyed." But how can science tell which authority is authentic? Maritain answers that, in order to be authentic, authority must be just. But what is just? If this is to be determined by "authority," we are faced with a circular argument. That justice and not numbers should govern is truly democratic, Maritain insists, because the origin of the democratic sense is not the Rousseauist desire "to obey only oneself," but rather the desire to "obey only what it is just to obey." Granted; but then again, what, in a conflict of opinions, is just? How can science decide among several claimants for authority? And with no scientific sanction available, what else but democracy, of some type or other, is the alternative to fighting it out or inviting despotism? Was it not this situation which led to the establishment of democratic constitutions?

As Maritain happens to be a friend of democracy, it does not fully appear in his writings what vistas are opened politically if his concept of transmission of knowledge through authority is accepted. There would be no limit then to the reestablishment of the authoritarian rule of any church, which might become quite totalitarian as it has been at times in the past, dominating science and the arts as well as the religious life; and all this with reference to "legitimate authority" (see the quotation, Chapter VIII, Section 8). Nor would non-religious authoritarian rule be excluded.[6]

Similar vagueness in point of transmissible knowledge is characteristic of Voegelin's writings. That there is knowledge of metaphysical truth he undoubtedly claims, as we have seen. But the question to what extent this truth can be demonstrated to those who oppose it in good faith he treats rather cavalierly. This problem does not interest him, it seems. As long as he does not claim intersubjective transmissibility, so long, as shown above, is there no contradiction to Scientific Value Relativism. Any scientific relativist may have convictions about the existence of God based on his own experience, or about the superiority of some values over others, the same as has Voegelin; and will nevertheless confess that he sees no way of intersubjective demonstration to others who differ in good faith.

---

[6] Maritain, to be sure, would have little of this. He would not abolish universal suffrage, whose "symbolic value" he recognizes. Nor would he suppress multiple parties, whose educational value he appreciates. Still, he would render the state and the government independent of political parties. He would reduce the role of elected assmblies to an advisory capacity and to the ratification of proposals made "by higher authority," including proposals on appointments. Final decision should lie with representative assemblies only "in certain cases concerning in a major manner the life of the nation," which is likely to mean especially the question of war (p. 115, n. 1). This scheme as such is a legitimate proposal, subject however to scientific examination of all its consequences and risks. It lies open to criticism, especially on behalf of democratic tradition in the name of eternal vigilance. For, where would be the limit of authority, and where would be the guarantee that men of Maritain's stature would wield it? And why should authoritarian proposals stop at the relatively modest limits of Maritain's proposals?

Most illuminating is the position taken by Alfred Weber. He refers to "consensus" on the significance of cultural factors and on the reverence given to "the sublime, the beautiful, the holy, etc., no matter in what essence, content, or form they may appear." He speaks of the "miracle" that among the recipients of such things "consensus about their existence and quality is possible," which indicates, he suggests, that "underneath (*unterirdisch*) we are all interconnected with one another." Sociological analysis here "hits upon facts of immanent transcendence, which it has simply to take, leaving their interpretation to philosophical contemplation."[7] But he does not claim that this consensus is universal in character. The cultural historian, he says, "demands recognition only from those who feel themselves to be tied to the same values" (*die sich in gleicher Wertbezogenheit fühlen*).[8] He thinks that this is a far cry (*liegt weit ab*) from Max Weber's views, which led the latter to a "fully conscious attitude of everywhere preferring the rational in interpreting history."

The two brothers have indeed pursued very different lines of approach. But while Alfred focused his attention on other aspects of history than Max had done, and refused to be neutral in his appraisal of cultural values as Max (sometimes) tried to be, Alfred's work is not in fundamental conflict with the theory of Scientific Value Relativism, which has room for both neutral relativists and avowed partisans. No verdict in that theory forbids us to proclaim our belief in definite cultural values, and to examine the role played by their recognition in history. There would be a decisive methodological difference only if Alfred had insisted that his chosen values could be established as scientifically valid even in the face of contradictory opinions held by others in good faith. But that he does not seem to claim, since he demands recognition "only from those who feel themselves tied to the same values." No facet of Scientific Value Relativism opposes him in this, nor in any attempt to explore how a more general recognition of these values and their approximation in practical life could be achieved. The whole methodological difference between him and his brother might then boil down to this: that Alfred is a "latent" and a "partisan" relativist, while Max is an "overt" and a "neutral" one (see on these differences above, Chapter III, Section 8).

---

[7] *Op.cit.*, pp. 31, 32. This was first published in 1931 (*Geschichts- und Kultursoziologie als innere Strukturlehre der Geschichte*).

[8] *Principles*, p. 109, reprinted from a 1930 essay ("Ideen zur Staats- und Kultursoziologie").

Certain remarks in Alfred Weber's writings, however, can be interpreted to mean that the superiority of cultural values, or of particular ones among them, could be scientifically established in an intersubjective manner. His reference to the miraculous character of the fact that a general consensus on the eminence of cultural values is possible and to the apparent "underneath" connection among all human beings points in this direction. Universal consensus would certainly be a factor of great bearing on our problem, as we shall see in Chapters ix ff. But is there really a universal consensus as to the paramount value of cultural phenomena in general and in particular? Is the typical European appraisal in cultural matters shared, for instance, by Americans in the United States? Is the typical Western appraisal shared by the communists, or by Asiatic peoples? Wherever there is a divergence of evaluations, are we there not scientifically thrown back from Alfred Weber to Max? Not that nothing would be left for science to do. The scientist can still examine the origins of contradictory evaluations and their consequences for the development of the human race, of an individual nation, or of the individual person. But we cannot simply point to our personal conviction as an adequate *scientific* ground for our own evaluation, or to the consensus of our, alas not universal, friends.

Contradictory evaluations, even concerning cultural elements, thus force the scientist to reconsider his own value judgments on a truly scientific basis, or to confess frankly that he has no other basis than his own intuitional preference and that of others he reveres, and that means, some type of religious faith. If it comes to that, I gladly confess my consensus with Alfred Weber, without, however, seeing therein a methodological contradiction to Max.

(e) CONCILIATION OF VIEWS

A few words may be added here to my earlier recommendation that different names or symbols be used to denote the different meanings which may be associated with the term science.[9] Adding Latin terms to the symbolic letters, I suggest the following basic distinctions, which leave ample room for further subcategories:

[9] The need for the use of different names for different kinds of knowledge has sometimes found direct or indirect expression, as, for example, in the following remark by W. Ernest Hocking "If ethics and aesthetics founded on purpose and choice are still to be called 'sciences,' they are of a different order from the sciences of nature founded on causality which have the first right to the name" (*Science and the Idea of God*, Chapel Hill 1944, p. 5).

Knowledge, intersubjectively transmissible *qua* knowledge	S₁	*Scientia transmissibilis*
Knowledge, considered such, but not intersubjectively transmissible *qua* knowledge	S₂	*Scientia (sive vera sive putativa) non transmissibilis*
Mere speculations, not claimed to be knowledge	S₃	*Scientia mere speculativa*

In terms of this scheme, Scientific Method certainly supplies *scientiam transmissibilem*. This is true at least if one keeps in mind (see Chapter I, Sections 5 and 7) that what is transferred are only basic data (reports) and strictly analytical reasoning (as in mathematics), not the "acceptance" of the correctness of the observations or of inductive inferences made from them.

Should other methods evolve that are able to perform the same function, they too would have to be listed here; this line will be pursued in Chapters IX and X, below.

Private knowledge based on unverifiable observations—such as memories that have no confirming evidence in their favor, or philosophical intuition whose certainty is claimed but cannot be intersubjectively passed on to others, or religious revelation considered certain —is *scientia non transmissibilis*. Without a good stock of it we could hardly live as human beings, because the stream of *scientia transmissibilis* runs dry in so many vital fields. We live by the individuality of our knowledge. It is quite possible, as a rule, to communicate this private knowledge to others by narrating it to them, and we are often driven to do so by an almost irresistible urge. But this communication does not transmit our own (real or putative) knowledge as knowledge; transmission is limited to the personal report, or "protocol," saying that we believe we have knowledge on such and such a basis (see Chapter I, Section 3).[10]

Mere speculations, as for example about the nature of God or about life after death, constitute no science in the sense of the two preceding categories, not even the second unless the author regards their results

---

[10] It is basically in line with this view when Leo Strauss writes (*op.cit.*, p. 12): "Philosophizing means . . . to ascend from public dogma to essentially private knowledge." Whether it is, however, always an "ascent" is a *petitio principii*; this depends obviously on whether the claim to have correct knowledge is warranted. Shallow philosophers, and even great ones in their not infrequent duller hours, do not ascend, they descend. Moreover, not everything in philosophy is *scientia non transmissibilis*. The efforts of modern philosophy to expand its intersubjectively transmissible portion (see Introductory, Section 5, and remarks on Husserl, Chapter IX, Section 8) should not be ignored.

as revealed or intuitive knowledge. They supply "knowledge" only insofar as they (1) clarify the meaning of the problems involved, or (2) lead to greater clarity about potential alternatives of truth and relative probabilities, as when a scholar speculates about the origin of the cosmos, about the structure of the atom, the nature of light, etc. They may influence the selection of problems and methods of inquiry in the pursuit of *scientia transmissibilis,* and may gain the standing of a scientific "working hypothesis" (Chapter II, Section 6). They have, therefore, a tremendous importance in the totality of the scientific process, although chiefly as auxiliary steps in our effort to gain knowledge of the first grade.

To speculate about things unknown is an activity so characteristic of human beings that it may be warranted to call it a necessity for them, as Kant rightly recognized (Chapter II, Section 5, above). Yet, it can hardly be denied that a distinction is necessary between *scientia mere speculativa* and *scientia plus quam speculativa.*

4. *Religious Truth Considered Scientifically Verifiable*

The writers mentioned in the preceding section did not base their objections to Scientific Method and Scientific Value Relativism exclusively or primarily on religious grounds. Although religion played a considerable role in at least Maritain's arguments, the protest of this group is a broader one; it is fundamentally directed against what they call the arbitrary restrictions of science by keeping it tied to "just one method."

Turning now to religious references in particular, it is generally recognized that Scientific Method is unable to present proof for God's existence (see Chapters II, Section 1, and XIII). Those who continue to consider God's existence scientifically verifiable, as that is generally done in official or approved pronouncements within the Roman Catholic Church on this subject, can do so only by using the term "science" in a broad sense, which admits evidence of a type that, however convincing it may appear subjectively, is intersubjectively inconclusive—that is to say, evidence of the S_2 category, *scientia sive vera sive putativa, sed non transmissibilis.* But even theologians have more and more refrained from attempts to offer "scientific" proof for God's reality, focusing attention instead on the inner experiences that cause men to choose God. On the Protestant side, Professor Paul Tillich built his great and constructive *Systematic Theology*[1] on scientifically un-assailable ground by explicitly "presupposing" or "assuming" the reality of God as the necessary basis of any theology, without attempting scientific verification.

I am not going to continue this discussion here in general terms. Instead I shall review a recent proposal to include Christianity among the scientifically verified truths on the ground that it explains the facts of human nature and existence better than any other theory, and that its fruits, i.e., its consequences, testify to its truth. Professor John Hallo-well of Duke University, reputed political scientist, argued in this way at a round table on the topic "Beyond Relativism in Political Theory," held at the 1946 annual meeting of the American Political Science Association.[2] Before turning to the question of values, he said, one must answer one prior question, namely: What is the nature and destiny of man? He related the answer given by Christianity in the following manner:

> Christianity regards man as a rational creature, but does not over-look the fact that his ability to reason is warped by sin (i.e., pride in his own self-sufficiency). Endowed by his Creator with reason, man is capable of distinguishing good from bad, justice from injus-tice. . . .
>
> It is through reason as a supernatural faculty that truth is dis-covered and reality revealed. By enabling us to distinguish good from evil, reason is the most reliable guide to action. We must re-capture our belief in man as a rational creature, and Christianity enables us to do so.
>
> But at the same time, Christianity teaches us that man (human nature) is warped by sin. It teaches us to approach the problems of political and social order, therefore, "not with a broken and dis-credited intellect," but with a "broken and contrite heart." It recog-nizes the evil in the world as the perversion of human will and urges men to repent and to bring their will into conformity with God's will.
>
> Only in this way can men realize their freedom. For freedom can be preserved and perpetuated only by linking our capacity to choose alternative modes of behavior with the faculty with which we were endowed by our Creator, reason. . . . Freedom is rational choice.

[1] Paul Tillich, *Systematic Theology*, vol. 1, Chicago 1951, vol. 2, 1957.
[2] See my report in *American Political Science Review*, vol. 41 (1947) pp. 470–88.

4. RELIGIOUS TRUTH VERIFIABLE

Thus far there is no difference between Dr. Hallowell's ideas and what many scientific relativists would affirm as their personal belief. But while the latter would say that the truth of what they believe cannot be intersubjectively demonstrated, Hallowell claimed that it could. Said he:

> The proof of Christianity is its correspondence to reality, i.e., the fact that it explains more adequately than any rival religion or philosophy all the facts of human nature and experience. In a sense, its truthfulness is derived, in part at least, from the inadequacy of all rival explanations of life. In another sense, its truthfulness is demonstrated by its practical fruits, i.e., that it does enable men to live serene and happy lives. It enables us to live in the present without either complacent optimism or helpless despair.

Thoughts like these may well have played a decisive role in converting or reconverting many men and women to religion in general, and to the Judaeo-Christian religion in particular. But there is still a gulf that separates them from an intersubjectively conclusive scientific proof. Religious belief always leaves room for scientific doubt, though not for scientific refutation. It leaves room for such doubt also in the believer's own mind, who has constantly to sustain his faith against the lack of scientific proof (see Chapter XIII).

Intersubjective demonstrability seems to fail us even when we do not go so far as to seek it for Christianity, or for the reality of God, but limit ourselves to some such contention as that presented by W. Ernest Hocking that every human being feels a "cosmic demand" reaching him.[3] Suppose it were indeed possible scientifically to verify that some demand to be good is felt by everyone, this still would not prove, in an intersubjectively conclusive manner, that its origin is "cosmic." It may be interpreted as coming from society rather than from heaven, in other words (if a pun be permitted in this serious question) that it is "cosmetic" rather than "cosmic." Society demands of us that we put on some ethical rouge, or else—

No less a man than Oliver Wendell Holmes can be called upon as a witness for this ambivalence of the nature of the moral demand we feel. He acknowledged that some rudimentary elements in our familiar institutions may be necessary in any civilized society ("that would seem to us civilized"). But he hesitated to see in such awareness an "Ought of natural law," finding in it rather the recognition of a neces-

[3] W. E. Hocking, *Science and the Idea of God*, Chapel Hill 1944, pp. 47, 49.

283

sary concession to others to be made by him who wishes to live with others. He could not even discover an a priori "duty" to live with others:

> I see no a priori duty to live with others . . . but simply a statement of what I must do if I wish to remain alive. If I do live with others they tell me that I must do and abstain from doing various things or they will put the screws on me. I believe they will, and being of the same mind as to their conduct I not only accept the rules but come in time to accept them with sympathy and emotional affirmation and begin to talk about duties and rights.[4]

This amounts to saying that what by some is praised as a cosmic demand is felt by others as a mere cosmetic demand.

My own personal convictions are of no scientific importance beyond their worth as one individual report. They are basically in line with those of Hocking and Hallowell. Yet if in a scientific discussion of these questions someone should raise Holmes' objections in good faith, and state that God's reality appears unlikely to him, I must admit that my opposite conviction is ultimately based not on transmissible items of knowledge alone, but in addition on subjective experiences, which I can relate, but which can be plausible only to one who has had similar experiences, and consequently generally plausible only with regard to elements that are experienced by every human being. The question whether there are such universally experienced elements and what they are will be taken up in Chapter ix and x.

5. Objectivity of Values Contended

Others emphasize what they call the "objective" character of values. They generally start with assailing the idea that every moral value is the mere reflection of some duty, of some Ought, of some norm. Moral values, the German philosopher Max Scheler (1874–1928) said, give rise to moral duties, not vice versa. They do "exist," they can be "perceived," "felt"; they "are."[1] The following typical quotations from another German philosopher, Nicolai Hartmann (1882–1951), foremost representative of this school of thought, best illustrate the point. Values, he wrote, "have self-existence" and subsist "independently of

---

[4] Oliver Wendell Holmes, "Natural Law," *Harvard Law Review*, vol. 32 (1918) p. 40.

[1] Max Scheler, *Der Formalismus in der Ethik und die materielle Wertethik*, first published in "Jahrbuch für Philosophie und phänomenologische Forschung," vol. 1 and 2 (1913, 1916); 3rd ed. in one vol., 1926; 4th ed., by Maria Scheler, Bern 1954. Hereinafter cited as *Formalismus*. See there, IV, 1, also I, 2; II, B, 1.

the consciousness of them." "Knowledge of values is genuine knowledge of Being."[2] "In this 'beholding' of them [values] the subject is purely receptive; he surrenders himself to them. He sees himself determined by the object, the self-existent value; but he himself, on his side, determines nothing."[3] "There is a realm of values subsisting for itself , . . capable of being grasped." "The sense of value is not less objective than mathematical insight."[4] If a person changes his preference and emphasis regarding values, it is the focus of his glance at values which is shifting; the values themselves do not change thereby. "When our look at values 'wanders' (*wenn der Wertblick 'wandert'*) then the look is the relative thing, not the values themselves. They are the same, where and however they are grasped."[5]

Objectivity of values has been claimed by many others, and not only by those classified, as are Scheler and sometimes Hartmann, as phenomenologists. It was actually the older theory, held about the turn of the century by men such as Brentano, Windelband, Meinong, G. E. Moore, Rashdall and Bosanquet,[6] and later espoused in various forms by Sheldon, Emge, Urban, Hocking, Laird, Garnett, Ross, Felix Cohen, Fuller, Coing, von Fritz, in some points also by Perry,[7]

---

[2] Nicolai Hartmann, *Ethik*, 2 vols., Berlin 1926; translated in 3 vols. by S. Coit, London, New York 1932, under the title *Ethics*, vol. 1, pp. 218, 219.

[3] *Ibid*. See also, N. Hartmann, *Zur Grundlegung der Ontologie*, Berlin and Leipzig, 1935, p. 308: "The feeling of value possesses no freedom in front of the value once grasped by it; since it is actually less a grasping of the value than a being grasped by it. . . . And the test [of this] is the fact that the will, if in making a decision it disregards the value, gets into conflict with the value-feeling, and experiences its [the will's] own condemnation in the voice of conscience."

[4] *Ethics*, vol. 1, pp. 226, 227.

[5] *Grundlegung der Ontologie*, p. 308.

[6] Franz Brentano, *Vom Ursprung sittlicher Erkenntnis*, Leipzig 1889; Wilhelm Windelband, *Präludien* (5th ed., Tübingen 1915) vol. 2, pp. 161, 295, *Lehrbuch der Geschichte der Philosophie* (1891; 14th ed., Tübingen 1950) p. 580; A. Meinong, "Für die Psychologie und gegen den Psychologismus in der allgemeinen Werttheorie," *Logos*, vol. 3, pp. 1, 9; George E. Moore, *Principia Ethica*, Cambridge 1903, p. 188; Hastings Rashdall, *The Theory of Good and Evil*, Oxford, 1907 (2nd ed. 1924) vol. 1, p. 166; Bernard Bosanquet, *The Principle of Individuality and Value*, London 1912, pp. 291 ff.

[7] W. H. Sheldon, "The Empirical Definition of Value," *Journal of Philosophy*, vol. 11 (1914) pp. 113, 122, 123; W. M. Urban, "Value and Existence" and "Knowledge and the Value Judgment," *ibid.*, vol. 13 (1916) pp. 449, 673, 682, and "Ontological Problems of Value," *ibid.*, vol. 14 (1917) pp. 309, 317, 329; C. A. Emge, *Über das Grunddogma des rechtsphilosophischen Relativismus*, Berlin and Leipzig 1916; W. Ernest Hocking, *Present Status of the Philosophy of Law and of Rights* (1926), pp. 74 ff., and "Outline Sketch of a System of Metaphysics" in Martin Farber (ed.), *Philosophical Essays in Memory of Edmund Husserl* (1940) pp. 251–61; John Laird, *The Idea of Value*, Cambridge 1929, pp. 182, 240 ff., 317 ff.; A. Campbell Garnett, *Reality and Value*, New Haven 1937, pp. 154 ff., 179, 180; W. David Ross, *Foundations of Ethics*, Oxford 1939, pp. 83 ff., 167 ff., 188; Felix Cohen, *Ethical Systems and Legal Ideals*, New York 1933, p. 115; Lon L. Fuller, *The Law in Quest of Itself*, Chicago 1940, pp. 7, 11, 64; Helmut Coing, *Grundzüge der Rechtsphilosophie*

and by many others.[8] Some of their fomulations may illustrate the trend:

Windelband: "Relativism is abdication of philosophy and its death. Hence philosophy can live on only as the theory of the universally valid values (*als die Lehre von den allgemeingültigen Werten*)."[9]

Rashdall: Moral judgments "possess an absolute truth or falsity, which is equally valid for all rational beings."

Urban: Value does not come and go with the subject that feels it. Value is real, valid, objective, as distinct from existent and subsistent.

Laird: "Excellence is objective"; "timology is our insight into values; and we have this insight, often imperfectly, to be sure, but authentically nevertheless."

Garnett: Values are "objective," "objectively real," "are there," "discovered rather than established"; "as immediately given they have that final reality which belongs to everything else with which we have direct acquaintance."

Coing: The ethical contents of emotions are given man "irrespective of external experience." Values are "no mere phenomena of consciousness; they are independent of a consciousness that apprehends them."

Recasens: "Values are not created by man; rather, man has to recognize values."[10]

Ross: There are no absolute, but there are *prima facie* obligations, e.g., to fulfill promises. These we know by intuition. Any prima facie obligation may be over-ridden by another that is more stringent. Yet even in such cases of conflict, objectivity may be attained.

Perry: Although a relativist regarding preference[11] he feels able to state objectively that the "most inclusive" goods are best, and to derive from this proposition the definition of the supreme good as

---

Berlin 1950, esp. pp. 104, 106; Kurt von Fritz, "Relative and Absolute Values" in Ruth N. Anshen, *Ethical Principles of Action,* New York 1952; Ralph B. Perry, *General Theory of Value,* New York 1926, pp. 27, 77 ff.

[8] See, for instance, Dietrich von Hildebrand, "Sittliche und ethische Werterkenntnis," *Jahrbuch für Philosophie und phänomenologische Forschung,* vol. 4 (1921) pp. 162 ff., and *Christian Ethics,* New York 1953; Herbert Spiegelberg, *Anti-Relativismus,* Zürich and Leipzig 1935, pp. 48, 89. See also literature given in Appendix B.

[9] Compare the remark by Roscoe Pound that the current value relativism must be rejected as a "give-it-up" philosophy (*Justice According to Law,* 1951, pp. 21, 22).

[10] See his article in *Natural Law Forum,* vol. 3 (1958) p. 151, and Appendix B, below.

[11] *General Theory of Value,* p. 640, and above, Chapter VI, Section 5.

"the object which satisfies all individuals, when individuals are both integrated and harmoniously associated." [12] At other times he has attributed to "agreement" objective, even absolute value. [13]

We must first separate what is controversial in these contentions from what is not. This compels me to repeat several points discussed in the systematic chapters (I to IV). In the first place, it is of course accepted by Scientific Value Relativism that things we consider valuable, such as food and money, or qualities we praise, such as fortitude or patience, or actions, like the display of generosity, are not necessarily matters of our subjective imagination only (unless everything else be so too), but are often "objectively there," and verifiable as such. Likewise, the interrelations between things and between them and us that cause us to like or dislike them are frequently verifiable as being "objectively there." Musical harmonies, for example, are harmonic in an objective sense, which can be described and explained with physical exactness: they are produced by periodically coinciding wave lengths, such as 2:1 in the octave, 3:2 in the fifth, and 4:3 in the fourth —old Pythagorean knowledge. All this is uncontroversial. It applies to things and relations; does it hold also for the "values" we attach to them? Are they too "objectively there"?

Two different meanings of this question must be distinguished. Objectivity of values may simply mean the same thing we have just understood by objectivity of the things themselves and their relations. Food is an objective value because it is objectively valuable for the preservation of health, and harmony because we enjoy it. If that is the meaning intended there is again no controversy. As W. H. Sheldon has said, "Any tendency furthering an existent tendency is a good for it." [14]

But the claim to objectivity of values may go beyond this by asserting that the value of the ulterior goal also can be objectively established, and that the rank of any value within the entire range of potential values is something objective, not merely a reflection of our thoughts on it. This is what the scholars mentioned above obviously wanted to say. Even here, there is no controversy whenever the ulterior goal in its turn is measured in terms of some more remote, supposedly higher goal. However, such dialectic recourse to ever higher

[12] *Ibid.*, p. 686. See also below, Chapter VIII, Section 14.
[13] "The Moral Norm of Social Science," *Journal of Social Philosophy*, vol. 5 (1939) pp. 16, 17, 20, 27.
[14] "The Empirical Definition of Value," *Journal of Philosophy*, vol. 11 (1914) pp. 113, 122, 123.

goals finally reaches some limit. Ultimate standards are used as yard-sticks for the "in-between" goals. Only with respect to these ultimate standards does Scientific Value Relativism hold that their value cannot be objectively established; it cannot be verified *scientifically* that these ultimate values "are there," nor that they are objectively valid in some absolute sense of the term.

Here we reach the decisive point. If there be a benign Creator who has made world and man and has set the standards which determine the value of everything, then these standards and the values that under-lie them or are in accord with them are objectively there, or at least objectively valid. No scientific relativist would deny that. Yet as long as science humbly accepts its inability to prove the reality of God with scientific means, this type of objectivity of values cannot be scientifically verified. Without assuming some suprahuman agent who sets up the standards it cannot be said that they are objectively there, independent of you and me; otherwise values would have to be considered like independent entities, or gods, organizing themselves on their own power in some definite pyramid. This is either polytheism, or absurd.

One of the most frequent arguments in support of the objectivity of values—an old stock in trade, going back to Plato—is reference to the objective validity of mathematics.[15] This reference is abortive as far as intersubjective proof is concerned because, as we saw in Chapter I, Section 6, the validity of mathematics can be sufficiently explained by the strictly analytical character of mathematical inferences. We can deal with ethics likewise in a strictly analytical manner, in such forms as *"If* we call the development of the individual the highest value, *then* . . . ,"* and thus obtain scientific objectivity in ethics too. But that would merely beg the question whether the development of the indi-vidual, etc., *is* the highest good.

More relevant than reference to mathematics is the argument that in certain fields, such as aesthetics, value judgments quite obviously reach different levels according to the competence of the evaluating person and that almost everyone experiences how his own faculty of

[15] See Plato, *Republic*, Bk. VII. Richard Price, *A Review of the Principal Questions and Dif-ficulties in Morals*, 2nd ed. 1767, pp. 63, 74 ff. made the same comparison: "Whatever a tri-angle or circle is, that it is unchangeably and eternally . . . the same is to be said of right and wrong." A reprint, ed. by D. Raphael, was published Oxford 1948. References to theoretical objectivity can also be found in Brentano, *op.cit.*, p. 17; Rashdall, *op.cit.*, p. 85; Rickert, *System der Philosophie, op.cit.*, p. 134; Husserl, "Philosophie als strenge Wissenschaft" (see below, Chapter IX) pp. 324–25. More recently, most elaborate and emphatic, Nicolai Hartmann, *Grundlegung der Ontologie*, as cited, pp. 242 ff.

evaluation improves under the influence of education and training.[16] It appears to be evident, too, that some people have a certain degree of "valuing blindness" (*Wertblindheit*)—evident at least to others, but in retrospect frequently even to themselves. All this seems to testify to the fact that values "are there," and need only to be grasped by us.

Here again, several aspects must be distinguished. There are certainly many objective elements in aesthetic values. Some such elements are automatic in their aesthetic effect, as for instance musical harmonies, already mentioned, and the progressing from disharmonies to their resolving in harmonies. (The final resolving, if well prepared, may even be left to the inner ear of the hearer.) Further illustrations are the phenomena of perspective and of complementary colors. The reasons for their automatic effect can be scientifically disclosed. Other factors have no automatic effect but can be recognized through some cooperative effort of the observer. Our youthful failures in art appreciation, for example, had their cause, as a rule, in our inability to distinguish between deep emotional feelings aroused by the subject matter of an art product and its artistic qualities apart from the story. Nor were we able to distinguish between mere imitations and new creations, between effects easily produced (as perspective after the scientific discovery of the laws underlying this effect) and those which require more than routine, even the full abandon of a creative personality. There are, therefore, many elements of "transmissible knowledge" in art appreciation. Once we have learned to discern them we feel "objective" progress. In addition, our growing older supplies us with more and more experience of a type similar to that expressed in the art products of others, and this again improves our ability to understand art. All this is an objective increase in transmissible knowledge.

There are more objective elements in art. One is the fact that we share the feeling expressed in art with others; first of all with the artist himself ("How is it that you know me?" we may be tempted to ask him), but then also with many other people, sometimes with almost all who are confronted with the work, in other cases at least with

---

[16] This argument can be found in Rashdall, *op.cit.*, pp. 84 ff.; Bosanquet, *op.cit.*; Scheler, *Formalismus, passim,* and *Abhandlungen und Aufsätze* (1915, 2nd ed. 1919 under the title *Vom Umsturz der Werte*) p. 74; von Hildebrand, *Werterkenntnis, op.cit.*, p. 486; Emge, *op.cit.*, pp. 28 ff.; Hartmann, *Ethics,* pp. 226 ff.; Haldane, *The Reign of Relativity* (*op.cit.,* Chapter VI, above) pp. 357 ff.; Perry, *General Theory of Value,* p. 640; Spiegelberg, *op.cit.,* p. 65; Garnett, *op.cit.,* pp. 154, 167–68; von Fritz, *op.cit.*

connoisseurs. This is as strikingly objective a fact as anything can be, and of deep scientific interest (see Chapter 1, Section 2, on consubjectivity).

Finally, the artist may have had and expressed a premonition of some objective knowledge that had not yet been secured by slow science, but was anticipated and communicated to the observer by the artist. So it was originally with the laws of perspective, and so it still frequently happens with regard to psychological interrelations and other facts of human existence. Such discoveries and disclosures by artists may some day be verified by science, and the artist's suggestion may be regarded as an expression of intuitional knowledge (S_2) and even as a scientific hypothesis, capable of becoming the basis of scientific inquiries that follow Scientific Method. "Art begins where science leaves off," as Walther Rathenau put it in one of his striking aphorisms.

Thus there are more objective elements in art than meet the eye. But deeper forms of art appreciation will go beyond all of them, transcending ascertainable objective factors. The enjoyment, at times even rapture, we then experience may cause us to assume that in this stage too we are being seized by great objective values which simply demand our recognition. But this is not the only possible explanation. Our emotion may also be explained as an entirely subjective reaction, fulfillment of a subjective desire, paralleled by similar emotions of the artist that prompted him in his work, and of other observers. These factors may be called objective; for my subjective feeling is objectively there as a feeling, and the parallelism with the feelings of others too may be objectively there. But these objectivities are entirely dependent on human beings, and do not exist independent of them. If this interpretation fails to satisfy us, if we insist that we feel like being confronted with suprahuman objective values that are such irrespective of their relation to human enjoyment and other emotions, then we testify to the subjective feeling that there are suprahuman, divine forces. This feeling may be right. Such forces may be there. But we cannot prove it conclusively to others in this manner. Neither, therefore, can we prove trans-human aesthetic values to be objectively there, independent of the observer, of human senses, human experiences, human emotions.

Like aesthetic values, no ethical ones can exist as objective entities independent of human beings, unless some suprahuman mind exists and has established them. If the reality of divine forces cannot be proved with purely scientific means, neither can the independent objective existence of ethical values be so proved. To reason that the objective existence of aesthetic and ethical values is explained by the reality of divine forces and that the reality of the latter is proved by the objectivity of the values is to reason in a circle.

It has been said that the objective existence of ethical values is borne out by history, because history is credited with having shown that "the process of winning higher insights of a spiritual-moral character is irreversible. Once higher values have been discovered they can no longer be ignored." Man cannot with a good conscience ever back away from a stage of ethical insight once reached.[17] But this argument too is scientifically inconclusive. As a matter of historical record, there have been many changes and reversals in ethical evaluations from the times of ancient Greek and Roman culture to those of the early Middle Ages, from the late Middle Ages to modern times, and within the latter, from nineteenth-century Liberalism to the various totalitarian ethics of the twentieth. The perseverance of those ethical evaluations that have survived without reversals can be explained by improved knowledge of objective factors in qualities and relations, and by tradition, without recourse to the idea of an independent existence of values.

We only fool ourselves when we speak of ethical values as "being there," independent of men, while expressing or admitting scientific doubt about divine forces. If values are objectively there, independent of men, then they are there by fiat of suprahuman forces. If science cannot establish, with scientific means, the reality of divine forces, neither can it verify the objective reality of ethical, or any other, values, independent of men. The objective interrelations of things may be independent of God and men, but human *values* can exist only in the minds of God or of men—or both.

6. *Quasi-Logical Arguments*

Max Scheler and Nicolai Hartmann, starting from their thesis that values "exist," can be "perceived" and "felt" (see preceding section), have offered elements of an absolute hierarchy, or order of rank, of values; they claim that this order is fully supported by "immediate evidence." Values, wrote Scheler, are higher than others if they (1) last

---

[17] Coing, *op.cit.*, p. 109. See also C. A. Emge, *Uber das Grunddogma des philosophischen Relativismus,* as cited, pp. 29, 30: "The history of culture has disclosed plenty of values regarding which error seems to be excluded," for example, "that it is valuable to learn to walk and to speak." But this latter insight is hardly ethical in character; the extrinsic advantages of the ability to walk and speak suffice to explain general agreement.

longer, (2) lose less by the sharing of others in them, (3) depend less on other values, (4) give a deeper satisfaction, and (5) depend less on a specific value-sense.[1] Hartmann tried to refine Scheler's classification. It is characteristic of the limited usefulness in scientific discussions of so-called "immediate evidence" (*Evidenz*), to which both appealed as to their authority, that he reversed Scheler's hierarchical order in No. 3, thinking it evident that values are the higher the more they depend on other values, not the less.[2] Yet, like Scheler, he did insist on the "objective existence of gradation," it not being "in the power of man to change this gradation."[3] "The historical relativity of morality cannot rest upon that of values but only on that of discernment."[4]

At first sight, there seems indeed to be self-evident truth in Scheler's hierarchy. It seems logical to say that a value is greater than an otherwise equal value if it lasts longer, or that of two values the one that gives deeper satisfaction is more valuable. Likewise, it seems logically self-evident to say with Ralph B. Perry (see preceding section) that the "most inclusive" goods are best. To the extent that such statements are merely analytical paraphrases of the meaning of terms, they have in their favor all the evidence that goes with a strictly analytical deductive logic. As soon, however, as they are meant to be synthetic, that is, to add something that is not already implied in the concepts used, self-evidence disappears.

Let us begin with Perry's contention that the "most inclusive" values are best. This sounds eminently logical. Yet is it really so? On a lovely summer evening four boys were playing poker on the porch of a charming country house, when another member of the party began to play Bach in the adjacent room. Then one of the card players, who was a musician himself, said with rapture: "Poker is wonderful, Bach is wonderful, and now—Bach *and* poker!" And he raised his finger in delight. Certainly, Bach plus poker is "more inclusive," quantitatively speaking. But is it a value higher than Bach without poker? That does not depend on the formula "more or less inclusive"; it depends on what can be included in the value of listening to Bach without diminishing its value. Are not some values so exacting that they are exclusive of other values? Certainly the value we attach to God is

---

[1] Scheler, *Formalismus*, II, 3 (3rd ed., pp. 88 ff.).
[2] Hartmann, *Ethics*, vol. 2, pp. 54 ff., 385 ff., 389.
[3] *Ibid.*, p. 60.
[4] *Ibid.*, p. 65.

exclusive of many things we consider valuable on earth. As Francis Thompson wrote in his "Hound of Heaven":

> I pleaded, outlaw-wise,
> By many a hearted casement, curtained red,
>   Trellised with intertwining charities;
> For, though I knew His love who followèd
>   Yet I was sore adread
> *Lest, having Him, I must have naught beside.*

This leads us almost to a reversal of Perry's criterion; values may grow the higher the more exclusive they are.

Similar criticism must be raised against the validity of Scheler's criteria. "Values that last longer are higher than equal values that last less long" sounds logical. But what does logic do to values? A rainbow that lasts forever is no more valuable than one that stands in the skies for only a few minutes. Many joys are such only because they do not last. A symphony of three-quarters of an hour seems to be the optimal length of symphonic values; to extend it through twenty-four hours would give diminishing returns. A good speech or lecture does not increase in value if extended. Abraham Lincoln's Gettysburg address was very short. The value of friendship may increase with time, that of sexual relations does not. Patience is considered by most of us a high value; but if it lasts too long it may lose its value and become a disvalue. No value remains the same with time; it diminishes or increases.

Next, Scheler says, a value is higher than another if it loses less by the sharing of others in it. He obviously had in mind the love of God. However, is the fact that all can share it the real reason for its superiority? Is not the love between two lovers, which no one can share, a greater value than the love of a whore which everyone can share? Is the love, shared by hundreds of millions, of a big country more valuable than the love of a small one, like Switzerland or Iceland? Logic cannot solve this riddle.

Scheler's third step, which places a value that depends less on other values higher than one that depends more on others, has already been challenged by Hartmann, who thought it necessary to reverse this order completely, since he felt it self-evident that a value that depends more on other values is on a higher level. One theory is as little founded as the other. Such abstractions provide no criteria of absolute validity.

That a value is the higher the deeper the satisfaction it gives is self-evident only when we define value as that which gives satisfaction and equate highest with deepest. Then the statement is merely analytical, adding no synthetic information to either side of the equation; it does not say which value is highest or which satisfaction is deepest. It is by no means self-evident, for instance, that religion gives the deepest possible satisfaction; if it were, all people would be religious.

Logic does not tell us what are values and what is their rank, and any attempt to make us believe that logic answers these questions is fallacious. Scheler and Hartmann did not mean to rely on logic, but their arguments had a logical flavor. There may be immediate evidence of the rank of values for us individually, that is, we may individually be certain that we know the truth about the rank of values, and we may even be right—but this is individual "intuitive knowledge" of the category S_2. We cannot transmit it conclusively to others who disagree in good faith. To what extent such intuitive knowledge is universal we may try to find out empirically (see Chapters IX and X).

7. Gestalt Psychology, a Supplier of Objective Values?

Gestalt psychology has developed an original approach to the value problem. In its terms, *that* is objectively valuable which is objectively "required" in a definite situation or field as a response to some existing or potential "lacuna" or gap, or as a release of forces directed toward the "correct" filling of that lacuna.[1] This view has taken an interesting psychophysical turn in Wolfgang Köhler's theory that physical processes within the cortex may account for, or correspond to, this urge (see Chapter XI, Section 1).[2]

No specific contribution to political problems has yet come from Gestalt psychology. Köhler excluded all ethical, political, and legal problems from his study on the place of values in the world of facts.[3] Max Wertheimer modestly admitted that it is necessary "to start with

---

[1] See especially Max Wertheimer's paper "Some Problems in the Theory of Ethics," *Social Research*, vol. 2 (1935) pp. 353–67, and Wolfgang Köhler, *The Place of Value in a World of Facts*, New York 1938. On Gestalt psychology in general see also Gardner Murphy, *Historical Introduction to Modern Psychology*, rev. ed., 1949, pp. 284 ff. (reprinted in Wiener, *Readings in the Philosophy of Science*, pp. 207 ff.). Further, Kurt Koffka, *The Growth of the Mind*, transl. by M. Ogden, New York 1924 (2nd ed. 1928); and *Principles of Gestalt Psychology*, New York 1935. Certain aspects of Gestalt theory had been developed independently earlier, e.g., by Bernard Bosanquet, *op.cit.*, and by Moore, *Principia Ethica*, *op.cit.*, pp. 27 ff., 213 ff.

[2] Köhler, *op.cit.*, pp. 185, 233, 329 ff.

[3] *Ibid.*, pp. 101, 339, 411.

the study of the most concrete, transparent examples," with "pure cases," and that most practical cases were "much more complicated." [4] One of the younger members of the Gestalt school, the late Karl Duncker, emphasized, on the basis of anthropological research, that there are invariant inner laws of ethical valuation and that only the different meanings of acts and situations becloud this invariant character. He pointed to the fact that justice has never been considered a vice.[5] Yet he made no attempt to tell us what inner laws of justice *are* invariant, a question to which we shall return later.

Looking at ethical problems from the Gestalt viewpoint would not necessarily contradict the Gulf Doctrine according to which purely logical inferences must not pass from statements of Is to those of Ought. Transcribed into formal logic, the approach of Gestalt psychology to ethics can be interpreted to operate on the basis of a major premise to the effect that what is objectively required in order to restore or complete a defective Gestalt (configuration, whole) ought to be done. Wertheimer, originator of Gestalt psychology, seems to have gone further, however, by envisaging the possibility that a revised code of logic would have to accept, as legitimate, logical inferences drawn from some Is to the "required" filling of a lacuna, without resorting to a major premise of the Ought form.[6] This, like J. S. Mill's thesis that all inferences are "from particulars to particulars," confuses psychology and logic (see above, Chapter v, Section 7).

It seems to me obvious that Gestalt psychology as such is unable to answer controversial ethical questions regarding what is objectively required in a situation. In order to know that, we cannot rely exclusively on a study, however ingenious, of psychological experience in the participants. We would need an additional theory to explain why a certain urge is objectively required where it actually is not forthcoming subjectively, or which states that certain ethical urges are actually alike in all persons. That these additional propositions cannot be supplied with the methods of Gestalt psychology will appear from the following illustration.

Suppose a man strolling through a park passes by a pond and observes how an infant, leaning over too far, is falling into the water

---

[4] Wertheimer, *op.cit.*, p. 364; also "A Story of Three Days" in Ruth Anshen (ed.) *Freedom —Its Meaning*, New York 1940, p. 555.

[5] Karl Duncker, "Ethical Relativity?" in *Mind*, vol. 48 (1939) pp. 39, 50, 51. See similar remarks at Nicolai Hartmann, *Zur Grundlegung der Ontologie*, *op.cit.*, p. 311; Clyde Kluckhohn, "Ethical Relativity: Sic et Non," *The Journal of Philosophy*, vol. 52 (1955) p. 666.

[6] Wertheimer in *Social Research*, *op.cit.*, p. 362, note 3.

and is about to be drowned. Suppose that no one else is around and that the pond is so shallow that the man, not being in a hurry, need only stretch out his arms in order to save the child from certain death, and that he is aware of all these facts. Then it is "objectively required," so it seems, that he lift the child from the pond; this would be the correct filling of the lacuna, the action which he ought to perform.

Now let us suppose that the man is one of the servants of Herod, sent out to Bethlehem with orders to kill all children two years or under.[7] Seeing that a child of less than two is about to be accidentally drowned in the pond, the man then would have within his psychological field not only the scene in the park but in addition the command of the king. Within his psychological field, therefore, there is no lacuna which requires action to save the child; rather the opposite. To say that in spite of the royal orders saving the child is "objectively required" in this situation is not warranted by Gestalt psychology; it could be justified only if we were able to introduce an additional thesis—which does not follow from Gestalt psychology—saying the king's order was so outrageous that disobedience was objectively required. In other words, we would have to establish the validity of an ethical postulate that saving children is a deeper duty than obedience to one's superior; and that is to say, we must establish a hierarchy of values.

We need only put Hitler or Stalin in lieu of Herod, and Jews or "capitalist counterrevolutionaries," respectively, in lieu of the infants to be killed, to see that we are dealing here with a practical problem of the greatest importance. Without referring to the idea that there is a law higher than the law given by the government, or a duty deeper than that of obedience to governmental orders, or at least that the inward urge to disregard governmental orders in such situations on the ground that they are flagrantly unjust is a universal human feeling, we cannot resolve the problem in favor of the persecuted group. These are questions to which we will return in another context (Chapters ix and x).

8. *Formal Standards*

Conceding the relativistic contention that no substantive ethical postulates can be scientifically established in absolute terms, some writers, following Kant's lead, have claimed that at least *formal* standards can be laid down as absolute postulates of justice. These efforts are closely related to the endeavor to find a correct *definition* of justice. They go

[7] Matthew 2:16.

beyond ordinary definitions, however, by claiming absolute validity for the formal standards.

Thus Karl Bergbohm, who in his main work of 1892 [1] administered what then was considered by many the knock-out blow to the old Natural Law school, did not go so far as to deny any invariant elements in justice. He held that the *concept,* or notion, of law and right (*der Rechtsbegriff*) was unchangeable, invariant and at all times the same.[2]

Rudolf Stammler, too, originally intended to offer no more than formal standards. Even in his violent attacks on Max Weber's relativism [3] he pleaded merely for the recognition of a "formal method which as a method is absolutely valid," and a few pages later [4] praised the *Weltanschauung* of the individual as the ultimate source of unity in all his mental endeavors and activities. His formal standard, however, saying that "just" is what is in line with "the objectively justified interests of others," is chiefly mere tautology, because only those interests are "justified" which, all things considered, it is "just" to respect. How we can "objectively" state which interests it is just to respect, without a circular reference to the question of what is just, he does not say. Actually, Stammler transgressed his allegedly formal standards by decidedly substantive statements (see above, Chapter v, Section 8). To that extent he abandoned the merely formal method.

Most attempts to lay down formal standards deal with law rather than justice. This involves a fundamental difference, since the concept of law, as distinct from "acts" on the one hand and "judgments" on the other, and as further distinct from "morals," "conventions," "customs," and "general conditions"—all of which may be just or unjust—includes several formal criteria that do not derive from the idea of justice and include no value judgments. Investigations bringing out these distinctions may be very elaborate and illuminating in other respects and still of no use for the investigation of the nature of justice. This applies, in particular, to the Vienna school of "pure law," which has endeavored to disclose universal formal elements of law, but has explicitly excluded from its work the question of what is just.[5]

---

[1] Karl Bergbohm, *Jurisprudenz und Rechtsphilosophie,* Leipzig 1892.

[2] *Ibid.,* vol. I, pp. 73, 74.

[3] Rudolf Stammler, "Rechtsphilosophie," *Das gesamte Deutsche Recht,* vol. I, Berlin 1931, p. 20.

[4] *Ibid.,* p. 42.

[5] See the literature cited in Chapter VI; also Felix Kaufmann, *Die Kriterien des Rechts,* Tübingen 1924, and "Juristischer und soziologischer Rechtsbegriff" in *Gesellschaft, Staat und Recht,* Wien 1931, p. 15.

9. *More, Not Less, Relativity Contended*

In contrast to the eight types of attack on Scientific Value Relativism so far discussed, a ninth insists that the error of value relativism is rather on the side of understating than of overstating relativity. *All* our scientific efforts, these critics say, not scientific value judgments alone, are necessarily marred by subjective prejudices. Within the social sciences, at least, there is no such thing as a *voraussetzungslose* (unprejudiced, nonconditional) science at all. Every scientific investigation is influenced, so it is argued, by at least four limitations of objectivity: first, by the historical, cultural, economic, social, or any other existential type of situation (caste, class, professional group, generation, etc.) within which the scholar lives and works; second, by his individual *Weltanschauung,* including his accepted myths from which he can never fully disentangle himself; third, by the fact that he makes his scientific decision at a definite date; and fourth, by the limitations of his individual capacity and maturity as a scholar.[1]

The first point has been elaborated in the sociology of knowledge, especially by Karl Mannheim;[2] it has been emphasized independently by others, such as the German philosopher Theodor Litt.[3] The second was given particular weight by R. M. MacIver,[4] the third by the religious philosopher Paul Tillich;[5] the fourth is self-evident.

This growing awareness of conditioning factors which hamper every scientific research is relevant in many respects, yet it is not apt to reduce the particular significance of Scientific Value Relativism. It is true that those general factors are not limited to value judgments but affect all our social knowledge, including the selection of problems and factual research. But to argue on this ground that there is no point in stressing relative elements in value judgments alone means disregarding fundamental differences. Factual research and strictly logical inferences offer

[1] See the able review given by Eduard Spranger, *Der Sinn der Voraussetzungslosigkeit in den Geisteswissenschaften,* Berlin 1929.

[2] Karl Mannheim's chief work, *Ideologie und Utopie,* was first published 1929 in Bonn. It was followed, among others, by his article "Wissenssoziologie" in *Handwörterbuch der Soziologie,* Stuttgart 1931. The latter article is included, as Chapter v, in the English edition, *Ideology and Utopia, an Introduction to the Sociology of Knowledge,* tr. by Louis Wirth and Edward Shils, London and New York 1936. This edition has been enriched also by an introductory chapter (I) written by Mannheim himself and by a good preface from the pen of Wirth. Other works include *Essays in the Sociology of Knowledge,* New York 1952; *Essays on Sociology and Social Philosophy,* ed. by Paul Kecskemeti, New York 1953, especially pp. 236 ff. See also R. K. Merton, *Social Theory and Social Structure,* 2nd ed., 1957, pp. 439 ff.

[3] Theodor Litt, *Wissenschaft, Bildung, Weltanschauung,* 1928, p. 106.

[4] R. M. MacIver, *The Web of Government,* New York 1947. See above, Chapter vi, Section 5, d.

[5] Paul Tillich, *Kairos, Zur Geisteslage und Geisteswendung,* Darmstadt 1926, p. 74.

possibilities of intersubjective verification that are not available in the case of ultimate value judgments. Regarding the former, we can at least try with every conceivable effort to overcome our dependence on historical and personal factors of the four types enumerated above, in order to present the facts and the logical inferences objectively. In dealing with ultimate value judgments, however, no scientific way is open to us when we wish to check upon their validity, beyond research on consequences, agreement, and the like. The more we try to disentangle ourselves from historical and personal conditions and prejudices, and the more we try to be objective, only the more will we recognize the particular obstacles which confront science in dealing with ultimate standards of values. Their validity seems to be outside the pale of possible intersubjective verification.

There is, in other words, more than a merely quantitative difference in the difficulty of verifying factual statements and value judgments. To argue that, because absolute validity cannot be guaranteed in factual statements, we may freely renounce our efforts toward objectivity everywhere, is like arguing with Valentin in Goethe's *Faust,* who says to Margarete, *"Du bist doch nun einmal eine Hur', so sei's auch eben recht"* (You are a whore now anyway, so be one fully and all right). In his 1929 essay on unprejudiced research in the social sciences,[6] Eduard Spranger rightly warned of the danger that would threaten scientific research if, out of recognition of the many difficulties that hamper our efforts toward objectivity, we should begin to think of these endeavors lightly or even abandon them. He hoped that three impulses would carry science to ever new levels, namely, first, the idea of truth, which has remained the unifying bond of all sciences; second, scientific self-criticism, which enables science at all times to criticize and revise its own foundations (*Voraussetzungen*); and third, when views remain different, the effort to lift the different systems to higher levels of unity through the uniform intention of following truth. Although the *reality* of scientific work may always be influenced or prejudiced by various conditions, the *idea* of science never permits us to cultivate such partiality and peculiarity, he wrote; it rather demands "that from those starting points we proceed under no ethical law other than that of objectivity. Accordingly it is the duty of philosophy, as the basis of science, to raise this law of objectivity to ever purer consciousness."

Spranger seems to have hoped that science might finally overcome those obstacles which still block its direct approach to ultimate value

[6] *Op.cit.*

judgments by an ascent to a synthesis on a higher level (see Chapter VI, Section 3 c, above). Such a synthesis is, of course, always open to religion and philosophy. But science is unable to establish the absolute validity of any proposed synthesis of ultimate values. Spranger himself refers with approval to Rickert's statement, quoted in Chapter VI, that "only when we have come to see all values as values can we successfully beware of onesidedly espousing specific values."

Mannheim ostensibly rejected relativism (*Ideology and Utopia,* pp. 145, 237, 254) as "sterile," but in so doing lumped historical, philosophical, and scientific relativism, and also relativism of general outlook and mere value relativism. This fusion is not conducive to clarity. Actually, he fully agreed that no absolute propositions regarding ultimate values can be proved valid with scientific means.[7] He characteristically wavered between a neutral and a partisan approach (without using these names, of course), declaring the former sometimes impossible, sometimes sterile, sometimes the most advanced, reserving it for "unattached intellectuals," or more especially, for "unattached sociologists." Then again he advised these free-floating glamor boys to attach themselves to some partial view on the basis of a free choice among alternatives, because only in participation and action would they obtain the deepest—although possibly partial—insights. In the course of his argument he gradually modified his original extreme formulations on the inevitable "existential determination" (*Seinsgebundenheit*) and "situational determination" (*Situationsgebundenheit*) of all human knowledge. Thus, in questions of value judgments his views became more and more similar to those of Scientific Value Relativism (see e.g., pp. 42, 166, 169, 254, 266 ff.; also R. K. Merton, *op.cit.*). In fact, he added many important observations in support of this approach.

10. *Conclusion*

Summarizing the results of this chapter, we are compelled to state, whether or not we like it, that Scientific Value Relativism, when understood as it is here presented, that is, minus the misrepresentations discussed in the first section, has not been refuted by any of the method-

[7] See e.g., p. 254, where he claims that his doctrine, which he calls "relationism," does not signify that there are no criteria of rightness and wrongness in a discussion, but immediately adds: "It does insist, however, that it lies in the nature of certain assertions that they cannot be formulated absolutely, but only in terms of the perspective of a given situation." Scientific Value Relativism teaches no more relativity than that, and even less, because it does not doubt that absolute criteria can be "formulated," but only that their validity can be proved scientifically.

ological attacks leveled against it: not by the contention that Scientific Method could deal with values precisely as with facts (Section 2), nor by the claim that other methods could solve value problems adequately in an intersubjectively verifiable manner (Section 3); not by the attempts to prove scientifically the validity of religious Truth (Section 4), or at least the "objectivity" of ultimate values beyond their relational aspects (Section 5); nor by quasi-logical arguments (Section 6), by Gestalt psychology (Section 7), or by the establishment of formal standards (Section 8); nor, finally, by the contention that all other scientific endeavors are as relative as the efforts to determine ultimate values (Section 9).

This debate has, nevertheless, contributed to a deeper understanding of the issue. It has shown, in particular (1) the necessity of clearly distinguishing among at least three types of knowledge—intersubjectively transmissible, not so transmissible, and merely speculative; (2) the considerable amount of objective contributions to the examination of values that can be made in various ways; and (3) the legitimacy of a frankly speculative discussion of metaphysical problems and alternatives by scientists who bring into these discussions their disciplined knowledge of the corpus of scientifically secured knowledge.

CHAPTER VIII

TWENTIETH-CENTURY ATTEMPTS TO IDENTIFY
HIGHEST VALUES

1. *Survey*

THE preceding chapter dealt with the methodological objections that have been raised against Scientific Value Relativism. It did not list the manifold attempts made by great scholars in this century actually to identify values, especially the highest and ultimately controlling among them. If we now turn to these attempts—concrete scientific propositions, that is, as distinct from the abstract scheme of theoretically possible differences of opinion on highest standards that was presented in Chapter VI, Section 6—the most striking feature is that the values served as supreme by contemporary scholars continue to vary greatly, almost as greatly as the systematic possibilities permit. And yet, self-evidence, or immediate evidence, has been claimed by all. Some have sought additional support in revelation as transmitted through holy books.

The accompanying schedule, which aligns the chief proposals in something resembling a systematic order, is likely to be more impressive and telling than any comment could be. What, we must ask, is the *scientific* weight of an alleged self-evidence that is in conflict with what appears self-evident to so many other excellent men?

It was no relativist, but one of the ablest fighters for the absolute, Austrian professor Johann Sauter, who wrote in 1932: "Who is authorized to behold (*schauen*) the Ideas—that, I admit, is the great question. Every one sees a different thing in the realm of Ideas, even among philosophers, nay much more among them than within any other vocation."[1] Whether it is really true that everyone sees something different in the realm of values, and does so in every respect, will be examined in later chapters. Yet insofar as top values are concerned, the differences are astounding indeed. Alas, the decisive ethical question in political controversies is usually precisely this: which of the values given top rank by the different apostles ought to be preferred?

The classification of the individual proposals given in the table's first column, "General Type," is admittedly rough. Details are discussed in the following sections. Before we move on to them, however, the following should be plainly remembered. Personal conviction that

[1] Johann Sauter, *Die philosophischen Grundlagen des Naturrechts*, Vienna 1932, p. 26, n. 4.

Top Values

in Twentieth-Century Political and Legal Philosophy

General Type	Representative Writers	Proposed Top Values	See Sec.
1. Equalitarian	Nelson G. Husserl	Equality	2
2. Individualist (Liberal)	Bosanquet	"Individuality within the whole"	3 and App.
	Hocking	"The right of the individual to develop the powers in him"	
	Wild	"Perfective tendencies"	
	Coing	Liberty takes precedence over equality	
	Recasens	"Humanism," or "Personalism"	
3. Revelationist	Cathrein Rommen Maritain Hallowell	God's will plus reason in its metaphysical reaches. The Decalogue. The basic principles of Christianity	4
4. Ethical naturalist	Del Vecchio	Human nature with its rational elements	5
	Gény	The "given facts," including history, reason, common ideals, and intuition	
	Radbruch III Northrop	The "nature of things" Nature in cultural interpretation	
	Fuller	Nature in collaborative discovery of purposes and principles	
5. Ethical evolutionist	J. Huxley	Evolution as a source of objective ethical standards	6
6. Conservative	de Tourtoulon Rommen	*Suum cuique* in a status-quo interpretation of *suum*, mitigated by a progressive interpretation of *cuique*	7
7. Democratic	Radbruch II	Tolerance, no violent enforcement of one's own value judgments (absolute principles derived from Relativism)	8

Top Values
in Twentieth-Century Political and Legal Philosophy (*continued*)

General Type	Representative Writers	Proposed Top Values	See Sec.
8. Hedonist	Felix Cohen	Happiness, as the surplus of pleasures over pains	9
	G. E. Moore (in part)	Personal affection, aesthetic enjoyment	17
9. Social idealist	Stammler	The "social ideal," i.e., the "community of men of free will"	10
Social func- tionalist	Duguit	Social solidarity and social function	
10. Nationalist	Binder Sauer	The nation	11
11. "Machiavellian"	E. Kaufmann Lasswell Catlin H. Morgenthau	Power, commonly striven after as a high value, though not necessarily by the author	12
12. Transpersonalist	Kohler Alfred Weber	*Kultur*	13
	Northrop	Cultural assumptions about na- ture	5
13. Harmonizer	Stammler Perry	Harmony Harmonious happiness	14
14. Fighter for the Golden Rule	MacIver	Do to others as you would have them do to you	15
15. Fighter for Justice	Radbruch IV	Human Rights, derived from the idea of justice	16

there is a difference in the weight of values, some ultimate goals toward which men strive being better than others and some deserving a neg- ative rather than positive evaluation, is not in conflict with Scientific Value Relativism. Its adherents, as shown, have at times professed their own faith in the preeminence of certain values.[2] What they have de- nied is solely the possibility for science in an intersubjectively trans-

[2] In addition to Max Weber and Gustav Radbruch (Chapter VI, Sections 2 and 3) see Hein- rich Rickert, *System der Philosophie* (cited *ibid.*, Section 1) pp. 150, 155, and *Grenzen der naturwissenschaftlichen Begriffsbildung* (*ibid.*) pp. 559 ff.; also Kelsen, *What Is Justice?* p. 24, see Appendix B.

missible manner to demonstrate the existence of an absolute order of values, or the validity of any proposed order, including the one accepted by themselves. Therefore, if we now proceed to review individual proposals made by twentieth-century philosophers, the question is not of our own personal agreement or disagreement with their personal convictions, or even of our denial that they *may* be right, but only of the transmissible proof they have offered or failed to offer.

Some uncontroversial points which, generally unexpressed but implied, underlie all proposals will be examined later. These points are important, both for theory and practice, but do not yield standards of the type here discussed.

Not infrequently, writers have presented observations of immaculate logic in order to show that their proposals follow strictly from some more general dogma accepted by them. But this does not spare us the trouble of asking for the scientific proof in support of the basic dogma itself.

I am ruefully aware of boresome redundance in my repetitive use of arguments within several sections of the present chapter. My only excuse is: that each of the specific values discussed hereafter has its own tremendous political and scientific significance and unsuppressible vitality, and that those arguments, though often substantially identical, apply to a characteristically different complex of ideas and feelings in each case. Moreover, it has been my main purpose here to show, from section to section, what great contributions science can render, and I could not do this without specifically restating the negative limitations.

2. *Equality*

There has never been any doubt that equality has something to do with justice. Equal treatment of equal cases has always appeared to be the very core of justice (see below, Chapter x). But almost as old as this postulate is the recognition that it does not decide what *is* equal, i.e., what cases are equal, and in particular, whether all human beings are equal. In claiming human equality one adds a second postulate to the former.

Can human equality be established in scientific terms? Aristotle stressed the inequalities of men at least as much as their equalities. The Stoics shifted the emphasis to equality as some of the Sophists had done before. Christianity proclaimed equality before God; but God's reality, being itself beyond scientific proof, cannot be made the basis for scientific demonstrations of its implications. Hobbes argued that human equalities were far more numerous and important than human inequalities, yet failed to offer a yardstick by which the relative weight could be measured.[1] Locke admitted that men were not, in fact, equal, but regarded nothing as more evident than that "creatures of the same species and rank . . . *should* also be equal one amongst another"; and that, though not born *in* equality, they were born *to* it.[2]

The Age of Enlightenment was dominated by the persuasion that human equality was "self-evident." This was most nobly expressed in the American Declaration of Independence: "We hold these truths to be self-evident, that all men are created equal, that they are endowed by their Creator with certain inalienable Rights, that among these are Life, Liberty and the pursuit of Happiness. . . ." But again, this assumption rested on the premise of a higher design ("Creator," "created"). If that premise lacked scientific proof, neither could the implication be sustained as a *scientific* statement; human equality then was a religious and political creed, to be either espoused or rejected, but not capable of scientific verification in absolute terms.

Approaching the problem not religiously but scientifically, we must distinguish (1) the fact, (2) the concept or idea, (3) the value or disvalue, and (4) the ideal, of equality. The first question is: what are the *facts* regarding the similarities and the differences between human beings in every sphere of their existence? The second: what, in speaking of non-identical things or beings, do we mean by "equal," both when we say that they are or are not equal and that the treatment they receive from others is or is not equal? Then the third question arises, whether equality of things or beings or of their treatment is not merely a neutral fact (actual or potential) but a *value* or disvalue; and finally, the fourth: whether equality is considered, or should be considered, an *ideal,* worthy of the highest place or, at least, of a high place in the list of values.

In observing the facts we are still confronted with the most obvious reality that human individuals are similar in many respects but different in many others. Whenever we claim that the features in which they are similar are the only "essential," the only "relevant," ones we must demonstrate more than the factual reality of such similarities; we must establish their relative "weight," "value," or "relevance" with regard to the problem under inquiry.

[1] *Leviathan*, ch. XIII.
[2] *Second Treatise of Civil Government*, Sections 4 and 55.

Anthropological research alone is unable to establish such relative weight. Anthropology can render—and has rendered—invaluable service by refuting the validity of the superficial appearance that ethnic or racial differences of external traits (such as color) mirror corresponding qualitative differences. While the books of science may not be definitely closed on this issue, positive contentions that such a hereditary correspondence exists—as distinct from merely environmental effects— have been refuted as scientifically unjustified or, at least, inconclusive. This is the greatest contribution anthropology could possibly render to the problem of human equality. The importance of it cannot be overemphasized. But, while racial differences may have nothing to do with the actual inequalities that otherwise exist between individuals, such other differences do remain obvious realities, within all human races, and anthropology can but confirm this fact. The ethical or political ideal that in spite of such individual differences all human beings should be treated as "essentially equal" is necessarily beyond the scope of anthropological determination.

Owing to this default in intersubjective demonstrability twentieth century scientific literature has, tacitly rather than overtly but nevertheless conspicuously, withdrawn from references to the "self-evidence" of human equality, although state documents, political addresses, and popular speeches have continued to use that old assertion. One important twentieth-century philosopher, however, bravely retackling the issue, has reverted to the claim of immediate evidence in favor of a broad equalitarian postulate. He is Leonard Nelson (1882–1927), professor of philosophy in Göttingen and Berlin, remarkable for his clear and beautiful style—a rare virtue with German philosophers—and for the broad sweep of his books, which include a major work under the hallowed Kantian title *Critique of Practical Reason*.[3] As regards equality, he presented a profound analysis of what real equality of treatment would mean and involve, in particular with reference to a redistribution of property.[4] But the important point for the present discussion is his derivation of the postulate of equality.

Nelson reaches it not from any empirical study of facts regarding the actual equality of all human beings, but through a rational deduc-

[3] Leonard Nelson, *Kritik der praktischen Vernunft*, Göttingen 1916; *Die Rechtswissenschaft ohne Recht*, Leipzig 1917; *System der philophischen Rechtslehre und Politik*, Leipzig 1926; *System der philosophischen Ethik und Pädagogik* (posthumously published), Göttingen 1932, the latter recently published in an English translation by N. Guterman under the title *System of Ethics*, New York 1956.
[4] See below, Chapter XII, Section 3, and vol. 2.

tion from another empirical fact, which he considers self-evident, namely, that men have ethical feelings which refer to some ethical norm. The "originally vague" meaning of this norm can be clarified, he holds, by "discursive argument" to the effect that it forbids any differentiations that are not due to qualitative differences. Therefore the criterion of the ethical norm must be equality, he concludes.[5]

So far so good. There seems indeed to operate some universal postulate in all men which demands equal treatment of cases that are qualitatively equal, as we shall go on to investigate in Chapter x below. Yet this fact, even if it could be verified scientifically, would not justify any conclusion as to what cases are qualitatively equal, and especially, whether and how far men are. In this respect however, Nelson slips into misleading formulations. Precisely because his books are written in such an admirably clear and logical language, which fills even a critical reader with confidence and finally lulls his critical independence, it is important to show exactly where the breach in Nelson's argument is.

At first he is on firm ground in stating that the human urge toward equality "by no means excludes preferences that are warranted by a difference in the situation of the one and the other"; [6] such a difference in the situation is rightly said to include differences in the quality of persons.[7] In the sentence following the first statement Nelson adds, however, that "individuals as such are equal. . . ," and he also speaks of the "equal claim of all persons to the recognition of their interests"; [8] this he calls their "equal dignity."

These formulations are likely to make us forget that according to Nelson's own point of departure there may be differences in the *quality* of persons. In the absence of any other limitative argument these differences might be considered so great as to warrant any kind of differential treatment, including such as has prevailed during periods of slavery and racial and religious persecutions. Nelson's demonstration unfortunately provides no argument against this possibility, although this shortcoming is clouded by the formulations quoted and Nelson's many adherents do not seem to be aware of it.

---

[5] *Praktische Vernunft*, pp. 469 ff., in particular pp. 503 and 518. Similarly Helmut Coing, *Grundzüge der Rechtsphilosophie*, Berlin 1950, p. 188: "The yardstick of *justitia distributiva* (as of justice altogether) is equality." Equality "forbids unjustified special advantages or disadvantages of individuals within the community."

[6] *Rechtslehre und Politik*, p. 85; this corresponds to the postulate of equal treatment of equal cases.

[7] *Praktische Vernunft*, p. 119.

[8] *Rechtslehre und Politik*, p. 85, and *Praktische Vernunft*, p. 520, respectively.

2. EQUALITY

It is methodologically important to note that Nelson did not try to prove the postulate of equal treatment in justice on purely logical grounds. He recognized, in explicit words, that a merely logical proof of ethical norms is impossible. Instead, he referred to empirical evidence as the indispensable basis of all his logical reasoning. This empirical evidence—not of human equality but of an ethical norm forbidding us to differentiate unless there are qualitative differences—he considered immediately given.[9] But even if this be conceded it does not bear out his conclusions regarding human equality, as we have seen.[10]

Sometimes the eighteenth-century argument that all men ought to be treated as equal on the ground that they are "born equal" is still heard today in the somewhat more precise form that equal treatment is evidently required on the ground that all men are by birth in "the same plight," because they had no influence on whether they were born at all, into what conditions they were born, and from whom they descended.[11] This way of arguing supplies a forceful emotional appeal, but no scientific proof that only equal treatment of all human beings is just, unless we have previously accepted a major premise to the effect that all those who are born into the same plight ought to be treated equally. This premise, in turn, needs proof in order to be scientifically acceptable. It is not self-evident. On the contrary, it obviously needs correction or modification, for it would prove much more than merely the equality of human beings: all animals are in the same plight from birth. In order to limit the postulate to man, one must add a rational ground on which men, and all of them, deserve such a distinction. If then reference is offered to the eminence of man because he alone is "endowed with reason," we are again up against the old objection that there are considerable differences in the breadth and depth of reason

[9] *Praktische Vernunft*, pp. 42, 504, 538. "No point of departure other than the facts of inner observation . . . no basis other than the data of descriptive analysis of ethical feeling" (pp. 505–6).

[10] Coing, *op.cit.* (Chapter VII, Section 5) p. 117, although a declared anti-relativist himself, is more consistent than Nelson when he writes: "The difficult question: where are the yardsticks regarding when something must be treated as equal and when as different, . . . cannot be answered from [the ideal of] justice alone; here justice fails us (*hier lässt uns die Gerechtigkeit im Stich*)." He helps himself by a recourse to Natural Law and intuition (S₂); see below, section 16. Carl J. Friedrich, in his German book, *Die Philosophie des Rechts in historischer Perspektive*, Heidelberg 1955, ends up his remarkable historical review with a more positive evaluation of Nelson's contribution than that here given, without, however, mentioning the gap in Nelson's argument (pp. 114–18). An English version of this book appeared in 1958 under the title *The Philosophy of Law in Historical Perspective* (Chicago).

[11] So Herbert Spiegelberg, with modifications, in his article, "A Defense of Human Equality," *Philosophical Review*, vol. 53 (1944) p. 101. See also his *Anti-Relativismus*, Zurich und Leipzig 1935, and "Justice Presupposes Natural Law," *Ethics*, vol. 49 (1939) p. 343.

in individuals and that these differences may justify any degree of differentiation, such as killing the least gifted people or enslaving them.

Gerhart Husserl, Edmund's son, has attempted to achieve results from the phenomenological concept of "essence" as a "something" that can be observed in the process of phenomenological observation (see below, Chapter ix, Section 6). He distinguishes four degrees of equality: first, equality of neutral qualities, such as length and width; second, "homogeneity," which involves some classification like bringing forth young alive; third, equality as to "essence," like that of dog and dog; and fourth, "similarity," like the correspondence between similar dogs. He emphasizes that the common "essence" of individual human beings is their common belonging to mankind, not their belonging to the same race or state.[12] All of us who believe in the essential equality of human beings in a religious or political sense or all who, at least, respect the potentiality of such essential equality, will go far toward emotional consent with him. But he has not added a single element of scientific proof. He has merely stated his assertion as based on immediate evidence—which evidence is denied by others, even by other leading phenomenologists.

Max Scheler, for instance, great phenomenologist himself, has pointed to the possibility, which to him is a probability, that races have different biological origins and respond differently in the sphere of inner evidence. He has, furthermore, refused to make the biological distinction between man and animal the discerning mark of what is "essential" in the hierarchy of animate nature, and has placed in its stead the recognition of the "value of the divine" (*Wert des Göttlichen*). Those who have come to feel the value of the divine, he said, regardless of whether they believe in a personal God, are essentially equal and different from the rest of animals and human beings.[13] This view not only doubts, but explicitly denies, that there is any essential equality of human beings as such.

Likewise, although for other reasons, Max Wertheimer, founder of Gestalt psychology, refused to accept the biological distinction between men and animals as the decisive criterion of essential equality.

[12] Gerhart Husserl, "Justice," *International Journal of Ethics,* vol. 47 (1937) pp. 271–307, in particular pp. 281, 283, 304.
[13] Max Scheler, *Der Formalismus in der Ethik* (cited in the preceding chapter) iii, end; v, 5 (3rd ed., pp. 159–61, 301 ff.). Also, *Vom Umsturz der Werte* (1915, 2nd ed. Leipzig 1923) vol. i, pp. 305 ff. Polygenesis of human races is still emphasized in his *Die Idee des Friedens und der Pazifismus,* Berlin 1931, p. 21.

The criterion to him was the ability to see, and to respond to, what he called the "objective requirements" of a situation (see Section 7 of the preceding chapter). He hoped that all men shared this quality. But he remarked that, if against his more optimistic hope part of mankind should be blind or inimical in its inner nature to objective requirements, there would then be two races, the one to whom these requirements are alive, the other which is blind or inimical to them.[14] This view too questions, if only conditionally, essential equality of all human beings.

One significant feature in which all human beings are alike may be their ability to choose to be good or evil in any moment of their lives. It makes sense to consider this feature so essential that all other differences, even those between high and low degrees of intelligence, are held negligible in comparison. This way of arguing (which is in line with my own convictions) would then lead logically to the proposition that all men are "essentially" equal. But in allotting such a high rank, and even top rank, to this one feature we render a value judgment which cannot be sanctioned by science. It may well be possible to prove empirically that all human beings make some distinction between good and evil and that all feel they have—always or generally—a choice between being either good or evil in their thoughts, and often in their action as well, although the yardsticks they use may be very different. But there the scientific possibilities end. Science cannot prove, although religion may teach and ethical volition may accept, that on this ground all men are "essentially" equal. The absolute value of this one feature cannot be ascertained by Scientific Method, and if asserted on the basis of intuition, or of any other source, its validity cannot be intersubjectively verified.

What possibly can be verified, among other universal human features, is the fact that all men not only distinguish good and evil but also are subject to some inner urge toward the ideal that equal cases ought to be treated equally. This line will be pursued in Chapter x. Apart from such, always tenuous, generalizations, science can continue to explore the interconnections, or the lack of interconnections, between physical and mental or moral traits, and to refute unscientific contentions as to racial differences in this respect. Science can, furthermore, do psychological and phenomenological research on the manner in which men become aware of equalities and inequalities, real or imaginary,

[14] Max Wertheimer, "Some Problems in the Theory of Ethics," *Social Research*, vol. 2 (1935) pp. 353 ff., 367.

for instance in the relations between in-group or out-group individuals.[15] It can distinguish various, mutually incompatible, yardsticks of equal treatment (need, ability, etc., see Chapter IV, Section 6), and point to the impossibility of establishing full equality (Chapter XII, Section 3). It can disclose ulterior motives in discriminations. Above all, science can predict the consequences and risks entailed by flagrant discriminations, from feelings hurt to violent uprisings. But when it comes to the question whether human beings are "essentially" equal, and whether all ought to be treated equally, science cannot claim authority to give a direct answer.

The soundest extra-religious basis of the claim to equality for all men can be found in the postulate of truth, or of veracity, which excludes from the title of justice any judgment that is based on actual falsehoods or on faked assumptions not truly believed in (see Chapter XI, below). But this argument does not hit evaluations founded on differences either real or at least truly believed to be real.

Insistence on truth and veracity can be efficiently supplemented by an appeal to volition, that is, free determination to treat all human beings as essentially equal in acknowledgment of the possibility, not to be refuted, that they may be so (argument from the absence of proof for the antithesis). In addition, the argument that equality is the only standard that can be accepted by all (Kant's argument) has retained some merit, although the privileged classes will be hesitant to accept it. But all such approaches fail to lead to a plain scientific conclusion that men are essentially equal and that their equal treatment is required regardless of consequences. To reach this democratic proposition, additional recourse must be had to religion or ethical volition. We merely confound the issues if we claim for science what science cannot do. Science itself should make this plain, while continuing in its efforts to (1) disclose universal features of human nature (Chapters IX ff.), (2) refute erroneous ideas about differences that are only apparent (racial issue), and (3) reveal the consequences of both unequal and of equal treatment of human beings in the various spheres and situations of community life.

---

[15] Alfred Schutz, in his paper "Equality and the Meaning Structure of the Social World," read at the fifteenth symposium of the Conference on Science, Philosophy, and Religion, has made constructive studies of this kind (*Aspects of Human Equality*, ed. by L. Bryson *et al.*, New York 1957, pp. 33–78).

3. *Liberty*

Historically speaking, the glorification of liberty preceded that of equality, and until recent times most philosophers continued to assign it higher rank and philosophical priority. Athenian ideals of liberty were not coupled with equality; not all men were free in Athens. When ideas of equality broke through, especially in the thought of the Stoics, there was only limited response. But ideals of freedom also faded. In medieval times it was considered a privilege rather than a natural thing to be free. Not until feudalism declined, when free cities rose with free citizens within their walls, when the Renaissance fashioned a new self-assertion of the individual and of his worth, when the Reformation insisted on freedom of conscience, and Locke planted Liberty as one of the three inalienable Rights (which did not include equality), was the ideal of freedom fully reestablished. Then its meaning was even deepened. Successful fights for political freedom, first in England, then in America and France, and the rise of a new economic doctrine which taught the superiority of economic freedom over government regulation finally led to a general apotheosis of liberty in Western thought at the end of the eighteenth century. Not of equality. Equality entered the picture only as a latecomer in the French revolution; it met with a great deal of suspicion and resistance, not merely in practice but also in philosophy.

Freedom continued to outrank equality in philosophical thought even when both were recognized as ideals. Freedom, not equality, stood out as the aboriginal right in Kant. Its absolute value he deduced from that of the individual, which he established in the hypothetical form that, *if* there should be any absolute value at all, it could only be found in the individual (see Chapter VI, Section 3c, above). Equality held only second place in his system of thought. He derived the claim to equality from that to freedom: since man as such had a right to freedom, the individual's right was limited by the equal right of all others.

In the twentieth century, with which we are specifically concerned here, Leonard Nelson, following earlier arguments by the German philosopher Jakob Friedrich Fries (1773–1843), attempted to reverse the Kantian order between freedom and equality. To Nelson, as we have seen (Section 1), equality was the fundamental postulate of justice, even its only postulate. Liberty was a mere implication of equality, he argued, because, if everyone had a legitimate claim to equality, he could claim also an equal share in liberty.[1] This reversal was not generally accepted, however, for its equalitarian premise was highly controversial. Those philosophers who in this century continued to absolutize the value of liberty have, therefore, followed the line of Locke and Kant rather than of Fries and Nelson.

Thus, the English philosopher Bernard Bosanquet (1848–1923) declared the ultimate criterion of value to be individuality, not in the transient states of consciousness but in all its potentialities; not isolated, but within the whole to which it belongs.[2] In America, Hocking wrote (1926) that the "only natural right" to be acknowledged is that "an individual should develop the powers that are in him" and "become what he is capable of becoming."[3] In post-Hitler Germany, Professor Coing declared in his highly praised *Introduction to the Philosophy of Law* (1950): "Wherever, in the individual case, freedom and social justice should be in conflict and a decision between the[se] two postulates of Right become necessary, there the decision must be made in favor of freedom. The dignity of man cannot be surrendered in exchange for equality of material goods. Here is the absolute and immovable limit which the idea of Right (*Rechtsidee*) sets to the community as a principle of organization."[4]

It is interesting to follow Hocking's argument more in detail. Like Kant he refuses to assign absolute value to liberty pure and simple, to liberty as such; he rather allots it to the dignity of the individual and to his right to grow. From this basic absolute right, however, he derives six particular ones which, in clear contradistinction to Nelson's equalitarian postulate, are apt to support political and economic liberalism (free enterprise) against socialism. They are: liberty in self-management, in seeking control of others, and of nature; and the right to the security of one's own person, to one's own agreements, and to one's own property.[5] On the other hand, Hocking does not flinch from pur-

---

[1] *Praktische Vernunft*, p. 528; *Rechtslehre und Politik*, pp. 110 ff. Nelson acknowledged that man's "interest in rational self-determination" must be inalienable because, if it were left to the individual to determine which interests he thinks to be of equal, superior, or inferior value as compared with others, he might bargain away his soul. The inalienable nature of the right to freedom, however, appeared to him as an "extra-juridical" ideal, not derivable from the idea of justice. This was the consequence of his doctrine that equality alone was a postulate of justice.

[2] Bernard Bosanquet, *The Principle of Individuality and Value*, London 1912, pp. 291 ff.

[3] W. E. Hocking, *Present Status of the Philosophy of Law and Rights*, New York 1926, pp. 71, 74 ff., 81, 84.

[4] H. Coing, *op.cit.* (Chapter VII, Section 5) pp. 197, 198.

[5] *Op.cit.*, pp. 87, 91.

suing to their last consequences all the implications of his premise that the fundamental right is not to liberty *per se,* but to development. There is, he says, no absolute right, then, forbidding slavery. If it were proved that an individual would better develop his powers in slavery, his enslavement would be justified. "In the case of an Epictetus or an Aesop, if tradition is to be credited, personal powers developed nobly in slavery; they might conceivably have developed less well under any less trying discipline. If that was the case, slavery was right for Epictetus and Aesop." But only God could answer this question in the affirmative, Hocking continued; the presumption is for liberty.[6]

To say that only God knows whether a person would profit from slavery is to acknowledge that science is unable to state so. Therefore, science cannot justify slavery on that ground. But science is likewise unable to establish the existence of a right to individual liberty, or free development. While dogmatic belief in such a right continues to underlie Western civilization, attempts to supply a scientific foundation for it in absolute terms have become rare in this century. Most writers, including Harold Laski,[7] have taken it simply for granted without caring for proof. Hocking himself argued ably against other propositions.[8] But, like Bosanquet, Coing, and everyone else in the field, he has been unable to produce for his own any ultimate proof other than intuition. This is meant to be a simple statement of fact rather than a reproach. Intuition, as has often been said in this book, may well be right. Yet as a scientific argument it fails if it meets with contradictory intuition. Simply to proclaim that something is the highest good may, as Leon Duguit once said,[9] "satisfy a believer, but is void of all scientific value."

However, although unable to verify the existence of a natural right to individual liberty and development in absolute terms, Scientific Method can contribute a great deal to the issue. First of all, it can clarify

---

[6] *Op.cit.,* p. 72.

[7] Harold J. Laski, *The State in Theory and Practice,* New York 1935, p. 138 (the end of the state *is* "satisfaction, at the highest possible level, of its subjects' demands") and passim. See also, Max Ascoli, "The Right to Work," *Social Research,* vol. 6 (1939) p. 255, and the "Discussions" thereafter; D. S. Robinson, *Political Ethics,* New York 1935, pp. 69 ff., and the little "difficulty" with which he meets on p. 108, in dealing with Communism and Fascism, because they do not recognize the absolute value of freedom; Gaston Gavet, "Individualism and Realism," *Yale Law Journal,* vol. 29 (1920) pp. 523, 526 ff.

[8] *Ibid.,* p. 75. Stammler and Kohler, with whom he mainly deals, have ceased to be typical representatives of the present status of legal philosophy; relativistic, functional, and equalitarian, if not national and racial principles have come to the foreground. On functional views, Hocking p. 70, and below, Section 10.

[9] "The Law and the State," *Harvard Law Review,* vol. 31 (1917) pp. 1 ff., 23.

the difference in meaning of the two questions whether human beings are free to think, to desire, or to will, on the one hand, and whether they are free to act as they like, on the other. Next, it can supply an adequate description and analysis of all data concerning freedom to act. Third, it can establish a number of important substantive points.

As regards the freedom to think, Scientific Method presupposes in line with common sense that such freedom exists at least to some extent (Chapter II, Section 1). If freedom of thought were a sheer illusion and all our thinking necessary, there could be no science, since any question, whether relevant or irrelevant, and any answer, whether true or false, would be equally necessary, and it would also be necessary that we consider true what is false whenever we think so, and false what is true (see also Chapter XII, Section 1).[10]

As regards the freedom to act, the scientist can clarify the numerous subcategories and subconcepts that are confusingly covered by the notion of freedom, such as religious, civil, political, economic, and social freedom, and the independence of nations from external interference; freedom *from* something and freedom *for* something, and from or for what; freedom to follow passion or freedom to follow reason. Science can point out that each type of freedom may be either merely negative or positive, either passive or active, and that some types are compatible with equality while others are not, as, e.g., economic freedom is incompatible with economic equality. Science can also examine whether there can be true freedom to be right unless there also is the freedom to err, and so forth.[11]

Beyond clarifying formal presuppositions and categories, Scientific Method can establish a number of important substantive points regarding freedom, especially the following three. First, it can be stated un-

---

[10] That the assumption of freedom is indispensable as a presupposition for the cognition of truth has been stated, for instance, by Georg Simmel (*Einführung in die Moralwissenschaft,* vol. 2, pp. 304–6) and Martin Heidegger (*Vom Wesen der Wahrheit,* Frankfurt 1943, 3rd ed. 1954). The latter's formulation "The essence of truth is freedom" (*Das Wesen der Wahrheit ist die Freiheit,* p. 12) distorts the matter, however, at least by its grammatical expression, because this way of stating it is as illogical as it would be to say that the essence of beer is the thirst, instead of saying that it is the essence of beer that it is apt to quench thirst in a particular manner. Freedom is the essence not of truth but of its recognition; in order to recognize and follow truth a man must be free to distinguish the true answer to his question from any other, and to prefer it to any other.

[11] Scientific analysis can also examine the truth of such statements as the following, taken from Coing, *op.cit.,* p. 149: "The idea of freedom excludes love. For, love is unconditional surrender (*Hingabe,* devotion, abandon), and freedom, unconditional self-assertion (*Selbstbehauptung*)." This type of arguing is inconclusive. When I love I may have no freedom as to whether or not I do love; but I still may have the freedom to act. On the other hand, freedom to act includes the freedom to self-limitation.

conditionally that the presumptive human ability, within limits set by nature, to think and act in accordance with reason is valuable in an objective sense because it enables humanity to reach stages of life and of knowledge not attainable without that freedom. Second, it can be stated unconditionally that no human being is *entirely* free to do what he likes because everyone is subject at least to the constraints imposed by nature; and third, that everyone considers freedom to do what he really and ultimately wants a positive value. As to this latter point, it is indeed but tautological to say that someone who without any reservations desires to do something wishes also to be free to do it and that, therefore, to be free to do what he wishes appears to him as something valuable. This statement may, therefore, be said to be "absolutely" true inasmuch as it merely expresses the *meaning* of the proposition that someone wants to do a particular thing (see Chapter 1, Section 6).

Whenever we proceed, however, to ask whether it is valuable from the standpoint of *other* people that some particular person be granted the freedom he might wish to have, or whether freedom of every human being is an "absolute" value, irrespective of desires, valid at all places and times, Scientific Method yields no unconditional answer. Scientists can list the conflicting interests of different persons, or of the same person at different times. They can gather ample data regarding the consequences of either granting or denying freedom. They can establish that the denial of freedom is bound, for psychological reasons, to stir up very deep feelings of resentment, feelings that tend to find an explosive outlet if they are not allayed in good time. They can point, on one hand, to the great achievements to which men can rise under freedom and the dampening effect which the denial of freedom may have on creative forces, and on the other, to the dangers that threaten from the abuse of liberty and from anarchy. They may compare the achievements possible and the setbacks that threaten under various forms of freedom or of its absence.[12]

Scientific labors may go far toward establishing the superior potentialities of freedom in the development of the human race as a whole in such and such directions under such and such conditions. Historical experiences can be used to illustrate the validity of such tentative theorems, or to modify them by disclosing conditions under which they are not valid. In addition, science can examine the limits

---

[12] The classic model of such a comparison is Friedrich Schiller's lecture "Lykurgus und Solon" of 1789, in which he compared the short- and long-range results of the laws given by Lycurgus in Sparta (denial of freedom) and by Solon in Athens (granting of freedom).

beyond which suppression of freedom is impossible, as is the suppression of the freedom to think and to believe as long as persons are fully conscious, that is, neither asleep nor doped; and it can reveal the interconnection between morals and freedom on the ground that a universal feeling seems to forbid us to blame someone for failing to do what he was not free to do (Chapters x and xii deal with these types of impossibility).

But with all this science cannot arrive at the generalizing conclusion that the freedom of every individual is an absolute value, a value not alone, subjectively speaking, for himself, but also objectively, for all and under all circumstances. On the contrary, science must admit that sometimes one person's or group's lack of freedom may be more valuable for reaching another person's or group's aims than would be full freedom for both. For science to maintain, in view of this situation, that the other fellow ought to be granted freedom to the same extent, irrespective of consequences, would require the scientific demonstration that all individuals are equal and should be treated equally. This demonstration, as we have seen, is beyond science to supply. It can only be grounded on religious convictions or ethical volition.

In particular, it is obvious that one person's freedom is rarely valuable for all others unless it is limited by some principle of regard for others, whether this limitation is effected by self-restraint or by constraint imposed from outside. The question, therefore, becomes important: what could or should be this limiting principle? It might be either equality, that is, the even division of freedom among all, or some principle of order not fully based on equality. In all historical examples, including those of the most democratically governed countries, order has never been based entirely on equality, and science is even able to state in advance that it would be impossible to do so (see Chapter xii). Ideas of how freedom should be limited under these circumstances vary greatly, both as to form (authoritarian rule, majority rule, etc.) and substance (see Chapter iv, above).

Some of these questions will be taken up in special contexts. My only intention here was to clarify two points. On the one hand, Scientific Method alone cannot lead to statements on the absolute value of freedom, or the existence of an absolute right to freedom, in general terms. Intuition (S$_2$), especially in its religious forms, may be able to provide such statements, and may be right, too; but reference to intuition deprives science of the transmissible character of its findings, unless all agree, and may be erroneous even then. On the other hand, science need not demonstrate an absolute right to liberty in order to contribute a great deal to the fight for it where it is denied and for its preservation where it is enjoyed. In addition, every scientist is free to engage in research under the "avowed assumption" that in the particular case under his investigation freedom *is* desirable or is actually being desired, and then concentrate on the methods by which it can be secured, broadened in substance, spread further, and best be defended, defended also from the consequences of its abuse.

4. God's Will. Human Reason's Metaphysical Insights

It would be a grave mistake to assume that religious revelation has been discarded today as a scientific basis in political and legal philosophy. Roman Catholic thinking, in particular, has never abandoned the claim that God's existence can be scientifically verified.[1] In order to sustain it, however, under the impact of Scientific Method, the latter had to be refused a position of exclusiveness; for it could hardly be denied that it was not feasible to prove God's existence in this way. It was necessary to refer to sources of knowledge that did not yield intersubjectively transmissible results in the sense in which this term has here been used.

Not only have all the representative Catholic philosophers of the twentieth century, from Victor Cathrein (1845–1931) to Jacques Maritain, Heinrich Rommen, and Jacques Leclerq,[2] continued to base their scientific teaching on God's reality, but so have many others, like John Hallowell, Eric Voegelin, and C. S. Lewis.[3] As this book devotes a special chapter (XIII) to the problem of whether God's reality can be established or refuted with scientific means, I shall refer presently only to two particular points.

Belief in God has led many philosophers, in line with St. Thomas, to distinguish between two kinds of unjust laws: those that merely go

---

[1] See especially the address by Pius XII to the Pontifical Academy of Sciences of November 22, 1951, in which the Pope maintained the claim in view of the recent advances, fully accepted by him, of astronomy and nuclear physics. Extended excerpts were published by the *New York Times*, November 23, 1951, p. 6.

[2] Victor Cathrein, *Recht, Naturrecht und positives Recht*, Berlin 1901 (2nd ed. 1909); Maritain, see Chapter VII, above; Heinrich A. Rommen, see Chapter IV; Jacques Leclercq, *Le fondement du droit et de la société*, 3rd ed., Namur 1947. See also Emil Erich Hölscher, *Sittliche Rechtslehre*, Munich 1928, and Karl Petrascheck, *System der Rechtsphilosophie*, Freiburg 1932.

[3] Hallowell and Voegelin, see Chapter VII. C. S. Lewis, *The Case for Christianity*, New York 1943.

beyond the authority of the lawgiver or fail to yield just results, and those that "order something that is sinful or wicked in itself." While one may obey the former, and as a rule should do so because their non-observance would involve greater damage than the opposite, one must never obey the latter. The reason given for this is "that one must obey God more than men and therefore rather die than sin." [4] Sometimes the reference to God and sin is circumvented by speaking of actions that are in themselves "immoral and unjust"; but what actions deserve this characterization is again explained by references to religious concepts, such as sin.[5]

Lacking means to demonstrate God's reality, Scientific Method cannot make use of this way of arguing. Other grounds must and can be found to deny juridic validity to "wicked" laws (see above, Chapter IV, Section 8, and below, Section 16). It is noteworthy, however, that even a scholar like Gustav Radbruch, who had always been careful to separate scientific and religious thinking, at the end of his life came close to the old distinction when he wrote: "It seems that the conflict between justice and certainty in law is to be solved in this manner: that the positive law, secured by the order that sets it (*Satzung*) and by power, must be accorded priority even when it is unjust and unreasonable (*unzweckmässig*), unless the conflict between the positive law and justice reaches such an unbearable degree that the law set (*Gesetz*) on the ground of its being 'incorrect law' (*unrichtiges Recht,* wrong law) must cede to justice." [6] This reasoning avoids any reference, direct or indirect, to God and to sin, putting in its stead a recourse to the idea of justice; it will be discussed below, Section 16.

The second point to be mentioned here is that the old Scholastic attempts to distill an ethical and social law from Nature and Reason as sources distinct from God's Will have gained new strength within the last one hundred years or so in Catholic thought, when Catholic politicians and representatives of the Church have tried to find common ground with non-Catholic fellow citizens in matters of government. This movement, substantially promoted by the writings of the authors already mentioned, and earlier by those of Theodor Meyer in

---

[4] Cathrein, *op.cit.,* pp. 300 ff. Moór, "Das Problem des Naturrechts" (1935), as quoted below, Chapter XII, Section 4.

[5] Rommen, *op.cit.* (Engl. ed.) pp. 255–56 (an immoral law is one that "prescribes a sinful action"). Pius XII, in an address to the first convention of Catholic Italian lawyers, put it more strongly: "The judge can never with any of his decisions oblige anyone to some action which is intrinsically immoral—that is, contrary to the laws of God or the Church" (quoted by d'Entrèves, *Natural Law Forum,* vol. 1, 1956, p. 51).

[6] In his 1946 article, "Gesetzliches Unrecht und übergesetzliches Recht," reprinted in *Rechtsphilosophie,* 4th ed., pp. 347, 356.

Germany (1821–1913),[7] became a powerful factor in the recent revival of Natural-Law doctrines. Yet it preserved some characteristic peculiarities. The old Scholastic treatises on Natural Law, which were legion, had been deeply entangled in the great mediaeval controversy whether will or intellect held the primacy in God, that is, whether or not God could will something that was against reason, such as changing the Decalogue. Primacy of will was the doctrine of Duns Scotus (d. ab. 1308) and especially of William of Occam (d. ab. 1349), primacy of intellect that of the majority of the late Scholastics, in particular of the Spaniards, Vittoria (d. 1546), Vasquez (d. 1604) and Suarez (d. 1617), and the Italian, Bellarmine (d. 1621).[8] This view gave principles of reason an independent validity, permeating God's will and unchangeable even for Him. Supported by it, the recent Catholic Natural-Law movement felt entitled to pursue the interpretation of reason independently of ideas of Divine Law.

Yet this has remained an enterprise fraught with great difficulties under modern scientific demands. Not only had some of the late Scholastics (Suarez and Bellarmine, against Vasquez) emphasized that for a reasonable act to be right it must *also* be God's will.[9] More important, whenever a scholar recognizes the existence of God and of Divine Law as scientifically verifiable, elements of this point of view are apt to enter also the principles he finds revealed in nature and by reason. Interpretations of the Law of Nature by philosophers of this group, consequently, have differed from those not based on the divine origin of nature.[10] For example, they have led to a reading under which marriage is indissoluble,[11] in contrast, e.g., to Stammler's, under which divorce must be possible;[12] or that abortion and mercy-killing are always wrong.[13] Quite generally, the principles revealed by reason have been identified with the second table of the Decalogue, in line

---

[7] Theodor Meyer, *Die Grundzüge der Sittlichkeit und des Rechts,* a special publication of *Stimmen aus Maria Laach,* 1869; the same author, "Naturrecht," *Staatslexikon der Goerresgesellschaft,* 1894; and *Institutiones Juris Naturalis,* Freiburg 1900. Cathrein, *Moralphilosophie,* Freiburg 1893, and *op.cit.* Maritain, *op.cit.,* and *The Rights of Man and Natural Law,* translated by Doris C. Anson, New York 1943. Rommen, *op.cit.* See also Edgar Alexander in J. N. Moody, E. Alexander, and others, *Church and Society in Germany, 1789–1950,* New York 1953 (also in German, *Kirche und Gesellschaft in Deutschland*); and E. Alexander, *Adenauer and the New Germany,* New York 1957, pp. 68 ff.

[8] See Rommen, *op.cit.,* pp. 42 ff.

[9] Rommen, *op.cit.,* pp. 63, 64.

[10] See, e.g. Cathrein, *Recht, Naturrecht und positives Recht,* pp. 66, 67, 311.

[11] *Ibid.,* p. 271. Others, like Rommen (pp. 65, 221, 239), find in the Natural Law only the condemnation of adultery and concubinage, but they too would object to the interpretation that according to nature and reason divorce must be possible.

[12] See above, Chapter v, Section 8.

[13] Rommen, *op.cit.,* p. 222.

with St. Thomas. Maritain, for one, is more circumspect when he writes that in interpreting the Natural Law (which he too recognizes) man runs "the risk of error here as elsewhere," adding that the "only practical knowledge all men have naturally and infallibly in common is that we must do good and avoid evil." [14] But other Catholic writers have objected to this modest withdrawal from claims to absolute rightness.[15]

If science is understood as intersubjectively transmissible knowledge, all attempts to reach a scientific clarification of the essence of justice from metaphysical sources are necessarily doomed to failure. The matter gains an entirely different aspect, however, if what is sought for in religion is no scientific clarification but merely religious directives for the interpretation of an ideal whose clarification by means of science alone is seen to be impossible. Attempts of this kind have been made by Professor Erik Wolf of Freiburg University in a small book entitled *The Idea of Right and Biblical Directives,*[16] in which he carefully scrutinizes the implications of Biblical pointers, including of course the Decalogue, for the meaning of justice. This is entirely meaningful for those who accept the reality of God and the divine character of Biblical revelation. It may obtain even scientific significance as a hypothetical basis for the examination of consequences involved in the acceptance or refutation of these directives.

5. *Nature*

Natural Law has staged its return not only in the wake of religious crusaders but also under its own power. Unabashed by scientific criticism leveled against the fusion of Is and Ought, or unaware of it, many secular philosophers have continued to derive absolute principles of justice from nature directly, with no reference to divine intercession.

The internationally best-known representative of this group is the Italian philosopher Giorgio del Vecchio (b. 1878). His views, insofar as they concern us here, appear purest in his earlier books, written before the fascist wave reached its crest and collapsed, but frequently republished and translated thereafter.[1] Some of the Natural-Law ideas

---

[14] *The Rights of Man*, pp. 62 ff.

[15] Rommen, *op.cit.*, p. 227, note 18.

[16] Erik Wolf, *Rechtsgedanke und biblische Weisung*, Tübingen 1948.

[1] See, in particular: *Il concetto della natura e il principio del diritto* (1908, 2nd ed., 1922, translated with other papers of the same author under the title *The Formal Bases of Law* in *Modern Legal Philosophy* series, vol. 10, 1914); *Sui principi generali del diritto*, Modena 1921 (tr. as *General Principles of Law* by F. Forte, Boston 1956; excerpts also in Ch. G. Haines, *The*

there expressed are merely paraphrases of necessary causal relations, enforced by nature (see Chapter XII, below). Others, like the postulate of equal treatment of equal cases, will receive special treatment (Chapters IX ff.), because they seem to be supported by universal human feelings and thus verifiably embedded in human nature. Many others, however, trespass considerably on grounds where neither naturalistic necessity nor universality of support by human nature can be demonstrated. They include: respect for the human being as a personality, and therefore for the essential equality of all human beings (see Section 2, above); the Kantian maxim that one should act as if mankind was acting through oneself (see Chapter IX, below); the absence of any intention to subdue other people; prohibition of slavery on the ground that slavery violates the "ideal law inherent in every human breast"; evolution from status to contract; freedom of contract; the right of property; duties toward the nation up to sacrifice of one's own life for it; and even such specific rights as that to one's own portrait.[2]

These certainly are substantive postulates, not merely formal ones as might be derived from the logical forms of law, to which the author refers at other places. Democratically minded people are likely to subscribe to all or most of these principles. But no reference to human nature alone can supply scientific proof of their absolute validity without the previous acceptance of other, scientifically undemonstrable, principles, such as what it means to be "essentially" equal, or that all men are equal before God, and the like.

Del Vecchio speaks repeatedly of the "a-priori character" of the most important postulates of right. Their source is what he calls the "natural *ratio* of right." Optimistically he asserts: "The natural *ratio* of right will reassert itself as an insuppressible and inexhaustible source of law, however much the inevitable imperfections and limitations of positive norms may sometimes obstruct its path."[3] But no insuppressible *ratio* of right in the broad sense in which del Vecchio speaks of it can be found in nature ready-made. It needs for its recognition either some type of nontransmissible, religion-like intuition, or a

Revival of Natural Law Concepts, Cambridge, Mass., 1930, p. 282); *Lezioni di filosofia del diritto*, 3rd ed., Rome 1936 (German tr., *Lehrbuch der Rechtsphilosophie*, with an introduction by C. A. Emge, Berlin 1937), 8th ed., 1952 (tr., *Philosophy of Law*, by Th. O. Martin, Washington 1952); and *La giustizia*, 4th ed., Rome 1951 (tr., *Justice*, by Lady Guthrie, notes by A. H. Campbell, Edinburgh 1952; German tr., *Gerechtigkeit*, by C. F. Darmstädter, Basel 1950). See below on his postwar publications.

[2] *Lezioni, op.cit.* (German ed., pp. 460 ff.), and *Sui principi generali, op.cit.*

[3] *Lezioni, op.cit.* See also *The Formal Bases of Law*, pp. 18, 258 ff., 328.

definite act of human volition, especially the determination to plan for peace and to build this plan on mutual respect. This volition, at least in its extension to all mankind, can hardly be proved to be ordained by human nature, and history has revealed profusely that it has not always been so considered.

After giving some support to the Mussolini regime in Italy for a while, a matter which does not interest us here, del Vecchio emerged after World War II as the leader of Italy's share in the general revival of Natural-Law thinking. His postwar publications,[4] although not entirely abandoning his original Neo-Kantian approach, were more definitely based on religious arguments. From the purely logical angle, this shift in emphasis made the soundness of his reasoning less questionable; for, as we have seen, once the operation of divine forces is accepted or assumed there is nothing illogical in our looking for intimations of moral laws in nature. At the same time, however, this turn has made his recent writings less representative of purely scientific attempts to extract moral laws solely from nature, without recourse to theology.

Following del Vecchio's example, many other Italian scholars also seem to have veered toward a theological foundation of Natural-Law ideas, among them Francesco Carnelutti, one of the most distinguished Italian jurists, who is said to have drawn gradually ever closer to the official line of Thomism. On the other hand, a marked resistance to this trend can be noted on the part of Italian positivists, who are wary of Catholic identifications of Natural Law with Divine Law in the Catholic interpretation of both.[5]

In *Germany,* until Hitler's access to power Natural-Law thinking had been definitely on the defensive under the blows of the scientific objections raised by the emergent group of brilliant German and Austrian value relativists. But it never surrendered fully, as my remarks on Cathrein, Stammler, Nelson, Binder, Sauer, etc., show (Sections 2, 4, 11, and 13 of this chapter, and 8 of Chapter v), and it even received fresh support from the philosophical side, especially from

---

[4] "Le concezione moderne del diritto naturale," *Justitia,* vol. 1 (1948) pp. 3 ff., reprinted under the title "Dispute e conclusioni sul diritto naturale," *Rivista Internazionale di Filosofia del Diritto,* vol. 26 (1949) pp. 155–62; "Essenza del diritto naturale," *Rivista, op.cit.,* vol. 29 (1952) pp. 18–24; "Mutabilità ed eternità del diritto," *Jus,* vol. 5 (1954) pp. 1–14.

[5] Guido Fassò, "Natural Law in Italy in the Past Ten Years," *Natural Law Forum,* vol. 1 (1956) pp. 122 ff.

Scheler and Hartmann (Chapter VII, Sections 5 and 6). Hitler's cruel domination led to a general revival of Natural-Law ideas, deeply inter-meshed with a religious renascence. Finally, Radbruch's recourse to the "nature of things" (see Chapter IV, Section 3), however guarded it may have been, became the signal for a general defection from value relativism. After the war, hardly any declared relativists were left in Germany. The former German theoretical interest in distinguishing science from religion, science from philosophy, scientific methods from reliance on intuition, declined sharply. Most contributions, like those of Coing (see Chapters VII, Section 5, and VIII, Section 3), were frankly based on a nonpositivistic interpretation of the functions of "science," admitting references to religious or intuitional evidence with little inhibition.

On the religious side, Neo-Thomist reasoning had to compete in Germany, more than in France and Italy, with Protestant arguments which,[6] however, were more decided in basing higher-law ideas ex-clusively on religious foundations, that is, on God's word rather than nature. On the secular side, which is at present our point of interest, a few Neo-Hegelians, seeking the source of Natural Law in history and in the laws ruling history, are outnumbered by the Neo-Kantians of various persuasions, who start out from formal logical reasoning but, more than in the past, are now trying to arrive from this formal basis at substantive principles by exploiting the "nature of things" to which logical reasoning is to be applied.[7] This increased emphasis on the "nature of things" has been the main result of the revival of Natural-Law thinking in the secular sector; see Chapter IV, Section 3.

[6] See, e.g., Emil Brunner, *Justice and the Social Order*, New York 1945, p. 39, and Klaus Ritter, *Zwischen Naturrecht und Rechtspositivismus*, Witten-Ruhr 1956.

[7] Freiherr von der Heydte in his short but fine report, "Natural Law Tendencies in Con-temporary German Jurisprudence," *Natural Law Forum*, vol. 1 (1956) pp. 115–21, enumerates the following: (1) Neo-Thomists—Johannes Messner of Vienna, Ernst von Hippel of Cologne, Günther Küchenhoff of Würzburg, Alfred von Verdross of Vienna (a former follower of Kelsen), Heinrich Kipp, Arthur Wegner, Adolf Süsterhenn, and Valentin Tomberg; (2) within the Protestant wing—Hermann Weinkauff (President of the Federal Supreme Court), Erik Wolf of Freiburg, Walter Schönfeld of Tübingen, Ulrich Scheuner of Bonn; also, Hans Lier-mann, Ernst Wolf, and Hans Dombois; (3) Neo-Hegelians—Gerhard Dulckheit and Karl Larenz of Kiel and, possibly, Erich Kaufmann of Bonn who, however, "has not written on the problem of natural law since he courageously professed the idea of law in his Hague lectures of 1935"; further, though one step removed, Heinrich Mitteis of Munich and Thomas Würtenberger of Freiburg; (4) Neo-Kantians—Jürgen von Kempski, Rudolf von Laun of Ham-burg, Hans Welzel of Bonn, Erich Fechner of Tübingen, and Werner Maihofer of Würzburg; also, with doubtful justification, Carl August Emge of Mainz (influenced by Nietzsche) and Helmut Coing of Frankfurt (wide off the Kantian line, see above). This list gives a good impression of the liveliness of the debate and of the prevalence of religious views.

French jurisprudence during the Third Republic was distinguished by its concentration on the positivistic approach. But this positivism was legal only; it was not philosophical. It did not extend to the legislative level. There was not much interest in philosophy of law. As a recent reviewer put it, "Studies of the philosophy of law have never known the same favor in France as in certain foreign countries. They are completely absent from the official curricula." [8] In particular, no overt system of thought in line with Scientific Value Relativism evolved. This may be surprising in view of the skeptical mood characteristic of many French intellectuals during the Third Republic. But it is explained by the fact that those Frenchmen who refused to adhere to the Natural-Law teachings of the Catholic Church or to absolutistic monarchic ideals, gave their loyalty to the "principles of 1789." This was generally true even of apparent skeptics, such as Anatole France. There was little room, therefore, for overt Scientific Value Relativism.[9] When French lawyers left the area of legal positivism and swerved toward transpositive meditations, their originality showed itself in the search for absolutes rather than in the formulation of relativistic doctrines.

Characteristic of attempts made in the first quarter of this century to establish absolute standards of justice at least in part on a secular basis was the work of François Gény (b. 1861). He referred to a variety of "given factors" (*données*).[10] His *données réelles* correspond roughly to the necessities of nature, and his *données historiques* include the traditional institutions.[11] If this were all, he could be classified as a naturalist and a traditionalist. But his *données rationales* and *idéales* go much further. The latter comprise all the "desiderata posited by public sentiment of the present state of civilization." They are, therefore, "neither universal nor immutable," but "somewhat subjective," based on "intuition." [12] Gény, for instance, would interpret them in such a way as to reject any extension of divorce legislation, even if public opinion demanded the extension. By thus reserving to the lawgiver the right to interpret the present state of civilization in contradiction

---

[8] René Théry, "Ten Years of Philosophy of Law in France," *Natural Law Forum*, vol. 1 (1956) pp. 104–14.

[9] See my correspondence with Radbruch on this question in Appendix B. But see also Chapter v, Section 3 on the French sociologists.

[10] François Gény, *Science et technique en droit privé positif*, 4 vols., Paris 1914–24; not available in English.

[11] *Ibid.*, vol. 2, pp. 371, 377.

[12] "One must rather speak here of an intuition, of an *expérience intégrale*, which merits . . . the influence that the universal testimony of humanity has assigned to it" (*ibid.*, pp. 385, 387).

to public opinion, without referring to any universal or immutable yardstick, Gény clearly abandoned scientific verification.

His most important category, however, within our present context was that of the *données rationales,* that is, what is "rationally given." These are the discoveries made by objective reason, which is to reveal the "objectively just." To this end reason is authorized to search "for what conforms to the nature of man as a social being, reasonable and free, and for what is in line with the origin and destiny which we assign to him." [13] This mixes together objective, subjective, teleological, and metaphysical elements. To illustrate, Gény derives from objective reason such postulates as that of a stable and permanent union of the sexes, with a certain subordination of the wife to the husband, and that of the "eminent value of the human personality," its inviolability, and free development in essential equality. In a further degree of specification he reaches prohibition of slavery and, in fact, a guarantee of all modern rights, civil and political, and of private property and contract—all this by mere application of objective reason. [14] "Is it not enough," he asks, "only to consider human nature to discover in it, by reason alone (*par la seule raison*), the principles of subjective rights to be acknowledged in order to permit man to develop his being and to pursue his ends?" [15]

There would, of course, be no quarrel here with his propositions if they were to be read as a religious or political creed or program. But they are presented as scientific truth. As such they are offered with a striking methodological naïveté. But, substantially, they are by no means startling. After setting out from the given facts it is, after all, small wonder that Gény finds himself, after a great detour, back at the given facts, ennobled by the addition of his own subjective ideals. [16]

From the methodological standpoint it is noteworthy that Gény avowedly adopts throughout a "metaphysical interpretation" of justice, because "no other satisfies." [17] Behind the positive law he sees a Natural Law as a "superior type of justice," which has an objective and independent existence. [18] It is based, not on reason alone, but also

---

[13] *Ibid.,* pp. 383, 392.

[14] *Ibid.,* pp. 383, 394, 396, 401, 403.

[15] *Ibid.,* p. 400.

[16] Nevertheless he complains of the "meager kernel of the *donné,*" as compared with the richness of what is construed by law or by human will (vol. 3, p. 520). To this process of legal construction he devotes the entire third volume of his work.

[17] *Ibid.,* vol. 2, p. 358.

[18] *Ibid.,* vol. 4, pp. 216, 241.

on faith.[19] Apart from this, it is a "necessity." The supreme end to which any other end is only a means, can be only God.[20] These sections of his work can claim scientific character, if any, only in an intersubjectively not transmissible sense.

During and after World War II, Natural-Law thinking was on the increase in France; but, as elsewhere, it was primarily *religious* thinking on rights and duties that gained from the anti-Fascist reaction, although with the remarkable innovation that religious loyalties more readily intermingled with adherence to the "principles of 1789." In the purely *secular* sector of Natural-Law doctrine, no major original contribution seems to have come forward, notwithstanding the efforts invested in the *Archives de philosophie du droit et de sociologie juridique* (annually, 1933–40; intermittently, since 1952, dropping sociology in the title). There was, however, a growing emphasis on universal elements in human reactions, especially by Marc Réglade,[21] and on "objective social value."

But not all the recent French writings support Natural-Law ideas. Some are outspokenly opposed. Paul Roubier, for example, explicitly rejects the doctrine of Natural Law in all its forms. He accepts the triad of top values among which men have to choose, as formulated by Radbruch (individual, group, transpersonal; see Chapters IV and VI, above), with a new emphasis on progress and security and some subsidiary reliance on the ideal of justice, this latter feature again quite close to Radbruch (see Section 16, below).[22] There are also countervailing political forces, precisely as in Italy. Anti-clerical sections are afraid that the elevation of Natural-Law principles to a supra-legislative level might be used someday for the strangling of reforms.

Nor has the vogue for Existentialism in Continental Europe, and especially in France, been favorable to Natural-Law ideas, since Existentialism joined Scientific Value Relativism in bringing the factor of human *choice* to the foreground. Existentialists are indeed first cousins of Scientific Value Relativists in this respect. Both teach three lessons: (1) Choose you *can*. (2) Choose you *must*. (3) Science alone cannot tell you *what* to choose, because it is unable to aver by what ultimate standards to make your decision. This is the human predica-

[19] Thus, explicitly, in vol. 2, p. 2; vol. 3, p. 22; vol. 4, p. 220. The war of 1914–18 was to Gény a war for the realization of Natural Law (vol. 4, pp. 264–65).

[20] *Ibid.*, vol. 2, p. 361, note 1.

[21] Marc Réglade, *Valeur sociale et concepts juridiques*, Paris 1950.

[22] Paul Roubier, *Théorie générale du droit—Histoire des doctrines juridiques et philosophie des valeurs sociales*, Paris 1946, 2nd ed. 1951. Likewise opposed to Natural Law, G. Ripert and J. Haesert; see App. B, Horvath, as there cited, and Théry, *op.cit.*

ment which faces all men, a predicament not of their own choosing. Both teachings, therefore, play up the responsibility of the individual and, through him, of society. Both are compatible with scientific attempts to warn people of the risks and the consequences of their choices. And both, although agreeing that science is unable to verify the existence of divine forces, leave people free to choose religion as their guide, because they are also agreed that neither can science disprove the existence of suprahuman forces.

In the *United States,* to turn finally to this country, the absence of direct experience with totalitarian governments in domestic affairs and the reassuring presence of the due-process clauses in the Constitution made the problem of the validity of Natural Law less pressing than it had become on the European Continent. But reflections on the European events, accentuated by American involvement in the Nuremberg trials, progressively stirred interest in the United States. Most appeals to Natural Law remained emotional, however, or referred to tradition or religion. Only a few penetrated more deeply into the scientific problems on a nonreligious basis.[23] In 1956, a new periodical, *Forum of Natural Law,* began to appear (annually), to which frequent reference will be made here.

A prominent example of secular Natural-Law thinking in the United States is Professor F. S. C. Northrop's book, *The Logic of the Sciences and the Humanities* (New York 1947). Northrop agrees (pp. 296 ff.) that it is not feasible to derive ethics directly from nature in empirical or intellectual terms. "Empirically and intellectually speaking," he writes, "there is no such thing as ethics. There is only the nature of things and one's basic theory of what it is." This basic theory is determined "by one's philosophical presuppositions." The problem of a good society is nothing more than the problem of getting an adequate conception of the "nature of things." If one knows a given people's philosophical conception of the nature of things, then one also knows what they regard as good. In order to have an idea of

---

[23] See Edgar Bodenheimer's report, "A Decade of Jurisprudence in the United States of America: 1946–1956," *Natural Law Forum,* vol. 3 (1957) pp. 44–67. He lists as Neo-Thomists, or "touching" upon their doctrines: John Wu, Thomas Davitt, Anton-Hermann Chroust, George Constable, Edward Barrett, Harold McKinnon, Robert Wilkin, and Miriam Rooney; as non-Thomist adherents of Natural-Law ideas: only Northrop and Fuller (see text) and Edmond Cahn (see Chapter x, Section 2, below), apart from a few remarks in Jerome Hall's writings (especially, *Living Law of Democratic Society,* 1949, p. 8) and the later writings of Roscoe Pound. All other authors listed in Bodenheimer's report either reject Natural Law or ignore the issue.

what is good for *all* people one must, therefore, have a "set of assumptions which consistently, in terms of a theory of the nature of things, gives meaning to all the diverse cultural assumptions, insofar as this is possible."

This far, Northrop does not request us to rely on the nature of things as such, but on the philosophical interpretation given it in the various cultures or in the latters' philosophical assumptions. In other places, however, he goes much further. Repeating that any given philosophy of culture is based on assumptions that make "certain assertions about the character of nature and man" (pp. 335 ff., 340), he adds, with a big jump in his argument, that for this reason all philosophies can be *empirically verified* by an appeal—not, as it would have been logically consistent for him to continue, to the "philosophies of nature," but to the "facts of nature" and to those "characteristics of men" which are "independent of any particular ideology." This does not follow from his premises. The facts of nature can supply empirical verification of *moral* social theory only on the assumption that they permit of no more than one philosophical (moral) interpretation, or that all men are led to the same interpretation. Where different interpretations are possible and are actually selected in good faith, with no undesired results, there the nature of things and men yields no "empirical verification" of moral philosophies. To say the opposite means either smuggling into science a divine will as scientifically established or succumbing to the fallacy of deriving an Ought from an Is.

This fallacy Northrop bitterly denounces elsewhere in his book (see Appendix B, below, notes to Chapter IX). But here he himself slips into it when he offers his own criterion of a true philosophy. A philosophy of *culture* is true, he says (pp. 338, 342), when the relation between its postulates and the postulates of the philosophy of *nature* is that of "identity," and "false or incomplete," when this relation is not that of identity. This is logically nonconclusive. To say that the results of natural science can ever yield *moral* principles is scientifically untenable without a reference to divine moral forces. A philosophy that offers moral principles, setting limits to actions other than those set by the implacable Must of nature, is no longer a natural science; it is a philosophy of culture, not of nature. If it permits or even asks us to do violence to nature, for instance, by destroying mosquitoes, using anesthetics or contraception, or even to the nature of man, for example, by forcing men to suffer and die for the nation against their own free will, it cannot be said on this ground alone to be "false or incomplete." Northrop's claim that through his philosophy "the gulf between the philosophy of value and the philosophy of science introduced by Immanuel Kant is resolved" (p. 344) is unfounded.

Among the few other twentieth-century writers in the United States who have contributed original ideas favorable to Natural Law in the nonreligious sector that concerns us here, Professor Lon L. Fuller of Harvard Law School merits special attention. He is a friend and well-wisher rather than a typical representative of Natural-Law thinking. For he explicitly states that he accepts no doctrine "which asserts that there is a 'higher law,' transcending the concerns of this life, against which human enactments must be measured and declared invalid in case of conflict," and, even in the secular sector, he rejects the doctrine that there is something called "*the* natural law capable of concrete application like a written code." [24] Indeed, he insists that he is "not, in any usual sense, advancing a 'theory of natural law'" at all.[25] Still, there is something in Natural-Law thinking with which he wants social scientists to become "more sympathetic." [26] What is it?

Fuller raises two major points. The one is that many human actions can only be understood—or, can be understood more quickly—if the observer knows what purposes (subjective "values") the actor is pursuing. This is nothing new, of course. No one—apart possibly from a small group of die-hard behaviorists [27]—denies that facts and valuations are simultaneously involved in many human actions; the facts of the action include the "fact" that subjective ideas are held by the actor about the "value" of its purpose and about the usefulness ("value") of the action and the tools used as means toward attaining that purpose. Even the objective usefulness which the action has or fails to have as a means is a factual component of the situation (see Chapters III and VII, above). This does not imply that facts and values really "merge," as Fuller suggests; they remain distinct aspects of the state of affairs.[28] But this is a minor matter of controversy in our present context because, as Professor Fuller admits, the fact that most human actions serve some intelligible purpose reveals nothing about

---

[24] Lon L. Fuller, "Human Purpose and Natural Law," *Natural Law Forum*, vol. 3 (1958) pp. 68–76 (reprinted from *Journal of Philosophy*, vol. 3, 1936, pp. 53 ff.) and "A Rejoinder to Professor Nagel," *ibid.*, pp. 82–104. The above quotation is from p. 84.

[25] *Ibid.*, p. 68.

[26] *Ibid.*, p. 75.

[27] See above, Chapter I, Section 2, and Appendix B thereto.

[28] See Ernest Nagel, "On the Fusion of Fact and Value: a Reply to Professor Fuller," *ibid.*, pp. 77–81. As to Fuller's views, see also his *The Law in Quest of Itself*, Chicago 1940.

the moral value of the purpose; it discloses no moral type of Natural Law.

Fuller's second point is more original, and its implications concern more directly the moral issue. He holds that "men, by pooling their intellectual resources, may come to understand better what their purposes are." This he calls the "collaborative articulation of shared purposes."[29] The recommendation here expressed must first be divested of a disturbing ambiguity, however, in order to render it fit for scientific debate. It may either mean that men should try through collaboration to clarify those purposes which they want to set for themselves; or it may mean that they should seek clarity on purposes that are set for them by suprahuman powers; or, finally, it may mean both. I have been unable to find out which of these possible interpretations of his advice Fuller intended. If only self-chosen human purposes are to be clarified, there is nothing controversial in his recommendation. Collaborative discourse may surely serve the quasi-scientific aim of attaining greater clarity on vague points in one's own yearnings, on their biological or psychological origin, and on the consequences and risks implied in the choice between alternative possibilities of action or of attitudes toward life. This includes common exploration of the wide area of *poena naturalis,* where a great deal can be discovered individually and collaboratively (see Chapter xii, below).

If, however, the aim of collaboration is to discover purposes set for man by suprahuman powers, success of the common enterprise presupposes that there *are* such powers. Whether inanimate nature in the nondivine sense of the term can be thought of as a power that sets purposes is highly questionable on logical grounds: nondivine nature presents aids for, or obstacles to, the achievement of human purposes, but it does not "set purposes" (see Chapter ii, Section i). Yet if God is thought of as the creator of nature, then a recommendation that we try to discover man's terminal purpose through collaboration involves no logical fallacy. The only trouble then is that the presupposition of God's existence and of his intention to speak to us through nature in moral matters is not verifiable scientifically, not even through collaboration, it seems (see Chapter xiii). In other words, collaboration can help us discover in nature intimations of terminal purposes set for man by God only on the twofold "hypothetical assumption" (scientifically speaking) that God is there and that he has incorporated

[29] Fuller, *op.cit.,* pp. 68, 74, 75, 84; see also the recapitulation by Joseph P. Witherspoon, *ibid.,* pp. 105–34.

moral purposes in nature. Should either of these two assumptions be wrong, the results of collaboration based on them could dismally miscarry. Only if both are true may efforts in this sector be successful; then they may even be very wholesome. My main point here is that, if Fuller's advice was meant to imply the second interpretation, he has failed to point to its doubly hypothetic character.[30]

But I am not certain that he wanted to put emphasis on purposes set by suprahuman powers. For elsewhere he avers that he discerns and shares one central aim common to all the schools of Natural Law, "that of discovering those principles of social order which will enable men to attain a satisfactory life in common." [31] This is a very human purpose, proclaimed in every democratic program, not necessarily dependent on divine orders. And Fuller himself is not sanguine on subsuming it under the title of Natural Law; for he proposes to give the study of "good order under workable arrangements" the name of "Eunomics" rather than Natural Law.[32] Scientific Method and Scientific Value Relativism certainly have no objections to such study. As a matter of fact, applied political theory is chiefly engaged in this kind of work.

In pleading that social scientists become "more sympathetic" with Natural-Law thinking Fuller refers only to the "essential aims" of the Natural-Law schools, he says. But this begs the question as to what the essential aims are. If they are to make us accept the doctrine that a moral law issues from nature without divine intercession, or that the existence of a divinely inspired Natural Law is scientifically established, they must be rejected. But if they are no more than to find out what limitations on human achievements nature imposes, what opportunities nature leaves open for man, what the natural consequences of human actions are bound to be, including *poenae naturales,* and what features of human nature are universal, then the scientific legitimacy of such inquiries is beyond doubt (see Chapters iv, ix to xii of this book). And if the Natural-Law schools, in addition, wish us to pay more attention to the possibility that there *may be* a divine moral law permeating nature, then my sympathy is entirely with them, provided the collaborative efforts are disciplined enough to

---

[30] Professor Witherspoon confuses religious and scientific aspects when (*op.cit.,* p. 111) he puts the burden of proof regarding the question whether men can know their God-set terminal end on the shoulders of those who doubt it. See Chapter xiii, below, on the burden of proof.

[31] *Op.cit.,* p. 84.

[32] "American Legal Philosophy at Mid-Century," *Journal of Legal Education,* vol. 6 (1954), p. 477.

keep scientific inquiries separated from religious dogma and that those who engage in these efforts are constantly aware that they conduct their inquiries under the two scientifically unproven religious hypotheses mentioned above.[33]

6. Ethical Evolution

In a remarkable attempt to make ethical thinking scientific, Julian S. Huxley in his *Evolutionary Ethics*[1] follows, first, psychoanalytic leads by tracing the development of conscience in the individual to guilt feelings aroused through the infant's experiences with his mother, with definite consequences for the distinction between "healthy" and "unhealthy" (or "perverted") forms of development. He then examines the biological and historical evolution of life from matter up to the highest forms of social life, with traceable consequences for the evolution of moral codes of society. He tries to gain objective moral standards from these two approaches, asserting that they teach us not merely facts but also by what standards science must rate values.

The weakness of Huxley's argument lies in this transition from facts to scientific standards of moral values. In deriving from the Is of evolution not only the inescapable Must whenever nature leaves us no way out, but also the moral Ought in situations in which we have some freedom of action, he elevates natural evolution to the position of moral god. This is fallacious thinking. By showing how evolution favors the type best fitted for survival we do not show that the type best fitted for survival on earth is the best also from a moral point (Jesus chose to die on the cross). And by showing how men, individually and socially, have come to consider things right or wrong, we do not show whether these things *are* right or wrong, except on those terms. In confounding these two questions Huxley tries in vain to escape from the problem whether science is capable of setting ultimate standards of right and wrong in moral terms, to escape, that is, over "Route Eight" (see Introductory, Section 4), substituting psychological and biological questions for ethical ones. He actually injects his own

---

[33] Regarding other American scholars who have expressed views in favor of certain aspects of Natural Law see the preceding and subsequent sections of the present chapter, Chapter VII (Strauss, Voegelin), Chapter XII (Felix S. Cohen), and Appendix B (*Natural Law Forum*, John Wild, Catlin, and others), where further literature is listed.

[1] Julian S. Huxley, *Evolutionary Ethics*, Oxford 1943; included also in *Touchstone for Ethics*, combining essays by T. H. and Julian Huxley, New York 1947. My own critical remarks are not meant to detract from the great merits of J. Huxley's article as a competent analysis of factors that contribute to the formation of moral judgments, and of the functions performed by ethics in social life. See also his "Conclusion" in *Touchstone*, pp. 193–257.

value judgments. As many of us Western scholars would do, he clearly favors the individual over the group, "complexity within unity" beyond merely evolutionary needs, and, especially, equality of opportunity for all individuals irrespective of the fact that, if this question is treated merely from the viewpoint of evolution, situations could well be conceived in which inequality might produce better evolutionary results by creating better breeding conditions for the most promising types.[2]

This is not to deny that the discoveries of psychoanalysis and of biological evolution provide us with important objective factors in the discussion of values. But they do so merely because they enable us to prove (1) what the natural origin and causes of certain human desires and inhibitions are, or may be; (2) what the consequences of certain actions are likely to be; and (3) what our chances to reach certain desired goals may be. This is what science can try to do. It is much, indeed, and very important. But beyond it, science cannot derive directions as to what men ought to desire, to do, or to approve, from either psychoanalysis or biological evolution.

7. *Suum Cuique*

This old definition of justice has often been branded as bare of substantial meaning, because the *suum* may be interpreted in either a conservative or a revolutionary sense, or in any other way, according to the individual creed. Therefore, it has been said, the postulate contains no definite norm. As Simmel wrote in 1892, it "naïvely presupposes the determination of the *suum* as previously given." It is merely analytical in character, because "we cannot define what is due [a person] otherwise than as that which we ought to give him." [1]

But the formula has kept cropping up also in the twentieth century. Thus, the French philosopher, P. de Tourtoulon (1867–1932) insists that it expresses a substantive postulate of absolute validity.[2] He does not hesitate to interpret the *suum* in the conservative sense, but modifies this basic interpretation by stressing the *cuique*. Thus he derives the idea of liberty from the fact that he who is restricted in his liberty has

---

[2] See the review of Huxley's book by C. D. Broad in *Mind*, vol. 53 (1944), reprinted in Feigl and Sellars, *Readings in Philosophical Analysis*, pp. 564 ff.

[1] Georg Simmel, *Einleitung in die Moralwissenschaft*, Berlin 1892, vol. 1, pp. 51, 52.

[2] Pierre de Tourtoulon, *Philosophy in the Development of Law* in Modern Legal Philosophy series, vol. 13 (New York 1922) pp. 478, 491. Rommen, *op.cit.*, p. 231 and *passim*, also resorts to *suum cuique*, as do in line with St. Thomas almost all Catholic writers, but also many others; for example, Emil Brunner, *op.cit.* (Section 5, above) p. 86.

not "his" *suum* (p. 492), reaching the conclusion that slavery is never just (p. 481); nor are anti-alcoholic laws, "for they sanction restraint upon individual liberty and make all pay for the excesses of some" (p. 493).

This argument does not refute the old objections. On the contrary, it serves to confirm their validity. Why should the line be drawn just where Tourtoulon cares to draw it? Why not allow a fully equalitarian interpretation? Or discriminations like those proclaimed and practiced by the National Socialists in Germany? In fact, Josef Goebbels ended an article of his with the postulate *"Jedem das Seine,"* the German translation of *suum cuique*,[3] and these words could be seen displayed on the gates of Nazi concentration camps.[4]

Although empty of meaning in the negative sense that it fails to say what the *suum* is, the old formula is not entirely bare of a positive meaning, I submit, because it does express to some degree that truth, generality, and equal treatment of equal cases are required in justice. This may explain why its spell is so enduring. That indeed truth, generality, and equal treatment of equal cases are universal postulates of justice will be discussed in Chapter x.

8. Democracy

When Hitler rose to power in Germany and began to transcribe the National Socialist table of values into positive law, Gustav Radbruch, driven from his university chair but keeping his residence in Heidelberg, used a brief presence at an international meeting in Lyon to express his views, not—as so many others who stayed within the reach of totalitarian power—in order to placate the tyrant, but to bolster the defense of democracy.

His courageous paper, read and published in French,[1] advanced the thesis that scientific relativism leads logically to the demand that values should not be forced upon any people against their will, and there-

[3] Joseph Goebbels, "Sozialismus und Eigentum" in *Der Angriff,* November 14, 1929, cited after K. D. Bracher, *Die Auflösung der Weimarer Republik,* Stuttgart 1953, S. 113, n. 64.
[4] Eugen Kogon, *Der SS-Staat. Das System der deutschen Konzentrationslager,* Frankfurt 1946, S. 42. Engl. translation under the title *The Theory and Practice of Hell* by H. Norden, New York 1950. This, however, was probably an intentional perversion in pursuit of the sadistic practice to make fun of misery. See the profound analysis in Fritz von Hippel, *Die Perversion von Rechtsordnungen,* Tübingen 1955, especially p. 107.
[1] Gustav Radbruch, "Le relativisme dans la philosophie de droit," *Archives de philosophie du droit et de sociologie juridique,* vol. 4 (1934) pp. 105–110. Now also in German, G. Radbruch, *Der Mensch im Recht* (selected papers, ed. by Fritz von Hippel, Göttingen 1957) pp. 80–87.

with to postulates of liberty (he enumerated freedom of thought, of science, of religious belief, and of the press), separation of powers, majority rule, and sovereignty of the people; in brief, democracy. Relativism, he said, in producing such "absolute consequences" (*nous avons tiré du relativisme même des conséquences absolues*), has at last succeeded in firmly vindicating the traditional natural rights, which philosophers had so often tried in vain to prove with other means. Thus the head of the school of relativism seemed to transform himself into an aggressive absolutist. As he himself exclaimed: *Un miracle logique s'est effectué: le rien a produit le tout* (a logical miracle has been effected: the nothing has produced the all).

But the values which Radbruch, in his honorable attempt to come to the aid of democracy in its darkest hour, lifted to the top position, were actually not proved by him to be absolute in the scientific sense, and a thinker who once had written, "No legal proposition could be excogitated that would necessarily and in all circumstances be right or wrong,"[2] could hardly have meant them to be so. Actually, it does not follow from Scientific Value Relativism that no values should be forced upon people: it follows only that this could not be done *under the authority of science*. True, science can warn against authoritarian revelationists or patriots who try to enforce scientifically unwarranted value systems, by pointing to the great mistakes and abuses of which they may be guilty, to ulterior motives, and to the impossibility of controlling a despot once he has been permitted to seize power (see Chapter XII). Science may bare all the "implied evils" of dictatorial regimes, and may try to demonstrate that better results may be produced through tolerance—meaning by "evil" and "better," what is so considered by the audience to which the scientist is speaking. But, with all this, science remains unable to prove that minorities, acting in good faith, are necessarily wrong when they apply intolerance and force in order to "pull the people back from an abyss," or when they reject majority systems as likely to be mediocre, immoral, or immature.

Radbruch, in the same paper, expressed the view that democracy presupposes relativism (*la démocratie, de son côté, suppose le relativism*). This statement, too, is not warranted. Kelsen had made a similar point before, adding: "Whoever knows with absolute certainty what the right social order is, must indignantly reject the demand to make the realization of this order dependent upon the fact

[2] Radbruch, *Grundzüge der Rechtsphilosophie*, 1st ed. 1914, p. 4.

337

that the majority . . . recognizes his order to be the best one. . . ." [3]
There is, of course, a certain psychological interconnection between
Scientific Value Relativism and democracy and between the belief
in absolute values and political absolutism. The latter alignment is
illustrated not alone by the totalitarian regimes of Communism (belief in the scientific truth of Marxian doctrines) and National Socialism
(belief in racial superiority), but also by the historical examples of
association between religious intolerance and absolute state power.
Such fellowships are not merely a matter of the past, as the following
contemporary statement shows:

> The Roman Catholic Church, convinced, through its divine pre-
> rogatives, of being the only true church, must demand the right to
> freedom for herself alone, because such a right can only be possessed
> by truth, never by error. As to other religions, the Church will
> certainly never draw the sword, but she will require that by legiti-
> mate means they shall not be allowed to propagate false doctrine.
> Consequently, in a state where the majority of the people are
> Catholic, the Church will require that legal existence be denied to
> error . . . In some countries, Catholics will be obliged to ask full
> religious freedom for all, resigned at being forced to cohabitate
> where they alone should rightly be allowed to live. . . . The Church
> cannot blush for her own want of tolerance, as she asserts it in prin-
> ciples and applies it in practice. [4]

But such views are not necessarily held by all people who have firm
convictions, and certainly not today by all Catholics, many of whom
are honest adherents of the democratic form of government, irrespective of their being within the majority or the minority. [5] It is precisely
one of the greatest merits of democracy that it does *not* presuppose
relativistic world views, or any other, but offers a haven to adherents

---

[3] Hans Kelsen, *Vom Wesen und Wert der Demokratie,* Tübingen, 2nd ed. 1929, and, almost
identical, *Staatsform und Weltanschauung,* Tübingen 1933. The quotation is from his *Allgemeine
Staatslehre,* Berlin 1925, p. 370. See also, *What Is Justice?* p. 204: "For, just as autocracy is
political absolutism—which is paralleled by philosophical absolutism; so democracy is political
relativism—which has its counterpart in philosophical relativism."

[4] Quoted by R. M. MacIver, "The Deep Beauty of the Golden Rule," in *Moral Principles
of Action,* ed. by Ruth N. Anshen, New York 1952, p. 46. The quotation is from *La Civiltà
Cattolica,* as rendered in *Christian Century,* July 1948. For further comment, see Section 15,
below.

[5] See, for example, Arthur Utz, "The Principle of Subsidiarity and Contemporary Natural
Law," *Natural Law Forum,* vol. 3 (1958) pp. 170–83, and Alfred L. Scanlan (Book Review),
ibid., pp. 189 ff.

of the most divergent absolute or relativist creeds. The founders of modern democracy—and, for that matter, of Athenian democracy too—were no relativists. It was the terrible experience of opposing views raging in mutual persecutions in the era of the religious wars, which led the adherents of these absolute views, *without abandoning them,* to establish political tolerance. Democracies today embrace millions of people whose value judgments are entirely absolute, but who are agreed to live together under the rule of mutual *political* toleration.[6]

From the democratic viewpoint it must be hoped that the day will come when the adherents of secular absolute creeds, like Communism, will also submit to democratic principles in the processes of government and community life. The historical experience that the adherents of the most intolerant religious views could finally be politically democratized shows that this is not a purely romantic speculation. But this much must be conceded to Radbruch and Kelsen: wherever adherents of absolute value judgments, religious or secular, dominate a nation's government, thinking that their judgments are scientifically warranted, there is a greater risk that they may try to enforce their judgments than where the government is run by adherents of Scientific Value Relativism. Let us not forget, however, that the latter too may become highly dogmatic in their private value judgments at times. Against the abuse of power there is ultimately no political remedy other than eternal vigilance.

9. *Happiness*

Proclamations of happiness as an absolute value, or even as *the* ultimate value, reached their climax in John Stuart Mill (Chapter v, Section 7, above). Then the anti-climax began. Georg Simmel, at the end of the nineteenth century, presented one of the most penetrating analyses of this question.[1] He acknowledged that pleasure is always felt as something valuable by him who experiences it, as long as it lasts, and even called it an "absolute" value in this context, a term

---

[6] Regarding intolerant puritans see below, Chapter XIII, Section 1. Against the identification of absolutistic philosophies and absolutistic forms of government, and of relativistic philosophies and democratic forms of government, see also René de Visme Williamson, "The Challenge of Political Relativism," *Journal of Politics,* vol. 9 (1947) pp. 147 ff., and Lon L. Fuller, *The Law in Quest of Itself,* Chicago 1940, pp. 120 ff. Further, R. B. Perry, *Realms of Value,* p. 219: "The adherent of democracy rejects skeptical relativism and claims truth."

[1] Georg Simmel, *Einleitung in die Moralwissenschaft,* Berlin 1892, vol. 1, Chapter IV, pp. 293 ff.

otherwise not used by him affirmatively.[2] But he declared that, if conceived of as an *ultimate* value or goal, the concept of happiness lacked definite meaning:

> No unambiguously defined idea of happiness can be found whose content could be proved to form the end of all human actions; and all [philosophy of] eudaimonism amounts to nothing more than calling the actual ends of actions, which are known from experience, happiness. Instead of a synthetic proposition, therefore, we get an analytic one, and instead of an explanation that penetrates below the surface, merely a collective name (*Sammelname*) for the totality of phenomena that had already been known before in some other way.[3]

Few would deny, even today, that happiness *as they understand it* is valuable. But what makes them happy is very multiform, and what they consider worthy of the name is even more so. After listening to an enthusiastic paper in honor of the pursuit of happiness, at a mid-century meeting in New York, a woman rose and asked, "Why, with all our pleasures, are we so unhappy?" She put the finger on the right spot. Most post-Millian philosophers have questioned, just as Simmel did, whether the praise of happiness as such has any justification other than that people like to feel happy, which is merely a tautological, analytic truth, undeniable as far as it goes, but no contribution to the problem of whether to feel happy has absolute value, and what feelings of happiness are worthy of our approval. Even an overall feeling of happiness would hardly be accepted as an ultimate value by most philosophers today, unless it were the "right type" of happiness. But what is the right type? This question can be answered only with the aid of religious or ethical references that are not derived from happiness or science, but rather are meant to establish preconditions of the right type of happiness.[4]

Matters would be different only if it could be established that goodness is *always* associated with happiness, or "true" happiness, and badness with unhappiness. The theory that this is indeed the case has been reiterated in this century by Felix S. Cohen. He maintains that surplus

---

[2] *Ibid.,* p. 317: "Pleasure is indeed an absolute value, which, considered separately (*an und für sich*), can never be put as equal to zero, but may be outweighed by others." Simmel said, with dubious validity, that one could not even repent the feeling of pleasure as such, but only the sacrifices of other values brought for it, and the consequences.

[3] *Ibid.,* p. 312.

[4] See, for example, R. M. MacIver, *The Pursuit of Happiness,* quoted above (Chaper VI, Section 5).

of pleasures over pains is an "outstanding characteristic" and "necessary concomitant" of the good. Put in another way, this amounts to saying that it is *impossible* to become unhappy by being good or just, or happy by being bad or unjust. This thesis will be discussed below, Chapter XII, in the pertinent context of theories based on impossibility. Suffice it to say here that Cohen admits he canot offer scientific evidence.

10. *Society. The Social Ideal*

The tendency to absolutize the value of the group is much older than the modern effort to secure top rank for the individual. Recent revivals of the older tendency have been supported on the one hand by Hegel's belief in the existence of a supra-individual "objective mind" and his glorification of the state, and on the other by the doctrines of the early French sociologists. Comte considered real only society as a whole; the individual, regarded separately, was a mere abstraction to him.[1] François Maine de Biran (1766–1824) went so far as to state, "The individual, the human being, is nothing; society alone exists." [2]

In the tremendous output of twentieth-century literature on the interrelations between the individual and society many writers have been concerned exclusively with the psychological or phenomenological inquiry into the manner in which the individual actually experiences otherness and his own interconnection with others. The absolute validity of value judgments could then remain entirely unexamined. Some, however, have gone beyond a merely descriptive examination in assigning ultimate value either to the individual alone—an alternative dealt with in Section 3, above [3]—or to society, at least in part.

When Georg Simmel, in 1892, interpreted the feeling of duty (*Sollen,* Ought) as a modified type of willing, namely, a willing that takes account of the interests of others, he could leave the question of the value of the social whole out of consideration. But when Emil Lask,

---

[1] *Cours de philosophie positive,* 2nd ed., Paris 1864, vol. 6, p. 590. Hayek, *op.cit.* (Chapter V, above) pp. 198, 248. Compare, John Dewey and A. F. Bentley, *Knowing and the Known,* Boston 1949, p. 142 n. 20: ". . . if one insists on considering individual and social as different in character, then a derivation of the former from the latter would, in our judgment, be much simpler and more natural than to produce a social by joining or otherwise organizing presumptive individuals. In fact, most of the talk about the 'individuals' is the very finest kind of illustration of isolation from every form of connection carried to an extreme of absurdity that renders inquiry and intelligent statement impossible."

[2] Maine de Biran, *Oeuvres Inédites,* 1859, vol. 3, pp. 207 f. See Salomon, *op.cit.* (Chapter V) pp. 100 ff.

[3] See also Theodor Litt, *Individuum und Gemeinschaft,* 2nd ed., Leipzig 1924.

in 1905, pointed to the impossibility of understanding the idea of justice merely from the point of the individual without a reference to the social idea (Chapter vi, Section 3, above), this recognition necessarily implied that the social group as such was valuable.

Rudolf Stammler absolutized what he called the "social ideal," defining it as the "community of men of free will." In this formula "free" was to mean free from subjective and selfish purposes. The social ideal was to imply that each makes the other's purposes his own "as far as they are objectively justified."[4] He thought that this was a merely formal concept; but he drew certain substantive postulates from it, which he formulated in four principles, two each concerned with "mutual respect" and with "co-operation."[5]

Léon Duguit stressed "social solidarity." From the *fact* of mutual interdependence he derived the postulate that everyone *ought* to fulfill his social function. This method of deduction we had to reject as logically defective; it could be allowed to pass only after interpolation of a number of premises that were not made explicit (see above, Chapter iii). These premises, in turn, cannot be verified exclusively with scientific means. But this is no objection to the possibility that society may have an absolute value of its own.

Ralph B. Perry came close to Stammler's view when he characterized as "best" that community "each member of which wills only what is consistent with the will of the rest."[6] He derived this proposition from the value of harmony, to be discussed in Section 14.

These and other rather tame attempts to assign independent value to ideal forms of society were crudely overtrumped by Communism, Fascism, and National Socialism, all three of which were at one in their totalitarian allotment of paramount value to the group, although at variance in the description of the group that mattered.

Scientific examinations of the value of society are complicated by the question whether there is a collective mind distinct from the individual mind. The great French sociologist, Emile Durkheim

---

[4] Rudolf Stammler, *Wirtschaft und Recht, op.cit.* (Chapter v, Section 8) pp. 552, 554, 572, and 350; *Die Lehre vom richtigen Recht*, Berlin, 2nd ed., 1926, pp. 208 ff. The latter work has been translated in the Modern Legal Philosophy series, under the title *The Theory of Justice.*

[5] Those regarding respect were: first, the substance of what someone wills should never be made subject to another person's arbitrary will; and, second, any legal demand must be compatible with the postulate that he who is bound by it can still remain his own "nearest neighbor." The principles regarding cooperation were: first, no member may be excluded from the community arbitrarily; and, second, authority granted by law may be exclusive only in the sense that those excluded from a share in authority can still remain their own nearest neighbors.

[6] Ralph B. Perry, *General Theory of Value, op.cit.*, p. 677.

(1858–1917), seems to have held in some period of his work that there was. So did Wilhelm Wundt (1832–1920), German physiologist and psychologist, founder of the first laboratory for experimental psychology; and later, Walther Rathenau (see above, Chapter III, Section 2). No intersubjectively transmissible verification of this hypothesis has been offered, however. All the phenomena of society can be reduced to such in the bodies and minds of the individuals that compose it. But neither does Scientific Method warrant a negative statement; the scientist can say no more than that the existence of a collective or otherwise supra-individual mind cannot be verified, and that to assume it is not necessary, or not the only alternative, for the explanation of societal phenomena.

Society may have an independent value, and be more valuable than the individual, even if it has no independent mind. To the extent that its value is meant to rest on metaphysical grounds, it cannot be established scientifically. Insofar as its grounds are sought for in the advantage which the individual, or the social group as a whole, draws from cooperation, scientific treatment is entirely possible. But science fails us again when the lines between the individual interest and that of others, or of society as a whole, are to be drawn. No more than the consequences of the different views, and in some degree their psychological and biographical origins, can be exposed by science. The choice among them is not the affair of science; it is up to those who compose society and to their governments. It cannot be made solely upon scientific grounds.

11. *The Nation*

Some twentieth-century writers have revived attempts to present scientific arguments in favor of the overruling rank, in the pyramid of values, not of the individual or of society as a whole, or of mutual cooperation, but of the nation. Among them was originally the German professor Julius Binder (1870–1939), author of the most voluminous works on legal philosophy in our time. He went through several periods. Starting from Kant, and later from Hegel's objective idea, he became one of the strongest opponents of Scientific Value Relativism. Mid-time during the Weimar regime he proclaimed the national state and a certain exclusiveness in political rights and in political leadership as necessary and objective postulates of justice, although along with the postulate of personal freedom.[1] After a few years of experience under Hitler, however, he had the honesty and

[1] Julius Binder, *Philosophie des Rechts,* Berlin 1925, pp. 391, 415.

courage to modify his earlier views. In avowed contrast with them he then wrote that "the idea of right (*Recht*) does not order men to anything, not even regarding the right way of organizing their community life." He refused to adopt any *Weltanschauung* as science, or as the basis of knowledge, and fought for objectivity against subjectivism and voluntarism.[2] This led him close to the scientific type of value relativism which he had so strongly attacked earlier in his life.

Wilhelm Sauer (b. 1879), in a book published at about the same time, upheld the paramount value of the nation as an absolute element.[3] While he combined it with the postulate of an increase in culture (see Section 13) he stressed the primacy of the national interests over the positive law.[4] The community of nations could be accepted only as a secondary and subsidiary aim, he said.[5]

While nationalists in the older European nations have frequently aligned themselves with anti-democratic forces, nationalists in dependent or recently liberated peoples, especially in Asia and Africa, but in part also, it seems, in Soviet-dominated Europe, have been attracted by democratic ideals of liberty, self-government, and popular sovereignty. These democratic values, however, are often thought of as subordinated to the value of national independence, which is given top rank.

Scientific Method warrants no such value judgments in absolute terms. It can examine the consequences and risks involved in their espousal or rejection. It can point to the vagueness of their concepts, which frequently lend themselves to incompatible interpretations. It can disclose the psychological or biological origin and the ulterior motives of theories that enhance the value of the nation at the cost of the individual, and analyze, on the other hand, the advantages which a strongly integrated, externally independent nation offers for the development of a country's culture and for the community life of its citizens. But it cannot refute, in absolute terms, either the contention that the nation's value is greater than that of the individual, or the opposite. To render such ultimate value judgments is not its business.

---

[2] Julius Binder, *System der Rechtsphilosophie* (being the 2nd ed. of the former book) pp. 6, 7 and x. See also his *Grundlegung der Rechtsphilosophie*, Tübingen 1935, preface and p. 163, rejecting natural law and the axiom of equality; there he wrote that justice can be conceived empirically only on the basis of the positive law, but insisted that the latter must present a "unity (*Einheit*, union) of the universal and the particular will"—a last Hegelian reminiscence.

[3] Wilhelm Sauer, *Rechts- und Staatsphilosophie*, Berlin 1936, pp. 401, 403, 406. He stressed practical and immediate tasks (p. 397) and warned against vagueness (p. 397). See also *Das juristische Grundgesetz*, Berlin 1923.

[4] *Rechts- und Staatsphilosophie*, p. 421.

[5] *Ibid.*, pp. 40, 400.

12. *Power*

Power, and the urge toward power, were extolled in the nineteenth century by writers as different in character and intention as the historian, Heinrich von Treitschke, and the philosopher, Friedrich Nietzsche. This power-current of thought has not run dry in the twentieth.

Prior to World War I, Erich Kaufmann, then a young German *privatdozent* of public law, of late a senior adviser of the German Foreign Office in Bonn, wrote in a book on international law that the essence of the state is *Machtentfaltung* (development, increase, and display of power) along with the will successfully to maintain and assert itself (*sich zu behaupten und durchzusetzen*).[1] In order to live up to these inherent postulates the state must develop also the mental and moral energies of the nation; but this, according to Kaufmann, was a by-product, not the primary purpose of the state. The state is a being "that wills power everywhere and precisely thereby produces what is highest" (p. 135). Kaufmann rejected the ideal of a world-wide state on the ground that it would lack the need for *Machtentfaltung* and hence the most essential element of a state (p. 136). He ridiculed Stammler's version of the social ideal (Section 10, above); the real social ideal, Kaufmann wrote, "is not the 'community of free willing men' [as Stammler had said], but victorious war." In war, "the state reveals itself in its true essence; war is the state's highest performance (*Leistung*), in which its special nature (*Eigenart*) reaches its fullest development" (p. 146). Victorious war is "the ultimate norm, which decides which of the states is right" (p. 153).

This has been called the "Power Theory of the State and of International Law."[2] As a historical fact, acquisition and aggrandizement of power were soon afterward to become the foremost aims of totalitarian governments, whereas neglect of the power factor played an undeniable role in the collapse of democratic regimes. Thus the high value of power came to be emphasized also by scholars of unquestionably democratic leanings, such as Charles Merriam, George Catlin, Harold Lasswell, Hans Morgenthau, and Bertrand Russell. Of

[1] Erich Kaufmann, *Das Wesen des Völkerrechts und die clausula rebus sic stantibus,* Tübingen 1911. Kaufmann, it should be noted, was an opponent of the Nazis when this movement made its appearance, and had to suffer persecution at their hands. His views of power were modified by his recognition of the value of law and justice. But he strongly opposed relativism, of course. See his *Kritik der kantischen Rechtsphilosophie,* 1921, where he chided Radbruch's "one-dimensional thinking" and lack of "understanding of social reality."

[2] See the scathing critique of Kaufmann's arguments, chiefly on logical grounds, by Leonard Nelson, *Die Rechtswissenschaft ohne Recht, op.cit.,* pp. 144 ff.

these, Morgenthau pursued his thoughts primarily in the field of international relations. He urged the United States to shape its foreign policy in line with the country's national interests rather than have it determined by idealistic and sentimental goals, and to grant power policy priority over what he called "scientific" policy. Power politics, he said, was "rooted in this lust for power which is common to all men," and for this reason was "inseparable from social life itself." He charged that "contemptuous of power politics and incapable of the statesmanship which alone is able to master it, the age has tried to make policy a science. By doing so, it has demonstrated its intellectual corruption, moral blindness, and political decay."[3] "International politics, like all politics, is a struggle for power. Whatever the ultimate aims of international politics, power is always the immediate aim."[4]

Merriam, Catlin, Lasswell, and Russell were interested also in the domestic aspects of power politics.[5] They pointed to the dominant role which the lust for power and the actual possession of power play in the game of politics. They would not necessarily give power top rank in their own scale of values; but they stressed that in the game of politics, power is commonly sought as a high value, if not the highest; that wielding power was necessary for good government too; and that the proper problem of politics was to see to it that power should be in the hands of the right type of person. For these reasons they even suggested that "power" or (Catlin) "control" constitutes the proper basic unit of political and social theory. Catlin went so far as to consider whether power was not indeed an ethically desirable goal, "far from ethically neutral as means, but actually valuable as a collective *end* and *to be admired*—in some measure"; and he raised the "nice theological point whether the omnipotence of God is part of the *virtue* of God."[6]

This tendency to absolutize power in the abstract as a high value is ambiguous on the ground that the term "power" lends itself to the most divergent interpretations. True, it always designates the ability to get one's own will done and opposing wills frustrated; but it fails to express unequivocally by what means and to what purposes

[3] Hans Morgenthau, *Scientific Man vs. Power Politics*, Chicago 1946.

[4] Hans Morgenthau, *Politics among Nations*, New York 1948.

[5] See Charles Merriam, *Political Power*, New York 1934; Harold Lasswell, *Power and Personality*, New York 1948; Harold Lasswell and Abraham Kaplan, *Power and Society*, New Haven 1950; George Catlin, *op.cit.* (Chapter VI, Section 5), and "Political Theory: What Is It?" *Political Science Quarterly*, vol. 27 (1957) pp. 1–29; Bertrand Russell, *Power: a Social Analysis*, New York 1934.

[6] In his article of 1957, just quoted. Italics not in the original.

this ability is desired and used. As regards its sources, power may be based on, or accrue from, facts as different as (1) brute force, or threat of its use; (2) prestige or authority, legal or otherwise; (3) pecuniary means that give their owner the "power" to buy what he wants in the market; or (4) personal attraction, fascination, charisma, love—phenomena that, in turn, may have their origin in highly divergent factors, such as external gifts, like beauty; mental qualities, like wit; popular actions, like heroic deeds or prominence in sports or arts; that particular something, called personal charm; or, finally, as with Buddha, Jesus, or Gandhi, humility and altruistic modes of life. All this is, or gives, "power."[7] We even speak of the "power of an idea," as when the leader of the German Social Democratic Party, Otto Wels said, in the courageous speech in which he denied his party's consent to Hitler's Enabling Act of March 1933: "We . . . know that mere protests cannot do away with facts that are based on power politics (*machtpolitische Tatsachen*). We do see that in terms of power politics your rule is an actual fact at present. Yet the people's sense of justice is a political power, too, and we shall never cease to appeal to it. . . . No enabling act can give you the power to destroy ideas that are eternal and indestructible."[8] Charles S. Peirce, in a similar vein, once wrote that he regarded "Truth and Justice as *literally* the most *powerful powers* in the world."[9] And, in again another sense, Whitehead wrote, "The power of God is the worship He inspires."[10]

Likewise, the ends for the sake of which power is sought may vary all the way from enjoyment for its own sake and use for selfish purposes, to the pursuit of the most unselfish aims.

These twofold ambiguities of means and of purpose render the general concept of power as inept to supply an adequate basic unit in political theory as for similar reasons the general concept of happiness has been found to be (Section 9, above). It may be vaguely true that happiness and power are striven after by everyone everywhere in the

[7] Fundamental is the distinction between the legal power to set juridically valid norms ("P"-power) and the factual power to influence the use of that legal power or to interfere with the norms set by it ("II"-power); see Arnold Brecht, "How Bureaucracies Develop and Function," *Annals of the American Academy of Political and Social Science*, vol. 292 (March 1954) pp. 1–10, and "Bürokratie" in *Herders Staatslexikon*, Freiburg 1958.

[8] See Arnold Brecht, *Prelude to Silence—The End of the German Republic*, New York 1944, p. 101.

[9] In the letter quoted in Appendix B, Notes to Chapter V, Section 6. Italics for "powerful powers" here added.

[10] *Science and the Modern World*, p. 276.

world, but the sense in which this is true is exceedingly different from case to case, and often mutually incompatible.

To sum up. If power is held up as an ultimate value, as an end desirable for its own sake, science can do three things. It can (1) criticize the lack of clarity in the concept of power, (2) question logical consistency in a theory that tries to isolate power from sources and purposes, and (3) point to the consequences which the enhancement of the value of power entails for other ideals, such as peace, harmony, freedom, equality.

The role which power plays as a *means* in the pursuit of ulterior ends will be dealt with in its proper context, especially in Chapter XII and in the planned second volume on special questions.

13. *Culture*

Some twentieth-century scholars have attached paramount value to culture, or *Kultur*. In order to understand this high appraisal correctly it is necessary to be aware of the different meanings associated with the continental European term "culture," or *Kultur,* and the Anglo-American concept of "civilization." Civilization is generally used so as to include indiscriminately three distinct factors, namely (1) intellectual and technical progress, (2) achievements in the development of community life and of governmental institutions, especially those tending toward freedom, equality, and tolerance, and (3) cultural expressions of what is traditionally called the "soul," as distinct from the "intellect," in religious phenomena, in the arts, or in any other manner. The European term "culture" or *Kultur* is now generally used in the third sense; it includes the other two categories only to the extent that they are influenced by the third.

This usage, it is true, has not always been strictly adhered to, and it has been counteracted by specific uses made of the same word in special contexts. Thus, Heinrich Rickert, in establishing his distinction between *Naturwissenschaften* and *Kulturwissenschaften* (Chapter VI, Section 1, above), defined *Kultur* as "reality related to value" (*wertbezogen*). Any chair or table then constitutes part of *Kultur*.

Culture in the narrower, soul-related, sense has often been listed by relativists among those ideals that may be chosen by individuals as their ultimate values (see Chapters IV, Section 6, and VI, Section 3). Some, like Radbruch, have indicated their own preference for it, without claiming ability to prove the validity of such selection scientifically. Other authors, however, have gone further, assigning some sort of *absolute* value to culture. Leading among these in the beginning of this century was the German philosopher of law, Joseph Kohler (1849–1919).[1] Ridiculing Kant's *Critiques* because of the substantive emptiness of their formal categories, and the sociological jurisprudence of Jhering because of its materialistic utility approach, Kohler glorified Hegel, with whom he believed in objective reason and its gradual historical realization ("unfolding"). He modified Hegel, however, by the concession that the "dialectic process of history" is interspersed with many unreasonable and accidental elements, varieties and detours in the way of evolution, so that not every stage can be called rational, although the general direction is toward "continuous perfection."[2] This belief in "objective reason" and the "objective *Geist*" led him to consider *Kultur* as the preeminent value, objective and absolute.[3] Ethics and "the good" have only subsidiary character, he maintained, not being themselves absolute values.[4]

Kohler, however, defined *Kultur* more broadly than was done above, namely, as "the totality of human achievements in the conquest of the universe through knowledge, creative art, and technical domination," which keeps it closer to the Anglo-American notion of civilization. Wilhelm Windelband's earlier definition, describing *Kultur* as "the spiritual substance ·common to a given society" was more in line with present usage. But Windelband also held that the "ethical value of any society stands and falls with its *Kultur* system; to engender and preserve the latter, society must stake its last drop of sweat and blood."[5] This too seems to allot absolute value to culture.

Gradually, the distinction between the spheres of the "soul" and those of the "intellect" came more to the foreground. Walter Rathenau, in his chief philosophical essay, in which he analyzed the phenomena of the mind, or spirit (*Geist*), taking this term in its broadest meaning, saw the decisive dichotomy in the presence or the absence of a *purpose*. Pursuit of a purpose is the province of the intellect; the soul is purposeless ·in its characteristic stirrings, he said.[6] His assigning of a

---

[1] Joseph Kohler, "Rechtsgeschichte und Universalgeschichte" in *Encyclopädie der Rechtswissenschaft*, Munich, 7th ed. (1913); *Lehrbuch der Rechtsphilosophie*, Berlin 1909, 3rd ed. 1923 (translated by A. Albrecht as *Philosophy of Law*, in Modern Legal Philosophy series, vol. 12).

[2] *Rechtsphilosophie*, pp. 28 ff.

[3] *Encyclopädie*, pp. 1 ff., 62; *Rechtsphilosophie*, p. 4.

[4] *Rechtsphilosophie*, pp. 4, 6. See also the careful analysis by W. E. Hocking, *op.cit.* (Section 3, above) pp. 24 ff.

[5] Wilhelm Windelband, "Vom Prinzip der Moral" (1883) in *Präludien*, 5th ed., Tübingen 1915, vol. 2, pp. 162, 191.

[6] Walther Rathenau, *Die Mechanik des Geistes oder die Geburt der Seele*, Berlin 1913, 19th ed. 1925. See Chapter iii, Section 3, above, and my article on Rathenau there quoted.

higher value to nonpurposive acts was not based on any attempt at scientific demonstration, but solely on intuition; he frequently expressed aversion to scientific research.

The contemporary scholar most representative of the distinction between civilization and culture and the allotment of absolute value to the latter was Alfred Weber, whose opposition to Scientific Value Relativism I discussed in Section 3 of the preceding chapter. To him, *Kultur* is "soul-spirit as expressed either in the substance of life or in the human attitude taken toward it" (*seelisch-geistige Ausdruckform in der Lebenssubstanz oder seelisch-geistige Haltung ihr gegenüber*); in other words, "the form in which at any given time the soul-elements express themselves and find their salvation (*Ausdrucks- und Erlösungsform des Seelischen*) within the given material and spiritual substance of existence."[7] This conception of culture derives, he explains, from phenomena, "whose roots cannot be comprehended naturalistically, but whose interwovenness within life can be watched and contemplated." Like Rathenau, he sees an essential difference between the realm of purposive, or useful, action—the "cosmos of civilization," which "carries no further than [at] what is in line with purpose and useful"—and *Kultur,* or the realm of the soul. "The cultural molding of human existence has nothing to do with the reasonable pursuit of some purpose (*Zweckmässigkeit*) and usefulness." He calls it the "great guilt" of the nineteenth century that, in examining the historical process, it "as it were, buried (*verschüttete*) the provinces of the human soul, the ultimate and deepest sphere of human life";[8] and its basic mistake that, with Hegel, it "lumped the spheres of intellect and soul within the one collective concept of the mind (*Geist, spirit*)," disposing of the entire process by treating movements of both civilization and *Kultur* indiscriminately as phases of "mental development" (*geistige Entwicklung*).[9]

No naturalistic approach can do justice to the phenomena of the soul in human history, Alfred Weber said:

No naturalistic approach is able to comprehend how the soul-elements in man, in nationalities, or in other historical bodies (*Geschichtskörpern*) have come to have the irresistible impulse to form the environmental substance of life after ultimate ideas that are not found

---

[7] Alfred Weber, *Prinzipien der Geschichts- und Kultursoziologie,* München 1951, pp. 24, 74. This part was first published under the title "Geschichts- und Kultursoziologie als innere Strukturlehre der Geschichte," *Handwörterbuch der Soziologie,* edited by Alfred Vierkandt, 1931.

[8] *Ibid.,* pp. 72, 73.

[9] *Ibid.,* p. 83.

within it—after notions and needs of the soul-spirit—and, intentionally or not, to mold the entire form (*Gestaltung*) of existence after them; or how, when this impulse fails in its effort or the effort seems not worth the trouble, man withdraws, seeking corresponding attitudes of the soul-spirit in such withdrawal from life (hope of personal happiness being only a minor by-impulse in this, and often quite unessential); and how, finally, the soul-spirit can ever arrive at those creations (*Gestaltungen*) of the sublime, the beautiful, the holy, etc.; in other words, at any cultural manifestation of a more or less universal effect, whatever this manifestation may be. Nor is it possible to understand through a naturalistic approach why there is a consensus among men about what is sublime, beautiful, holy, etc., no matter in what essence, content, or form these qualities may appear. And indeed, the essence, content, and form [in which they appeared] in the various historical bodies, in part even in various epochs, have been worlds apart. This consensus may have soft and elastic limits, but without it no historian can talk to us of the "greatness" of a man, a work, or a period, of the "sublimity" or the "dreadfulness" of an historical area or era. . . .

As a matter of consequence, Alfred Weber insisted that there can be no cultural "progress" in the sense in which there is progress in civilization, from stage to stage, and that it may be necessary to look upon our own time as on some historically perhaps quite singular epoch of immense "re-barbarization, some lapse into almost general naturalism," with the external re-barbarization constituting merely the correlate of the internal one. *Kultur,* he wrote, is always "spontaneous," is "unforeseeable creation in a new stage of life." And this type of creation will appear ever again, in one form or the other, as long as the human soul is not destroyed.[10]

He regrets that Max Weber, instead of engaging in overall interpretations of cultural history, stopped at applying his "dissecting" (*zerlegende*) methods to it, an approach that may easily lead to a situation where one "finally holds on his hands a plenitude of valuable conceptual schemes and a like ample wealth of—conceivable or real—causal interrelations among the parts of the whole of life, but nothing more." He thinks that Max Weber did not fully exploit the richness of his attention to "part-events" (*Teilvorgängen*).[11] He complained also of

---

[10] See *Prinzipien, op.cit.,* pp. 31–34.
[11] *Ibid.,* pp. 108, 109.

Max's individualistic method, which regarded the structure of society only from the point of the individual. This is not suitable in matters of *Kultur,* Alfred insisted, not on the ground of philosophical objections to be raised—he did not mean to express any philosophical preference for universalism as against individualism—but because the cultural historian desires to "illuminate a complex totality in its totality" and to achieve a "tolerable comprehension of indissolvable, fundamentally entirely irrational, historical collectivities in their very unity."

I have quoted Alfred Weber at length, because his eloquent and persuasive description puts the question squarely before us whether, as scientists, we recognize the significance of the cultural factor in human history, and its particular character. But the conclusion that, if we do so, we abandon Scientific Value Relativism is not warranted. In drawing it, Alfred Weber unjustly identified the attitude of individual adherents with the basic methodological theory (see Chapter vii, Section 3). Scientific Value Relativism cannot but welcome any careful description of the role which the cultural factor and its appraisal has actually played in history, and the quasi-universal esteem it has found. Nor does it object to the scholar's proclaiming his own preference for, and paramount interest in, cultural standards. On the other hand, when the value attributed to a definite cultural phenomenon is controversial, is contradicted by the value judgments of others, then the mere insistence on one's own appraisal is without scientific merit. But any serious attempt to bolster evaluations by an examination of the consequences of positive or negative cultural attitudes has great scientific merits in the eyes of Scientific Value Relativists.

As regards consensus, Professor Weber does not pretend that his own cultural judgments are universally shared (see Chapter vii, Section 3); he has been contented with the far more modest statement that he addresses his own writings to those who do share his value judgments, a starting point that, if made explicit, is entirely legitimate under Scientific Value Relativism.[12]

For an excellent American contribution to the distinction between civilization and culture I may refer to the writings of R. M. MacIver.[13]

---

[12] Alfred Weber's views were previously set forth in his article "Prinzipielles zur Kultursoziologie" in *Archiv für Sozialwissenschaft und Sozialpolitik,* vol. 47 (1921) pp. 1, 25 ff. His *Kulturgeschichte als Kultursoziologie* (1st ed., Leiden 1935, 2nd ed. München 1950) and his *Der dritte und der vierte Mensch,* München 1953, are based on his methodological principles, as explained above.

[13] R. M. MacIver, "The Historical Pattern of Social Change," *Journal of Social Philosophy,* vol. 2 (1936) p. 35, and *Society,* 2nd ed., New York 1937, pp. 272 ff. See also R. K. Merton, "Civilization and Culture," *Sociology and Social Research,* vol. 21 (1936) pp. 105–13. Neither MacIver nor Merton, however, absolutized the value of culture.

14. *Harmony*

Praise of harmony in human affairs goes back to Pythagoras and Plato. In the search for absolute values it has been reiterated through the ages, up to the present time. Thus, at the end of the nineteenth century, Franz Brentano (1838–1917) thought it possible to state with absolute certainty the superior value of a harmonious personality, not onesidedly developing either intellect or emotions; while it was impossible to measure the relative weight of the values of knowledge (*Einsicht*) and noble love, the sum of both was better than each in isolation; neither should be neglected at the cost of the other.[1] Rudolf Stammler, in conflict with his contention that scientific statements regarding justice could merely be formal, treated harmony as an absolute aim of justice; this view appeared in his first major work in 1896, but came more to the foreground in his later writings.[2] Perry, in his *General Theory of Value* (1926), too, gave harmony high rank; that will is best, he wrote, which is apt "to bring harmony through its universal adoption." [3]

A strictly scientific discussion of these proposals is particularly difficult because the term harmony today refers to music and can be applied to human personalities and the state of society only in a figurative sense, which leaves the meaning very vague. If harmony is used as a synonym for what is worthy of being desired, then it is merely tautological to say that it designates a high-ranking value. Likewise, when used as a synonym of peace, rest, and balance, it is merely tautological and analytic to say that harmony implies these things. It may well be possible, furthermore, to prove scientifically that a certain amount of harmony, both in a person's individuality and in social life, is a universal human need and desire, which generally grows in old age. This adds an important universal factor, which might be called absolute so far as human beings are concerned. It may also be conceded to Brentano that sometimes the combination of two qualities, both of which are considered valuable, like knowledge and love, is better than a onesided possession of either to the exclusion of the other, at least as long as neither suffers by the "harmonious" addition. Finally, harmony is, of course, valuable as a means, or indispensable condition, for the achievement of many other aims.

[1] Franz Brentano, *Vom Ursprung sittlicher Erkenntnis*, Leipzig 1889, pp. 29, 30.
[2] Rudolf Stammler, *Wirtschaft und Recht*, Leipzig 1896, 5th ed. 1924, p. 564; "Rechtsphilosophie" in *Das gesamte Deutsche Recht*, 1931, vol. 1, pp. 17, 42.
[3] Ralph Barton Perry, *General Theory of Value*, New York 1926, pp. 659 ff., 682, also pp. 102–04.

All this can be said with assurance. As soon, however, as we generalize such statements, proclaiming harmony an absolute value that should be striven after by all and in every situation, we are leaving the area of *scientia transmissibilis,* leaning either on our own preferences or on intuition—an intuition that, far from being shared by everyone, is certain to encounter strong objection. It must not be overlooked that harmony may exist on low intellectual or cultural levels; it may be found in households that include slaves and illiterates. Many will see in strife, even when it upsets existing harmony, a necessary and valuable element of human life and development (see Chapter IV, Section 6). Most will feel, with Hocking, that harmony is just only if achieved "on the right terms."[4]

More recently, Perry has attempted to combine happiness and harmony, because either alone was a defective ideal. Thus he recommends "harmonious happiness" as the highest standard. He does not pretend that its absolute and universal validity can be scientifically proved; he explicitly admits that this cannot be done (see above, Chapter VI, Section 3). But he thinks that there are "paramount reasons" why this standard should be chosen. They are, first, that it is "capable of being agreed on—both theoretically and practically"; second, that it is "impartial," because it "places itself in all points of view and fits them together"; and, third, that acceptance is *"to some extent* [italics in the original] to everybody's interest" and therefore obtains "a breadth of support exceeding that of any other good."[5]

Of these reasons, the first, that harmonious happiness is "capable of being agreed upon," could conclusively support selection as the highest standard only if it were simultaneously assumed that there *should* be universal agreement on some one standard, and that no other would do, as Kant had believed respect for human dignity and freedom to be the only standard on which universal agreement was possible. Perry's second reason, that his standard fits all points of view together, leaves us wondering how this could be done. How are we going to fit together the points of view of an adherent of white supremacy and of a Negro or an Asiatic; or of a National Socialist and a Jew; or of a man who glorifies violence and war and of a sweet Christian, Gandhian, or antimilitarist; or of a communist and of a liberal or Catholic; of worshipers of God and of Satan? Perry's third assertion, that support for his standard is to be expected by everyone in his own interest, is gravely limited

[4] W. E. Hocking, *op.cit.,* p. 78.
[5] Ralph B. Perry, *Realms of Value,* Cambridge, Mass., 1954, pp. 132 ff. Occasionally his statements are couched in quite absolute terms; for example, ". . . in short, war *is* moral evil and peace *is* moral good," *ibid.,* p. 219.

by the addition "to some extent." Indeed, what common support can be expected from both the haves and the have-nots? Perry, in an aside, admits that his standard may not reward everyone who accepts it. Why then are we entitled to suppose acceptance in the individual's own interest?

These critical remarks are not meant to disparage the ideals underlying Perry's standard and shared by many of us within democratically built societies; but only to remind the reader that his explicit reasons rest on three implied premises, namely, that a universal common standard is desirable, that human equality should be its basis, and that people who lose under the standard should be willing to put up with the loss. To accept these premises is a quasi-religious resolve, or an act of ethical volition, and not a matter of science alone. Even so, the objection that harmony may exist on low cultural levels would stand. Walther Rathenau once remarked that, if we knew that worms were perfectly happy, we still would not desire to be worms.

15. *The Golden Rule*

Professor MacIver agrees that no goal-value of absolute validity can be established by science (see the quotations in Chapter VI, Section 5, d). But, while "on the level of goals there is irreconcilable conflict" and "no possible agreement," he holds that there is "one universal rule, and one only, that can be laid down, on ethical grounds—that is, apart from the creeds of particular religions and apart from the ways of the tribe that falsely and arrogantly universalize themselves." This, he says, is The Golden Rule: Do to others as you would have others do to you.[1] It is the only rule that "stands by itself in the light of its own reason." The universal laid down in it is one of *procedure* only, he notes, since it describes a "mode of behaving, not a goal of action." It is "the only universal of ethics that does not take sides with or contend with contending values." It permits everyone to follow his own rule as it would apply "apart from the accident of his particular fortunes," especially apart from the accident that the one is up and the other is down, the one is strong and the other is weak, the one is large and the other is small.

These arguments are sure to have a strong appeal, in particular to Christian readers. For the Golden Rule is the fundamental law of

[1] Robert M. MacIver, "The Deep Beauty of the Golden Rule" in Ruth N. Anshen, ed., *Moral Principles of Action*, New York 1952, pp. 39 ff. See also his *Pursuit of Happiness* (discussed above, Chapter VI, Section 5, and below, Chapter XIII) pp. 85 ff.

Christian ethics and, if we define ethics by the Golden Rule, of all ethics. But does it "stand by its own reason"? Can we derive it, with merely scientific means, from observation, logical reasoning, and the like, in an intersubjectively transmissible manner? When men notice that they are up and others are down, that they are strong and others at their mercy, they may sincerely believe—as they have done in history—that this is either the consequence of their being right and the others wrong, or that fate has given them a chance to destroy their enemies and that they would be fools unless they used it.

We cannot refute such proud, wanton, callous views, whatever we may call them, merely with the means of science. Science can sound warnings as to the risks and consequences of recklessness, describe the benefits to be expected from kindness, and point to numerous nice things we can do *if* we want to be nice. But, unless science could establish with certainty either (1) that the Golden Rule is a command of divine origin or (2) that its violator will *always* suffer a kick-back and that kindness *always* has superior rewards (whether this can be demonstrated will be examined in Chapter XII), science must abdicate precisely where the ethical nature of the Golden Rule, as distinct from its utilitarian character, begins.[2]

That the Golden Rule cannot be derived from reason alone is shown by the simple reflection that few people will accept it in their behavior toward animals. We kill them in order to eat them or to avoid annoyances, let flies die miserably on glued paper, lobsters lie alive on ice blocks with their claws fettered, eat oysters alive, and hook fish in that "peaceful" sport which is the unfairest of them all if thought of under the Golden Rule. We do such things although we would not want others to do similar things to us. In thus limiting the validity of the Golden Rule to the behavior among men only, but extending it to all men, we implicitly recognize two principles, namely, that in this respect men are different from animals, but also that all men are essentially alike. This, as we saw in Section 2 above, cannot be established by science alone. It is not self-evident, without a reference to moral qualities of all men and to the essential significance of these qualities, propositions that cannot be scientifically verified. The Romans did not consider the Golden Rule a self-evident principle in their attitude toward conquered enemies, nor did the Greeks in theirs toward barbarians.

---

[2] See Section 8 (Democracy) above, and MacIver's own reference to certain Catholic views, there quoted, which he too easily brushes aside as lacking rationality and "mere childishness" (p. 47).

Only after we have previously defined ethics in line with the Golden Rule can we derive that rule from the concept of ethics. Then it becomes a merely analytical inference.

16. *Excursus on Radbruch vs. Radbruch*

Scientific Value Relativism originally meant to Radbruch much more than merely a necessary, though unpleasant, concession to be made to the requirements of logic and scientific honesty. Dedication to the deepest values which he himself recognized, but withdrawal from any attempts to assume commanding attitudes in matters of value judgments toward others were views that blended harmoniously within his benign personality, humane and mild-mannered, always willing to find the good points in other people's views, and unendingly engaged in a dialectic struggle within his own delicate conscience. This balance was cruelly upset by the advent of totalitarianism, which led him to an agonizing reappraisal of scientific relativism. He searched desperately for lines that could be drawn against totalitarian value theories under the full authority of science. In this effort he came to pursue three different ideas, two of which have been discussed earlier in this volume.

The first, publicly expressed in 1934 (here referred to as "Radbruch II") was the new emphasis he placed on the "aggressive" potentialities of relativism. This, as shown in Section 8, above, was entirely consistent with his former views insofar as he urged combating any arrogation of *scientific* authority for ultimate governmental value judgments; but it was inconsistent when he implied that such lack of scientific authority was a conclusive argument against the practical and political acceptance of value judgments and their enforcement. Radbruch has not to my knowledge in his later writings resumed the claim that aggressive relativism was apt to solve the problem. Instead, in the quiet years of self-scrutiny which he spent in "inner exile" during the Hitler regime, he began to pursue two other lines of approach. The one ("Radbruch III") was the increased attention he paid to the interrelation between the justice of governmental measures and the "nature of things," discussed in Chapter IV, Section 3. As shown there, this idea too fails to lead to a solution whenever the nature of things is susceptible to being changed, bent, or suppressed by human interference and the only question is whether or not this should be done.

The third of Radbruch's new approaches ("Radbruch IV"), not yet treated here, started from the thesis that, while the "goals" of governmental measures are relative, the requirement of justice itself is not. To this proposition we now turn.

Radbruch's basic conception of Right (*Recht,* or "right law") had always been, from the first edition of his *Rechtsphilosophie,* that the idea of Right was no simple one, but that it harbored a "triad" of ideals, namely (1) the ideal of justice, meaning the equal treatment of what is equal, (2) the ideal of utility (*Zweckmässigkeit*), that is, of a reasonable relation between measures and the purposes pursued with them, and (3) the ideal of certainty, that is, the possibility to be granted everyone to foresee the legal consequences of his actions and omissions. Of these three, he now stressed, only the second, the utilitarian one, was related to "purposes," whose value could not be established or denied scientifically. The first (justice) and the third (certainty of law) were independent of the particular purposes pursued. Some "tension" could arise between them, he admitted; for example, a minor violation of the principle of equality must not be regarded as rendering the law invalid because to do so would impair the certainty of law. But, at any rate, these two ideals were independent of any particular purposes pursued in legislative measures. Thus he tried to secure, via the postulate of justice, an absolute position for the postulate of equality.

Had he stuck to interpreting this postulate in the modest sense of equal treatment of what is equal, his position would have been very strong. For, as we shall see in Chapter x, this interpretation of the meaning of justice has universal and invariant support, as has also the exclusion of arbitrariness. But Radbruch went much further. He now read into the equal treatment of equal cases the meaning that all men are equal, not unlike Leonard Nelson had done. Here his emotional desire to get nonrelativistic results carried him beyond what was scientifically warranted. Science, as shown in Section 2, can warn against erroneous statements on human differences or their causes, against unwarranted generalizations, and against the risks and consequences of discriminations; it can expose insincerities, ulterior motives, inconsistencies, and false claims of scientific authority; but it is beyond science to say that all individuals, despite their many differences, are "essentially" equal and must be treated as such by legislation, and that, apart from historical conditions, they have any "rights" as distinct from natural impulses and needs. Here is the end of science; here begins the sphere of religious, ethical, political, or legal convictions and decisions. Most significantly, here begins the impact of *history*—cultural history, in particular—and of a *jurisprudence* that is based ultimately on history rather than science.

Much as the moral motives that caused Radbruch to modify his former views are worthy of praise, from the purely scientific point "Radbruch I" was right, and "Radbruch IV" was in error, as had been "Radbruch II" and "III." This is not to say that we are left without scientific support in the protection of human rights. Precisely by keeping within its own proper sphere science can render highly important contributions, as emphasized in this whole study time and again. But whether norms set by the government and capable of execution are juridically valid or invalid is ultimately a matter for jurisprudence to say, not for science. What science is unable to do—establish inalienable human rights—jurisprudence *can* do. Jurisprudence can establish the principle that acts of legislation which are in conflict with certain basic standards of civilization as they have developed in historical evolution are juridically not binding upon law-courts and citizens (see Chapter IV, Section 8). In other words, ultimate reference in the question of the validity of norms lies, not to abstract, universal science but to jurisprudence as a concrete historical phenomenon. Science can, in this context, play only the subsidiary role of the handmaiden of jurisprudence, supplying the lawyers with the relevant historical material to bolster their theories about the limits set to the juridical validity of legislation.

In view of the confusion wrought by Radbruch's retreat from his earlier views it is appropriate to add the following remarks. It is not easy to point out exactly where and when Radbruch began to read into the postulate that equal cases must be treated as equal the additional thesis or axiom that all men *are* equal. In his delightful *Fünf Minuten Rechtsphilosophie* (Five Minutes of Legal Philosophy), a brief statement which he distributed among his students in 1945,[1] he stated (Third Minute): "Right law (*Recht*) is will to justice. Justice means: to judge without regard of person, to measure all by the same measure." This could have been a mere paraphrase of the postulate that what is equal should be treated as equal; but the word "all" surreptitiously introduced the idea that all men are equal. This transformation became more obvious in the subsequent passage, where he called on the jurists that they should refuse to grant the character of law to legal acts which consciously deny the will to justice, for example, "by arbitrarily granting or denying *human rights to human beings*."[2] This would have been entirely in line with the views here taken, had Radbruch merely intended to appeal to the jurists that they should deny the *juridical*

---

[1] Published in an appendix to the 4th and 5th eds. of his *Rechtsphilosophie*, pp. 335–37.
[2] Italics not in the original.

validity of certain acts, without presenting the existence of human rights as a finding of science. But the latter was what he meant. This appears from another section (Fifth Minute) of the same piece, where he referred to principles of law that cannot be validly disregarded. He said that they have been called Law of Nature or of Reason, and continued: "Certainly they are subject to many doubts in detail; but centuries of labor have worked out a firm core and gathered it in so-called Proclamations of the Rights of Men and of Citizens with such general consensus that, with regard to some of these rights, only an intentional (*bewusste*) skepticism could maintain doubt."

His new views came out more plainly in an article of 1946, entitled *Gesetzliches Unrecht und übergesetzliches Recht,* which might be approximately rendered in English as "Legal Wrong and Higher Law." [3] Here he wrote that one line, at least, "can be drawn with all precision: where justice is not even intended (*erstrebt,* striven after), where the equality which forms the core of justice is intentionally denied in the proclamation of positive laws, there the law is not merely 'incorrect' (*unrichtiges Recht*), but entirely misses the nature of Right (*die Rechtsnatur*). For, one cannot define *Recht,* or even positive law (*positives Recht*) otherwise than as an order, or a set norm (*Satzung*), which according to its meaning is intended to serve justice." Then he proceeded to enumerate several measures of the National Socialist regime which were in conflict with these postulates and, therefore, invalid, including the establishment of the one-party state and all decrees that treated "men as undermen and *denied them the Human Rights.*" [4]

Once more, in *Vorschule der Rechtsphilosophie,* a transcript of his lectures published by students with his approval (Heidelberg 1948), Radbruch limited his—basically repeated—acceptance of scientific relativism by absolute postulates. He declared that the Human Rights are of an "absolute nature," because, and to the extent that, they are necessary to make the fulfillment of ethical duties possible. Although he emphasized that details must be left to the positive law, he summed up that "the complete denial of the Human Rights . . . is absolutely incorrect law" (*absolut unrichtiges Recht*). [5]

To repeat, this equation of justice with the recognition of human

[3] First published in *Süddeutsche Juristenzeitung,* reprinted in the 4th and 5th eds. of his *Rechtsphilosophie,* pp. 347 ff., and in *Der Mensch im Recht,* ed. by Fritz von Hippel, Göttingen 1957, pp. 111 ff.

[4] *Rechtsphilosophie,* p. 353. Italics not in the original.

[5] Pp. 27, 28. Compare Coing, *op.cit.,* p. 170: "The core of the modern theory of Natural Law is the human rights. They are grounded in the moral postulate (*Forderung*) to respect the dignity of man as a moral person; this postulate is contained in the idea of Right (*Rechtsidee*)."

rights was perfectly sound as a historical interpretation of the meaning of justice and as an appeal to jurists that they should apply this interpretation in granting or denying juridical validity to legal acts. But it was unwarranted insofar as it was meant to imply that science *qua* science can state, in absolute terms, that is, apart from historical conditions and from religious convictions, what rights men have or ought to have, that men are essentially equal, or even that there should be more than one party under every form of government. All this is not a matter for science to say in absolute terms.

Hence there is clearly a conflict between the first and the later stages of Radbruch's philosophy. This impression increases when the various formulations he used are promiscuously blended, as was done in the posthumous editions of Radbruch's other chief work, *Einführung in die Rechtswissenschaft* (Introduction to Legal Science).[6] The result is a rather inconsistent, self-contradictory, text without the old pith in the respective sections. But the conflict can be resolved when Radbruch's former views, those of Scientific Value Relativism, are regarded as statements on the interrelation between justice and *science,* statements that are still valid; and those of his last stage, are viewed as the—equally legitimate—statements of a great jurisprudent in which he appeals to his people, and all peoples, that they should deny *juridical* validity to any laws that flagrantly discriminate between human beings or violate other minimum standards of regard for fellow-men that have developed in the evolution of human civilization in the Western world within the last two thousand years and more.

Radbruch, therefore, was well inspired when he decided to have his *Rechtsphilosophie* republished *unchanged* despite the changes in his views. He believed this to be justified only on the ground that the book was a historical document. But here, once more, he was too modest.

17. *Conclusion*

The list presented in this chapter of writers who still in the twentieth century have offered absolute standards of justice, and of the standards offered, is meant to be representative rather than exhaustive. There are many more writers, and other standards, in addition. Personal affection and aesthetic enjoyment were declared greatest goods by no less a man than George Moore in his *Principia Ethica* of 1903 (p. 188);

---

[6] Gustav Radbruch, *Einführung in die Rechtswissenschaft*, 9th ed., ed. by Konrad Zweigert, Stuttgart 1952. See also Appendix B (Eric Wolf).

truth, by Rickert and others (see Chapter VI, above); reliability, veracity, and faithfulness (*Treue*) by Helmuth Coing in his post-Hitler text (pp. 145–47); self-respect, by Lasswell (see Appendix B). Social security, including the absence of anxieties over a person's adequate subsistence in times ahead, has advanced to a high position in the list of values.

It is not necessary here to deal with these additional items or further to enlarge the list. The following more general remarks, however, should be added in concluding this chapter.

As mentioned (Chapter III, Section 8), it is often not easy to decide whether a scientist who explicitly or implicitly allots high, or even highest, rank to some particular good or value is an "absolutist," who believes he has scientific knowledge regarding the validity of his appraisal, or a "partisan relativist," who makes no such claims but simply uses Scientific Method in the service of the values which he and his friends prefer. There I spoke of "latent relativists," who did not call themselves, but actually were, adherents of Scientific Value Relativism. Similarly, we might dub "latent dogmatics" those who, while ostensibly rejecting absolutism in the sphere of values, nonetheless adopt some value without question and even with unconcealed contempt of other scholars who confess other creeds. Many who have written in this century in support of equality, liberty, or other summary standards, should perhaps be classified as "latent dogmatists" rather than "partisan relativists," I suppose. But these two categories are difficult to sever.

However that may be, certainly not *all* scientific dogmatists among twentieth-century scholars have been merely latent ones. Many have stood up to be counted. They have opposed Scientific Value Relativism explicitly, although frequently mistaking its meaning. Unintentionally, however, the variety of their standards has offered a striking illustration for the relativistic thesis that basic values are chosen, not scientifically proved.

The examination of more than a dozen proposed ultimate standards, one by one, in this chapter should have made it plain that none can be upheld by science, and by science alone, without recourse to ideals based on religious, scientifically unverifiable sources, or to historical conditions, or to not-universal personal opinions and preferences. At the same time, however, our examination, point by point, has revealed that in each case strictly scientific analysis and research can contribute a great deal to the appraisal of certain aspects covered by the proposed standard. In particular, risks and consequences of its acceptance or repudiation can be disclosed in each case in an entirely empirical manner, with scientifically warranted results that, if fully presented, studied, and understood, in some cases may have a strong deterrent effect, not only on the respective victims of such a policy, but even on the masters themselves.

Thus, at least indirectly, the search for absolutes has enriched the social sciences. In addition, it must be acknowledged that some of the modern scientific absolutists, while unable to prove their chief point, have rightly objected to certain practices, indulged in by relativists, that were not necessitated by the theory of Scientific Value Relativism, especially the complete abstinence observed in the discussion of metaphysical questions, even when conducted on a merely hypothetic and speculative basis, a negative attitude that was not compelled by scientific theory. We have also seen that, although none of the proposed absolute standards is supported in its entirety by universal consensus, some do contain elements that apparently are so supported, and whose universal support may be capable of scientific, empirical verification to a relevant degree.

The next, and last, part of this volume will be dedicated to these and related questions.

PART FOUR

AT THE BORDERLINE OF

METAPHYSICS

CHAPTER IX

FACTUAL, NOT LOGICAL, LINKS BETWEEN
IS AND OUGHT

OREMOST among the factors that have contributed to the rise of Scientific Value Relativism has been the recognition that no logical inference can be drawn from statements in terms of Is to statements in terms of Ought-to-be. However, not every contention regarding moral laws is meant to be such a logical inference. The intention may be that of establishing a factual rather than a logical link between Is and Ought. This alternative calls for separate treatment and for a fresh look at its implications, which have not yet been fully explored in terms of twentieth-century science.

1. *God and the Inner Voice as Factual Links*

When Moses returned from Mount Sinai and reported he had heard the voice of God and God had given him then and there the Ten Commandments, he did not derive the Ought-content of the individual commandments logically from observed facts. He did not say: "There are human beings, hence they ought to be, hence thou shalt not kill," which would have involved a logical fallacy. Instead, he reported on what he considered a fact, that these commandments had been given him by God, and from this fact he derived the conclusion that whatever the content of the commandments they ought to be obeyed. The only logical premise of this inference was "If God says thou shalt, then thou shalt." Although we are not told that Moses stated this premise explicitly, his actions clearly showed that he accepted it as a matter of course, as does every reader of the report. There was, therefore, no logical fallacy involved. The modern scholar who today examines Moses' story naturally faces a number of other difficult questions, to which we shall revert in later sections of this chapter. But he cannot dismiss the story on the ground of logical fallacy.

Assertions of factual links between Is and Ought are not limited to divine references. It may be contended, and often has been, that if we observe our inner processes closely we can ascertain within ourselves some Is—an "inner voice" or "urge"—which directs us toward some ethical Ought. This inner voice or urge may order us to be good, or reveal to us some hierarchy of ethical values, placing, for instance, unselfish above selfish actions. In short, some ethical Ought may have its announcer in some Is, although an announcer who operates without station identification. This link between Is and Ought, too, would be factual rather than logical in character.

When Kant formulated his "necessary regulative principles" and his "categorical imperative,"[1] he did not mean to draw logical conclusions. He meant to state a *fact* that certain ideas are necessary forms of human thinking, or that they are conceived by the human mind as imperative orders or demands. As he wrote:

> Moreover, the moral law is given, as it were, as a fact (*Faktum*) of pure reason of which we are a priori conscious, and which is apodictically certain even if no case in which it was strictly obeyed could be ferreted out in experience. . . .[2] The objective reality of a pure will, or, what is one and the same thing, of pure practical reason, is given in the moral law a priori, as it were by a fact (*Faktum*); for it is thus that we may designate a determination of the will which is inevitable, although it does not rest on empirical principles.[3]

Now, Kant's thesis is not quite as simple as the assertion that all human beings feel an inner urge. The "fact" (*Faktum*) to which he referred was not some merely passive hearing of a voice or feeling of an urge. Rather, it was the active operation of "pure reason" and its "inevitable result." But pure reason, as Kant saw it, did not draw logical inferences from observed empirical facts; it worked "a priori," independently of empirical observation. Logically speaking, therefore, the situation appeared similar to him as in immediate references to an inner urge. In either case, the only major premise was: "If an inner urge—or, if pure reason—ordains Thou shalt, then Thou shalt." The minor premise, asserting what pure reason does ordain, was to Kant "as it were a fact," just as the contention that all human beings feel an inner urge of a certain kind asserts a fact.

It is not here the question whether Kant was right in stating that "the moral law is given, as it were, as a fact." Here it is merely intended to make clear that we must carefully distinguish between statements meant to be of a factual character and propositions meant

---

[1] See Chapter vi, above, and Section 6, below.

[2] Kant, *Kritik der Praktischen Vernunft, op.cit.,* Academy ed., p. 47; Cassirer ed., p. 53. Kant goes on here as follows: "Hence, the objective reality of the moral law cannot be demonstrated by any deduction or by any effort of some speculatively or empirically supported type of reasoning; and though we might be ready to renounce apodictic certainty it cannot be confirmed by experience and thus be proven a posteriori; and yet, it is itself certain (*und steht doch für sich selbst fest*)."

[3] *Ibid.,* p. 55 (Cassirer ed., p. 62).

to draw logical conclusions from facts. Once we accept his premises we cannot accuse Kant, any more than we could Moses, of having made unwarranted inferences from what is to what ought to be.[4]

2. *Ambiguous Theories*

It is often difficult to tell what the intention of an author is when he switches from Is to Ought. An illustration is offered by the following passage in Cohen and Nagel, *Introduction to Logic and Scientific Method,* one of the best texts in logic. In a chapter entitled "Logic of Moral and Practical Judgments," after introductory remarks on the necessity of distinguishing Is and Ought, the authors continue:

> What people *ought* to desire is what they *would* desire *if* they were enlightened and knew what they really wanted and what natural means would bring it about. Morality is thus wisdom applied to the conduct of life and yields rules which we would follow if we thought out all the implications of our choices and knew in advance their consequences.[1]

Here the authors flatly derive some Ought from some Is; for they say that a person ought to desire what he does desire when he knows all the consequences. Our desires and the consequences of our acts are both events in the realm of Is. Did the authors really mean a logical inference here? If so, they have succumbed to the very fallacy against which they had just warned in the introduction to the same chapter. However, the passage may be meant differently. It may merely be a restatement of the old hedonistic theory that the good is always identical with, or concomitant to, the pleasant. This would mean that there is a factual link between "good" (Ought) and "pleasant" (Is). Such a statement, and the implied denial of moral laws outside those natural laws which rule our pleasure or displeasure, our happiness or unhappiness, cannot be dismissed as a logical fallacy. Other objections can be raised, of course. No demonstration is offered, in the passage quoted, that there is no other moral law and that what the authors describe is a moral law at all. It may also be objected that their theory might morally sanction any mean action of a scoundrel who can get away with it. We shall return to this side of the hedonistic theory in Chapter XII. Here our purpose is again only to point to the importance of distinguishing between logical and factual links.

[4] See also Appendix B on the major premise.
[1] Morris Cohen and Ernest Nagel, *Introduction to Logic and Scientific Method*, New York 1934, p. 366.

In passing, it may be mentioned that there is another ambiguity in Cohen's and Nagel's proposition, because it is not clear whether they refer to consequences in this world only or also in a potential life after death, if such life there be, which the authors neither claim nor deny and which either to claim or to deny they would probably—and rightly—not consider to be within the reach of Scientific Method.

3. Actuality and Authenticity of the Outer Voice as a Scientific Problem

Whenever the argument used in support of a moral demand is based, not on the demand's content, but on its source—for example, an outer or an inner voice—there remain, of course, two questions to be answered: whether the alleged announcement ,and its source can be verified, and whether the premise that we ought to obey it is justified. Regarding both, there are noteworthy differences between the outer and the inner voice.

When the contention is that God's voice has been heard from outside, then a scientific examination would have to investigate whether the reported hearing was not an illusion and whether, if anyone spoke at all, it was God and not some imposter, human or suprahuman. As to illusions I may refer to the story of the chimney sweep who called down through the chimney the name of his assistant, to summon him up to the roof. It was the house of a clergyman, who happened to have the same name. When he heard the hollow sound of his name from above he fell on his knees, answering "Speak, O Lord, Thy servant is listening." If in this instance it was a chimney sweep who spoke, this does not disprove that it was God who spoke to Moses, and even in the good pastor's visitation God may have caused the incident as an accompaniment of what he was about to say with a more spiritual voice. Who knows?

As regards imposters, there are stories in the Bible in which the voice was that of Satan [1] or where Moloch imitated the voice of God.[2] Luther was once asked by some more radical religious reformers—the "Zwickauers"—whether he would allow them to prove their divine mission by telling him what he was just then thinking in his mind; and when he gave permission, they stated correctly that he felt inclined toward them in spite of the objections he had raised. Luther, however, at once exclaimed that this was a sign of Satan's and not one

---

[1] See I Chronicles 21:1.
[2] Micah 6:7. See the article by Buber quoted below.

coming from God.[3] There is obviously no scientific proof possible that Luther's interpretation was correct or that there was a transcendent sign at all. If there was one, however, then it mattered, of course, whether it came from God or from Satan.

Science, like religion, cannot accept without further questioning the equation of a suprahuman voice and a voice that ought to be obeyed. The early Gnostics taught that this imperfect world of ours had been created not by God, the supreme source of being, but by some bungling demiurge, who acted as a creator in ignorance and passion. His rules dominated the cosmos and even our *psyche;* only a small inner core of the latter, the *pneuma,* is still connected with God, who does not care for the rules governing the cosmos and allows them to take their course.[4] When the maker of this demiurgean cosmos speaks to us, or one of his associates or subordinates, ought we to obey?

In this Gnostic version a God whose voice ought to be obeyed was still assumed to exist on a higher level. Suppose for the matter of arguing that there is no such God of goodness and justice—only that demiurge, or only Satan, or only some dragon god, but equipped with infinite power. Ought his commands to be obeyed? Of course they ought in the sense of "You had better obey or else." But this is not the ultimate question. An inner voice seems to tell us that a god who is not identical with the good loses the ultimate claim to be obeyed.[5] What is this inner voice? What is its authority?

4. *Actuality and Authenticity of the Inner Voice*

If the ultimate criterion for the authentic character of an external voice claiming to be that of God—of a "good" God—is its accord with the inner voice within us, then the inner voice is the deepest source of our knowledge about good and evil, the ultimate judge.[1] The mere fact of its speaking seems to be a guarantee that, if there is an all-powerful God at all he must be good, because no dragon god would be likely to permit an inner voice that was antagonistic to him to rise; its very actuality then could be explained only by an oversight of the dragon god, or by deficiencies of his powers which enabled the human

---

[3] *Rankes Meisterwerke: Deutsche Geschichte im Zeitalter der Reformation,* München und Leipzig, 1914, vol. 2, pp. 33, 34.

[4] See Hans Jonas, "Gnosticism and Modern Nihilism," *Social Research,* vol. 19 (1952), p. 430. See now also his book, *The Gnostic Religion,* Boston 1958, pp. 42 ff.

[5] This footnote will be found on the following page.

[1] This conclusion has been drawn, for instance, by Eduard Spranger in his fine essay *Die Magie der Seele,* Tübingen 1947 (2nd ed., amplified, 1949).

race to outgrow him, or as his sophisticated invention of how to torture human beings by contrition. Such explanations would be flagrantly
inadequate. As the early Gnostics saw it, the *pneuma* section of the
psyche, where the inner voice spoke, seemed to require the assumption of an ultimate God far above their bungling demiurge.

However, a few reflections will show that the inner voice cannot
claim the role of ultimate judge with unquestionable assurance. When
a religious person has no doubt that the speaker is God, the inner
voice is dethroned as the ultimate judge. Thus Abraham, when God
ordered him to immolate Isaac, having no doubt that the order came
from God, gave no room to the natural inner voice which might have
rebelled against the human sacrifice as unethical.[2] Nor need we look
to this extreme example alone for illustrations of an imaginable discord between the external and the inner voice. The entire Bible is to
the believer the external voice of God; those who wrote it may have
relied on an inner voice for their inspiration, but their writings have
come to us from without. Who firmly believes in the Bible as God's
revealed word will tend to acknowledge the authority of the external
voice over any opposition cropping up from within. There are numer-

---

[5] (At previous page) A mnemonic poem which I wrote down in German may illustrate the
point; it describes, as poetry generally does, subjective knowledge of S_2, not of S_1 character:

> Gott ist das Gute und das Gute nur.
> Das Gute ist das Wunder der Natur.
>
> Das Gute will, dass ich, beglückt und frei,
> Nur ihm bedingungslos gehorsam sei.
>
> Es ist in diesem einzig freien Sinn,
> Dass ich noch einem Herrn gehorsam bin.
>
> Ein Gott, der nicht das Gute wär', verlöre
> So Macht wie Anspruch, dass ich ihm gehöre.
>
> Ich wollte höhnen bis zum letzten Hauch
> Solch' Drachengott, und seine Priester auch.
>
> Und für das Gute wollt' ich kämpfen hier,
> Selbst wenn das Gute lebte nur in mir.
>
> Doch überall seh' ich es spriessen, quellen,
> Und spüren tu' ich's wie in warmen Wellen.
>
> Richt' ich mich trotzig auf, verstockt und dumm,
> Die nächste Welle kommt und wirft mich um.

This means in English prose, approximately, that God is the Good, and only the Good;
the Good (i.e., the fact that there is something good) is the miracle within nature. The Good
demands that, happy and free, I be unconditionally obedient to it alone. It is in this sense
the only free sense, that I am still obedient to a master. A God who was not good would
have neither the power nor the right to ask that I be his. I would taunt, to my last breath,
such dragon god, and his priests also. And I would want to fight for the good even if it
should live in me alone. But everywhere I see it surging up, time and again, and it overwhelms me.

[2] See Martin Buber, "The Suspension of Ethics," in Anshen, *op.cit.*, p. 223.

ous stories in the Bible that challenge the "natural" human sense of justice, much as the sense of justice of the prodigal son's elder brother was gravely hurt when his father elaborately celebrated the home-coming of the sinner though no similar thing had ever been done in the elder's honor. The story of Job's sufferings and the doctrines of predestination and of eternal condemnation to Hell, may serve as examples. To the orthodox believer it is the external voice of the Bible which he thinks he has to follow and not his rebellious inner voice, although it may cost him great effort to adjust his inner voice to the holy text.[3]

Notwithstanding these reservations it is reasonable to assume that, if God is real and not just a product of our imagination, the inner voice and the external voice are meaningfully interrelated. Discords between them may be only seeming and temporary; we may learn to understand the outer voice's teaching, or may discard it as not authentic. We may also trust that God, if real, will forgive men who follow their inner voice to the best of their abilities when they rebel against his orders, as God forgave Job when he revolted. Since, fur-thermore, the reported incidents of external revelation are less ac-cessible to scientific verification than are processes within us, the study of the inner voice remains a matter of great importance for science as well as for religion. It would be so even if there were no God, as we shall see presently.

Suppose we could verify that within all human beings some inner voice speaks which orders them to do or not to do something. Whether its source is metaphysical or natural we are not able to state scientifi-cally. There are other alternatives, however, which we may be able to explore. The voice may differ in different individuals; it may differ even in the same person at different times; it may differ in different groups; or it may not differ at all but be universal. It may be universal in the sense that it is active in all human beings either at all times or at some times—not while they are sleeping, not always even when awake, but so that in a characteristic manner it often talks to all of them.

---

[3] Pope Pius XII, in a pronouncement sent to the Union of Catholic Jurists, February 1955, admitted that many people, including theologians, found the idea of eternal punishment hard to believe, but added that "the immutability and eternity of reprobation and of its fulfillment is beyond dispute." "The revelation and the teaching authority of the Church clearly establish that after the end of the earthly life those who are burdened with grave guilt will receive from the most high God a judgment and execution of penality from which there is no libera-tion or condonation. . . . Such Divine disposition is in no way contrary to any of God's attributes: neither to His justice nor His wisdom, neither to His mercy nor His goodness." Cited from the *New York Times,* February 6, 1955.

To the extent that the voice differs, some people may hear Truth announced where others hear falsehood, or some may hear a higher form of Truth than do others. Each one would be the sole witness of what he hears within him, and he may not tell, or not tell correctly; his report may be either sincere or insincere, and if the former, it may be adequate or fumbling in its expression.

Even if we were able to ascertain scientifically what the inner voice tells people, so long as it tells different things to different people the basic problem of Scientific Value Relativism would continue to be with us. Only if some of these characteristic announcements from within were alike in all persons would our problem acquire another aspect. Such universal and invariant factors would be relevant for political science, as well as for the other social sciences, in many respects. They would reduce the impact of Value Relativism at least to some extent. For we would then have a *human invariant* which links Is and Ought in human terms and might be significant enough for many practical purposes. We might safely draw the conclusion then —a strictly analytical inference—that an action which all human beings feel inescapably to be right or wrong, just or unjust, will find in all some inner support or opposition on the ground of its being felt to be right or wrong, just or unjust, respectively.[4]

As a matter of historical fact, such ideas formed one of various bases underlying Natural-Law theories, tacitly if not always explicitly. They were discredited on the ground that their fruits were ambiguous tautologies, as a rule, such as that just means *suum cuique* (to everyone his due—but what *is* his due, that is the question, see Chapter VIII) or, when more concrete, were conflicting in the variety of Oughts that were offered from inner observation. This, however, is not fatal to the thesis that some factual nexus between Is and Ought may exist in human nature. We may not have observed it carefully enough as yet.

To the task, therefore, of exploring whether this type of factual bridge between Is and Ought is a general human phenomenon we should apply ourselves with new energies, not in the manner of former centuries by mere speculations or by generalizing our own pet ideas or experiences, but under the severe controls of twentieth-century scientific research. Where the factual link comes from, science may not be able to tell with scientific means. Science may, however, be able to state empirically whether it is there.

---

[4] This would be an important political factor even if not all but most human beings felt that way, and inescapably so.

5. *Kant's Reading of the Inner Message*

Kant's statement, mentioned above, that a moral law could be found within us like a *Faktum,* was basically only a restatement of what had been held by theologians and Natural-Law philosophers before him for thousands of years. There was, however, this difference. They had focused attention on the *source* of the moral law—God or nature. Kant left the ultimate source out of focus, convinced as he was that it was beyond scientific knowledge. But while deliberately modest regarding the ultimate source he was bold enough to state in words what the moral law within us said. It said: "Act according to that maxim only by which thou canst will at the same time that it should become the universal law," or "So act as if the maxim of thy action should become, by thy will, the universal law of nature." [1]

This was not, of course, meant to be the literal text heard by everyone; it was the meaning of the message as brought into words by the philosopher. It did not establish any substantive directions as to what to do in any particular case. It has even often been said that it offered no more than formal standards for the decision. This is, I think, an understatement, because Kant's formula clearly condemns any arbitrary, whimsical, or purely selfish way of action. But it does not positively say what the action should be.

Does "conscience" tell us that in some other way? No, said Kant. He was sure that man had a conscience. But conscience does not give us any substantive directions, he held. It tells us to be scrupulously particular about right and wrong, but it does not tell us that anything is wrong as long as we think it right, and conversely. It merely urges us to test again and again whether we are really convinced beyond any doubt:

Whether an action is right or wrong, mind and not conscience judges. . . . Nor does conscience judge actions like cases under the law; that is done by reason inasmuch as reason is subjective and practical. But here [in the case of conscience] reason passes judgment on itself, whether it actually did undertake that judgment on actions with all caution (as to whether they are right or wrong), and sets man as a witness for or against himself that this has or has not been done.[2]

[1] *Grundlegung der Metaphysik der Sitten,* in *Gesammelte Schriften,* Academy ed., vol. 4, p. 421 (Cassirer ed., vol. 4, p. 279).
[2] *Die Religion innerhalb der Grenzen der blossen Vernunft,* 1793. Academy ed., vol. 6, pp. 185–86; Cassirer ed., vol. 6, pp. 336–37.

If that is so, then we cannot hope to find any direct and substantive answer to our question of what is right or wrong, just or unjust, in our conscience. Whenever fanatics are convinced beyond doubt that they are right, their conscience may even urge them to go ahead fanatically in the service of what they are convinced is the truth, as has often happened in history.

True, Kant himself has put forward propositions of a more substantive character elsewhere in his writings, such as his famous principle that man ought never to be used. merely as a means-to-an-end but should always be respected as an end in himself.[3] This is indeed a substantive principle. But his reference to the fact-character of the moral law did not extend to his own interpretations of its message. The command so to choose our maxims that we could will them "to become the universal law" did not logically imply acceptance of human equality and equal dignity. Other universal laws could be imagined. Kant's proof for his own interpretation was hypothetic. Unless we considered every reasonable being of absolute value, i.e. an end in himself, so he argued, nothing of absolute value could be found at all. Therefore, *if* there was to be something of absolute value, *then* it could only be beings endowed with reason. He himself pointed out that this was not "knowledge," but "belief." [4]

Kant's moral law conveyed the idea that some Is in human nature announces some principles of Ought, principles felt to be mandatory because of their unconditional form. There were other pointers in Kant that led in the same direction, especially his idea that there were "necessary" elements in human thinking, such as the assumption that some freedom was left us in thinking and reasoning because otherwise we would not feel able to think and reason at all. His illustrations of such "necessary regulative ideas," as he called them, were chiefly related to "theoretical" knowledge (knowledge of what is) rather than "practical" knowledge (of what ought to be). But they might have their parallel in the emotional sphere. Some nineteenth-century scholars, like Franz von Brentano [5] and Wilhelm Windelband,[6] suggested that such was indeed the case. But they failed to offer a detailed analysis.

---

[3] *Grundlegung der Metaphysik der Sitten*, Academy ed., vol. 4, pp. 427–29, 461–62, and *Kritik der Praktischen Vernunft, ibid.*, vol. 5, pp. 86–87.

[4] He called it a "useful and legitimate idea in behalf of a reasonable belief, *although all knowledge ends at its border"* (vol. 4, p. 262).

[5] Franz Brentano, *Vom Ursprung der sittlichen Erkenntnis*, Leipzig 1889, pp. 6, 20 ff.

[6] Wilhelm Windelband, *Präludien, op.cit.* (Chapter vi, Section 1, above).

Before we pursue this line of thought further, we should note a significant point in Kant's way of arguing. When he proclaimed his moral law as a categorical imperative that could be found within us, "as it were as a fact," he did not adduce any empirical evidence in order to prove that not only he and some other persons in Königsberg, and not only those who had written about it in the course of history, but that *all* human beings did find this call "as a fact" within them. The problem of generalization does not seem to have caused him any qualms. This was perhaps unobjectionable where he spoke of assumptions which he considered *logically* necessary, such as that of freedom in the process of thinking. Regarding the moral law, however, there was no logical necessity that it be found as a fact within us. If he found it in himself, he could have meaningfully raised the question whether that was so with all people and what degree of maturity was required, if any. He did not engage in that type of research, nor did he propose that others should. He was, after all, a son of the Age of Reason; notwithstanding his radical demolition of the over-confidence in pure reason then current, he definitely and outspokenly argued in this question from pure reason rather than from empirical research.

6. *A New Method: Husserl's Phenomenology*

Hope for more precise findings than those of the old Natural-Law schools and of Kant's categorical imperative and "necessary regulative principles" has been aroused by twentieth-century phenomenology. It is advisable for social scientists to be familiar with the basic approach of this school and with the general results of its labors. We shall outline both here to the extent appropriate to our context.

Under the name of "transcendental phenomenology" Edmund Husserl (1859–1938) advocated a new method of inner observation.[1] He insisted that it was possible to recognize, with absolute certainty,

[1] Husserl's main works are: *Logische Untersuchungen,* Halle 1900 et seq., 3rd ed. 1922; *Ideen zu einer reinen Phänomenologie und phänomenologischen Philosophie,* Halle 1913, 3rd ed. 1928 (transl. by W. R. Boyce Gibson under the title of *Ideas: General Introduction to Pure Phenomenology,* New York 1931, reprinted 1952) hereinafter cited as *Ideen;* "Philosophie als strenge Wissenschaft" in *Logos,* vol. 1 (1910) pp. 289–341; *Formale und transzendentale Logik* 1929, hereinafter cited as *Logik; Méditations Cartésiennes* (in French), Paris 1931, hereinafter cited as *Méditations;* "Die Krisis der Europäischen Wissenschaften und die transzendentale Phänomenologie" in *Philosophia,* vol. 1 (1936) pp. 77–176. All of Husserl's writings are republished, or posthumously published for the first time, in *Husserliana,* ed. by The Husserl Archives in Louvain under the direction of H. L. van Breda, Hague. This collection includes a second and a third volume of *Ideen* (*Husserliana,* vols. 4 and 5), carefully analyzed by Alfred Schutz, *Philosophy and Phenomenological Research,* vol. 13 (1953) pp. 394 ff., 506 ff., but with no immediate importance to us here. References hereafter are to the original publications cited above.

377

characteristic elements in our observing, feeling, and willing. In singling them out he took great pains to be exact, basing his research on a rigorously descriptive method.[2] All metaphysical speculation was discarded. So was psychology in the general broad sense of the term, where the existence of the outside world is not questioned and the entire person and his life story are taken into consideration.[3] Husserl wanted to describe what can be discovered by refined methods of inner observation, in an "immanent" manner, to lie at the rock-bottom of our *ego*. In this effort he proceeded, in the first place, to eliminate from direct attention (to "bracket") all external ("transcendent") elements, including the body. This was not to predicate that these external elements—for example, the flowers we are looking at, or our own bodies for that matter—were not there or were not what they seemed. They were merely "bracketed" in the procedure, that is, left out of consideration, because we could not be absolutely certain that they were there or were what they seemed.

This first step Husserl called "transcendental-phenomenological reduction" (*transzendental-phänomenologische Reduktion*), obviously because thereby we limit, or reduce, our field of observation to the phenomena on the inside which reflect, or react to, some "transcendent" thing (e.g., a flower) that causes or affects them but is itself supposed to be on the outside. In applying this method Husserl traced the ultimate elements of experience to certain active ("intentional") performances of the subjective ego. Through these performances, he said, the ego first of all marks off ("constitutes") the objectives of inner attention, for instance, some individual "real" thing, taken as real or existent, such as a person we are looking at; or some object of pure imagination, taken as such, for example, a centaur. The next thing we can state with certainty is that our ego is able to act upon these objectives in several characteristic ways, such as perception, remembering, and reflection.[4] This carried him to a distinction between the im-

---

[2] See *Ideen*, pp. 112, 290, 300. Also *Logische Untersuchungen*, vol. 2, p. 4.

[3] The distinction of transcendental phenomenology from customary psychology is most emphatically drawn in *Logik*, pp. 222 ff., and *Méditations*, pp. 26, 27, 122 ff.

[4] *Logik*, pp. 226, 244; *Méditations*, pp. 23 ff. This reduction could also be applied to our occupation with metaphysical questions. See *Logik*, p. 222, regarding God in the light of the phenomenological reduction: in that reduction, we can intentionally fix our attention on God as either a real or an imagined being, and reflect on him; likewise, we can fix attention on events that seem to us to intimate God's existence or his working; but God himself and the events that seem to intimate his existence remain "bracketed" in our operation; the one thing that remains certain is our intentional constitution of the objective of our attention and our reflecting on it, etc.

manent act of observing and the immanent "something" being observed.

Husserl frankly acknowledged that his method led ultimately to the "transcendental subjectivity" of the ego.[5] It could not possibly lead to anything else, as he had "bracketed" everything that did not belong to the subjective *ego*. Yet Husserl thought it was important enough to state what we could thus describe with certainty. He called for a systematic investigation of the ego's structure and characteristics.

In addition to the "phenomenological reduction" Husserl introduced a second step, which he called the "eidetic reduction." [6] He used the term *"Wesen"* (essence), or as an alternative the Greek *"eidos,"* to denote objects of inner observation that are not individual things but characteristics, or essentials, common to a group of them, e.g., "sound" or "color." *Wesen* in this sense, he said, is no mere verbal notion, no mere conceptual universal. It can be the actual objective of our immanent attention, no less than can the individual things themselves. Inner attention may shift at will from a "something" that presents only essential characteristics (e.g., color) to a particular something (e.g., red or blue) as an illustration, and vice versa. "What is invariant in all examples is *Wesen.*" [7] Occasionally he used also the term "type" as an explanation.[8] This faculty of focusing one's attention on *Wesen* rather than on particular things had its ultimate source in the "productive intentionality" of the ego, Husserl said, calling for an investigation of the manner in which the ego perceives *Wesen*. It was this transformation of particulars into *Wesen* that he called "eidetic reduction" or "ideation."

In using the suggestive but ambiguous term *Wesen* for his legitimate purpose, this ardent advocate of precision gave rise to fanciful misinterpretations. The German meaning of *Wesen* runs all the way from "some being," "some mystical being," "some phantom," "some ghost-like apparition" to the more philosophical meaning of "characteristic and essential features" or "essence," and from "meaning" to "significance." Husserl was quite definite in excluding any connotation of "mystical beings" or of "reality of ideas" in the Platonic sense.[9] To him,

[5] *Logik*, pp. 239, 240; *Méditations*, 1 ff., 16 ff., discussing Husserl's progress over Descartes, who was not consistent enough in excluding the external.
[6] For the following, see *Ideen*, pp. 8 ff., 12, 40, and *Logik*, pp. 219, 222, 226 ff. (also on the progress beyond Hume and Kant).
[7] *Logik*, p. 219.
[8] *Méditations*, pp. 58 ff.
[9] *Ideen*, p. 40.

his presentation was fundamentally a mere description of the way in which we may be "conscious of something." But in speaking of *Wesen* and even using this term in the plural, he could induce followers to hunt for objective truth through "eidetic reduction," where nothing more than some subjective combination could be expected if the method was applied strictly.[10]

7. Husserl in Plato's Cave. Limited Usefulness of His Phenomenology for Political Theory

It may well serve to help in understanding Husserl's place in philosophy if we imagine him to be one of the men in Plato's cave, chained against the wall and aware only of the shadows cast on the opposite wall, through an opening above the prisoners' heads, by things moving outside the cave. The cave-men stare at the moving shadows and try to interpret them. What would Husserl do as one of them? In his phenomenological reduction he would "bracket" even the shadows! This would guard him against taking their reality for granted. Instead, he would find what alone is certain: that his *ego* was fixing its attention on them, remembering others, thinking of them either as real things or otherwise, and reflecting on them. His reflections might have led him to free himself from the chains and to ascend through the entrance toward the light and toward Plato's "real" things. But then again, he would bracket both the light and the things and be fully certain only of the fact that his *ego* intentionally fixed its attention on such things as appeared to it, that it reflected on them, and so forth. Husserl's phenomenology, despite its great merits in the structural description of the ego, could not give us back even the certainty of Being,[1] at least not of the outer world. Could it then help us overcome Scientific Value Relativism?

True, Husserl insisted that evidence, yielded by his method of guarded inner observation, can be fully adequate and certain. But

[10] I submit that Husserl himself was not entirely consistent in his language. He used *Wesen* with at least a threefold meaning. While in the technical sense it was to him merely the "something" that to some subjective ego constitutes the invariant core of different particulars, he at other times also used it in the usual sense of the term, where it denotes the aggregate of essential properties in a more objective sense. In this sense it does not allow of a plural in German, while the plural is freely used for *Wesen* as phantoms or mystical beings or other ill-defined agents. Thirdly, in his later writings, Husserl sometimes referred to *Wesen* as something given a priori (see, e.g., *Logik*, p. 211), which rather suggests a more restricted use of the term, because if my ego intentionally constitutes the *Wesen* of several particular phenomena that it groups together, then the *Wesen* cannot be said to have been a priori given.

[1] Arnold Metzger, *Phänomenologie und Metaphysik, Das Problem des Relativismus und seiner Überwindung*, Halle 1933, pp. 211–12. See also Wolfgang Köhler, *The Place of Value in a World of Facts*, New York 1938, chapter "Beyond Phenomenology."

it can lead to certainty only regarding the fact that something happens to my own ego, or with it. How can I know for certain that it also happens to all other human beings, and in the same manner? Just as with Kant, I have not found this point discussed by Husserl. It seems clear to me, though, that what he wanted to describe was not merely the way things happened just to him. For he did not bring any of those specific phenomena into the picture which each of us has as his own private domain. He obviously wanted to describe only phenomena that were generally human. But he did not engage in any effort to prove the generality of the experiences described. He did not delve into any specific empirical research on this count. At the most, there is a tacit assumption of obviousness in this respect. When we do find his illustrations of immediate evidence convincing, it is because they describe noncontroversial elements in our activities of thinking, perception, remembering, imagination, and the like, and because it seems obvious that no human being functions differently. Should there appear differences in the experiences of different individuals, Husserl's method would not provide us with any means to decide between alternatives. Everyone would be right in referring to his own immediate evidence, but everyone would be right only for himself.

Even subjectively, there remains a sphere of vagueness and uncertainty as soon as we leave the sphere of what is universally admitted. Husserl himself speaks of "degrees" of clarity of perception, and of evidence "more or less" adequate or inadequate.[2] Dealing with the intuitive apprehension of immanent phenomena and their essentials (Wesen) he wrote: *"Insofar* as this intuitive apprehension is a pure one, which *does not include transitory opinions* with it, so far the apprehended *Wesen* are something adequately apprehended and absolutely given."[3] But how can we ascertain, and demonstrate intersubjectively, *that* no transitory opinions have crept into our own inner observations, if others arrive at different descriptions of theirs? In his later works, Husserl admitted explicitly that the "immediate evidence of experience implies the possibility of deception" and that "even an experience which pretends to be apodictic may be deceptive."[4] He ardently warned against the "usual, fundamentally wrong interpreta-

---

[2] *Ideen*, pp. 10, 127 ff.; *Logik*, pp. 139 ff.; *Méditations*, pp. 10, 12 ff., 19 ff.

[3] Husserl, "Philosophie als strenge Wissenschaft," *Logos*, vol. 1 (1910) p. 315. Italics not in the original.

[4] *Logik*, pp. 139, 140, 245, 253–54. Here he deviated from the sterner conception of *Evidenz* in his *Logische Untersuchungen*, 1st ed., vol. 1, pp. 190–91 (where there is no truth, there can be no *Evidenz* either) and vol. 2, pp. 592 ff., 599.

tion," which regards such evidence as an "absolute guarantee against deception," and against playing with "immediate-evidence feelings."[5]

After what has been said we cannot hope to find elements of absolute certainty in political questions, especially in questions of justice, law, and government, through Husserl's phenomenological method *alone*. He once observed, quite consistently, that law and government are factors in the external, transcendent world, which must be "bracketed," i.e., excluded from direct attention, in phenomenological research.[6] In his *Ideen* he failed to examine a single phenomenon of Ought, or to present us with a phenomenology of the sense of justice. There is merely a short remark to the effect that "theoretic" evidence of a full and immediate nature (*Evidenz*) may find its analogy in "axiological" and "practical" evidence of such nature, that is, in the fields of emotion (evaluation) and volition. But he added at once that these are "utterly difficult and far-reaching problems," all the elements of which are still in need of basic examination.[7] He is said to have gone more into details of these problems in unpublished lectures on ethics. However, what pupils like Theodor Lessing[8] have published with reference to such teachings is not regarded as a reliable reflection of Husserl's views. And indeed, how could he ever have arrived at statements on objective requirements of justice, or even only on universal postulates in these fields, through his investigations of the "subjectivity of the ego"? His original intentions had never been to ascertain even the reality of Is; how could he have claimed ability to reveal the validity of Ought? What he wanted to do, and succeeded in doing, was merely to lay bare the ultimate, original experiences which lie at the bottom of human consciousness, regardless of what certainty these inner experiences may give us as to the external world.[9] Here, he said, the question is "of a science which is as it were 'absolutely subjective' and whose object is independent of what we can decide regarding the existence or nonexistence of the world."[10] On occasions, he explicitly confessed to his own relativistic leanings.[11]

[5] *Ibid.*, pp. 140, 144, 245, 250. His investigation of intersubjectivity in *Méditations*, pp. 74 ff., contains nothing to detract from this reserved attitude. See also Alfred Schutz, "Das Problem der transzendentalen Intersubjektivität bei Husserl," *Philosophische Rundschau*, Tübingen, vol. 5 (1957) pp. 81–107.

[6] *Ideen*, p. 108.

[7] *Ideen*, pp. 290–91, acknowledging his indebtedness to Franz Brentano, *Vom Ursprung sittlicher Erkenntnis*, Leipzig 1889.

[8] Theodor Lessing, "Studien zur Wertaxiomatik," *Archiv für systematische Philosophie*, vol. 14 (1908) pp. 58–93, 226–57.

[9] See, e.g., *Méditations*, pp. 12, 25.

[10] *Ibid.*, pp. 27, 52.

[11] *Logik*, pp. 241, 245, 247.

8. *Husserl's Pupils Deviating from His Method*

In spite of Husserl's many sober and cautioning remarks, the "playing with immediate-evidence feelings" went ahead, supported by the vague connotations of the term *Wesen*. Max Scheler, greatest of his immediate pupils, contended in contrast to his teacher that full immediate evidence of what is good or evil can never deceive us, but hastened to add that we may be deceived as to whether there *is* full evidence. This leaves the matter pretty much as inconclusive as before. He poured more water into the wine by stressing that immediate evidence may differ among different individuals and races and may reveal only what is good "for me." [1] This, had he stuck to it, would have led him close to Scientific Value Relativism, except that the latter would not even concede that we can prove our subjective inner evidence regarding what is good for ourselves to be objectively correct. Phenomenology in Husserl's sense, too, could never have warranted such a statement on the objective validity of the ego's subjective observations and reflections.

Scheler, however, did not even stand by his cautious remark that inner evidence may reveal only what is "good for me." Disregarding it completely he contended that elements of an absolute hierarchy, or order of rank, of values could be ascertained. In this he was followed by Nicolai Hartmann. Both claimed that their presentations of such an objective order were fully supported by "immediate evidence." I examined this claim in Chapter VII, Section 6. At present my only purpose is to make it clear that their reference in this context to "immediate evidence"—a term which had played such a great role in Husserl's teaching—was in fact a fundamental deviation from the master's scientific endeavors, distinctly non-Husserlian, if not anti-Husserlian, in character. Hartmann spoke of the "phenomenon of preference." This he could certainly do in line with Husserl's method, because it is indeed obvious that our ego is able to observe feelings of preference; this much we can state with full certainty, at least everyone for himself. But when Hartmann continued, "In the phenomenon of preference we have an accompanying knowledge of the relative height of value," [2] he could no longer justify this statement with Husserl's method, which could at best have resulted in the finding that we have the accompanying phenomenon of a *subjective* feeling of a relative

---

[1] Max Scheler, *Formalismus* (cited Chapter VII, Section 5) v, 7 and 10 (3rd ed., pp. 333–36, 369). See also, A. C. Garnett, *Reality and Value*, New Haven 1937, p. 288.

[2] Hartmann, *Ethics*, p. 63. He added that "this accompanying knowledge has not the form of a criterion; it is not an ever-ready standard by which we can measure and test . . ."

height (or rank) of the respective value, and perhaps of a subjective feeling that presents itself as a feeling of certainty of knowledge. By no means could this method lead to the result that the feeling was *objectively* correct, objectively valid as to its content. Such a thesis, identifying subjective certainty with objective truth, adds a non-phenomenological proposition to the phenomenological observation.

Scheler, in contrast to Husserl, felt no inhibitions about entering the political field with phenomenological tools. He examined the fundamental political problem of the relation between the individual and the community. Every person, he stated, and quite correctly it seems, constantly finds himself to be not only an individual but also a member of various communities, with the two positions on an equal level of originality, neither appearing superior, or anterior, to the other.[3] This conclusion, however, is too general to serve as a guide for political decisions in conflicts between the individual and the community. Its vagueness was augmented by theological remarks Scheler inserted regarding the common subordination of the individual and the community to the Deity, or the Infinite.[4] This went far beyond what could have been stated on the basis of phenomenological research conducted strictly according to Husserl's method. Nor was this the end. In numerous political writings, Scheler dealt with war and peace, militarism, emancipation of women, the bourgeois, capitalism, and the like.[5] These essays were in fact psychological analyses, ethical speculations, and the political opinions of a philosopher interested in problems of the day, rather than attempts at accurate phenomenological demonstrations. They only tend to show how little the basic findings of phenomenology have as yet been able to narrow the bounds of individual speculations in the social sciences, as for instance when Scheler (in 1914) characterized a war for hegemony in Europe as a "just" war for Russia as well as for Germany, and perhaps also for Great Britain,[6] or when he described British cant,[7] or advocated "instrumental militarism."[8]

Whenever phenomenologists have taken a stand on controversial

---

[3] Scheler, *Formalismus*, VII, 4, d, *ad*4 (3rd ed., pp. 540 ff.).

[4] *Ibid.*, p. 546.

[5] Max Scheler, *Der Genius des Krieges und der Deutsche Krieg* (1914; 5th and 6th ed., Leipzig 1917); *Die Idee des Friedens und der Pazifismus*, Berlin 1931; *Abhandlungen und Aufsätze* (1915; 2nd ed., Leipzig 1919 under the title *Vom Umsturz der Werte*), especially in the final sections.

[6] *Genius des Krieges, op.cit.*, pp. 154 ff., 164 ff.

[7] *Ibid.*, pp. 354 ff.

[8] *Idee des Friedens, op.cit.*, pp. 33, 61.

political and juristic evaluations they have done so by abandoning Husserl's cautious methods.[9] His phenomenology is quite incapable of establishing the objective, universal, or absolute validity of values, because it is inherently a subjective method.

9. Summary and Conclusions Regarding Factual Links between Is and Ought

In this chapter we have been compelled to follow many different and winding pathways. It is advisable to summarize our findings before drawing our conclusions. This is what we have found:

Factual links between Is and Ought must be distinguished from logical links. Holy stories reporting that God's voice has spoken to some elected men from the outside and has told them what they ought to do or not to do are contentions of factual, not logical, links connecting Is and Ought; so are contentions that some elements of what we ought to do or not to do are announced by some inner voice, or urge, to some or all human beings (Section 1). Sometimes it is hard to tell whether apostles of absolute yardsticks for values mean to claim a factual or a logical link between Is and Ought; this ambiguity must be cleared up for a fruitful scientific discussion (Section 2). The correctness of reports that an external voice issuing from a suprahuman source was heard, and that this source was a good and almighty God, cannot be verified scientifically in an intersubjectively conclusive manner (Section 3). The contention, however, that some kind of inner voice making pronouncements about right and just, or wrong and unjust, operates in some or all human beings is verifiable by empirical research at least to some extent. If such a voice were found operative in all human beings, this would be relevant as proof for a factual link connecting Is and Ought in man; it would be so, even though we may remain unable to ascertain the ultimate nature of this link in scientific terms, because we could then rely on some "invariant factors" in human nature as a source of support for some judgments or actions and of opposition to others (Section 4). Kant assumed the activity of such an inner voice and rendered its message in ordinary language without engaging in empirical research regarding the universal and invariant occurrence of this phenomenon in all human beings (Section 5). Husserl's phenomenology could arouse hope that a more accurate description of the inner voice and of the forms in which

[9] See above, Chapter VIII, Section 2, on such an attempt made by Gerhart Husserl, Edmund's son.

it functions might be possible; but he did not examine this area himself, at least not in his published works, nor did he engage in empirical research into the universal and invariant nature of any of his findings (Sections 6 and 7). His pupils, abandoning his strict method, made generous statements about the inner voice and its message, but continued to neglect research on the universal and invariant character of the phenomena they described (Section 8).

The conclusions we may draw from these findings are simple and imperative. It still remains for science to inquire into what has never yet been established in strictly scientific terms: whether there are some elements in the human thinking or feeling about what is right and just, or what is wrong and unjust, that are universal and invariant. Our own individual intuition, if any, that some elements of thinking and feeling on right and just or wrong and unjust, which we discern within ourselves, are universal and invariant constitutes no sufficient scientific proof in the inter-subjective sense that these elements are actually universal and invariant. We must, therefore, add to our own phenomenological introspection empirical research about other people and even, within the limits of possibility, about so many of them, and such different types, that inductive generalizations of our factual findings appear warranted. In order to direct this research in a meaningful manner, however, we may predict its outcome by anticipation in a tentative fashion on the basis of all available information. To this task we shall turn in the next chapter.

CHAPTER X

UNIVERSAL POSTULATES OF JUSTICE

1. *The Scientific Search for Universal (Invariant) Elements Still Lagging*

EFFORTS to ascertain absolute ethical values and an absolute order of rank among them have so far always led into one of three impasses. Propositions have been derived from premises from which they did not follow; this was so especially when logical inferences were made from Is to Ought. Or they were deduced, even if in a logically unimpeachable manner, from premises that could not be verified scentifically; for example, from a divine order. Or they were based on intuitional evidence, with no verification offered other than obdurate insistence on the correctness of the intuition. All these attempts have failed to provide intersubjectively transmissible knowledge. This is not to say that the values presented were no values, or that their rank was lower than claimed. It means only that intersubjective verification was either not offered or when offered was not conclusive.

Some of the intuitionists have frankly acknowledged that their intuitions were not shared by others. It is only natural, they have argued, that some persons are farther advanced than others, especially the vulgar mass, in their ability to recognize absolute values. As Max Scheler said, the authority of the more advanced persons must be trusted by those who are less advanced, and the latter must at first obey the rules given by the former, without understanding them, because in such obedience they will gradually come to recognize the rightness of the rules.[1] That some persons should proceed to a more accurate intuition of the absolute order of values than others is indeed quite plausible, once the underlying premise that there *is* an absolute order is accepted. But when just this premise is at issue, then the reference to different abilities of apprehension is abortive as an intersubjective proof; it is then a fallacious *hysteron proteron,* i.e., an attempt to prove proposition *a* (the absolute order) by proposition *b* (different ability to recognize it), which presupposes the truth of *a*. Nor is this the only weakness of the argument. There remains the question whether science can find out—or can say how it could be found out—which of competing authorities whose intuitions are in conflict is right.

[1] Max Scheler, *Formalism, op.cit.,* v, 7 (3rd ed., pp. 339–40).

Unfortunately, professional philosophers have frequently dismissed this second question too easily. They have stated what they consider self-evident, and then period. But reference to authority without saying who is the authority or by what signs it can be found cannot be considered a satisfactory solution, not even philosophically, certainly not scientifically, and least of all, politically.

It is, in other words, not one but two problems that remain unsolved, namely, how to verify that there is an absolute order of values, and if so, how to find out scientifically which of the conflicting human intuitions regarding this order is correct. Individually we may feel certain regarding both and may be right, too. But if others feel differently, we are scientifically still confronted with the two problems.

From this array of impasses there may be, as we have seen in the preceding chapters, one exit which still holds promise for a further advance of science in the field of values. Could we verify that there are certain universal and invariant elements in the human way of thinking and feeling about values, then we would have some firm ground on which to stand. Not that we would then know for certain that there is a divine order. Strongly as such inference may suggest itself to believers, the origin of the universal elements might still be sought in other factors by nonbelievers. Yet the verification of such elements would provide us with an international and interdenominational yardstick in human terms.

Many great thinkers, from the religious prophets and apostles [2] and from the Greek and Roman philosophers to the medieval Scholastics, and again to Kant and Husserl, have indeed assumed, either explicitly or implicitly, that there are universal elements in human thinking and feeling, although each has described them in his own terms. But the only basis for this assumption was either revelation or intuition ("self-evidence"). No systematic empirical research has been undertaken. This omission has left a gap in scientific efforts up to this day.

2. *Prima Vista Evidence That There Are Such Elements*

Were it our intention here to inquire into values in general, or at least into ethical values in general, we would have to cover a tremendous field in our pursuit of this course of arguing. Whether it would lead us to results of sufficient concreteness to build on it a general theory of values we cannot here examine. We are dealing, not with ethics in general, but with political science and political ethics

[2] See Paul's Epistle to the Romans 2:14, 18 f.

388

in particular, and within this field we are justified in focusing attention on one particular topic, that of justice or injustice, because much
would be gained by the search for universal elements of ethical feelings
in the political sphere if we found such elements in human ideas or
feelings of justice.

Justice depends very greatly, as we have seen (Chapter iv), on factors
that have no universal character, such as traditional institutions or, in
transtraditional justice, subjective ideas. But we must beware of the
fallacy which would have us believe that for this reason necessarily
everything depends either on such extraneous or subjective factors
or on a scientific proof of metaphysical principles which is, a priori,
doomed to failure.

There are a number of *prima vista* indications that all ideas of justice,
all varieties of thinking and feeling regarding justice, have something
in common. First, such ideas exist everywhere as a distinct category
of ideas. Second, the term "justice" or its approximate equivalent exists
everywhere. Third, human longing for justice is so universal a factor
that no one in public life can neglect presenting his acts as just. And,
fourth, there is the negative indication that we can easily construe an
action which appears *not* just, which is unjust from *every* point of
view, for example, a parent's or teacher's punishing one child—knowingly and out of pure meanness—for what another has done.

A few observations may be added here regarding the third and the
fourth of these points. Dictators of old and recent times have constantly
appealed to the sense of justice, no less than have popular governments.
True, in so doing they have often falsified the facts. But that they
took such great pains to persuade people of the justice of their policies
testifies to the tremendous importance of the sense of justice. Caesar
tried to justify his crossing of the Rubicon by accusing Pompey of a
breach of the Roman constitution, William the Conqueror his crossing of the Channel by reference to his feudal rights. To choose one
of many examples from recent history, before invading Ethiopia in
1935 Mussolini ended his radio speech of October 2 with these words:
"It is the cry of Italy which goes beyond the mountains and the seas
out into the great world. It is the cry of justice and of victory." It was
the same with Hitler's speeches in support of his actions against Austria,
Czechoslovakia, and Poland, or versus the Jews.[1] And, of course, it
was the same with all governments on the other side.

The fact that some imaginable actions would be considered unjust

[1] A systematic content analysis of dictatorial publications for references to justice would be
of some interest in this context.

by everyone used to lead old-time theological philosophy to speculations on the limits that are set even to God's free will, since it seemed
obvious that not even God could make such actions just. In Leibniz'
view it is impossible that God should violate the basic norms of justice by ordaining against them; by ordaining, for instance, that someone should crucify innocent people for the mere satisfaction of his own
pleasure (*ut aliquis solius voluptatis suae causa . . . homines inno-
centes cruciet*).[2] There are similar observations in Grotius.[3] A contemporary writer has aptly spoken of the "sense of injustice."[4]

In view of these *prima vista* indications we have good cause for
supposing that the universal term justice responds to a universal human need of expression, not only in acquiescence with existing laws
but also in criticizing them for lack of justice, and that this universal
need relates to a feeling that has at least some elements in common.
We have good cause for supposing, further, that these elements must
be very important for human nature, since they are tied up with such
passionate feeling.

3. Inadequate Attempts To Find Them

Former periods have been very rash in formulating universal and
invariant postulates of justice under the heading of Natural Law. The
Stoics suggested that one should search for common notions which
are implanted in all men. This came pretty close to what we are after
here. But no one seems to have had the patience to keep within these
narrow boundaries—notions common to *all* men. The writers usually
set forth as universal their own individual postulates or those prevalent
in their period or their class. In this way, philosophers of the first order,
such as Aristotle and St. Thomas, included slavery under Natural Law,
as others excluded it or included institutions of feudalism, or absolute
kingship, of individual liberalism, of equalitarianism, or of Christianity. Only very few elements of these doctrines can be seriously considered here, since we are looking for inescapable postulates that are
common to all known or imaginable ideas of justice. The list of universal and invariant postulates in this sense is subject to the formidable

---

[2] *Leibnitii Opera Omnia*, ed. by Dutens, vol. 3, pt. 3, p. 273.

[3] See Julius Moór, "Das Problem des Naturrechts," *Archiv für Rechts- und Sozialphilosophie*,
vol. 28 (1935) pp. 325, 543.

[4] Edmond N. Cahn, *The Sense of Injustice*, New York 1949. I am not guilty of plagiarism
though, since my own remarks, as presented in this section, were first published ten years
before Cahn's book in my paper "Relative and Absolute Justice" in *Social Research*, vol. 6
(1939), pp. 58, 70 ff.

challenge that any utterance to the contrary would overturn any item of the list, provided only that the utterance were sincere, and the contradiction was not due merely to a conflicting use of terms. When, for example, Hobbes used the term "just" in a narrow positivistic sense this did not indicate that what we are calling here the idea or the sense of justice worked within him only in line with the positive law of the individual country. The opposite is clear from his writings.

Often attempts have been made to lay bare the ultimate principles underlying the positive law of individual countries; this is a useful preparation for further research, but does not provide us with evidence that we are hitting on universal and invariant principles, the opposite being frequently quite manifest. Early in the present century a French professor, R. Saleilles, tried to find objective criteria of justice through comparative studies from analogies in the positive law of various countries. This procedure he hoped might lead him to discover some "collective juridical conscience." But he himself did not attribute absolute universal or invariant character to the results of such endeavors; he only looked for a universal common law of "civilized humanity," derived from comparative law and subsidiary to the national law.[1] Starting from similar motives, Roscoe Pound has ably crystallized a number of "jural postulates" as characteristic of "civilized society."[2]

In the search for universal and invariant elements all these efforts can claim but a restricted significance. That mere comparison of existing laws or institutions does not lead to such elements is obvious; otherwise slavery and torture might have been considered absolute standards in ancient times, torture in the Middle Ages and beyond, and exploitation of labor in the nineteenth century. When investigations are confined to the views of lawgivers and public administrators and fail to include the views of those to whom the law is applied, as for example the slaves, they cannot possibly reveal universal and invariant elements of human thinking and feeling. Once we limit ourselves to what we call civilized countries, as did Roscoe Pound, we cannot hope to find more than illustrations of our own preconceived

[1] R. Saleilles, "Ecole historique et droit naturel d'après quelques ouvrages récents," *Revue trimestrielle de droit civil,* vol. 1 (1902) pp. 80 ff., 111; discussed by C. G. Haines, *The Revival of Natural Law Concepts,* Cambridge, Mass., 1930.

[2] Roscoe Pound, *An Introduction to American Law,* Cambridge, Mass., 1919. In a later paper, Pound dubbed those so-called "natural" principles that underlie the positive law of a number of countries "positive natural law," as distinct from "natural natural law" which is not incorporated in positive law and whose validity cannot be demonstrated; see his "Natural Natural Law and Positive Natural Law," *Law Quarterly Review,* vol. 68 (1952) pp. 330 ff.

definition of civilization; whenever the issue is that of the relative merits of different civilizations, this method leads to nothing.[3]

Contemporary anthropologists have examined the degree to which primitive and advanced cultures differ regarding ethical values. They have pointed to the fact that back of apparent differences identical ethical notions often could be found to operate in both primitive and advanced types. For example, in the case of a North American Indian tribe in which it was considered the duty of sons to kill their aging father in a ritualistic ceremony before his weakness caused too much trouble to him and to the tribe, the idea that children have ethical duties toward their parents could still be recognized. Or, to give another illustration, justice and courage have never been considered a crime.[4] Notwithstanding the great merits of such anthropological suggestions, they do not as yet permit us to tell what actually *are* the universal and invariant postulates of justice. What has been lacking is a systematic coordination between anthropology, philosophy, and political science in this matter. Political scientists have failed to formulate concrete questions relevant to our problem that can be put to a test through anthropological research.

4. A Working Hypothesis and Multiple Tests

It is neither necessary nor practicable to go blindly and haphazardly about the exacting task of trying to disclose what elements of the sense of justice can be found everywhere. A great deal of preparatory thinking can be done on the basis of the abundant material that is already available in order to focus research on meaningful questions and to lead it along promising paths. On the one hand, we must heed all encouraging signs regarding elements on which field research may lead to positive results; on the other, we must avoid wasting efforts on attempts to find universal and invariant elements of which we can already know that they are not there or that they are unlikely to be found. It is a complete misunderstanding of the requirements of scientific research to begin immediately with indiscriminate field research. Such research can and should be well prepared by hard thinking on the basis of available experiences, including those of the thinker himself. Such preparatory work may lead us to good guesses of what we can or cannot expect to find; in more technical terms, it may lead

---

[3] See the quotation from O. W. Holmes, Chapter VII, Section 4, above.
[4] See the quotation from Duncker, Chapter VII, Section 7.

us to a working hypothesis which, if well supported by the available material, may even be accepted by science as a tentative law until refuted through further research (see Chapters I, Section 1, and II, Section 6).

It is, of course, practically impossible to ascertain *everyone's* ideas and feelings regarding those elements of justice we have reason to suspect of having universal character. Therefore we must look for supplementary controls. If we personally regard some element as indispensable for justice and can empirically ascertain that many others, too, do so and have done so in the past with no exception known, we may ask ourselves, in addition, whether we can even imagine that someone could take another view in earnest. And we may go one step further, examining as far as our material permits whether anyone else can seriously imagine such a thing. This would lead us to four tests, or criteria, of universal and invariant elements: first, our own subjective experience regarding our feelings of immediate evidence; second, general confession to the same subjective evidence by others who are in earnest, without any exception; third, our own inability even to imagine a view that would not contain these elements; and fourth, inability of others to imagine such a deviation.

Although these four tests may not be fully independent of one another, in each one attention is focused on a different aspect. Our own idea of justice may be correct or incorrect; at any rate, in itself it presents no transmissible proof for its objective validity. The fact that it is shared by many others may help a bit, but cannot document the validity of our ideas, as has been said before with reference to slavery and exploitation of labor. Matters are different, however, if certain elements in our idea of justice are found time and again in other persons' thinking or feeling about justice without any exception; if, furthermore, these elements are considered obvious by those whose reactions we examine, and no deviation can even be imagined by us or them. This does not mean that no one is able abstractly to think of something else; there may be no limit to what we can "think" abstractly. We can say we are able to "think" that an event has no cause, but can we really imagine, grasp, believe it? Likewise, we may be able to "think" abstractly that a false accusation knowingly made is just, but it seems we cannot really believe it (see Chapter XI).

If inner evidence is contradicted by contrary inner evidence of other human beings and no misunderstanding, different use of terms, or bad will can explain away the contradiction, we must either abandon the effort to prove that the element is universal and invariant, or subdivide mankind into two species with different sets of invariants.[1]

The reader may ask why should we look only for feelings common to *all* human beings; why not limit ourselves to "reasonable" people. This was indeed the old Natural-Law idea, which for two thousand years tempted thinkers away from the search for universal elements. The trouble is that therewith our own interpretation of what is reasonable decides the outcome of our research in advance. We are naturally always inclined to consider our own ideas about justice reasonable and those of others that conflict with ours, unreasonable.[2] Whenever reasonableness is the issue, we cannot decide it in an intersubjectively plausible manner by referring to our own reason. We may be justified in leaving out of attention the thinking and feeling of persons who, according to objective medical tests, cannot be considered normal human beings on the ground that they are abnormally affected by physical or mental illness, provided we do not use this loophole to exclude as abnormal all those who do not share our own ideas. Likewise, we may exclude children (although their feelings may be particularly telling) and people who are asleep or not fully awake, or are in a state of excitement, and we may even decide to concentrate our research only on opinions held by people when in a state of contemplation or meditation. But beyond such objective limitations we cannot introduce the concept of "reason" here without running up the old blind alley where we are finally left alone with our own statements about what we consider reasonable and with no intersubjective means to prove our point to others who differ.

Reason has, of course, a tremendous intersubjective field at its disposal in analyzing the meaning, implications, and consequences of values that are espoused by ourselves or our opponents, and likewise when the question is whether the pursuit of the cherished values is conducive to the attainment of accepted ulterior goals. But we are not here dealing with such relations of means to ends, or with implications and consequences; we are dealing with ultimate standards. There reference to

---

[1] See the reference to Max Wertheimer in the section on equality in Chapter VIII above.

[2] As Mill put it: "Some particular mode of conduct or feeling is affirmed to be *unnatural;* why? because it is abhorrent to the universal and natural sentiment of mankind. Finding no such sentiment in yourself, you question the fact; and the answer is (if your antagonist is polite), that you are an exception, a peculiar case. But neither (say you) do I find in the people of some other country, or of some former age, any such feeling of abhorrence: 'Ay, but their feelings were sophisticated and unhealthy.'" (*Logic*, p. 541, under the heading "Fallacies of Confusion"; skipped in Nagel ed.).

reason loses its intersubjective meaning whenever people, after all implications and consequences have been explored, still prefer different standards in good faith. Whether they are in good faith we may try to find out; but if they are, scientific verification ends. Therefore it is most important to stick to the identification of those elements in the sense of justice that are universal and invariant in *all* people, and not only in those whom we call reasonable. Examinations as to whether persons are able to express themselves correctly, and whether they are not mistaken as to what they really mean, are of course in order, and must play a considerable role in our research.[3]

Even he who thinks that reason can be used as an intersubjective tool beyond what has been admitted here should see some advantage in the identification of elements that are actually universal and invariant in all people, regardless of whether we ourselves think other elements to be reasonable too and consider people unreasonable who feel otherwise.

The procedure here recommended, then, implies a combination of inner observation and comparison, or of phenomenology and comparative empiricism. We are starting not with an arbitrary concept but with an immanent phenomenon of human existence as we find it given in ourselves, characteristic and distinct as are the phenomena of hunger and love; we are starting, in other words, with a way of feeling, thinking, and judging which we denote by the general name of justice, or some other word applied to the same phenomenon, and which we wish to describe more exactly. Description rather than arbitrary definition is the starting point. The results are checked by comparison. Neither method alone—phenomenological description or comparison—can lead to a conclusive result of intersubjective science. Together they may.

5. *Tentative List of Universal Postulates of Justice*

In spite of the extremely severe requirements here posited, a tentative list of universal and invariant postulates of justice can be set down on the basis of the abundant material that is already available, with considerable confidence that it will be confirmed by whatever field research may be undertaken. The following five, it seems, can be regarded as universal and invariant postulates of justice in the sense here explained.

---

[3] See Socrates' treatment of Thrasymachus' erroneous statements regarding his own ideas about justice in Plato's *Republic*, Bk. 1.

First, *truth*. In the objective sense (as when we speak of an objectively just action) justice demands an accordance with objective truth; that is, all relevant statements on facts and relations must be objectively true. In the subjective sense (as when we speak of a just person) it demands an accordance with what is thought to be true; that is, the acting or judging person must honestly think (believe) that the relevant statements are true. The exact meaning and the immense importance of this postulate will be considered in the following chapter.

Second, *generality* of the system of values which is applied. It is unjust to select arbitrarily different systems of values in considering one case and another.

Third, *treating as equal what is equal under the accepted system*. It is unjust to discriminate arbitrarily among equal cases ("arbitrarily" signifying "in contradiction to the accepted system").

Fourth, *no restriction of freedom beyond the requirements of the accepted system*. It is unjust to restrict freedom arbitrarily ("arbitrarily" again meaning "in contradiction to the accepted system").

Fifth, *respect for the necessities of nature* in the strictest sense. It is unjust to inflict punishment or moral reproach for nonfulfillment of a law or command which is impossible of fulfillment.

The first and fifth postulates—truth and possibility—are independent of any particular system of values.

The second, third, and fourth can be traced to a more general postulate, which excludes *arbitrary* laws, actions, and judgments in the specific sense that they discriminate against persons in contradiction to the accepted system of values. It is advisable, however, to list the three separately, in order to bring them into sharper focus. Although in contradistinction to the other two they refer to a particular system of values, the prohibition of arbitrariness is a universal and an invariant element of the sense of justice.

The term "system of values" in the second, third, and fourth postulates is used, not in the severest sense of the word "system," but in its more general understanding of a basic scheme or order of values.

In setting forth these five postulates I mean to say that justice demands a conformance with all of them. Any law, action, or judgment anywhere can be branded as unjust, in an international and interdenominational language, if it violates any of the five. It can be branded as "objectively" unjust if it actually violates them, and as "subjectively" unjust if the lawmaker, acting agent, or judge *knows* that he violates them.

By summing up these postulates we would obtain a minimum definition of justice. It would claim to be more than an arbitrary or a convenient, or conventional definition to be used for some arbitrary and conventional purposes, and more than a merely historical definition. It would attempt to be the exact description of a human phenomenon, of a universal, invariant, inescapable form of human thinking and feeling, based on universal characteristics of human existence.

Whether the universal and invariant elements are transcendent in the sense that they are harbingers of a higher world, and if not that, whether they are nevertheless innate, or whether they are merely acquired, although universally and invariantly acquired, we cannot ascertain with scientific means. Even if merely acquired, the disposition to acquire them would be part of the human hereditary outfit; but whether that has its origin in God or, if there be no God, in natural evolution alone is beyond scientific verification in the sense in which that term is used in this book. However, we may be able to explore empirically whether these elements are actually universal and invariant. I shall presently adduce the available evidence in favor of the tentative hypothesis that they are.

6. *Tentative Evidence That These Postulates Are Universal and Invariant*

First of all, no statement can be found, as far as I can see, that is in substantial contradiction with any of the five postulates, unless the contradiction arises from a mere difference in the use of terms [1] or from lack of sincerity.[2] Hence we can refer to the entire literature on justice as testimony. Positive confirmations from literature are, however, only implicit and casual in most cases. Most writers have gone much further in some postulates, at the same time neglecting or overlooking others without contradicting them. The attempt has never been made to single out invariant elements in the literature on justice by cross-checking them in the way here recommended. Such an attempt leads to a core of universal and invariant elements which has been drowned in much more sweeping controversies.

Only one of the postulates, the third one, demanding equal treatment of equal cases and therefore in particular equality before the law, has been *explicitly* included in the meaning of justice by practically all writers in line with Aristotle.[3] Often this postulate is treated as the

---

[1] As in Hobbes' use of the term justice, see above.

[2] Thrasymachus in Plato's *Republic*, see above.

[3] *Nicomachean Ethics*, Bk. v, ch. iii.

very equivalent, synonym, translation, of the term justice. Thus to Radbruch, at least in his pre-Hitler writings, justice meant exactly this, equal treatment of equal cases, unequal treatment of unequal cases, and nothing else; he used other terms, like *Recht,* for some other requirements, such as expediency and certainty.[4] Max Scheler came close to our view of the inescapable nature of this postulate when he rightly declared that no one is able to deny (he said, inexactly, to disobey) it; everyone will immediately draw differentiations to justify unequal treatment, although he may act in bad faith.[5] In the latter case, I may add, he would violate the postulate of subjective truth (veracity).

Most writers have also proclaimed the second postulate, demanding generality, in explicit words, although as a requirement of law rather than of the evaluations underlying law.[6] This limitation to law is not warranted. The postulate of generality is not restricted to law. It belongs higher up where it includes the scheme of values expressed in law or in actions or in critical judgments. To be just, actions and judgments too must be based on a general scheme of values as distinct from one applied arbitrarily only to the case at hand. Moreover, under the criticism of the Vienna school[7] and of the American realists it has become doubtful whether all law is, or must and can be, general, while there is no doubt that every specific law, as well as acts and opinions outside the sphere of law, must in order to be just be directed by a general scheme of values not arbitrarily selected from case to case, if they hurt others.[8]

The fourth postulate—that freedom be not restricted unless in line with the accepted system of values—has hardly ever been mentioned in this form as an invariant element of justice. Either much more substantial postulates for freedom have been formulated (religious phi-

[4] *Rechtsphilosophie,* 3rd ed., p. 70; 4th ed., p. 168; Wilk tr., p. 107. About Radbruch's later stages, see Chapter VIII.

[5] *Formalismus, op.cit.,* II, 1, end (3rd ed., p. 82).

[6] For example, Kant, John Austin, R. von Jhering, T. E. Holland, L. Duguit, L. Nelson (see Chapter VIII above), Mirca Djuvara ("Sources et normes du droit positif" in *Annuaire de l'institut international de philosophie du droit et de sociologie juridique,* vol. I, 1934–35, pp. 82, 84) and many others.

[7] See W. Ebenstein, *Die philosophische Schule der reinen Rechtslehre* (Prague 1938) p. 120. English ed. under the title *The Pure Theory of Law,* Madison 1945.

[8] Which was first, law or justice? K. N. Llewellyn, *The Bramble Bush,* New York 1930, p. 121 (2nd ed., 1951) makes an able case for law, as did R. von Jhering, but I think the case for justice is better. Children feel actions to be just or unjust even when they know of no law or without reference to it, as for example when cake is distributed unevenly among them, or punishment. See also G. Jellinek, *Allgemeine Staatslehre* (3rd. ed., Berlin 1914) p. 352. Only if we stretch the term "law" to make it apply to any accepted hierarchy of values, even when the acceptance is not ordained by law but is only factual in character, would law be always prior to justice.

losophy, natural rights, Kant, Hegel, Stammler, Gény, Del Vecchio, Hocking, etc.) or freedom has been completely omitted (legal positivists, relativists). The former attitude collides with contrary ideas of justice, and, however firmly we may adopt it as a matter of personal conviction and confession, there is no way of intersubjectively demonstrating its ethical superiority over contrary convictions defended in good faith, except indirectly by analysis of consequences, etc. (Chapter VIII). All those, however, who approve of actions designed to suppress freedom in favor of other values—for example, the national interest, peace and order, or equality—will still admit that such actions in order to be just must pursue values considered higher under the accepted scheme, and that when applied arbitrarily, i.e., in contradiction to the accepted system, they are not just. This is one of the inescapable postulates of justice, and although it has not been proclaimed explicitly as such in the literature on justice, it has never been contradicted either. It has simply been overlooked. Leonard Nelson came closest to expressing it when he stressed that justice forbids restricting liberty beyond equality; equality being his accepted standard, the injunction conforms to the postulate as here formulated.

Universal and invariant recognition of these three postulates—the second, the third, and the fourth—follows indirectly also from the general acknowledgment that *arbitrary* actions of a discriminating effect are not just. At first sight one might be tempted to believe that this is merely a question of definition: arbitrary actions are unjust because we define justice so as to exclude arbitrary discrimination. But in this definition we are not free, any more than we are in the definition of the feeling of hunger or of love. Irrespective of how we define justice, or whether we define it at all, an arbitrary discrimination will inescapably hurt that type of feeling which we call the sense of justice and will arouse a feeling of an injustice being done, at least in the person against whom the discrimination works. But then, what is arbitrary? The minimal criterion to be applied for an action to avoid arbitrariness is that it should not be in conflict with the accepted system of values. What happens if the system of values itself is considered arbitrary we shall see in the following chapter. Its arbitrary application, at any rate, is always felt to be unjust, and inescapably so, even by those who believe in the system, although they may hide their feelings.

Until the 1930's the United States Supreme Court interpreted the clauses of the Constitution that no person shall be deprived of life, liberty or property without due process of law in such a way as to permit the court to fix substantive limitations on what legislatures can do. When thereafter the Court withdrew from this practice in the area of economic and social legislation it stopped at the point where a legislature had acted "arbitrarily." Whether the legislative action can be "regarded as arbitrary or capricious . . . that is all we have to decide," the Supreme Court said. "Even if the wisdom of the policy be regarded as debatable and its effects uncertain, still the legislature is entitled to its judgment." [9] The guarantee of due process "demands only that the law shall not be unreasonable, arbitrary or capricious, and that the means selected shall have a real and substantial relation to the object sought to be attained." "Price control, like any other form of regulation, is unconstitutional only if arbitrary, discriminatory, or demonstrably irrelevant to the policy the legislature is free to adopt, and hence an unnecessary and unwarranted interference with individual liberty." [10] It is characteristic that in these and many other opinions what remains of the more ambitious former theories of the court is the condemnation of arbitrary, capricious, or as it is sometimes called "whimsical," actions as flagrantly unjust. About the additional requirement that the means selected must have a real and substantial relation to the end sought we shall speak in the next chapter; it falls under the category of the postulate of truth, objective or subjective.

The fifth postulate—demanding respect for the necessities of nature—has often been explicitly recognized, and never been substantially contradicted, as we shall see in the special chapter dealing with Impossibility (Chapter XII).

The most important postulate of all five, however, is the first, that of *truth*—subjective or objective truth, according to whether we speak of subjective or objective justice. It has never been gainsaid in the literature. In many specific contexts it has been accepted explicitly or implicitly. In particular, the significance of factual truth for the administration of justice has always been noted. Yet, strange as it may seem, the postulate has hardly ever been stated as an invariant postulate of justice. Relativists, although none of them has ever contradicted it, have neglected formulating it as a limitation to relativism. One reason why they have failed to do so is the fact that in the old Natural-Law tradition truth played a bigger role than here attributed to it on the ground that right law was being held identical with right reason. This sweeping way of combining truth and justice was abandoned with the

[9] *West Coast Hotel Co.* v. *Ernest Parrish and Elise Parrish*, 300 U.S. 379 (1937).
[10] Both quotations are from *Nebbia* v. *New York*, 291 U.S. 502 (1934).

decline of Natural-Law ideas. In giving up the postulate of truth completely, however, positivists and relativists threw out the child with the bath. They brought truth back into the picture only indirectly by admitting scientific, and that means truthful, examinations about the consequences of proposed values and their meaning. But these attempts, important as they are, approach justice from the outside, with the yardstick of science, and pass by the question of the intrinsic relationship between justice and truth. It is one thing to give science some field of activity in the clarification of values, another to state that the phenomenon of the human urge for justice is inseparable from the requirement of (objective or, at least, subjective) truth as the basis of justice. I would therefore challenge Radbruch's statement that justice has direct relations only with the good and not with truth, which he says is the field of science.[11] I submit that the phenomenal feeling of justice directly requires truth—objective or at least subjective truth—as an indispensable element. It does so in its own right. Here is another factual bridge between Is and Ought in universal and invariant human thinking and feeling, which we shall explore in the next chapter.

7. Summary and Conclusions

What we have found in this chapter can be summarized as follows. With two problems unsolved and unsolvable—namely, how to verify intersubjectively that there is an absolute order of values, and if so, which of the conflicting human intuitions regarding this order is correct—there is one more intersubjective channel left for us to pursue: we can engage in empirical research whether there are universal and invariant "inescapable" elements in the human way of thinking and feeling about ethical values, and especially about justice (Section 1). Strong prima vista evidence indicates that there are (Section 2). Although this has often been contended, systematic research in twentieth-century terms regarding both the existence of such elements and their identification has been lagging, and most claims have obviously gone too far (Section 3). There is little use in starting with field research blindly, as it were from scratch; research can and must be carefully prepared by the formulation of pertinent questions which exploit the very considerable amount of positive and negative evidence already available. Four tests suggest themselves both in the analysis of the available material and for further research, combining phenomenological description of our own individual experiences and their categorical

---

[11] *Rechtsphilosophie,* 3rd ed., p. 51; 4th ed., p. 147; Wilk tr., p. 91.

character with research regarding the experiences of others (Section 4). On this basis a tentative list of five universal and invariant elements has been here proposed (Section 5). There is strong evidence available, especially in the entire literature, old and modern, that these five are indeed considered indispensable or unescapable by everyone (Section 6).

One question that requires a clarifying answer may have arisen in the reader's mind at this point. He may be inclined to add other postulates; to declare, for example, that the accepted system of values must not only be applied to all cases without arbitrary discrimination, but that it must be acceptable to everyone. However, not everyone considers only those standards just which can be accepted by all. He who sincerely believes in some system of values as absolutely true will consider its standards just, whether or not they are acceptable to others. Many group worshippers, many revelationists, many "pyramid builders," do not care whether their scheme of values is generally acceptable; *they* accept it, and that suffices to make actions conforming with it appear to them as just. Even in so deviating from other views, however, they would not be able to deny that the five elements enumerated above are indispensable elements of justice, in other words, that their own system must not be applied arbitrarily (in conflict with itself), that the distinctions must be carried through in line with truthfulness, etc. In going beyond this by demanding general acceptability of the system of values, we would switch from universal elements of the sense of justice to a postulate that certainly dominates many of us and has much to recommend it, but is obviously far from being universal.

Our list of five universal and invariant postulates of justice is, of course, tentative only, as are all scientific hypotheses. It is not meant to preclude the possibility that one or the other of the five must be modified or stricken from the list, nor that other universal elements may be found. The five, however, are so well supported by the available evidence even now that the question whether this evidence can be accepted as sufficient for elevating the hypothesis that they are universal to the rank of a scientific law—tentative as are all scientific laws but sufficiently founded to be called a law—is a matter of conventional agreement among scholars. Any attempt made by anthropologists, jurisprudents, political scientists, or others, further to test the hypothesis or law is welcome, and systematic research should be done thereupon as much as feasible. Contrary results, unless questionable as to their accuracy, would naturally have to lead to corrections of the postulates as here formulated, as always in Scientific Method.

In the following two chapters we shall discuss the meaning and the implications of two of the postulates at greater length—truth and impossibility.

CHAPTER XI

TRUTH AND JUSTICE

1. *The Postulate of Factual Truth*

ANY discriminatory statement, such as that someone has stolen, can be entirely just only when it is true. To say that a person has stolen who has not is "objectively unjust" in every case; it is so even when he who makes the statement acts in the best of faith and after the most careful investigation. In the latter case, to be sure, the statement although objectively unjust may be called "subjectively just"; in a broader sense we may speak of a subjectively just statement even when the speaker or writer has not engaged in a careful investigation, provided only that he believed what he said to be true. Yet when he himself thinks it is contrary to fact, then the discriminatory statement is "subjectively unjust" in every case; it is so even when it happens to be objectively true.[1]

The postulate of factual truth in discriminating statements applies not only to moral or juridical discriminations but to any other kind of discriminatory judgments as well, including those referring to abilities and achievements. Whatever may be the merits or failures of Alexander, Caesar, or Napoleon, of Lenin or Stalin, Mussolini or Hitler, of the Germans, the Jews, the Russians, or the Chinese, they have a claim to truth in the final judgment concerning them. This claim cannot be denied even to a Nero or a Judas Iscariot.

Factual truth, in other words, is a necessary condition of justice. Some of us may go further than calling it merely one condition among others. To correct a falsification of facts, to get the facts stated and acknowledged as they really are, may appear to us the most important aspect of justice, even more important than the redress of grievances and the punishment of the evil-doer. In the Last Judgment, as it is envisaged with deepest awe by religious feeling, when "the trumpet sounds," a voice will tell us all the facts about ourselves as they really were and not as we wish them to have been. For the religious this voice in itself, this statement, anticipated in hope and fear, constitutes justice. Not to everyone will truth have such dominating weight. But even if one thinks of truth very lightly and laughs at the idea of a Last Judgment, even if

---

[1] As regards its factual truth a discriminatory statement, therefore, may be (1) both objectively and subjectively just, (2) both objectively and subjectively unjust, (3) subjectively just but objectively unjust, or (4) subjectively unjust but obectively just.

one thinks that lying is natural and valuable, one's inner vocabulary will not call true what is a lie nor just what is contrary to truth. No one will be able to deny that his sense of justice, this ideal or feeling of justice, demands truth as the basis and as part of justice.

This remains true even though human nature builds everywhere on lies and illusions. Man, as has often been said, has a desire to conceal the truth not only from others but also from himself, be it for meanness or for shame or out of his limited capacity for looking truth in the face. We are seldom aware to what extent we lie to ourselves every day, as if bound to do so for self-preservation; consciousness of the whole truth would threaten to destroy us. In practice this passionate impulse toward falsehood (illusion) penetrates deeply into the realm of justice. The greatest crimes against truth and justice are generally committed in the name of truth and justice, and very often are really believed to be committed at the command of truth and justice. People lie to others and to themselves that they believe something to be true and, therefore, some cruel action to be just. But this does not affect the close connection between justice and truth. On the contrary, the very fact that the proclamation of the justice of a cause even when the facts are consciously distorted is always associated with the contention that the factual allegations are true, or at least that they are thought to be true, merely testifies to the inseparable connection between the ideas of justice and truth.

That truth is a necessary condition of justice appears so self-evident that it is difficult to enforce attention for an inquiry into the reasons why this is so. It may seem to be simply a matter of logic. No doubt it would be, once we had *defined* justice so as to include the postulate of truth. But why do we have to define it so? "Otherwise it would not be justice." Why not? This is not a question of logic.

We might, of course, refer to popular usage. Inclusion of the postulate of truth in the meaning of the term justice certainly corresponds to usage. Yet usage does not guarantee that the inclusion is necessary, or with other words that it is more than merely a usage. Should someone challenge the usage and contend that justice does *not* require factual truth of the judgment, then our reference to usage alone would prove nothing.

Nor would it help us if we pointed to the fact that to examine something scientifically means to examine it with the intention of seeking the truth. Surely, in examining justice scientifically we are after truth; but this does not imply that truth is a required element not only in science but also in its objects. Such transfer of a postulate from method to object would be logically untenable. This will become clearer when, for a moment, we consider Beauty rather than Justice. In a scientific investigation of what is beautiful we would be foolish to derive from the postulate of truth, which dominates our scientific effort, a postulate of truth in art, saying that a painting, or a piece of fiction, or a drama, such as Shakespeare's *Julius Caesar,* can be beautiful only when and insofar as it is true to the facts. It may well be that for other reasons the postulate of truth may play a role even in art. Indeed, if that were our topic, I would be prepared to submit that a piece of art to be great must be the *true* expression of something. Yet this, if it is so, must rest on grounds other than the fact that science requires veracity. Art need not be true to fact, while science must. That justice too must respect the facts, then, cannot be derived from the standards of science. It must have other grounds.

Most of the people who feel strongly about justice will derive their absolute certainty as to its essential postulates neither from logic nor from science but from the strength of their feeling that there is something transcendent from higher spheres in the majesty of the idea of justice. They may be right. Yet at this point we must be consistent. Once we have reached the conclusion that science cannot verify intersubjectively that there are divine forces, not even by reference to such strong feelings as love, sense of justice and of beauty—much as such feelings may have driven us individually to the acceptance of a divine order—then we must be consistent enough to dismiss references to divine forces and metaphysical transcendency in the scientific treatment of the phenomenon of justice. This is hard to do; but, again, science is no child's play.

Under these circumstances there remains only one ground which can justify our unconditional inclusion of the postulate of truth in a scientific definition of justice. This is the fact that we are dealing here with a universal phenomenon of human experience, of human thinking and feeling, which would not be correctly *described* if we omitted the postulate. Whether or not we are faced here with such a universal phenomenon has nothing to do with postulates of logic, of science, or of religion. It is exclusively a question of fact.

Several indications that the phenomenon is universal were given in the preceding chapter. No statement to the contrary, we have said, can be found in the entire literature on justice through the ages. None, it seems, can be found either in any other recorded human utterance made in earnest, with only some apparent exceptions that are not really in conflict with the principle; with them we are going to deal below (Section 4). If we asked, a minute ago, what could we say if someone should in good faith challenge the postulate of truth in justice, our reply now is that no one *will* challenge it. No one has ever done so in earnest, and no one will as long as men remain structured as they are, because he cannot do so. We cannot even *imagine* that anyone could, nor can anyone else imagine such a thing, it seems.

Whether there is a specific human "sense" of justice, or only a specific kind of "feeling and thinking" about justice, and whether this is "innate" or merely a product of experience may remain a matter for controversy.[2] I shall not undertake to answer these questions beyond saying that, if this way of feeling and thinking should not be innate, if it was merely a matter of response to experience, then this experience and the response to it must be of a universal character, *grounded in the human situation as such and quite inescapable,* just as memory of the truth is not escapable at will.

Why this is so I do not dare to state. It may be that psychophysical processes in our cortex provide some clue. This would mean that, once we have known the truth, its record in our cortex may make it impossible for us to ignore it at will, and that psychophysical forces beyond our control proceed to restore the record whenever it is being violated by lies, or to correct any untrue fiction which we ourselves may try to superimpose.[3] Hypothetically, one might take the stand that such psychophysical factors plus universal human experiences in group life are the only reasons for the inescapable equation of justice and truth in human feeling and thinking. Another explanation is that, with or without psychophysical intermediary, some metaphysical force, or God, operates. Yet whether this is positively so is beyond science in the meaning of the term as accepted here. At any rate, selfish interests alone cannot explain the inescapability of the postulate of truth in human feeling and thinking of justice. Our selfish interest often seems to require that we forget or ignore the truth, but we are unable to do that at will.

To state that the postulate of truth is universally felt is not the same as saying that it ought to be obeyed. Of course, it should if its source is

---

[2] See on this, Erwin Riezler, *Das Rechtsgefühl; rechtspsychologische Betrachtungen,* München 1921, 2nd ed., 1946.

[3] See on this field of research Wolfgang Köhler, *op.cit.* (Chapter VIII, Section 7), Chapters 6, 7, 9; also, Wertheimer, *op.cit.,* p. 365. Neither refers to the present problem, however. It should be noted that to the extent that such psychophysical processes play a role we would indeed be confronted with "innate" factors.

God. But if it has a different source, such as psychophysical processes, or environmental influences, then it is not feasible for science to infer from the fact of universality any moral duty of submission to the postulate; to do so would be a logically unwarranted inference from Is to Ought. There is, however, something else that Scientific Method can well do without violating its own rules. It can state that the very universality of the feeling will expose violations of the postulate to the charge not only of untruth but of injustice as well, and this reaction will be produced not only in the minds of opponents but even in that of followers, and ultimately also within some layer of the violator's own feeling and thinking.

To state this is no more than to spell out the logical implications of the universality of the postulate. Beyond this point, still other predictions are possible. The universal reaction can be predicted to entail further consequences, at least potentially (risks), such as an overt or clandestine opposition to the government that uses factual lies as a basis for cruel discriminations. Science, therefore, may be able to warn that he who wants to avoid these consequences or risks "ought to" avoid violating the postulate. This is no "categorical" (unconditional) imperative, it is true; but it still is an imperative, though a "hypothetic" one, hitched to a condition: *if* you want to avoid the consequences, *then* you must avoid the violation.

Science, *qua* science, may not be able to go further, but this far it can go, and this should not be overlooked.

2. *Implications of the Postulate of Factual Truth*

An enormous field is covered by the postulate of factual truth in justice. In most cases in which justice is questioned the real issue is the truth of a factual statement. An illustration from the political sphere is the Dreyfus case in France. When this Jewish officer, arrested in 1894 on the charge of selling military secrets to Germany, then condemned, publicly degraded, and deported to Devil's Island, was finally acquitted in 1906, at the second retrial, it was the factual statement—that is, that the first conviction had been based on forgery and that he had *not* sold secrets to a foreign power—which settled the case in its most important aspects. That Dreyfus was restored to office and promoted was a matter of secondary importance. What later became of him did not matter very much; only a few will remember that he served as a colonel in World War I and died in the nineteen-thirties. The important thing was the statement and acknowledgment of the facts.

After that the appeal to the idea of justice had a firm basis, at least as far as the new statement of the facts was accepted to be true.[1]

That a question of justice can thus be reduced to a factual question is the rule rather than the exception. In most cases it is only a factual controversy, a falsehood, that makes possible a difference in judgments.

The postulate of factual truth entails several procedural implications that have figured greatly in the history of justice. Here belong all those rules which are meant to facilitate an ascertainment of the true facts, such as the provisions designed to safeguard the evidence, and the demand that the litigants be granted a fair hearing ("fair" meaning that they should be granted an adequate share in the ascertainment of all relevant facts), that they be allowed to prove their contentions, that the judge be unbiased. These requirements are not based on separate ideas; they are but applications of the one postulate of truth. Their gradual refinement in the course of legal history reflects the progress from rough thinking to less superficial thinking, from ready credulity to watchfulness in regard to rash conclusions, the transition from the ideal of order and authority as highest values to that of respect for individual liberty. But throughout this development the idea that a judgment is objectively just only when it is based on truth has always been the same; it was so even when the procedure was rough and inadequate.

3. *Truthfulness of Evaluations*

The postulate of factual truth in justice, if taken alone, might be belittled on the ground that science is unable to prove or disprove the ultimate values, or standards, that underlie discriminations. Value standards accepted within a particular society may justify, and even require, discriminations, including such of the most brutal kind. The stranger, the Negro, or the Jew, the communist, the liberal, or the conservative, against whom discriminations are applied in line with a country's accepted system of values, is not helped by the postulate that there must be no factual distortion in the statement that he *is* a stranger, a Negro, a Jew, a communist, a liberal, a conservative. Should the standards accepted in a cannibal tribe permit eating its enemies, then the member of an enemy tribe caught and led to the fire for roasting is not comforted by the postulate of factual truth; alas, he *is* a member of that tribe.

[1] A recent book on the *affaire* is Guy Chapman, *The Dreyfus Case, A Reassessment*, New York 1956.

This would indeed be the deplorable situation if the human sense (feeling, idea) of justice were satisfied with truth or truthfulness regarding the *facts* of the individual case. Yet the inescapable association between justice and truth goes further. *Evaluations,* too, must be truthful; that is, they must be truly in line with convictions as to what *is* valuable, in order to support the sense of justice in discriminatory statements or actions. Alleged evaluations that actually are in conflict with what is truly felt to be valuable will necessarily lead into inner trouble if made the basis of action, because an inescapable postulate of the human sense (feeling, idea) of justice is violated.

That this is so was indirectly confirmed by the early advocates of neutral relativism when—in an apparent contradiction to their professed abstinence from value judgments—they insisted that the individual is not free to choose his ultimate values as he listeth, but that he must follow his "conscience" or his "feeling of right and wrong" (Chapter VI, Section 6, above). This implies that he must choose those values in which he truly believes.

The postulate of truthfulness penetrates into the selection of values in various ways. Many discriminating evaluations are based on assumptions concerning facts, such as that the stranger or the person of another race, nationality, or class is a bad character of evil intentions or of minor qualities. These underlying assumptions may be proved untrue by personal experience or by scientific investigation. Once a person comes to see, one way or the other, that there was no factual basis for his discriminative evaluation, his sense of justice ceases to support his discrimination to the extent that it had been based on this factual error; more, it now revolts against the discrimination. He cannot go on acting the old way with a "good conscience," in "good faith"; there is now some inescapable cross-current in his feeling.

A priest who wants witches burned alive may consider his actions entirely just as long as he believes that there are witches who make a contract with the devil, that God has ordained them to be burned, and that this is the only way to save their souls. But it may be attempted, first, to prove that the indicted woman is not a witch, so that even under the priest's system of values she ought not to be burned, and second, to prove that there are no contracts with the devil in the medieval concrete meaning of the transaction or that God never ordained the burning of witches. If this attempt is successful, and if it convinces the priest, or at least the bystanders, the valuation of certain actions as evidence of witchcraft and deserving the death penalty will *necessarily* change.

By such deeds science has often altered the people's sense of justice, and will continue to do so. Although it has been unable to prove or disprove the existence of God and of revelation, science was nevertheless able to prove that no Zeus, Hermes, Dionysus, or Aphrodite lived on the top of Olympus, behaving in the way people thought they did; and gradually justice could not continue to regard offenses against these gods as criminal. It was not the Jews or Christians, it was science which emptied Olympus of the old gods, preparing the way for the belief in one invisible God. Although science has not been able to prove how the world was created, it was nevertheless able to prove that sun and stars do not move at a distance of a few miles around a disk-like earth, that eclipses of sun and moon are not brought about by monsters swallowing them for a while; consequently it was no longer possible to maintain that burning those who denied these beliefs was objectively just. In the same way, a belief that another race consists of murderers and knaves may be proved wrong. To the belief that intermarriages produce inferior progeny science may contribute its statements.

If science is not able to contribute any conclusive statements or if the "believer" is not capable of understanding them or if his belief is not affected by them, he will continue to orient his sense of justice toward what he thinks to be the truth; we cannot, for that matter, even disparage his righteousness. But those who do modify their beliefs, their convictions, under the impact of science, change the responses of their sense of justice (although often they have several lines of defense against science).

This magic influence of truth on the ideas of justice is not restricted to the correction of the factual assumptions underlying evaluations. The latter may also be influenced by poor thinking, such as the confusion of several meanings of the same word, and other logical fallacies. Poor thinking may be corrected, and inevitably the ideas of justice will be affected apace. Here once more science comes into a broad field which is entirely open to its activities and assaults.

To illustrate, the fanatic equalitarian, valuing everything in terms of equality, is often deeply confused in his thinking. He has not yet understood (though he may be made to understand) that in his demand for equal distribution he must make up his mind whether he means equal distribution per capita or according to need or work, distribution of substance, happiness, or "opportunity" (and what that is to mean), equal distribution all over the world or only in his country. Further, in each case the feasibility, the sacrifice of other goods (also of other yardsticks of equality), and the consequences of every proposal must be considered. If the equalitarian, in trying to find answers to this demand for specification and articulation, finds himself hesitating and his belief turning uncertain, he will come to modify if not to change his ideas on highest values, and his ideas of justice will be changed correspondingly.

Again, the libertarian may be led to think over what he really means by liberty. Many an individual, because in a certain case he definitely desires liberty, thinks he desires it in all cases, whereas better thinking would convince him that actually he would wish to restrict liberty in many situations which he has not yet thoroughly considered. By articulate thinking the majority worshipper may modify his ideas on what he really worships. Not only may the group worshipper who disparages another group be corrected in his factual convictions, but also his thinking about the separation of groups, if any, may be made more articulate and considerate in regard to the means to be employed and the consequences of the application of the various means. These few illustrations may stand for a thousand others.

After going through all the turnings and readjustments of articulate thinking the individual still decides on his own evaluations; yet the more he thinks the less sweeping and disastrous his choices are likely to be. This is not to say that old and habitual evaluations will break down as soon as erroneous factual assumptions or faulty reasonings are corrected. Inveterate habits often have the effect that we continue to entertain positive or negative evaluations long after the reasons for them have gone. Yet our conviction as to the righteousness of our evaluation will be weakened, and our former assurance that we act righteously using the old standards in discriminating statements and actions will fail us accordingly.

Here is another link between truth and justice. It has often been stated by relativists that, even though ultimate values cannot strictly be proved, there is a certain field left for science in the discussion of values because science can clarify the meaning and the implications of values. But the link between truth and justice is still closer than this. Science, and truth through science, can do more than enter into such clarifying discussions from outside, can do more than prepare the ground for a more considerate choice from the list of potential values. If this were all, the individual, in his ideas of justice, would still be completely free to follow or not to follow the signposts put up by truth. But in this he is not free, at least not completely. The feeling of justice, as it seems to operate in all human beings, inescapably demands truthfulness; it demands, and enforces its demand at least inwardly, that we direct our choice according to our convictions or beliefs. Whenever we have been convinced by truth we cannot escape following its signposts in our transtraditional ideas of justice. When we come to see that our convictions or beliefs were based on erroneous assumptions concerning facts, or on poor thinking, they may gradually break down and change; and when they do so, even if we try to conceal it, our transtraditional ideas and feelings of justice will change apace. We cannot help it. Science, in fighting for truth, simultaneously remodels evaluations, *and along with them the ideas and feelings of justice.*

4. *Apparent Exceptions. The White Lie*

There are some apparent exceptions to the rule that everyone's sense of justice requires truth as the basis of justice, but they are only apparent. One may think of the white lie told a dying person to spare him the agonies of anxiety or adorning an obituary in honor of a deceased friend, meant to console his family, or—as a political lie—used in the interest of one's country or party. Such behavior may at times be accepted by those present, without their experiencing the slightest revolt of their sense of justice even where some harm to other persons is involved. If this be so, don't we have then an example here of a separation between truth and justice?

If we look a little closer we see, however, that truth and justice remain interlocked even in such cases. Falsehood is resorted to, not just for the purpose of doing harm to anyone but in the service of some overriding value—mercy, respect for grief, the country, a common cause, or the like. It is only because of this ulterior purpose that the discriminatory lie may lose its automatic repulsiveness. It will do so only when the action is thought of as being *truly* committed in the service of what is *truly* believed to be the higher cause. Thus the close association between justice and truth comes back into the picture; it is confirmed rather than refuted by these apparent exceptions.

The case of the doctor's white lie at the bedside of a dying person is typical of all others. Our sense of justice may not be hurt by the doctor's behavior should he even go so far as to denounce as a charlatan another physician who had told the truth. Yet it must at least have been *true* that the liar acted for what he *truly* believed to be the higher value, i.e., to help the dying person. Even so the derogatory denunciation may be felt to be "objectively unjust" toward the other doctor. In this respect our example may not be entirely conclusive because the interest of the other doctor may be so slight, comparatively, that the injustice committed against him can be regarded as negligible; perhaps he would agree. Other illustrations will bring out the objectively unjust character of a discriminatory type of white lie more clearly. Suppose a country's government conceals its own aggressive intentions and actions under the cover of a public lie that the troops of the enemy had begun the fighting. This will be inescapably felt by those who know the truth as objectively unjust toward the soldiers of the other country, no matter how much the lying officials had been motivated by love of their own. Likewise, if some government agency yielding to mob pressure declares a man guilty of a crime it knows he has not committed, this will be generally held objectively unjust toward him however strongly it may have been prompted by a true desire for the preservation of peace and order on the side of the government. Pilate at least washed his hands publicly when he surrendered Jesus to the mob, thus signifying that he did not consider his prisoner guilty.

Yet the "objective" injustice involved in discriminatory white lies is not the chief point here. The decisive thing is that such a lie and the discriminatory actions based on it will not be considered even "subjectively" just, unless it is at least true that the liar acted in the interest of what he truly believed to be the higher value. As soon as bystanders come to doubt the higher value of the ulterior purpose, the action automatically loses the appearance of justice for them. Thus justice and truth always remain associated.

5. *Summary and Conclusions*

The postulate of "truth in justice" is so obvious that, as we have seen, the necessity of stating it explicitly and inquiring into its grounds is easily overlooked, and actually has been overlooked by the early relativists. If attention is drawn to it, the interrelation is often mistaken for a logical requirement, a mere matter of definition, or otherwise a "matter of course." Thus the very obviousness of the postulate has kept even great scholars from seeing that we are faced here with something peculiar, something to be wondered at—nothing less, indeed, than a link, and as it seems even an unbreakable link, between

Is and Ought. Such a link, as we know, is never a logical necessity, nor is its acceptance justified by operations of a merely logical nature. Breakable or not, any link between Is and Ought can be only factual, not logical. The intertwining fact in this case is that apparently all human beings *do* feel and think that way, that they are unable to feel and think otherwise, even if they want to, or to imagine, concretely and realistically, that they could feel and think otherwise.

We have seen that this wondrous fact, as all the wondrous things of the world, can be theoretically explained in several ways, either divine or not, but that in trying to find the ultimate explanation we have to resort to mere speculations, scientifically speaking. In this respect I need not repeat what was said at the end of Section 1 above, nor anticipate the further reflections to be found in Chapter XIII. The important point here is that, while we may explain the fact in various ways, we cannot explain it *away*. The fact seems to remain.

Our contention that this is so has been supported by a great deal of observational evidence. Nevertheless it remains, in scientific terms, nothing better than an "inductive generalization from observed facts," that is, a *hypothesis* gained from multifarious observations and, like any other scientific hypothesis, open to challenge on the basis of contrary observations if any. What we are dealing with here is a question of general factual anthropology.[1] Put on a particularly significant track by the specific character of the hypothesis as here developed, anthropologists may subject it to further tests. This is indeed highly desirable. Yet the material already available is rich enough for us tentatively to assume that the hypothesis will be essentially confirmed by whatever further tests may be applied.

To conclude this chapter a few words may be added on the meaning of the term truth as here used, lest I be accused of evading that quasi-philosophical stand-by question asked by all would-be philosophers in such discussions: Pilate's question, What is Truth? The answer is that I have not used the concept of truth here in any abstract or metaphysical sense in which such philosophical debate might be in order (Chapter 1, Section 5), but have been dealing with things much simpler than that, namely, with the common-sense meaning of truth and falsehood, of truthfulness and lying. When I know that I spent my

[1] I am speaking advisedly of factual rather than philosophical anthropology. Our psychologists, philosophers, and theologians may do their part in looking for an explanation, and the psychologists and the theologians especially have good stuff here to put their fingers on. Yet the decisive concern for us is confirmation or refutation of the factual hypothesis, not its ultimate explanation, which must remain speculative anyway.

money on a spree and then say that it was stolen at home by the maid, this is untruthful (and therefore unjust), and it is inappropriate and irrelevant to interject the philosophical question here of what is Truth. The positive evidence for the validity of the factual hypothesis that all human beings feel the requiredness of truth in justice may be invalidated by tests with contradictory results; but it cannot be invalidated by the philosophical question of what is Truth.

Nor is it likely that it will be invalidated by contradictory tests. The fact seems to prevail. There *is* that link between justice and truth, so it seems. Even if *some* exceptions should turn up, this would not necessarily affect the sociological and political importance of the rule, much as it would affect its anthropological character (see above, Chapter x, Section 4). For, should there be no more than a few isolated exceptions, we could still rely in political theory on the presence of the link between truth and justice in the deepest feelings of the great majority of people everywhere, irrespective of nationality, ideology, or denomination. Yet it does not seem that there are any exceptions. The more assuredly can we base our scientific work in politics and jurisprudence on the existence of that link.

Here then, in the ocean of relativity, is an island where we can take foot. This island is no barren rock. It has been shown to have a fertile soil. Let us go to work and cultivate it, knowing what we are doing and how blessed we are to own that island. A precious wreath awaits science if it will wage a candid fight against superstition, against factual errors and poor thinking, and especially—against lies. *The triumph of truth will carry the triumph of justice.*

CHAPTER XII

IMPOSSIBILITY (LIMITED POSSIBILITY)

1. Positive and Negative Necessity.
Necessity and Freedom

IN Plato's Republic, at a crucial point of the argument about justice
and injustice, Socrates discusses "utility" and "possibility" as two
important aspects of any proposed reform of society. He speaks
ironically of daydreamers who neglect to think about possibility
when they advance what today we would call "utopian" proposals.
"Before they have discovered," Socrates says, "any means of effecting their wishes—that is a matter which never troubles them—they
would rather not tire themselves by thinking about possibilities; but
assuming that what they desire is already granted to them, they proceed with their plan, and delight in detailing what they mean to do
when their wish has come true. . . ."[1]

Nevertheless, Socrates postpones discussion of possibility when, on
the ground of obvious political utility, he voices the most utopian of
his own proposals: eugenically selected women should be held in common by the guardians in his ideal state, and their children be reared
in common without knowing their parents. Toward the end, Glaucon,
who agrees on the utility of such an arrangement, reminds Socrates
of the postponed examination of its possibility. But Socrates refuses
to take that up. We were searching after justice and injustice, he says.
Once we have discovered them, are we "to require that the just man
should in nothing fail of absolute justice; or may we be satisfied
with an approximation, and the attainment in him of a higher degree
of justice than is to be found in other men?" They agree that approximation will be enough. Their intention was only to obtain ideals
(paradeigmata). They did not look at the ideals "with any view of
showing that they could exist in fact," exactly as the painter is not any
worse because he is unable to show that the perfectly ideal man he
delineated could ever have existed. The actual must always fall short
of the truth. "Then," Socrates concludes, "you must not insist on my
proving that the actual state will in every respect coincide with the
ideal. If we are only able to discover how a city may be governed *nearly*
as we proposed you will admit that we have discovered the possibility

[1] Plato, *Republic* (Jowett translation. 1908) Bk. 5, p. 458.

417

which you demand; and will be contented." [2] Agreeing on this, too, they promptly turn to the question of what slightest change would be necessary to bring the perfect constitution they have in mind into existence. There follows the famous section wherein Socrates recommends, as such minimal amendment, vesting the philosopher with power by making him king.

This story sets the theme for an inquiry into more than one problem. At first glance it might seem as if Socrates at the end denied what he had so strongly stressed in the beginning, that impossibility is a relevant objection to proposals of action. But he did not disavow that. True, he emphasized that an "ideal" may be useful even when it cannot be fully attained. He still postulated, however, that some "approximation" at least must be possible. If it is impossible even to approximate the goal, or if approximation is not enough, then the objection of impossibility remains relevant. This obviously was the meaning of Socrates' words. What he said, therefore, was not inconsistent. But it was not enough. There is far more involved here than is tackled in this story. To bring out the significance of impossibility more fully is the purpose of the present chapter.

To begin with, the objection of impossibility may be raised in two different contexts, either as an objection to proposals or projects, as in Plato's dialogue, or as a defense against a moral reproach, an alternative not mentioned there. These contexts are essentially different, as we shall see; it is advisable, therefore, to deal with them separately. Before we do so, however, it is appropriate to cope with a more general question. What is impossible?

Impossibility is negative necessity. If all events were necessary—be it on grounds of the flawless operation of causality or because of metaphysical predetermination—then our feeling that we have some freedom of choice would be a sheer illusion. However strenuously we may ponder what to do and what not to do, and the value of alternative goals, our very pondering and its outcome would be mere links in the chain of necessity. Even our feeling that we are able to choose would be a necessity, for otherwise we would not have it; but it would be an illusion just the same. That I am writing this at this moment would be a necessity in every detail, and also that you read it and what effect it has upon you, if any. In other words, *everything* would be impossible except that which actually did happen, does happen, or will happen.

[2] *Ibid.,* pp. 472–73. Italics added.

If we reject this deterministic view, then there lurks the opposite extreme. If there be no complete necessity, is there any at all? Can we say, with scientific assurance, that *anything* is impossible, except, maybe, that which is logically inconsistent? Much that appeared impossible only yesterday no longer appears so today. Theoretical physics, as we saw, has reached a stage where it is no longer declared impossible that an unsupported stone will fly up rather than fall down, but only highly improbable, since the normal behavior is but the result of statistical laws regarding the probable outcome of a tremendous number of infinitesimally small movements of huge numbers of smallest bodies or waves. In macrocosmic history, too, events that had seemed impossible, such as the Nazi regime in Germany, became a formidable reality. *Nothing,* then, may be impossible; anything may happen.

Confronted with the first of these two extreme views—that necessity reigns absolute—Scientific Method answers that, although many events may be necessary and inevitable, it cannot be verified that all are. In the absence of such proof, as we saw in Chapters II, Section 1, and V, Section 2, the scientist is permitted tentatively to accept the common-sense interpretation of reality that between positive and negative necessities some freedom of choice is left human beings in what they think and do.

As regards the other extreme—that nothing is impossible [3]—the answer of science is that even if that were true actual possibilities would still be more or less *limited,* and the limitation may be so severe that for the purpose at hand it amounts to impossibility. In particular, scientific inquiry can often state that something is impossible "according to the present state of our knowledge," or that it cannot be achieved "with the type or the amount of exertion" the participants of the discussion have in mind, or that it is "logically impossible." We shall meet with many illustrations of practically unquestionable impossibilities in the following sections.

The doctrine that impossibility sets a limit to moral duties as well as to proposals of action has always constituted a sound kernel in the old ideas that there is a Law of Nature. Unfortunately the summary rejection of the classical Natural-Law doctrines covered up this solid cornerstone with everything else. It must be unearthed and relaid. Today we are only at the beginning. A brief restatement of the idea that duty presupposes possibility can be found in the writings of L.

[3] John Stuart Mill called fallacies "all propositions that assert impossibility" (*Logic,* p. 515).

Nelson,[4] M. Scheler,[5] and N. Hartmann.[6] More recently, Felix S. Cohen in the United States[7] and W. D. Ross in England[8] have emphasized this point. The Hungarian professor J. Moór devoted an illuminating article to natural limitations.[9] But the whole significance of impossibility for the social sciences is far from being plumbed.

2. *Impossibility as an Objection to Moral Reproaches*

No one has a moral duty to do what he cannot do; or, to express the same thing in slightly different terms, we cannot justly reproach someone for not doing what it is impossible for him to do.

This seems self-evident. But why is it so? At first sight one might be inclined to answer it is "illogical" to say that someone ought to have done what he could not do. But why should it be illogical? Whether or not I can do something is a question in the realm of Is; there is, as we have seen, no *logical* way of inferring from Is to Ought without recourse to some broader premise in the Ought-form. A logical inference would, of course, be warranted after we had previously defined the meaning of Ought so as to put into it some definite relation to what Is. We may, for example, define Ought, or Duty, so as to presuppose a choice between two alternatives of conduct that were both actually possible. Once we have done that, we can logically infer that where no such choice was open there was no duty. But why do we have to define duty this way? We all feel a strong impulse to define it so, I suppose. Where does this impulse come from?

Plato's story reminds us that we often permit ourselves to use the modes of ought-to-be, or ought-to-do, regarding the obviously impossible also. There ought to be eternal youth. We ought never to sin. Plato, however, wisely restricted this manner of speech to "ideals." Unattainable ideals may be valuable as goals toward which to exert our-

---

[4] Leonard Nelson, *Kritik der praktischen Vernunft*, Göttingen 1916, p. 270.

[5] Max Scheler, *Der Formalismus in der Ethik und die Materiale Wertethik*, *op.cit.* (Chapter VII, Section 5, above) I, 2, end; II, 2; IV, 2; 3rd ed., pp. 24, 83, n. 1, and 244).

[6] Nicolai Hartmann, *Ethics* (as cited Chapter VII, Section 5, above) vol. 2, p. 34.

[7] Felix S. Cohen, *Ethical Systems and Legal Ideals* (as cited Chapter VI, Section 5, above) pp. 140 ff.: ". . . every assertion of *right, wrong,* and *duty* involves an assertion of *can.* . . ." ". . . in calling a given act right we say simply that *it is a possible act which is not worse than any possible alternative.* . . ." Therefore definitions of ought and duty "require the addition of a nonethical concept which does not seem to be purely formal, namely the concept of possibility." See also *ibid.,* p. 262.

[8] W. David Ross, *Foundation of Ethics,* Oxford 1939. See also John Macmurray, "Freedom in the Personal Nexus" in R. Anshen (ed.), *Freedom, Its Meaning,* New York 1940, pp. 507 and 513 on the relation between freedom and possibility (loss of freedom = "A situation in which a real possibility is actually impossible to realize . . . the presence of an impossible possibility").

[9] J. Moór, "Das Problem des Naturrechts," *Archiv für Rechts- und Sozialphilosophie,* vol. 28 (1935) pp. 325 ff., 543 ff. See below, Section 4.

selves in an effort to "approximate" them as far as is possible. But our moral duty in such cases only can be the striving, the exertion, the *possible* approximation. Saying that it is our duty to do or achieve something while simultaneously stating that it cannot be done or achieved seems to involve a strong contradiction. As we have just seen, this is not a contradiction in *terms*, unless we define the terms so as to make it one. It is primarily a contradiction to a *fact*, namely, universal human experience of the difference that exists between freedom and necessity, between a situation where we can do or achieve a thing if we want to, and one where we cannot. It seems to be an invariant element in human thinking and feeling, due to this universal experience, that a person cannot be justly reproached for failing to do or to achieve what is impossible. The very universality of this experience and of the reaction to it has caused a profound need for a term to describe an obligation that relates to a situation where a choice is open, or is thought to be so. If we had not the terms Duty, or Thou Shalt, or You Ought To, for pointing to what a person is expected to do when faced with a choice-situation, we would have to invent such terms. But we do have, and use, these words predominantly for such situations. When in vague speech we apply them to impossible achievements we either think of the duty toward the closest *possible* approximation, as in Plato's case; or we present a postulate to God, to whom realization would be possible; or we merely state our opinion that the achievement, if it were possible, ought to be performed. If we go beyond this and insist on its being our duty to reach an unattainable goal, we change the meaning of the term, using, in fact, a different vocabulary. We cannot meaningfully conceive of a moral duty in the first and narrower sense to do or achieve what is impossible.

Several writers have hesitated to admit this. They have pointed to the deep sense which may lie in the submission to duty-conceptions independent of rational purposes and the possibility of reaching them. Thus, Max Weber referred to the moral importance that may be found in the action of a soldier who, without any conceivable military utility, blows himself up with his untenable redoubt rather than become a prisoner or flee. Or of the extreme Buddhist who condemns all purposive acts.[1] Professor W. M. Urban has made a similar point.[2] But such illustrations do not establish a conclusive counterargument. If all

---

[1] Max Weber, *Der Sinn der "Wertfreiheit" der soziologischen und ökonomischen Wissenschaften* (1917), now Weber, *Gesammelte Aufsätze zur Wissenschaftslehre*, Tübingen 1922, pp. 451, 467, 477, 492.

[2] W. M. Urban, "Ontological Problems of Value," *Journal of Philosophy*, vol. 14 (1917) pp. 309, 315.

purposes are condemned, as in the case of the Buddhist, the question of whether purposes can be achieved does not arise. Even if they are achievable, they are deemed unworthy of pursuit. The only end accepted as worthwhile is that of abandoning all purposes. This end, which may be said to be in itself a purpose, can be approximated to a certain degree and even reached. The moral duty then, in this case as any other, is to reach or approximate an end which can be reached or approximated, or at least is conceived in these terms. No impossibility is involved. Likewise, if the soldier thinks it his duty to die and "not to reason why," it is not impossible for him to do so. His government, educating him in such a spirit, may well pursue a meaningful purpose, such as establishing a formidable force of resistance. Whether and to what extent this goal may be attained by such means is open to scientific discussion.

Weber raised another objection. The effort to reach the impossible, he said, may have by-products of the highest cultural value. This is undoubtedly true. The effort may even in itself attract our admiration and love. In the second part of Goethe's *Faust,* the centaur Chiron brings Faust, who wants a union with Helena, long since deceased, to Manto, daughter of Aesculapius, that she may cure him of his madness. She answers, *"Den lieb' ich, der Unmögliches begehrt,"* i.e., him do I love who asks (demands, yearns, aspires, desires—the German term includes all these meanings) for the impossible.[3] Yet that which, when what is wanted cannot be had, may produce cultural values, admiration, or love, is the longing, the striving, the exertion, and they are not impossible. One may hope to wrest the impossible thing from God or from Destiny, and therefore think it meaningful, and even one's duty, to carry on. But that is to say that he still believes in the possibility. Once impossibility is definitely established and accepted as such by the parties to the argument, attaining *this* impossible end or doing *this* impossible deed can no longer be conceived of as a moral duty.

Impossibilium nulla obligatio est is the classical Roman formulation of this idea.[4] It is important to see that the Roman doctrine expressed a necessary, inevitable element of political, legal, and ethical thinking rather than an arbitrary statement of positive law. Just as we cannot expect someone to do what he cannot do, we cannot seriously bind or force him to do it. We may, of course, pledge and eventually force

[3] *Faust,* Second Part, Act 2, Scene 4.
[4] Justinian's *Digest* 50.17.185.

him to pay us damages, if he fails to achieve the desired effect. We may compel him to suffer a term in jail. Such impositions are not impossible for him to undertake or bear. But moral duty, in the last analysis, can never go *ultra posse*. For this reason, in fact, one's duty can never be, accurately speaking, to *perform* any act, or to *effect* any result, because impossibility may always intervene, but only to *exert* oneself to perform an act or effect a result eventually, and to exert oneself to pay damages and the like.[5] In Richard Wagner's opera *Rheingold* Wotan reminds Loge of his promise to free Freia, only to receive this answer:

> With the greatest of care to consider how to attain it,
> That is what I have pledged.
> Yet to find what never will happen nor ever succeed,
> How could that ever be pledged?[6]

This interpretation of an obligation's meaning is unassailable insofar as moral duty is concerned. Expectation may have been unduly aroused or fostered, however, or a guarantee of success given. Where this was the case, liability for damage or a penalty may be justly incurred, and no impossibility may interfere with their enforcement.

Naturally, there may be differences of opinion about what is and what is not possible. Then a reproach may appear just to one person, and unjust to the other. For example, the command in a national emergency to work exceedingly long hours or with exceedingly little food may be considered possible of execution by the dictatorial government in power, but impossible by the individual worker. This may make him a rebel for the cause of justice in cases where the hierarchy of values is not an issue, as both parties agree that extreme efforts should be made but also that the lives of the workers should be spared.

3. *Impossibility as an Objection to Political Proposals*

Impossibility does not limit only moral duties. It furnishes a relevant objection to any proposal, intention, plan or project, irrespective of moral values.

To start out with a fictitious illustration even more fantastic than

---

[5] I discussed this at length in one of my earliest papers, "System der Vertragshaftung—Unmöglichkeit der Leistung, positive Vertragsverletzung und Verzug" (System of Contractual Liability—Impossibility, etc.), *Jherings Jahrbücher*, vol. 53 (1908) pp. 213–302, where I advanced a detailed "Exertion Theory" (*Kraftanstrengungslehre*). W. D. Ross, *Foundations of Ethics*, Oxford 1939, has more recently made the same point with great force.

[6] My translation (see Jameson translation, New York 1904, pp. 82–83).

Plato's story but more graphic: a proposal to harness the moon to the earth in such a position that the United States would always have the benefit of a full moon can be countered with the relevant objection that it is impossible of execution. This involves no other value judgment. We need not examine whether it is at all "desirable" always to have full moon since that might help an enemy in air attacks, or whether it would not be "unethical" to deprive other countries of their fair share in moonlight. Impossibility is relevant *irrespective of such value questions.*

Why is this so? This time we need not search the human way of thinking and feeling for universal and invariant elements. The matter is far simpler here. The *meaning* of any proposal, if seriously made, implies the *meaning* that the proposed action is possible. On the face of it, a proposal seems to be no proposition that can be true or false. Its meaning, however, implies one or several such propositions. For example, the proposal that we do *a* to achieve *b* implies the meaning *"if* we do *a, then* we shall achieve *b,"* and "we *can* do *a"*; either of these two propositions can be true or false. It would be self-contradictory, therefore, to propose an action and at the same time to admit that it cannot be done. This inconsistency could be resolved only if the proposal was meant to reach some other end which actually could be reached through its pursuit, such as some possible approximation of the goal, or some attainable by-products of the exertion, or some ulterior end, as when a traitor makes the proposal only in order to weaken the country through useless exertion, or some Eulenspiegel is merely out for fun.

Glaucon, therefore, was quite in order when he reminded Socrates of the postponed examination of possibility regarding the philosopher's proposal that women and children should be held in common in the ideal state. Glaucon might well have gone further. He might have raised the question whether, even if the proposal could be carried through, it was possible to reach Socrates' ulterior purposes—the just and efficient state—in this manner. Aristotle, in the second book of his *Politics,* severely criticized Socrates' communism precisely from this angle.[1] It was *impossible,* Aristotle wrote, to reach the most important good, which was to him the self-sufficiency of the state, if all persons were equal. Moreover, if women and children were held in common, it would be *"impossible* to avoid men's supposing certain persons to be their real brothers and sons and fathers and mothers; for they

---

[1] Aristotle, *Politics* (Rackham translation in Loeb ed.) Bk. 2, p. 79. Italics added for emphasis.

424

would be found to form their belief about each other by the re-semblances which occur between children and parents." Were that not the case, so much the worse; community of children then would imply the *risk*—that is, would make it *impossible* to exclude the eventuality (see below)—of assaults on parents and of incest. Even if communism were restricted to the economic sphere, it would be *impossible* to avoid a number of undesired psychological consequences. In raising the issue of possibility regarding the final goal, Aristotle spoke the legitimate language of science.

The authority of science to interpose its verdict "impossible" may not seem at first sight to promise important results. It is, alas, not impossible to arrest and detain innocent people, and to flog, torture, and execute them for no cause, or even to cook one's enemies and eat them. Proposals to do such things, therefore, cannot be combatted with the objection that they are impossible. Yet many other things of practical importance *are* impossible and cannot be made possible by either persuasion or force. There are, in fact, an infinite number of logical, physical, biological, psychological, and legal impossibilities.[2] Science, in pointing them up, can objectively contribute to the selection of plans in which governments can properly engage. A few general illustrations will be given hereafter, merely to illustrate the surprisingly wide field of application. More concrete examples are examined in Sections 5 and 6. In going over these listings, the reader should keep in mind that their scientific significance is to be found, not in an irrelevant play with the concept of impossibility, but in the fact that such impossibilities can be stated without value judgments and that they are relevant whether or not one desires the performance in question.

It is impossible for people to work continuously for twenty-four hours a day, or to work without food, or to work hard when ill and underfed. Many a slaveowner has chafed in vain at this impossibility which no flogging could amend. There it was, and it did set limits to human arbitrariness.

It is impossible to make all human beings good and friendly all of the time, and to eradicate human corruptibility. On the other hand, it

[2] See Moór, *op.cit.*, who omits psychological and legal impossibilities, but adds sociological and ethical ones. It seems to me that a sociological impossibility would always have biological, psychological, physical, or legal causes, but not conversely. Legal impossibilities are explicitly included here because of their practical importance whenever the debate is conducted on the basis of a particular legal system. Regarding so-called "ethical" impossibilities, see Section 4, below.

is impossible to eliminate all metaphysical longings of all human beings. It is impossible not to think when fully awake, or to enforce a command not to think.

It is impossible to establish full equality. Even if economic conditions could be made equal—which they cannot (see below)—it would remain impossible to equalize physical and mental qualities of all individual persons, their state of health, the length of their lives, their character, the atmosphere of family life in which they grow up, the happiness of their matings, the number, length of life, health, and behavior of their children and friends, the satisfaction they find in their work, and many other conditions of personal happiness.

It may not be entirely impossible to establish full racial equality, i.e., a state of affairs where people make no distinctions according to race. To reach this goal is certainly very difficult; but there is no warrant for science to say that it is and will be impossible, always and everywhere. In particular, it is not impossible—at least not everywhere —to establish racial equality before the law courts, in business, employment, housing and education, including nonsegregation. On the other hand, it *is* impossible to establish full racial equality, with people generally making no racial distinctions in any respect, *by legislation alone,* because it is impossible to dominate by laws the way human beings think and feel, their preferences, ideals, images, hopes, and fears. What legislation is unable to do, education and example may be able to bring about in the long run under favorable circumstances; this, at least, cannot be declared equally impossible in scientific terms.

As regards economics, science is able to pronounce with absolute certainty that it is impossible to establish full economic equality between all human beings in the world or even within a large nation, because the personal differences that cannot be equalized—health, quality, family, etc. (see above)—entail ever-changing differences in economic conditions, necessarily defeating any attempt to set up a valid standard of economic equality even theoretically, and even more, to maintain it in practice over any length of time.

It is impossible—short of a miracle—so to distribute five loaves of bread among ten people that each one receives an entire loaf. Stated in slightly different terms this impossibility is at the bottom of the science of economics: it is impossible to supply goods to everyone who wants them when there are fewer goods than wanted. But it may not be impossible to reduce the demand so as to correspond to the supply, for example, by offering the goods only at a price high enough that all who want them at that price can get them, and low enough that all goods available will be wanted at that price; or by threatening those who purchase or own more than a certain amount with punishment.

It is impossible to have any two of the following at the same time within a large population: equality per capita, equality according to need, equality according to quantity of work, equality according to quality of work, equality of opportunity (see Chapters IV, Section 5, and VIII, Section 2).

While it is certainly not impossible to make economic conditions far more equal than they now are, it is impossible to do so without interfering in liberty. In other words, to the extent that economic equality *can* be established and maintained at all, it is impossible to have full economic liberty at the same time.

It may not be impossible to have the United States Constitution amended in a desired direction within a number of years even where public opinion at the present moment is strongly opposed to the change; yet it is certainly impossible to effect the change within a few weeks, since the rules require a longer time for the procedure alone.

Impossibility is the issue also whenever goals can be reached only in combination with some "undesired by-product," or means can be used only on condition of some sacrifice. If someone proposes that we pursue the goal A, it may be that according to logical, physical, biological, psychological, or legal conditions A is necessarily linked with B and that, therefore, only $A + B$, that is C, can be attained, not A alone, or at least, that the means, m, proposed for attaining A, will never attain A alone, but only $A + B$. If the parties to the conflict agree that B is undesired, we may speak of an *implied evil* in the sense of an evil which it is impossible to evade in pursuing an otherwise desired end. One cannot eat one's cake and have it too. One cannot live licentiously and remain young and fresh.

If the undesired by-product is not certain but likely to occur one may speak of an *implied risk* as a subspecies of implied evils. Here too impossibility is the issue, because whenever some undesired effect may materialize in the pursuit of a goal the question is whether it is possible or impossible to preclude this concatenation.

The risk can be called a *calculated risk* when it has been taken fully into account in the choice between possible alternatives of action. If the risk cannot be reduced to zero, it is often important to know whether the remaining possibility cannot at least be limited. This question turns research on probability into one on impossibility; for the problem then is whether it is possible or impossible to change, say, a fifty-fifty chance into one of sixty, ninety, or ninety-nine percent, or respectively the risk into one of only forty, ten, or one percent.

In all such studies one must bear in mind that he who prefers $A + B$ to *non-A* cannot be deterred from pursuing his goal by being reminded that B is certain or likely to enter. He will say: that is the price we pay. The fact that in war, even if victorious, many will be killed and mutilated, and great treasures of industry and art destroyed, may not disparage war for him who is prepared to accept these implied evils, and so in any other case. Science can, however, bring out the cost more exactly in advance and thereby influence preferences and reactions.

That implied evils offer a wide field for scientific research has always been recognized from antiquity to our time, as Aristotle's objection to the community of wives and children shows. In our century, Max Weber's papers have been particularly rich in this respect (see Chapter VI, above). Many other writers, both in Europe and America, have made statements to the same effect during the last fifty years.[3] It has hardly become clear, however, that impossibility is a relevant objection to social actions and purposes *irrespective of value judgments* about ends or means, and that this fact gives the category of impossibility its unique significance in the social sciences.

While abstaining from interposing his own value judgments, the scientist may well find that evaluations rightly or wrongly applied by the *people,* or groups of people, may make it impossible to reach some goal pursued, or to reach it with the means at hand, as illustrated by the resistance of the French nobility against encroachments on their privileges before the Revolution, or of Americans against the ban of alcoholic drinks, or against racial equality in the South. In other words, value judgments may play a causal role in making achievements impossible (see next section, below, regarding ethical value judgments).

That government should not attempt to achieve what cannot be done (or to approximate what cannot be approximated) seems so obvious that these elaborate statements may appear more boring than

[3] Felix Cohen, *op.cit.,* p. 121; Morris Cohen, *op.cit.,* pp. 421, 424; Ralph B. Perry, *General Theory of Value, op.cit.,* pp. 611, 638 ff.; Eduard Spranger, *Der Sinn der Voraussetzungslosigkeit in den Geisteswissenschaften* (*op.cit.* Chapter VII, Section 9) p. 18; John Dewey, "Theory of Valuation," *International Encyclopedia of Unified Science,* vol. 2, pp. 33 ff., 42; John Dickinson, "The Law Behind the Law," *Columbia Law Review,* vol. 29 (1929) pp. 285, 295, n. 22; Max Wertheimer, "Some Problems in the Theory of Ethics," *Social Research,* vol. 2 (1935) p. 353.

important. Will not even the worst government in its own interest avoid such stupid action? To be sure, it will try. Yet he would be mistaken who on that ground would overlook the import of impossibility. *Political history is a vast cemetery of plans and projects that were foredoomed to failure. Their success was impossible,* at least with the means applied in the effort.

In two later sections (5 and 6) illustrations will be given for the importance of the category of impossibility in the debate on present-day political problems of the first magnitude. But as these details would interrupt the general course of our present argument I shall first proceed with the latter.

4. *Impossibility on the Borderline of Metaphysics*

The preceding section referred to impossibility in strictly scientific terms, stripped of any metaphysical elements. It is, however, rewarding and clarifying to pursue ideas of limited possibility a little further, up to the borderline of metaphysics, and even to venture some speculative glances beyond that line.

(a) "ETHICAL IMPOSSIBILITY"

As a matter of fact, almost every writer who has cared at all to deal with impossibilities in the hope of some gain for the social sciences has ended with metaphysical value judgments. The fine paper by Professor Moór, quoted at the end of Section 1, serves well to illustrate this point.

Moór starts out from the fundamental difference between the Natural-Law conceptions of the old Aristotelian-Scholastic school and those entertained by the Continental school of the seventeenth and eighteenth centuries, the former resulting only in a few very broad principles, the latter deriving detailed codes from nature. He calls for a reversion to the earlier school, which distinguished between the "flagrantly immoral" and the "merely unjust" law, denying validity to the former only, while holding other laws laid down by proper authority to be valid even if unjust. Moór urges that this idea, "which indeed means the denial of boundlessness to law-giving power," ought to be salvaged and utilized for legal theory.[1]

This introduction, in itself competently written and designating a great legal problem, is entirely misleading as a preface to what the author actually did in his subsequent inquiry. For it intimated that

[1] Moór, *op.cit.*, pp. 543, 545. See on this view above, Chapter VIII, Section 4.

he intended to search for basic ethical standards. Instead, however, he turned to the exposition of naturalistic impossibilities such as discussed above, which do not yield ethical standards. But as though he wished to make good on the expectation he had aroused, he finally included among the various types of impossibility—physical, logical, etc.—a special category of "ethical" impossibility, which he defined as the violation of "those ethical laws the disregard of which makes the existence of society causally impossible." Therewith, however, the terms "impossible" and "causal" are made dependent on nonnaturalistic factors, namely, the ethical type of society the observer has in mind. What the liberal may regard as destruction of society, the equalitarian will not so regard, and so from type to type.

Moór tries to evade this relativistic complication. He thinks merely of that "ethical minimum," he assures us, without which human society would "commit suicide." With such restrictions, however, he reduces ethical impossibility to trifling importance, far from identifying the "flagrantly immoral" law of the Scholastics from which he had started. Indeed, he is led to question in an odd footnote whether that ethical minimum was violated even in Sodom and Gomorrha and to answer this question in the *negative,* because social life there was capable of sheer continuance.[2] His illustration of an act amounting to social suicide, and therefore invalid for ethical reasons, is a law ordering the invariable extermination of all newborn children, a law not likely ever to be enacted. Even so, he is forced to spoil his naturalistic argument by interposing surreptitiously a metaphysical value judgment, namely, that human society is a positive value that ought to be preserved in however rotten a state, an idea Schopenhauer would contradict and somewhat at variance also with the celibatarian laws of the Catholic Church and the doctrine of the Last Judgment. Einstein, for example, would not have agreed that this opinion could be supported by scientific reasons; for he wrote, as quoted in the Introductory above, that "if someone approves, as a goal, the extirpation of the human race from the earth, one cannot refute such a viewpoint on rational grounds."

Instead of intermingling metaphysical judgments that are either controversial or so narrow as to have no practical significance we had better keep the scientific basis (*scientia transmissibilis*) pure and unadulterated here, concentrating strictly on the question of what actually can or cannot be done or achieved. This will lead us further,

[2] *Op.cit.,* p. 563, note 57.

not less far. For, as we saw in Section 3, in estimating actual possibilities science must take into account value judgments held by the *people,* which frequently place serious obstacles in the path of governmental measures. In this context ethical ideas can play a significant role. For it may well be that it is impossible to achieve political goals—either at all or with the means proposed—on the ground that they are in conflict with deeply founded ethical ideas of the people. This may lead to genuine impossibility far earlier than at the point of Moór's "social suicide." But then the scientifically effective argument against the proposal is the impossibility of enforcing it in view of ethical convictions actually held—whether rightly or wrongly—by the people, rather than the plan's unethical character as such.[3]

The great question originally raised but not answered by Moór, whether and when "validity" should be denied to governmental orders on the ground that they violate basic standards, is—as I tried to show in Chapter IV, Section 8—not really a scientific question, but a juridical one, *and is solvable as such.*

The term "ethical impossibility" could be used with better scientific justification in another sense. We might call it ethically impossible to reproach a person for failing to do what he could not do, or to regard a lie as a just basis for discriminations, or to call arbitrary shifts in standards "just," because these are actions that are universally felt to be unjust. But the ethical impossibility of justifying them is, of course, no guarantee that they will not be committed.

(b) SELF-AVENGING LAWS OF CONDUCT

Whenever science can point out that it is impossible to reach a goal we are pursuing—to reach it at all, to reach it with the means and the knowledge at our disposal, or to reach it by the particular action we are contemplating—or that it is impossible to avoid undesired consequences or risks, then science assumes the role of a *great warner.* Its warnings may obtain an apparently ethical aspect at times, especially when they point to the possibility, probability, or certainty that the intended action, which is going to hurt others, will also hurt the actor himself. In such cases science seems to divulge "ethical laws,"

---

[3] Studies on impossibilities in law enforcement because of a conflict of legislation with public opinion have sometimes been made. See, e.g., Felix S. Cohen, *op.cit.* (Chapter VI) p. 252; Morris Cohen, *Reason and Nature,* New York 1931, pp. 422, 423; Karl Llewellyn, "The Effect of Legal Institutions on Economics," *American Economic Review,* vol. 15 (1925) pp. 665, 673; Roscoe Pound, "The Limits of Effective Legal Action," *International Journal of Ethics,* vol. 27 (1917) pp. 150, 153, 163, 167.

and it may well be that it actually does so. This has been contemplated from the beginnings of philosophy. Thus, Socrates is reported to have said, "But surely transgressors of the laws ordained by the gods pay a penalty that a man can in no wise escape, as some when they transgress the laws ordained by man escape punishment, either by concealment or by violence." [4] The two illustrations here used by Socrates were ingratitude and incest, and in both cases he described the consequences not by reference to the gods but in terms of physiological or psychological laws that make such transgressions unpleasant in their consequences. Likewise, in Plato's *Republic*, Socrates discoursed on the inevitable unhappiness that awaits a tyrant, whose relative unhappiness he calculated as 729 times greater than that of a ruler who governs under the ideal constitution, applying a queer mysticism of numbers but a very plausible psychological analysis.[5]

As late as the end of the ninteenth century, the Scottish professor James Lorimer (1818–1890) published a book on the principles of jurisprudence "as determined by nature," [6] in which he defined Natural Law as meaning just such self-avenging laws, although he amply trespassed on grounds far beyond this principle in his actual performance.

What science actually does, however, in all such cases is no more than to ascertain inevitable consequences of an act. To characterize an action as "unethical" because of the bad consequences it has for ourselves is not justified scientifically unless we either define ethics merely as the art of avoiding unpleasant consequences for ourselves or see in the fact that the act has such consequences the operation of metaphysical forces. The latter, of course, many of us do; but it is beyond science to ascertain the existence and operation of divine forces by some intersubjectively transmissible manner of proof. Therefore, science can do no more than point to the consequences.

That we cannot safely infer from evils resulting for the actor that the act is ethically wrong is illustrated by the nurse who catches a deadly disease in ministering to lepers, or by the martyr who incurs pain of death as a consequence of his refusal to do what is against his conscience.

For these several reasons we will do well to avoid the term "ethical laws" in this context and rather speak only of "implied evils," or even more neutrally of "undesired" implications or consequences. Even

---

[4] Xenophon, *Memorabilia* (Marchant translation, Loeb ed., 1923) Bk. iv, 4, 21.

[5] Plato, *Republic*, Bk. 9 (Jowett, p. 587).

[6] James Lorimer, *The Institutes of Law; A Treatise of the Principles of Jurisprudence as Determined by Nature*, Edinburgh, 1872 (2nd ed. 1880, especially pp. 4, 237).

so it is obvious that scientific research on "self-avenging laws of conduct" is apt to salvage some significant portion of the old Natural-Law ideas; the unpleasant consequences are held up as a warning to the individual not to commit a self-destructive act.[7]

An extreme form of the idea that there are self-avenging laws of conduct is the doctrine that *every* wrong action leads to unpleasant results for the author. This is what Goethe expressed in the "Song of the Old One," *Denn alle Schuld rächt sich auf Erden* (all guilt avenges itself on this earth).[8] Similarly, Lorimer wrote in his book just mentioned that *"every* sin or folly we commit is, in principle, an act of self-destruction."[9]

In recent times, preachers and poets rather than philosophers and scientists have pursued this view. A great part of the literary work of the Swedish poet August Strindberg was impressively dedicated to its illustration. Taken literally, the proposition that all guilt is an act of self-destruction would yield a definition of guilt to the effect that "guilt is what avenges itself on earth," or at least in the negative (since some self-destructive actions, as those of the martyr, do not involve guilt) that there is no guilt where there is no self-destruction. This, however, would hardly do justice to the essential meaning of the thesis, which obviously is not intended to present a naturalistic definition of guilt but is based, rather, on the assumption that guilt is primarily determined by metaphysical laws and that the bad consequences for the author are merely an additional factor. In other words, the proposition is meant to be synthetic, not analytic (see Chapter 1, Section 6).

It is entirely legitimate for scientific research to regard such a proposition as a "working hypothesis." There are many indications of its validity, both in the lives of individuals (at least when these lives are not accidentally shortened), and of groups. But any systematic research through observation is confronted with formidable difficulties, because the finer forms of self-avengement—such as inner restlessness, physical or mental consequences concealed for shame, loss of horizon, visionless materialism—are not readily verifiable from the outside. On the other hand, although there is certainly no scientific proof yet and none

---

[7] This is the soundest point in the revival of Natural Law ideas. See, e.g., Harry Jaffa's "Comment on Oppenheimer in Defense of the 'Natural Law Thesis,'" *American Political Science Review*, vol. 57 (1957) pp. 54 ff. But scientifically unwarranted metaphysical premises should be introduced, if at all, only hypothetically.

[8] *Wilhelm Meisters Lehrjahre*, Bk. 3, Ch. 13.

[9] *Op.cit.*, p. 238. Italics added.

to be expected, no conclusive counterevidence has been adduced either. Science, therefore, must keep in mind the possibility that such a law operates and should add any results of scientifically controlled observations to the intuitions of preachers and poets.

(c) NATURALISTIC HEDONISM

Hedonists have gone farther along naturalistic roads. Not content to associate the morally evil with ensuing pain they have equated also the morally good with a surplus of pleasure. Insofar as they have referred to pleasure and pain of the acting subject and not of third parties, their doctrine amounts to the proposition that it is *impossible* to be good and yet (preponderantly) unhappy, or to be bad and yet (preponderantly) happy.

Socrates is reported to have voiced such hedonism—or rather eudaimonism (this term allows better for joys more profound than ordinary pleasures)—as well as his belief in self-avenging laws of conduct. In this broader theory, too, he has had many followers down to modern times, not including Goethe here, however, who required Heaven to do justice to Margarete in his *Faust*. Jeremy Bentham gave the doctrine a new social meaning: it was not the happiness of the individual, it was that of the greatest number that counted. John Stuart Mill, too, declared that happiness was the proper standard for political action (see above, Chapter v, Section 7). At the end of the nineteenth century, however, under the impact of the idealistic objections from Kant to Hegel, hedonism seemed to peter out, except in some branches of religious philosophy where it was carried on in an ill-defined relation to rewards and punishment in another world.

In our own century, as mentioned in Chapter VIII, Section 9, Felix S. Cohen has tried to revive secularized hedonism in a new form.[10] True, he does not want to define "good" directly in terms of pleasure;[11] that would make it impossible even to ask whether the good is always pleasant. He prefers to hold good to be indefinable. But he adopts the view that nevertheless there can be identified naturalistic criteria which always attend "the good." In this sense he holds that a surplus of pleasures over pains, each taken in its finest connotations and ramifications, is an outstanding characteristic and necessary concomitant of

[10] Felix S. Cohen, *Ethical Systems and Legal Ideals,* New York 1933, pp. 161, 172, 174.

[11] In line with Moore, *Principia Ethica,* Cambridge 1903, p. 16. Cohen rejects also Perry's definition in terms of preferences.

the good. He offers this "absolutistic hedonism"—as he himself calls it—as an alternative to relativism. It is, he says, a doctrine "consistent with the writer's value judgments" and, although he admits that this "does not prove the truth of the theory," he thinks that "it is a sufficient ground for belief. . . ." [12] Lack of proof does not bother him, because to him it is the very characteristic of science that its results are always uncertain and subject to empirical refutation, and because "the ultimate appeal of an ethical system is to the immediate obviousness of its intelligible conclusions." [13]

These are rather loose and ambiguous passages in an otherwise carefully written book. Personal "belief" of an intelligent scholar may at times prompt the discovery of a useful "working hypothesis." If meant as such, a refined form of eudaimonism must be admitted, and even welcomed, to science. Thus far, there can be no quarrel with Felix Cohen's views. But personal belief is no scientific proof. Cohen explicitly states that the alternative between relativism and absolutistic hedonism is scientifically insoluble. [14] This equation is misleading. We must keep in mind that Scientific Value Relativism does not contend that all values *are* relative—there is surely no scientific proof for that —but merely that the absolute validity of values is beyond scientific proof. This is admitted by Cohen, so that we were able to state in Chapter VI that he himself actually is a Scientific Value Relativist, though *malgré lui*. But he is wrong when he equates the lack of scientific proof for value judgments, such as his own hedonistic ones, with the lack of full proof that is the general calamity in empirical science. These defects are, as discussed in Chapters III, Sections 4 and 7, and V, Section 2, on quite different levels regarding the intersubjective element. Transmissible proof can be presented with intersubjective adequacy, for example, in support of the proposition that men cannot live and work without eating and sleeping. But there is no such intersubjective proof or immediate obviousness in support of the thesis that the good ones enjoy a naturalistic surplus of pleasure. If there were, everyone would be good.

The most plausible form of "eudaimonistic parallelism"—as we may

---

[12] *Ibid.*, p. 188.

[13] *Ibid.*, pp. 117, 125, 186, 214.

[14] *Ibid.*, p. 227. He slips into saying: "The conclusion is not a pleasant one. But the stories philosophy tells do not always have happy endings." This, according to hedonism, would be identical with saying that the theory is not morally good, as it is a criterion of the good to be pleasant.

call it, in the sense of a necessary coincidence between being good and happy—seems to me Max Scheler's version, foreshadowed by Plato.[16] Scheler assumes that there are several layers or levels of feeling, each of a different "depth." At the most superficial level there are sensual feelings of a local character. Then there follow general feelings of the body (static) and of life (functional, active). Next, there are what he calls "soul" feelings, i.e., feelings of the Ego, the I. And, finally, at the deepest layer, there are the "purely spiritual feelings," or personality feelings. Only feelings of the first layer, and to a lesser extent, those of the second, can be reached intentionally. Feelings of the fourth, the deepest, layer are never the product of intentional endeavors directed toward their acquisition; they present themselves as the by-product, accompaniment, or aftermath, of worthy acts, and in their turn are the *source* of moral acts.

The decisive point in Scheler's theory is that different layers may be affected differently by the same event at the same time; for example, a person may feel a sensual pain and at the same time a positive happiness at the deepest layer of feeling, such as a mother feels who succeeds in saving her child from a fire while she suffers burns and bruises.

I, for one, "hope" and, to a certain extent, even "believe" that there is some endaimonistic parallelism. But does it go so far as to make it *impossible* for the good ones to fall into deepest grief? History has witnessed many atrocious cruelties maliciously applied to or accidentally striking individuals who finally broke down in utter torment although, to all outward appearances, they did not deserve such a fate on the ground of any particular failure of theirs. Confronted with these observations it would be rash for scientific conviction to take the universal and automatic rule of eudaimonistic justice for granted. One may think it obvious with Kant that there *ought* to be such compensatory justice. But one can hardly contend that the facts obviously conform to this desire. Close observation may offer many indications—as my personal observation indeed tends to confirm—that, with an almost faultless regularity, not only does guilt avenge itself on this earth in some way or other in the long run, if there be a long run, but as well that inner balance at the deepest layer helps a person in overcoming even very serious trials. But one may still feel that, beyond these two important

---

[16] Max Scheler, *op.cit.* (Chapter VII, Section 5) v, 8 and 9 b (3rd ed., pp. 344, 361 ff.). Compare Plato, *Republic,* Bk. 9. Scheler rejects the idea that happiness as such is a worthy goal that should be striven for and could be reached by such direct efforts.

elements, eudaimonistic parallelism is far from obvious, nay that, if not the wish but the facts are observed, obviousness can be said to be rather on the opposite side. This hostile evidence may be only apparent —I do "hope" it is. At any rate it need not constitute a final barrier for the believer. But *the scholar has to take stock of it.*

Moreover, there is no intersubjective standard of measurement wherewith to verify a perfect eudaimonistic parallelism. The obvious psychological relation which can be easily stated to exist between subjective self-contentedness and subjective happiness proves nothing for our case, because self-contentedness may rest on self-complacency as well as on real goodness, just as its opposite, contrition, may not necessarily rest on real badness, but be caused by oversensitiveness of conscience.

Thus we find ourselves moving toward the borderline of metaphysics with only limited possibilities of scientific verification. But all potentialities for more intensive research have hardly been exhausted yet. Whatever contributions have been forthcoming are scattered and sporadic, with no attempt at anything resembling unified effort and systematic reporting. Political science should watch such attempts and contribute to them wherever possible. The results may rarely provide a direct answer for political issues. But the disclosure of interrelations between goodness and happiness, and between badness and unhappiness, has a great educational bearing; it may influence the way in which people learn to pursue happiness—an eminently political factor.

5. *Impossibility in the Argument between Democracy and Totalitarianism*

A. Genuine Impossibilities in Totalitarian Regimes

In the Great Debate between democracy and totalitarianism references to alleged impossibilities have been widely used by both sides without much ado about theory. Just as it is the task of science to refute phony allegations of this kind, and therewith to point to hidden possibilities (see next section), so it is to disclose genuine impossibilities. In the present section several such genuine impossibilities will be discussed regarding transition to a dictatorial regime from freer forms of government. It is not yet the issue here whether a change-over from one social system to another, e.g., from capitalism to socialism, is possible *without* dictatorship—that will be examined in the next section—but merely what kind of impossibilities are involved in any grant of dictatorial powers, especially total ones, irrespective of whether the intended policy be communist, fascist, or of any other type. The only aspect here considered, it should be kept in mind, is the impact of impossibility. Other questions might be raised, but this one is basic.

Let it be first understood in its full gravity that it is *not* impossible, regrettable as that may be, for a democracy to break down. Democratic Athens, democratic Germany, democratic Italy, democratic Austria, democratic Spain did break down. Likewise, it is *not* impossible, repugnant though it be to admit it, that authoritarian methods at critical junctures may be able to tide a nation over a period of trouble while insistence on democratic procedures would result in catastrophe.[1] Next, if a country is about to surrender all power to one man, it is *not* impossible—unlikely though it may be—that the man who obtains all the power has high moral and intellectual qualities, or as we shall call it here more briefly, is both "good" and "wise."

Yet several other things *are* impossible in such a change of regime, and these impossibilities go to the core of the political problem. While it is, as we have just stated, not entirely impossible that a man who wields total power is both good and wise, it is *impossible*—

(i) To *ensure* that the particular person emerging in the dictatorial role actually will be a man both good and wise.

(ii) To ensure that, if he is so in the beginning, he will continue to be so later on—he may turn insane, senile, or corrupt, or become the puppet of corrupt wirepullers; for even if power should not always corrupt, it often does, and it is certainly impossible to guarantee that it will not do so.

(iii) To ensure that his successors also will be good and wise; benevolent dictators, from Pisistratus onward, and long before him, often had particularly cruel or stupid successors.

If this were all it would be bad enough in view of the tremendous mischief which a dictator who is either immoral or unintelligent or both can cause for country and people, and for other nations as well. Yet the worst impossibility is still to come. Once all legal powers, including command of the military and police forces, of the bureaucracy

[1] See the section on "Undemocratic Majorities" in my article "Democracy—Challenge to Theory," *Social Research,* vol. 13 (1946) p. 195; the discussion of the situation in Germany during the year of 1932 in my *Prelude to Silence,* New York 1944, and in Karl Dietrich Bracher, *Die Auflösung der Weimarer Republik,* Stuttgart 1955, especially pp. 529–734; and my review of the latter book, "Die Auflösung der Weimarer Republik und die politische Wissenschaft," *Zeitschrift für Politik,* Neue Folge, vol. 2 (1955) pp. 292–308. The present chapter went to the publisher before the birth of de Gaulle's (non-total) dictatorial regime in France in the spring of 1958; it has not been changed thereafter, as there was no reason for alterations.

and of lawgiving, have been surrendered to a totalitarian dictator without reservations, it *is impossible*—

(iv) To get rid of him without his own consent short of a violent revolt or revolution which, as the entire machine of the state and all legal powers are in his hands, has to be fought against tremendous odds, exposing the rebels and their families to the cruelest suppressive measures.

The decisive point in our present content is that these four scientific objections of impossibility are valid irrespective of the scientist's own value judgments. For the value judgments here employed—such as unwise, mean, dreadful, cruel—are meant not as those of the scientist but of the people, including persons who originally had approved the investment of total power in the dictator, or who theoretically recommend such a change in government. The question here, in other words, is not whether the effects are undesir*able,* but whether they are actually undesir*ed;* this is a question of fact, not of the scientist's personal value judgment.

Unwise and mean persons may wield power under democratic governments also. But there the power they hold is neither total in character nor unlimited in time. It is legally and actually limited in scope, in intensity, and in duration. There is division of powers. There are checks and balances. Periodic free elections give the people a chance to get rid of "unwise" and "mean" legislators and executives; they need not resort to violent revolution for that purpose.

It is incredible how often the elemental importance of the impossibilities inherent in the grant of total powers is overlooked in political as well as in scientific discussions. The argument always tends to swerve toward other points of greater emotional bearing, points that may indeed be very important too, but whose validity depends on controversial value judgments. Ever again, in the world's history, have people called for a strong man—meaning, of course, one who was good and wise in their own sense of the terms—without considering those four impossibilities. It seems as if each individual nation has to go through the hell of personal experience separately, as the British did in the seventeenth century, the French in the seventeenth and eighteenth, and the Germans in the twentieth, before they learn the lesson of the four impossibilities —if they ever do learn them.

Nine years after World War II, there appeared in Germany an eloquently and intelligently written book, highly critical of democracy, by an author whose record had been neither fascist nor communist.[2] Widely read and acclaimed, the book's main point of attack was the lack of stability to which the foreign policy of democratic nations is exposed because of its dependence on the vacillating moods of the people. This criticism is certainly not quite without foundation; it will be discussed along with other difficulties of long-range planning in democracies at its proper place (Part Five). But the remarkable fact was that the author devoted no more than a few pages at the end of his book to the crucial question of an appropriate alternative to democracy and there briefly suggested a form of government like that of present-day Portugal with a man of the character and the abilities of Dr. [Antonio de Oliveiro] Salazar as a dictator, generously adding that Dr. Heinrich Brüning, ex-chancellor of the Weimar Republic, would be a similar type of man. Not a single word was devoted to the four impossibilities, not even to the first one: how could it be ensured that the dictatorial powers would fall into the hands of a Salazar or a Brüning, and not of a Hitler, Mussolini, or Stalin? The fact that Socrates, too, in Plato's *Republic,* failed to put this question when he recommended making "the" philosopher the king, is no excuse for present-day writers when they continue to ignore or evade it after more than two thousand years of historical experience.

If the improbable but not entirely impossible thing should actually happen that a dictator proves to be that rare bird, a man with total powers who is both good and wise, and that he remains such, and his successors too, then there is a fifth impossibility of tremendous significance. It is impossible for one man, or a few of them, at the head of a large country, however good and wise he or they may be—

(v) To watch personally over the welfare of many millions of individuals.

This is a physical impossibility that can be stated by social scientists with the same exactness with which natural scientists proclaim their most certain laws. In fact, it is itself but a biological, i.e., natural law in the strictest sense of that term. Not even the strongest man can work more than a limited number of hours every day and every week, watch more than a limited number of persons individually, check the doings of more than a limited number of subordinates, have more than a limited number of personal visitors and of penetrating conversations with each of them, read and write more than a limited number of

[2] Winfried Martini, *Das Ende aller Sicherheit, eine Kritik des Westens,* Stuttgart 1954.

letters, reports, or decrees. Even Caesar, who won fame for his ability to dictate a great number of letters simultaneously, could not dictate a hundred or a million, or read them, at the same time.

Every executive, in other words, as a human being necessarily has only a limited "span of control." A dictator who is to rule a modern nation of a hundred million people or more, therefore, needs thousands or millions of captains and lieutenants who cannot all be supposed to be good and wise even if he is. These underlings—unless controlled by freedom of speech and of the press, and by independent courts or their equivalent—may commit in their own areas (which may be concentration camps) barbaric acts, which the potentially good and wise man at the top might condemn *if he learns of them* but which may never come to his knowledge. This fact has led to disastrous consequences even under well-intentioned dictators, as can be amply documented from the times of the Egyptian pharaohs and Roman emperors down to the present. In this respect it hardly makes a difference whether or not the dictator himself is a morally decent man.

Under Hitler, so it is reported, a woman came to the prison where her husband, having served his judicially fixed term, was about to be released, only to witness that he was being taken over by the Secret Police, who took him to an unidentified concentration camp. She wrote a letter of complaint to Hitler, whereupon she received a warning from the Secret Police, which had intercepted the letter, that she too would be taken to a concentration camp if she should dare to write again to the Führer.

In the Soviet Union, according to the *official* version of the story revealed in the purge trials of 1938, Henrich Yagoda, Chief of Police and one of the highest Soviet officers, confessed to having committed, behind Stalin's back, the most abominable acts of murder, including the assassination of the great poet, Maxim Gorki. Yagoda confessed that, in order to kill Gorki, he had summoned the latter's physician and ordered him to prescribe to the poet, who was suffering of tuberculosis, a "cure" that was sure to lead to his quick death. Yagoda terrorized the unwilling doctor into submission and threatened him with reprisals against himself and his family if he should try to appeal to Stalin.[3] It has been suggested that the official story was untrue and that actually Yagoda's confessions had been extorted by the prosecution. Yet this alternative would make no better case for dictatorship.

Again, in January 1953 it was officially stated in the Soviet press that a terrorist group of doctors had sought to cut short the lives of several

[3] *New York Times*, March 6, 9, and 10, 1938

leading personages through "sabotage medical treatment." Three months later, on April 4, the Soviet press announced that the accusation had been false and that the physicians were being released. The case against them was said to have been fabricated in the Ministry of State Security. Like Yagoda, his successor Lavrenti Beria was executed.

The new Stalin biography in the fortieth volume of the official *Great Soviet Encyclopedia* (1958) blames Yezhov, Yagoda, and Beria, the three leaders of the secret police under Stalin, for many other crimes against innocent people. It describes them as "sworn enemies of the people and the party," and says that they "wormed their way into his [Stalin's] confidence" and "slandered and executed many honest people who were faithful to the party" (*New York Times,* February 23, 1958, p. 9). The biography bitterly attacks those who contend that such events are an inevitable part of the Soviet system. But this is not the decisive point. Events like these may not be entirely "inevitable," even under a government of the Soviet type; it is not "impossible" that for a while they will not be repeated. But it *is* impossible to *ensure* that they will not happen again, or to provide remedies against this danger, without introducing constitutional guarantees that are alien to the Soviet system.

The difficulty of keeping top leaders informed merely "through channels" of arbitrary cruelties committed by their subordinates exists even in democracies whenever freedom of speech and control by independent courts are curtailed, as for example during military service, especially in wartime or in occupied countries. Complaints through channels are not sure to reach the leaders when the underlings themselves are involved. Instances have been reported where letters of complaint written by American soldiers in the Far East to the War Department and addressed as legally required through official channels "were never forwarded and the senders were threatened with punitive measures."[4] If this can happen in the world's most liberal army—though only for the duration of the military service, and even there occasionally exposed to public criticism by free press, as the report shows—what are the chances that complaints will reach the potential saint at the head of a totalitarian regime? What are the chances that people in conquered and occupied countries can bring their complaints up through channels? Stalin knew what the Germans had done in the Soviet Union during the war, but did he know equally well what wholesale plunder, rape, and murder Soviet soldiers later committed in Germany? Did even the commanding Soviet generals know the full story? Even in the

[4] Hanson W. Baldwin, *New York Times,* January 20, 1946.

Western zones of occupation, could the commanding generals and their civil governments at home know what was done by members of their occupation armies? Occupation is supposed to be a transient state of affairs. In totalitarian governments, however, such situations last as long as the totalitarian system is preserved.

No other remedy has ever been invented for these implied evils and risks of dictatorships than those which historically developed under the impact of bitter experiences and untold sufferings: constitutional limitations of autocratic power; the institution of law courts that are independent of the executive power; freedom of speech and of complaint; freedom of the press; and the writ of habeas corpus or its equivalent in cases of detention.

The interrelation between totalitarianism and persecution points to another impossibility. It is *impossible*—

(vi) To carry through a totalitarian regime without persecution.

Totalitarianism tolerates no opposition, and without persecution people cannot be kept from expressing opposition. It is dubious whether totalitarian dictators, after a long reign of terror, can liberalize their regime, even if they should like to, without destroying themselves and their most resolute supporters. As Professor Schumpeter put it: "For the really terrible point about the Stalin regime is not what it did to millions of victims but the fact *that it had to do it if it wished to survive.* In other words, those principles and that practice are inseparable." [5]

Two questions, however, must here be distinguished. The one is whether it is possible for a totalitarian dictator and his henchmen personally to survive the regime's liberalization; the other, whether the regime as such can survive. The first type of survival may be possible. To be sure, the pent-up resentment of millions of people, if given any chance to express itself, is likely to turn against the dictator and his radical supporters. But it cannot be said with scientific certainty that personal survival is impossible. The English revolution of 1688 has been rightly considered the more glorious because it was unbloody; the tyrant and his faithful survived. It may be highly unlikely that such an unbloody change-over may be made from totalitarian practices that were many times harsher than those of the Stuart kings. Hitler and his

[5] Joseph Schumpeter, *Capitalism, Socialism, and Democracy,* London 1943, p. 362, n. 10. Italics in the original. See also, Carl J. Friedrich and Z. K. Brzezinski, *Totalitarian Dictatorship and Autocracy,* Cambridge, Mass., 1956, especially pp. 288 ff., and my review, *Social Research,* vol. 24 (1957) pp. 482–86. This book is particularly good on changes in totalitarian ideologies.

chief executioners could hardly have escaped their fate had a popular upsurge succeeded. But it cannot be definitely said in general terms that a peaceful change is quite impossible.

The second question, however, can be answered in the negative without any reservations. For it is *logically* impossible that totalitarianism survives when it is being abolished. What then survives is no longer totalitarianism. Dictators endowed with total powers have, of course, always the theoretical possibility of introducing constitutional guarantees of freedom; but when they do so and survive personally, their regime ceases to be totalitarian, moving toward constitutionally limited, democratic government.

In concluding, it should be made clear that this list of impossibilities is not meant to be exhaustive, not even with regard to dictatorial regimes. Certain impossibilities are inherent also in nontotalitarian types of government, including democracies.[6] They will be discussed systematically in the chapters devoted specifically to the various forms of government (vol. 2). It will appear that they are of a different kind and magnitude. Nor are all those alleged impossibilities that have been ascribed to democracy really such, as we shall see presently.

6. *Democracy and Totalitarianism* (*Continued*)

B. Alleged, But Questionable Impossibilities in Democratic Regimes

Contentions of impossibility sometimes constitute the very core of a political theory, whose entire scientific validity then hinges on the validity of that allegation. If the impossibility is merely imaginary or at least questionable, that overthrows the theory, or puts its conclusiveness in doubt. The more important it is for science to examine such contentions.

In the fight of communism against democracy imaginary and questionable impossibilities have played a particularly great role and continue to do so. The extent to which this is true is so remarkable that extensive documentation is in order. In the following quotations the decisive words expressing impossibility will be freely italicized to show our point.

[6] See also Francis Coker, *Recent Political Thought*, New York 1934, pp. 328 ff., on "Impossibility of Democracy," dealing with Pareto, Michels, and Spengler.

(a) IMPOSSIBILITY OF HALTING THE WORKERS' IMPOVERISHMENT WITHOUT VIOLENT REVOLUTION

It began with the beginning—the Communist Manifesto by Marx and Engels of February 1848. There it was argued that "the proletariat, the lowest stratum of our present society, *cannot* stir, *cannot* raise itself up, without the whole superincumbent strata of official society being sprung into the air." This was followed by the contention that the modern laborer "instead of rising with the progress of industry, sinks deeper and deeper below the conditions of existence of his own class. He becomes a pauper. . . ." This thesis was strongly accentuated by the final statement that in a revolution "the proletarians have nothing to lose but their chains."

This amounted to saying that it was *impossible* for the workers to avoid further deterioration of their lot without a violent revolution. History has produced plenty of evidence meantime that the conditions of laborers have not deteriorated but improved in capitalistic countries. The allegation of impossibility was wrong. It was also wrong to say that it is impossible for workers to lose anything by a revolution but their chains. It is obvious that they have many precious rights to lose, economic and other, and above all their freedom of opinion, of speech, of assembly and association, of the press, of science, art, and religion, and the guarantees of these freedoms through independent law courts and through institutions such as habeas corpus.

(b) IMPOSSIBILITY OF IMPROVING WORKERS' CONDITIONS BY MEASURES OF THE BOURGEOISIE

The first thesis of impossibility was dovetailed with a second, which said that it was impossible for the bourgeoisie, even should it so desire, to avert or arrest the workers' doom by intelligent countermeasures. The bourgeoisie, so the Manifesto said, "is unfit to rule, because it is incompetent to assure an existence to its slave within his slavery, because it *cannot help* letting him sink into such a state that it has to feed him, instead of being fed by him. Society *can no longer* live under this bourgeoisie. . . ."

This contention, too, has been refuted by history; minimum wages, maximum hours, collective bargaining, old age and unemployment insurance, public health insurance in many countries, control (at least to some extent) of monopolies, and other measures have proved effective in the planned effort not to let the worker "sink" but to lift him up. This also has taken the original meaning out of the subsequent conclusion that "what the bourgeoisie therefore produces, above all, are its own grave-diggers. Its fall and the victory of the proletariat are equally inevitable." Whatever correct elements might be found in this latter prediction—such as that nineteenth-century society was fated to be superseded by other forms of society, as in fact it has already been superseded by modified types of liberal society deeply permeated by measures of social control [1]—these changes were not the consequence of the "inevitable" progressive doom of the workers.

(c) IMPOSSIBILITY OF A CHANGE-OVER TO SOCIALIST RULE THROUGH DEMOCRATIC PROCEDURES

Another questionable contention is the alleged "impossibility of Social-Democracy," that is, the impossibility of combining democracy (in the sense of freedom of elections, majority rule, and guarantee of human rights) with socialism (in the sense of socialization of the means of production and central control). Two stages of this argument must be distinguished: first, that it is impossible to attain a change-over to a socialist regime through democratic procedures, and, second, that after a change-over it is impossible with democratic procedures to implement socialism, to carry it through and maintain it.

These contentions refined the thesis that the impoverishment of the workers cannot be halted, in two ways; they said, more in particular, that at any rate *socialism* could not be peacefully attained, and secondly, that democratic majorities were no substitute for a violent revolution. This thesis, too, was adumbrated in the Communist Manifesto, whose last paragraph stated that "the Communists disdain to conceal their views and aims. They openly declare that their ends *can* be attained *only* by the forcible overthrow of all existing social conditions."

As a matter of fact, Marx did not entirely insist on the impossibility of winning socialism through democratic procedures. In a public address he delivered after the adjournment of the Hague Congress of the International in 1872 he said, "we do not deny that there are countries, like England and America, and if I understood your arrangements better, I might even add Holland—where the worker may attain his

---

[1] See Eduard Heimann, "The Interplay of Capitalism and Socialism in the American Economy," *Social Research*, vol. 24 (1957) pp. 87–111; also in German, "Was Amerika aus dem Sozialismus gemacht hat," *Hamburger Jahrbuch für Wirtschafts- und Gesellschaftspolitik*, vol. 2 (1957).

object by peaceful means. But not in all countries is this the case." [2] By mentioning Holland, in addition to England and America, this admission went further than a previous passage in a letter of 1871 where Marx wrote that to smash the bureaucratic and military machine was the precondition of any real revolution "on the Continent." [3]

Some thirty years later, however, Lenin restored the original theory that a violent revolution is necessary in all cases, even in democracies. In his *State and Revolution* (1917) [4] he wrote, "The liberation of the oppressed class is *impossible not only without a violent* revolution, but also without the destruction of the apparatus of state power, which was created by the ruling class" (p. 9). He called this a "theoretically self-evident conclusion" (p. 10). "The bourgeois state *can only* be put an end to by a revolution" (p. 17). Then, quoting from Marx, "Class struggle *necessarily* leads to the dictatorship of the proletariat," and "the working class *cannot* simply lay hold of the ready-made state machinery and wield it for its own purposes" (p. 31). He explicitly repudiated Marx's letter of 1871: "Today, in 1917 . . . this exception made by Marx is no longer valid. . . . Today, both in England and America, the 'precondition of any real people's revolution' is the smashing, the destruction of the 'ready-made state machinery.' . . ." (p.34). Similarly Lenin had written two years earlier, "It is impossible to annihilate classes without a dictatorship of the oppressed class, the proletariat." [5]

Another forty years later, however, Nikita S. Khrushchev, First Secretary of the Soviet Communist Party, in his great speech of February 14, 1956, at the opening of the Twentieth Congress of the Communist Party in Moscow, in his turn repudiated Lenin's doctrine. The importance of this change-back may be underlined by the following extensive quotation. Khrushchev said:

> In view of the fundamental changes that have taken place in the world arena, new prospects have also opened up with regard to the transition of countries and nations to socialism. It is quite likely that the forms of the transition to socialism will become more and more

[2] Quoted by Karl Kautsky, *The Dictatorship of the Proletariat,* 2nd ed., Manchester 1921, pp. 9 ff. See Hans Kelsen, *The Political Theory of Bolshevism,* University of California Publications in Political Science, Berkeley, vol. 2 (1948) p. 41 for a clear discussion of this matter.

[3] Letter to Kugelmann, *Neue Zeit,* vol. 20–21 (1901–02) p. 709; Kelsen, *op.cit.,* p. 40.

[4] *State and Revolution* (1917), International Publishers, Marxist Library, vol. 8, New York 1932.

[5] The United States of Europe Slogan," *Sotsial-Demokrat,* August 23, 1915 (No. 44), reprinted in *The Strategy and Tactics of World Communism* (80th Congress, 2nd Sess., H.D. 619), Suppl. 1, "One Hundred Years of World Communism, 1848–1948," p. 39.

variegated. Moreover, it is not *obligatory* for the implementation of these forms to be connected with civil war in all circumstances

The enemies are fond of depicting us, Leninists, as supporters of violence always and in all circumstances. It is true that we recognize the necessity for the revolutionary transformation of capitalist society into Socialist society. This is what distinguishes revolutionary Marxists from reformists and opportunists. There is not a shadow of doubt that *for a number* of capitalist countries the overthrow of the bourgeoisie dictatorship by force and the connected sharp aggravation of the class struggle is *inevitable*.

But *there are different forms of social revolution* and *the allegation that we recognize force and civil war as the only way* of transforming society *does not correspond to reality*.

Leninism teaches us that the ruling classes will not relinquish power of their own free will. However, the greater or lesser degree of acuteness in the struggle, the use or not of force in the transition to socialism, depend not so much on the proletariat as on the extent of the resistance put up by the exploiters and on the employment of violence by the exploiting class itself.

In this connection the question arises of the *possibility of employing the parliamentary form* for the *transition* to socialism. For the Russian Bolsheviks . . . this way was excluded. However, *since then radical changes* have taken place in the historical situation that *allows an approach to this question from another angle*. Socialism has become a great magnetizing force for the workers, peasants and intelligentsia of all lands. The ideas of socialism are really conquering the minds of all toiling mankind. At the same time, in *a number* of capitalist countries, the working class possesses in the present situation realistic opportunities of welding under its leadership the overwhelming majority of the people and of insuring the *transition of the principal means of production into the hands of the people*. . . .

In these conditions . . . the working class has the possibility of . . . *gaining a firm majority in Parliament,* and converting it from an organ of bourgeois democracy and into an instrument of genuinely popular will. In such an event, this institution, traditional for many highly developed capitalist countries, may become an organ of genuine democracy, of democracy for the working people.

The *winning of a stable parliamentary majority* . . . would bring about for the working class of *a number* of capitalist and former

colonial countries conditions insuring the implementation of fundamental social transformations.

Of course, in countries where capitalism is still strong and where
it controls an enormous military and police machine, the serious resistance of the reactionary forces is inevitable. There the transition to
socialism will proceed amid conditions of an acute class revolutionary
struggle.

He ended by resuming the old warning of the Communist Manifesto
that the necessary changes in society cannot be brought about by the
bourgeoisie itself but only by the working class:

> The political leadership of the working class, headed by its advance
> detachment, is the indispensable and decisive factor for all the forms
> of the transition to socialism. Without this the transition is *impossible*.

As a result of this speech and of its endorsement in the subsequent
speeches by other communist leaders and in the concluding resolution
of the twentieth Congress, communist theory now admits, if with a
number of reservations, that it is *not impossible* for the workers to
achieve a change-over to a socialist regime, at least to its initial stage,
through democratic means—thus in part abandoning a thesis that
since the begining of this century had distinguished European Social
Democrats from Soviet Communists.[6]

(d) IMPOSSIBILITY OF IMPLEMENTING SOCIALISM THROUGH DEMOCRATIC
PROCEDURES

To say that it is possible to achieve a change-over to socialist rule with
democratic means does not necessarily imply, however, that it is possible also to implement and maintain socialism with such means. Communist theory has persistently alleged—*and in this point it has not yet
changed*—that it is impossible to carry through socialism under a system
of free elections, freedom of speech, free association, and free majority
decisions. On two grounds Soviet theorists have held that a strictly
dictatorial regime by a communist "vanguard of the proletariat" is
necessary over an indefinite period of time; first, because the capitalist
opponents will put up a violent resistance if not against the transition

---

[6] See Francis W. Coker, *Recent Political Thought*, New York 1934: "It is chiefly in this
emphasis upon the impossibility of a free and democratic socialistic government . . . that the
Russian Communists may be said to differ from the orthodox Marxians in the Western states"
(p. 183).

·then at least against the subsequent implementation of socialism; and second, because the inertia of the victorious socialist majorities will induce them to vote for immediate benefits during a period where more rather than less work and less rather than more consumption are required.

Soviet theorists do not stand alone in their contention that the implementation and maintenance of socialism are impossible with democratic means. Right-wing liberals, like Friedrich Hayek, agree with them on that count. Their interest is, of course, the opposite; if democracy and socialism are incompatible, they hope to see democracy maintained and socialism abandoned. But on the chief point here under discussion—whether it is possible to have both, democracy and socialism—the two opponents are agreed. It is *impossible,* they say.

In his *Road to Serfdom*[7] Hayek predicts that socialism will inevitably lead to the abolition of democratic liberties, in other words that it will be impossible to avoid this, however much one may try. He pays no attention to the violent resistance to be expected from the vested interests—the first obsession of all Soviet theorists. But he goes more into detail than the latter have done to show why, irrespective of such a resistance, a democratic parliament must fail if it tries to carry through socialism with democratic procedures.

One of his chief points is that socialism requires centralized planning and that, even if there is a large majority for socialism, there frequently will be no majority able to agree on the particular ends and means. In this case, he says, a democratic parliament *"cannot* direct." "In a society which for its functioning depends on central planning . . . control *cannot* be made dependent on a majority's being able to agree; it will often be *necessary* that the will of a small minority be imposed upon the people, because this minority will be the largest group able to agree among themselves on the question at issue" (p. 69). "If 'capitalism' means . . . a competitive system based on free disposal over private property, it is . . . important to realize that *only* within this system is democracy *possible*. When it becomes dominated by a collectivist creed, democracy will *inevitably* destroy itself. . . . Planning *leads* to dictatorship, because dictatorship is . . . essential if central planning on a large scale is to be *possible"* (p. 70). "Formal equality before the laws is . . . *incompatible* with an activity of the government deliberately aiming at material or substantive equality of different people. . . . To produce the same result for different people, it is *neces-*

[7] Friedrich A. Hayek, *The Road to Serfdom,* Chicago 1944.

sary to treat them differently" (p. 79). And again: ". . . socialism *can* be put into practice only by methods [i.e., dictatorship] which most socialists disapprove" (p. 137).[8]

In appraising the Lenin-Hayek theory of incompatibility between democracy and socialism we must not underestimate the strength of their combined arguments. They competently point to grave difficulties and dangers. But they fail to prove impossibility. Their allegations are half-true at best. Let me briefly show why.

It is a strong argument that those who are to lose their privileges are likely to rise in violent resistance when a radically socialist legislation issues from a prosocialist majority in a democratic legislature. This was strikingly illustrated after the Spanish revolution of 1931, when the democratic majority in the newly elected parliament engaged in frontal legislative attacks simultaneously against all vested interests— monarchists, army, church, big landowners, and big industrialists—before it had built up sufficiently strong armed forces of its own for the support of the republican government. Although the reform measures then enacted could hardly be called socialist in character—most of them were no more than liberal reforms of a feudalist system—they led to a rally of all opponent groups in a violent revolt and eventually to the establishment of the Franco regime. However, there is no justification for a scientific verdict that it was impossible to avoid this historical sequence, and that it will always be impossible to avoid a similar outcome when an attempt is made to carry through socialism with democratic procedures. Once the danger has been fully understood it is conceivable that better results will be attained, for example, if the majority first builds up sufficiently strong military and police forces for the support of the democratic government, before it engages in measures that are likely to meet with violent resistance, and if it adapts its legislative program at every step to the actual power relations, never trying to do more than at that time can be enforced. This may imply gradualism, to be sure, and even permanent abstention from unnecessarily irritating and reckless measures, in which the history of Soviet communism has been so rich. But it may make the implementation of a truly democratic socialism possible.

It is another strong argument of the impossibility-theorists that workers who have won parliamentary majorities may be impatient

[8] See also the least tenable of his statements: "Both competition and central direction become poor and inefficient tools if they are incomplete: they are alternative principles used to solve the same problem, and a mixture of the two means that *neither will really work* and that the result will be worse than if either system had been consistently relied upon" (p. 42).

451

in their desire to secure tangible benefits quickly beyond reasonable limits. In order to cope with this danger it will be necessary to educate people in advance so as to prepare them for the meaningful exercise of majority powers. That may not be easy, but it is not necessarily impossible.

Finally, it is a weighty argument when Hayek warns that the majority is likely to split whenever major decisions on planning become necessary—such as the decision whether to give priority to investment in heavy industry or to the production of consumer goods, of which goods and in which order, or how much productive strength to allot to armament and how much to peaceful use. But once this danger has been well understood in advance, it may not be impossible to meet it by proper devices, such as a careful preparation of master plans and delegation of the power to make current economic decisions under such plans to some board or commission, even to one with powers so independent of the other branches of government as to raise its standing to that of a fourth branch. It may not become necessary for that matter— and this is the decisive point—to abolish noneconomic guarantees of personal freedom of speech, of elections, of the press, of art, science and religion, independent courts, habeas corpus, or equality before the law irrespective of religion, race, or political opinion.

The question of compatibility of democracy and socialism, therefore, is still an open one. There is good reason to believe that it is not necessary to go all the way along the totalitarian road if a majority should be bent on carrying through socialism, although certain modifications in the process of economic legislation and administration will be necessary.

If it were correct that democratic socialism is impossible, then those many people in many countries who ardently want socialism would have no choice but to abandon democracy. This is another reason why political science should give serious attention to the problem. To evade it because one hates socialism is very shortsighted. There is real danger that in a critical situation the masses will abandon democracy in favor of socialist dictatorship unless they are satisfied that it is possible to establish and maintain socialism through democratic means, and unless institutional devices apt to make democratic socialism workable without the wholesale abolition of the guarantees of human rights have been prepared in advance.[9] To be sure, the danger of a socialist majority

[9] Herman Finer's *Road to Reaction* (New York 1945) contributed to the critical part of the task by showing that Hayek's arguments against the possibility of democratic planning

making its appearance in the United States Congress seems remote; even in Great Britain, where Labour twice won majorities in Parliament and may win them again, the will to democracy among the masses is still stronger than that to socialism. But there are countries with less stability of democratic experience and a more acute urge toward socialism. Unless the workers there are convinced that socialism can be carried through with democratic means they may turn communist in theory and practice—as many have already done in their votes.

Establishment of a penetrating and reassuring political theory regarding the compatibility of socialism and democracy also could offer encouragement to whatever tendencies there may develop in the Soviet Union or some of its satellites toward introduction of more democratic institutions. It would make possible a stronger and more precise language in international political discussions about both democracy and socialism, and their coexistence.

(e) IMPOSSIBILITY OF COEXISTENCE OF CAPITALIST AND SOCIALIST COUNTRIES

Up to the Second World War communist leaders often proclaimed the impossibility of peaceful coexistence between capitalist and socialist countries. It began, relatively mildly, with Lenin's statement in his brief paper, "The United States of Europe Slogan" of 1915, that it is "impossible freely to unite the nations in Socialism without a more or less prolonged and stubborn struggle of the Socialist republics against the other states." [10] More poignantly, Lenin wrote later: "We live not in a State, but in a system of States, and the existence of the Soviet Republic next to a number of imperialist States for a long time is *unthinkable*. In the end either the one or the other will have the better of it. Until that end comes, a series of most terrible conflicts between the Soviet Republic and the bourgeois States is *inevitable*. This proves that the ruling class, the proletariat, if it wants to and will rule, must prove this also by its military organization." Stalin, in his "Letter to Comrade Ivanov" of 1938 [11] quoted these words of Lenin approvingly. He also quoted himself, from his *Problems of Leninism,* where he had

---

are not conclusive in the generalized form in which they were presented. Yet he weakened his own arguments by a highly personal form of polemics (which Hayek did not deserve) and by somewhat cavalierly ignoring the true elements in Hayek's warnings. Assuming that democratic planning will never try to be all-comprehensive in the Soviet manner, Finer failed to discuss whether all-out socialistic planning could be done democratically; this remains, therefore, an open question between him and Hayek (and Lenin).

[10] "One-hundred Years of World Communism" (*op.cit.,* above) p. 29. Italics added.
[11] *Ibid.,* p. 151.

said that "the support of our revolution on the part of the workers in at least some countries, is an *indispensable condition* of the final victory of Socialism." To these quotations from former writings Stalin added the remark that this problem of making the victory of Socialism in the Soviet Union complete *"cannot* be solved . . . by the unaided efforts of our country alone," but that it "can be solved *only* by combining a serious effort of the international proletariat with a still more serious effort of the whole of the Soviet people." [12]

Later, Stalin tried to make the world forget these views. He then proclaimed, on several occasions, the possibility of peaceful coexistence. This new theory was forcefully taken up by Khrushchev in his speech of February 14, 1956, referred to above. There he said:

> It is alleged that the Soviet Union advocates the principle of peaceful coexistence exclusively from tactical considerations of the moment. However, it is well known that we have advocated peaceful coexistence just as perseveringly from the very inception of Soviet power. Hence, this is not a tactical stratagem but a fundamental principle of Soviet foreign policy.

He disclaimed any intention of the Soviet Union to interfere in the internal affairs of countries where a capitalist system exists.

> It is ridiculous to think that revolutions are made to order. When we say that in the competition between the two systems of capitalism and socialism, socialism will triumph, this by no means implies that the victory will be reached by armed intervention on the part of the Socialist countries in the internal affairs of the capitalist countries.
>
> We believe that after seeing for themselves the advantages that communism holds out, all working men and women on earth will sooner or later take to the road of the struggle to build a Socialist society. [But] we have always asserted and continue to assert that the establishment of a new social order in any country is the internal affair of its people.
>
> Such are our positions, based on the great teachings of Marxism-Leninism. The principle of peaceful coexistence is gaining increasingly wider international recognition. And this is logical, since there is no other way out in the present situation. Indeed, there are only two ways: either peaceful coexistence, or the most devastating war in history. There is no third alternative.

[12] *Ibid.*

He added that just to coexist peacefully is not enough. "There must be progress to better relations, to stronger confidence among them, to cooperation." He blamed imperialism rather than the differences in the economic systems as such for the danger threatening peace, accusing capitalism of inherent imperialism without of course even mentioning the imperialism inherent in communist theory and practice:

As will be recalled, there is a Marxist-Leninist premise which says that *while imperialism exists wars are inevitable*. While capitalism remains on earth the reactionary forces representing the interests of the capitalist monopolies will continue to strive for war gambles and aggression, and may try to let loose war.

But again, he no longer considered coexistence impossible:

There is no fatal inevitability of war. Now there are powerful social and political forces, commanding serious means capable of preventing the unleashing of war by the imperialists. . . .

From the scientific point of view it can only be frankly admitted that the coexistence of unmitigated totalitarian communism in one part of the world and of democratic freedom in other areas, and the rivalry of the two power groups in their efforts to maintain or expand their present influence, are likely sooner or later to end in war. But to say that it is *impossible* to avoid a global war through any method is not warranted; in this admission Khrushchev was scientifically more correct than were Lenin and the earlier Stalin.

CHAPTER XIII

TWENTIETH-CENTURY POLITICAL SCIENCE AND THE BELIEF IN GOD

1. Dual Objective of Inquiries into Religion

(a) RELIGION AS A RELEVANT POLITICAL FACTOR

WESTERN political scientists are in agreement that religion has been a historical factor of great force in the genesis of modern society. It has given our society much of its character and coherence, permeating human behavior in various ways, either directly or, through codes of morals and through customs shaped under religious influences, indirectly. Despite the great secularizing process that has taken place during the last four centuries, belief in God has continued to play a relevant role in political ideas, motivations, and institutions up to the present, illustrated by religious resistance to totalitarianism, the rise of separate governments in India and Pakistan, the birth of the state of Israel, and the lingering conflict about the status of Jerusalem.

As regards, more in particular, religion's interrelation with democracy, it is undeniable that, historically speaking, the rise of modern democracy was strongly influenced by the Jewish-Christian religious heritage. Even Karl Marx, no friend of religious dogmas and inclined to trace historical events to economic rather than religious reasons, acknowledged that "democracy is based on the principle of the sovereign worth of the individual, which, in turn, is based on the dream of Christianity that man has an immortal soul." [1] This is in line with the general findings of historians and political scientists on the role actually played by Christianity in the genesis of democracy.

Not only was this influence an indisputable historical fact. It may be doubted whether modern democracy, with its emphasis on the dignity of the individual person, could ever have arisen without religious impulses, and it is a legitimate question of political science to ask whether, even today, the formal devices of democratic government alone could hold society together without the cement of a common religious belief.

---

[1] This quotation, taken from the Marx-Engels Historical-Critical Edition, Karl Marx Institute, Moscow, vol. I, no. I, p. 590, was aptly referred to in the statement on the dignity of man issued by the Roman Catholic Bishops of the United States, November 21, 1953 (*New York Times*, November 22, p. 84).

1. DUAL OBJECTIVE OF INQUIRY

The view that democracy depends for its successful operation on a religious basis was restated by Ernest S. Griffith in a symposium, published in 1956, on the "Cultural Prerequisites to a Successfully Functioning Democracy."[2] He enumerated seven "attitudes" which he held were necessary to sustain democratic institutions. They are: love for and belief in freedom; participation in community life; integrity of discussion; freely assumed obligation of economic groups to serve society; leadership and officeholding regarded as public trusts; passions to be channeled to constructive ends; and friendliness and co-operation among nations. Each of these seven "necessary attitudes," he wrote, were "best based" upon the fundamental elements of religion in the Jewish-Christian tradition. He did not precisely say that these attitudes could *only* be based on religion, but merely that they were *best* based on it. His emphasis, however, was in the direction that democracy would be doomed if belief in God and reverence for God's will ceased to animate the great majority of the people.[3]

The two other discussants, Professors John Plamenatz of Oxford University and J. Roland Pennock of Swathmore College, while fully recognizing the role actually played by Christianity in the historical evolution and as a stimulating force, doubted that religion was indispensable for the functioning of democracy. They stressed the importance of institutions, which may survive their moral and cultural conditions for a considerable time (Plamenatz), the "interplay between attitudinal and institutional factors," and the relevance of social and economic conditions (Pennock). They enumerated many attitudes in addition to those mentioned by Griffith that were prerequisites to the proper functioning of modern democracy, such as: the desire to be self-governing; respect for the rights of others, for privacy, and for

[2] *American Political Science Review*, vol. 50 (March 1956) pp. 101 ff.
[3] A few quotations from Griffith's remarks may serve to illustrate the above. "It is my hypothesis that the Christian and Hebrew faiths constitute a powerful matrix, a common denominator, of those attitudes most essential to a flourishing democracy. Moreover, it would appear that it is these faiths, and especially the Christian faith, that perhaps alone can cloak such attitudes with the character of 'absolutes'—a character which is not only desirable, but perhaps even necessary to democratic survival" (p. 103). "A democracy whose economic groups and peoples have freedom but lack altruism is weak at its very heart and may well be doomed" (p. 110). Reason and patriotism are no adequate substitutes. "There really remains then only a conditioned humanitarianism as an adequate and safe outlet for passion, and only religion has historically been able to evoke this on a sufficiently wide scale to be effective" (p. 111). "Will anything less [than religion] suffice as a cultural prerequisite for sustaining a democratic socio-political order? If not, for which religions may we claim adequacy to sustain the democratic way? These are *coldly objective questions*. Let those who resist the author's line of reasoning and conclusions, at least face the obligation to answer them" (p. 115, italics not in the original).

personal independence; lack of servility; less subservience to authority than to public opinion; tendency to "prefer the system to the leaders produced by it" (Plamenatz); a sense of justice; a certain consensus and community of values, plus respect for rules and procedures (Pennock); and above all a willingness to peaceful settlement.[4] They emphasized the independence of all these attitudinal postulates, including Griffith's, from the motivating forces back of them, and voiced doubt whether religion was even the major motivating factor. In addition, they eloquently referred to the fact that authoritarian societies too have profited from Christianity, and that "liberty has been more often suppressed than defended in the name of religion" (Pennock). "A good Christian need not be a democrat, nor a good democrat a Christian," said Plamenatz.

To deal with the latter objection first, it is obvious that Christianity has been a firm buttress of many an authoritarian government, including that of the late Roman emperors, who would hardly have espoused the Christian creed had not its teachings, especially of submission to earthly authorities, made government easier for them. But whether other regimes have benefited from Christianity and whether *they* could have functioned without a truly religious basis—modern totalitarianism seems able to do so, at least for some time—is quite irrelevant for an inquiry into the specific problem of whether *democracy* can get along without the religious impulse.

To answer this question in the negative without reservations would amount to setting up another of those claims of "impossibility" with which the preceding chapter dealt. That would be hard to prove beyond question. But if what is contended is not impossibility but merely the presence of a definite danger or *risk*—the danger or risk that the decay of religious loyalties may go hand in hand with a decadence of those ethical attitudes which are essential for the functioning of democracy—then it must be admitted that the evidence is substantial, since it can be shown, first, that democracy *is* in need of a constant injection of ethical impulses, and second, that these impulses—within the framework of the typically democratic institutions and attitudes—were supplied in the past, and are still being supplied, chiefly by religious feelings.[5] Griffith's opponents hardly did more than state—and

---

[4] Whether tolerance, too, was essential remained controversial; Plamenatz referred to the absence of *inner* tolerance in many democrats, as for example the typical puritan. See above, Chapter VIII, Section 8.

[5] See also W. E. Hocking, *The Coming World Civilization*, New York 1956, pp. 1–20, and Reinhold Niebuhr, *The Children of Light and the Children of Darkness*, New York 1944.

correctly so—that a genuine "impossibility" of adequate ethical support forthcoming from other than religious sources has not been shown. But until those other sources are proved ready to take over, and to be as universal and potent in character as the religious motive, the warning cannot be dismissed as unjustified.

Publication of the symposium in the official journal of the American Political Science Association shows professional recognition that such questions are within the scope of political science. In view of the important role played by religion in many public affairs, political science must indeed be concerned with religion. To disregard the religious factor would often mean to distort reality and to base analysis and conclusions on defective data. Whenever religion enters political motivations it becomes part of the subject matter of political science.

(b) RELIGION AS A SOURCE OF KNOWLEDGE

But to say that religion as a social phenomenon is a relevant factor for political science is not the same as saying that religion is a prerequisite for the scientist's own understanding of reality. However absurd a primitive tribe's religious ideas may be, the political scientist must take stock of the fact that the tribesmen entertain such beliefs and must study the influence this has on their political actions. But in doing so he must keep clear of their superstitions in his own scientific judgments and predictions if he wants to fulfill his scientific function well. Is it any different with the higher forms of religious belief?

It cannot be said that belief in God is "scientifically untenable"; to this point we shall revert in the next section since it is controversial. But neither can God's existence be scientifically established. Scholars who follow Scientific Method have, therefore, felt it their duty as scientists to take no stand in this matter. When special aspects of their political topics of inquiry have forced them to describe and analyze religious ideas and emotions, they have often tried to do so in a manner which did not reveal whether they themselves believe in God. Not only have many done so individually; they have come to consider it the professional duty of all scholars in their professional work to keep free from religious motivations, denouncing as unscholarly the attitude of any scientist who mixes religious arguments into his scholarly presentations.

This prevailing attitude of twentieth-century political science was epitomized by the impatient stricture with which a brilliant young social scientist not many years ago interrupted a colleague who had referred to God. "God, in a scientific discussion," exclaimed the listener, "is a superstition." We shall come back to this challenge below.

(c) RECENCY OF THE DISTINCTION

Let it first be noted, however, that our present radical distinction between religion as a subject matter of scientific inquiry and religion as a source of knowledge is a relatively recent development. Through the greatest part of recorded history the interconnection between knowledge (science) and religion was as close in method as it was in subject matter. At a time when the gods were thought of as entering the struggle between nations, or when the people of Israel were organizing their political and legal systems in accord with the law given them by the Lord, or when the early Roman emperors claimed to be gods and were being worshipped as such, God or the gods had their overt place in social theory. Again, when the medieval church claimed superiority in secular matters, God was placed right in the center of political thought, and when emperors and kings had themselves crowned and anointed by priests, when they assumed the attribute "by the grace of God" and strutted in the glory of the divine rights of kings, God remained a leading argument in the underlying theory.

Even when it had become fashionable to avoid direct quotations from the Bible as scientific proof, God's finger was hardly questioned in references to the Law of Nature, to a-priori principles, or to the World Spirit, the *Volk* Spirit, and the like. Most of the fundamental principles referred to in academic works on state and government until the end of the nineteenth century can easily be traced to the religious heritage. It was customary to reject as "Machiavellian" any frankly amoral scientific approach, to leave insistence on facts to the natural sciences, and to ignore as outsiders any author, such as Comte and Marx, who rejected metaphysical lines of thought. Actually, even Comte and Marx had remained under the influence of religious chiliastic ideas.

Of course, university professors could not equally ignore Immanuel Kant, this great insider of the academic world, who in his *Critique of Pure Reason* laid the foundations for what later came to be called scientific agnosticism, the impossibility of proving or disproving God with scientific means.[6] But in academic debates there emerged two Kants rather

---

[6] See the famous passage in the preface to the second edition: "Thus I had to remove (deny) *knowledge* in order to obtain room for *belief*" ("Ich musste also das *Wissen* aufheben, um zum *Glauben* Platz zu bekommen").

than only Kant I, the author of the theoretical Critique. Kant II, in his *Critique of Practical Reason* and elsewhere, had established his "categorical imperative," had formulated the moral law that was "as certain as if it were a factum," and had elaborated his doctrine of the "necessary regulative principles" (see above, Chapters v, Section 7, and ix, Sections 1 and 5). Therefore, religious absolutists as well as scientific relativists could refer to the sage of Königsberg, and both continue to do so to the present day.

It is true that legal positivism, which banned acceptance of religious dogmas as valid laws, spread among Western lawyers long before 1900, conquering also the academic lecture halls. But it did not interfere with religious elements in the theory of the state. It dealt with the *power* to make laws, not with the *motives* for making them, and hence did not question the pertinence of religious motivations in lawmaking. John Austin, one of the fathers of modern legal positivism, explicitly accepted the law of God as a standard for legislation, as we have seen in a different context (Chapter v, Section 3). Characteristically, this religious statement of his was relegated to a mere footnote within the two volumes of his famous work. But if only in a small footnote, God was still there in political theory a hundred years ago.

Only when, around the turn of the century, the radical dichotomy was evolving in the social sciences between propositions of Is and of Ought and between facts and value, only then did the methodic purification of the social sciences from all nonscientific elements gain momentum. And only thereafter did it become a professional convention that all direct and indirect references to religious revelation or religious intuition as evidence in scientific discussions must be avoided.

(d) HAS THE PENDULUM SWUNG TOO FAR?

Thus the pendulum swung to the other extreme, complete abstinence from any discussion of metaphysical questions. This went beyond what was required by Scientific Method and Scientific Value Relativism. For these would not have prevented scientists from engaging in "reflections" and "speculations" about the conceivable alternatives back of the sensually observable world, so long as such reflections and speculations were clearly marked as hypothetic (Chapter vii, Section 3). But typical twentieth-century scholars tended to avoid *any* discussions about the Beyond, even those of a scientifically unobjectionable character, at least to avoid them in their professional teachings and writings.

461

It is merely a graphic illustration of this carefully maintained abstinence that the symposium mentioned above, which came so close to
metaphysical issues, strictly limited itself to the problem whether popular belief in God was a prerequisite for the functioning of democracy,
without inquiring whether or not such belief was tenable in view of
modern scientific developments. It rather exposed the audience to the
fallacy that, if religious faith was necessary for true democracy, this
fact alone would vindicate such faith, since democracy was the most
desirable form of government. Scientifically speaking, of course, this
would not follow, any more than it should have followed at Cicero's
time that the traditional belief of republican Rome in the old gods and
rituals was scientifically tenable on the ground that its maintenance
had become a prerequisite for the coherence of Roman society. If democracy cannot function without a substantial dose of popular belief
in God, then this proves neither the scientific tenability of religious
faith nor the eminence of democracy. Other approaches are required
for an answer to either question.

The following sections will deal more closely with some aspects of
the scientific abstinence from discussions of God's reality, a certain
weakness of present-day social science resulting therefrom, and the
scientific dignity of such discussions. As in the title of this chapter,
I shall speak of "belief in God" rather than of "religion," since the latter term has come to be stretched to the extent that it does not presuppose belief in God.

2. The Scientific Convention of Bracketing
the Divine Alternative

(a) METHODOLOGICAL GROUNDS

The twentieth-century convention of condemning as unscientific any
contribution to scientific discussions that blends scientific and religious
arguments is rooted in the conviction, arrived at by some philosophers
in the eighteenth century or even earlier and now generally accepted
by professional social scientists, that it is impossible to prove the
existence of God in an intersubjectively conclusive manner.

Dealing with this subject one has to be particularly careful in the
use of words ("God," "existence") and other symbols of communication (intonation, style). There are obviously a number of sub-alterna-
tives on the side of God's existence according to the kind of God one
has in mind. As Ernest Hocking put it: "The question, Do you be-

lieve in God? will seldom get a direct answer from a thoughtful contemporary without the preliminary counter-question, What do you mean by God? And many a man, including many a scientist, . . . is ready to use the word God or Deity if you allow him to define it in his own way." [1] In our present context (denial of intersubjective demonstrability) the term "God" is meant to refer to any kind of a supreme (supra-human) being equipped with the power to think, to plan, and to act, and thought of as the creator either of the entire universe or, at least, of the moral world ("the good ")."

If someone calls the universe itself, or the laws governing it, "God," but denies that this God can think, plan, and act spontaneously, he uses the term in a meaning different from that attached to it here. He too, of course, denies the intersubjective demonstrability of God in the sense in which this chapter speaks of God. But the significant question in our present context is whether there is a Deity able, according to its own spontaneous decisions, to exercise some kind of influence on the happenings in the world, and that has actually used this power, should it even have done so only in the past and in advance. It is in particular the existence of such a Deity which it has been considered impossible to prove, and whose potential workings twentieth-century scientific convention, therefore, has excluded from scientific argument.

The term "existence" has sometimes been given the limited meaning of a finite and temporary phenomenon and can then, of course, not properly be applied to the infinite and eternal. Instead, one would have to speak of God's "being," of his "reality" or "actuality." For our present purpose, however, all these terms may be used interchangeably in distinction from the alternative that what we call God is merely a product of our imagination and that there actually is no God.

Another, though minor, point may be mentioned about symbols. It has become customary to capitalize words that refer to God, such as "He" and "Him." This I shall not do here, because the present chapter deals with the scientific question of God's reality and, therefore, should not give the answer surreptitiously in the style of printing. Even so, capitalizing the noun God is justified in order to distinguish the idea of one God from that of a plurality of gods.

In line with the widely accepted impotence of science to prove God's reality, all deductive arguments that start with the recognition of God and with the allotment of definite attributes to him, such as

---

[1] W. E. Hocking, *Science and the Idea of God*, Chapel Hill 1944, pp. 14, 15.
[2] For further discussion, see Appendix B.

absolute goodness, absolute knowledge, and absolute power, have come to be considered "not scientific." This negative predicate, as we have seen, was extended in due course to any absolute value judgments about good and evil, because they either referred in ultimate analysis to some metaphysical order whose ontological reality could not be demonstrated intersubjectively in a conclusive manner, or were unwarranted logical inferences from Is to Ought.

Twentieth-century science has equally recognized, however, that it is impossible to prove that there is no God and, consequently, to *dis*prove the absolute validity of ethical postulates founded in God's reality. Our scientific thinking, in other words, still faces two basic alternatives—that God is or that he is not—both beyond scientific demonstrability. In deciding to limit our scientific work to the negative alternative alone, and to keep the other "bracketed," we have not eliminated the latter. This is the fundamental situation.

The use of the term "bracket" in this context is not customary, but seems most appropriate. As discussed in Chapter ix, Section 6, the word was introduced into philosophical language by Edmund Husserl in the pursuit of his "phenomenological reduction"—the attempt to decribe what remains when we leave the external world out in the description of our reaction to it. Similarly, the term is here used for the intentional disregard of something (the divine alternative) the reality of which is neither affirmed nor denied but merely excluded from consideration.

Within the last sixty years political science has to such an extent assumed the habit of bracketing the divine alternative that it now seems to many students as if science is taking God's nonbeing for granted, and as if doing so was the only respectable scholarly attitude. But this amounts to a shallow fallacy, doubly objectionable when it is succumbed to by scholars who are proud of their logical severity. If there is a God, to bracket him out of our field of attention is not the same as to eliminate him from reality, however long we continue the bracketing technique.

(b) MATERIAL GROUNDS

This simple methodological situation is, however, complicated by the fact that the ascendancy of demands for greater methodological severity in the social sciences happened to coincide historically with the victorious expansion of astronomic, physical, chemical, and biological knowledge. The ensuing growth of confidence in science, along with the rise of Darwinism, materialism—Marxian or non-Marxian —and an optimistic belief in automatic progress, gravely shook traditional naïve conceptions of God.

This historical coincidence led to a fusion of purely methodological grounds for the bracketing of the divine alternative with substantive arguments against God's reality. Many people, including scholars of great reputation, have come to think that the disregard of the divine alternative in modern social theory is justified, not merely for methodological reasons, but also on the ground that, if the question is investigated with scientific honesty, the reality of a personal God, who thinks, plans, and acts independently, though it may not be completely disprovable, is highly *unlikely*.[3]

"Can anyone suppose," writes MacIver, "that the prophets and preachers of earlier days would have maintained their now sanctified doctrines of God and the universe had they known anything about the amazing cosmos revealed to us by modern science?" Obviously, their religious teachings would have been different, he argues. They would not have conceived of God as a tribal deity. But MacIver goes farther. "They would not, in a more audacious and magnificent feat of imagination, have conceived that the Universal God sent 'His only begotten Son' on earth in the form of a man, to be hung on a cross in order that, through some magical principle of compensation, the race of men might be 'saved.'" The author acknowledges that mankind has a "natural hunger for religion," that science is no substitute for religion, and that, therefore, religion "will not die." But, so he asks, "Can anyone believe that the creeds of today will be the creeds of men a thousand, a million years from now?" He rather waits for a new religion, a religion whose joys "lie in the contemplation of the style of the universe, searching out the heights and depths that everywhere within it may be found," and whose divinity is "immanent in the allness to which we humbly belong." This, though it still may be called religion in a broader sense, is no longer belief in God, in the sense of a God who can think, plan, and act spontaneously and independently. Belief in a personal God is being discarded, not merely

[3] So, e.g., Barbara Wootton in her *Testament for Social Science—An Essay in the Application of Scientific Method*, New York 1951, p. 87, where she speaks "of the two great superstitions of the Western world—Christianity and Marxism," also p. 185; and R. M. MacIver, *The Pursuit of Happiness—A Philosophy for Modern Living*, New York 1955. See also Albert Einstein, *Out of My Later Years*, New York 1950, p. 28.

for methodological reasons, but because it is considered unlikely that there is such a God.[4]

MacIver's explicit statement on this matter is one of the few that have been forthcoming from typical twentieth-century social scientists. Characteristically, he included it in a literary by-product from his pen rather than in one of his major scientific works. It seems, however, to express what is at the bottom of the thought of many other social scientists.

There can be no doubt that such thinking has tended to strengthen the inclination to interpret the bracketed God as a nonexistent God. We must be aware of this confusing mixture of methodological and material arguments and must try to disentangle them. This task we cannot leave to the theologians and philosophers, because we are dealing here, not primarily with the meaning of God, but with the meaning and scope of science, and of political science in particular.

It should first be noted, however, that there are today not only social scientists who consider it more likely that there is no God. Many hold the opposite view. Some of these, like Jacques Maritain, Eric Voegelin, and John Hallowell, are not "typical" representatives of twentieth-century social science, it is true; they oppose Scientific Method because of its exclusion of metaphysics from science (Chapter VII, Sections 3 and 4). But adherents of Scientific Method and Scientific Value Relativism, too, not infrequently confess to their belief in God in private conversations. One of the most amazing facts about personal religious convictions, however, is the following. Only a minority of people in present-day Western society, scientists as well as others, seem *always* to consider it certain or more likely that there is a God, or that there is none. Most people, so it seems, are sometimes certain while at other times they doubt; or they are sometimes certain of the one answer and sometimes of the other; or they are in doubt all the time. Not a few shift aimlessly between the two extremes.

Doubt has overcome not only many believers, but many atheists as well. While it has often been noted that modern science has led to confessions of doubt by people who classify themselves basically as believers, it seems to have escaped notice that modern science has also produced a large class of what may be called "doubting atheists"—people who once were atheists pure and simple, and who still today would

[4] The quotations are from *The Pursuit of Happiness* (cited above), pp. 153–54, 156, 160. See also MacIver's remarks on the unlikelihood that prayers can change events by causing God's intervention, pp. 149–50.

classify themselves basically as such, but who now admit to some degree of doubt because they have come to see the limitations of science. This doubt of atheists is as much a result of modern science as is that of believers, and science should receive as much credit for the one as it has attracted blame for the other.

To find out approximately how many people in a given society or group are in the various categories—those who always believe there is a God or always that there is none, or sometimes the one and sometimes the other, or sometimes believe and sometimes merely doubt or do not care—could well be made the objective of a research project based on a particularly careful type of interviewing and sampling. But not only would it be hard to get representative cross sections of the people to be honest in such matters, even with anonymity entirely guaranteed, there is the additional great obstacle that people themselves often do not know what they really believe or hold to be likely. Many have an indirect form of belief: they trust the Church, and the Church believes in God, so they indirectly believe in God without questioning.

If, in view of these difficulties, estimates are at all permissible, I would think that MacIver goes too far when he writes, "Men do not believe, but often dare not really disbelieve. They live and think in a twilight zone between belief and unbelief." [5] It is my own tentative estimate that in a big modern city like New York out of a hundred people an average of about twenty always believe in the existence of God, another ten to twenty always in his nonexistence, and the balance, i.e., about sixty to seventy, sometimes do and sometimes do not believe, or doubt always. In sections where people are not used to independent thinking in religious matters figures differ. I have often asked adult groups, graduate and others, whether they agreed with this estimate on the basis of their own impressions, and have never met with a determined challenge.

Whatever estimate may be correct, we obviously cannot count heads in order to determine the degree of likelihood. Can we speak of the greater likelihood of God's existence or of his nonexistence in some scientifically more meaningful sense?

(c) CRITIQUE OF ARGUMENTS FROM LIKELIHOOD

When we call some nonrecurrent fact or event "likely" we mean that there are stronger reasons for than against acceptance of a proposi-

[5] *Op.cit.*, p. 156.

tion asserting the truth of the alleged fact or the actual occurrence of the event. "It is likely that I shall travel to Europe next summer" means that the reasons according to which it can be expected that I shall travel outweigh those according to which the opposite must be expected. We often say "probable" instead of "likely" in such cases. This makes little difference; but as the former term has been used predominantly for statistical propositions regarding recurrent or repeatable events I prefer "likely" whenever reference to only one fact or event is intended.

Even in reference to a singular fact or event we may use figures to describe the respective weight of the reasons or causal factors, speaking of a fifty-fifty likelihood when the weight seems equal, or of ninety-ten where the likelihood is very strong. We may, in minor matters, emphasize our estimate by betting dollar against dollar, or nine dollars against one, that our assumption or prediction is correct. But we generally do not, when we are calling an individual fact or event likely, mean thereby that in a "series" of similar cases there will be fifty-one, sixty, or ninety, out of a hundred in which our assumption or prediction will prove correct. We generally do not think of such a series. At times we may be willing to see our estimate translated into statistical language for recurrent events, but in speaking of one individual event we generally do not intend that meaning, and in some cases such translation is hardly at all possible. So it is when we speak of the likelihood that there is a God, or that there is none. Here we do not even indirectly mean, and scarcely could mean, that in a series of similar problems there will be such and such an average of our being right. Nevertheless, even here we may speak of the degree of liklihood in the sense of the comparative weight of the reasons pro and con.

This distinction between the likelihood of individual factors or events and the probable distribution of factors in a *series* is not, however, our chief problem here. The major problem is the sense in which we can call any likelihood or probability "scientific."

When we speak of "scientific" likelihood we can only mean that the *scientific* reasons in favor of one answer are stronger than those in favor of the other. We are then compelled to distinguish between scientific and nonscientific reasons. In what sense can we do so? Scientific Method certainly does not entirely bar considerations of likelihood. A scientific problem is often chosen, an assumption made, a working hypothesis formed, on the basis of a mere hunch. Even the acceptance as "facts" of the results of careful observations, and the (final) acceptance as "law" of a hypothesis after observations and tests have confirmed it, is based in ultimate analysis on likelihood or probability in many if not all cases (Chapters I, Section 5, and II, Section 6). There can be no demurrer, therefore, to reflections on likelihood in general on grounds of scientific principle. But it is necessary to distinguish the various stages of the scientific process in which estimates of likelihood are used, and to separate what in each stage can or cannot serve as a legitimate base for such estimates.

In the initial, or preparatory, stages of scientific inquiry—those of choosing a problem, making an avowed assumption, forming a working hypothesis—the scholar's freedom to follow any hunches he entertains is almost unlimited. As soon, however, as he enters the specifically scientific operations of controlled observation, description, testing, and so on, and presents the results of his labors as science, he is—if he follows Scientific Method—constrained to limit the selection of factors which he uses for drawing his conclusions. He can then refer only to "intersubjectively transmissible data." As discussed in Chapters II, Section 7, and VII, Section 3, there are good reasons for this technical use of the term "science," although we cannot compel every scholar to submit to this terminology. I do not propose to repeat the argument here. I only wish to point to the necessity that, once we have decided to use the term "science" only for intersubjectively transmissible knowledge, we must be consistent and *keep to this use in discussing scientific likelihood*. That is to say that we must exclude from the argument regarding what is or what is not likely any data as nonscientific that are not intersubjectively transmissible, and especially any merely personal inclination to believe or disbelieve. If we do so, we shall find that Scientific Method fails not only to offer full proof for God's reality or for its opposite, but even to establish any higher degree of likelihood in either direction.

When we refer to our personal subjective estimate, based on our personal external and internal experiences, or choose to speak in terms of a science that admits intersubjectively nontransmissible arguments (S_2 = *scientia sive vera sive putativa sed non transmissibilis*), things may look very different. Then we may feel that we have reached, if not full certainty, at least an overwhelming indication of likelihood regarding the truth of either the one or the other alternative. Yet whenever it comes to intersubjective demonstration we cannot make our individual inferences of likelihood conclusive for someone who disagrees in good faith. However far we have penetrated into the expanding universe and into the inner life of atoms, the ultimate question of how all this came about cannot be answered by science except in alternatives. Forces were set going either by a creator, or by events that do not presuppose a creator and still were miraculously creative. If you reject the one alternative, you claim the other to be true, without offering any scientific proof for it. Any intersubjectively transmissible argument in favor of the one alternative can be matched by one for the other. Both are equally likely, or equally unlikely, in scientific terms. In other words, the question of God or no God is scientifically (in an intersubjective sense) still in the same fifty-fifty balance in which it has been as long as we have been able to examine the evidence with scientific means.

This is by no means necessarily so. If God is a reality and not merely a product of our imagination, he might make his reality known to us, not only individually, as religious persons claim he often does, but also in signs and acts that are intersubjectively unmistakable. Most creeds tell us that God once did so, and that he will do so again on the day of Last Judgment. Then there was, or then there will be, no fifty-fifty balance of the scientific scales.

"Then, if any one says to you, 'Lo, here is the Christ!' or 'There he is!' do not believe it. For false Christs and false prophets will arise and show great signs and wonders, so as to lead astray. . . . Lo, I have told you beforehand. So if they say to you, 'Lo, he is in the wilderness,' do not go out; if they say, 'Lo, he is in the inner rooms,' do not believe it. For as the lightning comes from the east and shines as far as the west, so will be the coming of the Son of Man." [6]

But within the span of our modern scientific age, the fifty-fifty balance has prevailed. To put it otherwise, we are confronted with the near-paradox that God's reality may some day be scientifically evident, but that if there be no God we shall never know that for certain. No discovery is even imaginable that would exclude the alternative explanation that there is a God back of all things and of all laws of nature. In popular parlance, we may some day know God's existence, but we can never know his nonexistence.

I shall not here go more deeply into the efforts of believers to offer

---

[6] Matthew 24:23–27. Similarly, Luke 17:22–24, where the last passage reads, "For as the lightning flashes and lights up the sky from one side to the other, so will the son of Man be in his day."

conclusive ontological evidence for the greater likelihood of the positive alternative. These arguments always cease to be scientific in the intersubjective meaning of the term at some relevant point. (See Chapters II, Section 7, and XII, Section 4.) In our present context—motivations for the professional habit of bracketing the divine alternative—it is not necessary to go more deeply into the positive arguments. But it is appropriate to discuss two pseudoscientific arguments that have been advanced for the greater likelihood of the *negative,* because they have been particularly influential.

In the first place, many students think that he who proposes to open the brackets must first prove the existence of God. He who contends that something is there, so it is argued, has the "burden of proof" for its being there. He is not permitted to shift the burden to those who deny that it is there. This is assumed to be a scientific principle, but wrongly so. It is a legal principle, not a scientific one. A defendant whose guilt is not proved ought not to be punished. Even if there be full evidence that one of two persons has committed some particular murder, but it cannot be proved which of the two, neither should be sentenced. This is not to say, however, that neither has committed the crime, and if only a few criminals can be condemned, this does not aver that there are only a few criminals. It says nothing about the factual truth.

Scientifically, we cannot speak of any particular burden of proof for one of two alternatives if both are mysterious. And this is precisely the situation with regard to the question of God or no God. If one could speak at all of a burden of proof—an obligation to present an intersubjectively conclusive scientific proof—for the How and Why of first things, we could only state that both, believers and nonbelievers, are in default. That burden would then rest on the shoulders of both, not merely of one.

Another pseudoscientific reason, often given for disregarding the divine alternative in scientific discussions, is the alleged likelihood that God would show himself more distinctly if he existed. The very fifty-fifty balance of scientific knowledge in religious matters is here used as an argument in favor of the greater likelihood of the negative alternative, because if there should be a God it is unlikely that he would leave it at that. He would tip the scientific scales in favor of his existence. It would be, so to speak, unfair of God to foil all our scientific efforts, all our searching for conclusive evidence.

But this argument leads us no further. It may be effective against the assumption of an "impatient" God, but has no force against the belief in a "patient" one, who operates from within. It is not difficult to conceive of an explanation why God, if real, does not allow the fifty-fifty balance of scientific (intersubjectively verifiable) research to be disturbed. Could his reality be proved scientifically, there would be no moral significance in our individually recognizing him from the bottom of our individual experience, or in our individually wrestling with the problem. If Heaven and Hell stood visibly before our scientific eyes, there would be little merit in our being good and avoiding evil. "It would be an unbearable sight," wrote Jakob Burckhardt at the end of his reflections on world history, "if owing to a consistent historical record of all good people always being rewarded and all bad ones always being punished down here below, all the bad people would begin to behave well on grounds of expediency. . . . One might well get into the mood then of asking Heaven to let some of the bad ones go unpunished on earth, so that at least the others might show their true character. . . . There is anyway enough make-believe in the world." [7]

Again, if only the advanced scholar could reach God with scientific methods, there would be a blatantly unfair difference between the fortunate few who are able to study toward the higher degrees and the masses who cannot understand the advanced ways of science. Hence, when we think of God as the creator who wants to test us individually, it seems almost necessary to conceive of him as leaving the fifty-fifty balance of *scientific* efforts undisturbed. It would be appropriate here to refer to Kierkegaard, who expressed some of his finest thoughts on this very question, and also to a passage in St. Paul's Epistle to the Corinthians (1:21), where he wrote: "In the wisdom of God, the world did not know God through wisdom," that is, through science. But we have elected to concentrate on twentieth-century political science, and it may, therefore, suffice to state that Scientific Method holds no warrant which could authorize it to attribute more scientific likelihood to God's nonexistence than to his existence, or vice versa.

The foregoing is not meant to say that every type of religious belief is exempt from scientific criticism. If someone should infer from the fact that the same people sometimes do and sometimes do not believe in God the conclusion that sometimes there is a God and at other times none, a sort of "quantum-god," as it were, now being, now not being; or that what there is is half-a-God-half-not-a-God; then science

[7] Jakob Burckhardt, *Weltgeschichtliche Betrachtungen*, Bern 1905, p. 266.

would be entitled to reject such inference as illogical and the conclusion as in conflict with likelihood. It is scientifically likely, to say the least, that there is a God either always or never. This is in itself quite important to realize, for a political scientist as much as for anyone else. It shows the radical type of alternative before us. But science cannot relieve us of the personal choice.

Likewise, we may reject as "scientifically unlikely" some low type of superstition whose human origin and primitive absurdity can be intersubjectively exposed, such as the belief that an eclipse of the moon is a sign of God's wrath, or that the future depends on our touching wood. We can reject as scientifically untenable the belief that the world is only four thousand years old. But we cannot summarily speak of any greater likelihood that there is a suprasensual Creator-God or that there is none, as long as we base our arguments exclusively on intersubjectively transmissible points.

It follows that scholars who fail to keep the two alternatives in their own mind as well as in the awareness of their students distort the basis of all our *scientific* work. If God is a superstition in science, no-God is as much of a superstition. Either alternative is indemonstrable; neither is scientifically more likely than the other; either is, scientifically speaking, a mere assumption, a mere hypothesis.

3. *Scientific Uses of Unbracketing the Divine Alternative*

Since the assumption of God's reality is, scientifically speaking, no worse than that of an entirely nondivine origin of world and man, the latter being as much a mere hypothesis as the former, we may unbracket the alternative of God's reality in our scientific work at any time. To do that does not in itself imply abandoning the merits of modern Scientific Method. It is scientifically justified to base reflection and research on some *avowed* assumption or hypothesis. We may, therefore, give the assumption, the hypothesis, of God's reality a scientifically legitimate place in our scholarly work. We expose ourselves to justified criticism unless we do so in proper measure in our corporate work as political scientists. But what is the use of such exercise? What difference does it make?

First of all, it helps us to correct the confusion caused by the methodological fallacy of equating the bracketed God with an eliminated God. It helps us to restore a sense of scientific honesty, of balance and of depth.

473

But this is not all. Many a scientific hypothesis that could never be completely verified has done great service in the development of science by drawing our attention to aspects that had been overlooked. Darwin's hypothesis drew our attention to the laws of heredity and to the significance of mutations; Hegel's, to the historical sequence of thesis, antithesis, and synthesis; Marx's to the influence of economic conditions on ideologies; Freud's to the subconscious; and others to other factors. Just so, and no less effectively, does the assumption of God's reality draw our attention to phenomena, to implications and consequences of actions or omissions, and to alternatives of action, that otherwise are easily overlooked.

The hypothetic assumption that there is a God may, for example, cause us to center attention on such factors or problems as these: the apparently irrepressible nature of metaphysical longings (see Kant's remarks, above, Chapter II, Section 5); the finest concatenations between evil and unhappiness (see Chapter XII, Section 6), between repentance and inward growth; the limits of psychoanalysis;[1] the inner moral logic of historical events; the long-range good effects versus the more obvious short-term failures of what we call goodness; the ultimate frustrations of many human ambitions; the lack of any sustained historical attempt to build political behavior on principles of goodness, love, and sympathy rather than on cleverness, selfishness, antipathy, and lust for domination; the over-evaluation of technical progress as a source of happiness; the possibility that the fate of nations and even of entire civilizations may be relatively insignificant before God—if God is real—as compared with the tests to which historical events constantly put each individual; the understanding of high-strung nationalism as an outlet of the yearning for unconditional devotion, as a poor ersatz-religion, and many more such vistas.

Speculative reflections of this kind—some perhaps more plausible than others, but scientifically all merely tentative as is every scientific hypothesis—may in turn lead to concrete research projects that are within the reach of scientific attack. They may inspire, for example, systematic efforts to disclose through competent empirical research inescapable elements in our human thinking and feeling, elements that by their omnipresence establish a factual bridge between Ought and Is in man (Chapters IX and X). Or they may stimulate research on

---

[1] See, e.g., the profound chapter "Psychology and the Cure of Souls" in W. E. Hocking, *Science and the Idea of God, op.cit.*, pp. 27 ff., and similar remarks in Maritain, *Scholasticism and Politics, op.cit.*

the influence of humility, of truthfulness, and of genuine friendliness in human relations, including international relations; or on the collapse of vanity and wantonness in short-term and long-term perspectives. They may lead to the distinction of spheres of success and of failure in revolutions or in ambitious five-year plans and the like; and to the consideration of hundred-year plans, more modestly conceived, that do not disregard either human corruptibility or human metaphysical yearnings.

Hence scientific reflections on the divine alternative and its implications are by no means foredoomed to infertility. They may act as a stimulus toward more subtle observations than those made before, as a prompter of meaningful scientific questions, and above all, as a protection from pseudoscientific lopsidedness.

The liberation of the social sciences from religious tutelage was a tremendous achievement, attained only after a long and heavy struggle against deeply entrenched forces, with innumerable and grave sacrifices. It is not difficult, therefore, to understand why the social sciences are watching over the preservation of their liberty from religious dogma with a jealous and suspicious zeal, always fearful lest they be reduced once more to a state of bondage under dogma. By now, however, this liberation has been secured to such an extent, and it has been so firmly guaranteed by constitutional and procedural devices in democratic countries, that we need no longer be afraid that every discussion of the divine alternative will tend to entangle us in some new dependence on religious dogma. There is greater danger today that science might become subservient to atheistic dogmas—they are dogmas too—or to some nationalistic substitute-dogma, than to any theistic doctrine.

It is, I submit, an absurd academic situation that students have to go today to professors of theology, to universities run by churches, to some Union Theological Seminary, or to holiday sermons, in order to engage in a discussion—sometimes shallow, but at other times profound and absorbing—of the alternative of God's reality and of the light it might shed on political events, while our secular schools of social sciences deal only with the other alternative. The great natural scientists of our time are more readily inclined to take account of the divine alternative than are social scientists, who seem to be duped by their own methodological conventions and thereby bereave themselves and their students of some of the greatest adventures of ideas.

This is no plea for a surrender of the negative religious alternative to the positive one; it is a plea only for due recognition of both. After fifty years of bracketing God we should by now be mature enough sometimes to remove the brackets, or to shift them occasionally from the positive to the negative alternative, therewith acknowledging God's latent place in twentieth-century political theory.

Yet whenever we do so we must continue to discharge our scientific function well—the function of the scientist to distinguish severely between mere speculations, hypotheses, assumptions, and personal beliefs on the one side, and scientifically established data, capable of inter-subjective transmission, on the other.

4. *Doubt and Faith in the Scholar*

Science is a stern mistress. Yet it might be said of her what Wordsworth said of Duty: "Nor know we anything so fair as is the smile upon thy face."

To give equal scientific weight to both alternatives, God's reality and his nonreality, is easy for the great number of doubting Thomases —both doubting theists and doubting atheists—but difficult for men with strong convictions, theists as well as atheists. Is it asking too much of them? The interrelation of doubt and faith in the twentieth-century scholar should be subjected to closer scrutiny than has been generally devoted to this problem. A few words may be added here under the assumption that the scholar believes in God.

Most believers would admit that their faith has different strength at different times. But the scholar seems to be compelled to doubt by the clock. When the class signal sounds, doubt time is there; when it sounds again, faith may return. Or does the believer, when in class, merely pretend to doubt in order to remain a scholar of acceptable standing in a twentieth-century university?

I would like to present a different phenomenological description. It seems that certainty and doubt can exist in the same person at the same time. This experience applies to many spheres of life, including the religious sphere. It sounds like a denial of the first axiom of logic, which states that if something is true—for example, that I am doubting—the opposite cannot be true at the same time—namely, that I am not doubting. Yet, axiom or no axiom, phenomenologically both can be observed to occur at the same time.

It seems to happen in the following manner, which I may be permitted to describe at first in poetic language. Two layers seem to feed the fount of subjective knowledge; knowledge surges up from two layers. In the one Doubt lives, the lad, in the other, Certainty (or Confidence), the dame. Certainty in her layer remains quite unaffected by the soliloquies of Doubt. Conversely, Doubt, in his, is not moved by the sound of the organ he hears in the heart down below. However much she beams and smiles, Certainty does not fully succeed in driving the other fellow out. He goes on doubting, in his layer, astonished that Certainty in hers remains undisturbed. After this has gone on for many years, both have abandoned all attempts at mutual conversion. They live like uninterested, but tolerant, neighbors in their separate layers. Doubt likes to muse that sometime soon there will be the great day when the long contest will be decided; after death either he or Certainty will be the victor. But then it occurs to him that, if he was right in doubting, he will not know his triumph. To realize this sad fact can make Doubt doubt doubt. Certainty is better off in this respect. "I shall not feel it, should I draw defeat. But, winning, bliss awaits me infinite," she might say.[1]

Methodologically speaking, what I have been doing in these figurative musings, as distinct from the preceding sections of this chapter, is to present the results of phenomenological self-observation regarding the interrelation between scholarly doubt and religious certainty. To

[1] The foregoing is a free translation from German verse which I wrote down as the shortest form of phenomenological description for documentation and memorizing rather than for poetic perfection. The German original may be added here for those who have a reading knowledge of the language.

> Empor quillt's aus zwei Schichten: eine Schicht
> Hegt Zweifel und die andre Zuversicht.
>
> Die Zuversicht bleibt völlig unberührt
> Von Selbstgesprächen, die der Zweifel führt.
>
> Der Zweifel seinerseits wird nicht betört
> Vom Orgelton, den er im Herzen hört.
>
> Wie sie auch lächelnd strahlt, die Zuversicht,
> Ihn gänzlich zu verjagen glückt ihr nicht.
>
> Er zweifelt fort in seiner Schicht und staunt,
> Dass drunten Zuversicht bleibt gut gelaunt.
>
> So sind sie längst gewöhnt schon, zu verzichten,
> Und wohnen, Nachbarn, in getrennten Schichten.
>
> Der Zweifel sinnt: "Einst kommt der grosse Tag,
> Wo sich der lange Streit entscheiden mag.
>
> Dann werd' ich siegen, oder Zuversicht.
> Doch wenn ich siege, ach, erfahr' ich's nicht."
>
> Der Zweifel zweifelt', als er dies bedachte,
> Am Zweifeln selbst. Doch Zuversicht, sie lachte:
>
> "Ich würd's nicht fühlen, müsst' ich unterliegen.
> Unendlich Glück erwartet mich im Siegen."

that extent I have produced no more than a "report" or a "protocol" on observations in one specimen (see above, Chapter 1, Section 3). There is no a-priori evidence that this is a general experience. Some people seem to observe nothing but doubts within them, and no certainty. Are they merely more accurate in their observations and more exacting in their demands on certainty, or do they overlook or suppress the fount of certainty that surges up from that other layer? My own self-observation cannot give the answer. Conversely, saints are said to be so certain as to have no doubts. Have they lost the faculty of doubting in that second layer, or don't they use it? My own observations cannot contribute to this question, as I am capable of doubt almost at will—but I can doubt many things only in one of the two layers, and some, such as that truth or veracity is required in justice, in neither of them.

Without generalizing my own experience I merely want to warn here against the axiomatic fallacy that doubt and certainty must be mutually exclusive. It has often been said, from Plato to Max Scheler, that we can feel pleasure and pain at the same time on various levels (see Chapter XII, Section 4, above). We also can feel doubt and no-doubt at the same time on various levels, I submit.

5. Summary and Conclusion

I have been using many words to say very little in this chapter. This little seems to me so important, however, that it must not be omitted in an essay that deals with the foundations of political theory today. Nor did I know how to say it in fewer words without courting the disaster of grave misunderstandings. But now that these things have been so broadly displayed, my summary may be short.

Religion is still today, in many political situations, a relevant factor and a strong motivating force, and as such must be studied closely. This is generally recognized by twentieth-century political scientists. But, is religion also a source of scientific knowledge? Separation of these two aspects of religion is a relatively recent achievement. Formerly, they were freely fused; now, the pendulum has swung to the other extreme, that of complete abstinence from any reference to religion as a potential source of scientific knowledge. (Section 1.)

The scientific convention of "bracketing" the divine alternative has arisen on two grounds. In the first place, it was the methodological consequence of general acknowledgment that God's reality could not be demonstrated in terms of Scientific Method. But, secondly, it seems to have been strongly supported by a widespread tendency to consider the nonexistence of God scientifically more likely than his existence. This argument from likelihood has been subjected to intensive scrutiny here with the result that nonscientific and scientific estimates of likelihood must be distinguished. Once we have decided to use the term "science" in the sense of intersubjectively transmissible knowledge, all those intersubjectively not transmissible factors that motivate people individually to consider the one or the other alternative more likely—with clashing results—must be eliminated from the argument. If that is done it appears that there is no greater scientific likelihood for either alternative. (Section 2.)

Under these circumstances, total abstinence from mention of the divine alternative in scientific discussions is not justified. Both alternatives should be given equal weight scientifically, since neither is capable of scientific proof and neither can even be awarded a higher degree of scientific likelihood. We should, therefore, occasionally unbracket the divine alternative in order to maintain scholarly honesty and scientific depth of perspective. Reflections that start out from God's reality as a hypothesis are by no means useless for our scientific work. They are apt to lead scholars to direct their attention to facts and interrelations that are otherwise easily overlooked. This in turn may inspire concrete research projects of a strictly scientific character, which —while holding no promise of affecting the scientific balance between the two alternatives—may enlarge our scientific knowledge about many socially and politically relevant factors and interrelations.

In other words, the lack of proof for the positive hypothesis should not deter us from using it at times as an eye-opener in our scientific study of facts, interrelations, and potentialities. We must only beware of succumbing to wishful thinking as if such experiments could give us greater scientific proof for the positive hypothesis or for its greater likelihood. In this respect, matters are no different from what they are when we use the negative hypothesis, which also never leads us nearer to a proof of its correctness or of its greater likelihood. The negative alternative is even more definitely doomed in this respect than is the positive; and yet we use it, and have unjustifiably done so to the exclusion of the other. (Section 3.)

The relationship between faith and doubt in the scholar can be better understood when we realize that faith and doubt can be present simultaneously in the same person at different levels. (Section 4.)

RESULTS

THE fascinating horizons and perspectives that have opened before us in the last several chapters—reflecting on those ultimate questions of political theory that touch on metaphysics and, in particular, the single metaphysical problem that surpasses all others in human concern, underlying them all, that of the existence of divine forces acting according to some plan and toward some goal—must not be permitted to mislead us into overrating the immediate practical bearing these reflections can have on the progress of science in general and of political science in particular. For one thing remains certain: the ultimate significance of these questions, great as it is, does not alter the grave fact that they cannot be answered in the language of intersubjectively transmissible knowledge.

All excursions into the border region between science and metaphysical speculation lead up to a point where the roads part, one branch drawing us back toward ever greater efforts to refine our observation of facts and of their interrelations, to clarify the consequences man's attitudes and actions have for himself and for others in the short run or the long; the other, enticing us to follow an orientation that relies on metaphysical intuition, on premises in which we may believe but whose correspondence to a surmised ulterior reality is beyond intersubjective verification, and which may lead our scientific work astray.

The two branches may run parallel for a while. Our chapters on political ideals (VIII) and on impossibility (XII) have shown that strictly scientific inquiries about the consequences of ideals and institutions can get us surprisingly far, now corroborating, now modifying our intuitional orientations. But the viability of the public road of science ends far sooner than that of the private road of esoteric intuition; when the going turns rough on the former, we can speed along the latter with seven-league steps toward something that may be either Truth or Error—science cannot tell which.

In concluding this volume, the following paragraphs sum up the results of our entire course of investigations; they make free use of the partial summaries presented in some of the individual chapters, but follow an independent arrangement.

It is a fundamental requirement in the pursuit of scientific political theory that scientific and nonscientific types of theory be consistently distinguished. There are several ways in which the distinction can be made. But there is one that cannot be ignored even by those who are unwilling to stop there: the distinction between knowledge that is intersubjectively transmissible *qua* knowledge, and knowledge, putative or real, that is not. (Introductory, Section 5; Chapter II, Section 7.)

Knowledge gained in adhering to the rules of Scientific Method *is* intersubjectively transmissible. This is not to say that it is entirely free from assumptions. Scientific Method permits us to accept some commonsense principles whose truth cannot, through its services alone, be demonstrated to someone who might care to deny them. Such "immanent methodological aprioris" include the assumptions, among others, that there is human consubjectivity regarding many types of experience, though not all; that there are interrelations between many successive events, but that human beings nonetheless enjoy some sphere of freedom in their decisions (Chapters I, Sections 2, 3, 7; II, Sections 1, 5; XII, Section 1). These assumptions—or, more precisely, the discretion which Scientific Method grants scientists to work under them—do not, however, impair intersubjective transmissibility.

Adherence to Scientific Method, as here understood, implies no denying the great significance of imagination and of genius in scientific research (Chapters I, Section 1, b and VI, 2, end). Nor does it prevent us from using metaphysical inspirations and speculations as pointers toward potentially relevant themes (Chapters VII, Section 3, and XIII). All attempts to disparage such nonscientific impulses to scientific activities, keeping science limited to a strictly positivistic, physicalistic, behavioristic approach even in the preparatory stage, have proved beside the point. They have led to some sort of negative metaphysics and to self-contradictory statements (Chapter V, Section 3, b).

Nor is there need to disbar from the bench of science scholars who prefer to use the term "scientific" in some broader sense, including metaphysical speculations, provided they avoid escapism regarding the fundamental difference between knowledge that, *qua* knowledge, is universally transmissible—if not in its results, at least in its constituent factors—and knowledge that is not universally transmissible (Chapter VII, Section 3).

Great strides have been made during the twentieth century in augmenting objective knowledge of an intersubjectively transmissible character in the social sciences, especially through the systematic production and collection of statistically useful data, developing and improving the techniques of tapping samples, conducting experimental tests, constructing useful "working hypotheses" and "models," and the like (Chapters I and II, with many details). But the novel techniques must not be overrated in comparison with the continuing great relevance of historical and anthropological research regarding the causes, purposes, and effects of political institutions and actions, and of psychological research regarding motives and their possible manipulation.

It is through the judicious use of a *variety* of techniques, not just one or two, that the political scientist is able to make relevant statements about the interconnection of events, past, present, and future.

The categories of cause and effect, motives and purposes, continue to play an eminent role in the social sciences, irrespective of the controversial place of causality in modern physics (Chapter II, Section 1). So does the category of "limited possibility," developed in this book in a more elaborate manner than usual. Scientific Method is frequently able to lead to definite statements regarding the extent to which the range of possible events has been narrowed or widened by events in the past, or will be by possible events in the future, especially by human actions. Moreover, the scientist can often show the impossibility of reaching some desired effect by the proposed means, or of reaching it at all, while in other cases he is able to refute alleged impossibility (Chapter XII; also VIII, Section 2, and *passim*).

Above all, it is always the legitimate function of the political scientist to inquire into the imaginable *alternatives* of political behavior and their respective implications and consequences.

Such are, among others, the *positive* contributions that are within the reach of political science. More on the *negative* side, legitimate approaches lie open to the political theorist in his fight against logical fallacies, such as unguarded inferences of what *ought* to be from what *is* (Chapter III, Sections 4 to 7); or against tendencies to overtax logic by elevating it to the rank of an independent master of nature or history. Logic deals with "meaning" and, therefore, can be applied only where there *is* a meaning. If nature or history sometimes appear "logical," it is because their course seems to agree with the "meaning" of what we either interpret as divine wisdom or formulate as "laws" intended to describe regularities in the interconnection of events. (Chapters I, Section 6; II, Section 1, e.)

Our "agreement" with a proposition, or our "acceptance" of it, is no substitute for science, not even when the agreement or acceptance is shared by many others (Introductory, Section 4, fourth argument); this does not make the proposition "scientific." Tentative acceptance is, of course a prerequisite of further scientific work based on a proposition (Chapter I, Sections 2, 3, 5). But acceptance *alone,* however unconditionally or enthusiastically given, is insufficient. It must be, above all, acceptance of a proposition that, under the rules of the scientific method applied, is scientifically acceptable (Chapter I, Section 7). If the method applied is "Scientific Method" in the strict sense of this term (Chapter I, Section 1), then substantive a-priori statements, contradictory propositions, and logically inconclusive deductions are barred from scientific acceptance. If a person reports that he saw a ghost while fully awake, we may accept his report as "subjectively honest"; but this does not justify scientific acceptance of the inference that what he thought he saw *was* a ghost, and that there *are* ghosts. To accept these propositions, additional evidence would be required: ghosts form no part of the "immanent methodological aprioris" of Scientific Method (Chapter II, Section 5).

The scientist must always be on the alert against the tendency to smuggle into scientific theory, through some back door, the unavowed assumption, ceremoniously ushered out through the front door as scientifically unverifiable, that divine forces do operate in the universe (Chapters III, Section 7; VIII, Section 2; and *passim*). Our acknowledgment that science is unable *qua* science, that is, in an intersubjectively transmissible manner to establish the operation of such forces as an actuality should be frank, honest, and consistent. No "smuggling" can be tolerated in this matter. If a scholar refuses to concede this limitation, he should say so explicitly and establish his conclusive intersubjective proof, if he can. Otherwise, references to divine forces are scientifically admissible only as an *avowed* "working hypothesis" (Chapter XIII, Section 3).

But equally frank, honest, and consistent should be our acknowledgment that science is unable to preclude the alternative that there *are* divine forces. It is one of the most significant effects of scientific thinking in the twentieth century that today not only believers in a personal God are exposed to inner doubts on the ground of lacking scientific proof—that has often been so before—but so are atheists as well. Another Nietzsche, who would today repeat this nineteenth-century philosopher's apodictic declaration "God is dead" (Chapter V, Section 6, a), without distinguishing between his own personal opinions or convictions and his scentific justification for expressing them in such apodictic form, could not qualify as a twentieth-century scientist (Chapter XIII, Section 2).

Distinction between transmissible and nontransmissible knowledge leads necessarily to a distinction, not simply between "facts" and "values," but between scientific statements regarding facts (events), including the fact that evaluations of a definite kind have occurred, or may or will occur, at definite times and places, and statements regarding the *validity* of the *ultimate standards* that underlie evaluations, or ought to underlie them. This necessary distinction does not imply that science is unable to contribute to a meaningful examination of evaluations. Our discussion of the many meanings of the term "valuable" has resulted in an extensive tabulation of significant steps which under Scientific Method can be legitimately and successfully taken regarding alleged values, even those in the moral sphere (Chapter III, Section 2). Yet there remains a gap which Scientific Method is indeed unable to close: the absolute validity of ultimate standards that underlie human value judgments cannot be established through this method (*ibid.,* Section 7). All attempts to overcome this calamity by other methods have failed, and must fail, unless the operation of divine forces is scientifically established (*ibid.,* and Chapter VII, Sections 3 and 4).

This limitation of what science can do, and can hope ever to achieve, does not hinder a scientist from orienting his own scientific research toward the question of how some particular end, considered valuable by him or by his country or by some other group whose ideals he shares, can best be reached or approximated ("partisan relativism," Chapter III, Section 8), nor on the other hand from pointing to actually *un*desired effects or side-effects of any particular decision either made or contemplated (Chapter XII, Sections 3, 5).

Statements about the justice or injustice of acts, judgments, and the like are statements about values—moral values, that is. Consequently, they are subject to all the limitations of scientific efforts regarding the validity of ultimate standards by which values are, or ought to be, measured. It seems, however, as though all human beings harbor some sense, or feeling, of justice, which at times influences their judgments. There are several conceivable sources of this universal sense or feeling. Some, like God or an immortal soul, are not accessible to scientific statements as to their reality. What science is able to study, however, as a possible source of universal elements in the human sense or feeling of justice, is the "nature of things" and the "nature of man." Of these, the "nature of things" does not lead to conclusive prescriptions regarding "just" behavior of man, unless nature is thought of as expressing a divine will, a thesis beyond scientific verification (Chapters

484

iv, Section 3, vii, Section 7, and viii, Sections 4, 5, 16). The "nature of man," however, might conceivably include moral tendencies common to all men. This is obviously not the case regarding the great controversial issues of the social and political sphere; the most divergent ideas and feelings of justice abound here as to the value of ultimate goals (Chapters iv, Section 6, and viii). To that extent, therefore, these ideas and feelings have certainly a "relative" character, not only on the ground that they refer to man rather than the universe, but because they are present only in particular individuals and groups. They are even relative twice over, namely, always to some potential "state of affairs" that is considered just (or "more" just), and secondly, to the particular ideas or feelings as to *what* state of affairs would be just. Different ideas or feelings of justice may prevail within the same person at different times, and even simultaneously, according to whether existing institutions are "accepted" or "criticized," and if the latter, whether the critique follows group opinions or is original. (Chapter iv, Sections 4 and 6). Ideas of "traditional" justice are relative to something that can be objectively ascertained, namely, the existing institutions, like family, property, inheritance, freedom of contract, where these *are* the existing institutions. But ideas of "transtraditional" justice, by contrast, reflect a great variety of preferences as to desirable conditions, with no possibility of an authentic choice among them to be effected by science, nor even of an exhaustive classification a priori (Chapters iv, Sections 5 and 6; and viii).

The calamity caused by this impotence of science to establish ultimate principles of justice is, however, more apparent than real; for it is greatly mitigated by four significant factors. First, science has an almost unlimited possibility of exploring the *consequences* of the different ideas of justice, after clarifying their meanings—their historical, individual, actual, or potential meanings. Second, *jurisprudence*, as distinct from science (although aided by scientific methods in exploring historical facts), may be able to declare maxims and other basic principles *legally* binding at a definite place and time, even in conflict with dictatorial decrees, although pure science is unable to establish the universal and invariant validity of the same principles (Chapters iv, Section 8, and viii, Section 16). Third, Scientific Method cannot, and does not, deny that there *may* be absolute standards of justice; it only insists that they cannot be scientifically verified. And fourth, empirical research seems to reveal a number of elements in human ideas and feeling of justice that are indeed universal and invariant characteristics of the "nature of man," and on this ground can be reckoned with as constant factors (Chapter VIII).

Recognizing certain elements of moral value judgments as universally present in human nature may be the closest science will ever come to verifying the absolute validity of moral values. Yet science must be conscientious enough to dismiss overambitious schemes that have been presented in this category in the course of more than two thousand years. This book has tried to identify some universal elements in the human sense of justice, that is, an inescapable interconnection between the feeling of justice and certain postulates, such as the postulate of truth or veracity, the postulate of equal treatment of what is equal under the scheme of values in question, and the postulate of respect for the necessities of nature in our moral demands on others. Even these elements can be classified as absolute only in the sense of their being "universally human." As such, however, they have a great bearing on the social sciences, and may be used as starting points in international and interdenominational policy. (Chapter X.)

Modern Scientific Value Relativism—as here presented it is no older than this century—is fundamentally distinct from earlier forms of relativism, of which there have been plenty in the history of human thought. It no longer refers to the current "stage of evolution," as did the relativism of the early French sociologists; nor to "historical conditions," as did (and does) the relativism of modern historicism; or to "economic conditions," as did (and does) the relativism of the Marxists. Instead, it refers to value judgments. It is no longer limited to the positive law, as was the relativism of nineteenth-century legal positivists; it is, rather, "transpositive" (legislative) in its essence. It is no longer "latent," as was the transpositive relativism of many philosophers of the nineteenth century; it is now "overt." It is not merely passive, as was (and is) the relativism of many skeptics, but rather "active" and militant in its attacks on political ideologies that try to present nonscientific value judgments as scientifically established or verified. And finally, although it *may* choose to be "partisan" in its selection of ends to the attainment of which it wishes to apply itself (admitting that this choice is nonscientific in character), it may rise to the level of strict "neutrality," and must do so if it wants to contribute through scientific analysis and research to the scientific comparison of contradictory value systems. (Chapters III, Section 8, and VI.)

486

The injunctions of Scientific Value Relativism are limited to the "scientific" approach as distinct from the "religious," the "philosophical," or the "juridical" approach. No postulate that relativity of values should be accepted as the ultimate limit of human thinking is raised by Scientific Method, as here understood, regarding human activities in any of these other spheres, provided the results are not handed down as being purely scientific. (Chapters II, Section 7; IV, Sections 7 and 8; VII, Sections 3 and 4; VIII, XII, XIII.)

As to the *genesis* of modern Scientific Method, its culmination in Scientific Value Relativism was reached in Europe not earlier than the beginning of this century, and on the American scene some fifteen years later. The American time lag is explained by two factors; first, that some, though not all, of the principles of Scientific Value Relativism had been anticipated by Anglo-American empiricism and pragmatism (Chapters V, Section 6, and VI, Section 5, a), and second, that an enviable homogeneity of basic political creeds at home made the need for scientific neutrality less pressingly felt (Chapter VI, Sections 4 and 5). When Scientific Value Relativism finally came to these shores, it remained more casual and more latent than its more systematic and overt European counterpart, and it was more often used in an avowed "partisan" manner than on the level of strict neutrality (Chapter VI, Section 5, e).

The European founding fathers of Scientific Value Relativism had, from the outset, put strong emphasis on its positive aspects, especially on the services science can render in analyzing logical implications and factual consequences of the espousal of any particular set of values and, therefore, on the practical usefulness of science in helping people to make reasonable choices among conflicting value standards. But the founders neglected (1) the search for universal and invariant elements in the human sense, feeling, or ideas of justice (Chapters IX to XII), and (2) the difference between jurisprudence and science, which may make it possible for jurisprudence to establish the legal validity of principles of justice at definite places and times when pure science is unable to establish their universal, invariant, or absolute validity (Chapters IV, Section 8, and VIII, Section 16).

Although the earlier founders (Simmel, Rickert, Max Weber) did not use the term "relativism" for their methodology, this name has gradually come to be connected with it (Radbruch, Kantorowicz, Kelsen, and thereafter in general). In order to avoid confusion with other types of relativism, the compound term "Scientific Value Relativism" or "Scientific Value Alternativism" has been used here. (Chapters III, Section 1, and VI, Section 7.)

When understood as here presented, that is, *minus* the misrepresentations discussed in Chapter VII, Section 1, Scientific Value Relativism has not been refuted by any of the ardent methodological attacks leveled against it during the Great Revolt: not by the contention that Scientific Method is apt to deal with values precisely as with facts; nor by the claim that other methods could solve value problems adequately in an intersubjective manner; nor by renewed attempts to prove scientifically the validity of religious truth, or at least the "objectivity" of ultimate values beyond their relational aspects (while many objective statements are possible, they do not decide on the ultimate standard to be applied); nor by quasi-logical arguments, or Gestalt psychology, or the establishment of formal standards; nor, finally, by the contention that all other scientific endeavors are as relative and subjective as are the efforts to determine ultimate values, which is not true. (Chapter VII.)

The lively debate kindled by the revolt, while leaving the revolters unsuccessful in their primary goal of refuting or overcoming Scientific Value Relativism, has yet contributed a great deal to a deeper understanding of the issues. It has, in particular, revealed (1) the necessity of clearly distinguishing at least three types of alleged knowledge: intersubjectively transmissible, not transmissible, or merely speculative; (2) the considerable amount of objective contributions that can be made by science in the examination of proposed value standards; (3) the legitimacy of a frankly speculative discussion of metaphysical problems by scientists who bring to these discussons their disciplined knowledge of the body of scientifically secured knowledge; and (4) the legitimacy of a scientific attitude which makes use of religious inspiration as a pointer directing attention to neglected areas of factual research and causal regularities, provided the ensuing scientific research itself is kept free from extrascientific religious opinions and convictions. (Chapters VII, VIII, XIII.)

The contention, always fallacious, that there are *logical* links between Is and Ought, must be distinguished from the—possibly meaningful—contention that there are *factual* links between them. Such factual links are envisaged in the idea of a perfectly good and powerful God, and also in the contention that some elements of what we ought to do or ought not to do are announced by some inner voice, or urge, to some or all human beings. Frequently, doctrines that teach an inter-connection between Is and Ought are ambiguous as to whether they mean the link is logical or factual. (Chapter ix, Sections 1 and 2.)

The correctness of reports that an external voice issuing from a suprahuman source had been heard cannot be verified scientifically in an intersubjectively conclusive manner. The contention, however, that some inner voice, making announcements about right and just, or wrong and unjust, operates in human beings is verifiable by empirical research at least to some extent. If such a voice was found to be announcing the same norm in *all* human beings, this would disclose the presence of a universal factual link connecting Is and Ought in man. Should we even remain unable to ascertain in scientific terms the ultimate source of this link, our empirically established knowledge that it is there, supporting some types of judgment and action and opposing others, would be relevant to the social sciences. (Chapter ix, Sections 3 to 8.)

In the pursuit of this research it is necessary to recognize at the outset that our own individual intuition, however imperative, to the effect that elements of thinking and feeling on right and justice which we discern within ourselves are universal and invariant, constitutes no sufficient scientific proof in twentieth-century terms (on this point very different from the eighteenth century) that they actually *are* universal and invariant. We must, therefore, add to our phenomenological introspection empirical research about other people—and even about so many and such different types that inductive generalizations of our factual findings appear warranted. However, in order to direct such research in a meaningful manner, we may formulate hypotheses predicting the outcome of further research by way of anticipation in a tentative fashion on the basis of all available information. (Chapter x, Sections 1 to 4.)

Among the potential (and likely) universal elements in the human sense of justice, one, the postulate of truth or veracity, plays a dominant role. The interrelation between justice and truth is so obvious that the necessity of stating it explicitly and inquiring into its grounds is easily overlooked; it was overlooked by the early relativists, and is generally still today. When attention is drawn to it, the interrelation is often mistaken for a logical requirement, a mere matter of definition, or otherwise a "matter of course." Thus the very obviousness of the postulate has kept even great scholars from seeing that we are faced here with something peculiar, something to be wondered at—nothing less, indeed, than a link, and, as it seems, even an unbreakable link between Is and Ought. Whether breakable or not, such a link can only be factual, it cannot be logical. (Chapter x.)

Put on a particularly significant track by the specific character of hypotheses regarding precisely defined universal elements of human thinking and feeling in matters of justice, anthropologists may subject them to further tests. It is highly desirable that they do so. But the material already available is rich and strong enough for political scientists tentatively to assume that these hypotheses will eventually be confirmed by whatever further tests will be applied. Too long has the philosophical discussion of universal elements in human moral feelings dabbled in generalities. We must finally come down to putting our fingers on such elements, singling them out and trying to verify them by empirical research.

Harking back, at the end of this volume, to the description of the contemporary scene in political theory given in the Introductory, we are now able, in a final effort to relieve the tension and suspense there aroused or registered, to sum up our results as follows.

It is undeniable that scientific political theory has been passing through an era of crises in our century. There has actually been not only one major crisis, but two. The first was caused by the stricter demands made on scientific research as distinct from nonscientific pronouncements of personal opinions, convictions, speculations. Maturing at the beginning of this century, these demands led to the withdrawal of scientific political theory from all substantive a-priori statements, including those which concerned the validity of ultimate standards underlying moral value judgments. The second, fanned if not kindled by the rise of nonscientific totalitarian ideologies, evolved from the revolt against the contracting effect which the stricter demands had on the area accessible to scientific operations.

The transition from the various nineteenth-century schools to a scientific method that was based on a stricter distinction between personal opinions and objectively transmissible knowledge was fundamentally sound, and has brought immense benefits to twentieth-century political science. The revolt against this development has been unquestionably inspired by the most noble motives. However, insofar as its goal was to refute Scientific Method and Scientific Value Relativism, it has failed or miscarried, and insofar as it was to preserve the art and the glory of metaphysical speculation, it was misdirected and unnecessary. It was justified only to the extent that it opposed the eccentric type of neopositivists who, in an ambiguous mannerism of speech, denied "meaning" to any proposition that cannot be verified in a physicalistic, behavioristic manner, and spread a sort of "negative" metaphysics (Chapter v, Section 3). Scientific Value Relativism as such has nothing to do with these positivistic eccentrics, if there are any left.

Recognition that ultimate standards of moral value judgments cannot be set or verified by scientific theory has been shown not to imply such devastating effects as had been feared. In particular, political science can often demonstrate that some type of political actions give the people a better guaranty than do alternative actions for getting what they actually desire and avoiding results that they actually do not desire; and also, that many ideological catchwords, if translated into practical policy, are bound to lead to results, or to include the grave risk of leading to results, which those who listen to these slogans with approval actually do not desire but, rather, abhor (see especially, Chapters viii and xii).

A more systematic concentration of political scientists on this legitimate type of work would have shown that scientific theory is by no means without weapons against nonscientific totalitarian theories. Nor does it impose its restrictive rules on those who wish to follow their own individual intuitions or religious inspirations, so long as they refrain from offering their theories as scientifically established, that is, as universally transmissible *qua* established knowledge. The scientist himself may join the intuitionists in their gropings, provided he keeps his speculative ideas or religious revelations clearly separated from those contributions for which he claims scientific rank.

Exploration of possible alternatives of action and of the foreseeable consequences and risks incurred by our choices—these are the broad areas where political science can render its greatest services. What concrete alternatives of possible action men actually did consider in definite situations of the *past*, and what their reasons were for choosing one rather than the other alternative, the historian rather than the political scientist must say. But regarding the *present* and the *future*, the historian cannot do the job, and even for the past he must rely on political theory (he may produce such theory himself) if he tries to indicate the causal relations between political institutions or actions and subsequent events, or the course history would have taken had other decisions been made (see Chapter ii, Section 1, e), and to examine possible alternatives of action other than those actually considered by the actors on the scene.

If political scientists apply scientific standards throughout, and do so not only with the required rigidity but with the utmost power and ingenuity they can muster, they will find a tremendous field for useful efforts before them. That this holds true for inquiries about political *means* and their factual adequacy in the pursuit of chosen ends, no one doubts. But it applies also to a critical inquiry of political *ends* and *values*. This has been brought out, I hope, in many sections of this book, especially those which deal with political ideals like equality, liberty, happiness, harmony, culture, power, or the nation (Chapter viii), and others that refer to the various rival systems of government (Introductory, Section 6; Chapters viii, Section 8, and xii, Sections 5 and 6).

Inescapable, universal elements in human feeling and thinking, such as the interrelation between justice and truth or veracity, are important accretions to the area of intersubjectively transmissible knowledge.

APPENDICES

APPENDIX A

NOTE REGARDING A PLANNED SECOND VOLUME

THE following of the author's publications refer to the particular subjects to be treated in the scheduled second volume. They are listed here provisionally, as explained in Section 7 of the Introductory.

PART FIVE: RIVAL FORMS OF GOVERNMENT

"Constitutions and Leadership," *Social Research*, vol. 1 (1934) pp. 265–286

Prelude to Silence—The End of the German Republic, New York 1944; also in German: *Vorspiel zum Schweigen*, Wien 1948. xxi and 156 pp.

"Die Auflösung der Weimarer Republik und die politische Wissenschaft," *Zeitschrift für Politik*, vol. 2 (1955) pp. 291–308

"The New German Constitution," *Social Research*, vol. 16 (1949) pp. 425–473; also published separately as on Occasional Paper of the Institute of World Affairs

"The New Russian Constitution," *Social Research*, vol. 4 (1937) pp. 157–190

Review of C. J. Friedrich and Z. K. Brzezinski, *Totalitarian Dictatorship and Autocracy*, in *Social Research*, vol. 24 (1957) pp. 482–86

"Democracy—Challenge to Theory," *ibid.*, vol. 13 (1946) pp. 195–224

Preussen contra Reich, proceedings of the Constitutional Court occasioned by the suit of the Prussian versus the German Government after the Papen putsch, 1932; with an introduction by A. B. and his speeches and pleas, Berlin 1932

PART SIX: POWER, RIGHTS, GOALS, TECHNIQUES

(in addition to incidental sections in the above publications and in the present volume, especially in its Chapters VIII and XII)

"The Concentration Camp," *Columbia Law Review*, vol. 50 (1950) pp. 761–82

Reviews of F. A. Hermens, *Democracy or Anarchy?* in *Social Research*, vol. 9 (1942) pp. 411–14, and of James D. Hogan, *Elections and Representation, ibid.*, vol. 15 (1948), pp. 123–24

"Bureaucratic Sabotage," *The Annals of the American Academy of Political and Social Science*, vol. 189 (January 1937) pp. 48–57

"How Bureaucracies Develop and Function," *ibid.*, vol. 282 (March 1954) pp. 1–10

"Bürokratie," in *Herders Staatslexikon*, Freiburg 1958

"Walther Rathenau and the German People," *Journal of Politics*, vol. 10 (1948) pp. 20–48; also in German: *Walther Rathenau und das deutsche Volk*, München 1950

"The German Army in Retrospect," *Social Research*, vol. 20 (1953) pp. 358–65

"United States Defense in Europe," *Social Research,* vol. 19 (1952) pp. 1–22
Commentary on the laws concerning freedom of association and public
meetings, the protection of the Republic, and presidential emergency
decrees in the Weimar Republic, in Brauchitsch, *Verwaltungsgesetze,*
vol. 2 (22nd ed. 1932) pp. 259–426, Berlin 1932 (in German)

PART SEVEN: GOVERNMENT ORGANIZATION

"Federalism and Business Regulation," *Social Research,* vol. 2 (1935) pp.
337–362
Federalism and Regionalism in Germany—The Division of Prussia, Mono-
graph Series of the Institut of World Affairs, with a preface by Adolph
Lowe, New York 1945, 202 pp. Also in German: *Föderalismus und Re-
gionalismus—Die Teilung Preussens,* Bonn 1949
"Civil Service," *Social Research,* vol. 3 (1936) pp. 202–221
"Democracy and Administration," in M. Ascoli and F. Lehmann, ed., *Po-
litical and Economic Democracy,* New York 1937, pp. 217–228
The Art and Technique of Administration in German Ministries, with Com-
stock Glaser, Cambridge, Mass., 1940, 191 pp.
"The Relevance of Foreign Experience," in Fritz M. Marx (ed.), *Public
Management in the New Democracy,* New York 1940, pp. 107–29
"Three Topics in Comparative Administration—Organization of Govern-
ment Departments, Government Corporations, Expenditures in Relation to Population," *Public Policy,* vol. 2 (1941) pp. 289–318
"Smaller Departments," *Public Administration Review,* vol. 1 (1941) pp.
363–375
"Organization for Overhead Government," correspondence with Paul Ap-
pleby, *ibid.,* vol. 2 (1942) pp. 61–66
Regional Coordination, Memorandum by the Special Committee on Comparative Administration, Social Science Research Council, March 1943
(mimeogr.)
"Personnel Management" in E. H. Litchfield, ed., *Governing Postwar Germany,* Ithaca 1953, pp. 263–293
"Government Departments" in *Encyclopaedia Britannica*

PART EIGHT: SOVEREIGNTY AND INTERNATIONAL ORGANIZATION

"Sovereignty" in H. Speier and A. Kähler, *War in Our Time,* New York 1939,
pp. 58–77
"European Federation—The Democratic Alternative," *Harvard Law Review,*
vol. 55 (1942) pp. 561–594
"Limited-Purpose Federations," *Social Research,* vol. 10 (1943) pp. 135–151
"Distribution of Powers between an International Government and the Governments of National States," *American Political Science Review,* vol.
37 (1943) pp. 862–872

Review of R. M. MacIver, *Towards an Abiding Peace,* in *Social Research,* vol. 10 (1943) p. 495

"Regionalism Within World Organization," in *Regionalism and World Organization,* American Council on Public Affairs, Washington, D.C., 1944, pp. 11–26

"The Idea of a 'Safety Belt,'" *American Political Science Review,* vol. 43 (1949) pp. 1001–09; German transl. in *Gegenwart* (Frankfurt), June 1953

"Struggling for Peace," *World Alliance News Letter,* vol. 25 (December 1949) pp. 3 ff.

"United States Defense in Europe," *op.cit.*

"Gangbare und Ungangbare Wege," in *Aussenpolitik* (Stuttgart 1955) pp. 685–694

Wiedervereinigung, three lectures on German reunification, delivered at the University of Heidelberg, München 1957, 64 pp.

APPENDIX B

MISCELLANEOUS NOTES
ON SPECIAL QUESTIONS
AND ON
LITERATURE

THESE notes serve three purposes. They fill gaps that the structure of the essay has induced me to pass over in the main text; they discourse on a select number of writings, chosen for the particular light their virtues, their defects, or their special approaches are apt to throw on our problems; and they add simple bibliographical references to other publications.

Many of the latter would have merited specific treatment, but I had to stop somewhere. The references have been added as a service to the reader. For listings in this group I am greatly indebted to the bibliography presented by Jean M. Driscoll and Charles S. Hyneman in their "Methodology for Political Scientists: Perspectives for Study," *American Political Science Review,* vol. 49 (1955) pp. 192–217, and to the report on "World Trends in Political Science Research" by C. B. Macpherson, *ibid.,* vol. 48 (1954) pp. 427–49.

Books and articles cited in the main text are, as a rule, not listed here; bibliographical inquiries should, therefore, always refer to the text first.

General reference books and articles include the following:

UNESCO, *Contemporary Political Science,* Paris 1950
UNESCO, *The Teaching of the Social Sciences in the United States,* based on reports by M. Dimock, A. Ehrenzweig, H. Ehrmann, E. Furniss, Jr., John Hazard, J. Manis, B. Meltzer, W. Ray, H. Taylor, and Erminie Voegelin, Paris 1954
UNESCO, *The Teaching of the Social Sciences in the United Kingdom,* based on reports by A. H. Campbell, G. L. Goodwin, R. H. Graveson, C. W. Guillebaud, H. C. Gutteridge, C. J. Hamson, A. H. Hanson, W. J. M. MacKenzie, D. L. MacRae, J. L. Montrose, and D. R. Stanford, Paris 1953
UNESCO, *The University Teaching of Social Sciences: Political Science,* by William A. Robson, Paris 1954
UNESCO, *Political Science in the United States, a Trend Report,* Paris 1956
UNESCO, *International Bibliography of Political Science (Bibliographie internationale de science politique),* prepared by the International Political Science Association in cooperation with the International Committee for Social Sciences Documentation, and with the support of the International Studies Conference, published annually, Paris 1953 ff.
International Political Science Abstracts (Documentation Politique Internationale), compiled by the International Political Science Studies Conference, published quarterly, with the assistance of UNESCO and the Committee for Social Sciences Documentation, Oxford 1953 ff.
American Political Science Association: Committee for the Advancement of Teaching, *Goals For Political Science,* New York 1951; and the comments thereon by J. W. Fesler, L. Hartz, J. H. Hallowell, V. G. Rosenblum,

W. H. C. Laves, W. A. Robson, L. Rogers, *American Political Science Review*, vol. 45 (1951) pp. 996–1024, and by M. E. Dimock, C. Rossiter, J. P. Roche, J. C. Donovan, *ibid.*, vol. 46 (1952) pp. 494–503
C. E. Hawley and L. A. Dexter, "Recent Political Science Research in American Universities," *American Political Science Review*, vol. 46 (1952) pp. 470–85

Helpful collections of reprints are presented (in addition to the more historically oriented readings edited by Francis Coker, Margaret Spahr, W. Y. Elliott and N. A. McDonald, William Ebenstein, and others) in

Herbert Feigl and William Sellars, *Readings in Philosophical Analysis*, New York 1949
Herbert Feigl and May Brodbeck, *Readings in the Philosophy of Science*, New York 1953
Philip P. Wiener, *Readings in Philosophy of Science; Introduction to the Foundations and Cultural Aspects of the Sciences*, New York 1953

NOTES TO THE INTRODUCTORY CHAPTER

Section 4. Professional Escapes. To sever legitimate from fallacious uses of historical arguments is often quite difficult and even painful. Take, for example, appeals to the "Grand Tradition of Values," which have occurred frequently in the recent fight against totalitarianism as, for instance, in the writings of George Catlin ("Political Theory: What Is It?" *Political Science Quarterly*, vol. 72, 1957, p. 26), of Ernest Barker, and of Leo Strauss. Such references are entirely legitimate when used (1) as *descriptive* of the remarkable fact that there is a historical continuity in commitments to certain moral values; (2) as *political* and *cultural* arguments, with the Burkean understanding that what has a grand tradition should, as a matter of political "prudence" or cultural "pride," not be lightly abandoned;[1] (3) as a *religious* argument in support of the belief that moral values are divinely revealed, although this piece of evidence, however important we may consider it, does not suffice to establish the reality of God and divine revelations "scientifically"; or (4) as a *juridical* argument in support of the thesis that dictatorial decrees should be denied juridical validity if they violate basic humanitarian principles (see Chapter iv, Section 8). But, when the question is whether some of the traditionally honored values, if challenged, can be *scientifically confirmed,* then the contention that what has a grand tradition must be supposed to be true amounts to an escape from the scientific issue over "Route Six"—the historical fallacy. The question

[1] In this sense, the argument constitutes the cornerstone of conservatism, also of the "New Conservatism" that has arisen during the last period, represented, for example, by the writings of Professor Michael Oakeshott of the University of London. See his "Rationalism in Politics," *Cambridge Journal*, vol. 1 (1948) pp. 145–57; "Rational Conduct," *ibid.*, vol. 4 (1950) pp. 3–27; his inaugural address *Political Education*, Cambridge 1951; and the comments by Thomas P. Peardon, "Two Currents in Contemporary English Political Theory," *American Political Science Review*, vol. 49 (1955) pp. 487 ff. Further, Samuel Huntington, "Conservatism as an Ideology," *ibid.*, vol. 51 (1957) pp. 454–83. Francis G. Wilson, *The Case for Conservatism*, Seattle 1951.

whether a traditional evaluation is right cannot be answered scientifically by reference to tradition.

Section 5. What Is a Theory? The term "theory" has here been used exclusively for propositions that try to "explain" something. Other writers employ it more broadly. Thus William J. Goode and Paul K. Klatt, in their praiseworthy textbook on *Methods in Social Research* (New York 1952), call a "theory" variedly a proposition that serves as (1) orientation, (2) conceptualization, (3) classification, (4) summarizing observations, (5) prediction, or (6) pointing to gaps (pp. 8, 9); or they equate theory with (7) "facts assembled, ordered and seen in relationship," or with (8) "a logical relationship between facts" (p. 56). I think this is rather confusing. A theory as I understand the term is never "facts," although the operation of devising or proposing it is a fact, of course. A theory is not even facts "assembled and ordered," although it may be very useful for assembling and ordering them. Nor is it ever a "logical relationship," least of all one "between facts." There are no logical relations between facts, only between meanings (see Chapter 1, Section 6), and a theory is no "relationship," although it always must point to one. This relationship can be "logical" only where the theory deals with meaning, as in logic and mathematics; otherwise the theory points to factual (causal or otherwise existential) relations or regularities, not to logical ones. The specific operations enumerated by the authors (orientation, conceptualization, classification, etc.) are purposes to which a theory may be advantageously applied; but they do not define the meaning of the term.

The word "theory" is sometimes so used that it designates an entire system of thought on a certain subject, for example when we speak of the political theory of Plato, Locke, or Rousseau, or generally of the history of political theory in the sense in which this topic is usually dealt with in Anglo-American colleges. The term then comprehends, in addition to the theoretical "explanation" of facts or proposals, the presentation of the facts themselves, as seen by the respective writer, and of his proposals, including goals and moral principles.[2] Thus, David Easton (*The Political System, an Inquiry Into the State of Political Science,* New York 1953, pp. 309 ff.) says that every political theory consists of "factual, moral, applied and theoretical" propositions. This broad use is not recommendable for technical language. It is inconsistent to say that a theory includes other things in addition to theoretical propositions. Of what, then, do these "theoretical" propositions consist, we ask; and we can only answer by using a narrower definition

---

[2] See George H. Sabine, "What Is a Political Theory," cited below. Thomas P. Jenkin (*The Study of Political Theory,* Garden City, N.Y., 1955, p. 80) thinks a majority of theorists would agree that at bottom political theory is an ethical study. See also H. Eckstein (*rapporteur*), "Political Theory and the Study of Politics: a report of a Conference," *American Political Science Review,* vol. 50 (1956) pp. 475–87.

of theory, preferably one that refers to the "explaining" function of theory. In particular we should not, in strict language, call a "theory" what actually is a "proposal of policy," especially of goals and moral principles; proposals of policy are theories only to the extent that they offer explanations in their own support, as the classical writings on Natural Law and Natural Rights generally did. Whether the explanations are "scientific" in the modern sense is a separate question.

The reader who remembers Burke's ire in contrasting "theory" and "practice," his almost contemptuous indictment of theory and his glorification of practical wisdom (see the precise references in Leo Strauss, *Natural Right and History*, Chicago 1955, last chapter) should realize that the type of theory Burke rejected was not the modest effort now called "scientific political theory," always tentative and open to corrections. Rather, his objections were directed against (1) *non*scientific theories, especially nonscientific speculations about desirable ends (Plato's *Republic*, the French Revolution) and (2) *defective* scientific theories that did not take due account of all the relevant facts, consequences, etc. Scientific political theory today neither sets goals nor condones speculations that overlook facts; it supplies premeditated thought for the exercise of practical wisdom.

Some contemporary writers use the term "theory" only when the explanatory proposition is *true*. This is not recommendable, because it makes it impossible even to ask whether some theory *is* true. Others call every "law" a "theory," therewith ignoring the difference between (1) laws as factual regularities of nature (see below), and (2) explanatory theories that *refer* to these factual regularities. For both deviations, see Carl G. Hempel and Paul Oppenheim, "The Logic of Explanation," *Philosophy of Science*, vol. 15 (1948), reprinted in Feigl and Brodbeck, *Readings*, pp. 319–52.

What Is a Law? As discussed in the text, the term "law" means either a "norm" set by someone (or by custom), or the actual ways things go on with more or less regularity. In the latter sense, laws are descriptions of facts (events) in general terms (if . . . then). Whenever we mean by the term "law" not the description but that which is described, then *laws are facts*. To this extent, therefore, Charles S. Peirce was not wrong when he ascribed "being" to laws (*Collected Papers*, vol. 1, No. 27, vol. 2, No. 249). This need not imply philosophical realism beyond the type of realism which is contained in pure empiricism.

Laws need not be causal. Quite apart from the question whether there *are* any causal laws or merely statistical laws (see Chapter II Section 1), regularities can also be found in the association of attributes (e.g., blond hair and blue eyes), regardless of whether we are able to explain the regularity by causal laws. Thirdly, there are laws of a merely analytical nature, for instance the law that the square of the hypotenuse of a right-angled triangle equals the sum of the squares of its sides, or that the squares of even numbers are always even numbers too, and the squares of uneven numbers, uneven.

Section 6. Importance of Theory. Driscoll and Hyneman (*op.cit.,* p. 207) summarize their impressions of the orientation of American political scientists toward political theory as follows: "First, there is a tendency to look to the great writings as the main repository of theoretic effort. And, second, the study of theory is mainly directed to criticism and evaluation of the contributions of other people; there is little effort to make the study of theory an exercise in theory construction." These are the main points made also by David Easton and by Andrew Hacker, as cited.

Additional Literature to the Introductory Chapter:

W. W. Willoughby, "Value of Political Philosophy," *Political Science Quarterly,*
   vol. 15 (1900) pp. 75–95
Norman Campbell, *What Is Science?* 1921 (Dover Publications, New York
   1952) pp. 52 ff
George H. Sabine, "What Is a Political Theory?" *Journal of Politics,* vol. 1 (1939)
   pp. 1–16
————, *History of Political Theory,* 2nd ed., New York 1950 p. ix
Mulford Sibley, "Apology for Utopia," *Journal of Politics,* vol. 2 (1940) pp.
   57–74, 165–88
Leo Strauss, "On Classical Political Philosophy," *Social Research,* vol. 12 (1945)
   pp. 98–117
Benjamin E. Lippincott, "Political Theory in the United States," in UNESCO,
   Contemporary Political Science (cited above).
J. R. Pennock, "Political Science and Political Philosophy, *American Political
   Science Review,* vol. 45 (1951) pp. 1081–85
Andrew Hacker, *op.cit.* (Section 4)
Alfred Cobban, "The Decline of Political Theory," *Political Science Quarterly,*
   vol. 68 (1953) pp. 321–37
William A. Glaser, "The Types and Uses of Political Theory," *Social Research,*
   vol. 22 (1955) pp. 275–96
Max Weber, *On Law in Economy and Society,* ed. with introduction and annota-
   tions by Max Rheinstein, translated by E. Shils and M. R.; 20th Century
   Legal Philosophy Series, vol. 6, Cambridge, Mass., 1954

NOTES TO CHAPTER I

(Theory of Scientific Method: Facts and Logic)

Section 2. Immediate and Inferential Knowledge. F. S. C. Northrop (*The Logic of the Sciences and the Humanities,* New York 1947, p. 48 and *passim*) calls the direct type of observation which relies exclusively on the senses, "aesthetic," as distinct from the indirect type, which is based on inferences; this he calls "theoretic." "Aesthetic" observation, almost entirely neglected by the West in favor of "theoretic" observation, has remained the basis of philosophy in the East, at least until recently, he says. The access of a purely "aesthetic" observation to facts is best represented by the art of the early Western impressionists and of the Chinese (p. 326). However, Professor Northrop concedes that no sharp line of distinction can be drawn between the two types; there is, rather, a broad "twilight zone," e.g., common-sense observations, which rest on inferences; for it is only by inference that we recognize what we see aesthetically as colors and lines to be a chair, and assume that it is the same chair we saw yesterday and will remain the same when we do not look at it (p. 93). I think we must go further. Whenever the observer breaks through what Northrop calls the "aesthetic continuum" by some act of "differentiation" (p. 98) he necessarily interrupts the purely immediate aesthetic impression.

There is still no established terminological usage to distinguish what in observation is "affected by cognitive action" from what is "immediate." C. I. Lewis (*Analysis of Knowledge and Valuation,* La Salle, Ill. 1946, p. 30) includes all directly given data of sense, even if noncognitive or illusory, in his use of the concept "apprehension"; this concept, however, is to cover also those data which, although not given by the senses, are empirically verifiable, i.e., inferential data, and, thirdly, the apprehension of "meaning." A. N. Whitehead, on the other hand, uses for noncognitive apprehension the term "prehension"; then, perception is "cognitive prehension" (*Science and the Modern World,* New York 1925, pp. 101, 104).

Common Sense. For the interrelation between common sense and science, see William James, *Pragmatism* (Perry ed.) pp. 165 ff. and 379 ff.; and John Dewey in his and Arthur F. Bentley's *Knowing and the Known* (Boston 1949) pp. 270–86, where he writes: ". . . the expression 'common sense' is a usable and useful name for a body of facts that are so basic that without systematic attention to them 'science' cannot exist, while philosophy is idly speculative apart from them" (p. 272). Also, William K. Clifford, *The Common Sense of the Exact Sciences,* prefaced by Bertrand Russell (Dover publ.); James B. Conant, *Science and Common Sense,* New Haven, 1951; Carl J. Friedrich, *The New Belief in the Common Man,* Boston, 1941; 2nd ed. (titled *The New Image of the Common Man*) 1951.

Modifications of Behaviorism. In the course of time Behaviorism has lost much of its original rigidity. Behaviorists have generally admitted that what people say they think is part of their behavior. Sample surveys about what people say they think have, therefore, not met with Behaviorist opposition. On the contrary, the growing popularity of such surveys has contributed to modifying the controversy between the opposed schools, since these surveys made "subjective data objectively observable, recordable, measurable, analyzable" (Bernard Berelson, "The Study of Public Opinion," in Leonard D. White, ed., *The State of the Social Sciences,* Chicago 1956, p. 309). Most Behaviorists, furthermore, admit that a person can observe the inner state in which he finds himself, e.g., that of anger, and that, at least to some extent although never completely, others can often confirm his inner state on the ground of its external characteristics. Some Behaviorists are even inclined to go further. Thus Rudolf Carnap writes in his paper "Testability and Meaning" (as cited in Chapter v, Section 3), that "the majority of philosophers, including some members of our [Vienna] Circle in former times, hold that there is a certain field of events, called the consciousness of a person, which is absolutely inaccessible to any other person. But we now believe, on the basis of physicalism, that the difference, although very great and very important for practical life, is only a matter of degree and that there are predicates for which the directness of confirmation by other persons has intermediate degrees. . . . We may formulate the fact mentioned by saying that the psychological predicates in a physicalistic language are intersubjectively confirmable but only *subjectively* observable" (No. 16). See Chapter v, Section 3, on Neopositivism.

That it is often more important to know what things mean to people than what they really are (see text) has been stressed especially by Schutz (*op.cit.,* Chapter II, Section 6, above), Howard Becker (*Through Values to Social Interpretation,* Durham, N.C., 1950, pp. 188 ff.), Robert K. Merton (*Social Theory and Social Structure,* Glencoe, Ill., 1957 ed., pp. 421, 22) and F. A. Hayek (*The Counter-Revolution of Science, Studies on the Abuse of Reason,* Glencoe, Ill., 1952, p. 44).

Section 3. Limited Usefulness of Formalized Techniques of Opinion Research. A certain healthy retreat from the original enthusiasm with which sociologists have sought to reform the social sciences by capturing attitudes and opinions through questionnaires and interviews can be noticed in some recent writings, e.g., Goode and Hatt (*op.cit.,* pp. 330 ff.), Speier and especially, Berelson. Hans Speier (*German Rearmament and Atomic War,* Evanston, Ill., 1957, p. 10) pleads for the advantages which the old-fashioned art of conversation between equals holds over formal interviews in appropriate cases. Berelson (*op.cit.,* pp. 317, 318) criticizes the latter-day vogue of novel techniques in opinion research on three grounds: first, their abrupt breach with the intellectual past in the study of public opinion; second, their isolation from other disciplines; third, their neglect of the question of "importance." Regarding his first complaint, he says: "The new studies have driven out the old—too fully, too quickly. There is a good deal in what the earlier writers said and the way they went about saying it, and the study of public opinion today is poorer for the absence of such macrocosmic considerations . . . here may be an instance of what happens when research crowds out reflection." As to the second point he holds that historians and political theorists and social philosophers "have more to offer to the student of public opinion than they have been willing or prepared in recent years to say or he to hear." He relates that he and some colleagues of his, when they included some "big" considerations of political theory in their remarks, were criticized for engaging in "high thinking"—"not that we could do it, but as though it were bad in itself." And finally, to the third complaint, he suggests that in some parts of the behavioral sciences now "there seems to be an inverse correlation between the importance of the problem and the technical proficiency with which it is, or can be, attacked." Too often, he feels, people in the public opinion field have "forgotten that the word 'significance' has more than a statistical meaning." All this tends to support my own remarks in Sections 3 and 6.

Additional Literature. The following are listed by Berelson (*op.cit.*) as the ten most important books on public opinion research published since 1935:[1]

Lasswell and Blumenstock, *World Revolutionary Propaganda, 1939*
Gosnell, *Grass Roots Politics, 1942*
Newcomb, *Personality and Social Change,* 1943
Cantril *et.al., Gauging Public Opinion,* 1944
Lazarsfeld *et.al., The People's Choice,* 1945; *Voting,* 1954
Mosteller *et.al., The Pre-election Polls of 1948,* 1948
Stouffer *et.al., The American Soldier,* 1949
Adorno *et.al., The Authoritarian Personality,* 1950
Cantril and Strunk, *Public Opinion, 1935–46,* 1951
Hovland *et.al., Communication and Persuasion,* 1953

Research Techniques: General Books, in addition to those mentioned in the text:
F. Stuart Chapin, *Experimental Designs in Sociological Research,* New York 1947
Pauline Young, *Scientific Social Surveys and Research,* New York, 2nd, 1949
Wilson Gee, *Social Science Research Methods,* New York 1950
Marie Jahoda, Morton Deutsch, Stuart W. Cook, *Research Methods in Social Relations,* New York 1951
Rusell L. Ackoff, *The Design of Social Research,* Chicago 1953
Arnold M. Rose, *Theory and Method in the Social Sciences,* Minneapolis, 1954

See further:
Francis G. Wilson, "Public Opinion in the Theory of Democracy," *Thought,* vol. 20 (1945) pp. 235–52; and "Public Opinion and the Intellectuals," *American Political Science Review,* vol. 48 (1954) pp. 321–39

---

[1] He contrasts them with older works, such as Tocqueville, *Democracy in America* (1935); Bryce, *The American Commonwealth* (1899); Lowell, *Public Opinion and Popular Government* (1913); Dicey, *Lectures on the Relation of Law and Public Opinion in England in the Nineteenth Century* (1914); Lippmann, *Public Opinion* (1922); Toennies, *Kritik der oeffentlichen Meinung* (1925); Angell, *The Public Mind* (1926); Dewey, *The Public and Its Problems* (1927); Bauer, *Die oeffentliche Meinung in der Weltgeschichte* (1930). Only three of these were written by Americans, all had individual authors, and none dealt with techniques.

Alfred de Grazia, "The Process of Theory-Research Interaction," *Journal of Politics,* vol. 13 (1951) pp. 88 ff.

David Truman, "The Implications of Political Behavior Research," Social Science Research Council, *Items,* vol. 5 (1951) pp. 37–39

M. Brewster Smith, J. S. Brunner, and R. W. White, *Opinions and Personality,* New York 1956

M. B. Smith, "Opinions, Personality, and Political Behavior," *American Political Science Review,* vol. 52 (1958) pp. 1–17, and "Comment" by Alexander L. George, *ibid.,* pp. 18–26

Herbert McClosky, "Conservatism and Personality," *ibid.,* pp. 27–44

Section 4. Measurement and Classification, Additional Literature:

Stuart A. Rice, *Quantitative Methods in Politics,* New York 1928

Emory S. Bogardus, "Social Distance and Its Practical Implications," *Sociology and Social Research,* vol. 17 (1933) pp. 265–71

Paul Lazarsfeld, B. Berelson, and H. Gaudet, *The People's Choice,* New York 1945

Helen Hall Jennings, *Sociometry in Group Relations,* Washington, D.C. 1948

Lyman Bryson, "Circles of Prestige," *Political Science Quarterly,* vol. 69 (1954) pp. 481–501

James G. March, "An Introduction to the Theory and Measurement of Influence, *American Political Science Review,* vol. 49 (1955) pp. 431–51

Section 5. Correspondence Theory of Truth. William James, too, was fundamentally an adherent of the correspondence theory. "An experience, perceptual or conceptual, must conform to reality in order to be true," he wrote in "Humanism and Truth," *Pragmatism* (Perry ed.) p. 148. But he modified this concession considerably, by adding that by reality he meant "nothing more than the other conceptual experiences with which a given present experience may find itself in point of fact mixed up," which was again quite subjectively formulated. Also, "conforming" was to mean "taken account-of in such a way as to gain any intellectually and practically satisfactory results," and to "take account-of" was called a term that permits of "no definition, so many are the ways in which [it] can practically be worked out."

True Statements vs. Stated Truth. Arthur F. Bentley analyzes the difference between Carnap's "truth" and Kaufmann's "true" (see text) in a paper included in Bentley, *Inquiry Into Inquiries, Essays in Social Theory* (ed. by Sidney Rattner, Boston 1954, pp. 325 ff.). Kaufmann's goal, says Bentley, is "the true; Carnap's the (semantical) truth." He obviously sides with Kaufmann. But if truth is defined with reference to assertions and their verifiability, as it is with Kaufmann, Dewey, and with Bentley himself, this has the disadvantage that truth is never a matter of the past or the present but always of the future. See my remarks in the text, and William Savery in *The Philosophy of John Dewey* (R. A. Schilpp, ed., New York 1939 and

1951) p. 501. Once the dual meaning of the term truth is clearly recognized, the two approaches are not irreconcilable, I believe.

Coherence Theory of Truth. There is a third theory of truth, which defines truth as coherent scientific propositions. If taken in isolation, this is the weakest of the three, because it is equally unsatisfactory with regard to the criterion of truth which is to apply to previously established coherent knowledge and that according to which a conflict between the established body and new additions must be judged. If, however, conceived not in isolation but in combination with either of the other theories, the coherence theory establishes a useful postulate, in accord with No. 9 of the basic scheme of Scientific Method given in Chapter I, Section 1.

Reality. Modern science can be said historically to rest on the stubborn faith that facts are facts. It does so although this faith cannot be accounted for by Scientific Method; it is an "immanent methodological a priori" of this method (see Chapters II, Section 5, and V, Section 2). If, in conflict with common sense, one means by "fact" only the *statement* about a phenomenon, not the phenomenon itself (thus, Talcott Parsons, *The Structure of Social Action,* New York 1937, p. 41, note), or some belief or state of mind, then one arrives ultimately at artifical definitions, like the one that a fact is an "empirically verifiable statement about phenomena in terms of a conceptual scheme" (Parsons) or "a logical construct of concepts" (Goode and Hatt, *op.cit.,* p. 42). I doubt that the fact that there were several big wars in this century can be adequately disposed of as a "statement" or as a "logical construct of concepts." I admit, of course, that "war," "this century," and "big" are logical constructs. But the fact that the wars took place is, unfortunately, more than a "logical construct."

Additional Literature

Alfred N. Whitehead, *Process and Reality, an Essay in Cosmology,* New York 1929 [1]

Kurt Riezler, *Physics and Reality, Lecture of Aristotle on Modern Physics at an International Congress of Science,* New Haven 1940 (a critique of modern concepts of reality fictionally ascribed to Aristotle)

Karl Jaspers, *Von der Wahrheit,* vol. 1, München 1947 (1103 pages)

Martin Heidegger, *Vom Wesen der Wahrheit,* Frankfurt 1943; 3rd ed., 1954

Wilbur M. Urban, *Language and Reality; the Philosophy of Language and the Principles of Symbolism,* London 1939, New York 1951

Louis Katsoff, *Logic and the Nature of Reality,* New York 1956

Maurice Natanson, *A Critique of Jean-Paul Sartre's Ontology,* Lincoln, Neb., 1951

---

[1] For the purposes of this book I have considered references to *Science and the Modern World* more appropriate than to the technical details and speculative elaborations of Whitehead's philosophy of organism in *Process and Reality.*

Charles N. R. McCoy, "The Logical and the Real in Political Theory: Plato, Aristotle, Marx," *American Political Science Review,* vol. 48 (1954) pp. 1058–66

Section 6. Logic or Logics? There have been several types of logic offered from Aristotle and the Aristotelians (ontological) to Hegel and the Hegelians (dynamic), and several others, more recently produced, compete in the market today. The logics of Russell and G. E. Moore, of Morris Cohen and Felix Kaufmann, of Charles Morris and Carnap, of Dewey and J. R. Kantor follow four divergent lines of thought on logic, and further differences appear within each of these rather loosely grouped pairs. Arthur Bentley has given useful skeleton-outlines of most of them in two chapters, titled "Logic in an Age of Science" and "A confused Semiotic," in his and Dewey's book, *Knowing and the Known* (Boston 1949, pp. 205–69), interspersed with acid criticisms. He characterizes the logics of Russell and Moore as "so simple-minded it is remarkable they have survived at all in a modern world," those of Morris and Carnap as hopelessly confused, and those of Cohen and Kaufmann as "heroic efforts to escape from the old confusions, yet futile because they fail to pick up the adequate weapons." He sees promise for the future only in the logics of Dewey and, to a lesser degree, of Kantor. They consider man in action, and his use of logic in the action of inquiry, as inseparable parts of nature in the process of mutual "transaction" between organisms and their environment (Kantor speaks of "interaction," which fails to point out the totality of what Dewey calls "transaction," see below).

This plurality of logics may look very discouraging for students of social theory. But insofar as sheer logic is concerned, matters are not so bad as they appear at first sight. For the greatest part of the embittered controversy is not primarily about logic in the sense in which this term has been used here; rather, it reflects deeper differences regarding conceptions the authors entertain about facts, truth, reality, or knowledge (i.e., their ontological, epistemological, or procedural views); or, and this seems to hold for most of it, the controversy is about the use of terms (i.e., terminological). Dewey and Bentley have in fact turned their particular scorn on any terminological vagueness and inconsistency they could lay hands on, and there were many indeed that deserved criticism. In order to cleanse scientific language from impurities the two reformers eliminated from their own use many currently employed terms, such as "definition" and "meaning," substituting other terms for them (see below), or invented new terms for new concepts, such as "transaction" (see below). Their own terminologies at times lie open to criticism. All this, however, should not be permitted to veil the fact that the basic elements of logical reasoning as described in the text of this book are, *apart* from questions of terminology, hardly controversial. Where they are, due mention has been made of the controversial points (see remarks

509

on Dewey, Kaufmann, Carnap, Morris, and others, in Chapters I, Sections 5, 6, and 7; II, Section 7; V, Section 3; VIII, Section 2; and in the notes hereafter). To do more cannot be the function of the present chapter, which is to describe and demarcate Scientific Method—but not to apply it immediately to every unsolved problem.

Larger and Smaller Logic. Occasionally, writers have taken the view that, although the generally recognized rules of deductive and inductive logic are valid, there is another area of logic which is governed by additional rules. Thus, John Stuart Mill held that the "Smaller Logic" which is concerned with the conditions of consistency constitutes but a part of a "Larger Logic," which embraces all the general conditions of the ascertainment of truth. This "Larger Logic" of his was—chiefly or entirely—identical with methodology (see Mill, *An Examination of Sir William Hamilton's Philosophy,* London 1867, p. 461; Nagel ed., p. xxxi). This view is similar to the one later taken by Dewey (see our text). More recently, Professor Recasens-Siches announced that he has begun to explore a "logic of the reasonable" as different from the pure "logic of the rational" (*Natural Law Forum,* vol. 3, 1958, p. 156). Like Mill, he does not seem to question the validity of rational logic; but unlike Mill's "larger logic," Recasens' "logic of the reasonable" is to justify intuitional acceptance of "given ends," religious values, and moral taboos (see notes on Recasens to Chapters VII and VIII). If his plan is carried through in line with rational logic, no Ought can be inferred from any Is without a major premise of Ought form. Such a major premise—for example that harmonious happiness (Perry) or the Golden Rule (MacIver) or the evolution of society (Comte, Huxley) or God's revealed will ought to be pursued, or, as Recasens himself teaches, that the value of every individual person is greater than that of any group (see at Chapter VIII)—may of course be proposed, and may be "supported" by reasoning. But this type of reasoning leads necessarily beyond the area of intersubjectively transmissible knowledge; in other words, it is of S_2 and not of S_1 character (see Chapter II, Section 7); it is not intersubjectively conclusive.

Definition. A particularly clear analysis can be found in C. I. Lewis (*op.cit.,* pp. 30 ff.). He distinguishes a term's "denotion," "comprehension," "signification," and "intension." *Denotion* is the class of all actually existent things to which the term applies; the term "unicorn," therefore, has zero denotion, since no unicorns exist. *Comprehension* includes all consistently thinkable things to which the term would be correctly applicable; thus the term "unicorn" has a definite comprehension, though no denotion. *Signification* of a term means *that* property in things the presence of which indicates that the term correctly applies, as the possession of one horn, and one horn only, in the case of unicorns. *Intension* is the conjunction of all other terms each of which must be applicable to anything to which the term would be correctly applicable; for example, other qualities of an animal in the case of unicorns. "The intension of a term represents our intention in using it." Abstract terms are those which name what some other term signifies; the abstract term "roundness" names that which the term "round" signifies. "The sole function of a real definition is to explicate the intensional meaning of the expression which is defined." I put these specifications down here as a good illustration of analytic thinking. Whether the names are well chosen might be questioned, but the distinctions are valid.

Dewey and Bentley (*op.cit.*) wish to avoid the term "definition" as too vague, except in mathematics, where it has a precise meaning. They divide it up into *characterization* for the broader type of definition, i.e., the "greater part of the everyday use of words," and *specification* for the "more highly perfected naming behavior, as best exhibited in modern science." Preceding the phase of characterization there may be an earlier phase, called *cue* by them. *Designation* they keep for the "naming phase," which to them is a "knowing-naming" phase, always including both knowing and naming, and always to be viewed as a (mutual) "transaction" between organism and environment (see below). Use of the word "name" they reluctantly permit wherever one can "safely expect to hold it to behavioral understanding."

Additional Literature. N. S. Timasheff, "Definitions in the Social Sciences," *American Journal of Sociology*, vol. 53 (1947) pp. 201–09.

Meaning. In their iconoclastic fury Dewey and Bentley proposed to eliminate the term "meaning" altogether, as too confused, from scientific language (*op.cit.*, p. 297). They hold that more direct expressions can always be found, recommending that we speak, whenever possible, in terms of "is" or "involves." This is not always feasible, however. I have generally used "meaning" in the sense of what is designated by a word or other sign, or involved, or implied in its use, i.e., its *Sinn*. As words (signs) are used with different intentions as to what they designate, involve, or imply, and are interpreted differently, it seems to me artificial to avoid saying that they can have different "meanings." Dewey rightly combats the tendency to think of meaning as separate from the word (sign); he "wants to do away with that split between disembodied meanings and meaningless bodies [i.e., signs without meaning]." But even though a sign without meaning and a meaning without sign are senseless, this does not alter the fact that some particular sign can have different meanings according to situation, intention, or interpretation. This cannot be expressed fluently without using the term "meaning" or its equivalent.

Concept. The term "concept" found mercy in the eyes of Dewey and Bentley. They use it as a "current phrasing for subject matters designed to be held under steady inspection in inquiry" (*op.cit.*), which seems to me a very good definition whether "characterization" or "specification" must be left to more legitimate students of Dewey to decide.

Northrop (*op.cit.*, p. 59 and *passim*) distinguishes concepts by "intuition" and concepts by "postulation." This distinction is valid, but the terminology is confusing because, ignoring the divinatory connotation generally associated with this term, he uses "intuition" exclusively for concepts that rely solely on immediate ("aesthetic") perception, such as "red" (see above, Section 2), with no inkling of "hunch, wild guess, axiom" (p. 113). He calls concepts like "electrons," which rely on theoretical hypotheses, concepts "by postulation." This is more in line with accepted usage. Northrop's main point in emphasizing his substantially valid distinction is that it is illogical to switch from concepts of immediate perception to concepts by postulation; it is "nonsense" to say "electrons are pink" (p. 128). In order to interrelate the two types of concepts (e.g., a definite wave length with a definite color) an intermediate process is required, which he calls "epistemic correlation" (p. 114).

Transaction. This term, placed by Dewey and Bentley in the center of their inquiry into *Knowing and the Known* (*op.cit.,* especially pp. 103–43), seems to me one of the most unfortunate, least suggestive, and most misleading names ever given a needed concept. The prefix "trans" is here understood not in the sense of "beyond" but of "across, from side to side." Transaction is to refer to organisms and their environments as observed in integration with, and within, their integrated fields (i.e., in "transaction," which term D. and B. prefer to field), not in separation or isolation, not as things acting under their own power ("self-acting"), nor as balanced against other things in causal relations ("inter-action"), but in such a way that none of the constituents of a fact can be adequately specified apart from the specification of other constituents of the full subject-matter. The authors' emphasis on the transactional aspects is the logical consequence of their philosophy which, more radically than others, discards the traditional basic differentiation of mind vs. matter, subject vs. object, self vs. non-self, and, of course, "tolerates" no entities or realities of any kind "intruding as if from behind and beyond the knowing-known events, with power to interfere," no "ultimate" truth or "absolute" knowledge (p. 120).[2] They do not, however, entirely object to the use of "mind" or "mental" if employed merely as a "preliminary word in casual phrasing." Then it "is a sound word to indicate a region or

---

[2] This "intolerance" appears quite "absolute" in itself as expressed by the authors. It is tenable merely if meant as a *postulation* for *scientific* inquiry, not as a negative scientific assertion. See note 25 on p. 145: "Many a man is confident in saying that he knows for certain (and often with a very peculiar certainty) what is behind and beyond his personal knowledge. We are well aware of this. Nevertheless, we do not regard it as good practice in inquiry when dependable results are sought"—intersubjectively transmissible knowledge, as I would call it. Also, Chapter XIII of this book.

at least a general locality in need of investigation"; as such it is "unobjectionable." But mind or faculty or the like as an "actor in charge of behavior is a charlatan, and 'brain' as a substitute for such a 'mind' is worse. Such words insert a name in place of a problem, and let it go at that. . . ." As a derivative from the old immortal soul mind is "wholly redundant. The living, behaving, knowing organism is present. To add a 'mind' to him is to try to double him up. It is double-talk; and double-talk doubles no facts" (p. 132). But to come back to transaction. "Transaction," Dewey and Bentley say, is "the knowing-known when as one process . . . the knowns and the named . . . taken as phases of a common process in cases in which otherwise they have been viewed as separated components, allotted irregular degrees of independence, and examined in the form of interactions" (p. 304). In all fairness I feel it must be said that concentration on the transactional as distinct from inter-actional (causal) aspects of events in social life is as yet a vague program rather than an achievement.

Fallacy of Reification. The mere fact that we use a concept with a definite "comprehension" and "intension" (Lewis' terms) does not guarantee the existence of the thing so defined; it is fallacious to follow from the terms "unicorn" and "centaur" that there are such creatures. This type of fallacy occurs frequently in handling abstract concepts such as "society," "nation," "capitalism," "collective mind." Many a scientist "uncritically assumes that when there are commonly used concepts there must also be definite 'given' things which they describe," as F. A. Hayek puts it (*The Counter-Revolution of Science*, pp. 54 ff.). He calls this attitude "conceptual realism"; Whitehead spoke of it as the "fallacy of misplaced concreteness." See also Goode and Hatt, *op.cit.*, p. 42, for the same objection under the more usual name of "reification."

The Search for Basic Concepts; Additional Literature

General:
Vilfredo Pareto, *The Mind and Society*, 4 vols., New York 1935
Talcott Parsons, *The Structure of Social Action*, New York 1937
———, *Essays in Sociological Theory*, Glencoe, Ill., 1949
Robert K. Merton, *Social Theory and Social Structure*, Glencoe, Ill., 1949; 2nd ed., revised and enlarged, 1957

"Signs" and "Language": see notes to Chapter V, Section 3

"Power," "Control," and "Influence": see Chapter VIII, Section 12, and March's article cited above, notes to Section 4

"Groups" and "Equilibrium":
A. F. Bentley, *The Process of Government, a Study of Social Pressures*, Chicago 1908; 3rd ed., Bloomington, Ind., 1949
Harold Lasswell, *passim*; e.g., *Power and Personality*, New York 1948, pp. 123, 146

David Truman, *The Governmental Process,* New York 1951

David Easton, *The Political System, An Inquiry into the State of Political Science,* New York 1951

Oliver Garceau, "Research in the Political Process," *American Political Science Review,* vol. 45 (1951) pp. 69–85

Earl Latham, "The Group Basis of Politics: Notes for a Theory," *ibid.,* vol. 46 (1952) pp. 376–97; also, *The Group Basis of Politics: A Study in Basing Point Legislation,* Ithaca 1952 (chapter on methods)

Murray S. Stedman, "A Group Interpretation of Politics," *Public Opinion Quarterly,* vol. 17 (1953) pp. 218–29

Richard W. Taylor, "Arthur Bentley's Political Science," *Western Political Science Quarterly,* vol. 5 (1952)

Phillip Monypenny, "Political Science and the Study of Groups: Notes to Guide a Research Project," *ibid.,* vol. 7 (1954) pp. 183–201

Gabriel A. Almond, "Comparative Study of Interest Groups," *American Political Science Review,* vol. 52 (1958) pp. 270–82

"Elites":

Vilfredo Pareto, *Mind and Society,* as cited above

Harold Lasswell, Daniel Lerner, and C. Easton Rothwell, *The Comparative Study of Elites; Introduction and Bibliography,* Stanford 1952

Harold Lasswell, "The Political Science of Science" *American Political Science Review,* vol. 50 (1956) pp. 961–79

Milovan Djilas, *The New Class, an Analysis of the Communist System,* New York 1957

"Action":

Talcott Parsons, *The Structure of Social Action, op.cit.*

Talcott Parsons, Edward A. Shils (eds.), *Toward a General Theory of Action,* Cambridge, Mass., 1951

"Anticipated Reaction" and "Game":

Carl J. Friedrich, *Constitutional Government and Democracy,* 2nd ed., Boston, 1941, pp. 589–91, also 462 (anticipated reaction)

J. von Neumann and O. Morgenstern, *Theory of Games and Economic Behavior,* Princeton, 3rd ed., 1953

Martin Shubik, *Readings in Game Theory and Political Behavior,* New York 1954

"Field" and "Transaction":

Kurt Lewin, *Field Theory in Social Science,* New York 1951

John Dewey and A. F. Bentley, as cited above ("transaction")

"Decision Making":

Ward Edwards, "The Theory of Decision Making," *Psychological Bulletin,* vol. 51 (1954) pp. 380–417

Jacob Marshak, "Toward a Preference Scale for Decision Making," reprinted in Shubik, *Readings (op.cit.)* pp. 22–32

Felix Oppenheim, "Rational Choice," *The Journal of Philosophy,* vol. 50 (1953) pp. 341–50

R. C. Snyder, H. W. Bruck, and Burton Sapin, *Decision-Making as an Approach to a Study of International Politics,* Princeton 1954

"Function," either "manifest" or "latent" (in the sense of the function or dys-
function performed, either purposively or without purpose, for or against
society or some part of it by any social or cultural factor, such as usage,
belief, behavior pattern, or institution):

Robert K. Merton, *Social Theory and Social Structure, op.cit.,* esp., pp. 19–120,
and literature there given, pp. 47, n. 50, and 82 ff.

Talcott Parsons, *The Social System,* Glencoe, Ill., 1951

M. J. Levy, Jr., *The Structure of Society,* Princeton 1953

Ralf Dahrendorf, "Struktur und Funktion," *Kölner Zeitschrift für Soziologie
und Sozialpsychologie,* vol. 7 (1955) pp. 492–519

Georges Gurvitch, "Le concept de structure sociale," *Cahiers Internationaux de
Sociologie,* vol. 19 (1955) pp. 3–44

The Postulates of Arithmetic. Credit for first formulating the postulates
must go to the Italian mathematician G. Peano (1858–1932). He used three
terms as given without definition ("o," "number," "successor"), and five
postulates, built from these primitives, namely (1) "o is a number," (2)
"the successor of a number is a number," (3) "no two numbers have the
same successor," (4) "o is not the successor of any number," and (5) "every
number has the property P if o has it and the property is such that whenever any number has it then its successor has it too." The missing definition
of the three primitive terms was provided by the German logician G. Frege
(1848–1925), whose work was completed by Russell and Whitehead (see
text). They describe a "number" as a characteristic of a certain class of objects, as, e.g., "two" is characteristic of the legs of healthy men, "three" of
certain geometric figures, and "five" of the fingers of a hand. The common
characteristic of the "class of all those classes" which share that characteristic
(e.g., man's legs, husband and wife, day and night, return trip, etc.) is the
respective "number." From there, one can reach a definition also of "o" and
of "successor." I cannot go into further details. For a good presentation, apart
from Russell's *Introduction* and from Tarski's book (both cited in the text),
see Carl G. Hempel "On the Nature of Mathematical Truth," (*American
Mathematic Monthly,* vol. 52, 1945, reprinted in *Readings* by Feigl and
Sellars, p. 222, also by Feigl and Brodbeck, p. 148). These definitions and
postulates I hold to be not quite satisfactory; they seem to me unnecessarily
artificial and still deficient. It may be right to describe the number "two" as
the class of all those classes that are united by the characteristic of twoness;
but with regard to high numbers, say, 1,257,812, this approach is artificial.
A number's meaning, especially beyond the first ten, twelve, or twenty,
refers to the process of *counting,* and to *relations,* not to the ontological property of a class of things that have this number in common. Furthermore, the
definitions omit the essential postulate that the units within the classes (the
individual legs, fingers, sides of a triangle, objects in a room) are considered
equal among themselves *for the purpose at hand.* My own definition, given
in the text, is oversimplified, on the other hand, because it omits Peano's

postulates Nrs. 4 and 5, and the proper definition of 0. But for our present purpose, which is merely to show that arithmetic is analytic and not synthetic, the indications given in the text and in these notes may suffice.

Induction. Use of this term has sometimes been restricted to reasoning that infers the composition of a whole *class* from samples (thus, e.g., by Peirce, *Collected Papers,* vol. 1, No. 68, vol. 2, No. 640), while different names are used for reasoning that infers a *hypothesis* from observed facts; this latter type has then been called variously "presumptive" (Peirce), "abductive," or "retroductive" reasoning. See Ernest Nagel, *Sovereign Reason* (Glencoe, Ill., 1954) p. 82. In a broader sense, the term "inductive" inference may, however, well be used for both types. They can hardly be distinguished in a strict manner, since the conjunction of events in clusters of so-called causal relations constitutes them as members of a class, e.g., the "class of things subject to gravitation." This seems to be Nagel's view too.

Probability. Empirical and analytical factors in probability judgments are frequently confused. The proposition, "The probability that a 'four' will turn up in the throw of a die is one-sixth," may have one of several meanings. In making explicit the particular sense in which I am using these words in a given case and all the implications of this sense I do not enter into any synthetic, empirical reasoning, but keep strictly within analytical deductive reasoning. The meaning may be, and often is, that

(1) "As seen at present, there are six possibilities, neither more nor less," and
(2) "As seen at present, there is no ground on which to presume that any one of them will materialize rather than any other."

This dual meaning implies the further contention that

(3) "There is no ground at present for presuming that, if the same process (throwing a die) is repeated several times, the four will appear more often than in *exactly* one-sixth of the throws, nor that it will come out in less than exactly one-sixth."

There may, of course, be good reasons for assuming that the four will not turn up in *exactly* one-sixth of the throws; if the number of tries is 7, 13, or 38, that would even be impossible. But there must be no good ground for presuming that the four will turn up in *more* than exactly one-sixth of the cases, nor that it will appear in *less* than that. Otherwise it could not be said that there is at present no ground for presuming that the chance is exactly equal to that of any of the five other possibilities.

All this is merely analytic. It states the meaning of a proposition. The proposition itself, however, is not merely analytic, unless it deals with purely logical or mathematical operations (as, for example, when it states that in multiplying any number by five the probability of the last digit being five is one-half). Whenever the proposition deals with empirical events, such as throwing dice (and even drawing the number with which to multiply five), it is not merely analytic; then it contains empirical elements in both of its principal statements (1) and (2). These statements may be in conflict with the actual facts. There may be more than six possibilities; the die may, in one out of a million cases, end its motion by standing on one of its edges. Or there may be grounds for expecting that one of the faces will be up more often than others, e.g., because the die is loaded. These are empirical questions. Unfortunately, in most practical cases of the social sciences the number and the weight of the possibilities are much harder to check than in the case of throwing dice (see below).

Be that as it may, we are free to continue in our purely analytical procedure by arguing on the *assumption* that the two principal statements (1) and (2) are correct. Then the meaning of (1), (2), and (3) implies another contention, namely, that

(4) "There is good reason to presume that the 'four' will turn up in *approximately,* or close to, one-sixth of a large number of throws."

This follows from the meaning of the other three statements on grounds that are merely analytic. We may list all possibilities of what under the postulates (1), (2), and (3) may happen in a series of, say, twelve throws of a die, beginning with the possibility that the "one" will appear in every one of the twelve; next, that it will appear the first time, followed by the "two" at the second throw, but again by the "one" at all other ten throws; and so on. There are actually more than two billion—precisely speaking, 2,176,782,336—such possibilities in the case of twelve throws. Hence we had better not count them, but use a simple mathematical formula (6^{12}) to calculate them—a good illustration of the value of analytical procedure. With the number of all possible combinations thus stated and likewise the number of those combinations counted or calculated in which the four appears in near to one-sixth of twelve throws (say, at least once), it will be seen that the four does so in the overwhelming majority of all possible combinations; in fact, it occurs at least once in about 89 percent[3] of the possible sequences, if there are twelve successive throws. This is why we have good grounds for predicting that the four *will* turn up in "approximately" one-sixth of the throws. But there is, analytically speaking, no *certainty* that it will do so. Nor is it certain that even the queerest of the many possible combinations, e.g., an unbroken sequence of four turning up in every one of the twelve throws, will not happen. Analytically, this combination has the same chance as any other of the two billion-odd *specific* sequences that are equally possible.

[3] Precisely speaking, in 1,932,641,711 of the 2,176,782,336 possible sequences, i.e., 6^{12} *minus* 5^{12}.

It is hard to realize that, although you can throw a die twelve times and write down the results within five minutes, the particular result you got had only one chance in more than two billion of materializing. What you have brought about, therefore, is something near a miracle: the materialization of this particular sequence. Try to get it again, tossing a die from morning to night to the end of your life—and you will in all probability not succeed.

I have chosen the small number of twelve throws as an illustration, although a larger number of, say, sixty or six hundred would have shown the significance of this analytical procedure more strikingly; but in that case the number of possibilities is beyond the human power of imagination. With sixty throws the number of possible sequences is over six million multiplied by one trillion multiplied by another trillion and by a third trillion, i.e., more than a six followed by forty-two zeros, or 6 times 10^{42}. *One* of these possibilities is that the four will turn up at every one of the sixty throws; but this possibility is infinitesimally low, and there is no certainty that it or any other particular sequence will ever occur, even if try-outs be infinitely prolonged. The opposite does not follow from analytical reasoning. It can be distilled only from some synthetic hypothesis, such as "Anything that *can* happen (in the sense that there are no grounds for assuming that it will not happen) *will* happen in the long run." But whether this hypothesis is true or false depends on empirical confirmation. That something will happen does not follow *logically* from the fact that there is no ground for assuming that it will not happen. We may decide upon postulating the validity of the "what-can-happen-will-happen" hypothesis for some scientific purpose; there is nothing illogical or self-contradictory in it. But it does not, like our statements (3) and (4), follow logically from the meaning of the propositions (1) and (2).

All the foregoing is predicated on the assumption that the proposition, "The probability that a four will turn up in the throw of a die is one-sixth," was to have the meaning (1) and (2). Sometimes the same sentence is used with a different meaning, namely, that *according to previous tests* it is probable that a four will turn up in approximately one-sixth of a long range of throws (see Rudolf Carnap, "The Two Concepts of Probability," *Philosophy and Phenomenological Research,* vol. 5, 1945, reprinted in Feigl and Sellars, *op. cit.,* pp. 330 ff.). This meaning is externally identical with No. (4) above, but based on different, purely empirical and inductive grounds.

In most practical cases, as just mentioned, the number of possibilities and their relative weight are far less evident than in throwing up a coin or a die. Then statistical frequency observations alone can provide the data on which to base contentions of probability. So it is, for example, with mortality rates, which are to answer questions such as, how many children born this year will live less than one year, or more than thirty, or sixty, or eighty. Here we have no base other than frequency tables grounded on statistical observations, subject to corrections suggested by particular factors which we assume to influence the results, as, e.g., war. In such cases, therefore, only the "Frequency Theory" of probability can serve as a suitable starting point; the "Analytical Theory" alone would not be useful.

C. I. Lewis (*op.cit.*, p. 305) says that a full statement of a probability judgment should be in the following form: "That c, having the property ψ, will also have the property ϕ, is credible on the data D, with expectation a/b and reliability R." In other words: that a thrown die, having the property of six numbered faces, will also have the property that the face numbered four will be on the upside, is credible on the data concerning the actual structure of the die with expectation one-sixth and reliability R. Lewis says correctly that the "reliability" can be stated only empirically. His tendency is to play down the analytical elements. It follows from my presentation above that this is not justified, although his formulation is faultless.

The principles here discussed have often been mixed up even by great authorities, especially regarding the difference between the implications stated in propositions (3) speaking of "exactly" one-sixth, and (4) speaking of "approximately" one-sixth of the throws of a die. I cannot here go into further details of probability, or the far-flung literature, except that I may refer to Chapter XIII for a discussion of likelihood of single events.

Additional Literature on Sampling: M. J. Hagood, *Statistics for Sociologists,* New York 1941; Mildred Parten, *Surveys, Polls, and Samples: Practical Procedures,* New York, 1950.

Section 7. Acceptance. How cautious we must be not to overrate as an indication of truth the fact that an observation or a theoretical explanation is widely accepted is illustrated by the entire history of science. All attempts, therefore, to limit the individual scholar in his freedom to accept or refuse to accept an observation or inference are futile; he is free to decide either way as long as he stays within the rules of Scientific Method and its underlying postulates of veracity and good faith. As Whitehead put it, "Heaven knows what seeming nonsense may not tomorrow be recognized truth" (*op.cit.*, p. 166). Whereas in formal logic a contradiction cannot be tolerated, he added, "in the evolution of real knowledge it marks the first step in progress towards a victory," and "A clash of doctrines is not a disaster— it is an opportunity" (pp. 266, 267). Campbell goes too far when he defines science as "the study of those judgments concerning which universal agreement can be obtained" (*op.cit.*, p. 27), and insists that, although a theory may be doubted for some time, "in the end it is always either definitely accepted or definitely rejected" (p. 165). This is more than we can promise. But, of course, it might be called the ideal aim.

NOTES TO CHAPTER II

(Scientific Method, Continued: Causation, Tests, Prediction)

Introductory Remarks on Explanation. Literature: see Emile Meyerson, *De l'explication dans les sciences,* Paris 1921, 2 vols.; Hayek, *op.cit.,* p. 195; John Hospers, "On Explanation," *Journal of Philosophy,* vol. 43 (1946) pp. 337–56; David L. Miller, "Explanation vs. Description," *Philosophical Review,* vol. 56 (1947) pp. 306–12; E. W. Strong, "Criteria of Explanation in History," *Journal of Philosophy,* vol. 49 (1952) pp. 57–67; Carl G. Hempel and P. Oppenheim, "The Logic of Explanation," *op.cit.* (notes to Introductory, above). Also, A. N. Whitehead, *Process and Reality, op.cit.,* pp. 33 ff.; R. M. MacIver, *Social Causation,* Boston 1942.

Section 1. Causality. The fallacious inference that quantum physics has refuted causality, to which I objected in the text, has also been rejected by one of the most brilliant stars in the skies of quantum mechanics, Louis de Broglie, in his paper *La physique quantiste restera-t-elle indéterministe?* (Paris 1953, pp. 21 ff., cited by Kelsen, *What Is Justice?* p. 394), and by the Neo-Kantian philosopher Ernst Cassirer (*op.cit.,* pp. 135 ff.). Northrop (*op.cit.,* pp. 212, 216, 223) formulates pointedly that "if there are certain laws in science which are statistical then there must also be laws in that science which are not statistical." Max Planck remarked soberly that causality can be neither demonstrated nor refuted (*Vorträge und Erinnerungen,* Stuttgart 1949, pp. 268 ff.). He called it a "heuristic" principle, i.e., a principle that serves well in research. Similarly, Kelsen calls causality a "useful" epistemological postulate; this, he says, is enough to justify it (*op.cit.,* p. 342). An intermediate view is taken by Philipp Frank, *Between Physics and Philosophy* (*op.cit.,* pp. 98, 99). He holds that no definite distinction can be drawn between probability and causality. Physics looks for symbols "among which there exist rigorously valid relations, and which can be assigned uniquely to our experiences." If these symbols conform to our experiences "in a very detailed manner" we speak of causal laws; if the correspondence is "of a broader sort" we call them statistical. The fact that with the help of positions and velocities we are today unable to set up any causal laws for single electrons does not exclude the possibility, however, that we shall perhaps someday be able "to describe the behavior of these particles in greater detail than by means of the wave function, the probabilities."

History of the Idea of Causality. As indicated, the ancient Greeks thought originally that all laws of nature were norms set by the gods. Thus, Heraclitus said that the sun will not overstep his prescribed course; otherwise "the Erinyes, the handmaidens of Justice (Dike), will find him out." Only after Leukippos and Democritus had replaced these older ideas with their atomistic theory did Greek thinkers cease to see natural laws merely as norms. The Greek word for "cause," *aitía*, originally had the meaning of "guilt"; the change of its meaning from "guilt" to "cause" mirrors the change from thinking in terms of norms to those of causation. See for the foregoing Kelsen, *op.cit.,* pp. 205, 309 ff.

Additional Literature:

Albert Einstein, *Relativity, The Special and General Theory, a Popular Exposition,* London 1920, 3rd ed.
P. W. Bridgman, *The Logic of Modern Physics,* New York 1927
Max Planck, *Where Is Science Going?* New York 1933
———, *The Philosophy of Physics,* New York 1936
A. S. Eddington, *The Philosophy of Physical Science,* Cambridge Engl., 1939
James B. Conant, *Understanding Science,* New Haven 1947
———, *Case History in Experimental Science,* Cambridge, Mass., 1948
W. H. Werkmeister, *The Basis and Structure of Knowledge,* New York 1948 (also has a good chapter on Hans Driesch)
Henry Margenau, *The Nature of Physical Reality,* New York 1950
Hans Reichenbach, *From Copernicus to Einstein* (popular), New York Wisdom Library, no date
John Dewey, *The Influence of Darwin on Philosophy, and Other Essays on Contemporary Thought,* New York 1910 (new ed., 1957)
Julian Huxley, "The Vindication of Darwinism," *Touchstone for Ethics,* New York 1947, pp. 167–92
Samuel Alexander, *Space, Time, and Deity,* 2 vols., 1920
Arthur O. Lovejoy, "The Meanings of 'Emergence' and Its Modes," paper read at the Sixth International Congress of Philosophy, Harvard University, 1926, reprinted in Philip P. Wiener, *Readings,* pp. 585–96
C. G. Hempel and P. Oppenheim, "On the Idea of Emergence," *op.cit.* (notes to Introductory, above) pp. 331–37
E. Nordenskiold, *The History of Biology,* New York 1928
Emanuel Radl, *The History of Biological Theories,* London 1930
Ludwig Bertalanffy, *Modern Theories of Development: an Introduction to Theoretical Biology,* New York 1933
———, *The Problems of Life,* New York 1943
Kurt Goldstein, *The Organism, a Holistic Approach to Biology,* New York 1939 (German ed., 1934)
Mary S. McDougall, *Biology: The Science of Life,* New York 1943
R. G. Coolingwood, *The Idea of Nature,* Oxford 1945 (pp. 158–77 reprinted in Wiener, *Readings,* pp. 570 ff.)
———, *The Idea of History,* Oxford 1946
Henri Irénée Marrou, *De la connaissance historique,* Paris 1954
Jacques Maritain, *On the Philosophy of History,* New York 1957
R. M. MacIver, *Social Causation,* Boston 1942

Section 3. Fallacies in Testing Hypotheses. The fact that the expected consequences actually occur does not logically warrant the conclusion that the hypothesis is correct. This has often been rightly stressed, e.g., by Northrop, *op.cit.,* pp. 108, 148–49.

Section 4. Prediction. Kelsen (*op.cit.,* p. 271) expresses doubt whether prediction is an essential task of science. It certainly is one of its most important *tools,* because the process of forming hypotheses would be pointless but for the prediction of the results further observations and experiments (future events, that is) will have; such prediction is essential for checking the correctness of hypotheses. But prediction is essential, also, for clarifying the significance of alternative actions before they are taken, and the influence which the potential reaction of other persons may have. In political science anticipation of developments and prediction of consequences of alternative courses of action are among the most important functions of science. One cannot analyze democracy, dictatorship, or even an election system adequately without describing predictable consequences (see especially Chapter xii). An extreme illustration is offered by Harold Lasswell's presidential address of 1956 at the annual meeting of the American Political Science Assocation ("The Political Science of Science," *American Political Science Review,* vol. 50, 1956, pp. 961–79); predicting a great number of technical developments he exhorted his colleagues to anticipate the political problems involved, so as to be prepared and not caught as unaware as when the first nuclear bombs were dropped.

Section 5. A Priori. The American fight against arguments a priori was led by William James. "The whole fabric of a priori sciences can thus be treated as a *man-made* product," he wrote ("Humanism and Truth," reprinted in *Pragmatism,* Perry ed., pp. 401–3). See also Chapter v, Section 6, of this book. Recent Literature, see: Moritz Schlick, "Is There a Factual A Priori?" first published in German, 1932–33, translation in Feigl and Sellars, *op.cit.,* p. 277; Ernest Nagel, *Sovereign Reason,* New York 1954, pp. 211 ff.; Felix Kaufmann, *Methods of the Social Sciences, op.cit.;* Bertrand Russell, *Human Knowledge: Its Scope and Limits,* New York 1948.

Section 6. Theory and Hypothesis. A "theory" explains something. In order to do so it may make use either of some "law" already firmly established, or of some "hypothesis," e.g., the hypothesis that such a law exists although it has not yet been firmly established, or of some other hypothesis to the effect that certain regularities prevail. A "theory," therefore, is not itself a "hypothesis"; but it may make use of one, or propose one in the course of its own endeavour to "explain" something. Contrarywise, a "hypothesis" is not itself a "theory"; but it may, and generally will, constitute an important item within a theory. Goode and Hatt (p. 56) define a hypothesis as the "formulation of a deduction." This is misleading. As a rule, a hypothesis formulates some tentative generalization reached by *induction,* or analytically derived from another hypothesis (or established theory) which in turn was gained by induction. If specific events are explained by deducing them from an hypothesis, this deduction is logically only the second step. If the general law is already well established and the hypothesis merely meant to point out the relationship between the problematic situation and the general law, it is permissible to say that the hypothesis is just the formulation of a deduction. But this is the exception rather than the rule.

It would be useless to look to ancient authorities for a good modern terminology, because Aristotle, Euclid, Archimedes, and other ancient writers used the terms "hypothesis," "axiom," and the equivalents of "assumption" and "postulate" with a great variety of meanings, often even within their own writings. See Kurt von Fritz, "Die ΑΡΧΑΙ in der griechischen Mathematik," *Archiv für Begriffsgeschichte*, vol. 1 (1954) pp. 13–103.

Analogy. Analogies are frequently instrumental for the birth of hypotheses. In watching mechanical operations, for example, the biologist may by "analogy" hit upon a "hypothesis," which in turn enables him to formulate a "theory," which tries to "explain" biological phenomena. Or, in watching embryonic stages, he may by analogy find a useful hypothesis, which enables him to explain the evolution of higher from lower forms of life. But what analogy leads to is merely a "hypothesis"; it is no proof for the latter's correctness (see Darwin's cautious remarks quoted in Chapter II, Section 1). The hypothesis must first be submitted to tests regarding all its implications. Herbert Simon and Allen Newell, "Models: Their Uses and Limitations" (L. White, ed., *The State of the Social Sciences*, Chicago 1956, pp. 66 ff.) oversimplify the interrelation when they say that "all theories are analogies, and all analogies are theories." Analogies are theories only to the extent that they are used for "explaining" something. The analogies, e.g., that exist between the game of chess and the game of politics are not in themselves "theories"; only if used to "explain" political phenomena do they become "theories," and then they serve as no more than one item, a "hypothesis," within the "theory."

Usefulness of Unrealistic Hypotheses. A good illustration can be found in G. J. Warnock, "Analysis and Imagination" (Gilbert Ryle ed., *The Revolution in Philosophy*, London 1957, p. 119). He asks us to suppose that our senses of sight and touch are very much less acute than they are, while our senses of hearing and smell are immensely sharpened, and then to imagine how such changes might modify our concepts. Other illustrations are offered in essays dealing with the logical structure and meaning of "contrary-to-fact conditional statements"; see, e.g., Roderick M. Chisholm, "The Contrary-to-Fact Conditional" (Feigl and Sellars, *Readings in Philosophical Analysis*, pp. 482 ff., reprinted with slight alterations from *Mind*, vol. 55, 1946).

Models. Abstract wholes, such as "society," "economy," "markets," "capitalism," the "nation," the "collective mind," are "never given to our observation but . . . constructions of our mind." They exist only if, and to the extent to which "the theory is correct which we have formed about the connection of the parts which they imply and which we can explicitly state only in form of a model built from those relationships." The social sciences, in such cases, do not deal with "given wholes"; rather, their task is to *"constitute"* these wholes by constructing models from the familiar elements." Hayek, *op.cit.,* pp. 54–56. Simon and Newell go too far, however, when they assert (*op.cit.,* pp. 66 ff.) that in contemporary usage the term "model" is simply a "synonym for theory." There are theories that make no use of "models," unless we call every generalization a model.

Additional Literature:

Theodore Newcomb, "An Approach to the Study of Communicative Acts," *Psychological Review,* vol. 60 (1953) pp. 393–404
Karl Deutsch, "On Communication Models in the Social Sciences," *Public Opinion Quarterly,* vol. 16 (1952) pp. 356–80
Paul Kecskemeti, *Meaning, Communication and Value,* Chicago 1952

Section 7. Knowledge. The term "knowledge" is used here broadly, so as to be applicable to both "verified" and "putative-but-not-verified" claims to knowledge. However, if the claim to knowledge is not scientifically warranted but merely putative, I have always expressed this through an added qualifying adjective. Some writers like Perry (*Realms of Value,* p. 300) and C. I. Lewis (*op.cit.,* pp. 9, 10, 29, 30) use the term "knowledge" only when a cognition is correct, i.e., when it corresponds to or accords with what is meant. Lewis calls an apprehension which is in error a "cognition." Knowledge, he says, "claims correctness." It certainly does. But the claim may be wrong. It seems to me more useful, rather, to start from the *claim* to knowledge and then to distinguish whether this claim can be verified, refuted, or must be left standing neither verified nor refuted. There is another difference between my use and that chosen by Lewis, because he does not extend the term "knowledge" to cover awareness of the sensuously given. Knowledge is to him "inferential" knowledge only. This leads him to some tortuous definitions, such as, "Only that with respect to which some misapprehension could occur, is here classed as knowledge. And whatever *is* subject to such possible mistake, will here be classified as *cognition,* and as *knowledge* if it is correct or veridical." Even Dewey and Bentley cannot get along entirely without the word "knowledge." They apply it only in a "loose" sense, considering it convenient and not objectionable "where there is no stress upon its accurate application and not great probability that a reader will assume there is; at any rate we shall thus occasionally risk it. We shall list it as No. 1 on a list of 'vague words'" (*Knowing and the Known,* p. 48).

Literature on Scientific Method. In addition to the essays cited in the main text or in these Notes; to the *Encyclopedia of the Social Sciences;* to Morris R. Cohen and Ernest Nagel, *An Introduction to Logic and Scientific Method,* New York 1934; and to D. D. Runes, ed., *The Dictionary of Philosophy,* New York 1942:

A. D. Ritchie, *The Scientific Method,* New York 1923
W. F. Ogburn and A. Goldenweiser, *The Social Sciences and Their Interrelations,* New York 1927
Abraham Wolf, *The Essentials of Scientific Method,* London, 2nd ed., 1928
Brookings Institution, *Essays on Research in the Social Sciences,* Washington, D.C., 1931
Morris R. Cohen, *Reason and Nature, an Essay in the Meaning of Scientific Method,* New York, 1931; 2nd ed., 1953
———, *American Thought, A Critical Study,* ed. by Felix Cohen, Glencoe, Ill., 1954; see review by Barna Horvath, *American Journal of Comparative Law,* vol. 5 (1956) pp. 157 ff.
R. M. MacIver, *Social Causation,* Boston 1942
George H. Sabine, *Democracy and Preconceived Ideas,* Columbus, Ohio, 1945
George Lundberg, *Can Science Save Us?* New York 1947
Bertrand Russell, *Human Knowledge, Its Scope and Limits,* New York 1948
Stuart Chase, *The Proper Study of Mankind,* New York 1948
C. West Churchman and R. L. Ackoff, *Methods of Inquiry, an Introduction to Philosophy and Scientific Method,* St. Louis 1949
Bernhard Bendix, *Social Science and the Distrust of Reason,* Berkeley 1951
Hans Reichenbach, *The Rise of Scientific Philosophy,* Berkeley 1951
Paul Kecskemeti, *Meaning, Communication, and Value,* Chicago 1952
Ernst Cassirer, *The Philosophy of Symbolic Forms,* translated by Ralph Manheim, New Haven 1953–57

Articles:
Joseph Mayer, "Social Science Methodology," *Journal of Social Philosophy,* vol. 1 (1936) pp. 364–81
Alexander Goldenweiser, "Nature and Tasks of the Social Sciences," *ibid.,* vol. 2 (1936) pp. 5–34
Peter A. Carmichael, "Limits of Method," *ibid.,* vol. 45 (1948) pp. 141–52
Marion Levy, "Some Basic Methodological Difficulties in the Social Sciences," *Philosophy of Science,* vol. 17 (1950) pp. 287–301
Louis W. Beck, "The Distinctive Traits of an Empirical Method," *Journal of Philosophy,* vol. 43 (1946) pp. 337–56
———, "The Natural Science Ideal in the Social Sciences," *Scientific Monthly,* vol. 68 (1949) pp. 386–94
Robert Redfield, "The Art of Social Science," *American Journal of Sociology,* vol. 54 (1948) pp. 181 ff.
Jessie Bernard, "The Art of Social Science: A Reply to Redfield," *ibid.,* vol. 55 (1949) pp. 1–9
Felix Kaufmann, "Cassirer's Theory of Scientific Knowledge," in *The Philosophy of Ernst Cassirer,* ed., by P. A. Schilpp, Evanston, Ill., 1949, pp. 185–213
David Riesman, "Some Observations on Social Science Research," *Antioch Review,* vol. 11 (1951) pp. 259–78

Harold D. Lasswell, "Impact of Psychoanalytic Thinking on the Social Sciences," in L. D. White, *The State of the Social Sciences, op.cit.*, pp. 84 ff.

David Riesman, "Some Observations on the 'Older' and the 'Newer' Social Sciences," *ibid.*, pp. 319 ff.

Albert Salomon, "Symbols and Images in the Constitution of Society," in L. Bryson *et.al.*, ed., *Symbols and Society*, New York 1955, pp. 103–32

Maurice Natanson, "A Study in Philosophy and the Social Sciences," *Social Research*, vol. 25 (1958) pp. 158–72

Especially: Political Science

Robert N. Gilchrist, *Principles of Political Science*, London 1916; 6th ed., 1938

H. J. Laski, *A Grammar of Politics*, New Haven 1925

John Dewey, *The Public and Its Problems*, New York 1927, Chicago 1946

W. Y. Elliott, *The Pragmatic Revolt in Politics*, New York 1928

James W. Garner, *Political Science and Government*, New York 1928

Raymond G. Gettell, *Political Science*, New York 1933; rev. ed., 1946

Francis Coker, *Recent Political Thought*, New York 1934

Hermann Heller, *Staatslehre*, ed. by Gerhard Niemeyer, Leiden 1934

Max Ascoli, *Intelligence in Politics*, New York 1936

Karl Mannheim, "The Prospects of Scientific Politics," in his *Ideology and Utopia*, London, New York 1936, ch. iii (pp. 97–171)

Francis G. Wilson, *The Elements of Modern Politics; an Introduction to Political Science*, New York 1936

Ernest Griffith, *Research in Political Science*, Chapel Hill 1948

T. D. Weldon, *The Vocabulary of Politics, An Enquiry into the Use and Abuse of Language in the Making of Political Theories*, Penguin Books, 1953

William Ebenstein, *Modern Political Thought*, New York 1954, pp. 1–124

Thomas P. Jenkin, *The Study of Political Theory*, Garden City, N.Y. 1955

William Esslinger, *Politics and Science*, with a foreword by Alfred Einstein, New York 1955

Robert A. Dahl, *A Preface to Democratic Theory*, Chicago 1956

————, "A Rejoinder," *American Political Science Review*, vol. 51 (1957) pp. 1053–61

Woodrow Wilson, "The Law and the Facts," *American Political Science Review*, vol. 5 (1911) pp. 1–11

Reports of two National Conferences on the Science of Politics, *ibid.*, vol. 18 (1924) pp. 119–66, and vol. 19 (1925) pp. 104–62

Charles Beard, "Time, Technology, and the Creative Spirit in Political Science," *ibid.*, vol. 21 (1927) pp. 1–11

W. B. Munro, "Physics and Politics, An Old Analogy Revised," *ibid.*, vol. 22 (1928) pp. 1–11

E. S. Corwin, "The Democratic Dogma and the Future of Political Science," *ibid.*, vol. 23 (1929) pp. 569–92

Harold F. Gosnell, "Statisticians and Political Scientists," *ibid.*, vol. 27 (1933) pp. 119–66

William Anderson, "The Role of Political Science," *ibid.*, vol. 37 (1943) pp. 1–17

Joseph E. McLean, "Areas for Postwar Research," *ibid.*, vol. 39 (1945) pp. 741–56

Pendleton Herring, "Political Science in the Next Decade," *ibid.*, vol. 39 (1945) pp. 757–66

John Gaus, "Job Analysis of Political Science," *ibid.*, vol. 40 (1946) pp. 217–30

Paul Appleby, "Political Science: The Next 25 Years," *ibid.,* vol. 44 (1950) pp. 924–32

Inter-University Seminars, "Research in Political Behavior," *ibid.,* vol. 46 (1952) pp. 1003–45, and "Research in Comparative Politics," *ibid.,* vol. 47 (1953) pp. 641–57

David G. Smith, "Political Science and Political Theory," *ibid.,* vol. 51 (1957) pp. 734–46

D. E. After, "Theory and the Study of Politics," *ibid.,* pp. 747–62, and comment on Smith and After by A. A. Rogow, *ibid.,* pp. 763–75

E. E. Schattschneider, "Intensity, Visibility, Direction and Scope," *ibid.,* vol. 51 (1957) pp. 933–42

J. A. Fairlie, "Politics and Science," *Scientific Monthly,* vol. 18 (1924) pp. 18–37

Arnold Brecht, "Democracy, Challenge to Theory," *Social Research* vol. 13 (1946) pp. 195–224

———, "A New Science of Politics," *ibid.,* vol. 20 (1953) pp. 230–35

W. A. Glaser, "The Types and Uses of Political Theory," *ibid.,* vol. 22 (1955) pp. 273–96

Carl J. Friedrich, "Policy—a Science?" *Public Policy,* vol. 4 (1953) pp. 269–81

Alfred Cobban, "The Decline of Political Theory," *Political Science Quarterly,* vol. 68 (1953) pp. 321–37

Avery Leiserson, "Problems of Methodology in Political Research," *ibid.,* vol. 68 (1953) pp. 558–84

Hans Morgenthau, *Scientific Man vs. Power Politics,* Chicago 1946 (see Chapter VIII, Section 12 of this book)

———, "The Dilemma of Freedom," *American Political Science Review* vol. 51 (1957) pp. 714–23; and comment by Howard B. White, *ibid.,* pp. 724–33

Thomas I. Cook and Malcolm Moos, "Foreign Policy: The Realism of Idealism," *ibid.,* vol. 46 (1952) pp. 343–56

Kenneth Thompson, "The Study of International Politics," *Journal of Politics,* vol. 14 (1952) pp. 433–67

———, "Toward a Theory of International Politics," *American Political Science Review,* vol. 49 (1955) pp. 733–46

Individual Countries

Th. I. Cook, "The Methods of Political Science, Chiefly in the United States," in UNESCO, *Contemporary Political Science,* as cited at the beginning of this Appendix

B. E. Lippincott, "Political Science in the United States," *ibid.,* pp. 208–24

Ch. E. Merriam, "Political Science in the United States," *ibid.,* pp. 233–48

P. Odegard, "Factors in the Study of Pressure Groups and Political Parties in the United States," *ibid.,* pp. 515–26

H. D. Lasswell, "Psychology and Political Science in the U.S.A.," *ibid.,* pp. 526–38

William Anderson, "Political Science North and South," *Journal of Politics,* vol. 11 (1949) pp. 298–317

Robert G. McCloskey, "American Political Thought and the Study of Politics," *American Political Science Review,* vol. 51 (1957) pp. 115–29; comments by Martin Diamond, *ibid.,* pp. 130–34, and by John P. Roche, pp. 484–88

Lewis Rockow, *Contemporary Political Thought in England,* London 1925

George Catlin, "Contemporary British Political Thought," *American Political Science Review,* vol. 46 (1952) pp. 641–59

Thomas P. Peardon, "Two Currents in Contemporary English Political Theory," *ibid.*, vol. 49 (1955) pp. 487–95

W. A. Robson, "Political Science in Great Britain," UNESCO, *op.cit.*, pp. 294–313 *and the other contributions on individual countries, ibid.*,

A. R. L. Gurland, *Political Science in Western Germany, Thoughts and Writings* 1950–1952, Washington, Library of Congress, 1953

For Literature on Values and on Natural Law, see notes to Chapters vi, vii, and viii.

NOTES TO CHAPTER III

(Scientific Value Relativism)
will be found in Chapters v to viii and the notes thereto.

NOTES TO CHAPTER IV

(The Theory of Justice)

Section 1. Law and Political Science, Additional Literature

W. W. Willoughby, *The Fundamental Concepts of Public Law,* 1924

Jerome Frank, *Law and the Modern Mind,* New York 1930

Ranyard West, *Conscience and Society; a Study of the Psychological Prerequisites of Law and Order,* New York 1945

Edward H. Levi, *An Introduction to Legal Reasoning,* Chicago 1949

George H. Sabine, "Political Science and the Juristic Point of View," *American Political Science Review,* vol. 22 (1928) pp. 553–75

My Philosophy of Law, Northwestern University Studies, Evanston, Ill., 1941

G. Lowell Field, "Law as an Objective Political Concept," *American Political Science Review,* vol. 43 (1949) pp. 229–49

Karl N. Llewellyn, "Law and the Social Sciences, especially Sociology," *Harvard Law Review,* vol. 62 (1949) pp. 1286–1305

David Riesman, "Toward an Anthropological Science of Law and the Legal Profession," *American Journal of Sociology,* vol. 57 (1951) pp. 121–35

Wolfgang Friedman, *Legal Theory,* London, 3rd ed., 1953

Edwin Patterson, *Jurisprudence: Men and Ideas of the Law,* New York 1953

Jerome Hall, "Unification of Political and Legal Theory," *Political Science Quarterly,* vol. 69 (1954) pp. 15 ff.

John Ching-hsiung Wu, *Fountains of Justice,* New York 1955

Barna Horvath, "Field Law and Law Field," *Östrreichische Zeitschrift für öffentliches Recht,* vol. 8 (1957) pp. 44–81

Section 2. History of Natural-Law Ideas. No detailed, comprehensive history of Natural-Law ideas from antiquity to the present time has yet been published. It would fill several volumes (see the project of the Swiss Professor Flückiger below). The best work in English on the entire history of the subject is Rommen's one-volume book *The Natural Law,* of 1947 (cited in the text), translated from the German original. There are a number of older publications that cover relatively long historical periods in more detail. They include

Charles H. McIlwain, *The Growth of Political Thought in the West, from the Greeks to the End of the Middle Ages,* 1932; although embedded within the general history of thought, this presentation, enriched by an appendix on absolute and particular justice in Plato and Aristotle, is still one of the best English introductions to the earlier periods;

Otto Gierke, *Das deutsche Genossenschaftsrecht* (4 vols., Berlin 1868–1913), in particular the parts translated into English and edited by F. W. Maitland (*Political Theories of the Middle Ages,* Cambridge 1900) and E. Barker (*Natural Law and the Theory of Society,* 1500 to 1800, Cambridge 1934), and, *Johannes Althusius und die Entwickelung der naturrechtlichen Staatstheorien* (Breslau 1880), tr. by B. Freyd (*The Development of Political Theory,* New York 1939); these works present a detailed picture of the bearing which Natural-Law ideas had on medieval thought and institutions, and the change both underwent in the early modern age;

D. C. Ritchie, *Natural Rights,* London 1894 (3rd reprint 1924); covers the development of thought on rights. The history of ideas on Natural Law and Natural Rights (esp., Plato, Aristotle, Cicero, Hobbes, Locke, Rousseau, Burke) has been illuminated recently by Leo Strauss in his book *Natural Right and History,* as cited in the text above.

See further:
J. W. Salmond, "The Law of Nature," *Law Quarterly Review,* vol. 11 (1895) pp. 121 ff.
Frederick Pollock, "History of the Law of Nature," *Columbia Law Review,* vol. 1 (1901) pp. 11 ff.; vol. 2 (1902) pp. 131 ff.; also, *Essays in the Law* (1922)
J. Dickinson, *Administrative Justice and the Supremacy of Law* (1927)
E. S. Corwin, "The Higher Law Background of American Constitutional Law," *Harvard Law Review,* vol. 42 (1928) pp. 149 ff., 365ff.
Anton-Hermann Chroust, "On the Nature of Natural Law," as cited below in the notes to Chapter VIII
A. Passerin d'Entrèves, *Natural Law, an Introduction to Legal Philosophy,* London 1951 (126 pp.)
C. J. Friedrich, *The Philosophy of Law in Historical Perspective,* Chicago 1958; this being a revised English version of his German book, *Die Philosophie des Rechts in historischer Perspektive,* Heidelberg, 1955

and the discussion of Natural-Law ideas in the standard works on the history of political ideas, especially those written by W. A. Dunning (3 vols., 1902–20), R. Gettell (1924), and G. H. Sabine (1937).

Three books in German should be mentioned because of their particular merits (in addition to Friedrich, see previous paragraph):

Johann Sauter, *Die philosophischen Grundlagen des Naturrechts,* Wien 1932; covers the history from the early Greeks to Thomasius and Wolff, with a preference for Platonian philosophy;
Felix Flückiger, *Geschichte des Naturrechts,* first vol., *Altertum und Frühmittelalter,* Zürich 1954, reviewed in great detail by Anton-Hermann Chroust in *Natural Law Forum,* vol. 1 (1956) pp. 135–146;

Erik Wolf, *Das Problem der Naturrechtslehre, Versuch einer Orientierung,* Karlsruhe 1955.

Wolf's book, although only a little over a hundred pages long, deals with the entire history of Natural-Law ideas. He groups the many interpretations of Natural Law within twice nine categories, according to nine different interpretations given the concept of Nature and another nine given the concept of Law. This ingenious arrangement, with its many subcategories, reveals most strikingly the multiplicity of revelations philosophers have thought to obtain from the study of nature. My review in *Natural Law Forum,* vol. 3 (1958), pp. 192–96, includes an English translation of Wolf's categories (see also below, notes to Chapter VIII).

For recent literature on the revival of Natural-Law ideas in the twentieth century, see notes to Chapter VIII.

The Role of the Sophists. The Greek Sophists are often referred to as ancient precursors of modern value relativism. But this is only half true. The Sophists believed in some sort of Natural Law and were even the creators of the theory of Natural Law and gave it its name (*physei dikaion*). They referred, first, to a god-given share of all Greeks in justice (Protagoras), later to a natural way of life (Hippias), next, to the natural equality of all men (Antiphon, Lykophron, Alkidamas), and finally, to the natural right of the strong (Thrasymachus and Callicles). Relative elements entered their varied theories because, in the first two stages, they distinguished the nature of the Greeks from that of the barbarians, and in the fourth, because of the relative nature of strength. But the basic reference, if not to the gods, was to nature and to its law. For the various teachings of the Sophists, see especially Erik Wolf, *Griechisches Rechtsdenken,* vol. 2 (1952) pp. 18–171, and more briefly, *Das Problem der Naturrechtslehre, op.cit.;* George H. Sabine, *A History of Political Theory,* New York 1938, pp. 25 ff.; A. H. Chroust, *op.cit.* Only Skepticism (Carneades) went so far as to teach that there was no Natural Law at all, at least none that we could perceive (Rommen, *op.cit.*).

St. Augustine. I have said advisedly in the text that St. Augustine pushed the Natural Law into the background, not that he rejected it. For he did not deny its existence. But to him it was merely "divine law with reference to man". He projected Plato's "ideas," i.e., Reality proper, into the thoughts of God, and the universal reason of the Stoics into his wisdom. Thus, supreme reason, eternal truth, and eternal law became identical. This complete oneness of God, supreme reason, and omnipotent will, sustains and governs the universe. While in nature the eternal law operates as necessity, it is inscribed in the heart of man as norm. Therewith, the impersonal part of nature was divested of any share in the origin of moral Natural Law. (See for the foregoing, Rommen, *op.cit.,* pp. 37, 38; Chroust, *op.cit.*) Ideas about the divine origin of all laws of nature, both physical and moral, had been at the bottom of Greek thought also, but the reference to nature had gained a more independent status with them than was conceded by St. Augustine.

Scholasticism. Scholasticism, in contrast to Augustinian doctrine, emphasized the dualism of God and created nature. It thus abandoned the unlimited monism and Platonic realism (according to which only the "ideas" are real) that were characteristic of Augustine. This made it possible for the Scholastics to ascribe at least part of Natural Law to the laws operating in created Nature rather than to direct commands of God. Thus Scholasticism could eventually become, at least in part, what a contemporary American scholar has called "common-sense knowledge critically examined and philosophically vindicated" (Celestine N. Bittle, *Reality and the Mind,* Milwaukee 1936, p. 146, quoted by Rommen, *op.cit.,* p. 39 n. 3).

Sections 3 ff. See the notes to Chapters v ff.; for additional literature on Natural Law, to Chapter VIII.

NOTES TO CHAPTER V

(Precursors and Cousins)

Section 1. Genesis of Scientific Method. Students not familiar with the history of philosophy are often misled by the various meanings with which the term "rational" is used. In ordinary language today a man's attitude is called "rational" if he pursues attainable goals with reliance on facts, causal relations, and logical reasoning. The opposite then is "irrational" action. In the history of philosophy, however, "Rationalism" refers to the belief that reason is capable of finding ultimate truth without experimental tests. Rationalism, hence, was the typical method of *medieval* scholars, with some residues of reliance on pure reason prevailing through the Age of Enlightenment. This rationalism was progressively undermined by Galileo's experimental and Newton's mathematicophysical methods, by Locke's empiricism, Hume's skepticism (see below, notes to Chapter VI), Kant's *Critique of Pure Reason* (see Chapter II, Section 5), and later, by Positivism, Pragmatism, and Scientific Method. In the philosophical sense of the term, therefore, Galileo acted not rationally but anti-rationally when he relied on experiments; he was one of the first great opponents and destroyers of medieval Rationalism. Consequently, Whitehead (*op.cit.,* p. 74) could correctly say that, after Newton, physicists emphasized the "anti-rationalism" that had made its appearance in the historical revolt of the Renaissance and the Reformation; and (p. 12) that it is a great mistake to conceive of the Renaissance and Reformation as an "appeal to reason"; on the contrary, this double-pronged historical revolt was "through and through an anti-intellectual movement," a return to the "contemplation of brute fact," and a "recoil from the inflexible rationality of medieval thought," and (p. 23) "science" to this day has remained an "anti-rationalistic" movement. Likewise, William James called "Rationalism" that approach against which Pragmatism was principally directed; see the first chapters of his *Pragmatism* and his letter to Münsterberg, quoted below (Section 6). In this philosophical use, therefore, the opposite of rationalism is not irrational behavior, but reliance on science and experiments. In again another, a third, sense "rationalism" is used to denounce unhistorical, utopian, or ideological political theories grounded in the confidence that reason all by itself is capable of determining salutary ends of politics. The opposite of rationalism in this third sense is neither irrational action nor reliance on science and experiments, but prudential reliance on traditional values and institutions (Burke). See the writings by Michael Oakeshott, cited in the notes to the introductory chapter for this third approach.

Additional Literature on the History of Science

William Cecil Dampier, *History of Science*, New York 1949
Herbert Butterfield, *The Origins of Modern Science, 1300–1800*, New York 1951
William P. D. Wightman, *The Growth of Scientific Ideas*, New Haven 1951
James B. Conant, *Science and Common Sense*, New York 1951
Alfred N. Whitehead, *Adventures of Ideas*, New York 1933 (Mentor Book 1955)
Ernst Cassirer, *The Problem of Knowledge, Philosophy, Science, and History since Hegel*, translated by W. H. Weglone and Ch. W. Hendel, New Haven 1950
Elmer Barnes (ed.), *The History and Prospects of the Social Sciences*, New York 1925
Floyd N. House, *The Range of Social Theory, A Survey of the Development, Literature, Tendencies, and Fundamental Problems of the Social Sciences*, New York 1929
Louis Wirth (ed.), *Eleven Twenty-Six: A Decade of Social Science*, Chicago 1946
Florian Znaniecki, *The Cultural Sciences, Their Origin and Development*, Urbana, Ill., 1952

History of Political Science, in particular:
Frederick Pollock, *An Introduction to the History of the Science of Politics*, London 1893
Anna Haldow, *Political Science in American Colleges and Universities, 1636–1900*, New York 1939
UNESCO surveys cited at the beginning of this Appendix

Section 3 (a). The Positivism of the French Sociologists. The term "positivism" was first used in *Doctrine de Saint Simon, Exposition*, published by his disciples, Paris 1831, which also contains the first use of the term "individualism" (see Hayek, *op.cit.*, pp. 147, 152). Comte's belief in Progress found its most absolute expression in two letters, originally included in a work of Saint Simon (whose secretary Comte was in the last seven years of

S. S.'s life) but later republished over Comte's own name in an appendix to his *Système de politique positive* (1854). There he said that "the law of human progress guides and dominates all; men are only its instruments . . . all we can do is consciously to obey the law." This was a far cry from present-day Scientific Method and Value Relativism. It is true that at other times Comte spoke the language of extreme relativism. Thus, in another of his contributions to Saint Simon's works, he even wrote: "There is nothing good and nothing bad, absolutely speaking. Everything is relative, that is the only absolute thing" (*tout est relatif, voilà la seule chose absolue*). But this passage dealt with the best methods of government, not with values in general, and the relativity was, here as always with Comte, to refer to the stage reached in the evolution of progress. The absolutistic foundations of Comte's philosophy appear clearly in his frequent insistence that positive philosophy is always characterized by the "necessary and rational subordination of man to the world." "L'étude positive n'a pas de caractère plus tranché que sa tendance spontanée et invariable à baser l'étude réelle de l'homme sur la connaissance préalable du monde extérieur" (*Cours de philosophie positive,* published Paris 1830–42, 2nd ed., Paris 1864, vol. 3, pp. 188–89). It is in line with his absolutizing of progress that Comte was not primarily interested in the preservation of liberty; unlimited freedom of conscience had to be abandoned with the establishment of positivism, he thought. For the foregoing, see Hayek, *op.cit.,* pp. 130, 133, 147, 152, 183, 242 n., 347. There is a condensed English translation of Comte's *Cours de philosophie positive* by H. Martineau, *The Positive Philosophy of A. Comte,* 2 vols., 2nd ed., London, 1875.

Additional Literature: J. B. Bury, *The Idea of Progress,* New York 1932.

Section 3 (b) Neopositivism, Moderate Types. Herbert Feigl, one of the early members of the Vienna circle, now a United States citizen, represents the moderate type of those Neopositivists who abandon physicalism and admit introspection. Although he preserves the postulate that sentences to be meaningful must be reducible to empirical verifiability, he recognizes that the "danger of a fallaciously reductive use of the meaning-criterion is great, especially in the hands of young iconoclasts. It is only too tempting to push a very difficult problem aside and by stigmatizing it as meaningless to discourage further investigation," as in questions of instincts, the unconscious, and the like. ("Logical Empiricism," in D. D. Runes, ed., *Twentieth Century Philosophy,* New York 1943, reprinted in Feigl and Sellars, *Readings* pp. 3 ff.) He describes the different approaches within the Neopositivists: . . . "in their choice of a basis for logical reconstruction, Wittgenstein, followed by Schlick, Waisman, and others, remained experientialistic [i.e., they admitted any type of experience], whereas Neurath, Carnap, Hempel, and others became physicalistic."

Northrop and Dewey Opposed. Northrop (*op.cit.,* pp. 99, 113) criticizes the Logical Positivists on the ground that they recognize only concepts by immediate apprehension. This criticism is not quite fair I think, because most Neopositivists admit, and even encourage, the forming of tentative hypotheses based on instances of immediate perception but not yet fully confirmed. More to the point is Northrop's second objection that Neopositivists by basing science on "atomic concepts by inspection" ignore what he calls the "aesthetic continuum." John Dewey is usually counted as a positivist. But actually he expressed severe objections. Like Northrop he charged that the logic of positivism has no recognized place for hypotheses which "at a given time outrun the scope of already determined 'facts' " and, indeed, "may not be capable of verification at the time or of *direct* factual verification at any time" (*Logic,* p. 519). He went on to point out that many hypotheses have played a great role in the advancement of science which were "at the time of their origin merely speculative." Consistent positivism would have condemned such hypotheses as metaphysical, he wrote, and this objection would have applied to such trail-blazing hypotheses as the conservation of energy and evolution. No important scientific hypothesis has ever been verified "in the form in which it was originally presented." Whether this is a correct description of positivism may be doubted (see above); but at any rate, it is a significant admission from Dewey's side. William Savery, *op.cit.,* p. 509, sees in these remarks even a hint of a "realistic" view, i.e., a view that presumes a reality beyond appearances.

Oxford Ordinary Language Philosophers. The flash of insight that motivated Intuitionists, such as G. E. Moore, and Neopositivists or Scientific Empiricists, such as Carnap, Ayer, or Morris, alike to pay attention to ordinary language as the ultimate basis to which all scientific concepts, even the most abstract and technical ones, must refer as primitive building stones, culminated in the work of a group sometimes referred to as Oxford Philosophers of Ordinary Language. They see in the actual use of words within the living language the necessary starting point for every philosophical analysis. "Use," rather than "meaning" is their key concept. For instance, they remark that the evaluative use of the word "good" is to commend or to prescribe; no philosophical analysis, therefore, is worthwhile that ignores this use of the word (see below, notes to Chapter VI, on C. I. Lewis). For an introduction to the differences between this group and other positivists see George Nakhnikian, "Contemporary Ethical Theories and Jurisprudence," *Natural Law Forum,* vol. 1 (1956) pp. 4–40. But the Oxford group agrees with the Neopositivists that ultimate values cannot be scientifically known or proven, only selected by an act of decision, and that there is no Natural Law.

Additional Literature on Neopositivism and Oxford Philosophers

A. J. Ayer, *Language, Truth and Logic,* London 1936; 2nd ed., 1946
Rudolf Carnap, *The Logical Syntax of Language,* London 1937, also New York
    1951, originally in German, *Logische Syntax der Sprache,* Wien 1934
————, "Rejection of Metaphysics," in Morton White, ed., *The Age of Analysis,*
    New York 1955
Charles W. Morris, "Logical Positivism, Pragmatism, and Scientific Empiricism,"
    International Encyclopedia of Unified Science, Chicago, 1938, vol. 1, pp. 63–75
————, "Foundation of the Theory of Signs," *ibid.,* vol. 2, pp. 1–59
————, *Signs, Language, and Behaviorism,* New York 1946
Charles L. Stevenson, *Ethics and Language,* New Haven 1944 (see G. Nakhnikian,
    op.cit., on the differences between Stevenson and the others)
S. S. Stevens, "Psychology and the Science of Science," *Psychological Bulletin,*
    vol. 36 (1939) pp. 221–62, reprinted in Wiener, *Readings,* pp. 158 ff.
David L. Miller, "The Unity of Science Movement," *South-Western Social
    Science Quarterly,* vol. 26 (1945) pp. 252–59
Hans Reichenbach, *The Rise of Scientific Philosophy,* Berkeley 1951 .
Richard von Mises, *Positivism,* Cambridge 1951 (essentially a translation of the
    author's *Kleines Lehrbuch des Positivismus,* 1939)
T. D. Weldon, *The Vocabulary of Politics,* Penguin Books 1953; it seems to him
    "meaningless to say that the world was created" (p. 81)
Ludwig Wittgenstein, *Philosophical Investigations,* London, New York 1953
Paul Feyerabend, "Wittgenstein's Philosophical Investigations," *Philosophical Re-
    view,* vol. 64 (1955) pp. 449 ff.
A. J. Ayer *et al., The Revolution in Philosophy,* with an introduction by Gilbert
    Ryle, London, New York 1957 (contains analyses of Frege, Russell, Wittgen-
    stein, Moore, and the Vienna Circle)

Oxford Philosophy of Language, see further
S. Toulmin, *An Examination of Reason in Ethics,* Cambridge 1950
R. M. Hare, *The Language of Morals,* Oxford 1952
H. P. Nowell-Smith, *Ethics,* Pelican ed., 1954
H. L. A. Hart, "The Ascription of Responsibility and Rights," in *Essays in Logic
    and Language,* ed. by A. Flew, New York 1951
————, "Definition and Theory in Jurisprudence," *Law Quarterly Review,* vol. 70
    (1954) p. 37

Section 3 (c). Legal Positivism. The fact that Kelsen is a transpositivistic
value relativist, whereas Austin was not (see text), is not the only difference
between the two standard bearers of legal positivism. Austin was not interested in an analysis of the concept of the state; he took state and sovereignty for granted. Kelsen teaches that what is usually called the "legal
order of the state" or "set up by the state," is the state itself. He proposes to
abandon the concept of state sovereignty, on which Austin built, and to
accept instead the concept of global sovereignty. Furthermore, Kelsen has
made it a point that legal rules are not, as Austin taught, identical with
"commands," since legal rules continue to be valid after the will of command has ceased to be there; the true character of law as a sanction becomes

apparent precisely when the command fails. Kelsen defines a legal norm as a norm by which a sanction is decreed for illegal conduct. *What Is Justice?* pp. 272 ff.

The Basic Norm. Kelsen's final teaching on the "basic norm" can be summarized as follows: (1) There is no scientific necessity to presuppose a basic norm. (2) But without postulating it, the validity of a country's constitution and of the legal rules derived therefrom cannot be logically established. (3) As regards this logical need of some basic norm, there is no difference between Natural Law, Divine Law, and Positive Law. See especially, *What Is Justice?* pp. 226, 260, 262, and my critical comment regarding the content of the basic norm as postulated by Kelsen (Chapter IV, Section 8, of this book).

Section 4. Historicism. Much emphasis within the debate on the unique character of every historical situation has been placed on the fact that history rarely or never moves as intended by men but is the result, unintended by any individual or group, of myriad individual actions. These arguments have not deterred a number of philosophers from looking to history for general laws of development. Not only Comte, Hegel, and Marx in the nineteenth century, but also Schmoller, Sombart, Spengler, Toynbee in the twentieth believed it possible to derive general laws of development from the study of history, although they did not go so far as did Hegel, who held that mere empirical research in the sense of description and discovery, useful as it might be at times, did not deserve the name of science because it was unable to explain and to construct the laws of the universal history of mankind, the only subject whose mastery was real science to Hegel (see Hayek, *op.cit.,* pp. 64 ff., 194 ff., 199). This reliance on history for the discovery of universal laws of human development, too, has been called "historicism" at times. Then again, there are others, like David Easton, (*op.cit.*), who call "historicism" the habit of substituting historical research for theoretical inquiry. Modern historians have pointed to the inevitable use of generalizations in the work of the historian (see Louis Gottschalk, "The Historian's Use of Generalization" in L. D. White, ed., *The State of the Social Sciences,* Chicago 1956, pp. 436 ff.). This is quite correct. It should lead, I submit, to the recognition that insofar as the historian does use generalizations he is actually a social scientist and should be as careful in generalizing as any other scientist is expected to be, or should plainly avow that he relies on guesses or speculation.

Additional Literature

Charles Beard, *Theory and Practice in Historical Study,* a report delivered as chairman of a Social Science Research Council Committee, New York 1946

————, "Neglected Aspects of Political Science," *American Political Science Review*, vol. 42 (1948) pp. 211–22

Howard Becker, *Through Values to Social Interpretation*, Durham, N.C., 1950, pp. 128 ff., with comments on Max and Alfred Weber, Toynbee, and Spengler

Charles Frankel, "Philosophy and History," *Political Science Quarterly*, vol. 72 (1957) pp. 350–69

Section 6. Pragmatism: Precursors, Origin, and Name. As has often been remarked, even by Peirce and James themselves, some type of pragmatic method had been frequently applied by others long before the full-fledged formulation of Pragmatism at the end of the nineteenth century. The first articles by Peirce which described his views appeared in 1868, 1871, and 1877–1878, but in none of them was the name "pragmatism" used, although Peirce, Wright, James, and their associates referred to these views informally under that name among themselves, especially in their so-called Metaphysical Club, from about 1876 on. Philip P. Wiener's *Evolution and the Founders of Pragmatism* (Cambridge, Mass., 1949), now the best work in the field, considers the existence of the club a myth (pp. 18 ff.). At any rate, it is certain that the name "pragmatism" was not introduced into the philosophical literature until 1898, in James's paper, "Philosophical Conceptions and Practical Results," read before the Philosophical Union at Berkeley, California. Peirce did not use it in any of his own publications until 1902. In the following year, John Dewey took it up in *Studies in Logical Theory*. Peirce said that both the term and the idea of pragmatism or "pragmaticism," as he called it later, had been suggested to him by Kant's *Critique of Pure Reason*. He explained that he had not called it "practicism" or "practicalism" on the ground that Kant preempted the term "practical" for *moral* questions, using for counsels of prudence and welfare, which today we would rather call practical, the term "pragmatic" (Dewey, "The Pragmatism of Peirce" in Morris R. Cohen, ed., *Ch. S. Peirce, Chance, Love, and Logic*, New York 1923, 1949, pp. 301 ff.).

While Peirce thus maintained some connection with Kantian thought, James sweepingly rejected any such association. "As Schiller, Dewey and I mean pragmatism," he wrote to Professor Münsterberg on March 16, 1905, "it is *toto coelo* opposed to either the original or the revived Kantism. What similarity can there possibly be between human laws imposed a priori on all experience as 'legislative,' and human ways of thinking that grow up piecemeal among the details of experience because on the whole they work best? It is the rationalistic part of Kant that Pragmatism is expressly meant to overthrow" (Perry, *Thought and Character of W. J., op.cit.,* vol. 2, p. 469). Here James did less than justice to the liberating role which Kant's *Critique of Pure Reason* had played in the fight against the traditional sweeping forms of Rationalism (see Chapter 1, Section 6). But certainly, there were remnants of belief in pure reason in Kant (see *ibid.,* and Chapter ix).

Pragmatism and Meaning. Peirce confined the significance of Pragmatism, as he understood it, to the determination of the "meaning" of terms or propositions. His theory was not yet a theory of the "truth" of propositions, or of their "testing." See Dewey, *op.cit.* Ernest Nagel, *Sovereign Reason* (New York 1954, p. 90), observes correctly that many of the views propagated by the Vienna Circle "have been taken for granted for some time by American colleagues, largely because the latter have come to intellectual maturity under the influence of Peirce."

Peirce as Metaphysician. The sixth volume of Peirce's *Collected Papers* deals with "scientific metaphysics." He considered it the task of metaphysics to inquire how the universe had come into existence. Once he complained in a letter that modern psychologists are "so soaked with sensationalism" that they "cannot understand anything that does not mean that." Such sensationalism was alien to his own views. "How can I, to whom nothing seems so thoroughly real as generals [universals], and who regards Truth and Justice as *literally* [P.'s emphasis] the most powerful powers in the world, expect to be understood by a thoroughgoing Wundtian?" (Letter to Mrs. Ladd-Franklin, quoted in *Chance, Love, and Logic,* cited above.) Thus he expressed (1) his belief in the reality of universals, (2) his own high evaluation of truth and justice (he capitalized both terms), and (3) his belief that justice and truth were actual powers, and even the most powerful ones. Since Peirce failed to separate such metaphysical convictions and value judgments from his strictly scientific contributions, he was certainly not a Scientific Value Relativist.

Pragmatism and Valuations. James gave a graphic illustration of the different value the same fact may have for different people in his story of the cut-down forest, which looks fine to the pioneer in his log cabin but offensive to the visiting aestheticist ("On a Certain Blindness in Human Beings" in *Talks to Teachers on Psychology, and to Students on Some of Life's Ideals,* New York 1899, pp. 231 ff.). See also the following passage (*ibid.,* p. 265): "The first thing to learn in intercourse with others is non-interference with their own peculiar ways of being happy, provided those ways do not assume to interfere by violence with ours. No one has insight into all the ideals. No one should presume to judge them off-hand. The pretension to dogmatize about them in each other is the root of most human injustices and cruelties, and the trait in human character most likely to make the angels weep." These like other utterances of James have a distinctly relativistic note; but again it could not be said that they established a clear type of Scientific Value Relativism. For the conclusion James drew from the varieties of value judgments, the need of tolerance, does not follow unless a basic value judgment is previously accepted, namely, that our own personal happiness is not the only value which counts but that the happiness of other people also ought to be valued and that, at least in this respect, equality is a valuable ideal or aim. James did not care to state, either here or elsewhere, that this basic moral standard, insofar as it intends to be more than the prediction of social pressures and other consequences, has no scientific status but is the result of a fundamental religious or democratic decision of nonscientific character (see Chapter VIII, Section 2 and 15 of this book).

Pragmatism and Progress. There is a good deal of faith in progress in American Pragmatism. While it is distinguished by its "trial-and-error approach" and its rejection of the absolute belief in progress from other nineteenth-century movements (French sociologists, Hegelianism, Marxism), it is not entirely without its own taint of unbounded optimism. William Savery (*The Philosophy of John Dewey, op.cit.,* p. 513), quoting Buddha's "So the world is afflicted with death and decay, therefore the wise do not grieve, knowing the terms of the world," observes that Dewey, with his "passion for social change and improvement, seems strangely silent about that feature of the world which finally sweeps all values away."

Additional Literature: Horace M. Kallen (ed.), *The Philosophy of William James, Selected From His Chief Works,* with an introduction by H. M. Kallen, The Modern Library, New York (no date), very useful as an initiation to the fascinating personality of W. J. Also Kallen's article, "Pragmatism," in *Encyclopedia of the Social Sciences,* vol. xii.

Section 7. "Desired" and "Desirable." Surprisingly, T. D. Weldon seems to reiterate Mill's fallacy in a passage of his own *Vocabulary of Politics (op.cit.,* pp. 176–77) where he says that the only criterion for something being "desirable" is that it is actually "desired." The meaning of the word "desirable" can perhaps be said to presuppose that the desirable thing is either actually desired by *someone* (e.g., the observer) or can at least be conceived of as being actually desired. But the mere fact that it is desired (e.g., by the acting person) offers no criterion for its being desirable in the moral sense of the word.

NOTES TO CHAPTER VI

(Rise of Scientific Value Relativism)

Section 1. Hume. Whether Hume should be enumerated among those who established the modern doctrine of the logical gulf between Is and Ought and of the scientific relativity of all value judgments is debatable. I have not done so for the following reasons. It is true that Hume expressed his objection to the switching from Is to Ought in *deductive* reasoning in no uncertain terms. Said he [1]

In every system of morality which I have hitherto met with, I have always remarked, that the author proceeds for some time in the ordinary way of reasoning, and establishes the being of God, or makes observations concerning human affairs: when of a sudden I am surprised to find, that instead of the usual copulations of propositions, *is,* and *is not,* I meet with no proposition that is not connected with an *ought,* or an *ought not.* This change is imperceptible; but it is, however, of the last consequence. For as this *ought,* or *ought not,* expresses some new relation [2] or affirmation, it is necessary that it should be observed and explained; and at the same time that a reason should be given, for what seems altogether unconceivable, how this new relation can be a deduction from others, which are entirely different from it.

But there he stopped. He did not go beyond asking for reasons why the authors felt entitled, after establishing to their own satisfaction, for instance, the Is of God, deductively to derive therefrom any proposition in terms of Ought. He did not build his own theory of morals on this distinction. On the contrary, changing the subject immediately, he turned to his elaborately presented doctrine of the "moral sense" in men and the source of this sense in passions and conventions.

Now, the question whether God's being, if established, automatically implies that we ought to obey his commands is of a somewhat special character (see below, notes to Chapter ix). It is not the decisive point either in the Gulf Doctrine or in Hume's teaching, because both agree that God's being *cannot* be proved scientifically. The decisive point of the Gulf Doctrine, as explained in the text, is that it extended the ban on switches from Is to Ought beyond deductive to *inductive* reasoning, i.e., deriving major premises of Ought-form from observations of facts. This side of the matter, however, was no particular concern of Hume's because his attack on reasoning about external facts went much further. He limited the possibility of knowledge to facts observed or remembered. His attack, therefore, was concentrated, not on fusions of Is and Ought, but on the belief that we even know much about the Is of external facts, especially that we could know (1) the matters of fact that were neither now observed, nor earlier observed and now remembered, (2) causality (see Chapter ii, Section 1, above) and, especially, (3) the truth of religious doctrines, miracles and the like. He denied that we could even know the *existence* of any external objects apart from what we observe when we observe; or that other people have minds or feelings. Only "custom" makes us think we know these things.

---

[1] David Hume, *Treatise of Human Nature* (London 1739) Book iii, titled "Of Morals," last paragraph of Section 1. A.P. d'Entrèves in his fine paper "The Case for Natural Law Re-Examined," *Natural Law Forum,* vol. 1 (1956) p. 29, sees evidence in the above passage that the Gulf Doctrine goes back to Hume. But it does so only in a very general sense, not characteristic of the doctrine's particular significance for the distinction between facts and values.

[2] Hume speaks of "relation of ideas" where we would speak of meaning and logic.

In effect, therefore, Hume taught that if we saw a thing two days ago and see it again today we could not know whether it existed yesterday. He had no reason to raise the question whether what is in the external world ought to be; he questioned even the Is. (Regarding some inconsistencies and changes in Hume's views, see G. E. Moore's chapter on "Hume's philosophy" in *Philosophical Studies,* London, 1922, reprinted in Feigl and Sellars, *op.cit.,* pp. 351 ff.).

Hume's skepticism, therefore, went beyond present-day Scientific Method and Value Relativism, both built on faith in the order of nature, a faith which alone, as Whitehead said (*op.cit.* pp. 73, 37), has made possible the growth of science; a type of "deeper faith" that cannot be justified by any inductive generalization and has "remained blandly indifferent to its refutation by Hume." See Chapters II, Section 7, and V, Section 2, of this book for the fact that belief in external objects, in other persons too having minds, and in the regularities of interrelations in nature constitute an "immanent methodological a priori" of Scientific Method, although subject to further inquiry; the reasons therefor, and why this methodological a priori cannot be extended to value judgments.[3]

Julius H. von Kirchmann. This remarkable outsider, self-made man among German philosophers, was by profession a judge, appointed vice president in a court of appeal in 1847, and also elected to the second Prussian chamber and, later, to the German Reichstag. His public speeches brought him into conflict with the Prussian government. Dismissed from his juridical office without a pension in 1867 he withdrew to his private country seat and there engaged in farming and in pursuing his chief hobby, philosophy. Later he moved to Berlin. He translated Bacon, Descartes, Spinoza, Locke, Berkeley, and Hume into German, in addition to portions of Aristotle, Plato, and Cicero.[4] From 1872 on a member of Philosophische Gesellschaft, Berlin, he gained so much respect that in 1878 he was elected its president, the first non-Hegelian to preside over this body. At a memorial meeting held after his death in 1884, the idealistic philosopher Prof. Adolf Lasson— who had once addressed him with the words, "My distinguished opponent believes he is surrounded by a world of *things;* I know myself surrounded by a world of *ideas* and I know of no other world than that"—delivered the main speech; subsequently, an abstract on Kirchmann's philosophical thinking was read to the audience. Lasson said: "Kirchmann called his point of view realism, and rightly so: for he stressed this above all that the sensory perceptions show us the things as they really (*an sich*) are. Yet he

---

[3] It should be noted, however, that Hume's skepticism regarding continuity of existence has obtained new significance lately in microcosmic quantum theory.

[4] *Philosophische Bibliothek,* Berlin 1868 ff., gradually growing to 94 vols. As a strange co-incidence it may be noted that Arnold Kitz (see text) likewise was a vice president in a German court of appeal.

explicitly rejected empiricism and sensationalism, because they were only crude beginnings of realism, and likewise materialism, which he called a mere aberration (*Auswuchs*)." Indeed, Kirchmann's philosophy cannot easily be classified. He preserved some formal a-priori concepts of the type of the Kantian categories (see Chapter II, Section 5 of this book), and he wanted the humanistic sciences to take account of the fact that men were motivated by feelings of respect (*Achtungsgefühle*), distinct from those of pleasure and pain. Feelings of respect he traced to the human capacity of marveling (*Staunen*), which entailed forgetting one's own self. Fundamentally he was what would now be called an empirical realist or a scientific positivist. He believed in God; but this was to him not a matter of scientific thought. "To realism," he said, "religion is not a source of knowledge (*Erkenntnis*) but merely an *object* of knowledge," and God was "merely a matter of faith." In the field of non-religious ethics he was a "full skeptic," the printed report tells us, noting with ill-concealed concern that he sympathized with the ethics of the Greek skeptics and published a translation of Sextus Empiricus. One of the minor speakers regretted that Kirchmann had never fully understood idealism.

Literature: Philosophische Vorträge, edited by *Philosophische Gesellschaft,* Berlin, vol. 9 (report on the memorial meeting of December 27, 1884), Halle 1885, pp. 141 ff. Also, E. von Hartmann, *J. H. von Kirchmanns erkenntnistheoretischer Realismus,* Berlin 1875.

Section 2. The Term "Value." Until the last quarter of the nineteenth century "value" was rarely used abstractly in the general sense that has become characteristic of the twentieth, so as to refer to anything that men consider valuable for whatever reasons, including ideal goods, such as beauty, justice, liberty, equality, and especially ethical aims and attitudes. While the adjective "valuable" was readily applied to all of these, the noun "goods" rather than "values" was used for noneconomic objects. One impulse for a broader use in philosophy and the social sciences came from the German philosopher Hermann Lotze (1817–81), who placed the notion "value" in the center of his ethics (see especially his *Kleine Schriften,* 3 vols., ed. by David Peipers, and the references given there in an elaborate analytical index, vol. 3, pp. 906 ff., at the word "Wert"). Lotze's philosophy was basically conservative. His main philosophical work, *System der Philosophie,* ended with the author's confession (2nd ed., Leipzig 1886, vol. 2, p. 604) that he had looked "for the ground of that which is, to that which ought to be (*sein soll*)"; that this was meant in a theistic sense was shown by the work's last words: "God knows better" (*Gott weiss es besser*). The linguistic influence he had on a broader and deeper use of the term "value" was soon duplicated, and gradually outranked, by the debates over Nietzsche's revolutionary and atheistic call for *Umwertung aller Wert* (revaluation of all values). Nietzsche's attack on traditional ethical "values" were chiefly voiced in four of his works written in the late 1880's (*Die Genealogie der Moral*, 1887; *Götzendämmerung, Der Antichrist*, and *Ecce Homo*, 1888), apart from a fifth, *Der Wille zur Macht*, which was published only after his death in 1900. Thus, in the 1890's it had become quite customary to speak of moral and aesthetic ideals as (controversial) "values." Simmel seems to have been the first social scientist who, in his *Introduction* (1892), applied the noun "value" throughout in this wider sense.

Section 2(c). Max Weber. A second edition of Weber's *Gesammelte Aufsätze zur Wissenschaftslehre*, carefully edited by Johannes Winckelmann, has been brought out recently by the old publisher (J. C. B. Mohr, Tubingen 1951). A synoptic table of page numbers makes it easy to look up references to the original publication in this new edition. The story of Weber's life is beautifully presented in Marianne Weber, *Max Weber, Ein Lebensbild* (Tübingen 1926). A leading German monograph on Weber's methodology is Alexander von Schelting, *Max Weber's Wissenschaftslehre*, Tübingen 1934. See also Talcott Parsons' introduction to Max Weber, *The Theory of Social and Economic Organization*, tr. by A. M. Henderson and T. P., New York 1947.

Section 3 (d). Kelsen. His relativistic formulations occasionally go beyond what is scientifically warranted, as when he writes (*What is Justice?* pp. 357-58) that science must destroy the "illusion" that there are immanent values in reality. Actually, science is unable to state with certainty that God did not set values, or that there is no God. Science can only assert that ultimate values cannot be deduced "logically" from reality, or otherwise be revealed with the tools of science in an intersubjectively transmissible manner. Conversely, as if to compensate for this negative slip in formulation, Kelsen at other times presents the reader with fairly apodictic interpretations, as when he writes: To say that a social order is just "means" that this order regulates the behavior of men in a way "satisfactory to all men, so that all men find their happiness in it. . . . Justice is social happiness" (in Paul Sayre, ed., *Interpretations of Modern Legal Philosophies*, New York 1947, pp. 390-91). The term "social justice" *may* mean just that in an individual case; but whether it always does—for instance, is always meant to include all people—cannot be established thus apodictically (see Chapter VIII, Section 2).

Summarizing his teaching on relativity of justice in his farewell lecture at the University of California in 1952, Kelsen said that, as a relativist, he cannot answer the question, What is Justice? He can only say what Justice is *to him*. This question he answers as follows: "Since science is my profession, and hence the most important thing in my life, justice, to me, is that social order under whose protection the search for truth can prosper. 'My' justice, then, is the justice of freedom, the justice of peace, the justice of democracy—the justice of tolerance" (*What Is Justice?* p. 24).

Section 4. Einstein. Although the relativity theories in physics and in the scientific handling of values in the social sciences have little more in common than insistence on clarity, accuracy, and logical precision, the father of the physical Relativity Theory has variously confessed his adherence, also, to Scientific Value Relativism. The latest of these testimonies can be found in his *Out of My Later Years* (New York 1950). It is clear, he wrote there, "that knowledge of what 'is' does not open the door directly to what 'should be.' One can have the clearest and most complete knowledge of what 'is,' and yet not be able to deduct from that what 'should be' the goal of our human aspirations" (p. 22). "Intelligence makes clear to us the interrelation of means and ends. But mere thinking cannot give us a sense of the ultimate and fundamental ends." Agreeing with the limitation of value relativism to the *scientific* as distinct from the religious or philosophical approach he added: "To make clear these fundamental ends and valuations, and to set them fast in the emotional life of the individual, seems to me precisely the most important function which religion has to perform in the social life of man" (*ibid.*). Religion, yes, or if the reader prefers, philosophy; but not science (S_1). Science may help in the process, though. Logical thinking is not "irrelevant" for ethics, Einstein said. Ethical directives, although they cannot be produced by scientific statements of facts and relations, can be made "rational and coherent by logical thinking and empirical knowledge" (p. 114).

Section 5 (a). European Theories and American Practice. Bernard Berelson (*op.cit.,* p. 317) writes that in the field of public opinion "European scholars supply the basic theoretical ideas and American scholars the technical apparatus and knowhow. Certainly some of the major theorists in the social sciences in the modern period have been European, and it is difficult for America to match them." He mentions Freud, Pareto, Durkheim, Weber, Simmel.

Section 5. (b). Catlin. His article *"Political Theory: What Is It?"* (*Political Science Quarterly,* vol. 72, 1957, pp. 1–29) repeats in the beginning what he stated thirty years earlier: political science deals with means, political philosophy with ends (p. 9). But later on, in the same paper, turning from science to philosophy, he confessed, "My personal position is that this age needs desperately a revival of Natural Law." He even adds, *"Properly stated the theory of Natural Law is not only defensible but essential"* (italics in the original). However, he immediately reduces this apparent concession to the opponents of Scientific Value Relativism to scientific proportions by (1) insisting that subjectivism, wishful idealism and the notion of "natural rights" must be "dismissed," and (2) explaining that the question is only one of "recognizable rules of behavior . . . not to be confounded with natural law" (which he had just declared to be desperately needed, defensible, and essential). These rules, he finally admits, lead only to "prudential commands . . . they can be broken at will. But the penalty will be paid." No scientific relativist denies that (see notes to Chapter XII).

Lasswell. An analysis of the development of Lasswell's thinking has been attempted by David Easton in his article, "Harold Lasswell: Policy Scientist For a Democratic Society," (*Journal of Politics,* vol. 12, 1950, pp. 450–77, partly incorporated in Easton's later book, *The Political System,* New York 1955). He describes correctly that Lasswell first passed through an "amoral" phase, when he was "reluctant to state that he prefers one political system or set of rules to another," but later, since about 1939, through a second, a "moral" phase, when he began to hold that the special sciences were "doomed to sterility unless they accept the contemporary challenge and say something about our ultimate social objectives." This shift, I would say, was the entirely legitimate change from a "neutral" to a "partisan" scientific relativism, as explained in Chapter III, Section 8, of this book. As far as I am able to judge, Lasswell has always upheld the basic doctrine of Scientific Value Relativism that goals and ends are chosen by individuals or groups, and cannot be verified scientifically in nonrelative terms (see my quotations in the text from his 1951 book with Lerner). Easton admits that Lasswell as yet offers no answer to the question how science can establish correct ends and goals, but he sees "evidence that if in the future Lasswell was to develop his thinking along one path already visible, an affirmative answer might not be ruled out" (p. 452). What he refers to here is Lasswell's various intimations (e.g., in his *The Analysis of Political Behavior* and *Power and Personality,* p. 118, both New York 1948) that a fundamental "craving for self-respect" may be part of human nature true for all times and places. The pursuit of this suggestion, I submit, may well contribute to the list of "universal elements" in human ways of thinking and feeling, discussed in Chapter X of this book. But unless this universal craving for self-respect can be shown to be paralleled by an equally universal feeling that we ought to respect this feeling *in others,* it would prove no more than that its disregard will lead to resentment and, perhaps, to resistance and revolution. It is true that Lasswell, in his later writings, defined justice as "respect for the dignity of man" (Easton cites *Democracy Through Public Opinion,*

1941, p. 7; *Power and Personality*, p. 107; *Analysis of Political Behavior*, p. 2).[5] This, however, may mean no more than that Lasswell accepted the Western democratic interpretation of justice and basic values as *avowed* basis of his own scientific labors. He was entitled to do that. I do not read him as claiming that he was now able to furnish "scientific" proof for the absolute validity of Western basic values beyond analysis of the consequences and risks, etc., implied in the acceptance of other ideologies, for example, those confessing the superiority of the "group" or of "achievement" as ultimate values. Another issue raised by Easton (p. 459)—shifts in Lasswell's attention to "elites" and to psychoanalysis—is outside our present concern. Easton points out that Lasswell pursued the concept of elite until the beginning of World War II, and only thereafter took a decided interest in the people, veiling this shift by associating the concept of elite with the masses from which the leaders are drawn. This turn is noticeable also in *Power and Personality*, where Lasswell wrote (p. 108): "The elite of democracy ('the ruling class') is society-wide." But Lasswell's presidential address of 1956 (cited in the notes to Chapter i, Section 6) was still replete with "elites," with no mention of the people. Nor did he hint there at the possibility of scientific value judgments; when he used the word "value" he spoke of "our" values.

Section 5 (c). Clarence I. Lewis. The term "good," as everyone agrees, can be used two ways; sometimes it serves to indicate conduciveness to personal satisfaction (Is), sometimes to moral praiseworthiness (Ought). The apple is "good"; to give one's life for one's friends, is "good." These meanings differ, of course, unless it is held, as it was by Felix Cohen, that everything conducive to satisfaction is morally praiseworthy, or everything morally praiseworthy is conducive to satisfaction and nothing else is (see Chapter viii, Section 9, and xii, Section 4, on naturalistic hedonism). If a writer concentrates solely on satisfaction, ruling out all ethical questions from his inquiry, then analysis of goodness becomes comparatively simple. This is the trick, if I may call it so, which C. I. Lewis uses in his voluminous work, *An Analysis of Knowledge and Valuation* (La Salle, Ill., 1946). Through some five hundred pages he gives the appearance of a scholar who is able to make highly authoritative, and even absolute, empirical statements on values, until at the end it turns out that he has meant to exclude the *ethical* meaning of values from his study. There he warns against the "fatuity" of confusing facts about what gratifies human beings, with an "ultimate and transcendental standard of values which is fixed by the metaphysical nature of reality" (p. 531); there he concedes that he has failed to resolve the

[5] See also *Power and Society*, 1950 (co-author, A. Kaplan): "There is in our [*sic*] culture a vast and increasingly intense concern with *respect* (both from self and others) as a major human value—the Kantian treatment of human beings as ends, never merely as means."

crucial problems of the relation between the social and the personal interest (p. 553); and, after inserting one single paragraph about justice, ends his book with these words: "Valuation is always a matter of empirical knowledge. But what is right and what is just, can never be determined by empirical facts alone" (p. 554).

With ethical and juridical questions thus shoved aside, everything Lewis said earlier in his book on the identification of satisfaction and value obtains a different aspect, less baffling than before. All those full-sounding, absolutistic statements, such as the following: "the only thing intrinsically valuable is a good immediately found or findable and unmistakable when disclosed" (pp. 397, 400, and passim); a good's *esse is percipi* (to be is to be perceived); there can be "no illusion of present enjoyment or present pain" (p. 407); nothing has really intrinsic and ultimate value except such goodness "as might characterize a life found good in the living of it" (*ibid.*)—all these statements would be highly questionable if they were to apply to ethical values. If, however, they are meant to apply to evaluation only *apart* from their ethical justification, then there is little to quarrel about.

Lewis does not mind if his view is called "subjectivism" (p. 413). He explicitly admits that he preserves at least one relativity, namely, the limitation of our evaluations to the "anthropocentric," and ignoring of what is good or bad "for other animals" or, as I may add, for other planets, or for God and the angels if such there are. But this means admitting too little. Not only does Lewis refer to *human* values solely; he excludes, as we have just seen, all *ethical* human values of right and wrong, just and unjust, from empirical scientific verification, and he regards nonethical goodness as relative to personal satisfaction in the most unambiguous language.

This would leave us in the case of Professor Lewis with one more scientific relativist, at least in questions of justice and ethics. A subsequent little book of his (originally Woodbridge lectures at Columbia University) *The Ground and Nature of Right,* New York 1955 (97 pp.) keeps me doubting, however, whether this characterization would be correct. There he gave to justice and to ethical values a little more space (13 pp.) than in his major work. Starting from the necessarily social nature of human existence and its evolutionary history as a "basic datum for ethics"—an entirely legitimate approach—he jumped to the conclusion (p. 91) that the Golden Rule is the "basic imperative for individuals in their relations to one another." This basic imperative he then divided into two—the "law of compassion" and the "law of moral equality." This way of arguing is, of course, fully in line with Christian ethics and democratic ideals. But the universal extension of the Golden Rule and of the two imperatives underlying it is based on religious grounds or voluntary ethical decisions; science alone is unable to establish the validity of these principles in their universal extension, as shown in Chapter VIII, Sections 2, 6, 9, and 15.

Section 5 (e). Peculiarities of American Political Science. According to the UNESCO survey of 1950 (cited at the beginning of this Appendix), as ably summarized by Macpherson (*ibid.*), there was in the United States during the second quarter of this century increasing emphasis on quantitative research, increasing interest in psychological methods, and a vast amount of collection and clearance of data (statistical, observational, and experimental) by public and private agencies. There was an effort to collect specialized data which would serve for the testing of hypotheses about particular relations within the process of attempts to define concepts and hypotheses, and construct theories of political structure, pattern, and action; there was a growing concern with the management and manipulation of the people, and a hope of contributing to policy formation. But American political science was so "intent on empirical analysis that for the most part it eschews any inquiry into adequacy, since that would involve 'value judgment.'" Its focus of attention was "the mechanics rather than the purposes or potentialities of the political process." Although interest in political philosophy seemed to be growing, "political theory was almost entirely empirical and intent on avoiding value judgment." Work in the direction of systematic political theory "is so far rather limited, but . . . there is increasing awareness of the need for it." (Macpherson, *op.cit.*, especially pp. 433, 435; and the papers by Thomas I. Cook, Benjamin Lippincott, Charles Merriam, and Harold Lasswell in the UNESCO report.)

Additional Literature on U.S.A. Benjamin Lippincott, "The Bias of American Political Science," *Journal of Politics,* vol. 2 (1940) pp. 125–39.

British Political Science showed "much less anxiety and perturbation about research aims and methods . . . less emphasis on purely empirical research and more inclination to examine political institutions and processes from the point of view of purpose—the purposes they serve, and the purposes they ought to serve" (Macpherson, p. 436). W. A. Robson notes in his contribution to the UNESCO report that there was in Great Britain, in contrast to the United States, little work on parties and the party system, the electoral process, or the formation of public opinion. Englishmen have been accustomed to thinking in terms rather of the sovereignty of parliament than of the sovereignty of the people or the general will. ·

France. Shortly before the outbreak of World War II, I corresponded with Professor Radbruch on relativism in France, expressing surprise that I had found no typical scientific value relativists among the French philosophers of law. He answered (July 2, 1939): "I too know of no representative of relativism in French literature (which I do not know very well, though), although one should really expect to find relativism there in view of the skepsis characteristic of French mentality (Anatole France!). Claude du Tasquin (University of Neuchatel) gives an elementary survey of the various lines pursued in the philosophy of law, especially in France, in his *Introduction à la théorie générale et à la philosophie du droit* (1937) but mentions as a relativist only me. One should indeed find relativism in France, also, in the theory of Democracy, since Kelsen has shown convincingly, I think, that relativism is presupposed in democracy.[6] But I have learned nothing to confirm this expectation. (Rousseau introduces into his theory of democracy an absolute factor in the form of his *volonté générale.*) Those who don't believe in Catholicism believe in the 'Ideas of 1789'—even skeptics such as Anatole France included." At the end Radbruch reiterates that it would be interesting to explore "what general character traits of the French nation explain the absence of a principled relativism (although in a non-principled instinctive sense it seems to be deeply inherent in the French character). But I can only paraphrase my ignorance with many words, and therefore prefer leaving that topic."[7]

Section 7. The Term "Relativism." What in this book has been named Scientific Value Relativism is sometimes referred to as "noncognitivism," thus by Felix E. Oppenheim ("The Natural Law Thesis: Affirmation or Denial," *American Political Science Review,* vol. 51, 1957, pp. 41–53 and 65). But this term fails, at least in its negative form, to indicate that it refers to values only, and even only to intrinsic or ultimate values. Its positive form, "value cognitivism," sometimes used for the adherence to Natural-Law Doctrines, is more useable, but again nonexpressive of the important fact that no one denies the possibility of "value cognitivism" with regard to *extrinsic* values, such as the value of food for health, and of health for work or longevity or for the profits of life insurance companies. Among those who get along with their relativistic approach to values without using any particular name for it (and also without mentioning Max Weber, Simmel, Radbruch, *etc.*) are Barbara Wootton (*op.cit.,* Chapter IV, above) and T. D. Weldon (*Vocabulary of Politics, op.cit.*).

NOTES TO CHAPTER VII

(The Revolt)

Section 2. Misunderstandings. Leo Strauss resumed his objections in his paper "Social Science and Humanism" (in L. White, ed., *The State of the Social Sciences,* Chicago 1956, pp. 415 ff.). The relativists hold, he asserts, that "civilization is not intrinsically superior to cannibalism" (p. 422); hence, speech for the cause of civilization will be to the relativist "not rational discourse but mere 'propaganda,' a propaganda confronted by the equally

[6] See, however, my comments on this point in Chapter VIII, Section 8, of this book. A.B.
[7] Quoted by permission of Frau Lydia Radbruch, Heidelberg.

legitimate and perhaps more effective 'propaganda' in favor of cannibalism" (p. 423). Relativists teach, he further contends, that "the absolute truth of value systems, such as Plato's, has been refuted unqualifiedly, with finality, absolutely" (p. 428), and he contrasts the "apparent humility" of relativists with their "hidden arrogance," considering all people "provincial and narrow" except themselves (p. 425).

This squarely put challenge is particularly helpful if it is neither ignored nor ridiculed but met in equally forthright language. And it can be met. For each of Strauss' statements is in conflict with the facts, insofar as Scientific Value Relativism is concerned. First of all, where and when has a scientific relativist ever asserted as a fact that civilization *is not* superior to cannibalism? Such apodictic negative statements would be quite contrary to the principles of Scientific Method. The only question that could be raised by some pedantic relativist or for the matter of methodological argument is, What is the scientific *evidence* for the superiority of non-cannibalistic civilization? How about civilizations that abhor the eating of cattle or hogs? But here too Dr. Strauss would have no valid point. Scientific Value Relativism, although not satisfied with easy references to intuition, is at no loss to show the superiority of noncannibalism, once "superiority" is defined, as it generally is, in terms other than selfish satisfaction of personal or tribal passions and with references to humanity (see Chapter III, Section 7; also, Paul Edwards, *The Logic of Moral Discourse*, Glencoe, Ill., 1955, pp. 62, 214, regarding bull-fighting). Even if the term "superior" were used in a strictly selfish sense (which Strauss certainly would not do) Scientific Method would not be at the end of its resources; the long-run superiority of one pattern of behavior over another can often be demonstrated even when the question is solely that of personal satisfaction (Chapter XII, Section 4, self-avenging conduct). Nor does Scientific Value Relativism deny that there may be absolutely valid, divine standards of moral values; it merely negates that this can be shown with scientific means in a serious controversy conducted in good faith. In other words, Scientific Value Relativism teaches none of the things Strauss says it does.

On the other hand, Scientific Value Relativism may indeed be too humble to offer a *scientific* decision on a question like this: whether the captain of a marooned crew ought to be condemned if he permitted his men to eat the flesh of other men killed in battle or by accident, when this was the only alternative to starving. Religious feeling and traditional education may tell us they should rather have starved, but this is no *scientific* decision.

There may still be some "philosophical" relativists abroad, although I have never met one among scholars, who make apodictic negative statements about cosmos, God, and values. It should not be difficult for a man of the great scholarly faculties of Dr. Strauss to distinguish Scientific Value Relativism from such self-contradictory philosophical aberrations, and even to resist the pleasure of exploiting occasional slips in formulations as arguments against the essence of Scientific Value Relativism (see notes to Chapter VI, Section 3 for such a slip on the part of Kelsen).

Reproaches of arrogance are mutual. Wolfgang Friedmann, for example, in a review of Del Vecchio's philosophy (*Natural Law Forum*, vol. 3, 1958, pp. 208–10) writes that the claim of the Natural-Law philosophers "to speak in the name of absolute truth, although millions of people differ . . . appears to [him] as an example of human arrogance clothed in supernatural wisdom."

Section 3. Special Methods Available for Value Judgments? Professor Northrop (*op.cit.*, pp. 273 ff.) agrees that the methods suited for factual research are incapable of leading to scientific results in inquiries about the validity of ultimate standards of value. But, like Maritain, Voegelin, Alfred Weber, and Strauss, he chides the value relativists for overlooking that other methods are available. The method he recommends is the following. Each culture is "based on assumptions," he says. He admits that these assumptions, as the relativists emphasize, are often different fom culture to culture. But, says Northrop, if the different assumptions are not contradictory, as oriental and occidental cultures are different but not contradictory, they should be combined. But what if they *are* contradictory? This, of course, is the crucial question. Northrop's advice is that in such a case we ought to "pass to a new set of assumptions which takes care of leading to the two traditional theories without contradiction" (*ibid.*, also p. 325, and passim). But what if no such synthesis is possible? And even if theoretically possible, why ought we to accept it on principle? Why ought we to come to a synthesis between good and bad, between God and Satan, National Socialism and Democracy? Northrop fails to answer these questions. Granted that if two sets of value judgments are incompatible both may be evil; but not always and necessarily are both wrong. Is harmony and agreement always the highest good, regardless of the costs? See on this question Section 14 of Chapter VIII.

Intuition. The fact that if Scientific Method is followed the nature of things and of man alone yields but ambiguous clues regarding ultimate moral questions or none at all (see Chapters IV, Section 3, and VIII, Section 5) has caused some contemporary legal philosophers who are aware of the epistemological situation frankly to refer, for a correct interpretation of nature, to "intuition." Luis Recasens-Siches of the University of Mexico, formerly of the New School for Social Research, is one of those who have done so (see his writings cited in my notes to Chapter VIII, below). His claim that there are "ideal objective values," although gained from the study of nature, is explicitly based on intuition. Juridical values, Professor Recasens says, are "objective ideas," whose objectivity is founded "in the existence of man." But intuition is needed to discover them; they cannot be derived from nature logically ("Ideas and Historical Conditioning," *passim,* and "Human Life," p. 21). The world of pure phenomena, "without adding to it anything that is not natural phenomena, can never furnish a criterion of preference or valuation"; what we call health is as natural as what we call sickness (*Natural Law Forum, op.cit.,* p. 150). But these reflections do not lead him to relativism. Rather, he infers from them that the "root or primary foundation of an axiology is an a priori," not a subjective but an objective one. "A priori values," he insists, are "not only formal" (Stammler) but include "many with content." These latter remarks are close to the philosophy of Del Vecchio; see my comments in Chapter VIII, Section 5. As regards "intuition" I can only repeat that intuitive interpretation of nature *may* be right, especially if divine forces operate within or back of nature. Even irrespective of divine powers, intuitive feelings may at times prove correct as pre-scientific, or scientifically inarticulate, anticipations of consequences involved in human conduct. But like all intuitionists, Recasens has been unable to offer any method through which we can decide scientifically which of two or more contradictory intuitions about ultimate values is correct, beyond the possibility of clarifying factual conditions and factual consequences. See below, notes to Chapter VIII, on his own top values. For an able recent critique of intuitionism see Paul Edwards, *The Logic of Moral Discourse* (cited below) pp. 85 ff.

Section 5. Objective Values. C. I. Lewis recognizes as I have done in the text that often objective factors can be found which explain *why* certain things satisfy and hence are considered valuable. Therefore, he feels justified in applying the term "valuable" to objects; but he does so solely with the meaning that these objects are capable of conducing to satisfaction in some "possible" experience (*Analysis,* p. 414) and remarks that it would even be "a little difficult" to find any object which has "no potentialities whatever for conducing to satisfaction and is absolutely without value of any kind" (p. 525). Not quite in keeping with this broad interpretation, he makes a distinction elsewhere between "objective" and "subjective" data in such a way that he calls objective only those which have the character of a "normal and common human apprehension in the presence of the object in question," and subjective those which "deviate" from this by something that is "personal or a temporary characteristic of the individual object" (pp. 420, 528). In the framework of his essay this amounts to saying that, although the good is not good unless it is immediately and unmistakably felt (see above, notes to Chapter VI), certain objects have qualities that by "normal and common human apprehension" do convey this good feeling. This almost looks as though Lewis wanted to use the popular distinction between "normal" and "abnormal" valuations as a yardstick for an objective distinction between good and bad. But he states explicitly that this is not what he has in mind: he rightly warns against identifying what is genuinely valuable with that in which "satisfaction is—or 'ought to be'—universally found," as this view is "one philosophical root of totalitarianism" (p. 527).

Aesthetic Values. Northrop (*op.cit., passim*) pleads impressively that the West adopt from the East some measure of greater devotion to aesthetic observation and use this approach, as does the East, even in philosophizing.[1] This might indeed be all to the good if seen as a counterweight against onesided overevaluation of technical progress. But any particular *philosophical* results from this aesthetic and contemplative approach would partake of the *nonscientific* characteristics of putative knowledge based merely on intuition or speculation and, therefore, not be intersubjectively transmissible *qua* knowledge beyond its purely observational and strictly logical inferential elements. Northrop does not, of course, recommend that the West entirely abandon "theoretic" studies. He wants a *synthesis* between West and East. "Were science the mere description of what is immediately observable, poetry, rather than physics, would be the better science of the brook," he says (p. 170).

Additional Literature

John Dewey, *Art as Experience*, New York 1934
Horace M. Kallen, *Art and Freedom*, a historical and biographical interpretation of the relation between the ideas of Beauty, Use and Freedom in Western Civilization, New York 1942 (2 vols.)
Barbara Wootton, *Testament for Social Science, op.cit.*, pp. 160 ff.
Julie Braun-Vogelstein, *Art—Image of the West*, New York 1955

Section 6. Quasi-logical Arguments. C. I. Lewis (*op.cit.*, p. 491) rightly states that the pleasure we find in the combined experience of two factors "may not accord with the results of summing them." He gives another good illustration of faulty logic in value judgments in pointing to the failure threatening the attempt to get a better symphony than any Beethoven ever wrote by putting together the three movements from all his symphonies that are rated highest (p. 491). But then he slips into a fallacy himself by saying that "an object is twice as good if it affords the same satisfaction to twice as many people" (p. 546)—a good excuse for a prostitute.

Section 10 (Conclusion). Does Recent Ontology Hold Promise for the Cognition of Ultimate Values? Presenting a good sketch of incompatible value judgments (p. 500) in a paper called "Das Problem des Relativismus" (in *Systematische Philosophie*, ed. by N. Hartmann, Stuttgart 1942, pp. 431–559) Hermann Wein admits that all attempts to base ethics on logical or even on cosmic laws have completely failed (p. 464) and that relativism

[1] See also his *The Meaning of East and West*, New York 1946.

cannot be overcome by absolutism, which, he says, is merely the "formal logical counterpart" of relativism and offers no philosophical solution of the problems put by it (p. 493). But he sees hope in the "recently developed type of ontology" (see Chapter 1, Section 5 of this book), which he considers the "first major complex of newly won land that is emerging from the relativistic high tide (p. 525)." Relativism, he sums up, "was perhaps a necessary transitional stage between the sequence of great philosophical systems —the alchemist stage of philosophizing—and a more sober and more profitable style of philosophy" (p. 552). It is certainly true that the relativistic critique of absolutizing philosophic systems has led to a more sober style of philosophy and that this greater sobriety in turn has produced some new and useful results. But this does not imply that the final outcome will be abolition of Scientific Value Relativism. The scientific usefulness of the new style was brought about precisely by the growing eagerness of contemporary philosophers to exploit the resources of Scientific Method and by their growing sense of responsibility in distinguishing the functions of *scientia transmissibilis, non transmissibilis,* and *mere speculativa.* This seems to indicate that the methods of Scientific Value Relativism, as understood in this book, far from being on the way of becoming obsolete, have rather come to be applied more and more widely in modern philosophy, even by its opponents. As regards ontological "intuition" and "speculation," let it be remembered that Scientific Method and Scientific Value Relativism refer to *scientia transmissibilis* only; they claim no control of *scientia sive vera sive putativa non transmissibilis* or *mere speculativa,* except in rejecting false pretenses of scientific transmissibility.

The Scholar as a Teacher. The functions of education and of scholarly work overlap. In the round-table discussion "Beyond Relativism in Political Theory" (pp. 486–87 of the report cited below) I suggested that pupils in "pre-scholarly age groups" should be educated in the spirit of fundamental democratic ideals regardless of the limitations of scientific demonstrability, but that work done with students in "scholarly age groups" should be marked by a decisive difference in this respect. It should be based on scholarly methods, and the limitations inherent in scholarly work should, therefore, constitute an ever-present factor. All students in democratic countries should be taught how to support democratic ideals with scientifically impeccable arguments in discussions with opponents who believe in other ideals, and to beware of fallacious platitudes that can be turned against them. For details see the report.

Additional Literature on the Value Problem

Louis T. More, *The Limitations of Science,* New York 1915
L. T. Hobhouse, *Morals in Evolution,* New York 1919

————, *The Elements of Social Justice*, New York 1922

W. W. Willoughby, *The Ethical Basis of Political Authority*, New York 1930

Morris R. Cohen, *Reason and Nature*, New York 1931

Henri Bergson, *Les deux sources de la morale et de la religion*, Paris 1932, tr. by R. A. Andra and C. Breveton, Doubleday Anchor Books, 1954 (the two sources are social pressure and creative aspiration)

J. W. N. Sullivan, *The Limitations of Science*, New York 1933

Charles A. Beard, *The Nature of the Social Sciences in Relation to Objectives of Instruction*, New York 1934

Francis G. Wilson, *The Elements of Modern Politics*, New York 1936

Walter Lippmann, *An Inquiry into the Principles of the Good Society*, Boston 1937

Charles Hartshorne, *Beyond Humanism; Essays in the Philosophy of Nature*, Chicago 1937

Robert S. Lynd, *Knowledge For What?* Princeton 1939

Arthur Compton, *The Human Meaning of Science*, Chapel Hill 1940

Ernest Barker, *Reflections on Government*, Oxford 1942

Arthur Murphy, *The Uses of Reason*, New York 1943

Emil Brunner, *Justice and the Social Order*, New York 1945 (especially pp. 8, 39, 60)

Karl R. Popper, *The Open Society and Its Enemies*, London 1945, Princeton 1950

E. F. Carritt, *Ethical and Political Thinking*, Oxford 1947

T. D. Weldon, *States and Morals*, New York 1947

————, *The Vocabulary of Politics*, Penguin Books, 1953

George A. Lundberg, *Can Science Save Us?* New York 1947 (especially pp. 97 ff.)

N. O. Lossky, *The Intuitive Basis of Knowledge*, London 1949

Max Otto, *Science and the Moral Life*, New York 1949

Jerome Hall, *Living Law of Democratic Society*, Indianapolis 1949

Ray Lepley, ed., *Value, a Cooperative Inquiry*, New York 1949

Aloys Wenzl, *Wissenschaft und Weltanschauung*, Leipzig, 2nd ed., 1949

G. D. H. Cole, *Essays in Social Theory*, London 1950

Eliseo Vivas, *The Moral Life and the Ethical Life*, Chicago 1950

Howard Becker, *Through Values to Social Interpretation*, Durham, N.C., 1950

Kurt Riezler, *Man Mutable and Immutable*, Chicago 1950

John H. Hallowell, *The Moral Foundations of Democracy and Main Currents in Modern Political Thought*, New York 1950

Ernest Barker, *Principles of Social and Political Theory*, Oxford 1951 (especially p. 117)

Hans Reichenbach, *The Rise of Scientific Philosophy*, Berkeley, Calif., 1951; especially pp. 287 ff.

James B. Conant, *Modern Science and Modern Man*, New York 1952

F. Finding Kruse (Professor of Jurisprudence, Copenhagen), *The Community of the Future*, New York 1952

A. H. Hobbs, *Social Problems and Scientism*, Harrisburg 1953

Dietrich von Hildebrand, *Christian Ethics*, New York 1953

Ernest Nagel, *Sovereign Reason and Other Studies in the Philosophy of Science*, Glencoe, Ill., 1954

Paul Edwards, *The Logic of Moral Discourse*, with an introduction by Sidney Hook, Glencoe, Ill., 1955 (excels in good illustrations)

C. I. Lewis, *The Ground and Nature of the Right*, New York 1955

Edmond N. Cahn, *The Moral Decision, Right and Wrong in the Light of American Law*, Bloomington, Ind., 1955

555

Articles

John Dewey, "Theory of Valuation," *International Encyclopedia of Unified Science* (Chicago 1939), vol. 2, No. 4

George H. Sabine, "What Is a Political Theory?" *Journal of Politics*, vol. 1 (1939) pp. 1–16 (against the fusion of facts and values in Hegel and Dewey)

Arnold Brecht, "Relative and Absolute Justice," *Social Research*, vol. 6 (1939) pp. 58–87

———, "The Rise of Relativism in Political and Legal Philosophy," *ibid.*, pp. 392–414

———, "The Search for Absolutes in Political and Legal Philosophy," *ibid.*, vol. 7 (1940) pp. 201–28; *erratum*, p. 385

———, "The Myth of Is and Ought," *Harvard Law Review*, vol. 54 (1941) pp. 811–31

———, "The Impossible in Political and Legal Philosophy," *California Law Review*, vol. 29 (1941) pp. 321–31

Morris D. Forkosch, ed., *The Political Philosophy of Arnold Brecht*, New York 1954 (includes reprints of the aforementioned five articles, and "The Latent Place of God in Twentieth-Century Political Theory," extract of a paper read at the general seminar of the Graduate Faculty, New School for Social Research, March 1, 1950, and at the American Political Science Association, September 11, 1953)

Brand Blanchard, "Fact, Value, and Science" in R. N. Anshen, ed., *Science and Man*, New York 1942, pp. 185–203

Frank H. Knight, "Fact and Value in Social Science," *ibid.*, pp. 325–45

Wilbur M. Urban, "Axiology," *Twentieth-Century Philosophy, Living Schools of Thought*, ed. by D. D. Runes, New York 1943, pp. 51–74

John Hallowell, "Politics and Ethics," *American Political Science Review*, vol. 38 (1944) pp. 639–56

J. Roland Pennock, "Reason, Value Theory, and the Theory of Democracy," *ibid.*, vol. 38 (1944) pp. 855–75

———, "Political Science and Political Philosophy," *ibid.*, vol. 45 (1951) pp. 1081–85

Gabriel Almond, Lewis Dexter, William Whyte, John Hallowell, "Politics and Ethics—a Symposium," *ibid.*, vol. 40 (1946) pp. 283–312

Arnold Brecht, "Beyond Relativism in Political Theory," Report on Panel Discussion, *ibid.*, vol. 41 (1947) pp. 470–88

Felix Oppenheim, "Relativism, Absolutism, and Democracy," *ibid.*, vol. 44 (1950) pp. 958 ff.

Howard B. White, "Commentary on Prothro's Content Analysis," *ibid.*, vol. 50 (1956) pp. 740–50

Kurt Riezler, "Some Critical Remarks on Man's Science of Man," *Social Research*, vol. 15 (1948) pp. 462–93

Felix Kaufmann, "The Issue of Ethical Neutrality in Political Science," *ibid.*, vol. 16 (1949) pp. 344–52

Horace S. Friess, "Methods in Social Philosophy," *Journal of Social Philosophy*, vol. 3 (1938) pp. 325–41

Ralph Barton Perry, "The Moral Norm of Social Sciences," *ibid.*, vol. 5 (1939) pp. 16–28

Thomas I. Cook, "Politics, Sociology, and Values," *ibid.*, vol. 6 (1940) pp. 35–46

R. L. Warren, "The Place of Values in Social Theory," *ibid.*, vol. 7 (1942) pp. 223–39

D. W. Gottschalk, "Value Sciences," *ibid.*, vol. 19 (1952) pp. 183–92

Hornell Hart, "A Reliable Scale of Value Judgments," *American Sociological Review*, vol. 10 (1945) pp. 473–81

Stuart C. Dodd, "On Clarifying Human Values," *ibid.*, vol. 16 (1951) pp. 645–53

Charner Perry, "Relation Between Ethics and Political Science," *Ethics*, vol. 47 (1937) pp. 163–78

Hans J. Morgenthau, "The Evil of Politics and the Ethics of Evil," *ibid.*, vol. 56 (1945) pp. 1–18 (best discussion of the problematic distinction between personal and political morals)

and many other articles published in Ethics

Luigi Sturzo, "The Influence of Social Facts on Ethical Concepts," *Thought*, vol. 20 (1945) pp. 101 ff.

Frank E. Hartung, "The Social Function of Positivism," *Philosophy of Science*, vol. 12 (1945) pp. 120–33

David L. Miller, "Norms, Values, and the Social Sciences," *Southwestern Social Science Quarterly*, vol. 32 (1951) pp. 26–34

Paul F. Schmidt, "Some Criticism of Cultural Relativism," *Journal of Philosophy*, vol. 52 (1955) pp. 780 ff.

Arnold M. Rose, "Sociology and the Study of Values," *British Journal of Sociology*, vol. 7 (1956) pp. 1 ff.

Carl August Emge, *Über das Grunddogma des rechtsphilosophischen Relativismus*, Berlin, Leipzig, 1916 [1]

———, *Geschichte der Rechtsphilosophie*, Berlin 1931, especially pp. 28–55

———, *Sicherheit und Gerechtigkeit, ihre gemeinsame metaphysische Wurzel*, Abhandlungen der Preussischen Akademie der Wissenschaften, Berlin 1940, No. 9

———, *Über den Unterschied zwischen "tugendhaftem," "fortschrittlichen" und "situationsgemässen" Denken, ein Trilemma der praktischen Vernunft*, Abhandlungen der Akademie der Wissenschaften und der Literatur, Mainz 1950, No. 5

Further Literature on Natural Law, see notes to Chapter VIII.

NOTES TO CHAPTER VIII

(Attempts to Identify Highest Values)

Section 2. Equality in the Soviet Union. Both Lenin and Stalin dissociated themselves from ideals of full equality. The former stated that "any demand for equality which goes beyond the demand for abolition of classes is a stupid and absurd prejudice" (*Collected Works*, Moscow, 3rd ed., 1935, vol. 24, p. 293; see C. J. Friedrich and Z. K. Brzezinski, *Totalitarian Dictatorship and Autocracy*, Cambridge, Mass., 1956, p. 180, also p. 93). Stalin said at the 17th Congress of the Communist party (1934): "To conclude that socialism demands equality and leveling of members of society, leveling of their tastes

---

[1] This was the first major critique of legal value relativism. Emge admitted that no bridge leads from the data of Is to the realm of Ought, but hoped for a higher form of logic under which both Is and Ought can be deduced. He conceded that this desirable philosophy did not yet exist. Should it not be forthcoming, then relativism would be the inevitable consequence, he wrote (p. 45).

and personal lives; to conclude that according to Marxism everyone must walk in the same type of suit, and eat the same dishes and the same amount of food—that is to talk rubbish and slander Marxism." See my paper, "Democracy, Challenge to Theory," *Social Research*, vol. 13 (1946) p. 199, n. 5. On the actual degree of inequality in the Soviet Union, see *ibid*. and "The New Russian Constitution," *Social Research*, vol. 4 (1937) pp. 157, 168, 170; Friedrich and Brzezinski, *op.cit.*, p. 93 and bibliography; and Milovan Djilas, *The New Class*, New York 1957.

Additional Literature

C. Bouglé, *Les idées égalitaires*, Paris 1899 (see above, Chapter v, Section 3)
Richard H. Tawney, *Equality*, London 1931; 4th ed., with a new chapter, 1952
Levi D. Gresh, "The Legal and Political Philosophy of Leonard Nelson," *American Political Science Review*, vol. 35 (1941) pp. 437 ff
Robert A. Dahl, *A Preface to Democratic Theory*, Chicago 1956
George Catlin, *On Political Goals*, New York 1957, ch. v, "Born Equal," p. 94
Charles A. R. Crosland, *The Future of Socialism*, London 1957

Section 3. Liberty. "Humanism," or "Personalism." Professor Luis Recasens-Siches (see above, notes to Chapter vii) calls himself a follower of José Ortega y Gasset's "ratio-vitalistic philosophy of life, a sort of existentialism, not pessimistic or nihilistic, but optimistic and full of hope" (*Natural Law Forum*, vol. 3, 1958, p. 148). He claims to have "provided reasons, strictly philosophical, to prove that humanism or personalism is the only correct doctrine." His reasons are: the central position of individual consciousness; the fact that human life is the point of departure of philosophy; that the authentic and genuine human life is always an individual's life, society not being an entity in and for itself; and that culture has meaning only for man. He adds that in the axiological hierarchy "those values that are to be fulfilled within the individual conscience, namely, moral values, and those that lift the individual spirit, have a rank higher than values that are to be materialized in things such as works of art, tools, etc., higher also than values to be embodied in social institutions, including nation, state, and law" (*ibid.*, pp. 154–55). These are succinct statements of the liberal-democratic creed; but in the conflict with opposing tenets they offer no proof for what they state. Recasens calls his proof "strictly philosophical." If he means by this that his proof is "strictly nonscientific" (that is, S_2 and not S_1), he is correct; but if he means that, though philosophical, it is a strict type of proof, he is not. There is no strict philosophical proof of the hierarchy of values. See above on Intuition, notes to Chapter vii.

Tendencies Toward Perfection or Completion. John Wild (*Plato's Modern Enemies and the Theory of Natural Law*, Chicago 1953) sees the sources of a moral Natural Law in the capacity of human reason to apprehend the "tendencies toward fulfillment and completion," or "perfective tendencies," characteristic of the human species. This is close to Hocking's view as discussed in the text. Wild admits that not every "accidental tendency" deserves respect as a Law of Nature, but only "essential" tendencies, such as the desire for food and education. Most Liberals will agree with the ethical views expressed in such a doctrine. But this is not the same as saying that its validity can be demonstrated *scientifically* in conflict with opposing views. In order to do that one would have to show not only that every human being desires to see his *own* essential tendencies respected (do not animals desire that, too?) but that nature distinctly requires of us to respect these tendencies also in *all other* human beings including strangers and enemies, although not in animals, unless we follow Albert Schweitzer's more comprehensive philosophy of kindness. Such a commandment of all-round respect for all human beings, however, we are unable scientifically to extract from human nature alone (see Section 2, on equality) unless we assume that nature expresses some divine will (which we are fully entitled to believe religiously, but cannot verify scientifically) or endows every human being with some "voice within" that tells him to respect not only himself but all other human beings as well (which we may surmise to be the case, and assume hypothetically, but cannot demonstrate scientifically, see Chapter ix), or finally, that any disregard of this norm is always followed by consequences that are undesired by the actor himself (which we can verify to be a fact in many instances but not so regularly as to warrant complete scientific generalization, Chapter xii). Furthermore, the question which tendencies are "essential" cannot be decided without engaging in additional value judgments, whose verification again cannot be undertaken by science.

Liberty and Progress. Worshippers of progress are always suspect of absolutizing their own opinions of what is progress and being ready and even eager to sacrifice Liberty on the altars of Progress as they see it. This point has been made forcefully by Salomon and by Hayek; see Chapter v, Section 3(a).

Additional Literature

John Hallowell, *The Decline of Liberalism as an Ideology,* Berkeley 1943
Michael Polanyi, *The Logic of Liberty,* Chicago 1951
T. D. Weldon, *The Vocabulary of Politics,* Penguin Books 1953, pp. 69 ff.
Frank E. Hartung, "The Social Function of Positivism," *Philosophy of Science,* vol. 12 (1945) pp. 120–33
Lon L. Fuller, "Freedom—A Suggested Analysis," *Harvard Law Review,* vol. 68 (1955) pp. 1305 ff.
Carl J. Friedrich, "The Political Thought of Neo-Liberalism," *American Political Science Review,* vol. 49 (1955) pp. 509 ff.

Sections 4 and 5. Particular Natural-Law Norms. In addition to the general norm that men ought to be good and avoid evil, Rommen mentions as particular norms of Natural Law: to honor one's parents, to condemn murder and theft, to recognize private property and inheritance, the prohibition of abortion, of mercy killing, and of incest, the principles of *suum cuique;* furthermore, regarding states, their right of existence, of freedom, and of self-determination for the purpose of the common good (*op.cit.,* p. 222, n. 10, 226 ff.). Luther and Melanchthon considered bigamy not against nature since it was permitted in the Old Testament (Kelsen, *op.cit.,* p. 27). Jerome Hall wants to see the requirement of consent of the governed included in any redefinition of Natural Law (*Living Law of Democratic Society,* 1949, p. 8). On the other hand, Professor d'Entrèves warns us to be "quite chary in drawing conclusions from 'natural law' which might turn into a highly controversial political program." He asks us not to forget that the organic theory of society has in recent days been "a welcome excuse for the suppression of individual freedom." He goes even so far as to exclaim: "Let us, above all, practice a healthy distrust of any persons or groups who claim to have a clear insight into the nature of goodness" (*Natural Law Forum,* vol. 1, 1956, p. 39). This is not very different from denying *scientific* rank to any absolute statements regarding ultimate values in controversial questions.

Natural Law and Divine Will. My various arguments in this and previous chapters (especially III and IV) all converge upon the one point that nature cannot be logically regarded as a fount of moral laws unless it is seen as a documentation of divine will and divine planning. All classic advocates of Natural-Law doctrines have indeed seen nature as a divine creation; so did not only the Church Fathers, but also Grotius, Hobbes, Pufendorf, and later, Hegel (see Kelsen, *op.cit.,* pp. 138, 167; Rommen, *op.cit.;* Erik Wolf, *op.cit.*). If reference to a suprahuman will is omitted, the derivation of moral laws from nature amounts to a logical fallacy.[1] But no such fallacy is involved, of course, if the reference to nature is merely meant as a historical report on the influence which human thnking about nature has had on the rise and growth of moral and juridical convictions. See Chapter IV, Section 8.

Erick Wolf's Four Questions. In his *Problem der Naturrechtslehre* (cited in the notes to Chapter IV) Professor Wolf writes that we may ask four questions about the Natural Law. We may inquire (1) ontologically, about the Natural Law that *is,* i.e., its Being, its Reality, as found in ever-recurrent

---

[1] This seems to be the opinion also of Jacques Leclercq. He concedes that Natural Law is not law, "since law is not the same as morality, and natural law is the same as morality" ("Suggestions for Clarifying Natural Law," *Natural Law Forum,* vol. 2, 1957, pp. 64–87, especially p. 70).

institutions, like marriage and property, (2) ethically, about the "true" Natural Law that *ought to be,* in the sense of asking whether, e.g., institutions of marriage and property ought to exist, (3) logically, about the *logical* meaning of Natural Law, i.e., what the basic concepts of law are, and (4) metaphysically, about the *transcendent* character of Natural Law as an order of being that has its origin not in man but either (philosophically speaking) in the cosmos, or (theologically speaking) in God, with sanctions provided either in immanent retribution (*poena naturalis*) or in the Last Judgment. The important point for us is that Wolf holds that *all four* approaches are necessary in order to establish (*begründen*) Natural Law (p 113). This amounts to the admission that metaphysical transcendence is of the essence of Natural Law and that, therefore, the latter's existence beyond the casuistry of *poena naturalis* presupposes the existence of suprahuman divine forces. This view is in harmony with Scientific Value Relativism, which does not deny God's existence, but merely insists that it cannot be scientifically demonstrated and that, therefore, the existence of an ethical Natural Law cannot be scientifically demonstrated, although it can be believed in, speculated about, and by voluntary decision in some form or other be made the standard of justice in practical life (see my review in *Natural Law Forum,* vol. 3, 1958, pp. 192–96).[1]

Section 6. Evolutionary Ethics. An earlier attempt to explain ethics and morals objectively as "social regulatives of behavior patterns" (*soziale Verhaltensregulatoren*) that were the evolutionary result of the human "vital energy" (*Lebenskraft*) in the pursuit of social and individual aims (*Zielgründe*) was made by Christian von Ehrenfels in his *System der Werttheorie,* 2 vols., Leipzig 1897, 1898, especially vol. 2, pp. 224 ff.

Neopositivism and Natural Law. Even Neopositivists have tried to meet the value problem by introducing self-evident or quasi-naturalistic standards. Herbert Feigl (*op.cit.,* notes to Chapter v, above) thinks we can avoid metaphysical absolutism when in the spirit of an "empirical and naturalistic humanism" no other procedure is acknowledged than the "experimental" and no other standards than those prescribed "by human nature and by our own insights into the possibilities of improving human nature" (p. 25). But, as we have seen, no standards of how to treat our enemies are prescribed

[1] My own views have been erroneously rendered at the place given above (p. 195), owing to an editorial misunderstanding, as though it was my opinion that Wolf's ideas "enhance greatly the importance of the theory of natural law." Rather, I wanted to say only that they have great significance *for* that theory because Wolf admits that recognition of Natural Law is inseparable from a recognition of its transcendental source, which is beyond scientific demonstrability. Furthermore, my manuscript spoke of "transmissible," not of "communicable" knowledge in this context, because metaphysical knowledge may be "communicable" in the sense of "relatable," but is not transmissible *qua* knowledge. As the reader of the present book knows, I use "transmissible" as a technical term in distinction from "relatable."

by human nature alone, unless we first accept either divine commandments or some other higher principle, such as equality and dignity of every individual. Furthermore, the intention to improve human nature presupposes value judgments on what *would* improve it. Value judgments are presupposed also when Feigl, like Wild, demands that the "basic needs" of all individuals should be fulfilled, or, like Duguit, asks for "cooperation" and recognition of "mutual dependence"; or when he calls for reforms "democratically undertaken," yet holds, like Scheler or Maritain, that "breaking through old and majority-endorsed standards to a new form of morality" may be envisaged, first achieved by a few, but nevertheless "justifiable on the basis of the expected results of the new measures for the totality of mankind." This latter remark sounds almost like an invitation for experiments by some totalitarian vanguard. If, however, merely meant as a program for voluntary choice, it is completely compatible with Scientific Value Relativism.

Section 8. Democracy. As evidence for the inherent conflict between belief in absolute truth and acceptance of democratic government Kelsen refers to the story of Jesus, who insisted before Pilate that it was his (Jesus') mission to bear witness to the truth (the absolute truth, that is), and was met by Pilate with (1) the relativistic query, What is truth? and (2) the democratic process of submitting the decision to the majority, which demanded crucifixion. The story shows, says Kelsen (*op.cit.,* p. 208), that Jesus did not recognize the authority of the majority. Modifying his own former views (see the main text of this section) Kelsen does not suggest here that all those who believe in absolute truth must necessarily oppose democracy. On the contrary, he ends his analysis by admonishing the reader that we can accept the biblical story as an argument against democracy "only under one condition: that we are as sure of our political truth, to be enforced, if necessary, with blood and tears—that we are as sure of our truth as was of his truth, the son of God." Even so the story cannot be offered as a valid illustration. What Jesus refused to recognize was the decision of earthly authorities in *religious* matters, not their demand that to Caesar be rendered what is Caesar's. Moreover, the political procedure applied against Jesus was not democratic, since freedom of conscience and teaching and discussion free from pressure were not politically guaranteed.[1]

Section 9. Happiness. Aristotle, too, absolutized happiness, but he equated it with virtue and, therefore, actually distinguished true from false happiness.

[1] Regarding the interrelation between political and philosophical absolutism, see P. Kecskemeti, *op.cit.,* p. 313, who calls the notion that those who affirm absolute beliefs by the same token countenance absolute rule an absurdity. "Absolute rule can be combated only on the basis of absolute principles."

Section 11. Additional Literature on Nationalism

G. Gentile, "The Philosophic Basis of Fascism," *Foreign Affairs*, vol. 6 (1928) pp. 290 ff.
Charles Maurras, *Au Signe de Flore*, Paris 1931
Hans Kohn, *The Idea of Nationalism, a Study in Its Origins and Grounds*, New York 1944
————, *Nationalism and Liberty, the Swiss Example*, New York 1956
————, *American Nationalism, an Interpretative Essay*, New York 1957

Section 12. Power. Lasswell-Kaplan (*op.cit.*, p. xiv) say: "Political science, as an empirical discipline, is the study of shaping and sharing of power." Similarly, Russell (*op.cit.*, p. 10) offers proof that "the fundamental concept in social science is Power, in the same sense in which Energy is the fundamental concept in physics." But Lasswell soon narrows the concept of power, using it only to designate those relations in which *severe* deprivations are expected to follow the breach of the pattern of conduct; this, he concedes, eliminates an enormous range of relationships in which a breach is assumed to be of trivial importance (*Power and Personality*, p. 12). That men want power "is a statement we can accept as true in every society where power exists. . . . For the purpose of analyzing the social process, power is unmistakably a value, in the sense that it is desired, or likely to be desired" (*ibid.*, p. 16). Similarly, Russell: ". . . love of power is the chief motive producing changes which social science has to study," and "the laws of social dynamics are . . . only capable of being stated in terms of power in its various forms" (*op.cit.*, p. 13). It is my thesis that all this is too general to be useful. Only when we limit the reference to "power" to "governmental" power and to the pressure on it are we getting concepts concrete enough to serve the needs of political science; but then we must refer to "purpose" and "use" of power as well as to its existence.

Additional Literature

Guglielmo Ferrero, *The Principles of Power; the Great Political Crises of History*, tr. by T. R. Jaeckel, New York 1942
Lord Radcliffe of Werneth, *The Problem of Power*, London 1952
John K. Galbraith, *American Capitalism—The Concept of Countervailing Power*, Boston 1952
Martin Kessler, "Power and the Perfect State: a Study in Disillusion as Reflected in Orwell's 1984 and Huxley's Brave New World," *Political Science Quarterly*, vol. 72 (1957) pp. 565–77
Robert K. Merton, *Social Theory and Social Structure*, 2nd ed., 1957, ch. on "Patterns of Influence," pp. 387 ff.
David Spitz, "Power and Personality," *American Political Science Review*, vol. 52 (1958) pp. 84–97
T. W. Adorno *et al.*, *The Authoritarian Personality*, New York 1950; critically discussed in *Studies in Scope and Method of "The Authoritarian Personality*," ed. by R. Christie and M. Jahoda, Glencoe, Ill., 1954

Carl J. Friedrich (ed.), *Authority,* Cambridge 1958, vol. 1 of the yearbook *Nomos;* especially Friedrich's own paper, "Authority, Reason, and Discretion" (pp. 28 ff.) and the contributions by Hannah Arendt, Charles W. Hendel, Jerome Hall, Frank H. Knight, Herbert J. Spiro, George Catlin, Bertrand de Jouvenel, David Easton, Talcott Parsons, Norman Jacobson, Wolfgang Kraus

Section 16. Radbruch. Professor Erik Wolf of Freiburg University, in a careful analysis which appeared after this book had gone to the publisher, emphasizes that there was no revolutionary breach in Radbruch's ethical convictions; the ideals he announced in the last decade of his life had formed an integral part of his thinking since his earliest days ("Revolution or Evolution in Radbruch's Legal Philosophy," *Natural Law Forum,* vol. 3, 1958, pp. 1–23). I can but fully confirm this testimony from my own personal acquaintance. But this emotional continuity is in no contradiction to the fact that Radbruch's *scientific* approach to ethical questions did change, as documented in the text of this section.

Additional Literature on Radbruch: Lon L. Fuller, "American Legal Philosophy at Mid-Century," *Journal of Legal Education,* vol. 6 (1954) pp. 457 ff., 481 ff.

Additional Literature on Natural-Law Ideas in the Twentieth Century

Charles G. Haines, *The Revival of Natural Law Concepts,* Cambridge, Mass., 1930 and 1946
Lon L. Fuller, *The Law in Quest of Itself,* Chicago 1940
Jerome Hall, *Living Law of Democratic Society,* Indianapolis 1949
A. P. d'Entrèves, *Natural Law,* London 1951 (also in Italian tr.)
Axel Hägerström, *Inquiries into the Nature of Law and Morals,* ed. by K. Olivecrona, tr. by C. D. Broad, Uppsala 1953
John Ching-hsiung Wu, *Fountains of Justice,* New York 1955

Articles
Georges Gurvitch, "Natural Law," *Encyclopedia of the Social Sciences,* vol. 11
Roscoe Pound, "The End of Law as Developed in Juristic Thought," *Harvard Law Review,* vol. 30 (1917) p. 201
———, "How Far Are We Attaining a New Measure of Values in Twentieth-Century Juristic Thought?" in *West Virginia Law Quarterly,* vol. 42 (1936) p. 81
———, "Fifty Years of Jurisprudence," *Harvard Law Review,* vol. 50 (1937) pp. 557 ff., vol. 55 (1938) pp. 444 ff. and 777 ff.
Felix S. Cohen, "Transcendental Nonsense and the Functional Approach," *Columbia Law Review,* vol. 35 (1935) pp. 809–49
Friedrich Kessler, "Natural Law, Justice and Democracy—Some Reflections on Three Types of Thinking About Law and Justice," *Tulane Law Review,* vol. 19 (1944) pp. 32–61
Myres S. McDougal, "Fuller v. The American Legal Realists: an Intervention," *Yale Law Journal,* vol. 50 (1941) pp. 827–40 (with a concluding footnote, p. 840, which is based on an erroneous reading of one of my own articles)

Anton-Hermann Chroust, "On the Nature of Natural Law," in Paul Sayre, ed., *Interpretations of Modern Legal Philosophies*, New York 1947, pp. 70 ff. (with valuable notes on literature)
———, "Natural Law and Legal Positivism," *Ohio State Law Journal*, vol. 13 (1952) pp. 178 ff.
Luis Recasens-Siches, "Ideas and Historical Conditioning in the Realization of the Juridical Values," Sayre, ed., *Interpretations* (*op.cit.*) pp. 611 ff.
———, "Human Life, Society and Law: Fundamentals of the Philosophy of Law," in *Latin American Legal Philosophy*, ed. by J. L. Kunz, Twentieth Century Legal Philosophy Series, Cambridge, Mass., 1948
Max M. Laserson, "Positive and Natural Law and Their Correlations," *Interpretations* (*op. cit.*) pp. 434 ff.
Jerome Hall, "Concerning the Nature of Positive Law," *Yale Law Journal*, vol. 58 (1949) pp. 545–66
W. K. Frankena, "The Concept of Universal Human Rights," in *Science, Language, and Human Rights*, Philadelphia 1952
F. S. C. Northrop, "Contemporary Jurisprudence and International Law," *Yale Law Journal*, vol. 61 (1952) pp. 623 ff.
———, "Ethical Relativism in the Light of Recent Legal Science," *Journal of Philosophy*, vol. 52 (1955) pp. 649 ff.
Helen Silving, "The Twilight Zone of Positive and Natural Law," *California Law Review*, vol. 43 (1955) pp. 477 ff.
Edgar Bodenheimer, "Law as Order and Justice," *Journal of Public Law*, vol. 6 (1957) pp. 194 ff.

Natural Law Forum, annually since 1956, all articles, especially the following, in addition to those discussed in the text:
A. P. d'Entrèves, "The Case for Natural Law Re-Examined," *Natural Law Forum*, vol. 1 (1956) pp. 5–52
Myres S. McDougal, "Law as a Process of Decision: A Policy-Oriented Approach to Legal Study," *ibid.*, pp. 53–72
Vernon J. Bourke, "Two Approaches to Natural Law," *ibid.*, pp. 92–96
George W. Constable, "The False Natural Law, Professor Goble's Straw Man," *ibid.*, pp. 97–103
George Nakhnikian, "Contemporary Ethical Theories and Jurisprudence," *ibid.*, vol. 2 (1957) pp. 4–40 (discusses the differences between naturalism, intuitionism, non-cognitivism, and Neo-Kantianism)
Jacques Leclercq, "Suggestions for Clarifying Natural Law," *ibid.*, pp. 64–87
Helen Silving, "Positive Natural Law," *ibid.*, vol. 3 (1958) pp. 24–43

Individual Countries

United States

B. F. Wright, *American Interpretations of Natural Law*, Cambridge, Mass., 1931
Lon L. Fuller, "American Legal Philosophy at Mid-Century," *Journal of Legal Education*, vol. 6 (1954) pp. 457 ff.
Edgar Bodenheimer, "A Decade of Jurisprudence in the United States of America, 1946–1956," *Natural Law Forum*, vol. 3 (1958) pp. 44–67

Great Britain

H. L. A. Hart, "Philosophy of Law and Jurisprudence in Britain (1945–52)," *American Journal of Comparative Law*, vol. 2 (1953) pp. 335 ff.

Germany (in addition to Radbruch, Wolf, etc., cited in the text or notes)

Helmut Coing, *Die obersten Grundsätze des Rechts, ein Versuch zur Neu-gründung des Naturrechts,* Heidelberg 1947

Hans Welzel, *Naturrecht und materiale Gerechtigkeit,* Göttingen 1951

Carl August Emge, *Einführung in die Rechtsphilosophie,* Frankfurt 1955

Thomas Würtenberger, reports on German writings since 1949, *Archiv für Rechts- und Sozialphilosophie,* vol. 38 (1949), pp. 98–138, vol. 40 (1952) pp. 576–97, vol. 41 (1954) pp. 58–87

Freiherr von der Heydte, "Natural Law Tendencies in Contemporary German Jurisprudence," *Natural Law Forum,* vol. 1 (1956) pp. 115–21

Italy (in addition to Del Vecchio's writings, cited in Chapter VIII, Section 5)

Guido Fassò, "Natural Law in Italy in the Past Ten Years," *Natural Law Forum,* vol. 1 (1956) pp. 122–34

France and Belgium

J. Charmont, *La renaissance du droit naturel,* Montpellier 1910

Louis Le Fur, *Les grands problèmes de droit,* Paris 1937

Jean Haesert, *Théorie générale du droit,* Brussels 1948

Marc Réglade, *Valeur sociale et concepts juridiques,* Paris 1950

Paul Roubier, *Théorie générale du droit,* Paris 1946, 2nd ed., 1952

Georges Ripert, *Les forces créatrices du droit,* Paris 1955

Georges Gurvitch, "Droit naturel ou droit positif intuitif," *Archives de philosophie du droit et de sociologie,* vol. 3 (1933) pp. 55 ff.

Barna Horvath, "Social Value and Reality in Current French Legal Thought," *American Journal of Comparative Law,* vol. 1 (1952) pp. 243–55

René Théry, "Ten Years of the Philosophy of Law in France," *Natural Law Forum,* vol. 1 (1956) pp. 104–14

Latin-American Countries

Josef L. Kunz, "Latin-American Philosophy of Law in the Twentieth Century," *New York University Law Quarterly Review,* vol. 24 (1949) pp. 282 ff.

Luis Recasens-Siches, "Juridical Axiology in Ibero-America," *Natural Law Forum,* vol. 3 (1958) pp. 135–69

NOTES TO CHAPTER IX

(Factual Links Between Is and Ought)

Section 3. Ought We To Obey God? And If So, Why? Both questions sound silly, and for good reason as we shall see. But if they be asked, what are we to answer? Kelsen has made it a special point that we cannot logically derive our duty to obey God from God's own commandment but need a "basic norm" other than God's word for reaching that conclusion. He calls this, logically postulated, norm "the basic norm of theology" (*What Is Justice?* pp. 260, 354). His insistence would be correct if the two questions failed to contain the term "God" or used it in an uncommon sense, for instance, that of an ancient godhead, or of *any* type of suprahuman being, including a Satanic one. Then, indeed, as shown in the text, the question whether and why we ought to obey such a being's commands would make sense, and could not logically be answered by mere reference to that entity's own words. However, the usual meaning of the term "God" is that of designating the one godhead *whose will should be done*. The link between Is and Ought, therefore, is already presupposed when we apply the term "God." The sentence, "We ought to obey God," then, is tautological. It means: we ought to obey him whom we ought to obey. And we ought to obey him because, calling him "God," we have already recognized that we ought to obey him. We can meaningfully ask, "Why do you think that such and such commandment has been given by God?" Or, "Why do you call him who gave it God?" Or, "Why do you believe that there is a God at all, that God is real?" But we cannot meaningfully ask, "Why ought God's commandments be obeyed?" It is just like asking, "Is a chair a chair?" The Gulf Doctrine tends to obscure the real problem here. We are making a factual statement rather than drawing a logical conclusion when we say that there is a God. And after making it we can no longer meaningfully ask whether we ought to obey him because we have already accepted that by calling him thus.

Section 4. Ought We To Obey the Inner Voice? And If So, Why? The logical problem here is similar, but not identical. Northrop (*op.cit.,* pp. 280, 284) blames Kant, G. E. Moore, Urban, and others for having succumbed to the fallacy of deducing an Ought from an Is when they tried to make the sense of intrinsic goodness which man *actually feels* a criterion for the goodness he *ought to have*. From the strictly logical angle this objection is correct. Nor can we say here, as in the case of God's command, that we had already recognized the obligation by using the term "God." But here, too, the objection loses weight if emphasis is shifted to the factual link between Is and Ought to be found in the (hypothetic) universal presence of a feeling of moral obligations in human beings. The logical function of the link may be explained as follows: Logic deals with meaning. Reference to the inner voice (a merely pictorial term) means that, as a matter of *fact,* we do feel an urge *to do a thing as that which ought to be done*. There is no logical fallacy, then, involved in the statement that "according to the feeling of that inner urge, what is commanded by it ought to be done." But the question *why* it ought to be done remains meaningful here, as it has not been preempted by the terms used. This question has been discussed, therefore, in the text.

Section 5. Readings of the Inner Voice. Kant (*Die Religion . . . , loc.cit.*) defined "conscience" as a type of "consciousness that is a duty to itself," i.e., a consciousness which to have is a duty of the consciousness itself. He asked how is it possible that we can form an idea of such a thing (*sich ein solches zu denken*). In the course of his reflections on this question he held it to be a moral principle "which needs no proof" that one should dare nothing at the risk that it is morally wrong. Therefore, he said, it is man's absolute (*unbedingte*, unconditional) duty in acting to have the consciousness that the action is morally right (*recht*). It is not necessary, he added, that I know of all possible actions whether they are right or wrong; but of that action which I am about to take "I must not alone judge and opine, but be certain that it is not wrong." This is a postulate of conscience, he said, to which "Probabilism" is opposed, which holds that the mere opinion that my action *may* be right (*könne wohl recht sein*) is enough for action. All this makes edifying reading. But if a man in a responsible public position tried to follow Kant's maxim literally (that is, dare nothing at the risk that it is morally wrong) he could in many situations neither act *nor abstain from action,* as it is often not "apodictically certain" whether the action or its omission is morally right. Who acts, sins, it has been said; but he who is responsible may sin also when he fails to act. Such is life on earth.[1]

C. I. Lewis (*Analysis,* p. 482) wrote that a moral sense may be "presumed" in humans, and that "where it exists" it may be clarified to mean that no rule of action is right "except one which is right in all instances, and therefore right for everyone." Such interpretation would include the principle that all human beings are to be treated as equal, in line with Nelson's interpretation of the moral sense (see Chapter VIII, Section 2). But Lewis, unlike St. Paul, Kant, and Nelson, did not go so far as to contend apodictically that all human beings do have a moral sense; he only said that this may be "presumed," adding that if the moral sense is lacking then moral argument on any principle of action would be pointless.

NOTES TO CHAPTER X

(Universal Postulates)

Shortcomings of the Current Treatment. Any honest analysis of the recent revival of Natural-Law ideas (see, especially, Chapter VIII, Sections 4, 5, and the notes thereto, above) tends to show that there are relatively few believers in moral laws of nature today who do not base their acceptance, directly or indirectly, on the assumption of supra-human divine forces; but who seriously try to find moral laws in nature itself irrespective of the existence of divine forces and without being guilty of fallacious reasoning. These few apostles of a strictly secular Natural Law always end up—though generally only after a long detour around the history of ideas—by pointing to one or both of the following two avenues of approach. The one leads to the area of *poena naturalis,* that is, of the self-avenging laws of conduct, a subject of study whose scientific legitimacy no one denies (see Chapter XII); the other, to inquiries about the universal character of certain types of hu-

---

[1] See on this problem also the profound article by Hans J. Morgenthau, "The Evil of Politics and the Ethics of Evil," *Ethics,* vol. 56 (1945) pp. 1 ff.

man reactions or of human ways of thinking and feeling, the subject of the present chapter. This outcome is characteristic also of most of the studies published in the new American periodical, *The Natural Law Forum*.[1]

Although the general convergence upon these two approaches from the side of both adherents and opponents of secular Natural Law seems to augur well for a possible conciliation of views, two shortcomings in the recent literature on universal features of humanity—our present topic—give cause for criticism and regret. The first is that almost all authors leave us with no more than the general assertion that there *are* such universal elements in human reactions, elements that imply moral laws of conduct, without saying *what* they are. As I have emphasized in the text, the time has come that such generalities should no longer be allowed to pass as adequate scientific contributions; scholars should finally settle down to the business of finding out *what* these universal elements are, and what our evidence is that they are universal.

The second, and more serious, shortcoming is that many authors seem to think they can logically deduce from the fact that all human beings resent certain actions if committed against *themselves* the inference that nature forbids such actions against *others*. This is fallacious since it presupposes what was to be demonstrated. The only inference logically permitted is that such actions are likely to meet with resistance, and possibly with revolt, revolution, and revenge (see above, notes to Chapter vi, 5 b, Lasswell). That for this reason they should not be undertaken even if the acting agent is strong enough to suppress the hostile forces loosed against him does not follow logically unless the principle of human equality or of equal dignity of all men is previously accepted. This key principle cannot be derived as obligatory from nature directly without reference either to divine will or to historical determination on the part of the human race or of sections of it (see Chapter viii, Section 2).

Impartiality. The two postulates of truth (veracity) and of equal treatment of what is equal under the accepted system of values imply, as one of their various derivatives, the postulate of impartiality. Paul Kecskemeti places the latter concept in the foreground, calling impartiality even *"the* formal principle of justice," the only principle that is unalterable (*Meaning, Communication, and Value,* Chicago 1952, pp. 286, 312). On the significance of this principle we are, of course, in full agreement. But I think it important that the two postulates from which that of impartiality is a mere derivative are listed separately. As a matter of logic, impartiality even presupposes the acceptance of one or several principles that are to be applied with impartiality. It has been the thesis of this chapter that a number of such principles are universally associated with justice. They go beyond impartiality.

[1] See, for example, the articles by d'Entrèves in vol. 1, p. 45, and by Nakhnikian, vol. 2, p. 34.

NOTES TO CHAPTER XI
(Truth)

Sections 1 to 3. Truth in Science and in Justice. The subject of this chapter is not whether the pursuit of truth is a postulate of *science*—which is generally recognized; see Chapters VI, Section 2 (Rickert), and VII, Sections 1 and 2 (Dewey, Strauss)—but whether it is a postulate of *justice*. Within science, truth has frequently been called even an "absolute" value. In line with this emphasis, Kecskemeti has recently declared it to be a complete misunderstanding that "the scientific attitude excludes all absolutes." On the contrary, he writes, "it is based on an absolute" (*op.cit.,* p. 312). Whether the term "absolute" is here in order can well be questioned, even with regard to science. All that can be said with certainty is that the term "science" is conventionally used exclusively for activities that pursue truth. This convention is obviously useful, and even necessary, for the systematic exploration of truth. But that does not make the requirement of truth an "absolute" value. It could even be questioned whether the pursuit of truth in every sphere of human interests is universally held to be a top value. In the case of justice, however, it is the stated assumption of the present chapter that the postulate of truth (veracity) *is* a universal element of human feeling and thinking.

Section 4. The White Lie. Plato supplies another illustration of a white lie. He taught that the most just life was also most pleasant (see Chapter XII, Section 4 c), but recommended that the government should say so even if it were not true; this would be a "useful lie" (*Laws,* 662 b). Kelsen, referring to this passage, suggests that the Natural-Law doctrine, although he considers it untrue, might be allowed to pass as a useful lie. Wrote he: "That the natural-law doctrine, as it pretends, is able to determine in an objective way what is just, is a lie; but those who consider it useful may make use of it as of a useful lie" (*What Is Justice?* p. 173; see also pp. 6 and 376). At least in Kelsen's example, however, the word "lie" is not appropriately used, since those who teach the Natural-Law doctrine unquestionably do so in good faith. Nor can anyone prove that they are wrong; only, they are unable to prove that they are right, because of the metaphysical factors involved.

Additional Literature. Giorgio del Vecchio, "Truth and Untruth in Morals and Law," in Paul Sayre, ed., *Interpretations of Modern Legal Philosophies,* New York 1947, pp. 143 ff.

NOTES TO CHAPTER XII

(Impossibility)

Section 1. Necessity and Freedom, Additional Literature

Lyman Bryson, *Science and Freedom*, New York 1947
Frank H. Knight, *Freedom and Reform*, New York 1947
John D. Bernal, *The Freedom of Necessity*, London 1949
Michael Polanyi, *The Logic of Liberty*, London 1951

Section 4 (b). Self-avenging Laws of Conduct. George Catlin seems to have had merely this category in mind, when he declared that "this age desperately needs a revival of Natural Law" (see above, notes to Chapter VI, Section 5). For he proposes no more than further inquiry into "recognizable rules of behavior," which are "empiric and can be tested" and "can be broken at will," but only on condition that "the penalty will be paid." He thinks that a rule of this kind will be observed *"also* as a moral rule or moral norm." ("Political Theory: What Is It?" *Political Science Quarterly,* vol. 72 (1957) pp. 21, 22. The word "also" is italicized in the original.)

Hesiod. Historically, the doctrine that all evil conduct entails its natural penalty received perhaps its strongest expression by one of its earliest announcers, Hesiod, who long before Socrates and Plato warned: "He does mischief to himself who does mischief to another, and evil planning harms the plotter most" (*Works and Arts*, Evelyn-White tr., Loeb ed., p. 265).

Section 4 (c). Hedonism. Aristotle, like Socrates and Plato taught that no virtuous man could ever be unhappy; but unlike his predecessors he added the realistic proviso that in order to be happy a man must also have sufficient earthly goods. See Kelsen's comment, *What Is Justice?* p. 116.

NOTES TO CHAPTER XIII

(Political Science and the Belief in God)

Section 1. Metaphysical Foundations of Democracy? See also T. D. Weldon, *The Vocabulary of Politics* (1953) p. 97.

Section 2. Scientifically Verifiable Religions? Northrop (*op.cit.*, p. 100) describes oriental religions as purely empiristic, limited to immediate apprehension. They "identify the Divine," he says, with the "timeless undifferentiated aesthetic continuum" (see notes to Chapter I, Section 2, above). On this ground he calls these religions "scientifically verifiable." But what is scientifically verifiable here is only the fact that the aesthetic continuum is there and that it is being worshipped, not that it is "divine."

Arguments from Likelihood. In view of the great number of conceivable variants of human ideas about the nature of God, I have limited discussion of scientific likelihood to the one alternative of whether or not there is a supra-human being capable of thinking, planning, and acting. My thesis was that no greater likelihood could be assigned in scientific terms to one or the other side of this alternative. Instead of stopping here, we may, of course, make the concept of the "thinking-planning-acting" God more specific, and then repeat the question. After reading an abridged version of my present chapter [1] the German philosopher, Professor Theodor Litt (Bonn), wrote to me: "It all depends on what content the respective idea of God has. It can be so conceived that there are no contradictions between it and man's world-immanent experiences. Then your 'fifty-fifty' holds. It is different when the idea's content involves such a collision. Illustration: the 'hypothesis' of an 'all-benevolent' (*allgütigen*) God seems to me to collide strongly with our worldly experiences. Faith does not mind this. But can science, too, disregard such contradiction? Or must it not hold this contradiction against an idea of God which has *this* content?" [2] Similar differentiations between more or less plausible ideas of God's nature can be frequently encountered (see the references to MacIver and Einstein in the text). A. N. Whitehead (*op.cit.,* p. 258) complains that an unfortunate habit has prevailed among medieval and modern professors of paying God "metaphysical compliments." If God is conceived as the all-powerful creator of the world and of the metaphysical situation, so Whitehead argues, then there can be no alternative except "to discern in Him the origin of all evil as well as of all good." He is then "the supreme author of the play, and to Him must therefore be ascribed its shortcomings as well as its success." If, on the other hand, God be conceived only as "the supreme ground for limitation," i.e., especially of limitation through ethical commandments, then it stands "in His very nature to divide the Good from the Evil and to establish Reason 'within her dominion supreme.'"

Now, the relevant question in our present context is not which of several ideas of God is more likely to be true than others, but whether it is scientifically more likely that no thinking-planning-acting God exists at all than "such a one" *or any other Deity* capable of thinking, planning, and acting. These are different questions. If, nonetheless, I should allow myself to be drawn into a debate on more concrete ideas, I would hesitate to admit that in appraising *scientific* likelihood we could, even then, legitimately

---

[1] "Gottes latenter Platz in der politischen Theorie des zwanzigsten Jahrhunderts," *Zeitschrift fur Rechts- und Sozialphilosophie,* vol. 42 (1956) pp. 465–78.
[2] Quoted by permission.

make the distinction Litt, Whitehead, and others indicate should be made. The fact that events often look bewilderingly unjust and cruel to men shows definitely, it is true, that, if there is an all-powerful God, he is not "kind" in the *human* everyday sense of this term, and this is obviously a type of reasoning that has motivated many people to doubt God's all-benevolent character, or his power or will to interfere with human events, or his existence altogether. As John Stuart Mill put it challengingly ninety years ago:

If, instead of the "glad tidings" that there exists a Being in whom all the excellencies which the highest human mind can conceive, exist in a degree inconceivable to us, I am informed that the world is ruled by a being whose attributes are infinite, but what they are we cannot learn, nor what are the principles of his government, except that "the highest human morality which we are capable of conceiving" does not sanction them; convince me of it, and I will bear my fate as I may. But when I am told I must believe this and at the same time call this being by names which express and affirm the highest human morality, I say in plain terms that I will not. Whatever power such a being may have over me, there is one thing which he shall not do; he shall not compel me to worship him. I will call no being good, who is not what I mean when I apply that epithet to my fellow-creatures; and if such a being can sentence me to hell for so calling him, to hell I will go.[3]

But this linguistic (semantic) refusal to apply the human term "kind" or "good" to the Deity does not dispose of the religious counter-argument that events may gain another aspect if an all-powerful God permits them to happen within a plan that extends infinitely beyond the individual's life-span on earth and includes the design of keeping men aware that earthly happiness is precarious, of stirring their moral will to care for their own virtues and for helping their suffering fellow-creatures rather than looking after pleasures, and of granting those who suffer unjustly inner comforts (see Chapter XII, Section 4, c) and even heavenly rewards. This is what most religions teach.

On the strictly scientific level (*scientia transmissibilis*) I can concede a conclusive disturbance of the "fifty-fifty" balance only when science can point to such faults in religious arguing as a gross lack of proportion between ideas of God's greatness, wisdom, and power on one side, and trivial acts, such as table-rapping, appearance of ghosts under ridiculous circumstances (and only then), or touching of wood being required to avert evil, on the other. Whenever religious teaching violates this scientific postulate of adequate proportions, then we can classify the correspondence of such a creed with reality as scientifically unlikely. We may also, of course, engage in a critical analysis of the historical or psychological origins and sources of particular teachings.

---

[3] John Stuart Mill, *An Examination of Sir William Hamilton's Philosophy,* London 1867, pp. 123–24. See Nagel ed., pp. xxx, xxxi, note.

Additional Literature: Charles Hartshorne, *Man's Vision of God and the Logic of Theism,* Chicago 1941; Charles Hartshorne and W. L. Reese (ed.), *Philosophers Speak of God,* Chicago 1953

Distribution of Believers and Nonbelievers. Questionnaires have sometimes been applied in research on religious attitudes, but none that have come to my knowledge have tried to form the categories listed in Section 2 of the text. Harvard undergraduates were asked in 1957 whether some religion or faith was necessary to their philosophies of life. Sixty percent replied that it was, twenty-three percent that it was not (*The New York Times,* March 26, 1957). These figures gibe well with my own estimates given in the text: but the questions asked were too different from mine to permit valid conclusions. Someone may consider religion necessary for his philosophy of life without himself being able to believe. There is a story of two famous Christian theologians debating intricate details of their religion when one of them interrupted the running argument with the question, "Say, why don't you believe in God?"

Section 3. Unbracketing the Divine Alternative. The following passage from Whitehead's *Science in the Modern World* (p. 275) may serve to illustrate what I have called the irrepressible nature of metaphysical longings:

Religion is the vision of something which stands beyond, behind, and within, the passing flux of immediate things; something which is real, and yet waiting to be realized; something which is a remote possibility, and yet the greatest of present facts; something that gives meaning to all that passes and yet eludes apprehension; something whose possession is the final good, and yet is beyond all reach; something which is the ultimate ideal, and the hopeless quest.

The immediate reaction of human nature to the religious vision is worship. . . . The vision claims nothing but worship; and worship is a surrender to the claim for assimilation, urged with the motive force of mutual love.

Section 4. Pascal's Wager. The concluding lines of the little German poem inserted in the text may remind the erudite reader of Pascal's wager. Pascal argued that, since we must choose between believing either that God does or that he does not exist we had best wager he does, because then we gain all if we win and lose nothing if we lose. But this is not the essential point of my German stanza. A belief based merely on such opportunistic calculations would never yield subjective "certainty." My intention was, rather, to point out the human capacity of feeling certainty and doubt *at the same time,* in different layers of the ego. The acid inquisitiveness of the doubting part of the ego and the carefree certainty, in some cases even jubilance, of the confident part may both be present simultaneously, neither quite to be suppressed.

SUPPLEMENTARY NOTES
ON LITERATURE

Addenda to APPENDIX A, Pages 495-497

Publications by Arnold Brecht on Special Problems of Political Theory:

Internationaler Vergleich der öffentlichen Ausgaben, Vorträge des Carnegie-Lehrstuhls, Hajo Holborn (ed.), vol. 2, Leipzig-Berlin 1932

"Fairness in Foreign Policy: The Chinese Issue," *Social Research*, vol. 28 (1961) pp. 95-104

Aus nächster Nähe, Lebenserinnerungen eines beteiligten Beobachters, 1884-1927, Stuttgart 1966, especially chapters 23 and 30

Mit der Kraft des Geistes, Lebenserinnerungen, zweite Hälfte, 1927-1967, Stuttgart 1967, especially chapters 35 and 50

"Political Theory," article in *International Encyclopedia of the Social Sciences*, especially the sections on Sovereignty and on Theory of Democracy

Addenda to APPENDIX B

Page 503. *General Reference Books*:
Charles S. Hyneman, *The Study of Politics. The Present State of American Political Science*, Urbana, Ill. 1959

Page 504. *Common Sense*:
Hans-Georg Gadamer, *Wahrheit und Methode*, Tübingen 1960, pp. 16-26

Pages 505-506. *Research Methods*:
Thomas C. M. Cormick and Roy G. Francis, *Methods of Research in the Behavioral Sciences*, New York 1958
James C. Charlesworth (ed.), *The Limits of Behavioralism in Political Science: A Symposium*, Philadelphia 1962

Pages 508-509. *Truth, Reality*:
Michael Polanyi, *Personal Knowledge: Towards a Post-critical Philosophy*, Chicago 1958
Hans-Georg Gadamer, *Wahrheit und Methode*, Tübingen 1960, pp. 16-26
Jean-Paul Sartre, *L'Etre et le néant*, Paris 1943
———, *L'Existentialisme est un humanisme*, Paris 1946
Alfred Stern, *Sartre, His Philosophy and Psychoanalysis*, New York 1953
Karl Löwith, *Heidegger, Denker in dürftiger Zeit*, Frankfurt 1953 (on Heidegger's concept of truth see also the German ed. of this book *Politische Theorie*, Tübingen 1961, p. 611)

Pages 509-510. *Logic*:
Karl R. Popper, *The Logic of Scientific Discovery*, New York 1959; in German, *Logik der Forschung*, 1934
Karl Jaspers, *Von der Wahrheit*, München 1949, pp. 1 ff., 10, 11 (distinguishes "philosophic" from "scientific" logic, the former based on metaphysical assumptions. For details see the German ed. of this book, p. 615)

Page 513. *Basic Concepts. General*:
Carl G. Hempel, *Fundamentals of Concept Formation in Empirical Science*, Chicago 1952

Gabriel A. Almond, "Political Theory and Political Science" (presidential address), *American Political Science Review*, vol. 60 (1966), pp. 869-879 (discusses the recent ascendancy of "Political System" as a basic concept, broader and deeper than the old-time concept of "forms of government")

Page 513. *"Signs" and "Language"*:
Hans-Georg Gadamer, *Wahrheit und Methode*, Tübingen 1960, pp. 361-465

Page 514. *"Elites"*:
Seymour Martin Lipset, *Political Man*, New York 1960
————, Introduction to Robert Michel's *Political Parties*, Collier Books, New York 1962
Robert Dahl, *Who Governs?*, New Haven 1961
Jack L. Walker, "A Critique of the Elitist Theory of Democracy," and Dahl's reply, *American Political Science Review*, vol. 60 (1966), pp. 285 ff.

Page 514. *"Action"*:
Hannah Arendt, *The Human Condition*, Chicago 1959, pp. 175 ff.

Page 514. *"Decision Making"*:
Herbert Simon, *Administrative Behavior: A Study of Decision-Making Processes in Administrative Organization*, 2nd ed., New York 1957
James G. March and Herbert A. Simon, *Organizations*, New York 1958
Dwight Waldo and Martin Landau, *The Study of Organizational Behavior: Status, Problems and Trends*, Papers in Comparative Administration, American Society for Public Administration, Washington, D. C. 1966

Page 520. *Causality*:
(For Kant's thought on causality see also the German ed. of this book, pp. 87, 88; for the great number of atoms in a single egg cell see *ibid.*, p. 86, n. 17)
Max Planck, *Religion und Naturwissenschaft*, 7th ed., Leipzig 1938
Werner Heisenberg, *Wandlungen in den Grundlagen der Naturwissenschaft*, Leipzig 1935
————, *Das Naturbild der heutigen Physik*, Hamburg 1955
————, *Physics and Philosophy: the Revolution in Modern Science*, New York 1958
Erwin Schrödinger, *What is Life*, Cambridge 1944; in German, *Was ist Leben*, Bern 1946
Hans Jonas, *The Phenomenon of Life, Toward a Philosophical Biology*, New York 1966
Ethel M. Albert, "Causality in the Social Sciences," *Journal of Philosophy*, November 1954
Theodor Litt, *Die Wiedererweckung des geschichtlichen Bewusstseins*, Heidelberg 1956

Page 524. *Knowledge*:
Michael Polanyi, *Personal Knowledge: Towards a Post-critical Philosophy*, Chicago 1958
Adolph Lowe, *On Economic Knowledge: Toward a Science of Political Economics*, New York 1965
Hans Neisser, *On the Sociology of Knowledge*, New York 1965

Page 525. *Scientific Method*:
Joseph S. Roucek (ed.), *20th Century Political Thought*, New York 1946
Theodor Litt, *Wissenschaft und Menschenbildung im Lichte des West-Ost-Gegensatzes*, Heidelberg 1958

Thomas S. Kuhn, "The Structure of Scientific Revolutions," *International Encyclopedia of Unified Sciences*, vol. 2, no. 2, Chicago 1962
Page 526. *Especially: Political Science:*
Jean Meynaud, *Introduction à la science politique*, Paris 1959
Maurice Duverger, *Méthodes des sciences sociales*, Paris 1961, first published as *Méthodes de la science politique*, 1959
Georges Burdeau, *Méthode de la science politique*, Paris 1959
James C. Charlesworth (ed.), *The Limits of Behavioralism in Political Science: A Symposium*, Philadelphia 1962
————, *Mathematics and the Social Sciences*, Philadelphia 1963
————, *A Design for Political Science: Scope, Objectives, and Methods*, Philadelphia 1966
George E. G. Catlin, *Systematic Politics; Elementa politica et sociologica*, Toronto 1962
Carl J. Friedrich, *Man and His Government, An Empirical Theory of Politics*, New York 1963
Harold D. Lasswell, *The Future of Political Science*, New York 1963
Gabriel A. Almond, "Political Theory and Political Science," as cited above (at Page 513)
Theodor Heuss, *Formkräfte der politischen Stilbildung*, Berlin 1952
Ossip K. Flechtheim, *Politik als Wissenschaft*, Berlin 1953
H. B. Mayo, *An Introduction to Democratic Theory*, New York 1960

Page 527. *Individual Countries*:
Bernard Crick, *The American Science of Politics, Its Origins and Contributions*, Berkeley 1959

Page 528. *Law and Political Science*:
Ilmar Tammelo, "Law, Justice, and Social Reality," *Österreichische Zeitschrift für öffentliches Recht*, vol. 8 (1957), pp. 373-384 (decisions motivated by anticipated future needs may appear unjust at the time being)
Roscoe Pound, *Jurisprudence*, St. Paul 1959

Page 530. *History of Natural-Law Ideas*:
Erik Wolf, *Das Problem der Naturrechtslehre, Versuch einer Orientierung*, 2nd enlarged ed., Karlsruhe 1959

Page 532. *History of Science*:
Hans-Georg Gadamer, *Wahrheit und Methode*, Tübingen 1960, pp. 162 ff.
William Anderson, *Man's Quest for Political Knowledge: The Study and Teaching of Politics in Ancient Times*, Minneapolis 1964, and A.B.'s review in *American Political Science Review*, vol. 59 (1965), pp. 449-451
Bernhard Crick, *The American Science of Politics, Its Origins and Contributions*, Berkeley 1959
Gabriel A. Almond, as cited above (at Page 513)

Page 536. *Historicism*:
Theodor Litt, *Die Wiedererweckung des historischen Bewusstseins*, Heidelberg 1956

Page 553. *Aesthetic Values*:
Hans-Georg Gadamer, *Wahrheit und Methode*, Tübingen 1960, pp. 31-51

Pages 554 ff. *The Value Problem*:
Victor Kraft, *Die Grundlagen einer wissenschaftlichen Wertlehre*, 2nd ed., Wien 1951

Alfred Verdross, *Abendländische Rechtsphilosophie*, Wien 1958; 2nd enlarged ed., 1963

Gunnar Myrdal, *Value and Social Theory*, New York 1958

Kenneth Thompson, *Christian Ethics and the Dilemma of Foreign Policy*, Durham, N.C. 1959

Arnold Brecht, "Fairness in Foreign Policy: The Chinese Issue," *Social Research*, vol. 28 (1961), pp. 95-104

Heinz Hartmann, *Psychoanalysis and Moral Values*, New York 1960

George E. G. Catlin, *Systematic Politics: Elementa politica et sociologica*, Toronto 1962, *passim*

Carl J. Friedrich, *Man and His Government. An Empirical Theory of Politics*, New York 1963, *passim*

Carl August Emge, *Einführung in die Rechtsphilosophie*, Frankfurt 1955

Pages 557-558. *Equality*:

Gerhard Leibholz, *Die Gleichheit vor dem Gesetz*, 2nd. ed., München 1959

Ralf Dahrendorf, *Über den Ursprung der Ungleichheit unter den Menschen*, Tübingen 1961

Arnold Brecht, "The Ultimate Standard of Justice," *Nomos*, vol. 6 (1963), pp. 62 ff.

Giorgio Del Vecchio, "Equality and Inequality in Relation to Justice," *Natural Law Forum*, vol. 11 (1966), pp. 36-47

Page 558. *Liberty*:

Sidney Hock, *Political Power and Personal Freedom*, New York 1959

Arnold Brecht, "Liberty and Truth," *Nomos*, vol. 5 (1961), pp. 243-261

Benjamin E. Lippincott, *Democracy's Dilemma: The Totalitarian Party in a Free Society*, New York 1965

Page 562. *Happiness*:

Ursula M. von Eckardt, *The Pursuit of Happiness in the Democratic Creed, an Analysis of Political Ethics*, with an introduction by Carl J. Friedrich, New York 1959

Page 563. *Power*:

Wright Mills, *The Power Elite*, New York 1956

Karl Loewenstein, *Political Power and the Governmental Process*, Chicago 1957 (also in German, *Verfassungslehre*, Tübingen 1959)

Harrington Moore, *Political Power and Social Theory*, Cambridge 1958

David Spitz, *Democracy and the Challenge of Power*, New York 1958

Theodor Eschenburg, *Über Autorität*, Frankfurt 1965

Page 564. *Literature on Radbruch*:

Wolfgang Friedman, "Gustav Radbruch" in *Vanderbilt Law Review*, vol. 14 (1960), pp. 191-209, and A.B.'s review in *American Political Science Review*, vol. 55 (1961), pp. 607-610.

Pages 564 f. *Natural-Law Ideas in the 20th Century*:

Alf Ross, *On Law and Justice*, Berkeley 1959, and A.B.'s review in *Natural Law Forum*, vol. 5 (1960), pp. 160-163

Johann Messner, "The Postwar Natural Law Revival and Its Outcome," *Natural Law Forum*, vol. 4 (1959), pp. 101-105

Page 566. *Natural-Law Ideas in Germany*:

Heinrich Rommen, "Natural Law in Decisions of the Federal Supreme Court

and of the Constitutional Courts in Germany," *Natural Law Forum*, vol. 4 (1959), pp. 1-25.
Ernst von Hippel, "The Role of Natural Law in the Legal Decisions of the German Federal Republic," *ibid.*, pp. 106-118

Page 569. *Arbitrary Interference With Equality or Liberty*:
For a slightly different description of what makes an interference "arbitrary" see the German ed. of this book, pp. 477, 685. An interference is arbitrary whenever it is "not justified" by the accepted value system, even though it may not be in direct "contradiction" to it.

Page 570. *The Useful Lie*:
See also the German ed. of this book, p. 686, and Karl Jaspers, *Von der Wahrheit*, München 1947, pp. 484 ff., 550, 556 ff.

Pages 571 ff. *Science and the Belief in God*:
Jacques Collin, *God in Modern Philosophy*, Chicago 1959
Horace M. Kallen, *Why Religion*, New York 1927
Ernst Topitsch, *Vom Ursprung und Ende der Metaphysik, eine Studie zur Weltanschauungskritik*, Wien 1958
Harlow Shapley, *Science Ponders Religion*, New York 1960
Herbert Muschalek, *Gottesbekenntnisse moderner Naturforscher*, Berlin 1952

Page 574. *Pascal's Wager*:
Blaise Pascal, *Pensées et opuscules*, Léon Brunschvieg (ed.), 11th ed., Paris, p. 439. See German ed. of this book, p. 691, where the French text is quoted and explained.

In a few cases in the index, the correct page reference may be one page preceding or following the one given.

I. INDEX OF NAMES

II. SUBJECT INDEX

methodology (*continued*)
priori, 99; immanent m. a priori, 99, 481;
m. axiom, 99; m. dualism, 124, 126ff, 231;
and relevance, 272; "dissecting," 351; individualistic, 352
militarism, 384
military service, 442
mind, term, 512; objective, 341
minimum, standards of human rights, 160;
definition of justice, 397; wages, 445
misery, as a subject of scientific research, 5;
of empiro-logical science, 272
misrepresentation, of Sc. Value Relativism,
262ff, 488, 549f
misunderstandings, caused by the term "relativism," 257
mob, and mob pressure, 414
models, 111, 482; and theory, 524; stage or
development m., 112
Moloch, 370
money, 127
monogamy, 149, 560
monopolies, control of, 445
Monte Cassino, 154, 269
monuments, destruction, 154
moral(s), values, 117ff, 284ff, 297, 484; decisions, 171, 267; the m. law as a fact, 200,
368, 375f, 460; equated with surplus of
pleasures, 250, 339f, 434f; faith in, 253;
m. factors in natural science, 267; m. and
freedom, 318; evolution, 334; duty, reproach, not *ultra posse*, 396, 418, 420,
425; deepest personality feelings as a source
of moral acts, 436; principles, 501; sense,
540, 568. See *also* law, norm, Ought
moralism, doctrinal, 191
moralists, 139
morality, new forms of, 562
"more" valuable, 124
mortality rates, 518
mosquitoes, 145
motivation, 81f, 122, 456, 478
motives, of choices, 254, 482
multiphase sampling, 64n
multiple, realities, 53; tests, 392
multistage sampling, 64n
musical harmonies, 287, 353
murder, 560
must, 210
mutations, 474
mutual, respect, 324, 342; dependence, 562
"my country, right or wrong," 153n
mystical experiences, 196
myth, 9, 251, 257

name, 511
nation, 304, 343, 474, 529; duties toward, 323

national interests, 131, 344, 399
National Socialism, 7, 153, 156, 342, 360,
419; concentration camps under, 336. See
also dictatorship, totalitarianism
nationalism, 156, 304, 474; aligned with
democratic forces, 344; with antidemo-
cratic forces, 344; as dogma, 475; literature, 563
natural, science, 27f, 213; selection, 84; evolution, 334; rights, 139, 337, 545, 558ff (*see
also* human rights, Natural Law)
Natural Law, 3, 136, 161, 183, 243, 283, 321,
333, 360, 374, 390, 433, 561; history of,
138ff, 528f; eclipses and revivals, 138ff,
167, 324, 544; with variable content, 205;
intertwined with divine law, 319f, 324,
328, 560; *N. L. Forum,* 320, 565; secular,
322, 328f, 568; in Italy, 322; Germany,
324; France, 326; United States, 334;
"positive" and "natural" N.L., 391; and
basic norm, 536; schools, aims, 333; particular norms, 560; Neopositivism and,
561f; a "useful lie"?, 570
natural-history stage of inquiry, 43
naturalism, 104, 351
naturalistic, approach unable to comprehend
soul, 350; criteria of "the good," 434; hedonism, 434
nature, and logic, 68; n. of things, 192ff, 161,
303, 325, 329, 357, 484; and culture, distinguished, 213, 350f; free-of-value, 213;
related to value, 213; philosophy of, 272;
n. of man, 282, 284, 286; in cultural interpretation, 303; respect for the necessities of, 396, 420ff; concept of, 530. See
also Natural Law
naturwissenschaftliche Methode, 27
Nazi, *see* National Socialism
Nebbia v. New York, 400n
Nebenfolgen, see by-products
necessary, regulative principles, 140, 368,
376; elements in human thinking, 376,
387ff
necessity, 54n, 81, 417f, 421; respect for, 396;
positive and negative, 417; and Scientific
Method, 419
negative, metaphysics, 177, 491; necessity, 417
Negroes, 409. See *also* equal, equality, racial
Neo-Kantians, 206, 209, 324f
Neo-Hegelians, 140, 325, 348
Neo-Thomists, 271f, 319, 325
Neopositivism, 78, 174ff, 177, 181, 491, 533f;
retreat from original positions, 177ff;
natural-law ideas, 361f; literature, 182, 535
Neovitalism, 86
neutral relativism, *see* Scientific Value Relativism
next step, 150

Brecht, Arnold, 1884–   . Political theory; the foundations of twentieth-century political thought. Princeton, N. J., Princeton University Press, 1959. 603 p. 25 cm. Includes bibliography. 1. Political science—Methodology. 2. Political science—Hist. 1. Title. JA71.B73

(320.1)   59–5591 ‡ Library of Congress